Handbook of Research on Enterprise 2.0:

Technological, Social, and Organizational Dimensions

Maria Manuela Cruz-Cunha
Polytechnic Insitute of Cavado and Ave, Portugal

Fernando Moreira
Portucalense University, Portugal

João Varajão
Universidade de Trás-os-Montes e Alto Douro, Braga, Portugal

A volume in the Advances in Business Information Systems and Analytics

BUSINESS SCIENCE Reference
An Imprint of IGI Global

Managing Director:	Lindsay Johnston
Editorial Director:	Joel Gamon
Production Manager:	Jennifer Yoder
Publishing Systems Analyst:	Adrienne Freeland
Development Editor:	Joel Gamon
Assistant Acquisitions Editor:	Kayla Wolfe
Typesetter:	Lisandro Gonzalez
Cover Design:	Jason Mull

Published in the United States of America by
Business Science Reference (an imprint of IGI Global)
701 E. Chocolate Avenue
Hershey PA 17033
Tel: 717-533-8845
Fax: 717-533-8661
E-mail: cust@igi-global.com
Web site: http://www.igi-global.com

Library of Congress Cataloging-in-Publication Data

Handbook of research on enterprise 2.0 : technological, social, and organizational dimensions / Maria Manuela Cruz-Cunha, Fernando Moreira and Joao Varajao, editors.
pages cm
Includes bibliographical references and index.
Summary: "This book collects the most recent developments in evaluating the technological, organizational, and social dimensions of modern business practices in order to better foster advances in information exchange and collaboration among networks of partners and customers"--Provided by publisher.
ISBN 978-1-4666-4373-4 (hardcover) -- ISBN 978-1-4666-4374-1 (ebook) -- ISBN 978-1-4666-4375-8 (print & perpetual access) 1. Information technology--Management. 2. Web 2.0. 3. Communication in organizations--Technological innovations. I. Cruz-Cunha, Maria Manuela, 1964- II. Moreira, Fernando, 1969 August 16- III. Varajao, Joao, 1972-

HD30.2.H36425 2014
658'.05--dc23

2013015165

This book is published in the IGI Global book series Advances in Business Information Systems and Analytics (ISSN: 2327-3275; eISSN: 2327-3283)

British Cataloguing in Publication Data
A Cataloguing in Publication record for this book is available from the British Library.

Advances in Business Information Systems and Analytics (ABISA) Book Series

Madjid Tavana
La Salle University, USA

ISSN: 2327-3275
EISSN: 2327-3283

Mission

The successful development and management of information systems and business analytics is crucial to the success of an organization. New technological developments and methods for data analysis have allowed organizations to not only improve their processes and allow for greater productivity, but have also provided businesses with a venue through which to cut costs, plan for the future, and maintain competitive advantage in the information age.

The **Advances in Business Information Systems and Analytics (ABISA) Book Series** aims to present diverse and timely research in the development, deployment, and management of business information systems and business analytics for continued organizational development and improved business value.

Coverage

- Big Data
- Business Decision Making
- Business Information Security
- Business Process Management
- Business Systems Engineering
- Data Analytics
- Data Management
- Decision Support Systems
- Management Information Systems
- Performance Metrics

IGI Global is currently accepting manuscripts for publication within this series. To submit a proposal for a volume in this series, please contact our Acquisition Editors at Acquisitions@igi-global.com or visit: http://www.igi-global.com/publish/.

The Advances in Business Information Systems and Analytics (ABISA) Book Series (ISSN 2327-3275) is published by IGI Global, 701 E. Chocolate Avenue, Hershey, PA 17033-1240, USA, www.igi-global.com. This series is composed of titles available for purchase individually; each title is edited to be contextually exclusive from any other title within the series. For pricing and ordering information please visit http://www.igi-global.com/book-series/advances-business-information-systems-analytics/37155. Postmaster: Send all address changes to above address.

Titles in this Series

For a list of additional titles in this series, please visit: www.igi-global.com

Uncovering Essential Software Artifacts through Business Process Archeology
Ricardo Perez-Castillo (University of Castilla-La Mancha, Spain) and Mario G. Piattini (University of Castilla - La Mancha, Spain)
Business Science Reference • copyright 2014 • 355pp • H/C (ISBN: 9781466646674) • US $185.00 (our price)

A Systemic Perspective to Managing Complexity with Enterprise Architecture
Pallab Saha (National University of Singapore, Singapore)
Business Science Reference • copyright 2014 • 327pp • H/C (ISBN: 9781466645189) • US $185.00 (our price)

Frameworks of IT Prosumption for Business Development
Małgorzata Pańkowska (University of Economics in Katowice, Poland)
Business Science Reference • copyright 2014 • 347pp • H/C (ISBN: 9781466643130) • US $185.00 (our price)

Handbook of Research on Enterprise 2.0 Technological, Social, and Organizational Dimensions
Maria Manuela Cruz-Cunha (Polytechnic Insitute of Cavado and Ave, Portugal) Fernando Moreira (Portucalense University, Portugal) and João Varajão (Universidade de Trás-os-Montes e Alto Douro, Braga, Portugal)
Information Science Reference • copyright 2014 • 603pp • H/C (ISBN: 9781466643734) • US $325.00 (our price)

Managing Enterprise Information Technology Acquisitions Assessing Organizational Preparedness
Harekrishna Misra (Institute of Rural Management Anand, India) and Hakikur Rahman (University of Minho, Portugal)
Business Science Reference • copyright 2013 • 344pp • H/C (ISBN: 9781466642010) • US $185.00 (our price)

Information Systems and Technology for Organizations in a Networked Society
Tomayess Issa (Curtin University, Australia) Pedro Isaías (Universidade Aberta, Portugal) and Piet Kommers (University of Twente, The Netherlands)
Business Science Reference • copyright 2013 • 432pp • H/C (ISBN: 9781466640627) • US $185.00 (our price)

Cases on Enterprise Information Systems and Implementation Stages Learning from the Gulf Region
Fayez Albadri (ADMO-OPCO, UAE)
Information Science Reference • copyright 2013 • 370pp • H/C (ISBN: 9781466622203) • US $185.00 (our price)

Business Intelligence and Agile Methodologies for Knowledge-Based Organizations Cross-Disciplinary Applications
Asim Abdel Rahman El Sheikh (The Arab Academy for Banking and Financial Sciences, Jordan) and Mouhib Alnoukari (Arab International University, Syria)
Business Science Reference • copyright 2012 • 370pp • H/C (ISBN: 9781613500507) • US $185.00 (our price)

IGI GLOBAL
DISSEMINATOR OF KNOWLEDGE
www.igi-global.com

701 E. Chocolate Ave., Hershey, PA 17033
Order online at www.igi-global.com or call 717-533-8845 x100
To place a standing order for titles released in this series, contact: cust@igi-global.com
Mon-Fri 8:00 am - 5:00 pm (est) or fax 24 hours a day 717-533-8661

Kathryn Cormican, *National University of Ireland, Ireland*
Carolina Costa, *University of Aveiro, Portugal*
João Crisóstomo Weyl Albuquerque Costa, *Federal University of Pará, Brazil*
Esmeralda Crespo-Almendros, *University of Granada, Spain*
José Carlos Martins Delgado, *Technical University of Lisbon, Portugal*
João Gonçalo Gomes de Paiva Dias, *University of Aveiro, Portugal*
George Drăgoi, *Polytechnic University of Bucharest, Romania*
João Pedro Vaz Pinheiro Estêvão, *Polytechnic Institute of Guarda, Portugal*
Paulo Fazendeiro, *Instituto de Telecomunicações, Portugal*
Maria João Ferreira, *Universidade Portucalense, Portugal*
Carlos Figueroa, *University of Turabo, Puerto Rico*
Sandra Filipe, *University of Aveiro, Portugal*
Carlos Renato Lisboa Francês, *Federal University of Pará, Brazil*
Roberto Berjón Gallinas, *Universidad Pontificia de Salamanca, Spain*
Monique Goepel, *Berlin Institute of Technology, Germany*
Fotios I. Gogoulos, *National Technical University of Athens, Greece*
Luís Gouveia, *University of Fernando Pessoa, Portugal*
Martin Heitmann, *Berlin Institute of Technology, Germany*
Damjana Jerman, *International Business School Ljubljana, Slovenia*
Dimitra I. Kaklamani, *National Technical University of Athens, Greece*
Francisco J. Liébana-Cabanillas, *University of Granada, Spain*
Georgios V. Lioudakis, *National Technical University of Athens, Greece*
V. Cruz-Machado, *Universidade Nova de Lisboa, Portugal*
Dalton Lopes Martins, *University of Sao Paulo, Brazil*
Francisco Vitorino Martins, *University of Porto, Portugal*
Sandra Morley, *National University of Ireland, Ireland*
Matjaz Mulej, *University of Maribor, Slovenia*
Francisco Muñoz-Leiva, *University of Granada, Spain*
João Negreiros, *University of Saint Joseph, China*
Juan Agustín Fraile Nieto, *Universidad Pontificia de Salamanca, Spain*
Abraham Otero, *University San Pablo, Spain*
Carmen Caba Pérez, *University of Almería, Spain*
Joaquim Sousa Pinto, *Universidade de Aveiro, Portugal*
Vojko Potocan, *University of Maribor, Slovenia*
Cláudio Alex Jorge da Rocha, *University of Amazônia, Brazil & Federal University of Pará, Brazil*
Mário Jorge Ferreira Rodrigues, *Institute of Electronics and Telematics Engineering of Aveiro, Portugal*
Ricardo Gouveia Rodrigues, *University of Beira Interior, Portugal*
Arturo Haro de Rosario, *University of Almería, Spain*
Sebastian Marius Roşu, *Special Telecommunications Service, Romania*
Montserrat Mateos Sánchez, *Universidad Pontificia de Salamanca, Spain*
Neide dos Santos, *State University of Rio de Janeiro, Brazil*
Jacqueline Gladys Guzmán Sequeira, *University of the Republic, Uruguay*
Alberto Manuel Rodrigues da Silva, *Technical University of Lisbon, Portugal*
Aleksandra do Socorro da Silva, *Federal Rural University of Amazônia, Brazil*

Ana Isabel Machado Silva, *Porto Business School, Portugal*
Marisa Carla Barros Fonseca Silva, *Escola Superior de Tecnologia e Gestão de Lamego, Portugal*
Dora Simões, *University of Aveiro, Portugal*
Fawzy Soliman, *University of Technology Sydney, Australia*
Ana Filipa Martins de Sousa, *University of Aveiro, Portugal*
Simona Sternad, *University of Maribor, Slovenia*
António Joaquim da Silva Teixeira, *University of Aveiro, Portugal*
Leonor da Conceição Teixeira, *University of Aveiro, Portugal*
Ana Isabel Perdigão Lopes Pereira Torres, *University of Porto, Portugal*
Iakovos S. Venieris, *National Technical University of Athens, Greece*
Miguel Angel Sánchez Vidales, *Universidad Pontificia de Salamanca, Spain*
Jelena Zascerinska, *Centre for Education and Innovation Research, Latvia*
Bruno Završnik, *University of Maribor, Slovenia*

List of Contributors

Table of Contents

Detailed Table of Contents

Small and Medium-Sized Enterprises (SMEs) are socially and economically important, since they represent 98% of all enterprises, providing around 90 million jobs in the European Union, and contribute to entrepreneurship and innovation. However, SMEs face particular difficulties in order to be competitive in a global world. In recent time, technology applications in different fields, especially Business Intelligence (BI) have been developed rapidly and considered to be one of the most significant uses of information technology. BI is a broad category of applications and technologies for gathering, storing, analyzing, and providing access to data to help enterprise users make better business decisions. This represents a tremendous competitive advantage that allows achieving and exploring the collective intelligence of the organization, enabling contextual, agile, and simplified information exchange and collaboration among distributed workforce and networks of partners and customers, which can be defined as Enterprise 2.0. Despite these advantages, the companies applying such systems may also encounter problems in decision-making processes because of the highly diversified interactions within the systems. Hence, the choice of a suitable BI platform for SMEs is important to take the great advantage of using information technology in all organizational fields. The authors analyze seven open source Business Intelligence tools, free of charge, given that one of the main objectives is to reduce costs and enhance Enterprise 2.0 using new open source technologies.

A wealth of research is associated with virtual teams and collaboration technologies; however, no integrated model is available to guide decision-makers at large organisations in the strategic implementation and management of "virtuality." Whilst collaboration through technology has become commonplace in modern teams, it is not yet clear if Enterprise 2.0 organisations have made changes to accommodate and support this new mode of work. In other words, managing "virtuality" requires supporting tools and research in order to maximise the benefits and diminish the challenges inherent in it. This chapter presents findings of research relating to managing "virtualtiy" that culminates in the development and evaluation of a management model that guides large organisations in implementing and managing virtual teams. The findings demonstrate that there are benefits associated with virtual teamwork; however, a structured approach is essential to realise and maximise such benefits. The authors uncover several critical success factors in managing virtual teams, and they also learned that the implementation of enabling technologies must be carefully planned to ensure successful adoption by the intended audience. This chapter provides practitioners with a structured approach to implementing and managing virtual teams in an Enterprise 2.0 environment. Essential conditions for success are identified, specific organisational level tasks are presented, a process to ensure the introduction of new technologies is documented, and the critical success factors to create and manage virtual teams are synthesised and presented.

Until recently, a company's communications with the public were unidirectional and mostly limited to advertisements in mass media. This gave companies almost complete control over their brand and image. Nowadays, a new set of media, in which the public has similar capabilities for creating content as companies has emerged: social media. The growth of this medium has been exponential, endowing it with a reach that can dwarf traditional mass media. Having or not having a presence in such media is not just a choice of the company. The company's customers and the general public can generate content related to a company without the company's consent. There is no way for the company to avoid it. All they can do is listen to the conversations, engage in them, and try to dampen negative feelings while steering the overall conversation in positive directions. Given the size of social networks and the large number of conversations that they support on a daily basis, manual monitoring is impossible. In this chapter, the authors review and evaluate various tools to support the tasks of monitoring and managing the content of social media that is relevant for a company, a brand, or a product.

To some authors and scientists the concepts effectiveness and efficiency are significantly different. To others, they mean the same; while to a third group the truth about them lies somewhere between these two extremes. This chapter provides an overview of efficiency theories. It finds that the term efficiency covers both doing the right thing and doing the thing right. Efficiency is not limited to internal factors of success, nor should effectiveness only be seen as a term pertaining to the outer factors of success of a human origin, organization source, or inherent in national, local, or international regions.

Before the development of the Internet, there were only a few major media outlets that organizations could use to reach their target audiences. Subsequently, public relations practitioners were able to carefully control all forms of communication. The arrival of new media in the past few years has posed an array of new opportunities but also threats. The public has developed a need to access news and information practically before it exists, and so there is a growing desire to find out what's new via social network sites. With the introduction of social networks, business organizations should identify those social networks representing their target audiences; they should control and participate in them. This chapter describes basic characteristics of social networks and their role for public relations.

Values of individuals, culture of groups, ethics of communities, and the resulting influential norms (i.e. VCEN) are interdependent. VCEN tend to crucially influence development and application of knowledge, skills, talents, and other resources. In the current very competitive and increasingly global economy, organizations and countries become more successful if their economic culture is innovation friendly. Economic culture reflects itself in the economic part of VCEN of nations as well, because organizations, such as enterprises, play a crucial role in a nation's life. National resources are no longer enough, neither is investment, if it is not innovation enhancing. Thus, a new concept of economic VCEN is going to become necessary for people to find a new positive direction beyond the worrisome blind alley of the current economic crisis. The innovation of VCEN is, again, becoming more important than the technological innovation for development of countries and, indeed, for humankind. The contribution discusses two theses: (1) VCEN in organizations is importantly interdependent with the economic culture, and (2) the change of the economic culture in an organization is connected with the changes of the organizing methods and their management.

The past few years have seen a revolutionary transition in the field of project management that enlightened the strength of agile methodologies as a strategic attack towards the progressively faster development rhythms and growing innovation requirements. In this chapter, the authors present a study developed under this context that aims to discuss the suitability of agile project management to multimedia production through a case study focused on an academic context depleted in management formalities, the Laboratory SAPO/UA. The most prominent project of this setting is the SAPO Campus, and its team is analyzed and subjected to an agile project management model. Consequently, the authors anticipate an enhancement to the studied project and the gathering of arguments that empower a clear perspective on the fitness of agile project management to the context of multimedia development.

Web 2.0 technologies have fundamentally reshaped everyday users' perceptions regarding online services by strengthening the importance of individual participation. This profound change is expanding to substantially affect modern enterprise operations and especially corporate information management practices. Well-established business models are upgraded to capture value from the establishment of dynamic coalitions and virtual organizations among remote stakeholders. However, these collaboration formulations dictate the concentration, use, and circulation of corporate information and sensitive personal data, and thus ignite severe security and privacy concerns. Enterprises against this background are more than willing to invest in terms cost and time in order to enforce the necessary countermeasures and thus build and maintain the trustworthiness of involved operations. This chapter studies how legislation and inherent characteristics of this new collaboration paradigm affect the qualities of trust and highlights prominent features of security and privacy protection measures that can deal with emerging trust issues.

Knowledge management systems are a way to help tracking and keeping organizational knowledge. Typically, organizations value is greater than their tangible assets value. Human, structural, and relational capital is essential knowledge but difficult to evaluate because it tends to be tacit and spread in different organizational elements. The relational capital, as tacit knowledge, is not possible to capture its value as from accounting systems. There is a lack of models to evaluate the relational capital of organizations in a network perspective and this research question is: What is the value of this social network? SNARE (Social Network Analysis and Reengineering Environment) is a framework with engineering artifacts that can answer this question. With the aim of evaluating the relational capital of organizations, the authors develop three SNARE components: (1) SNARE-Language – a descriptive UML-based method

new approach in the design of their offices ("bank branch 2.0") and Websites as a way to innovate and diversify business. This chapter explains the innovative strategies of the Urban@ program at the Caja Rural of Granada (Granada, Spain). The history and consolidation of the program, the internal institutional response, and the competition within the banking sector are described and analyzed. In general, the main strategies and achievements of this initiative are: (1) active customer listening, resulting in increased confidence and commitment from the staff; (2) use of up-sale strategies (cross-selling, reduced dropout rates, increased membership advantages), which increase both customer loyalty and customer satisfaction; and 3) a modern, more positive perception of the entity among the general public.

This chapter examines how the concept of social networks can be effectively transferred to a business context and why some of the promises associated with network use might be misleading. Special emphasis is given to the issue of co-determination within social networks in the light of networks' proposed benefits for modern companies. The chapter draws relevant insights from literature research and provides a comparison of social networks, user innovation communities, and company requirements. Findings are illustrated by three respective cases from the context of different networks, communities, as well as from network use in business contexts.

Volume II

Web 2.0 represents the second generation of the Web applications, based on online services collaboration and sharing that promote different ways of interaction between people. These applications provide several collaboration and communication opportunities, like social interaction, feedback, conversation, and networking, thus being a perfect environment for the teaching and learning context. The main goal of this chapter is to present the most used Web 2.0 tools, their major advantages and disadvantages, and their specificity when used in the teaching and learning process. It is believed that their use can greatly improve the teaching and learning process and, consequently, the need to adjust the traditional practice to the new technological paradigm emerges.

necessarily lead to successful ERP usage. ERP systems benefit organizations only to the extent that users accept and utilize them frequently and extensively. To improve the efficiency and effectiveness of ERP systems in the operation phase, organizations need to research the factors that impact user satisfaction. In this area, the Technological Acceptance Model (TAM) proposed by Davis (1989) has been widely used as it can enhance understanding of the influences that increase the efficiency and effectiveness of ERP system use. Regardless of ERP complexity and ERP implementation failure, very few studies have been conducted to examine technology acceptance, especially when dealing with autonomous ERP users and including more external factors, which can influence users' acceptance of ERP system. Because ERP solutions are implemented by different methodologies and some are more present at large organizations than at small and mid-sized organizations, the authors research and compare the importance of external factors of two global solutions—namely, SAP and Microsoft Dynamics NAV—regarding user acceptance. The chapter contributes to the body of knowledge in this specific area.

Many innovative companies pass through a number of transformation stages. The transformation is considered a chain of activities that begins with information that leads to knowledge, then into learning before it can finally be used for innovation. The chapter shows that transformational leadership is a key factor for moving the organisation from being information-based into knowledge-based and then into a learning organisation and an innovative company. The six important characteristics of the transformational leaders for the transformation are shown to be courage to switch off or terminate projects, rewarding performing staff, ability to appropriately time release of products to the market, ability to release products to the market within budget, and ability to inspire and be a role model for other staff. The chapter also shows that there are fourteen transformational leadership attributes that may be considered less critical than the above-mentioned six characteristics. Those non-critical characteristics include: degree of passion for the job, attracting talent, ability to build teams, coaching subordinates, communicating at all levels, driving projects successfully, enabling project-supporting environments, advising others managers, advocating for improvement, encouraging self-goal setting, ability of self rehearsal, ability of self reinforcement, ability of self-observation, and ability of self-expectation.

Technology is fundamental to the youth culture of today and high schools need to integrate it into live classes. This research hopes to provide a better understanding of the present learner styles and the technology impact towards enhancing and enriching the conventional learning process. Hence, the central focus of this writing is based on the four Index Learner Styles (Active VS Reflective, Sensing VS Intuitive, Visual VS Verbal, Sequential VS Global) of Felder and Soloman (1993, 2011) and on the teaching strategies impact that integrates technology (online lessons, blending learning topics, and collaboration software use) as a vehicle in the differentiation of the traditional learning curriculum. The field of experiment is the Portuguese language subject of the 8th grade students at the Portuguese School of Macau, China.

The knowledge era redefines companies' scenarios and workers' profiles, requiring models and tools for Knowledge Management (KM) and Organizational Learning (OL) to respond to external demands. The growth of the Internet and the emergence of Web 2.0 created the conditions for Enterprise 2.0. This chapter analyzes Web 2.0 usefulness in the workplace and presents a software application for KM and OL that aims to support the software development process in software houses. The conclusion discusses controversial issues related to collaboration and competitive markets and presents some reasons for the apparent negative reaction of companies to adopt systems based on social networks.

In this chapter, the authors analyze and discuss how the activity inside a social network impacts on the value of a Learning Object (LO) used in a collaborative e-learning platform. Recent works propose metrics for measuring LO reusability based on a variety of approaches. In this work, they combine and extend these approaches in order to design a valuation strategy which helps to identify the usage of LOs inside a social network. Their proposal is to identify the factors that are relevant for the valuation of a LO and determine which of them can be computed automatically from its context of usage, the level of success of its authors and its metadata. The authors' analysis was performed on a particular social network called LOP (LO Poll) system, which strongly motivates the creation and collaborative valuation of LOs. They present preliminary conclusions obtained from an experiment performed in order to analyze the feasibility of the proposal.

Bearing in mind the new Supply Chain Management (SCM) paradigms, it is important that supply chains be aware of the implementation level of the main practices associated to each SCM paradigm (Lean, Agile, Resilient, and Green, hereafter referred as LARG). The main objective of this chapter is to propose a framework, based on Enterprise 2.0 approach, for global supply chains to assess their LARG index in order to evaluate the leanness, agility, resilience, and greenness of their practices. Enterprise 2.0 technologies and Fuzzy Logic techniques are used as enablers to the proposed LARG evaluation model in the following assessment tasks: 1) determination of an adequate set of Lean, Agile, Resilient, and Green practices; 2) consensual definition of the relative weights of the considered practices; 3) adjustment of the evaluation policy to the particular supply chain; and 4) effective follow-up of the assessment results.

Current enterprise architecture frameworks are inherently committed to the process paradigm by separating the data and application architectures. The N-tier architectural style is a good match to those methods, since it is based on the same separation principle. However, the process paradigm does not satisfy the information hiding and low semantic gap principles heralded by the object-oriented paradigm. This chapter presents an enterprise architecture framework that emphasizes the motivations (stemming from the business), the ends (expectations, what the business needs to achieve), and the means (what is needed to accomplish the ends), as the basis for a method to develop architectures better prepared for changes, either due to maintenance, adaptation, or enterprise integration and interoperability. The main tenets are to refine the ends into goals and objectives, increasing the level of concreteness as much as possible before delving into the design, and to adopt the service paradigm, for which a tierless architectural style is a more suitable match.

Engineering education is facing a challenge to bring e-business closer to student engineers. Enterprise 2.0 application in engineering education advances engineering students' enterprise for the development of innovative products, processes, and services. The aim of the research is to analyze student engineers' Enterprise 2.0 application underpinning elaboration of pedagogical guidelines on student engineers' Enterprise 2.0 application in engineering curriculum. The meaning of key concepts of Enterprise 2.0 and engineering curriculum is studied. Moreover, the study indicates how the steps of the process are related following a logical chain: Enterprise 2.0 → engineering curriculum design → modelling Enterprise 2.0 application in engineering curriculum → empirical study within a multicultural environment. The present empirical research was conducted during the Baltic Summer School "Technical Informatics and Information Technology" in 2009, 2010, and 2011. The findings of the research allow drawing the conclusions that student engineers' Enterprise 2.0 application in engineering curriculum is efficient.

This chapter summarizes several previous studies on the analysis of social networks and presents some challenges in monitoring and evaluating large-scale training programs that make use of social networks. The main objective is to understand the dynamics and identify how information is shared among the participating agents of the training program. In this regard, the authors present various algorithms that apply metrics to social network analysis to assess the evolution of networks throughout the training process, and specifically, to discuss the application of these metrics in the evaluation of large-scale training programs for digital inclusion.

Enterprise 2.0 aims to help employees, customers, and suppliers collaborate, share, and organize information. As governments are relevant partners for enterprises (legislation, contracts, etc.) e-government platforms need to be ready for Enterprise 2.0 to what concerns e-government interactions. The public sector holds huge quantities of information and just a small proportion is relevant to each enterprise. Enterprises should only be confronted with relevant information and not flooded with lots of data. This implies data organization with semantic description and services using open standards. The goal is to build a durable information infrastructure for government that can be readily accessed by enterprises. The authors propose a conceptual model for government information provisioning. The rationale for this proposal is to motivate the creation of durable, standard, and open government information infrastructures. The model acquires information from natural language documents and represents it using ontology. A proof-of-concept prototype and its preliminary results are presented.

Preface

This handbook of research represents a collection of the most recent developments on the technological, organizational, and social dimensions of Enterprise 2.0 that dictate a paradigm shift in organizations, society, and people. It covers the following dimensions:

- The technological dimension, addressing: emerging technologies, emerging architectures, Web 2.0 tools, standards and reference models, apps and platforms technology, and security.
- The impact on organizations, society, and individuals, covering: new business models, collaborative work, culture and internal communication, mobile enterprise people, social networks, studies on adoption, studies of impact, critical success factors, and level of preparedness of SME.
- Applications and solutions: application to different sectors, from business to government services, from education to eHealth, relevant developments, and technical considerations.

ORGANIZATION OF THE HANDBOOK

This handbook is a compilation of 33 contributions to the discussion of the main issues, challenges, opportunities, and developments related with Enterprise 2.0. They are arranged in a very comprehensive way in order to disseminate current achievements and practical solutions and applications. These 33 chapters are written by a group of 76 authors that include many internationally renowned and experienced researchers and specialists in the e-Business field and a set of younger authors, showing a promising potential for research and development. Contributions come from all over the world and from academia, research institutions, and industry, representing a good and comprehensive representation of the state-of-the-art approaches and developments that address the many dimensions of this quickly evolving theme.

The *Handbook of Research on Enterprise 2.0: Technological, Social, and Organizational Dimensions* is organized in three sections:

- **Section 1:** The Technological Dimension
- **Section 2:** Impact on Organizations, Society, and Individuals
- **Section 3:** Applications and Solutions

The first section, "The Technological Dimension," addressing technologies supporting Enterprise 2.0 applications, comprises five chapters that address relevant research and development contributions to the field of Enterprise 2.0, summarized below. Contributions include: "Emerging Business Intelligence Technologies for SMEs," "Managing 'Virtuality': An Integrated Model for the Implementation and Management of Virtual Teams," "A Review of Tools for Overcoming the Challenge of Monitoring of Social Media," "E-Health Sites Development Using Open Source Software and OMT Methodology as Support for the Family Doctors Activities: A Romanian Case Study," and "CommunicaME: A New Proposal for Facilitating Communication using NFC."

"Emerging Business Intelligence Technologies for SMEs"

Small and Medium-Sized Enterprises (SMEs) are socially and economically important, since they represent 98% of all enterprises, providing around 90 million jobs in the European Union, and contribute to entrepreneurship and innovation. However, SMEs face particular difficulties in order to be competitive in a global world. In recent time, technology applications in different fields, especially Business Intelligence (BI) have been developed rapidly and considered to be one of the most significant uses of information technology. BI is a broad category of applications and technologies for gathering, storing, analyzing, and providing access to data to help enterprise users make better business decisions. This represents a tremendous competitive advantage that allows achieving and exploring the collective intelligence of the organization, enabling contextual, agile, and simplified information exchange and collaboration among distributed workforce and networks of partners and customers, which can be defined as Enterprise 2.0. Despite these advantages, the companies applying such systems may also encounter problems in decision-making processes because of the highly diversified interactions within the systems. Hence, the choice of a suitable BI platform for SMEs is important to take the great advantage of using information technology in all organizational fields. The authors analyze seven open source Business Intelligence tools, free of charge, given that one of the main objectives is to reduce costs and enhance Enterprise 2.0 using new open source technologies.

"Managing 'Virtuality': An Integrated Model for the Implementation and Management of Virtual Teams"

A wealth of research is associated with virtual teams and collaboration technologies; however, no integrated model is available to guide decision-makers at large organisations in the strategic implementation and management of "virtuality." Whilst collaboration through technology has become commonplace in modern teams, it is not yet clear if Enterprise 2.0 organisations have made changes to accommodate and support this new mode of work. In other words, managing "virtuality" requires supporting tools and research in order to maximise the benefits and diminish the challenges inherent in it. This chapter presents findings of research relating to managing "virtualtiy" that culminates in the development and evaluation of a management model that guides large organisations in implementing and managing virtual teams. The findings demonstrate that there are benefits associated with virtual teamwork; however, a structured approach is essential to realise and maximise such benefits. The authors uncover several critical success factors in managing virtual teams, and they also learned that the implementation of enabling technologies must be carefully planned to ensure successful adoption by the intended audience. This chapter provides practitioners with a structured approach to implementing and managing virtual teams in an Enterprise 2.0 environment. Essential conditions for success are identified, specific organisational level tasks are presented, a process to ensure the introduction of new technologies is documented, and the critical success factors to create and manage virtual teams are synthesised and presented.

"A Review of Tools for Overcoming the Challenge of Monitoring of Social Media"

Until recently, a company's communications with the public were unidirectional and mostly limited to advertisements in mass media. This gave companies almost complete control over their brand and image. Nowadays a new set of media in which the public has similar capabilities for creating content as companies has emerged: social media. The growth of this medium has been exponential, endowing it with a reach that can dwarf traditional mass media. Having or not having a presence in such media is not just a choice of the company. The company's customers and the general public can generate content related to a company without the company's consent. There is no way for the company to avoid it. All they can do is listen to the conversations, engage in them, and try to dampen negative feelings while steering the overall conversation in positive directions. Given the size of social networks and the large number of conversations that they support on a daily basis, manual monitoring is impossible. In this chapter, the authors review and evaluate various tools to support the tasks of monitoring and managing the content of social media that is relevant for a company, a brand, or a product.

"E-Health Sites Development Using Open Source Software and OMT Methodology as Support for the Family Doctors' Activities: A Romanian Case Study"

E-health is the generic term used for the set of tools based on information and communication technology used to help prevent, diagnose, treat, and monitor the health and lifestyles and to improve these processes. These considerations are the starting point of this chapter, which presents a Website development solution for family doctors' consulting-rooms to meet the needs of potential patients, based on Object Modeling Technique (OMT) and Open Source Software (OSS) in a metropolitan area network infrastructure. Development of ICT leaves much more freedom to the consultants to accommodate organizations to other influences, both internal and external.

"CommunicaME: A New Proposal for Facilitating Communication Using NFC"

In a society that is clearly influenced by new technology, new advances in mobile technology have yielded important changes in the way users interact with information systems and contextual information. There is a need to provide technological solutions that help users communicate more easily. In this chapter, a novel solution that makes it easier for the elderly to use mobile phones is proposed. The senior population is rapidly growing; they represent 16-17% of the total population in developed countries. The use of a mobile device presents two large obstacles for this group: problems from disabilities due to age and problems associated with the lack of familiarity with mobile technology. The combined use of contactless technologies such as NFC and MiFARE eliminates the barriers encountered by older individuals. These technologies make it possible to use basic services of a mobile telephone, such as placing a call or sending a message, in a way that is easy, user friendly, and intuitive. The CommunicaME system makes it possible to place a call or send a SMS on a mobile by simply moving it closer to a contactless tag. The use of contactless technologies helps the user to carry out their daily tasks, and it also provides a new method of mobile communication that is both quick and secure. The results obtained with the defined and implemented prototype are presented in this chapter.

The seventeen chapters of section 2, "Impact on Organizations, Society, and Individuals," introduce the efficiency and impact of Enterprise 2.0 theories and practices. Section 2 consists of: "The Impact of Enterprise 2.0 Principles on Business Processes: Emphasizing Human Decisions," "Efficiency Theories: The State of the Art," "Use of Social Network for Business in Public Relations," "Impact of Economic Culture on the Development of Enterprises," "Agile Management for Multimedia: A Case Study," "Trust in an Enterprise World: A Survey," "How to Value and Monitor the Relational Capital of Knowledge-Intensive Organizations," "Critical Success Factors in Enterprise 2.0: The Importance of Business Performance," "The Influence of (Online) Social Networks on Workers' Attitudes and Behaviours in Higher Education Institutions," "Innovation and Diversification Policies in the Banking Sector: The Case of the Urban@ Program," "Internal Social Networks: The Danger of Misleading Promises," "The Impact of Web 2.0 in the Teaching and Learning Process," "Experts vs. Novices: Influence of Promotional Benefit Type on their Online Purchase Intention," "The Importance of ICT in the Social Support Networks and in the Citizenship of the Portuguese Elderly," "Impact of 2.0 on Contemporary Marketing," "Comparative Analysis of Acceptance Factors for SAP and Microsoft Dynamics NAV ERP Solutions in their Maturity Use Phase: Enterprise 2.0 Issues," and "Attributes of Innovation Leaders."

"The Impact of Enterprise 2.0 Principles on Business Processes: Emphasizing Human Decisions"

The impact of Enterprise 2.0 principles on business processes is a hot research topic and involves several aspects. In particular, this chapter addresses knowledge-intensive processes in which participants are not considered as mere resources needed to carry out tasks that are not automatable, but their involvement is required at a higher level where they can take decisions that affect the control flow of the process. Participants must be given as much information as possible on the decisions they have to take and on the business entities to be acted on and produced by the tasks they have to perform. For this reason, this chapter proposes a business process notation that integrates the data flow and the control flow and focuses on three kinds of decisions, referred to as data selection, task selection, and performer selection. It also illustrates the structure of to-do lists, which are the major interface between the participants and their tasks.

"Efficiency Theories: The State-of-the-Art"

To some authors and scientists the concepts effectiveness and efficiency are significantly different. To others, they mean the same; while to a third group the truth about them lies somewhere between these two extremes. This chapter provides an overview of efficiency theories. It finds that the term efficiency covers both doing the right thing and doing the thing right. Efficiency is not limited to internal factors of success, nor should effectiveness only be seen as a term pertaining to the outer factors of success of a human origin, organization source, or inherent in national, local, or international regions.

"Use of Social Network for Business in Public Relations"

Before the development of the Internet, there were only a few major media outlets that organizations could use to reach their target audiences. Subsequently, public relations practitioners were able to carefully control all forms of communication. The arrival of new media in the past few years has posed an array of new opportunities but also threats. The public has developed a need to access news and information practically before it exists, and so there is a growing desire to find out what's new via social network sites. With the introduction of social networks, business organizations should identify those social networks representing their target audiences; they should control and participate in them. This chapter describes basic characteristics of social networks and their role for public relations.

"Impact of Economic Culture on the Development of Enterprises"

Values of individuals, culture of groups, ethics of communities, and the resulting influential norms (i.e. VCEN) are interdependent. VCEN tend to crucially influence development and application of knowledge, skills, talents, and other resources. In the current very competitive and increasingly global economy, organizations and countries become more successful if their economic culture is innovation friendly. Economic culture reflects itself in the economic part of VCEN of nations as well, because organizations, such as enterprises, play a crucial role in a nation's life. National resources are no longer enough, neither is investment, if it is not innovation enhancing. Thus, a new concept of economic VCEN is going to become necessary for people to find a new positive direction beyond the worrisome blind alley of the current economic crisis. The innovation of VCEN is, again, becoming more important than the technological innovation for development of countries and, indeed, for humankind. The contribution discusses two theses: (1) VCEN in organizations is importantly interdependent with the economic culture, and (2) the change of the economic culture in an organization is connected with the changes of the organizing methods and their management.

"Agile Management for Multimedia: A Case Study"

The past few years have seen a revolutionary transition in the field of project management that enlightened the strength of agile methodologies as a strategic attack towards the progressively faster development rhythms and growing innovation requirements. In this chapter, the authors present a study developed under this context that aims to discuss the suitability of agile project management to multimedia production through a case study focused on an academic context depleted in management formalities, the Laboratory SAPO/UA. The most prominent project of this setting is the SAPO Campus, and its team is analyzed and subjected to an agile project management model. Consequently, the authors anticipate an enhancement to the studied project and the gathering of arguments that empower a clear perspective on the fitness of agile project management to the context of multimedia development.

"Trust in an Enterprise World: A Survey"

Web 2.0 technologies have fundamentally reshaped everyday users' perceptions regarding online services by strengthening the importance of individual participation. This profound change is expanding to substantially affect modern enterprise operations and especially corporate information management practices. Well-established business models are upgraded to capture value from the establishment of dynamic coalitions and virtual organizations among remote stakeholders. However, these collaboration formulations dictate the concentration, use, and circulation of corporate information and sensitive personal data, and thus ignite severe security and privacy concerns. Enterprises against this background are more than willing to invest in terms cost and time in order to enforce the necessary countermeasures and thus build and maintain the trustworthiness of involved operations. This chapter studies how legislation and inherent characteristics of this new collaboration paradigm affect the qualities of trust and highlights prominent features of security and privacy protection measures that can deal with emerging trust issues.

"How to Value and Monitor the Relational Capital of Knowledge-Intensive Organizations"

Knowledge management systems are a way to help tracking and keeping organizational knowledge. Typically, organizations value is greater than their tangible assets value. Human, structural, and relational capital is essential knowledge but difficult to evaluate because it tends to be tacit and spread in different organizational elements. The relational capital, as tacit knowledge, is not possible to capture its value as from accounting systems. There is a lack of models to evaluate the relational capital of organizations in a network perspective and this research question is: *What is the value of this social network?* SNARE (Social Network Analysis and Reengineering Environment) is a framework with engineering artifacts that can answer this question. With the aim of evaluating the relational capital of organizations, the authors develop three SNARE components: (1) SNARE-Language – a descriptive *UML-based* method that provides a representation of an abstract social network structure able to be extended and applied to organizations; (2) SNARE-RCO – a model to determine the relational capital of organizations; and (3) SNARE-Explorer – based on SNARE-Language, is a tool for social networks visualization able to simulate or use real social network scenarios. It also uses SNARE-RCO model to compute the value of the organizational relational capital. The chapter presents an approach for the measurement of the value of organizations' networks.

"Critical Success Factors in Enterprise 2.0: The Importance of Business Performance"

While evangelists and enthusiasts of Enterprise 2.0 praise the benefits of the use of social software in the workplace, the sceptics are not that convinced and some draw attention to the failures of the Knowledge Management concept and tools that were trendy some years ago. In parallel, board members and top management question the true business benefits of Enterprise 2.0 and demand proof of the potential business value prior to giving a green light to this type of investment. If it is true that some of the benefits of Enterprise 2.0 are intangible and therefore harder to measure, the impact on business performance should be observable and consequently measurable. This chapter reflects on the importance of addressing the topic of business performance when it comes to social software in the enterprise. It also discusses the importance of integrating social software into the flow of work in order to drive adoption and sustained use.

"The Influence of (Online) Social Networks on Workers' Attitudes and Behaviours in Higher Education Institutions"

According to the literature, social relationships have a positive influence on work-related attitudes and behaviours. Taking into account that Online Social Networks (OSNs), brought about by Web 2.0, have become an international phenomena and have a considerable impact on the way people communicate and interact with each other, the chapter's purpose is to evaluate the effect that the use of OSNs has on the worker's attitudes and behaviours. In this way, the authors use a questionnaire to evaluate the attitudes of 157 faculty members in Higher Education Institutions (HEI). To assess the use of OSNs by faculty members, they use a binary variable. After analysing and discussing the results, the authors conclude that the use of OSNs influences the workers' performance traits. The relations they propose in what concerns the workers' attitudes are all empirically proven. At last, the authors describe the study limitations and suggest some perspectives for future research.

"Innovation and Diversification Policies in the Banking Sector: The Case of the Urban@ Program"

This chapter describes innovation and diversification policies (i + d) and analyzes the main drivers of innovation in financial institutions. In addition, recent examples of financial innovations and their effect on banking policies are discussed. Specifically, the Internet has been the key to enabling financial institutions to extend and optimize their business by improving the information and services they can offer to their customers and prospects. Due to innovations and changes, the banking sector now takes a new approach in the design of their offices ("bank branch 2.0") and Websites as a way to innovate and diversify business. This chapter explains the innovative strategies of the Urban@ program at the Caja Rural of Granada (Granada, Spain). The history and consolidation of the program, the internal institutional response, and the competition within the banking sector are described and analyzed. In general, the main strategies and achievements of this initiative are: (1) active customer listening, resulting in increased confidence and commitment from the staff; (2) use of up-sale strategies (cross-selling, reduced dropout rates, increased membership advantages), which increase both customer loyalty and customer satisfaction; and 3) a modern, more positive perception of the entity among the general public.

"Internal Social Networks: The Danger of Misleading Promises"

This chapter examines how the concept of social networks can be effectively transferred to a business context and why some of the promises associated with network use might be misleading. Special emphasis is given to the issue of co-determination within social networks in the light of networks' proposed benefits for modern companies. The chapter draws relevant insights from literature research and provides a comparison of social networks, user innovation communities, and company requirements. Findings are illustrated by three respective cases from the context of different networks, communities, as well as from network use in business contexts.

"The Impact of Web 2.0 in the Teaching and Learning Process"

Web 2.0 represents the second generation of the Web applications, based on online services collaboration and sharing that promote different ways of interaction between people. These applications provide several collaboration and communication opportunities, like social interaction, feedback, conversation, and networking, thus being a perfect environment for the teaching and learning context. The main goal of this chapter is to present the most used Web 2.0 tools, their major advantages and disadvantages, and their specificity when used in the teaching and learning process. It is believed that their use can greatly improve the teaching and learning process and, consequently, the need to adjust the traditional practice to the new technological paradigm emerges.

"Experts vs. Novices: Influence of Promotional Benefit Type on their Online Purchase Intention"

As each year sees an increase in the number of Internet users, so too the percentage of purchases made online increases. It is for this reason that firms are showing a growing interest in designing effective communication strategies that help to achieve their online business objectives. Online sales promotion is one of the most widely used communication tools on the Internet. However, there is little research into its effect on purchase intention and how this effect may vary depending on the type of incentive offered and the consumer's level of experience in using the Internet. This chapter seeks to analyze which types of online sales promotions (utilitarian vs. hedonic) are most effective at triggering online purchasing and whether the user's past experience of the Internet is capable of moderating the effect of the type of incentive on online purchasing.

"The Importance of ICT in the Social Support Networks and in the Citizenship of the Portuguese Elderly"

The Information and Communication Technologies (ICT) contain properties that easily convert into solutions for people with special needs, contributing to their inclusion in everyday life. The possibility to intervene and participate in acts of communication in interpersonal settings and distance learning, or simply the possibility of using a device that simulates the vocalization of requests, greetings, and caresses gain a redoubled sense in the efforts to include citizens with special needs, as it does to the senior citizens, in societies attempting to promote equal opportunities among its members. This chapter focuses on the interaction between the elderly and the information and communication technologies and the impact that that interaction has on their participation in society.

"Impact of 2.0 on Contemporary Marketing"

Contemporary marketing recognizes the scope and complexities of marketing activities. It is a multi-dimensional and a dynamic concept, known as holistic marketing, that asks and allows for the support systems in order to permanently connect to the parties, to create value and long-term relationships among all. In this context, this chapter presents a wide review about conceptualization of relationship marketing and its evolution and integration within the broader concept of contemporary marketing. It highlights that the development of a program for implementing and managing a successful Customer Relationship

Management (CRM) system is an essential part of a strategic contemporary marketing plan. Additionally, it is imperative to assess it to better demonstrate its success or failure. The metrics to do this are also revisited in this chapter. Still, the emerging capabilities of CRM systems using Internet technologies are putting tremendous challenges on organizations and their human resources. Reference is made to some social media tools that can be a cheap and useful support in marketing strategies.

"Comparative Analysis of Acceptance Factors for SAP and Microsoft Dynamics NAV ERP Solutions in their Maturity Use Phase: Enterprise 2.0 Issues"

Enterprise Resource Planning (ERP) systems have been implemented in numerous organizations over the last decade. However, research indicates that successful implementation of ERP solutions does not necessarily lead to successful ERP usage. ERP systems benefit organizations only to the extent that users accept and utilize them frequently and extensively. To improve the efficiency and effectiveness of ERP systems in the operation phase, organizations need to research the factors that impact user satisfaction. In this area, the Technological Acceptance Model (TAM) proposed by Davis (1989) has been widely used as it can enhance understanding of the influences that increase the efficiency and effectiveness of ERP system use. Regardless of ERP complexity and ERP implementation failure, very few studies have been conducted to examine technology acceptance, especially when dealing with autonomous ERP users and including more external factors, which can influence users' acceptance of ERP system. Because ERP solutions are implemented by different methodologies and some are more present at large organizations than at small and mid-sized organizations, the authors research and compare the importance of external factors of two global solutions—namely, SAP and Microsoft Dynamics NAV—regarding user acceptance. The chapter contributes to the body of knowledge in this specific area.

"Attributes of Innovation Leaders"

Many innovative companies pass through a number of transformation stages. The transformation is considered a chain of activities that begins with information that leads to knowledge, then into learning before it can finally be used for innovation. The chapter shows that transformational leadership is a key factor for moving the organisation from being information-based into knowledge-based and then into a learning organisation and an innovative company. The six important characteristics of the transformational leaders for the transformation are shown to be courage to switch off or terminate projects, rewarding performing staff, ability to appropriately time release of products to the market, ability to release products to the market within budget, and ability to inspire and be a role model for other staff. The chapter also shows that there are fourteen transformational leadership attributes that may be considered less critical than the above-mentioned six characteristics. Those non-critical characteristics include: degree of passion for the job, attracting talent, ability to build teams, coaching subordinates, communicating at all levels, driving projects successfully, enabling project-supporting environments, advising others managers, advocating for improvement, encouraging self-goal setting, ability of self rehearsal, ability of self reinforcement, ability of self-observation, and ability of self-expectation.

Finally, Section 3, "Applications and Solutions," consists of a comprehensive collection of eleven chapters presenting relevant applications to different sectors of activity and target uses, such as "The Portuguese School of Macao, China: A Traditional/Web 2.0 Assessment Facing Different Learning Styles," "Visibility of the Airport Sector: Web 2.0 and Social Communication Networks," "Online Social Networks: Recommendation Diffusion and Co-Consumption Influence," "The Evolving Value of eTourism for Suppliers and Visitors," "Organizational Learning and Web 2.0 Technologies: Improving the Planning and Organization of a Software Development Process," "Valuing Learning Objects Shared in an Online Community," "A Framework Proposal to Assess the LARG Index of a Supply Chain in a Fuzzy Context," "Objective-Oriented Modeling of Enterprises under the Service Paradigm," "Enterprise 2.0 in Engineering Curriculum," "Brazilian Government's Training Network for Digital Inclusion: Analysis of Strategies for Improving Interactivity," and "Towards E-Government Information Platforms for Enterprise 2.0."

"The Portuguese School of Macao, China: A Traditional/ Web 2.0 Assessment Facing Different Learning Styles"

Technology is fundamental to the youth culture of today and high schools need to integrate it into live classes. This research hopes to provide a better understanding of the present learner styles and the technology impact towards enhancing and enriching the conventional learning process. Hence, the central focus of this writing is based on the four Index Learner Styles (Active VS Reflective, Sensing VS Intuitive, Visual VS Verbal, Sequential VS Global) of Felder and Soloman (1993, 2011) and on the teaching strategies impact that integrates technology (online lessons, blending learning topics, and collaboration software use) as a vehicle in the differentiation of the traditional learning curriculum. The field of experiment is the Portuguese language subject of the 8th grade students at the Portuguese School of Macau, China. One online survey and four tests (two for each class) are carried out to check whether the e-Learning perspective will benefit student learning in this new surrounded generation of mobile devices. Still, the main purpose relies on the learning style identification of high school scholars and to raise awareness of those personal characteristics to facilitate future development on personal learning strategies. Some other related topics are also highlighted such as Web 1.0 to Web 4.0 evolution and learning distance topics.

"Visibility of the Airport Sector: Web 2.0 and Social Communication Networks"

The aim of this chapter is to analyse the use of social communication media and Web 2.0 tools at airports to determine whether these technologies are being used as a means of raising the airports' visibility, enhancing their level of e-participation and improving corporate dialogue. In addition, the authors seek to determine which variables influence the use and development of these tools. The results obtained reveal a moderate use of Web 2.0 tools by airports, with the most noteworthy finding being their presence in social networks and the use of the latter as channels through which to increase e-participation.

"Online Social Networks: Recommendation Diffusion and Co-Consumption Influence"

The chapter is conceptual, based on analysis and synthesis of social network theory and e-consumer literature. Despite a broad spectrum of disciplines that investigate social networks and the interest of marketing practitioners in the consequences of social networks, there are still areas open for research into networked-consumer behavior in marketing. Based on previous theoretical and empirical research, this study examines and discusses the influence of social network structure and ties in matched dyads, recommendation diffusion, social contagion and co-consumption influence, and individual motivations to spread market information. The chapter proposes a theory of matched dyadic ties in close networks of connections as a proxy for information about the potential market that is difficult and expensive for businesses to measure or access directly.

"The Evolving Value of eTourism for Suppliers and Visitors"

The tourism industry is known to have an extensive use of the Internet, both on the supply and on the demand side. The steady and fast emergence of the Internet has dramatically changed the business processes within the sector, forcing suppliers and intermediaries to adapt to a scenario in which visitors have multiple and more flexible choices regarding the search, planning, booking, and purchase of tourism services and products. This chapter explores the main impacts and trends that the dynamic use of the Internet within the tourism sector—the so-called *eTourism*—has originated in each of the sector's main stakeholders, including suppliers, intermediaries, destination management organizations, and tourists.

"Organizational Learning and Web 2.0 Technologies: Improving the Planning and Organization of a Software Development Process"

The knowledge era redefines companies' scenarios and workers' profiles, requiring models and tools for Knowledge Management (KM) and Organizational Learning (OL) to respond to external demands. The growth of the Internet and the emergence of Web 2.0 created the conditions for Enterprise 2.0. This chapter analyzes Web 2.0 usefulness in the workplace and presents a software application for KM and OL that aims to support the software development process in software houses. The conclusion discusses controversial issues related to collaboration and competitive markets and presents some reasons for the apparent negative reaction of companies to adopt systems based on social networks.

"Valuing Learning Objects Shared in an Online Community"

In this chapter, the authors analyze and discuss how the activity inside a social network impacts on the value of a Learning Object (LO) used in a collaborative e-learning platform. Recent works propose metrics for measuring LO reusability based on a variety of approaches. In this work, they combine and extend these approaches in order to design a valuation strategy which helps to identify the usage of LOs inside a social network. Their proposal is to identify the factors that are relevant for the valuation of a LO and determine which of them can be computed automatically from its context of usage, the level of success of its authors and its metadata. The authors' analysis was performed on a particular social network called LOP (LO Poll) system, which strongly motivates the creation and collaborative valuation of LOs. They present preliminary conclusions obtained from an experiment performed in order to analyze the feasibility of the proposal.

"A Framework Proposal to Assess the LARG Index of a Supply Chain in a Fuzzy Context"

Bearing in mind the new Supply Chain Management (SCM) paradigms, it is important that supply chains be aware of the implementation level of the main practices associated to each SCM paradigm (Lean, Agile, Resilient, and Green, hereafter referred as LARG). The main objective of this chapter is to propose a framework, based on Enterprise 2.0 approach, for global supply chains to assess their LARG index in order to evaluate the leanness, agility, resilience, and greenness of their practices. Enterprise 2.0 technologies and Fuzzy Logic techniques are used as enablers to the proposed LARG evaluation model in the following assessment tasks: 1) determination of an adequate set of Lean, Agile, Resilient, and Green practices; 2) consensual definition of the relative weights of the considered practices; 3) adjustment of the evaluation policy to the particular supply chain; and 4) effective follow-up of the assessment results.

"Objective-Oriented Modeling of Enterprises under the Service Paradigm"

Current enterprise architecture frameworks are inherently committed to the process paradigm by separating the data and application architectures. The N-tier architectural style is a good match to those methods, since it is based on the same separation principle. However, the process paradigm does not satisfy the information hiding and low semantic gap principles heralded by the object-oriented paradigm. This chapter presents an enterprise architecture framework that emphasizes the motivations (stemming from the business), the ends (expectations, what the business needs to achieve), and the means (what is needed to accomplish the ends), as the basis for a method to develop architectures better prepared for changes, either due to maintenance, adaptation, or enterprise integration and interoperability. The main tenets are to refine the ends into goals and objectives, increasing the level of concreteness as much as possible before delving into the design, and to adopt the service paradigm, for which a tierless architectural style is a more suitable match.

"Enterprise 2.0 in Engineering Curriculum"

Engineering education is facing a challenge to bring e-business closer to student engineers. Enterprise 2.0 application in engineering education advances engineering students' enterprise for the development of innovative products, processes, and services. The aim of the research is to analyze student engineers' Enterprise 2.0 application underpinning elaboration of pedagogical guidelines on student engineers' Enterprise 2.0 application in engineering curriculum. The meaning of key concepts of *Enterprise 2.0* and *engineering curriculum* is studied. Moreover, the study indicates how the steps of the process are related following a logical chain: Enterprise 2.0 → engineering curriculum design → modelling Enterprise 2.0 application in engineering curriculum → empirical study within a multicultural environment. The present empirical research was conducted during the Baltic Summer School "Technical Informatics and Information Technology" in 2009, 2010, and 2011. The findings of the research allow drawing the conclusions that student engineers' Enterprise 2.0 application in engineering curriculum is efficient.

"Brazilian Government's Training Network for Digital Inclusion: Analysis of Strategies for Improving Interactivity"

This chapter summarizes several previous studies on the analysis of social networks and presents some challenges in monitoring and evaluating large-scale training programs that make use of social networks. The main objective is to understand the dynamics and identify how information is shared among the participating agents of the training program. In this regard, the authors present various algorithms that apply metrics to social network analysis to assess the evolution of networks throughout the training process, and specifically, to discuss the application of these metrics in the evaluation of large-scale training programs for digital inclusion.

"Towards E-Government Information Platforms for Enterprise 2.0"

Enterprise 2.0 aims to help employees, customers, and suppliers collaborate, share, and organize information. As governments are relevant partners for enterprises (legislation, contracts, etc.) e-government platforms need to be ready for Enterprise 2.0 to what concerns e-government interactions. The public sector holds huge quantities of information and just a small proportion is relevant to each enterprise. Enterprises should only be confronted with relevant information and not flooded with lots of data. This implies data organization with semantic description and services using open standards. The goal is to build a durable information infrastructure for government that can be readily accessed by enterprises. The authors propose a conceptual model for government information provisioning. The rationale for this proposal is to motivate the creation of durable, standard, and open government information infrastructures. The model acquires information from natural language documents and represents it using ontology. A proof-of-concept prototype and its preliminary results are presented.

EXPECTATIONS

Within these 33 chapters the reader is faced with the discussions and confirmation of the relevance and impact of this hot topic, providing professionals, researchers, and scholars with some of the most advanced research developments, solutions, state-of-the-art enabling technologies, discussions, and case studies on mobility and computing.

The handbook is expected to support a professional audience of top managers, IT professionals, technology solution providers, and an academic audience (teachers, researchers, and students, mainly of post-graduate studies). As an academic tool, it can be a support to disciplines of post-graduate studies on IT/IS.

We hope you find it useful. Enjoy your reading and study!

Maria Manuela Cruz-Cunha
Polytechnic Insitute of Cavado and Ave, Portugal

Fernando Moreira
Portucalense University, Portugal

João Varajão
Universidade de Trás-os-Montes e Alto Douro, Portugal

Acknowledgment

Editing a book is a hard but compensating and enriching task, as it involves a set of different activities, like contact with authors and reviewers, discussion and exchange of ideas and experiences, process management, organization and integration of contents, and many more, with the permanent objective of creating a book that meets the public's expectations. This task cannot be accomplished without the help and support of many sources. As editors, we would like to acknowledge the help, support, and belief of all who made this creation possible.

First of all, this book would not have been possible without the ongoing professional support of the team of professionals at IGI-Global. We are grateful to Dr. Mehdi Khosrow-Pour, Jan Travers, Kristin Klinger, and Erika Carter for the opportunity and belief in this project. A very special mention of gratitude is due to Joel Gamon, Development Editor, for his professional support and friendly words of advice, encouragement, and prompt guidance. We also address our recognition and appreciation to all the staff at IGI Global, whose contributions throughout the process of production and making this book available all over the world was invaluable.

We are grateful to all the authors for their insights and excellent contributions to this book. We are also grateful to the authors who simultaneously served as referees for chapters written by other authors, as well as to the external referees and to the members of the editorial advisory board for their insights, valuable contributions, prompt collaboration, and constructive comments. Thank you all, authors and reviewers, you made this book! The communication and exchange of views within this truly global group of recognized individuals from the scientific domain and from industry was an enriching and exciting experience!

Thank you.

Maria Manuela Cruz-Cunha
Polytechnic Insitute of Cavado and Ave, Portugal

Fernando Moreira
Portucalense University, Portugal

João Varajão
Universidade de Trás-os-Montes e Alto Douro, Portugal

Chapter 17
The Impact of Web 2.0 in the Teaching and Learning Process

Carolina Costa
University of Aveiro, Portugal

Leonor Teixeira
University of Aveiro, Portugal & Institute of Electronics and Telematics Engineering of Aveiro (IEETA), Portugal

Helena Alvelos
University of Aveiro, Portugal & Governance, Competitiveness and Public Policies (GOVCOPP) Research Unit, Portugal

ABSTRACT

Web 2.0 represents the second generation of the Web applications, based on online services collaboration and sharing that promote different ways of interaction between people. These applications provide several collaboration and communication opportunities, like social interaction, feedback, conversation, and networking, thus being a perfect environment for the teaching and learning context. The main goal of this chapter is to present the most used Web 2.0 tools, their major advantages and disadvantages, and their specificity when used in the teaching and learning process. It is believed that their use can greatly improve the teaching and learning process and, consequently, the need to adjust the traditional practice to the new technological paradigm emerges.

INTRODUCTION

In recent years, the use of Information and Communication Technologies (ICTs) has grown drastically in education, providing access to information in an easier and more convenient way. These ICTs support the process of teaching and learning, and are the usual source of the modalities of Distance Education (DE). The diversity of interactive multimedia equipment, as well as the existence of the broadband communication networks, provide students with a set of endless information and education arrangements underpinned by new ICTs. On the other hand, the evolution of Web technologies from Web 1.0 to Web 2.0 has also been an important factor for

DOI: 10.4018/978-1-4666-4373-4.ch017

the study of new models of teaching and learning. Nowadays, teachers must not only transmit knowledge using traditional methods, but must use appropriate methods adapted to the new learning standards of new students, called digital natives (Prensky, 2001a). This new phenomenon is not intended to underestimate the role of teachers in the classroom, but rather to adjust the traditional approaches to the new technological paradigm, in order to contribute to the improvement of teaching and learning process. In this context, ICTs in education are able to highlight the role of education platforms or Learning Management Systems (LMS) (such as Moodle) as tools to support the teaching and learning process. In most cases, these platforms are used as a repository of documents available for consultation by teachers and students.

Web 2.0 is a second generation of Web based on services online, collaboration and sharing and represents a paradigm shift in the way the Internet is used. It involves a more open approach to the Internet, and user generated contents, that are posted using tools such as Blogs, Wikis, Social Networks, Social Bookmarks, RSS and Media Sharing. Web 2.0 applications reflect different ways of promoting interaction between people, supporting social interaction, feedback, conversation and networking.

The Web 2.0 tools have great potential on the educational context, improving the teaching and learning process, and consequently contributing to the adjustment of the traditional approaches to the new technological emergent paradigm. The main goal of this chapter is to present the most used Web 2.0 applications related to the teaching and learning activity and to discuss their major advantages and disadvantages.

It starts by analyzing the new paradigm in teaching and learning processes. Next, the main Web 2.0 tools are presented through a brief description, including their pros and cons. Afterwards the authors analyze the use of Web 2.0 in teaching and learning process, their advantages and disadvantages and their use by e-learning platforms. Finally, some conclusions and future work are presented.

TEACHING AND LEARNING PROCESS: THE NEW PARADIGM

Most students today in higher education are considered digital natives. The fact that on their day-to-day live, students are native users of the Web tools facilitates greater interactivity (Collis & Moonen, 2008). According to Prensky (2001a, 2001b) digital natives are everybody that were born after 1980, and those who were born before that year are considered digital immigrants. The digital natives think and process information differently from their predecessors (Prensky, 2001a). Therefore, teachers today can not assume that students learn through the same methods that they learned. ICTs that have emerged in the 1990's caused a shift in the way of communicating and data transmission, and have also caused changes in the people own thought patterns and an how they learn the content (Prensky, 2001a).

Currently, universities have these new students and therefore, they should adapt teaching methods, which include the adoption of ICTs for the transmission of knowledge. In fact, digital natives and students of technical subjects use more technology when compared to digital immigrants and student of non-technical subjects (Margaryan, Littlejohn, & Vojt, 2011). However, despite the facts showing a clear need for the adoption of ICTs in new teaching methods, the decisions of teachers and administrators should not be based exclusively on students' preferences and on the trends in technology. There must be an understanding of the educational value of these technologies, in order to improve the process and learning outcomes. In this sense, it is necessary to explore the different technologies in teaching, to evaluate their effectiveness in practice within each institution (Kennedy, Judd, Churchward, Gray, & Krause, 2008; Margaryan, *et al.*, 2011), and based on this, adopt them in a prudent and progressive way.

In general, universities are concerned about motivating students based on methodologies of teaching and learning using the ICTs, as well as attracting other students based on a paradigm of DE. In this sense, the choice of a methodology that promotes the study autonomy, could provide a more student-centered education and thus promote the creation of students' own knowledge. ICTs and the variety of tools that characterize the Web 2.0 can be used to support this new paradigm for the benefit of students, teachers and institutions.

THE WEB 2.0 TECHNOLOGY: THE MAIN TOOLS

The concept of "Web 2.0" emerged in a brainstorming session between O'Reilly and MediaLive International in October 2004, being presented as "a revolution" in the business of the computer industry. It was caused by the change of the Internet as a platform for content management (O'Reilly, 2005). Besides being motivated by technology, it portrays a social phenomenon that involves an approach to content generation and distribution, characterized by open communication, decentralization of authority and freedom to share and reuse information (Alexander, 2006). The aim is to create applications that take advantage of network effects to get better benefits for people who use it. According to O'Reilly (2006) the Web 2.0 means "harnessing the collective intelligence" and is referred as the social use of the Web that allows people to collaborate and to have an active involvement in content creation, in order to generate knowledge and sharing information (Grosseck, 2009).

The Web 2.0 tools support social interaction, feedback, conversation and networking, but these are also endowed with a flexibility that enables collaboration. This paradigm redefines the interaction between Internet and users, allowing building virtual applications using data and functionality from a number of different sources.

Brief Description of the Main Web 2.0 Tools

Blogs, Wikis, Social Networks, Social Bookmarks, Syndication of Contents through RSS and Media Sharing are some of the most popular tools, and therefore a brief description of each of them is presented in this section.

Blogs

Blogs represent one of the most used Web 2.0 tools and the first one appeared in the late 1990s (Top, Yukselturk, & Inan, 2010), before the appearance of the Web 2.0 concept. The term Weblog was introduced by Jorn Barger in December 1997 and in early 1999, Peter Merholz shortened it 'Blog' (Blood, 2000). Blog refers to a simple Webpage consisting of brief paragraphs of opinion, information, personal diary entries in the form of text, images, video, audio, or links, called *posts*, arranged chronologically with the most recent first (Anderson, 2007; Franklin & Harmelen, 2007; Grosseck, 2009; Halic, Lee, Paulus, & Spence, 2010; Virkus, 2008). It allows users to express their opinion about a subject or a topic as well as to create a topic and document it (Sousa & Gomes, 2010), and allows feedback from the audience by means of successive comments on the main entry, with the possibility to preserve the old posts in addition to new entries (Grosseck, 2009; Halic, *et al.*, 2010; Top, *et al.*, 2010). More and more people are publishing in Blogs and in 28 September 2011, there were 172,360,000 identified Blogs in http://www.blogpulse.com/. There are various formats and the most popular is Blogger.com (Williams & Jacobs, 2004).

Blogs allow to keep the interaction with external environments using, for instance, videos, photos, bookmarks, and network (Kim, 2008). In this context the RSS technology can be useful to help users in managing contents (Kim, 2008).

Wikis

The concept of Wiki was created by Ward Cunningham in 1995 (Zeinstejer, 2008), and represents a system that allows to build up a corpus of knowledge in a set of interlinked WebPages, using a process of creating, writing and editing pages (Franklin & Harmelen, 2007; Grosseck, 2009; Kear, Woodthorpe, Robertson, & Hutchison, 2010). These pages can be created and modified by any user utilizing simple text editing facilities (Kear, et al., 2010), and any person can see and / or modify the information of the document (De Pedro et al., 2006). The philosophy of Wikis is one of complete openness, with any Web user being able to modify the content, as mentioned by Kear, et al. (2010): "Wikis allow for Web documents to be structured and organized in different ways, and to be updated regularly".

According to Lai & Ng (2011), Wikis are one of the many popular Web 2.0 tools that facilitate collaborative work, being the Wikipedia the most popular Wiki.

The concepts of Blogs and Wikis are different (Zeinstejer, 2008). However, the concept of Bliki, also known as wikiLog, conceived in 2003 by Martin Fowler and Ward Cunningham, combines features and advantages of Blogs and Wikis (Huang & Yang, 2009; Wan & Zhao, 2007) and is defined by Fowler (2003) as "a cross between a wiki and a blog". The same author refers "Like a blog, it allows me to post short thoughts when I have them. Like a wiki it will build up a body of cross-linked pieces".

Social Networks

Social Networks are tools that support collaboration, knowledge sharing, interaction and communication of users from different places with a common goal (Franklin & Harmelen, 2007; Grosseck, 2009; Usluel & Mazman, 2009). The Facebook, MySpace and LinkedIn represent the most popular examples of Social Networks, allowing the creation of a personal 'space' (Anderson, 2007).

Dwyer, Hiltz & Passerini (2007, p. 1) characterize features the Social Networks as present in the following statement: "When people join social networking sites, they begin by creating a profile, then make connections to existing friends as well as those they meet through the site. A profile is a list of identifying information. It can include your real name, or a pseudonym. It also can include photographs, birthday, hometown, religion, ethnicity, and personal interest. Members connect to others by sending a "friend" message, which must be accepted by the other party in order to establish a link. "Friending" another member gives them access to your profile, adds them to your social network, and vice versa. Members use these sites for a number of purposes. The root motivation is communication and maintaining relationships. Popular activities include updating others on activities and whereabouts, sharing photos and archiving events, getting updates on activities by friends, displaying a large social network, presenting an idealized persona, sending messages privately, and posting public testimonials."

Social Bookmarks

A social bookmarking service provides users the ability to record WebPages and consequently to tag those records with meaningful words that describe the pages recorded (Anderson, 2007; Franklin & Harmelen, 2007; Grosseck, 2009). These tools allow users to create lists of favorites, to store and to share them with other users (Anderson, 2007), and may be tagged with keywords. There is an important difference from the traditional categorization based on favorite's lists in the browser (Anderson, 2007) as Social Bookmarks allow users to explore connections between their own bookmarks and the others' ones, and thus enable discovering new items and people with similar interests (Rethlefsen, 2007).

The social bookmarking phenomenon was launched by Joshua Schacter with *del.icio.us* Website (Anderson, 2007). Ma.gnolia and BlinkList, represent other examples of this tool (Rethlefsen, 2007). These tools allow to build up reading lists and resource lists, using of multiple tags and structured into sub-categories (Anderson, 2007). Groups of users with a common interest can team together using the same service to bookmark items of common interest (Anderson, 2007). Social bookmarking systems allow individuals to discover what others find interesting and useful, without spending too much effort on it (Gray, Parise, & Iyer, 2011). With this service it is possible to check what other people are reading in two ways: searching on a certain tag to find what bookmarks others have associated with it or seeing the complete set of tags and bookmarks created by another person. This allows coming across information that may be interesting and relevant but which users may not have known to search for directly. These online resources visited by the user are influenced by the prior actions of others (Gray, *et al.*, 2011). A bookmark can be made visible to others if a user chooses to make it public, otherwise the act of accessing a bookmark in contemporary social bookmarking systems is not visible to others at all (Gray, *et al.*, 2011).

Syndication of Content through RSS

Really Simple Syndication (RSS) or Rich Site Summary is a format for delivering regular changing Web content (http://www.whatisrss.com/) (Anderson, 2007). RSS feeds can potentially replace traditional email lists, reducing email overload and to keep specific WebPages current and relevant (Grosseck, 2009).

It allows users to find out about updates to the content of RSS-enabled sites, Blogs or Podcasts without actually having to go and visit the site (Anderson, 2007). A feed reader (sometimes called an aggregator) has to be used in order to centralize all the recent changes in the sources of interest of the user (Franklin & Harmelen, 2007).

Media Sharing

Media Sharing is a service store of user-contributed media that allows sharing for and displaying contents. Users can create their personal resources for trading and networking (Anderson, 2007). Media Sharing tools can be divided into four categories: Podcasting (audio), Video Sharing (video) Photo Sharing (photo) and Slide Sharing (presentation), as described next.

Podcasting refers to the publication of audio content on the Internet and may be available to download for aggregators such as iTunes (the most popular) or other mobile devices such as mobile phones and iPods, allowing hearing regardless of place and time (Usluel & Mazman, 2009).

The Video Sharing enables the sharing of videos as clips from movies, television programs, video clips, and amateur content. YouTube is the most popular sharing service.

The Photo Sharing allows creating, manipulating, and disseminating images. There are dozens of photographic applications on the Web and Flickr represents one of the most innovative (Sadik, 2009). Flickr is a Website to host and share images, drawings, illustrations and photographs and allows the creation of albums to store, organize and sort out photos, which can be seen in different parts of the world (Cress & Kimmerle, 2008; Grosseck, 2009).

The Slide Sharing allows sharing presentations posting this material available anywhere, anytime and for any person (Grosseck, 2009).

In the next section, the main advantages and disadvantages of the above referred tools are presented.

Advantages and Disadvantages of the Different Web 2.0 Tools

The literature presents a set of benefits and weaknesses related to usage of the Web 2.0 tools. There are more essays and studies about Blogs and Wikis than about the other tools. In this sense, it is difficult to find literature referring to the advantages and disadvantages of the other tools for people and organizations. Table 1 presents the advantages and the disadvantages of the main Web 2.0 tools. The numbers in the table represent the studies where the advantages / disadvantages of the Web 2.0 tools are referred. As some of the studies only analyze few tools, and the advantages / disadvantages of those tools can be common to some of others, some new links between the advantages / disadvantages (lines) and the tools (columns) were represented in the table by an '*'.

As it can be seen in Table 1, the Web 2.0 tools are very easy to use as they are intuitive and user-friendly. They can be accessed "anytime-anywhere," they are open systems, they present high level of interactivity and they promote creative collaboration and the possibility of sharing digital contents. They also allow communication and collaboration, as well as experiences sharing. Some of the obstacles to the use of the tools are the basic requirements needed, such as Internet connection and JavaScript activation. The need of time for using, updating, and organizing the contents as well as for selecting sources is also a constraint that should be highlighted.

TEACHING AND LEARNING THROUGH THE USE OF WEB 2.0 TOOLS BY E-LEARNING PLATFORMS

Web 2.0 Tools in the Educational Context

Today's teaching and educational institutions don't need huge budgets to develop a global educational program, in the technological context (Jabbour, 2011). The Web 2.0 tools and the expansion of its capabilities, provide opportunities for teaching and learning (Jabbour, 2011).

Connection, collaboration, and engagement can be achieved instantly to remote devices virtually anywhere in the world. Technology solutions can support learning experiences in different ways (Jabbour, 2011), facilitating the education processes. For example, the students and teachers can publish content, create knowledge from scratch or combine online content and then share and exchange their ideas. On the other hand, the technology tools, in a specific class, can involve more people than traditional forms of classroom interaction (Jabbour, 2011).

Once connected to the Internet, any user can share and explore ideas, thoughts and knowledge. Web 2.0 software is an open-ended tool that provides a lot of opportunities to explore new forms of teaching and learning (Jabbour, 2011). Web 2.0 aims at reducing barriers to entry and may influence diverse cultural environments with strong implications on education (e.g. on teaching in the classroom or on individual learning) (Alexander, 2006). Specific technologies and services such as Blogs, Wikis, identification of content through RSS, Social Bookmarking (favorites or bookmarks online), Media Sharing (Podcasts, videos, photos, presentations) and Social Networks can contribute to the creation of new models of teaching and learning (Anderson, 2007; Dabbagh & Reo, 2010; Franklin & Harmelen, 2007; Grosseck, 2009).

The top management of the educational institutions has the responsibility of creating and maintaining an appropriate environment for the use of these tools (Divitini, *et al.*, 2005). Besides, it is believed that the positive impact on the teaching and learning process outcomes is greater when the Web 2.0 paradigm is present in the organizational culture.

The following paragraphs briefly analyze the possible use of each of the tools referred in the previous section in the educational context.

Table 1. Advantages/disadvantages of web 2.0 tools

Advantages	Web 2.0 Tools					
	Blogs	Wikis	Social Networks	Social Bookmarks	RSS	Media Sharing
They are open system	5	*	*	*	*	*
Do not depend on the used platform (a computer with browser and Internet connection is enough)	12	12	12	12	12	12
Allow anytime-anywhere access	4	*	*	*	*	*
It is easy to create and use contents (user-friendly)	1, 2, 4, 5, 12	6, 8, 12	12	12	12	12
Allow communication on the Web in an interactive way	1, 2, 3		*			
Provides fast access to information		12		*	*	
Allow joint, de-centered authorship / Enable contents sharing and creative collaboration	2	7	15			
Allow creating digital contents	*	*	*			12
Enable sharing accumulated experiences	12	12	*			12
Make possible organizing and presenting ideas and information		7, 11				
Allow controlling access to resources by authenticating users	12	12	12	12	12	12
Allow the redistribution of the effort, so that less and less time and energy are spent on the search and information management				12, 14	12, 13	
Enable the notification of the updates of the pre-selected sites					13	
Allow the individual evaluation of the participation in work group		9, 10				
Allow easy visualization of the changes introduced in a document		10				
It is possible to recover contents that have been erased or modified		10				
Allow access to the historic information of the content (who, when and what)		10				
Facilitate meeting people			15			
Disadvantages / Obstacles						
Dependence on Internet connection	12	12	12	12	12	12
Dependence on JavaScript activation	12	12	12	12	12	12
Limited security	12	10, 12	12	12	12	12
Possibility of different interpretations according to browser in use	12	12	12	12	12	12
Difficulty of some users on moving from passive readers to active contributors of information	16	*	*	*	*	*
Hard to get an overview of all the provided information	16	*	*	*		*
Difficulty on filtering and organizing contents	*	6	*			*
Difficulty on understanding the contents posted by others	*	6	*			*
Time consuming on reading, understanding, selecting, organizing and maintaining contents	*	6	*			*
Lack of clear contributions ownership and possibility of users to change each others' contributions		7				
Lack of functionality / Time consuming to learn to use the editing tools		7, 10, 9				
Fear of other people seeing the non-finished work		10				
Do not allow discussion		1				

Legend: 1 - (Meyer, 2010); 2 - (Brescia & Miller, 2006); 3- (Williams & Jacobs, 2004); 4- (Huffaker, 2005); 5 – (Kim, 2008); 6 - (Lai & Ng, 2011); 7 - (Kear, *et al.*, 2010); 8 - (Wan & Zhao, 2007); 9 - (Chu, 2008); 10 - (De Pedro, *et al.*, 2006); 11 - (Grace, 2009); 12 - (Grosseck, 2009); 13 - ("What Is RSS? RSS Explained,"); 14 - (Gray, *et al.*, 2011); 15 - (Anderson, 2007); 16 - (Divitini, Haugalokken, & Morken, 2005); * - Aditional link.

Teachers seem to have adopted the use of Blogs for class assignments, but few studies have been completed on educational uses of Blogs (Meyer, 2010). Some teaching and learning activities in higher education make use of Blogs due to their popularity among young people (Halic, *et al.*, 2010). There are several ways by which teachers use Blogs as a teaching and learning tool (Paulus, Payne, & Jahns, 2009). When the teacher knows and acknowledges the barriers and constraints of students he / she can use the Blog as a starting point for finding ways to break through the identified barriers (Paulus, Payne, & Jahns, 2009). The Blog conversations offer opportunities to reflect on concepts related to the lessons outside the class and share different perspectives on the lessons material (Halic, *et al.*, 2010). Unanswered questions in Blog conversations are a valuable source of information for teachers as they provide a means for gathering information about what is known and not yet understood. Furthermore, teachers can create more learning environments based on the needs expressed by students and verified through blog conversations (Paulus, *et al.*, 2009). In large classes, there is usually not enough time for students to answer or participate in the discussions but when performing a content analysis of a simple conversation on the blog the teacher can get information on the themes and the frequency of discussion of the students (Paulus, *et al.*, 2009). In fact, students have already recognized the beneficial effect of the blog activity on their overall learning (Halic, *et al.*, 2010). The Blog appears to be an effective tool when included in the e-learning environment (Lin, *et al.*, 2006).

Wikis help to create a dynamic and collaborative learning environment where, through open discussion and exchange of ideas and opinions, students can have an active participation in the creation and consolidation of knowledge (Meyer, 2010; Su & Beaumont, 2010). Wikis provide a valuable way for groups of students and their teachers to collaboratively develop learning resources offering, at the same time, a way for learning in a more student centered system and in a more democratic logic (Kear, *et al.*, 2010). The Wiki-based activities give teachers a new way of teaching that can be an alternative or a complement to traditional classroom-based learning (Lai & Ng, 2011).

Social Networks allow students to participate in an informal and creative learning. At the same time, they allow developing their digital literacy (McLoughlin & Lee, 2007). As an example of Social Networks, it can be noted that *Elgg* is an open source social networking system designed specifically for teachers and students that plays nicely with LMS like WebCT and Moodle (Rethlefsen, 2007). "Elgg is an award-winning social networking engine, delivering the building blocks that enable businesses, schools, universities and associations to create their own fully-featured social networks and applications" (Elgg, 2011).

Using Social Bookmarks, teachers and students can create a set of sites' references that can be accessed by any computer connected to the Internet (Anderson, 2007; Grosseck, 2009). Teachers can use these tools to save helpful Web resources, search for other Web resources with similar tags and share those resources with students and other instructors (Luo, 2009), as well as help students on deciding the usefulness of resources.

RSS are a useful tool that can help on having the information in the teaching area updated allowing sharing work with other educators (Grosseck, 2009). Feeds can be used to keep specific courses' WebPages up to date. They can be created from search engines, bringing the most current information (such as text, images, audio or video) on a topic and are, thus, a useful research tool for class studies and projects (Rosen & Nelson, 2008).

Media Sharing services represent a valuable educational resource (Franklin & Harmelen, 2007). For example, in the teaching and learning process, the Podcasts is not considered a synchronous activity, but can help students connecting to learning communities, which can be pedagogically appropriate in specific contexts, enabling students to create their own Podcasts (Beldarrain, 2006). The TeacherTube, useful for teachers, educators and schools (Cress & Kimmerle, 2008) represents a kind of Video Sharing tool, using the educational potential inherent in the Web. The use of YouTube as a supplement to learning is not necessarily a new phenomenon, allowing a more active participation of students and improving their visual literacy (Smith & Peck, 2010). The Photo Sharing, other type of Media Sharing tool, allows teachers sharing images that can be used on developing visual literacy through critical analysis and visual information (Sadik, 2009). With Slide Sharing, students can post presentations to an audience and get feedback from around the world (Grosseck, 2009).

Advantages and Disadvantages of the Use of the Web 2.0 Tools in the Teaching and Learning Process

In addition to the advantages/disadvantages of the Web 2.0 tools listed in Table 1, there are a set of benefits and weaknesses on the use of the Web 2.0 tools analyzed in this paper on the teaching and learning context, that are summarized in Table 2.

The Web 2.0 tools allow costs reduction and students motivation. Some examples of their most positive aspects are the democratic nature which allows building on opinions and research by students. The possibilities of sharing contents and collaborate outside class hours. Besides, it should be stressed that sometimes the Web 2.0 tools are used by students on the leisure and learning contexts simultaneously, what can cause loss of attention and of concentration in the learning tasks. To overcome some of the constraints presented, it should be noted that the successful use of the Web 2.0 in these teaching and learning context critically depends on the teachers having knowledge about the tools, being aware of how they should be used and being capable of organizing all the communication process.

E-Learning Platforms and Web 2.0 Tools

The Distance Education (DE) is a practice that demonstrates the powerful resources and new capabilities, providing complementary ways of teaching and learning through the use of new ICTs. Despite the various definitions presented in the literature, the concept of Distance Education (DE) can be understood as a planned educational experience, using ICTs, in order to encourage interaction in teaching and learning (Deperlioglu & Kose, 2010; Greenberg, 1998).

E-learning is one of several ways of DE that involves the Internet as the main channel on mediating the teaching and learning support process. Several studies reveled the existence of strong advantages on using e-learning platforms (Mahmoud, 2008; Mellow, 2005; A. Moura & Carvalho, 2009). However, their implementation involves some challenges that require clear and effective answers from the institutions that intend to adopt them, as well as an appropriate choice of the technologic platform.

The e-learning platforms, also known as Learning Management Systems (LMS), provide a set of configurable features, in order to allow creating courses online, pages of subjects, work groups and learning communities (Paulsen, 2003). In these systems, students can access course content/course unit, as well as interact with teachers and/or colleagues. In addition to the pedagogical dimension, such systems also have features for registration, monitoring and evaluation activities of students and teachers, enabling the contents' management via Internet.

There are different types of LMS, some of them are commercial, such as Blackboard or WebCT, and others represent open source solutions, as Moodle. In addition, there are proprietary solutions developed by the institutions themselves, called self-development technologic solution.

Table 2. Advantages/disadvantages of web 2.0 tools in the teaching and learning process

Advantages	**Web 2.0 Tools**					
	Blogs	**Wikis**	**Social Networks**	**Social Bookmarks**	**RSS**	**Media Sharing**
Reduction of costs and reliability in continuous usage, when used over an extended period of time	12	12	12	12	12	12
Compatibility with the elements of the educational field and the existing contextual dynamics	12	12	12	12	12	12
Democratic nature	*	1	*	*	*	*
Provide students with an e-learning environment and allow motivating their continuous participation	17	*	*	*	*	*
Leverage teaching and learning outside class hours	2, 4	*	*	*	*	*
Students can comment and ask questions outside the classroom and can be tasked to provide contents	2, 3		*			
Can be used to track students' behavior	2	*				
Allows the easy and fast follow-up by the teaching staff of the development of the collective work		10				
Heighten learning and help students integrating theory into practice	1	*	*			
Allow the existence of a database of topics and the integration of class materials	5					
Possibility to follow up the experts' work	*		*	*	*	
Disadvantages / Obstacles						
The process execution presuming teacher's good organization	18	*	*	*	*	*
Difficulty for some teachers to get familiar with the tool	18	*	*	*	*	*
Difficulty on selecting the technology to be used among the large offer	12	12	12	12	12	12
Possibility of teachers' and students' expectations about course objectives and learning processes not being aligned	16	*	*			*
Low quality of some contents	12	12	12	12	12	12
Demands specific students' abilities as self-learning, self-control, collaborating and communicating	18	*	*	*	*	*
Difficulty in aligning the assessment criteria with the learning process	16	*	*			
Final product may not be representative of all students' perspectives because of failure to participate by some of them		7				
Texts with very complex formats are difficult or impossible to put online		9, 10				
Cannot be edited by several students simultaneously		1				
Can give a false idea of the complexity level of the information	*	*	*			*

Legend: 1 - (Meyer, 2010); 2 - (Brescia & Miller, 2006); 3 – (Williams & Jacobs, 2004) ; 4 - (Huffaker, 2005); 5 - (Kim, 2008); 7- (Kear, et al., 2010); 9 - (Chu, 2008); 10 – (De Pedro, et al., 2006); 12 - (Grosseck, 2009); 16 - (Divitini, et al., 2005); 17 - (Lin et al., 2006); 18 - (Paulus, et al., 2009); * - Aditional link.

In the literature, some studies present the classification of platforms according to same characteristics and type of users (Alexander, 2006; Bremer & Bryant, 2005; Campanella *et al.*, 2008; Cavus & Momani, 2009; Coates, James, & Baldwin, 2005; Machado & Tao, 2007; Miyazoe, 2008; Paulsen, 2003; Santo, Colace, Santo, & Vento, 2003). In the referred studies, the Moodle (Modular Object-Oriented Dynamic Learning Environment) emerges as an easy to use platform, as well as the most used in secondary and higher education, with 55,000 registered sites in June 2011 (Moodle, 2011).

Table 3. Web 2.0 tools in the e-learning platforms

E-Learning Platforms		Web 2.0 Tools								
	Open-source	**Blogs**	**Wikis**	**Social Networks**	**Social Bookmarks**	**RSS**	**Podcasting**	**Photo Sharing**	**Slides Sharing**	**Video Sharing**
ATutor (1)	X	X		X			X			
Blackboard (2)		X	X			X	X	X	X	X
Claroline (3)	X		X							
Dokeos (4)	X		X	X			X			
Moodle (5)	X	X	X							
Sakai (6)	X	X	X				X			

Legend: (1) http://atutor.ca/atutor/; (2) http://www.blackboard.com/; (3) http://www.claroline.net/; (4) http://www.dokeos.com/; (5) http://moodle.org/; (6) http://sakaiproject.org/ (accessed in October 2011).

The Moodle is a platform for content management, distribution free (Open Source), and allows the exchange of information among geographically dispersed users through synchronous (chat and discussion rooms) and asynchronous communication (e-mail and discussion forums). In addition, this platform has features easily configurable, allowing the creation of student assessment processes (quizzes, online testing, and surveys) as well as the system management tasks and calendar (Itmazi, Megías, Paderewski, & Gutiérrez, 2005; Legoinha, Pais, & Fernandes, 2006; Mahmoud, 2008). Furthermore, the Moodle platform allows easy integration with other systems involving Academic Management, based on relational databases and supported by Web services infrastructure (R. Moura & Bernardino, 2010).

Based on the Websites of providers of some e-learning platforms (referred, for example by (Bremer & Bryant, 2005; Coates, *et al.*, 2005; Khan, 2010; Machado & Tao, 2007; McLoughlin & Lee, 2007; Miyazoe, 2008)), it was performed a content analysis in order to verify the existence or not of the more common Web 2.0 tools. Table 3 presents the results of the content analysis.

The results reveal that Social Bookmarks tools do not exist in any platform and that RSS, Photo Sharing, Slides Sharing, and Video Sharing are only present in Blackboard. Although Social Bookmarks and RSS are almost absent from platforms studied, it believed that, due to their characteristics they can be successfully used in the teaching and learning process as they allow to share bookmarks between colleagues, teachers and students. Photo Sharing, Slides Sharing and Video Sharing, though present only in one platform are accessible on other platforms (eg Flickr, slidesharet, YouTube) through a link that can be used in the e-learning platforms. Blogs and Wikis are present in all platforms, which confirm its usefulness and importance in the teaching and learning process. Social Networks are incorporated in two platforms. However, it is noted that, as mentioned, it is possible to use the social networks, in particular Elgg through other platforms (Rethlefsen, 2007).

Halic *et al.* (2010), Lai and Ng (2011), Meyer (2010), and Pop (2010) present studies on the practical application of the Web 2.0 tools in teaching and learning context that reveal a very positive impact on the motivation of the students and on their participation on the activities and assignments proposed by the teachers. It is though obvious that e-learning platforms should incorporate the maximum number of Web 2.0 tools that is possibly, namely those the students are used to use in their day-to-day lives. It can be noticed that the open-source platforms (more used by the education institutions) incorporate less tools that some of the commercial ones.

CONCLUSION AND FUTURE RESEARCH DIRECTIONS

The Web 2.0 became more mature and popular in education; thus, it is imperative to develop further and new strategies and methodologies. The functionalities of the Web 2.0 (construction, interaction, collaboration, communication) provide users with mechanisms to create digital contents and assessment materials. Blogs, Wikis, Social Networks, Social Bookmarks, Syndication of Contents through RSS, and Media Sharing represent some of the most popular tools. The Web 2.0 tools allow, on the one hand, reliability in continuous usage and reduction of costs, when used over an extended period of time. On the other hand, these tools are compatible with the elements of the educational field and existing contextual dynamics.

The Blog is a good way to provide direct student/teacher communication, allowing students to place their doubts, and the teacher to answer them. The Wiki is extremely valuable for sharing accumulated experiences, providing a repository to place common solutions, FAQ (Frequently Asked Questions) answers, etc. Social Networks facilitate content sharing, while Social Bookmarks offers extensive opportunities of collaboration and information management. The RSS features allow the redistribution of effort, so that less and less time and energy are spent during the search and information management process. Media Sharing also facilitates the creation of digital contents.

In a nutshell, the use of the Web 2.0 tools can be an extremely valuable asset for learning and can be encouraged by the students' motivation, which is a very important factor for the successful use of these tools in the teaching and learning process. The new paradigm in education may involve the adaptation of teaching and learning methods used with Web 2.0 tools.

Regarding future work, it is intended to promote a pilot study, where the Web 2.0 tools incorporated in Moodle and Educast platforms can be tested and evaluated in a real context of teaching and learning. The procedure of introducing the tools requires analyzing studies and essays, and, accordingly, the positive aspects highlighted in these studies, should be incorporated in the project, and the less positive aspects have to be overcome considering the reality of teachers and students in the case study.

It is also intended to analyze an online graduate course and compare it with two correspondent face-to-face courses (one in working hours and another after working hours) in order to identify success factors and possible disadvantages of the new approach that can help to improve existing courses, as well as in preparing the future. These courses are taught at the University of Aveiro (UA), Portugal.

The results of the experiments and of the analysis of the courses will be evaluated through information collected from primary and secondary sources.

REFERENCES

Alexander, B. (2006). Web 2.0: A new wave of innovation for teaching and learning? *Educause Review, 41*(2), 32-44. Retrieved May 28, 2011, from http://www.educause.edu/ir/library/pdf/erm0621.pdf

Anderson, P. (2007). *What is web 2.0? Ideas, technologies and implications for education*. JISC Technology & Standards Watch.

Beldarrain, Y. (2006). Distance education trends: Integrating new technologies to foster student interaction and collaboration. *Distance Education, 27*(2), 139–153. doi:10.1080/01587910600789498.

Blood, R. (2000). *Weblogs: A history and perspective*. Retrieved September 28, 2011, from http://www.rebeccablood.net/essays/Weblog_history.html

Bremer, D., & Bryant, R. (2005). *A comparison of two learning management systems: Moodle vs Blackboard.* Paper presented at the 18th Annual Conference of the National Advisory Committee on Computing Qualifications. New York, NY.

Brescia, W., & Miller, M. (2006). What's it worth? The perceived benefits of instructional blogging. *Electronic Journal for the Integration of Technology in Education, 5*, 44-52. Retrieved September 11, 2011, from http://ejite.isu.edu/Volume5/Brescia.pdf

Campanella, S., Dimauro, G., Ferrante, A., Impedovo, D., Impedovo, S., & Lucchese, M. G. et al. (2008). E-learning platforms in the Italian universities: The technological solutions at the University of Bari. *WSEAS Transactions on Advances in Engineering Education, 5*, 12–19.

Cavus, N., & Momani, A. (2009). Computer aided evaluation of learning management systems. *Procedia - Social and Behavioral Sciences, 1*(1), 426-430.

Chu, S. K.-W. (2008). TWiki for knowledge building and management. *Online Information Review, 32*(6), 745–758. doi:10.1108/14684520810923917.

Coates, H., James, R., & Baldwin, G. (2005). A critical examination of the effects of learning management systems on university teaching and learning. *Tertiary Education and Management, 11*(1), 19–36. doi:10.1080/13583883.2005.9967137.

Collis, B., & Moonen, J. (2008). Web 2.0 tools and processes in higher education: Quality perspectives. *Educational Media International, 45*(2), 93–106. doi:10.1080/09523980802107179.

Company, T. N. (2011). *BlogPulse*. Retrieved September 28, 2011, from http://www.blogpulse.com/

Cress, U., & Kimmerle, J. (2008). A systemic and cognitive view on collaborative knowledge building with wikis. *International Journal of Computer-Supported Collaborative Learning, 3*(2), 105–122. doi:10.1007/s11412-007-9035-z.

Dabbagh, N., & Reo, R. (2010). Back to the future: Tracing the roots and learning: Affordances of social software. In Lee, M., & McLoughlin, C. (Eds.), *Web 2.0-Based E-Learning: Applying Social Informatics for Tertiary Teaching* (pp. 1–20). Academic Press. doi:10.4018/978-1-60566-294-7.ch001.

De Pedro, X., Rieradevall, M., López, P., Sant, D., Piñol, J., Núñez, L., et al. (2006). *Writing documents collaboratively in higher education using traditional vs. wiki methodology: Qualitative results from a 2-year project study.* Paper presented at the 4th Internacional Congress of University Teaching and Innovation. New York, NY.

Deperlioglu, O., & Kose, U. (2010). The effectiveness and experiences of blended learning approaches to computer programming education. *Computer Applications in Engineering Education.*

Divitini, M., Haugalokken, O., & Morken, E. M. (2005). *Blog to support learning in the field: Lessons learned from a fiasco.* Paper presented at the Fifth IEEE International Conference on Advanced Learning Technologies. New York, NY.

Dwyer, C., Hiltz, S., & Passerini, K. (2007). *Trust and privacy concern within social networking sites: A comparison of Facebook and MySpace.* Paper presented at the Americas Conference on Information Systems (AMCIS). New York, NY.

Elgg. (2011). *Elgg - Open source social networking engine.* Retrieved October 4, 2011, from http://elgg.org/

Fowler, M. (2003). *What is a bliki*. Retrieved October 6, 2011, from http://martinfowler.com/bliki/WhatIsaBliki.html

Franklin, T., & Harmelen, M. V. (2007). *Web 2.0 for content for learning and teaching in higher education*.

Grace, T. P. L. (2009). Wikis as a knowledge management tool. *Journal of Knowledge Management*, *13*(4), 64–74. doi:10.1108/13673270910971833.

Gray, P. H., Parise, S., & Iyer, B. (2011). Innovation impacts of using social bookmarking systems. *Management Information Systems Quarterly*, *35*(3), 629–643.

Greenberg, G. (1998). Distance education technologies: Best practices for K-12 settings. *IEEE Technology and Society Magazine*, *17*, 36–40. doi:10.1109/44.735862.

Grosseck, G. (2009). To use or not to use web 2.0 in higher education?. *Procedia - Social and Behavioral Sciences*, *1*(1), 478-482.

Halic, O., Lee, D., Paulus, T., & Spence, M. (2010). To blog or not to blog: Student perceptions of blog effectiveness for learning in a college-level course. *The Internet and Higher Education*, *13*(4), 206–213. doi:10.1016/j.iheduc.2010.04.001.

Huang, S.-L., & Yang, C.-W. (2009). Designing a semantic bliki system to support different types of knowledge and adaptive learning. *Computers & Education*, *53*(3), 701–712. doi:10.1016/j.compedu.2009.04.011.

Huffaker, D. (2005). The educated blogger: Using weblogs to promote literacy in the classroom. *AACE Journal*, *13*(2), 91–98.

Itmazi, J., Megías, M. G., Paderewski, P., & Gutiérrez, F. L. (2005). *A comparison and evaluation of open source learning management systems*. Paper presented at the IADIS International Conference on Applied Computing. Retrieved September 21, 2011, from http://www.iadis.net/dl/final_uploads/200501C014.pdf

Jabbour, K. K. (2011). Web 2.0 tecnology tools for global education in Lebanon. *International Journal of Advanced Engineering Sciences and Technologies*, *7*(1), 151–168.

Kear, K., Woodthorpe, J., Robertson, S., & Hutchison, M. (2010). From forums to wikis: Perspectives on tools for collaboration. *The Internet and Higher Education*, *13*(4), 218–225. doi:10.1016/j.iheduc.2010.05.004.

Kennedy, G. E., Judd, T. S., Churchward, A., Gray, K., & Krause, K. L. (2008). First year students' experiences with technology: Are they really digital natives? *Australasian Journal of Educational Technology*, *24*(1), 108–122.

Khan, Z. H. (2010). *ICT and the changing face of higher education*. Paper presented at the International Conclave of Scientists on Regional Cooperation in Science & Technology: Opportunities and Challenges in the Context of Globalization. New Delhi, India.

Kim, H. N. (2008). The phenomenon of blogs and theoretical model of blog use in educational contexts. *Computers & Education*, *51*(3), 1342–1352. doi:10.1016/j.compedu.2007.12.005.

Lai, Y. C., & Ng, E. M. W. (2011). Using wikis to develop student teachers' learning, teaching, and assessment capabilities. *The Internet and Higher Education*, *14*(1), 15–26. doi:10.1016/j.iheduc.2010.06.001.

Legoinha, P., Pais, J., & Fernandes, J. (2006). *O Moodle e as comunidades virtuais de aprendizagem*. Paper presented at the VII Congresso Nacional de Geologia. New York, NY.

Lin, W.-J., Liu, Y.-L., Kakusho, K., Yueh, H.-P., Murakami, M., & Minoh, M. (2006). *Blog as a tool to develop e-learning experience in an international distance course*. Paper presented at the Sixth International Conference on Advanced Learning Technologies. New York, NY.

Luo, L. (2009). Web 2.0 integration in information literacy instruction: An overview. *Journal of Academic Librarianship, 36*(1), 32–40. doi:10.1016/j.acalib.2009.11.004.

Machado, M., & Tao, E. (2007). *Blackboard vs. Moodle: Comparing user experience of learning management systems*. Paper presented at the 37th ASEE/IEEE Frontiers in Education Conference. New York, NY.

Mahmoud, S. S. (2008). *A proposed model for distributing e-courses content through mobile technology architectures*. Paper presented at the word academy of science, engineering and technology. New York, NY.

Margaryan, A., Littlejohn, A., & Vojt, G. (2011). Are digital natives a myth or reality? University students' use of digital technologies. *Computers & Education, 56*(2), 429–440. doi:10.1016/j.compedu.2010.09.004.

McLoughlin, C., & Lee, M. J. W. (2007). *Social software and participatory learning: Pedagogical choices with technology affordances in the web 2.0 era*. Paper presented at the Ascilite. Singapore.

Mellow, P. (2005). *The media generation: Maximise learning by getting mobile*. Retrieved May 27, 2011, from http://www.ascilite.org.au/conferences/brisbane05/blogs/proceedings/53_Mellow.pdf

Meyer, K. A. (2010). A comparison of web 2.0 tools in a doctoral course. *The Internet and Higher Education, 13*(4), 226–232. doi:10.1016/j.iheduc.2010.02.002.

Miyazoe, T. (2008). *LMS-based EFL blended learning: Blackboard vs. Moodle*. Paper presented at the JALT2007. New York, NY.

Moodle. (2011). *Moodle*. Retrieved June 2, 2011, from http://moodle.org/

Moura, A., & Carvalho, A. A. (2009). Mobile learning: two experiments on teaching and learning with mobile phone. In Hijón-Neira, R. (Ed.), *Advanced Learning* (pp. 89–100). Academic Press. doi:10.5772/8105.

Moura, R., & Bernardino, J. (2010). Um modelo para a integração de serviços: Moodle e sistemas de gestão Académica. *RISTI- Revista Ibérica de Sistemas e Tecnologias de Informação,* (5), 31-44.

O'Reilly, T. (2005). *What is web 2.0: Design patterns and business models for the next generation of software*. Retrieved May 18, 2011, from http://oreilly.com/Web2/archive/what-is-Web-20.html

O'Reilly, T. (2006). *Web 2.0 compact definition: Trying again*. Retrieved May 18, 2011, from http://radar.oreilly.com/archives/2006/12/Web-20-compact.html

Paulsen, M. (2003). Experiences with learning management systems in 113 European institutions. *Journal of Educational Technology & Society, 6*(4), 134–148.

Paulus, T. M., Payne, R., & Jahns, L. (2009). Am I making sense here? What blogging reveals about undergraduate student understanding. *Journal of Interactive Online Learning, 8*(1).

Prensky, M. (2001). Digital natives, digital immigrants: Do they really think differently? *Horizon, 9*(5), 1–6. doi:10.1108/10748120110424816.

Rethlefsen, M. L. (2007). Social networking. *Medical Reference Services Quarterly, 26*(supl), 117-141.

Rosen, D., & Nelson, C. (2008). Web 2.0: A new generation of learners and education. *Computers in the Schools, 25*(3-4), 211–225. doi:10.1080/07380560802370997.

Sadik, A. (2009). Improving pre-service teachers' visual literacy through flickr. *Procedia - Social and Behavioral Sciences, 1*(1), 91-100.

Santo, C. D., Colace, F., Santo, M. D., & Vento, M. (2003). *Evaluating on-line learning platforms: A case study.* Paper presented at the 36th Hawaii International Conference on System Sciences. Hawaii, HI.

Smith, A., & Peck, B. (2010). The teacher as the 'digital perpetrator': Implementing web 2.0 technology activity as assessment practice for higher education innovation or imposition?. *Procedia - Social and Behavioral Sciences, 2*(2), 4800-4804.

Sousa, L., & Gomes, R. (2010). Strategy 2.0 to a teaching and learning process in higher education. In *Proceedings of the 2010 International Conference on E-Education, E-Business, E-Management and E-Learning: Ic4e 2010,* (pp. 484-489). Los Alamitos, CA: IEEE Computer Soc.

Su, F., & Beaumont, C. (2010). Evaluating the use of a wiki for collaborative learning. *Innovations in Education and Teaching International, 47*(4), 417–431. doi:10.1080/14703297.2010.518428.

Top, E., Yukselturk, E., & Inan, F. A. (2010). Reconsidering usage of blogging in preservice teacher education courses. *The Internet and Higher Education, 13*(4), 214–217. doi:10.1016/j.iheduc.2010.05.003.

Usluel, Y. K., & Mazman, S. G. (2009). Adoption of web 2.0 tools in distance education. *Procedia - Social and Behavioral Sciences, 1*(1), 818-823.

Virkus, S. (2008). Use of web 2.0 technologies in LIS education: Experiences at Tallinn University, Estonia. Program: Electronic Library and Information Systems, 42(3), 262 - 274.

Wan, L., & Zhao, C. (2007). Construction of a knowledge management framework based on web 2.0. *Wireless Communications. Networking and Mobile Computing, 12*, 5341–5344.

What Is, R. S. S. (n.d.). *RSS explained.* Retrieved October 14, 2011, from http://www.whatisrss.com/

Williams, J. B., & Jacobs, J. (2004). Exploring the use of blogs as learning spaces in the higher education sector. *Australasian Journal of Educational Technology, 20*(2), 232-247. Retrieved September 28, 2011, from http://www.ascilite.org.au/ajet/ajet20/williams.html

Zeinstejer, R. (2008). The wiki revolution: A challenge to traditional education. *TESL-EJ, 11*(4). Retrieved September 28, 2011, from https://tesl-ej.org/~teslejor/ej44/m1.html

ADDITIONAL READING

Ajjan, H., & Hartshorne, R. (2008). Investigating faculty decisions to adopt web 2.0 technologies: Theory and empirical tests. *The Internet and Higher Education, 11*(2), 71–80. doi:10.1016/j.iheduc.2008.05.002.

Albion, P. R. (2008). Web 2.0 in teacher education: Two imperatives for action. *Computers in the Schools, 25*(3-4), 181–198. doi:10.1080/07380560802368173.

Berger, P., & Trexler, S. (2010). *Choosing web 2.0 tools for learning and teaching in a digital world.* Libraries Unlimited.

Borza, S., Bondrea, I., & Simion, C. (2010). Create tutorials with multimedia elements, used in the education process in higher education. *Quality Management in Higher Education, 1*, 527–530.

Buffington, M. L. (2008). Creating and consuming web 2.0 in art education. *Computers in the Schools, 25*(3-4), 303–313. doi:10.1080/07380560802365898.

Carmichael, P., & Burchmore, H. (2010). Social software and academic practice: Postgraduate students as co-designers of web 2.0 tools. *The Internet and Higher Education, 13*(4), 233–241. doi:10.1016/j.iheduc.2010.05.002.

Cukušić, M., Alfirević, N., Granic, A., & Eljko, G. (2010). e-Learning process management and the e-learning performance: Results of a European empirical study. *Computers & Education*, *55*(2), 554–565. doi:10.1016/j.compedu.2010.02.017.

Danciu, E., & Grosseck, G. (2011). Social aspects of web 2.0 technologies: Teaching or teachers' challenges?. *Procedia - Social and Behavioral Sciences*, *15*, 3768-3773.

Dawson, S. (2010). 'Seeing' the learning community: An exploration of the development of a resource for monitoring online student networking. *British Journal of Educational Technology*, *41*(5), 736–752. doi:10.1111/j.1467-8535.2009.00970.x.

Glogoff, S. (2003). Blogging in an online course: A report on student satisfaction among first-time bloggers. *E-Learning in Corporate, Government, Healthcare, and Higher Education*, 2160-2162.

Gomes, R., & Sousa, L. (2010). Contributions to a strategy 2.0 in higher education. In *Proceedings of the International Conference on Information Management and Evaluation* (pp. 116-121). Academic Conferences Ltd.

Hsu, I.-C. (2011). Web 2.0-based SaaS for community resource sharing. *International Journal of Digital Content Technology and its Applications*, *5*(5), 132-141.

Huang, Y.-M., Yang, S. J. H., & Tsai, C.-C. (2009). Web 2.0 for interactive e-learning. *Interactive Learning Environments*, *17*(4), 257–259. doi:10.1080/10494820903195108.

Hung, S. T. (2011). Pedagogical applications of vlogs: An investigation into ESP learners' perceptions. *British Journal of Educational Technology*, *42*(5), 736–746. doi:10.1111/j.1467-8535.2010.01086.x.

Lau, K., Ip, R., Kwok, R., Wong, S., So, J., & Wong, E. (2010). An internet-based social technology blended learning. *Internet Computing*, *14*(3), 33–41. doi:10.1109/MIC.2010.74.

Lee, M. J. W., & McLoughlin, C. (2008). *Harnessing the affordances of web 2.0 and social software tools: Can we finally make student-centered learning a reality?* Paper presented at the World Conference on Educational Multimedia, Hypermedia and Telecommunications 2008. Retrieved September 11, 2011, from http://www.editlib.org/p/28915

Lim, S., & Palacios-Marques, D. (2011). Culture and purpose of web 2.0 service adoption: A study in the USA, Korea and Spain. *Service Industries Journal*, *31*(1), 123–131. doi:10.1080/02642069.2010.485634.

Maag, M. (2005). The potential use of blogs in nursing education. *Computers, Informatics, Nursing*, *23*(1), 16–24. doi:10.1097/00024665-200501000-00005 PMID:15681990.

Maldonado, U. P. T., Khan, G. F., Moon, J., & Rho, J. J. (2011). E-learning motivation and educational portal acceptance in developing countries. *Online Information Review*, *35*(1), 66–85. doi:10.1108/14684521111113597.

Mason, R., & Rennie, F. (2008). *E-learning and social networking handbook: Resources for higher education*. New York: Routledge.

Pettenati, M. C., & Ranieri, M. (2006). *Informal learning theories and tools to support knowledge management in distributed CoPs*. Paper presented at the European Conference on Technology Enhanced Learning. New York, NY.

Pop, A. (2010). The impact of the new technologies in foreign language instruction our experience. *Procedia - Social and Behavioral Sciences*, *2*(2), 1185-1189.

Reyes, N. R., Candeas, P. V., Galan, S. G., Viciana, R., Canadas, F., & Reche, P. J. et al. (2009). *Comparing open-source e-learning platforms from adaptivity point of view*. New York: IEEE. doi:10.1109/EAEEIE.2009.5335482.

Roca, J. C., Chiu, C. M., & Martinez, F. J. (2006). Understanding e-learning continuance intention: An extension of the technology acceptance model. *International Journal of Human-Computer Studies*, *64*(8), 683–696. doi:10.1016/j.ijhcs.2006.01.003.

Sanchez, R. A., & Hueros, A. D. (2010). Motivational factors that influence the acceptance of Moodle using TAM. *Computers in Human Behavior*, *26*(6), 1632–1640. doi:10.1016/j.chb.2010.06.011.

Solomon, G., & Schrum, L. (2007). *Web 2.0: New tools, new schools. ISTE*. Internet Soc Tech Educ.

Uribe-Tirado, A., Melgar-Estrada, L. M., & Bornacelly-Castro, J. A. (2007). Moodle learning management system as a tool for information, documentation, and knowledge management by research groups. *Profesional De La Informacion*, *16*(5), 468–474. doi:10.3145/epi.2007.sep.09.

Wang, H. C., & Chiu, Y. F. (2011). Assessing e-learning 2.0 system success. *Computers & Education*, *57*(2), 1790–1800. doi:10.1016/j.compedu.2011.03.009.

Wu, J., Tennyson, R. D. T., & Hsia, T. L. (2010). A study of student satisfaction in a blended e-learning system environment. *Computers & Education*, *55*(1), 155–164. doi:10.1016/j.compedu.2009.12.012.

Wu, L., Xu, J. C., & Qu, X. L. (2009). *Exploration of Moodle-based collaborative learning for the deaf*. Los Alamitos, CA: IEEE Computer Soc..

Yan, L., Yang, J. M., & Wang, W. J. (2008). Using web 2.0 for knowledge management in higher education. In *Proceedings of the International Symposium on Knowledge Acquisition and Modeling,* (pp. 419-423). Los Alamitos, CA: IEEE Computer Soc.

KEY TERMS AND DEFINITIONS

Blog: It is a Web 2.0 tool that represents a Webpage with brief paragraphs of opinion, information, personal diary entries in the form of text, images, video, audio, or links, called *posts*, arranged chronologically with the most recent first.

E-Learning: It is one type of Distance Education that involves the Internet as the main channel to mediate the teaching and learning process.

E-Learning 2.0: It is the combination of e-learning and Web 2.0 concepts.

Learning Management Systems (LMS)/E-Learning Platforms: They represent platforms used to create courses online; to register, monitor and evaluate activities and content management; as well as to exchange of information among geographically dispersed users through synchronous and asynchronous communication.

Media Sharing: It is a Web 2.0 tool that allows to store, search, display and share media files.

Really Simple Syndication (RSS): It is a Web 2.0 tool that allows delivering regular changing Web contents to the user.

Social Bookmarks: It is a Web 2.0 tool that provides users the ability to record WebPages and consequently to tag those records with significant words that describe the pages recorded.

Social Networks: It is a Web 2.0 tool that supports collaboration, knowledge sharing, interaction and communication of users from different places with a common goal.

Web 2.0: Represents the second generation of the Web applications, based on online services collaboration and sharing, that promote different ways of interaction between people.

Wiki: It is a Web 2.0 tool that allows one person or more people to build up a corpus of knowledge in a set of interlinked WebPages, using a process of creating, writing and editing pages.

Chapter 18

Experts vs. Novices: Influence of Promotional Benefit Type on their Online Purchase Intention

Esmeralda Crespo Almendros
Universidad de Granada, Spain

Salvador del Barrio García
Universidad de Granada, Spain

ABSTRACT

As each year sees an increase in the number of Internet users, so too the percentage of purchases made online increases. It is for this reason that firms are showing a growing interest in designing effective communication strategies that help to achieve their online business objectives. Online sales promotion is one of the most widely used communication tools on the Internet. However, there is little research into its effect on purchase intention and how this effect may vary depending on the type of incentive offered and the consumer's level of experience in using the Internet. This chapter seeks to analyze which types of online sales promotions (utilitarian vs. hedonic) are most effective at triggering online purchasing and whether the user's past experience of the Internet is capable of moderating the effect of the type of incentive on online purchasing.

1. INTRODUCTION

The Internet constitutes something of a revolution, both for its users and for firms. The resources it offers individuals and organizations facilitate communication and foster commercialization between people and entities. Each year witnesses growth in the numbers of individuals and firms adopting the medium. Over 2,044 million people world-wide now use the Internet, or 29.7% of the world's population (ONTSI, 2011). For firms in the European Union (EU), online commerce rep-

DOI: 10.4018/978-1-4666-4373-4.ch018

resents 14% of their billing. Over 40% of the EU's population uses the Internet to acquire products and services, representing a 3% increase on 2010, and 20% on 2004 levels (Eurostat, 2011). This growth is also reflected in the $689,635 million generated by e-commerce (JP Morgan, 2011).

This scenario explains the extensive interest amongst researchers and the volume of research projects focusing on the Internet that are currently emerging.

The Internet is being used for increasingly complex and sophisticated purposes, having evolved from being almost exclusively used as a messaging system (email), to now being used for keeping up to date with current affairs, instant messaging, social networks, videos, gaming, or as a shopping channel – to name but a few. In short, the Internet is used, above all, as an information source, a direct and instantaneous communication medium, and a shopping channel.

Figure 1 outlines the evolving percentage of individual users world-wide, by the type of activity they carry out online. In general terms, social networks are expanding in their reach and in fact represent one of the most rapidly growing online activities in terms of volumes of users.

Amongst the many activities that can be carried out over the Internet is the acquisition of products and services. In 2010, 40% of EU Internet users made some sort of purchase online (European Parliament, 2011). These data reveal that there is still a long way to go in terms of increasing confidence levels around electronic commerce and fostering online purchasing.

It would seem undeniable that the Internet is now a part of our everyday lives and that the benefits it brings to each user are increasingly regarded as essential. It also appears inevitable that people, regardless of who they are, what they do for a living or what age they are, will have some kind of contact with the Web. Yet the importance

Figure 1. Worldwide evolution of active use of the internet by activity undertaken. Sample: Active internet users (going online daily or every other day). Source: "The Socialisation of Brands: Social Media Tracker Wave 5," Universal McCann (2010).

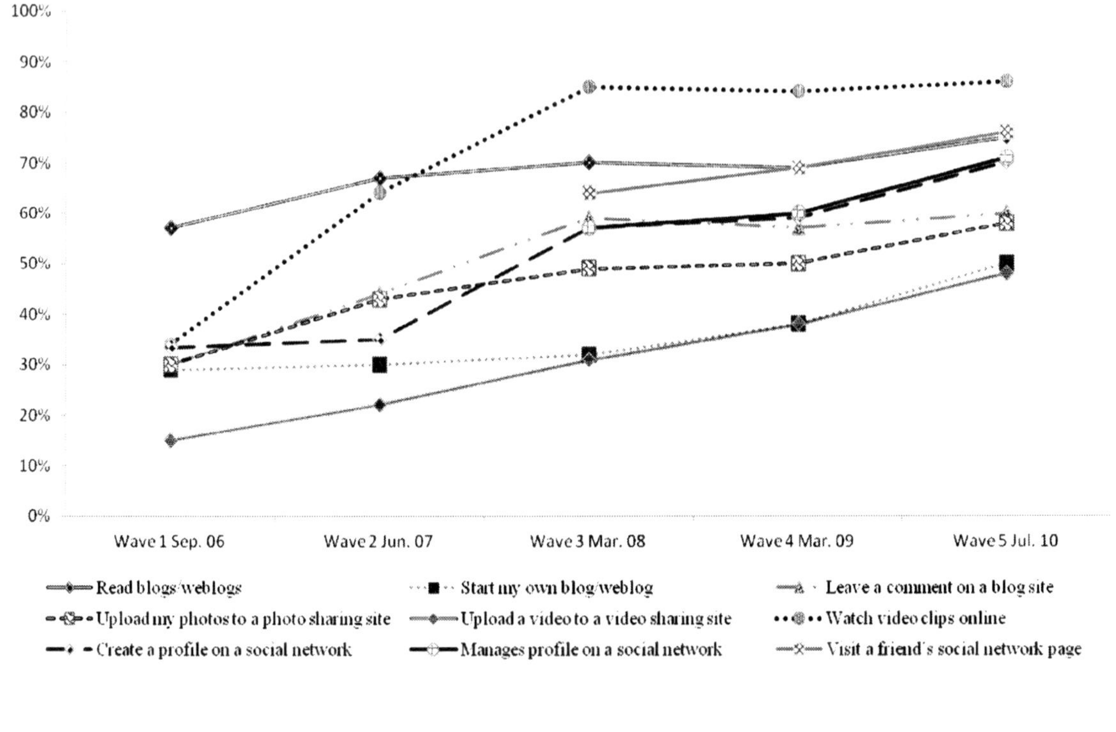

of this medium in our everyday activities is not only based on the use we put it to, but also, as alluded-to earlier, on the major income source it represents for firms operating online.

This, then, gives rise to two key questions:

- How effective are the marketing techniques used online?
- Are the online tools currently used online sufficient?

From a marketing perspective, the Internet enables communication campaigns to be created and aimed at very specific market segments, as well as delivering benefits related to information and interactivity:

- **Information:** The Internet gives consumers access to a vast quantity of information with just one click. Thanks to its flexibility in terms of content, available space, time, and so on, it also enables information to be permanently updated. According to Brackett and Carr (2001), when a Website is regarded as an information source, attitudes towards that site are positive.
- **Interactivity:** This refers to the degree of involvement experienced by the Internet user. The Internet's capacity to enable the user to interact with the online source means that the user is employing a greater number of cognitive resources to process the information they are receiving (Ariely, 2000). For this reason, the degree of involvement will be much greater than that experienced with other, non-interactive, media.

In the USA, to take advantage of these benefits and capture millions of Internet users, firms invest approximately $7,880 million annually in online advertising, a 22% increase on 2010 (IAB, 2011). In Europe the corresponding figure is €14.7 billion, a 4.5% increase on 2008 (IAB, 2010), and the tool attracting the heaviest investment is search-based advertising (46%), followed by display advertising (30%) (IAB, 2010). More specifically, in Spain, the key objectives pursued by firms when investing in Internet advertising is to raise awareness of their products or services, to capture customers, and to provide corporate information as a means of generating brand image and customer loyalty (AGEMDI, 2011).

Focusing the budget on activities that foster the capturing of new clients and convey corporate information is particularly relevant for two main reasons: the need for the consumer to find the brand when browsing online, and the need to generate online confidence as a means of incentivizing the acquisition of products via this medium.

One of the main differences between online and offline marketing is to be found precisely in matters relating to the brand. On the Internet, the primary objective should be to bring the consumer in contact with the brand. However, this medium comprises millions of sources that an individual can consult to gather more information or acquire a product that satisfies their needs. This process of information-search followed by product acquisition can be fast, agile and simple, or it can be arduous, slow and complicated, obliging the user to devote considerable time to it. Hence, the purpose of online communications should be to stand out from other offers and facilitate the user's information-search.

However, while advertising spend increases, its effectiveness declines, as consumers, both in the EU and the US, find the never-ending barrage of advertising messages increasingly wearisome. Their disapproval and displeasure at so much online promotion is becoming more and more evident, particularly when it is invasive (European Parliament, 2011). This is reflected in a gradual decline in the effectiveness of online advertising. In the early days of the Internet, banner advertising was effective at generating awareness and positive attitudes (Briggs & Hollis, 1997). Since then, however, online advertising has been the target of numerous criticisms, for instance that it is not informative, it is not targeted a specific public, it is impossible to segment and, overall, it is ineffective (Bulik, 2000; Hwang & Kranhold, 2000; Goldsmith & Lafferty, 2002). The lack of useful information it provides is reflected in a lack of interest on the part of the consumer, and can often confuse the Internet user or generate a negative attitude (Bulik, 2000; Mathews, 2000; Gaffney, 2001). This typically translates into a low click-through rate (≤1%), indicating that this advertising approach is ineffective (see Figure 2).

The marked growth in other techniques such as sponsored links or positioning in search engines is a further reflection of the symptoms of saturation in the sphere of online advertising. Logically, then, in the Internet medium budgets should be redistributed towards activities that enable the firm to promote itself online and generate brand image, but that do not irritate or inconvenience the consumer, so that they have a motive to purchase or to visit the firm's Website.

It is in this context online sales promotion may constitute a valid and appropriate tool for boosting online competitiveness as it facilitates the purchase decision-making process and also helps increase client satisfaction. What is more, this particular tool is able to deliver the most important competitive elements of the Internet medium: convenience and enjoyment (Hoffman & Novak, 2000).

Sales promotions can attract the customer's attention and direct it towards the product. They also have a direct influence on customer behavior in the short term as they deliver added value, in the form of an incentive together with information on the firm in question. When applied online, this tool attracts visitors to the Website of the brand in question, thus fostering awareness of, and familiarity with, the brand. Online promotion also provides an incentive for acquiring the product, which may help the consumer to overcome any perceived risk associated with the purchase, and it can generate feelings of surprise and pleasure

Figure 2. Evolution of click-through ratio (CTR) at international level. Source: International Advertising Bureau (IAB) (2010).

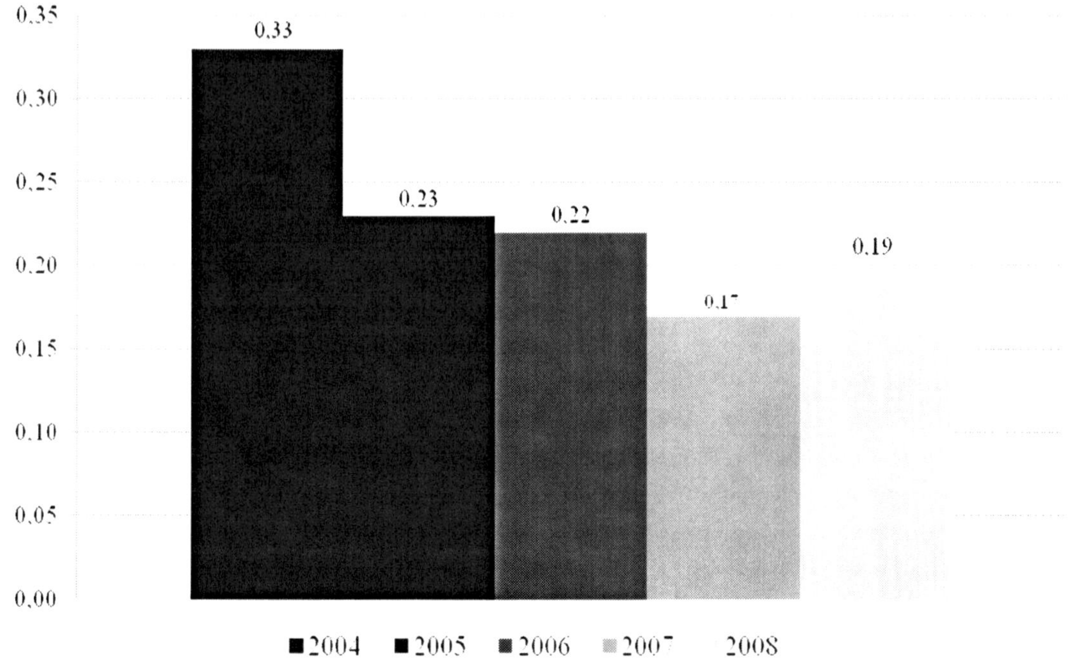

for the consumer that transfer onto the brand and thus increase satisfaction.

Meanwhile the entertainment provided by a sales promotion can go some way towards reducing users' rejection of online advertising, thus generating a higher click-through ratio and heightening the effectiveness of the message. This is reflected in the impact of sales promotions on online purchase decision-making, according to the study 'Trends in Online Shopping' (Nielsen, 2008). The study reveals that 30% of Internet users world-wide are guided in their online purchasing by special offers they have seen on the Internet, compared to just 18% who are influenced by online advertising.

However, the effectiveness of a sales promotion will depend on, amongst other variables, the particular type of promotion used (DelVecchio et al., 2006), as its hedonic or utilitarian nature will be a determining factor in the consumer's reactions and selection processes (Hirschman & Holbrook, 1982; Dhar & Wertenbroch, 2000; Jones, 2008; Palazón & Delgado, 2009). This phenomenon is widely studied in the context of traditional media, the conclusion of most authors being that differences in the processing of sales promotions are due to the type of benefit on offer (Shi, Cheung & Prendergast, 2005; DelVecchio et al., 2006; Mittal & Sethi, 2011). However, there is no relevant literature analyzing this concept in the context of online promotions. Academic research has underlined the fact that sales promotion has a positive effect on online purchase intention (Foxall, Goldsmith, & Brown, 1998), as it reduces the perceived risk associated with the Internet (So, Wong, & Sculli, 2005). Nevertheless, there is no literature that analyzes whether this effect could be moderated by the type of benefit offered. It is of interest therefore to address this gap in the literature by analyzing whether it may be the case that there are differential effects relating to hedonic and utilitarian incentives, as regards their impact on online purchase intention.

It is also accepted that past experience of using the Internet medium is a major moderator of the user's response, affecting their decision-making and processing of online communications stimuli (Hoffman & Novak, 1996; Koufaris, Kambil & Labarbera, 2002; Thorbjornsen & Supphellen, 2004). Past experience of using the Internet is known to be one of the key moderators of online behavior (Hoffman & Novak, 1996; Thorbjornsen & Supphellen, 2004) as it has a major impact on the consumer's preferences and evaluations of brands and products (Alba & Hutchinson, 1987; King & Balasubramanian, 1994), and above all, on the perceived risk associated with online purchasing (Stanforth et al., 2000). According to Reisenwitz et al. (2007), for users who are more experienced in using the Internet their perception of risk associated with this technology is lower than for those with less experience, hence they will make more use of it. Therefore it would be logical to expect that a novice Internet user would be less prone to respond to an online promotional activity as they would first have to overcome their fear of the medium itself. However, once that fear is overcome, newcomers will be more likely to respond to online sales promotions than expert users, as the latter are less susceptible to such communications activities.

That said, there is a lack of research in the literature regarding how past experience of Internet use may affect the consumer's response to online sales promotion. The present research therefore seeks to analyze which type of on sales promotions (utilitarian *vs.* hedonic) is the more effective in triggering online purchasing, and whether the user's past experience of the Internet medium is capable of moderating the effect of incentive type on online purchasing.

2. BACKGROUND

Considerable analysis has been undertaken into consumer behavior, from a marketing perspective. There are innumerable studies on the variables that influence the consumer's response to different stimuli, and many theories attempting to explain that response. Meanwhile, with the Internet increasingly finding its way into the home, studying online consumer behavior has also become an important line of research. However, although the Web makes purchasing easier for consumers, it hampers attempts to understand their behavior (Lyons & Henderson, 2005). More specifically, one of the most widely-studied aspects is that of browsing behavior. Studies endeavor to analyze browsing patterns, site traffic, the most commonly searched products, the most widely explored area of the Web, and consumer profiles by browsing pattern (Barrett, Maglio & Kellem, 1997; Yang & Lai, 2006).

The great majority of the components of consumer behavior theory have already been applied in the study of online behavior (Cheung et al., 2003), and there are numerous studies that aim to understand the factors that affect purchase intention, use intention, adoption of a system or purchase, and repeat online purchase or repeat site visit.

The Internet provides a number of advantages that lead the consumer to behave differently than in traditional media. For example, aspects such as interactivity, or the consumer's control over what they want to see and do at any point, mean that the firm must continually innovate, identifying ways of communicating that are both appealing and useful, attracting the consumer's attention and then leading them to process the content. On the other hand, issues such as security of the medium, the absence of a physical establishment and lack of sensory features mean that the user may perceive risks in purchasing online that they do not associate with traditional media. Perceived risk is the key limiting factor in online behavior (Castañeda et al., 2005). The means to reduce that risk is to generate familiarity with, and experience of, the online medium, whilst building confidence in the medium, the product and the brand (Mitchell & Vassos, 1997; Shimp & Bearden, 1982; Sood & Adams, 1984; Tan, 1999; Rodgers et al., 2005). In this scenario, in order to convince the consumer to make their purchases online, firms must implement communication techniques that generate confidence and security whilst also incentivizing the purchase itself, and online sales promotions may be an effective tool for achieving these objectives. This approach is capable of building brand awareness, image and loyalty, whilst at the same time driving the consumer towards specific behaviors in the short term.

There are numerous definitions of sales promotion as a strategic variable. Amongst these, the following should be noted:

It is that part of the firm's communications process in which there is, or can be, direct, immediate feedback, in other words it is possible for the consumer or user of the goods and services being commercialized to respond, and this effect achieves significant growth in sales compared to the level achieved by other Marketing activities. (Rabassa, 1987, p. 25)

In this definition, it can be observed that sales promotion is regarded as a communication tool capable of influencing the other variables of the Marketing Mix, and as such should be planned.

In the Internet medium, it is more difficult to define sales promotion per se, because of the conceptual complexity of separating out the major communication instruments, namely advertising, direct marketing and sales promotion (Calvo & Reinares, 2001). Offline, these instruments use different communications media to achieve their objectives, whereas online communication can combine, in real time, all of these tools at once. The Internet enables firms to distinguish a range of target publics and address each of them directly, delivering a banner advertising campaign that effectively communicates a promotional incentive. It is precisely because of this characteristic of the Web—its capacity to overcome the barriers of space and time—that sales promotions have a special potential in online applications.

Table 1. Differences between online and offline sales promotion

On-Line Promotion	Off-Line Promotion
Individual as promotional target.	Mass targets and traditional channels.
All activities are managed as if there were aimed at the end-consumer.	Activities are differentiated depending on the public they are being aimed at (channel or consumer).
The Internet is the communication channel for the promotion.	Need to use mass communication media, direct marketing and point-of-sale to communicate the promotion.
Ease of segmentation of activities.	Difficulty of segmenting activities other than by channel.
Low fixed costs, low cost per contact.	High fixed costs.
Use of Data Mining and Data Warehouse.	Conventional tracking of effectiveness by analyzing the 'sales' variable.
Need to make prior investment in the technology.	High implementation and logistics costs.
High level of control over activities, both quantitatively and qualitatively.	Low level of control over activities due to complexity of the process and the volume of players involved.
Offers the possibility of delivering incentives based on information, services and other intangibles.	Preponderance towards tangible incentives.
High quality information on the target beneficiary of the promotion.	Limited information on target publics of the promotion.
Synergies in communication thanks to ease of coordination with other online communication instruments.	Difficult and costly coordination of promotion with other communication instruments.
High response rate to the promotion.	Low-to-medium response rate to promotion.
Short planning-to-implementation timescales.	Long planning-to-implementation timescales.

Source: Adapted from Calvo and Reinares (2001)

Table 1 summarizes the key differences to be borne in mind when planning to implement this communication tool in either the offline or the online medium.

3. IMPACT OF ONLINE SALES PROMOTION TYPE ON PURCHASE INTENTION: KEY DIFFERENCES BETWEEN NOVICE AND EXPERT INTERNET USERS

As already mentioned at the beginning of this chapter, academic research has underlined the fact that sales promotion has a positive effect on online purchase intention (Foxall, Goldsmith & Brown, 1998), as it reduces the perceived risk associated with the Internet (So, Wong & Sculli, 2005). Some authors assert that differences in the processing of sales promotions are due to the type of benefit on offer (Shi, Cheung & Prendergast, 2005; DelVecchio et al., 2006; Jung & Lee, 2010; Mittal & Sethi, 2011). That is to say, each type of sales promotion is capable of satisfying different needs, as each one delivers a different benefit (Buckinx et al., 2003; Palazón & Delgado, 2009). Such benefit may be utilitarian in nature or hedonic (Chandon et al., 2000; Liao, 2006). While the former helps the consumer to maximize the utility, efficiency or value for money of their purchase, the latter provides intrinsic motivation such as fun, entertainment or self-esteem (Hirschman & Holbrook, 1982). Each type of sales promotion provides one or more of these benefits, although typically those which are monetary in nature or based on price tend to deliver utilitarian benefits, whilst non-monetary promotions tend to provide hedonic benefits (Hirschman & Holbrook, 1982; Chandon et al., 2000).

The literature covering traditional media finds that monetary incentives are most appropriate when the objectives in question are conative in nature, except when the individual does not feel the need to justify their choice, in which case hedonic incentives are more efficient (Palazón & Delgado, 2009). Monetary incentives, in the main, lead consumers to buy faster, buy more, and spend more, whilst the non-monetary type are more effective at encouraging consumers to try out the product for the first time (Shi et al., 2005; Mittal & Sethi, 2011).

Meanwhile, according to benefit congruency theory (Chandon et al., 2000), the effectiveness of a sales promotion increases when the benefits it delivers are compatible with the brand (Roehm, Pullins & Roehm Jr., 2002) and with the value proposition of the product (Dowling & Uncles, 1997). When the consumer evaluates a sales promotion associated with a utilitarian product, they give more weight to the utilitarian benefits on offer, and are therefore more easily influenced by monetary promotions. However, when evaluating the sales promotion for a hedonic product, they will give more weight to the hedonic benefits of the sales promotion, hence non-monetary promotions will tend to have a greater influence on their decision (Chandon et al., 2000). In those situations in which the utilitarian or hedonic incentive is congruent with the product, it is easier to assess the value delivered by the utilitarian incentive than that of the hedonic one, and the consumer will choose the sales promotion that offers utilitarian value – as explained by the compatibility principle (Tversky, Sattath & Slovic, 1988). In light of this, the following hypothesis is proposed:

H1: A non monetary utilitarian online sales promotion will have a greater influence on the online purchase intention than non monetary hedonic online sales promotion or monetary online sales promotion.

Meanwhile, one of the variables that has been extensively analyzed in academic research is that of experience in using the Internet. This can be regarded as a person's skill at carrying out activities related to products (such as information searches), interacting with sellers, making decisions, purchasing products and, ultimately, using the product (Sicilia, Ruiz, & Munuera, 2005).

This variable has been addressed in the literature as a moderating variable of online consumer behavior (Bruner & Kumar, 2000; Morris & Venkatesh, 2000; Koufaris, Pambil & LaBarbera, 2002; Venkatesh et al.,2003; Castañeda et al., 2005), and as a determinant of that behavior (Bruner & Kumar, 2000; Stevenson, Bruner & Kumar, 2000; Johnson, Bellman & Lohse, 2003).

Past experience of using the Internet is known to be one of the key moderators of online behavior (Hoffman & Novak, 1996; Thorbjornsen & Supphellen, 2004) as it has a major impact on the consumer's preferences and evaluations of brands and products (Alba & Hutchinson, 1987; King & Balasubramanian, 1994), and above all, on the perceived risk associated with online purchasing (Stanforth et al., 2000). According to Reisenwitz et al. (2007), for users who are more experienced in using the Internet their perception of risk associated with this technology is lower than for those with less experience, hence they will make more use of it.

According to various authors, experience of using the Internet can influence an individual's browsing behavior (Hoffman & Novak, 1996; Hammond et al. 1998; Novak, Hoffman & Yung, 2000; Wolfinbarger & Gilly, 2001; Pedersen & Nysveen, 2003; Castañeda et al. 2005). For those who have only recently started to use the Internet, it is likely that they will undertake online activities for the experience of it, whilst those with a longer history of use will do so with specific aims in mind (Novak, Hoffman & Yung, 2000; Pedersen & Nysveen, 2003). This latter group responds less to unexpected stimuli (Dahlén, 1998) and is less easily swayed by competing stimuli (Bruner & Kumar, 2000). These Internet 'experts' will also plan their online behaviors and searches in light of their own experience and not in response to what they see on the Web, unlike their novice counterparts (Novak, Hoffman & Yung, 2000; Perdensen & Nysveen, 2003).

For novice and expert users alike, their particular way of evaluating and processing information will be duly affected and this, in turn, will influence their purchase intention (Stevenson, Bruner & Kumar, 2000; Thorbjornsen & Supphellen, 2004).

In this regard, Balabanis and Vassileiou (1999) and Pedersen and Nysveen (2003) found that past experience of using the Internet had a direct influence on purchase intention. Amongst the causes they identified, they assert that the level of complexity perceived by novice and expert users respectively is not the same. Novice users tend to perceive a given Website to be more complex to use than do expert users, and hence their intention to repeat purchase via that site is reduced. However, other authors consider that there is no such direct effect, but rather an indirect effect via attitudes towards the Website and towards online advertising (Bruner & Kumar, 2000).

In summary, consumers will only undertake more complex online activities related to information-search and purchasing of products once they have acquired significant experience of using the medium (Liang & Huang, 1998), as the learning process they undergo reduces the perceived risk and increases online purchase intention. Therefore, it would be logical to expect that a novice Internet user would be less prone to respond to an online promotional activity as they would first have to overcome their fear of the medium itself. However, once that fear is overcome, newcomers will be more likely to respond to online sales promotions than expert users, as the latter are less susceptible to such communications activities.

On the other hand, according to prospect theory (Kahneman & Tversky, 1984), each kind of promotional incentive is assimilated by the consumer as a loss or a gain. Monetary online sales promotions are generally seen as reducing losses, whilst non-monetary online sales promotions are seen as gains (Diamond & Campbell, 1989). If novice Internet users perceive a greater risk in acquiring a product online than their expert counterparts, then it is likely that they will prefer those sales promotions regarded as a reduction in the loss the purchase will entail, as their sense of risk will decline. By contrast, expert users will prefer those sales promotions regarded as an additional gain, as their confidence in their own capacity to take decisions relating to online purchases is greater (Sanchez & Villarejo, 2004). This confidence enables them to dispense with the need to reduce the level of risk. However, as established by Han, Yoon and Cameron (2001), their need to put themselves to the test, to take on new challenges and to overcome them will lead them to prefer those sales promotions that are regarded as a gain and that consequently make them feel as if they have 'passed the test' and that they have the highest possible level of skill. In light of this, the following hypotheses are put forward:

H2: Expert Internet users display a greater online purchase intention, when presented with an online sales promotion, than novice users.

H3: The capacity of each type of online sales promotion to trigger a purchase will depend on the degree of past experience in Internet use.

4. EMPIRICAL STUDY

In order to test the proposed hypotheses, an experiment was conducted that was based on observation of individuals' behavior and completed with a computer-assisted survey. The experiment consisted of three banners promoting an airplane ticket on the Website of a national daily newspaper. The independent variable was the type of promotional incentive – that is, monetary, non-monetary hedonic or non-monetary utilitarian. These three types of incentive were chosen for the study with a view to ensuring that they were in line with the benefits that Internet browsers seek (enjoyment, fun, and so on), and that they were perceived to be worth the same in monetary terms. A pre-test amongst 90 students confirmed that the incentives on offer were indeed perceived to be worth the same amount of money (roughly €120). The three specific incentives finally chosen for the experiment were a discount of €120 on the flight (monetary promotion), two free nights' accommodation with a national hotel chain (non-monetary hedonic promotion) and a gift, in the form of a luggage set from a well-known brand (non-monetary utilitarian promotion). Those surveyed were randomly classified into three groups and then exposed to one of these incentives.

The experiment consisted of asking each individual to visit the Website of a Spanish national daily newspaper (www.elmundo.es) and browse it at their leisure for a maximum of ten minutes. During this time the individual was exposed to one or other of the promotional banners and could decide whether to click on it or not. If they decided to do so, this was registered in the online database and a pop-up survey then appeared, designed to measure their shopping intentions, their Web experience, and their personal socio-demographic characteristics. For those who did not click on the banner, this same survey appeared after ten minutes.

In order to avoid the findings being dependent on the particular Web user's profile and therefore not being possible to generalize across the whole population, the individuals in the sample were chosen at random on the street, not via the Internet. Therefore the sample – which ultimately comprised 676 individuals – was based on age and gender quotas proportional to the Spanish population.

To measure buying behavior the purchase intention scale was used, as applied many times before by various authors, based on a single item (Belch, 1981; Grossbart, Muehling & Kangon, 1986; Chatterjee & McGinnis, 2010; Goodrich, 2011). To measure Web experience a combination of different objective measures was chosen. Firstly, subjects were asked a series of questions regarding the number of hours per week spent browsing the Web, the frequency of Internet use, and the type of online tools used. Secondly, immediately following the experiment, subjects were asked to find the solution to a specific problem, using the Internet, and were given a maximum of 6 minutes for the task. In line with the recommendations of Yun and Lee (2001), the time in seconds that each individual took to ascertain the correct solution would be indicative of their skill in using the Internet.

5. FINDINGS

Prior to testing the hypotheses, a hierarchical segmentation analysis was carried out using the measurements of experience (a priori and a posteriori) with a view to classifying the sample in terms of true level of experience in use of the Internet. The analysis revealed three groups, namely: high level of experience (56.6%); moderate level of experience (31%); and low level of experience (12.4%). The sample was composed of 56% men and 44% women, whose ages ranged between 20-34 years (50%), 14-19 years (18%) and over 34 (32%). The majority had monthly incomes of less than €1,500, and used email, social networks and the Internet several times a week, every day, or even several times a day.

To test the proposed hypotheses various different univariate general linear models were applied, using online purchase intention as the dependent variable in all cases. Prior to each analysis the statistical assumptions behind this type of model were checked to ensure they were fulfilled. The results for hypothesis H1 revealed that promotional incentive type had no direct significant effect on the online purchase intention ($p \geq 0.05$) (see Table 2).

Table 2. ANOVA: promotional incentive type – online purchase intention

	SS	gl	QS	F	Sig.
Inter-group	5.46	2	2.73	0.80	0.44
Intra-group	2239.28	659	3.39		
Total	2244.75	661			

The three promotional incentives used reached very similar average levels of purchase intention, at around 4.5 points, meaning that H1 could not be confirmed.

Next, H2 and H3 were tested, namely whether past experience of Internet use influenced the purchase intention, and whether this experience could moderate the influence of the sales promotion type on that intention. Contrary to what was proposed under H2, it was found that past experience of Internet use, in and of itself, does not influence the online purchase intention ($p \geq 0.10$) (see Table 3). This finding is congruent with those of Bruner and Kumar (2000).

However, past experience does seem to moderate the relationship between the sales promotion type used and the purchase intention, the effect of the interaction being significant ($p \leq 0.05$). Thus H3 can be confirmed (see Figure 3). These findings reveal that the most effective type of sales promotion to incentivize online purchasing amongst novice Internet users is monetary in nature, and for experienced users it is non-monetary utilitarian. However, when the latter is applied to novice users, it is the least effective type of sales promotion of all at encouraging the individual to make an online purchase.

6. SOLUTIONS AND RECOMMENDATIONS

It can be concluded from the findings of the present work that online sales promotion is an effective tool for achieving online purchasing, thus confirming the findings of earlier studies (So, Wong & Sculli, 2005). However, neither the type of online sales promotion nor the user's level of past Internet experience alone can influence the online purchase intention. The present work finds that the three promotional incentives used in the study achieve similar levels of purchase intention ($p \geq 0.05$). This finding does not enable the results of studies into tradition media to be corroborated, as monetary incentives are not always better at incentivizing online purchasing, but rather the purchase will depend on the characteristics of the consumer in question and, more specifically, on their experience of using the Internet.

*Table 3. Online purchase intention by promotional incentive type *web experience*

	SS type III	gl	QS	F	p	Partial η^2	NCP	η^2
Corrected model	39.16	8	4.89	1.44	0.17	0.01	11.59	0.66
Intersection	8544.17	1	8544.17	2529.64	0.00	0.79	2529.64	1.00
Web Exp.	2.73	2	1.36	0.40	0.66	0.00	0.80	0.11
Sales promotion type	0.30	2	0.15	0.04	0.95	0.00	0.09	0.05
Web Exp.* Sales promotion type	30.96	4	7.74	2.29	0.05	0.02	9.17	0.66
Error	2205.58	653	3.37					
Total	14523.00	662						
Corrected total	2244.75	661						

Figure 3. Online purchase intention (promotion type x internet experience)

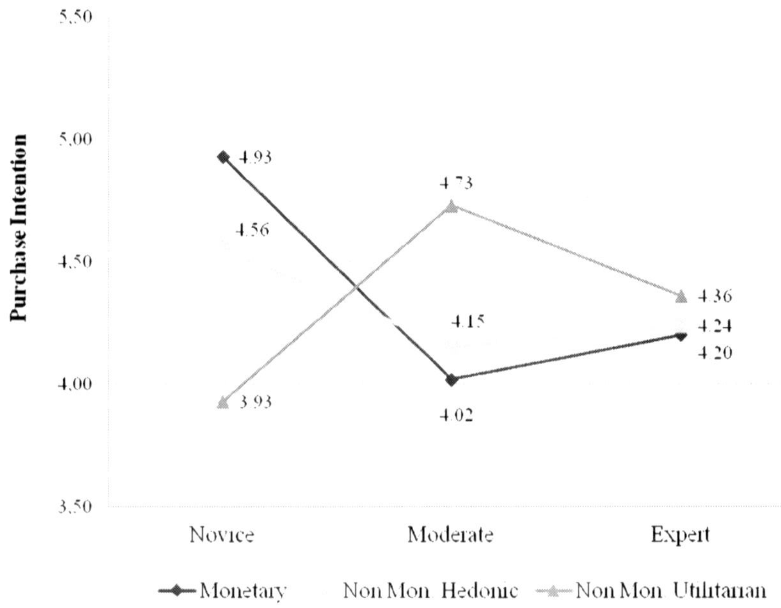

The findings show that when the underlying aim of the promotional strategy is to increase volumes of online sales, the most effective type of sales promotion is that which is monetary in nature and designed for novice users of the Internet, whilst for this same group, non-monetary online sales promotions offering a utilitarian incentive is the least effective. However, for those users with a moderate level of Internet experience, online sales promotions that are non-monetary and utilitarian in nature are the most influential, whilst for experts in the use of the Internet, the three types of incentives appear to be equally effective.

The overall preference for online sales promotions offering utilitarian benefits (either monetary or non-monetary) is congruent with the work of Chandon et al. (2000). These authors submit that when the product is utilitarian in nature—as is the case here—the consumer will place greater importance on the utilitarian benefits derived from the sales promotion and hence will prefer those sales promotions that deliver this type of benefit. It should be borne in mind that the incentives offered in the present work were compatible and congruent with the chosen product, and thus the findings can be said to be in line with the compatibility principle (Tversky, Sattath, & Slovic, 1988) that was later demonstrated by Palazón and Delgado (2009) for traditional media.

On the other hand, and in keeping with the work of Dahlen (1998) and Hoffman and Novak (1996), it has been demonstrated that novice users of the Internet are more susceptible to online marketing than expert users in terms of being driven to make online purchases. It is highly likely that this result is due to what is established under Optimal Stimulation Level Theory (Raju, 1980; Holbrook & Gardner, 1993; Steenkamp & Baumgartner, 1992). The degree of familiarity with the stimulus that expert Internet users have means that the stimulus is rendered 'routine' and does not arouse the level of surprise that it does amongst novice users, hence losing its effectiveness.

It can be concluded, then, that online sales promotions are particularly appropriate when designed with novice Internet users in mind. For this group, those online sales promotions offering a monetary benefit are the most appealing, whilst for those users with a moderate level of experience of the Internet, non-monetary utilitarian online sales promotions will be the most effective. Lastly, it has been shown that all three types of online sales promotion are equally effective for expert users of the Internet. As outlined in the Literature Review, it may be that these effects are due to the way in which information on each type of sales promotion is integrated into the product information. That is, these findings are congruent with prospect theory (Kahneman & Tversky, 1984), which was subsequently demonstrated by Diamond and Campbell (1989).

In light of the above, it is recommended that when designing an online promotional campaign aimed at generating online sales, the potential consumers' degree of past experience in using the Internet should be analyzed. The different sales promotions should be designed according to the level of experience and the relationship between the user and the brand. It is advisable to use non-monetary utilitarian incentives for expert Internet users or those with a moderate level of experience, and to use monetary incentives exclusively for novice users.

7. FUTURE RESEARCH DIRECTIONS

The findings of the present study make it patently clear that there is the need to continue researching the question of how online sales promotion can help firms to meet their business objectives. The following future lines of research are of particular note:

1. Analysis of the effectiveness of online sales promotion by product category.
2. Analysis of the effect of promotion-proneness on online promotional effectiveness.
3. Analysis of the effect of the credibility of the promotion on online purchase intention, and how this credibility is affected by the value of the incentive in question.
4. Analysis of the effectiveness of online sales promotion by awareness of the brand in question.
5. Analysis of the effect of product engagement on online promotional effectiveness.
6. Analysis of online promotional effectiveness by Internet users' degree of online experience and familiarity with the brand.
7. Analysis of the impact of online sales promotion on intention to repurchase and revisit the Website.
8. Analysis of the effect of attitudes towards the Internet, towards the banner, and towards the Website, on online promotional effectiveness.

8. CONCLUSION

It can be concluded from this chapter that promotional incentive type alone cannot explain the differences in purchase intention amongst consumers. It is only when incentive type combines with the variable 'experience in using the Internet' that it affects online purchase intention. Monetary online promotions will only be effective in those cases where the consumer is new to the Internet, and even so they must be sufficiently appealing so as to reduce the consumer's risk aversion and encourage them to make an online purchase.

By contrast, for users with a moderate level of Internet experience and those considered expert users, non-monetary utilitarian sales promotions will be the most effective. In this case, the promotions should be designed in the most appealing and innovative way possible in order to incentivize, stimulate and entertain these users, who need to feel they are somehow being put to the test and are successfully overcoming fresh challenges. In such a way, the effectiveness of the promotional activity is assured.

REFERENCES

AGEMDI. (2011). *IV estudio sobre marketing y publicidad en medios interactivos*. Retrieved November, 20, 2010 from http://www. agemdi.es

Alba, J. W., & Hutchinson, J. W. (1987). Dimension of consumer expertise. *The Journal of Consumer Research*, *13*(4), 411–455. doi:10.1086/209080.

Ariely, D. (2000). Controlling the information flow: Effects on consumers' decision making and preference. *The Journal of Consumer Research*, *27*(2), 233–248. doi:10.1086/314322.

Balabanis, G., & Vassileiou, S. (1999). Some attitudinal predictors of home-shopping through the internet. *Journal of Marketing Management*, *15*, 361–385. doi:10.1362/026725799784870315.

Barrett, R., Maglio, P. P., & Kellem, D. C. (1997). How to personalize the web. In *Proceedings of Human Factors In Computing Systems*. New York: ACM Press.

Belch, G. E. (1981). An examination of comparative and noncomparative television commercials: The effects of claim variation and repetition on cognitive response and message acceptance. *JMR, Journal of Marketing Research*, *18*, 333–349. doi:10.2307/3150974.

Brackett, L. K., & Carr, B. N. (2001). Cyberspace advertising vs. other media: Consumer vs. mature student attitudes. *Journal of Advertising Research*, *41*(5), 23–32.

Briggs, R., & Hollins, N. (1997). Advertising on the web: Is there response before click-through? *Journal of Advertising Research*, *37*(2), 33–45.

Bruner, G. C. II, & Kumar, A. (2000). Web commercials and advertising hierarchy-of-effects. *Journal of Advertising Research*, *40*(1/2), 35–42.

Buckinx, W., Moons, W., Van Den Poel, D., & Wets, G. (2003). *Customer-adapted coupon targeting using feature selection*. Gent, Belgium: Universiteit Gent, Faculteit Economie En Bedrijfskunde.

Bulik, B. (2000). Ad nauseum. *Business 2.0*, *12*, 112.

Calvo, S., & Reinares, P. (1999). *Comunicación en internet: Estrategias de comunicación y marketing interactivo*. Madrid: McGraw-Hill.

Castañeda, J. A., Muñoz, F., Luque, T., & Alcántara, J. M. (2005). *Experience moderation effect on the relationship between usefulness, ease of use and website acceptance*. Paper presented at Network and Electronic Commerce Conference. Riva Del Garda, Italia.

Chandon, P., Wansink, B., & Laurent, G. (2000). A benefit congruency framework of sales promotion effectiveness. *Journal of Marketing*, *64*(4), 65–81. doi:10.1509/jmkg.64.4.65.18071.

Chatterjee, P., & McGinnis, J. (2010). Customized online promotions: Moderating effect of promotion type on deal value, perceived fairness, and purchase intent. *Journal of Applied Business Research*, *26*(4), 13–19.

Cheung, C. M. K., Zhu, L., Kwong, T., Chan, G. W. W., & Limayem, M. (2003). *Online consumer behavior: A review and agenda for future research*. Paper presented at 16th Bled eCommerce Conference. Bled, Slovenia.

Dahlen, M. (1998). *Controlling the uncontrollable: Towards the perfect web sample*. Paper presented at the Worldwide Internet Seminar. Amsterdam: Esomar Publications.

DelVecchio, D., Henard, D. H., & Freling, T. H. (2006). The effect of sales promotion on post-promotion brand preference: A meta-analysis. *Journal of Retailing*, *82*(3), 203–213. doi:10.1016/j.jretai.2005.10.001.

Dhar, R., & Wertenbroch, K. (2000). Consumer choice between hedonic and utilitarian goods. *JMR, Journal of Marketing Research*, *37*, 60–71. doi:10.1509/jmkr.37.1.60.18718.

Diamond, W., & Campbell, L. (1989). The framing of sales promotions: Effects on reference price change. *Advances in Consumer Research. Association for Consumer Research (U. S.)*, *16*, 241–247.

Dowling, G. R., & Uncles, M. (1997). Do customer loyalty programs really work? *Sloan Management Review*, *38*(4), 71–82.

European Parliament. (2011). *Consumer behavior in a digital environment*. Retrieved 20 November, 2010 from http://www.europarl.europa.eu/document/activities/cont/201108/20110825ATT25258/20110825ATT25258EN.pdf

Eurostat. (2011). Retrieved from http://epp.eurostat.ec.europa.eu/portal/page/portal/eurostat/home/

Foxall, G. R., Goldsmith, R. E., & Brown, S. (1998). *Consumer psychology for marketing* (2nd ed.). London: International Thomson Business Press.

Gaffney, J. (2001). The battle over internet ads. *Business 2.0*. Retrieved from http://www.business2.com/articles/Web/0,1653,16546,00.html

Goldsmith, R. E., & Lafferty, B. A. (2002). Consumer response to web sites and their influence on advertising effectiveness. *Internet Research*, *12*(4), 318–328. doi:10.1108/10662240210438407.

Goodrich, K. (2011). Anarchy of effects? Exploring attention to online advertising and multiple outcomes. *Psychology and Marketing*, *28*, 417–440. doi:10.1002/mar.20371.

Grossbart, S., Muehling, D., & Kangun, N. (1986). Verbal and visual references to competition in comparative advertising. *Journal of Advertising*, *15*(1), 10–23. doi:10.1080/00913367.1986.10672984.

Hammond, K., Mcwilliam, G., & Narholz, A. (1998). Fun and work on the web: Differences in attitudes between novices and experienced users. *Advances in Consumer Research. Association for Consumer Research (U. S.)*, *25*, 372–378.

Han, K. H., Yoon, D., & Cameron, G. T. (2001). *Web users' attitude and behavior toward online coupons*. Paper presented at 2001 Annual Conference of American Academy of Advertising. New York, NY.

Hirschman, E., & Holbrook, M. (1982). Hedonic consumption: Emerging concepts, methods and propositions. *Journal of Marketing*, *46*(2), 92–101. doi:10.2307/1251707.

Hoffman, D. L., & Novak, T. P. (1996). Marketing in hypermedia computer-mediated environments: Conceptual foundations. *Journal of Marketing*, *60*(3), 50–69. doi:10.2307/1251841.

Hoffman, D. L., & Novak, T. P. (2000). How to acquire customers on the web. *Harvard Business Review*, *78*(3), 179–188. PMID:11183979.

Holbrook, M. B., & Gardner, M. P. (1993). An approach to investigating the emotional determinants of consumption duration, why do people consume what they consume for as long as they consume it? *Journal of Consumer Psychology*, *2*(2), 123–142. doi:10.1016/S1057-7408(08)80021-6.

Hwang, M. I., & Lin, J. W. (1999). Information dimension, information overload and decision quality. *Journal of Information Science*, *25*(3), 213–218. doi:10.1177/016555159902500305.

IAB. (2010). *Interactive advertising bureau*. Retrieved from www.iab.net

In Goldsmith, R. E., & Lafferty, B. A. (2002). Consumer response to web sites and their influence on advertising effectiveness. *Internet Research*, *12*(4), 318–328. doi:10.1108/10662240210438407.

Johnson, E. J., Bellman, S., & Lohse, G. L. (2003). Cognitive lock-in and the power law of practice. *Journal of Marketing*, *67*, 62–75. doi:10.1509/jmkg.67.2.62.18615.

Jones, J. (2008). An exploratory study on attitude persistence using sales promotion. *Journal of Managerial Issues*, *20*(3), 401–417.

Jung, K., & Lee, B. Y. (2010). Online vs. offline coupon redemption behaviors. *International Business & Economics Research Journal*, *9*(12), 23–36.

Kahneman, D., & Tversky, A. (1984). Choices, values and frames. *The American Psychologist*, *39*, 341–350. doi:10.1037/0003-066X.39.4.341.

King, M. F., & Balasubramanian, S. K. (1994). The effects of expertise, end goal, and product type on adoption of preference formation strategy. *Journal of the Academy of Marketing Science*, *22*(2), 146–159. doi:10.1177/0092070394222004.

Koufaris, M., Kambil, A., & Labarbera, P. A. (2002). Consumer behavior in web-based commerce: An empirical study. *International Journal of Electronic Commerce*, *6*(2), 115–138.

Liang, T. P., & Huang, J. S. (1998). An empirical study on consumer acceptance of products in electronic markets: A transaction cost model. *Decision Support Systems*, *24*, 29–43. doi:10.1016/S0167-9236(98)00061-X.

Liao, S. (2006). The effects of nonmonetary sales promotions on consumer preferences: The contingent role of product category. *The Journal of American Academy of Business*, *8*(2), 196–203.

Lyons, B., & Henderson, K. (2005). Opinion leadership in a computer-mediated environment. *Journal of Consumer Behaviour*, *4*(5), 319–329. doi:10.1002/cb.22.

Mathews, A. W. (2000). Advertisers find many web sites too tasteless.

Mitchell, V. W., & Vassos, V. (1997). Perceived risk and risk reduction in holiday purchases: A cross-cultural and gender analysis. *Journal of Euromarketing*, *6*(3), 47–79. doi:10.1300/J037v06n03_03.

Mittal, M., & Sethi, P. (2011). The effectiveness of sales promotions tools among Indian consumers: An empirical study. *Journal of Promotion Management*, *17*, 165–182. doi:10.1080/10496491.2011.580693.

Morgan, J. P. (2011). *Annual report forecasting trend*. Retrieved from http://www.jpmorgan.com

Morris, M. G., & Venkatesh, V. (2000). Age differences in technology adoption decisions: Implications for a changing work force. *Personnel Psychology*, *53*(2), 375–404. doi:10.1111/j.1744-6570.2000.tb00206.x.

Nielsen. (2008). *Trends in online shopping*. Retrieved January 01, 2009 from http://www.nielsen.com

ONTSI. (2011). *La sociedad en red 2010*. Retrieved January 01, 2011 from http://www.ontsi.red.es/estudios-informes

Palazon, M., & Delgado-Ballester, E. (2009). Effectiveness of price discounts and premium promotions. *Psychology and Marketing*, *26*, 1108–1129. doi:10.1002/mar.20315.

Pedersen, P. E., & Nysveen, H. (2003). *Search mode and purchase intention in online shopping behavior*. Retrieved March 10, 2004 from http://citeseer.ist.psu.edu/article/pedersen03search.html

Rabassa, B. (1987). *Promoción de ventas: Cómo se prepara una campaña*. Madrid, Spain: Editorial Pirámide.

Raju, P. S. (1980). Optimum stimulation level: Its relationship to personality, demographics and exploratory behavior. *The Journal of Consumer Research*, *7*, 272–282. doi:10.1086/208815.

Reisenwitz, T., Iyer, R., Kuhlmeier, D., & Eastman, J. (2007). The elderly's internet usage: An updated look. *Journal of Consumer Marketing, 24*(7), 406–418. doi:10.1108/07363760710834825.

Rodgers, W., Negash, S., & Suk, K. (2005). The moderating effect of on-line experience on the antecedents and consequences of online satisfaction. *Psychology and Marketing, 22*(4), 313–331. doi:10.1002/mar.20061.

Roehm, M. L., Pullins, E. B., & Roehm, H. A. Jr. (2002). Designing loyalty-building programs for packaged goods brands. *JMR, Journal of Marketing Research, 39*(2), 202–213. doi:10.1509/jmkr.39.2.202.19085.

Rugimbana, R. O., & Iversen, P. (1994). Perceived attributes of innovations. *International Journal of Bank Marketing, 12*(2), 30–35. doi:10.1108/02652329410052955.

Sánchez, M. J., & Villarejo, A. F. (2004). La calidad del servicio electrónico: Un análisis de los efectos moderadores del comportamiento de uso de la web. *Cuadernos de Economía y Dirección de la Empresa, 21*, 121–152.

Shi, Y. Z., Cheung, K. M., & Prendergast, G. (2005). *The effectiveness of sales promotion tools: A Hong Kong study*. Hong Kong: Hong Kong Baptist University.

Shimp, T. A., & Bearden, W. O. (1982). The use of extrinsic cues to facilitate product adoption. *JMR, Journal of Marketing Research, 19*(2), 229–240. doi:10.2307/3151623.

Sicilia, M., Ruiz, S., & Munuera, J. L. (2005). Effects of interactivity in a web site: The moderating effect of need for cognition. *Journal of Advertising, 34*(3), 31–45. doi:10.1080/00913367.2005.10639202.

So, W. C. M., Wong, T. N. D., & Sculli, D. (2005). Factors affecting intentions to purchase via the internet. *Industrial Management & Data Systems, 105*(9), 1225–1244. doi:10.1108/02635570510633275.

Sood & Adams. (1984). Model of management learning styles or predictor of export behavior and performance. *Journal of Business Research, 12*, 169–182. doi:10.1016/0148-2963(84)90004-3.

Stanforth, N. F., Lennon, S. J., & Moore, S. (2000). *Perceived risk and purchase intent associated with television shopping*. Paper presented at Frontiers in Direct and Interactive Marketing Research. New York, NY.

Steenkamp, J. E. M., & Baumgartner, H. (1992). The role of optimum stimulation level in exploratory consumer behavior. *The Journal of Consumer Research, 19*, 434–448. doi:10.1086/209313.

Stevenson, J. S., Bruner, G. C. II, & Kumar, A. (2000). Webpage background and viewer attitudes. *Journal of Advertising Research*, (January): 29–34.

Tan, S. T. (1999). Strategies for reducing consumers' risk aversion in internet shopping. *Journal of Consumer Marketing, 16*(2), 163–180. doi:10.1108/07363769910260515.

Thorbjornsen, H., & Supphellen, M. (2004). The impact of brand loyalty on website usage. *Journal of Brand Management, 11*(3), 199–208. doi:10.1057/palgrave.bm.2540166.

Tversky, A., Sattath, S., & Slovic, P. (1988). Contingent weighting in judgement and choice. *Psychological Review, 95*, 371–384. doi:10.1037/0033-295X.95.3.371.

Universal McCann. (2010). *The socialisation of brands – Social media tracker wave 5*. Retrieved December 01, 2011 from www.mccannworldgroup.com/

Venkatesh, V., Morris, M. G., Davis, G. B., & Davis, F. D. (2003). User acceptance of information technology: Toward a unified view. *Management Information Systems Quarterly*, *27*(3), 425–445.

Wolfinbarger, M., & Gilly, M. (2001). Shopping online for freedom, control, and fun. *California Management Review*, *43*(2), 34–55. doi:10.2307/41166074.

Yang, T., & Lai, H. (2006). Comparison of product bundling strategies on different online shopping behaviours. *Electronic Commerce Research and Applications*, *5*, 295–304. doi:10.1016/j.elerap.2006.04.006.

Yun, T. W., & Lee, W. (2001). *Psychological antecedents of amount of attention to web sites – An exploratory study*. Paper presented at 20th Annual Advertising and Consumer Psychology Conference, Online Consumer Psychology: Understanding and Influencing Consumer Behavior in the Virtual World. Seattle, WA.

ADDITIONAL READING

Park, D.-H., Lee, J., & Han, I. (2007). The effect of online consumer reviews on consumer purchasing intention: The moderating role of involvement. *International Journal of Electronic Commerce*, *11*(4), 125–148. doi:10.2753/JEC1086-4415110405.

Puto, C. P. (1987). The framing of buying decisions. *The Journal of Consumer Research*, *14*, 301–315. doi:10.1086/209115.

Raghubir, P. (2004). Free gift with purchase: Promoting or discounting the brand? *Journal of Consumer Psychology*, *14*(1&2), 181–195. doi:10.1207/s15327663jcp1401&2_20.

Ram, S., & Sheth, J. N. (1989). Consumer resistance to innovations: The marketing problem and its solutions. *Journal of Consumer Marketing*, *6*(2), 5–14. doi:10.1108/EUM0000000002542.

Shimp, T. A., & Kavas, A. (1984). The theory of reasoned action applied on coupon usage. *The Journal of Consumer Research*, *11*, 795–809. doi:10.1086/209015.

Shoemaker, R. W., Hardy, K. G., & MacKenzie, F. (1989). *Measuring and evaluating sales promotions from the manufacturer and retailer perspectives*. Cambridge, MA: Marketing Science Institute.

Swaminathan, S., & Bawa, K. (2005). Category-specific coupon proneness, the impact of individual characteristics and category-specific variables. *Journal of Retailing*, *81*(3), 205–214. doi:10.1016/j.jretai.2005.07.004.

Tellis, G. J., & Redondo, I. (2002). *Estrategias de publicidad y promoción*. Madrid, Spain: Pearson Educación.

Thaler, R. (1983). Transaction utility theory. *Advances in Consumer Research. Association for Consumer Research (U. S.)*, *10*, 296–301.

Thaler, R. (1985). Mental accounting and consumer choice. *Marketing Science*, *4*, 199–214. doi:10.1287/mksc.4.3.199.

Vaughn, R. (1986). How advertising works: A planning model revisited. *Journal of Advertising Research*, *26*(1), 57–66.

Vyas, P. H. (2005). *Measuring consumer preferences for sales promotion schemes through conjoint design in FMGC sector*. New Delhi, India: IIMA.

Walters, R. G., & MacKenzie, S. B. (1988). A structural equations analysis of the impact of price promotions on store performance. *JMR, Journal of Marketing Research*, *25*(1), 51–63. doi:10.2307/3172924.

Walters, R. G., & Rinne, H. J. (1986). An empirical investigation into the impact of price promotions on retail store performance. *Journal of Retailing*, *62*(3), 237–266.

KEY TERMS AND DEFINITIONS

Click-Through Ratio: This ratio measures the percentage of clicks made on an online banner or advertisement, compared to the total number of individuals who have received it.

Convenience: This refers to the additional benefits perceived by the consumer, in terms of attributes such as the location of the establishment, 24-hour availability, time saving, compatibility with lifestyle, and privacy (Rugimbana & Iversen, 1994).

Hedonic Benefits: All those benefits derived from the use and enjoyment of the product. Principally they refer to entertainment, exploration, and expression of value, given that these provide pleasure, emotions and self-esteem (Chandon, Wansink, & Laurent, 2000).

Monetary Sales Promotions: These promotions offer a monetary stimulus and are capable of capturing the attention of the individual as they represent a cost saving, because they deliver either a price discount or an additional quantity of the product. This type of tool typically aims to fulfill short-term objectives, such as increasing the sales volume of the product, incentivizing re-purchase, and/or triggering a change of brands.

Non-Monetary Sales Promotions: These promotions offer a non-monetary stimulus and they attract the individual's attention because of the additional benefit they provide, above and beyond the product itself. This may be in the form of a tangible or intangible gift, presented immediately or following some time after the purchase, or via a competition. This type of tool typically aims to fulfill objectives such as generating brand image and awareness, retaining customers, generating Web traffic, and facilitating the capturing of information about the target public.

Online Sales Promotion: A combination of communication instruments designed to communicate (to an individual or entity) the addition of some kind of bonus to the product during a defined timescale, as a means of achieving certain pre-planned communication objectives.

Utilitarian Benefits: All those benefits derived from the utility of a product. Principally they refer to saving, quality, and convenience, as these help the consumer to increase the utility of the acquisition derived from the purchase and the efficiency of the purchasing experience (Chandon, Wansink, & Laurent, 2000).

Web Experience: The skill of carrying out activities related to products, such as information-search, interacting with sellers, decision-making, purchasing products, and, ultimately, using the product (Sicilia, Ruiz, & Munuera, 2005).

Chapter 19
The Importance of ICT in the Social Support Networks and in the Citizenship of the Portuguese Elderly

Marisa Carla Barros Fonseca Silva
School of Technology and Management of Lamego, Portugal

ABSTRACT

The Information and Communication Technologies (ICT) contain properties that easily convert into solutions for people with special needs, contributing to their inclusion in everyday life. The possibility to intervene and participate in acts of communication in interpersonal settings and distance learning, or simply the possibility of using a device that simulates the vocalization of requests, greetings, and caresses gain a redoubled sense in the efforts to include citizens with special needs, as it does to the senior citizens, in societies attempting to promote equal opportunities among its members. This chapter focuses on the interaction between the elderly and the information and communication technologies and the impact that that interaction has on their participation in society.

INTRODUCTION

According to what was proposed by several authors throughout this work as well as through the analysis of obtained results, we can infer that the senior individual has advantages when using the Internet as a communication intermediary. When they use the virtual space to improve the physical space, they improve the communication in distance. They also realize that the social support provided online is likely to be more accessible and visible to any hour, which allows a greater enjoyment of it. Besides, the Internet allows effective participation, which transforms seniors in active citizens with the ability to increase their sociocultural capital.

DOI: 10.4018/978-1-4666-4373-4.ch019

The presented analysis allowed inferring that senior citizens in the sampled group want to learn and use ICT in the promotion of their personal networks and citizenship. We conclude, therefore, that the use of this tool is a strong improver of senior citizen's quality of living as well as their social inclusion/participation and as a consequence, a powerful tool of sociocultural capital.

The relevance of Internet used by seniors under study and its importance on active citizenship, advises us that we need to pay special attention to the systematic teaching of this tool. This kind of teaching in institutions that support these age groups, is used as a tool that is useful in fighting isolation and loneliness.

The study sample consists of 351 seniors who attend computer classes at Senior Universities in Portugal, individuals over 50 years using ICT. Nowadays there are about 120 Senior Universities in Portugal where computer courses are taught. Each class comprises about 40 students, which makes a population of about 4,800 seniors.

To evaluate the study variables it was used a questionnaire. This questionnaire will provide the description of the sample regarding the social characteristics and the use of ICT by the older. It was also used the Instrumento de Análise da Rede Social Pessoal (IARSP) which allowed to analyze the social network which could be improved by ICT use.

Issues for which the study aims to address:

Can the computer and the Internet use help seniors to feel included as members of the community as their age and needs increase? Does this use promote the development of their social networks?

BACKGROUND

The impact of ICT use, and more specifically the computer and the Internet's impact has on the increase of seniors social capital and in the promotion of their (re)integration into society was a theme already studied in some works, especially in the international context, such as Spain, the United States, Ireland and Scotland (the latter by comparing the Swedish senior). In the Portuguese case there is a certain hiatus of research on this subject.

Among the work carried out in the international context we can highlight the study of Manuel Area Moreira (1998), entitled *Desigualdades, educación y nuevas tecnologías*, which states that ICTs have harmful side effects on the social system, including, target and increase cultural and economic distances between sectors integrated in the technological development and the population excluded from this development, since a certain economic and cultural level to acquire these tools is an essential factor for this type of inclusion.

According to him, the use of ICT is contributing to a change and a better society as a whole and is a consequence of the quality of life of citizens. It would be naive not to recognize that the economic, social and cultural ICT benefits for those who use them are undeniable (Moreira, 1998). ICTs have also substantive effects on the citizenship policy formation, in the configuration and transmission of ideas and ideological values, in the development of attitudes towards inter-relationship and interaction with others. According to the study, access to culture conveyed by these technologies will become a reality for those whose economic level enables them to acquire them and those who have adequate knowledge to understand and use them. The article looks at ICT as a specific communication system and compares it with the means of traditional mass communication (television, for ex.), concluding that in today's societies are set up two parallel networks of different information both the content and convey the same culture as the way to store, organize and access to information: A network is represented by the traditional media (press, radio, movies and especially television) and the other shaped by technology information and digital media (mobile, digital television, Internet, etc.). Each one offers different opportunities and cultural experiences, and it is expected to be used only for a given network communication

can take in the short term, a situation of cultural marginality, but currently this membership still identifies himself with socioeconomic profile of each individual and according to his experience of life and professional experience.

Antonio Bautista García-Vera published in 2001 an article *Desigualdades sociales, nuevas tecnologias y política educativa* (Bautista García-Vera, 2001) that, following the previous one, makes an analysis of the nature of links that may exist between the current technology products and the inequalities that exist in the countries and peoples, and between the layers of the population of a society or a country. It also presents a historical perspective on the issue of inequalities in the world, covering concepts such as poverty, hunger, and misery.

Given this approach, the author aims to distinguish the inequalities between developed and developing countries, highlighting the main variables that may contribute to this distinction and can even help to maintain this gap at the development level.

As a theoretical framework for understanding the replication and scaling up of social inequalities, the author focuses on the assumptions of Basil Bernstein (this explains the reproduction of social inequalities through the mechanisms that, through the symbolic control and identity provided by codes and speeches, increase that reproduction) and Michael Foucault (this, based on the construction of knowledge, present some regulatory and disciplinary techniques as mechanisms used by the power to keep the governance and inequality, as relevant elements of these techniques are new technologies).

As main conclusions, the author presents the concern shown by several authors with regard to the danger involved in the increase of inequalities mediated by uneven growth of technology and the access to them, depending on the region and the socio-economic benchmark of every social class.

Also in 2001, Melanie Lewin prepared a study entitled "Equal with Anybody: Computers in the Lives of Older People" (Lewin, 2001). According to this study, there is much more to study when we talk about the computer used by seniors than what is commonly studied, and that concerns to the need of support that older people find by that way, like a form of maintenance of their contact with society and continue to participate actively as citizens.

Speaking of seniors is, according to this study, speak of losses. Being able to use the computer is a way to offset some of the losses that accompany old age. It is also mentioned in the study that there are those losses that result in the exclusion of this group of people.

For those people who are left alone or have health problems/mobility that invite them to the isolation, this study argues that the computer provides companionship and distraction, and that increases their social networks and, in our opinion, in a way of promote self-esteem of these people, as they continue to be able to validate/share their contribution to the community.

Those who have some health problems, age characteristics, answered that the computer can function as a valuable help in everyday life, bridging some gaps inherent to these ages (e.g., larger font than the one that is handwritten facilitates reading) and even serving as a form of contact with social institutions. In addition, the computer allows them to retain some autonomy in some areas and, in some cases, provide skills.

Some have referred that it has been given them a second chance to learn, provided them the opportunity to develop and perfect new capabilities/skills that, until then, had not developed because they are unnecessary for their social life and/or professional. It seems that also offered them the opportunity to look forward instead of being stuck in the past, planning how they will use their free time and feeling as useful to society.

Computer use has made these people that would be finished for life active and participatory citizenship, to gain new respect for their family, the younger generation and their friends and neighbors, and those who actively contributed in their local community, can use the computer to continue to do so. Computer use has another advantage that translates into the need of older people have to stay rooted in the modern world, giving up the convenience and comfort of the knowledge acquired and that it had been sufficient throughout their lives and achieve their objectives.

The seniors in the study showed that they do not accept the bias given to them to be technophobes. Some with greater will power, others encouraged by some others. Everyone learned to use the computer because they feel it as a need for not being socially excluded.

In his turn, the British Educational Communications and Technology Agency (BECTA) published a study in 2001 entitled The "Digital Divide": A discussion paper (BECTA, 2001) where, through a desk review, the authors argue that the introduction of ICT serve the purpose to prevent and end social divisions and provide new opportunities for all, by ensure that new knowledge economies include everyone. However, the construction of powerful communication networks introduces new social disparities. Once ICTs proliferate, begins to verify the need for a reformulation of concepts of poverty and social exclusion. This study argues that the main factors contributing to the "digital divide" are: the segmented offer of the market, the equipment cost, lack of relevance, interest and aspirations towards ICT, lack of access to ICT or training for its use, the lack of sufficient levels of literacy for the use of ICT, the lack of working together to share best practices in using ICT, and barriers to ICT access in the community.

Another author, with some relevance in the study of this issue, is Susannah Fox. Her study is titled Wired seniors: a fervent few, inspired by family ties (Fox, 2001) and was conducted through telephone interviews.

This study shows that seniors who use the Internet are usually healthier and with a higher level of education. Regarding gender, there are more men using the Internet. We can also see in this study that 84% of older Americans first used the Internet for reasons that are related to their work or school. Of these, 48% said they were encouraged by their relatives using the Internet. About 3 in 5 seniors using the Internet (56%) say that this form of communication has increased its contacts with the family. The utility that seniors seek on the Internet more often relates to the use of electronic mail (93%).

In 2002, David Segarra Mediavilla (2002) published a study based on structured in-depth interviews, entitled *Vivir al margen de Internet: los ancianos en la sociedad de la information.*

Data analyses and interviews allowed the author to observe an effective relationship between age and Internet use. Older people are the least that use. The percentages of connection of the elders in Western societies are so low that it can be stated, the author says, that this is a population segment most part outside the information society. However, the intensity of this "gray gap" varies widely between countries and contexts. In the U.S., for example, Internet use declines precipitously from 65, while in Catalonia connection levels decay more smoothly.

A very important conclusion that this study reached was that this exclusion (digital) is closely linked to other types of exclusions that are concentrated in these age groups. The fact that these people are no longer working (end of active life) is another factor for not using ICT, even if they have had some contact with these tools before.

Another study produced in the theme "use of ICT in specific countries" is the one conducted by the National Council on Ageing and Older People (sd). This study - ICT and Older People in Ireland: evidence from a study by the National Council on Ageing and Older People (People, sd) begins by stating that the information and communication technologies have come to form a Second Industrial Revolution.

According to the authors, the Internet offers tremendous potential for people to participate in society, economy, politics and, above all, to share experiences and knowledge with others, contributing to social change and evolution. It also allows to overcome the traditional disadvantages translated, for example, by geographic isolation or the possible limitations in terms of physical mobility.

However, the study also points to the effect that the increase in information and communication technologies can make that some groups occupy a position of serious disadvantage, particularly those with low education and low wages/earnings, which usually include the most seniors.

The aim of this study was, through the seniors for their own, know what kind of information they would like to see made available, by what means and where. The study concluded that the means by which the most Irish senior received information was the press, being the Internet placed second to last. The reason given for this was the little confidence that the Irish senior lay in the use of new technological tools.

Senior Net also publishes a paper in 2002 where the U.S. population is studied. This study is entitled The Age Wave Meets the Technology Wave: Broadband and Older Americans (Adler, 2002) and presents some benefits that information and communication technologies can bring to Americans seniors, as well as some barriers that still need to be overcome for the full enjoyment of these benefits.

As for benefits, the study shows the following: a close connection with family and friends, even though geographically separated, a long life learning, even for those who have limitations in terms of mobility, the fact that they have an enormous impact on the lives of seniors with regard to health (provides services such as tele-medicine), the fact that they allow seniors to remain independent and that the creation of new entertainment options to combat loneliness.

However, the study points out some obstacles that need to be overcome, among which stands out the fact to ensure that these new services are easy for seniors to learn, use and ensure that online applications are private and safe (to ensure confidence in these applications).

Older people and Information Society Technology (2002) was a Senior Watch study that used a comparative analysis between the European Union Member States (Watch, 2002). Thus, this study provides precise information about the member states with regard to seniors and to information technology and communication.

Initially, the article analyzes the infrastructure that each member state makes available to older people who are interested in using information technology and communication. Later, it describes the policies that are being practiced on this subject in all Member States, also doing a detailed comparison of the current use and potential demand of information technology and communication by seniors and how policies have sought to promote increased adherence to these tools.

BT (BT Group - United Kingdom Company that works with telecommunications, telephone lines, mobile phones, digital TV, online security, etc.) published in 2004 a study about the impact of "New Technologies in Social and Cultural Capital in the British population" (BT, 2004), making a projection of the Technologies impact on the year 2025, entitled The digital divide in 2025. This study is carried out, based on interviews addressed to experts, documentary analysis and forecasting methods.

The study defines digital exclusion as not having Internet access at home. On this basis, according to the study, 51% of the adult British population can be considered digitally excluded. Therefore, this percentage is still away from the opportunities presented in terms of access to information, access to services, increasing their social and cultural capital and the many ways to communicate with friends, family, business and government, even using the full potential of electronic commerce on the various stakeholders.

According to the study, the most frequently problems found that hinder digital inclusion are those who are relate to wages/low income, that unfeasible the payment of information technology and communication, deficiencies and/or lack of skills for its use, and, finally, the fact that people still see no need to use these technologies and do not perceive their benefits.

Taking into account the projections in this study, we can say that these problems will grow in importance and the access will be limited to certain groups of society.

Recently, in 2010, Farah, Rosa Maria; Arantes, R. Pillar, Baptist, Fabio Luis, et. al., present an article entitled, New technologies in aging, which refers to the importance that ICT has in filling the "vacuum" left by the inherent reduction of the personal network, as well as the fact that they are powerful tools for seniors social and cultural inclusion.

The longevity achieved by promoting health in our days brings as consequences the sharp change routines and life itself, imposing new challenges that society needs to respond urgently and effectively. Factors such as the family nuclearization, the distance from neighbors, make the social life of the senior restricted and limited, and their chances of human encounters and exchanges increasingly rare and occasional, because of their conditions attached to their own age/condition, or because of the speed of life in our modern society (Farah & Arantes, 2010).

The longevity above coincides with the period when the work stops, which does not imply, that these individuals can't stay active since their physical and psychological capacities still intact and because of that they can continue to contribute as citizens pro-active and involved. It is a fact that the maintenance of social activity and/or family, work through volunteering and/or educational activity by Senior Universities are relevant factors to the preservation of health. It is precisely this "empty space" left by the circumstances of the life of this age group (death of loved family, friends, retirement, etc.), that ICT can be adopted as a powerful tool for social and cultural integration for this population (Farah & Arantes, 2010).

The technology evolution, no one doubts, revolutionized the lives of everyone and is now part of our experiences, providing a significant improvement in our quality of life. Although the generation of "digital immigrants" (digital immigrants, according to Small & Vorgan, 2009, are those people who were not born in the technologies era, i.e., they have to learn to use a tool that is not "of his time") (Small, 2009) be afraid to let themselves be influenced by the computer age, not because they don't want to take advantage of ICT but mainly because these devices are unfamiliar and perhaps even an impediment to the routine they're used to, seniors are no exception when they can, through this use, be part of the world, get to it and feel part of it.

Until a few years ago people were "old", now become elderly in the mood to feel active participants in a social context where they are located and mainly collaborative and interactive.

Interactivity, then, is the keyword on the Internet, we are called on it to change, build relationships, to listen and be heard, to share information and give us a little to the development of social capital and the efficient social change .

Social networks that now reach us via the Internet may, indeed, be a "cibersocial" inclusion channel accessible to all ages, since already provide resources to overcome some possible difficulties in the older ages.

By allowing the senior to beinformed in real time, inserted in the world and participant, this tool, may turning their participation in an active and effective participation and important for the strengthening of social capital. This communication channel, which opens doors to people of all ages, is a networks system that is expanding rapidly.

The creation of new relations is one of the possibilities presented by this tool that may provide the growth of the individual networks. The Internet and the computer can adduce unique opportunities for seniors to socialize and establish social networks that help them to overcome the moments of solitude and to foster their emotional and societal well-being (Sum SM, 2008).

In a life time when the changes are large and the phase of the "empty nest" is installed, with major losses in familiar terms (widow and children independence) and also important employment losses (retirement), the seniors are driven to seek alternative that make them continue to participate in life and that make them continue to feel useful to the environment where they are inserted.

Learning to use a considered cutting-edge technology as the computer and the Internet has broken with the idea that old is past and have no possibility of being renewed with new acquisitions.

Several studies (as mentioned earlier) show the reasons why seniors want to learn informatics. Among these we can point: curiosity, the need to be updated and track progress, grandchildren and children who appear as supporters and as a mean to help them occupy their leisure time better and feel integrated.

THE LANGUAGE OF RELATIONS: SOCIAL SUPPORT ON THE INTERNET

Seniors and Computing: The Virtual Networks

If we refer to how this technology affects social relations in terms of possibilities and opportunities, we conclude that the Internet enables a greater number of relationships between members that are spaced, including elements that are in different temporal rhythms, because of the possibility of everyone do not need to be simultaneously on-line, which demonstrates the role of the Internet and ICT in general for the maintenance of pre-existing social networks (Boase & Wellman, 2004). Therefore provides the possibility of a less discrimination among the stakeholders in the relationship, allowing individuals belonging to a greater variety of social cycles and still allow it at a speed never reached through the relationships face to face. This way the Internet allows relationships to flourish in an environment of equality and respect, looking ahead to a stronger interaction in the future (ibid.).

One is also the fact that there are evidences (Boase & Wellman, 2004) that most relationships taken through online contacts are far beyond this type of contacts and are run by people who also know each other offline or that, sooner or later, they can feel the need for overstepping mere contact distance.

Having regard to the study by Katz and Riee in 2002, entitled The Social Consequences of Internet use (Katz & Riee cit. By Boase & Wellman, 2004), the social consequences of Internet use can be conceptualized with respect to the interaction with family and friends, the formation of new friends online and the neighborly relations. The same study examined whether the maintenance of personal relationships online is associated with changes in the lives of these people offline.

In this same study was examined the item "Civic and Community Participation," the results did not show a direct correlation between the Internet and more or less civility, or between the extreme positions and manipulation, nor has this tool as a source of society democratization, may even be understood as a tool that complements and reinforces (to toast the community with a new mean of communication) the existing physical communities.

Therefore, the Internet cannot be considered a decisive tool of political socialization, but for those who already have a motivation or a civic community involvement, that is, allows those who already holds a participatory and responsible citizenship to society where it operates see potentiated its options and its ability to interact with the use of this tool. In the words of the authors (Katz & Riee cit. by Boase & Wellman, 2004) "the Internet does not create or diminish on its own the social capital."

Also, in the text are offered many examples of cases that demonstrate how groups of people or collectives with similar interests or needs have become true communities, thanks to these technological resources (Katz & Rice, 2006).

We consider, therefore, that social networks online are, more and more, to get people into the virtual world, are providing the motivation for global engagement with a medium that until very recently, was considerate little attractive or inaccessible, for the costs or the lack of preparation for their use as a daily tool.

This desire that most people have to be in contact with others (either know them or not know) can be used to strengthen relationships offline, since online social networking can offer a perspective of life (a possible resumption) for those who are isolated and disconnected from family, friends and communities for various reasons, such as seniors (difficulty of mobility, migration of elements belonging to their social networks, loss of contact, end of professional life, etc.).

Social networks can also offer the possibility of involvement in public services and organizations in a very different ways and have the potential to involve those who usually see the public sector as a system that is far and impenetrable. The bets on e-government in the field of the Administration-to-citizen interaction by the Public Administration in many states demonstrates the importance attached to these tools to transform the relationship between the citizens and the public sector and in the modernize of the provided services (Government, 2008).

Seniors and Computing: The Promotion of Citizenship

Through the global communication means such as television and the Internet, many barriers have been overcome with the goal of defining global phenomena.

The Information society refers itself to a new status quo and the new paradigm resulting from the socio-economic and technological change process observed worldwide and all-encompassing. In a narrower plan, with direct relation to the use of technology, this phenomenon is expected to influence the interaction in computer-mediated activities, human behavior at the individual level, the collective consciousness, the social and the economic environment and the citizens' quality of life.

Without a great effort we can detected that the information and communication technologies are being included in the various activities called "worldly" of our daily lives.

The link, which will increasingly be identified as the dependency between communication technologies, information and the user, opens itself like an umbrella that will gradually cover everything. Professional, personal and recreational strands of the individual life intersect with the technological tools, transforming the activities and the associated processes.

The individual functional capabilities in their communication, professional and entertaining strands, just to name a few, gain new levels of performance and success for those who follow the evolution of new technologies.

Therefore, we must follow the evolution of times surpassing the risk of being left out of society.

This rapid evolution that brings, on the one hand the progress, the ease of communication and the ease in obtaining information that we could not reach before, but in the other hand opens the door to new types of exclusion for those who do not want, cannot or do not know how to accompany such changes.

Computer networks have the high potential that is to bring people together and because of that they promote social networks. However, this concept of social networking exceeds the telematics links allowed through a computer network. A fundamental principle of any network defines that its real value is based on relations between people of this network, relations-oriented to multiple activities that extend themselves from leisure to work.

The social networks that are connected with the Internet today certainly can be a "ciberso-

Table 1. Statistics on age by gender

Age Gender	N	Min	Max	$\overline{X}$	$\bar{s}$	Sk	Std. Error	K	Std. Error	CV (%)
Males	108	53	82	66.69	7.080	-0.039	0.233	-0.367	0.461	10.62
Females	243	53	83	67.39	6.544	0.237	0.156	-0.290	0.311	9.71
Total	*351*	*53*	*83*	*67.18*	*6.711*	*0.127*	*0.130*	*-0.293*	*0.260*	*9.99*

cial" inclusion channel that enables the seniors to promote their contacts, meet new people with common interests, and avoid social exclusion state that seniors are normally voted, since this powerful tool is provided with equipment and resources that enable the overcome of possible limitations that exist in this population.

This possibility of "e-Inclusion" aims not offer a "godly" to "spend time," but rather the possibility of expanding their "active life" and creative life (Farah & Arantes, 2010), i.e., an effective social participation. Basically, the maintenance of their citizenship rights (informing, interacting, providing real-time news, entering by this way the senior in to the world events, could well invite them to continue giving valid opinions and be a member of a society still under construction).

With greater access to information and active participation in different experiences, different brand of globalized society, the elderly has had opportunities in various fields (...) to reframe their existence, their learning, their importance as a citizen holder of rights and legal safeguards, his age, his own old age and the levels of their effective participation in society. (Gaspari, Schwartz, 2005 cit. Farias & Miranda, 2009).

Then the technology appears as a contribution in the isolation reducing, in the mental stimulation, and finally, in promoting the welfare of senior citizens, facilitating the process of communication with relatives or friends, fostering by this way, interpersonal relations or promoting new generational encounters on the Web.

Table 2. Participation and citizenship

		n	%	Descritive mesures
Participates actively in an organization	No	120	34.2	Mode = 2
	Yes	231	65.8	
If so, which?	Senior Academy	79	22.5	Mode = 1
	Senior Academy; Cultural; Sports	3	0.9	
	Senior Academy; Sports	5	1.4	
	Senior Academy; Religious	8	2.3	
	Scouts	3	0.9	
	Red Cross	31	8.8	
	Cultural	2	0.6	
	Cultural; Sports; Civic	3	0.9	
	Cultural; Sports	7	2.0	
	Cultural; Religious	18	5.1	
	Sports	3	0.9	
	Partisan	36	10.3	
	Partisan; Sports; Cultural; Senior Academy	3	0.9	
	Partisan; Religious	3	0.9	
	Religious	3	0.9	
	Religious; Cultural	3	0.9	
	Religious; Sports	9	2.6	
	Religious; Humanitarian	3	0.9	
	Missing values	9	2.6	

Table 3. Descriptive statistics of the factor analysis

	Average	Standard Deviation	N
People to talk	1.58	.495	345
Friends	1.47	.500	345
A way to pass time	1.32	.469	345
Familie and friends contact	1.34	.473	345
Stay active in the community	1.50	.501	345
Stay informed	1.39	.489	345
Sort things out without help	1.68	.467	345
Feeling of being equal to all	1.66	.475	345
Opportunity to learn something new	1.10	.295	345

Seniors and Computing: The Study

Table 1 analysis shows us that the sample used in our study consists of 351 seniors, 243 females and 108 males. We note also that the age of the 351 elements of the total sample ranges from a minimum of 53 years and a maximum of 83 years, accounting for a current average age of 67.18 years, standard deviation of 6.71 years and a coefficient variation of 9.99%, which indicates the existence of a low dispersion around the average.

Analyzing the statistics for age by gender, we found that the average age for males ($\overline{X} = 66{,}69$) is higher than for females ($\overline{X} = 67{,}39$), presenting both a weak dispersion ($0\% < CV \leq 15\%$).

Analyzing the asymmetry or bias measures (Skweness/Std. Error) and flatness or kurtosis (kurtosis/Std. Error), we conclude that the distribution of ages in both sexes, is symmetric.

The study sample is divided between those who participate actively in an organization (66%) and those who not participat (34%), the first representing the majority (Table 2).

Of those who actually participate we can say that the vast majority (23% and 10% respectively) participate in the Senior Academy and in an organization of partisan nature. All other values were insignificant (Table 2).

Table 4. Correlation matrix of factor analysis

	People to talk	Friends	A way to pass time	Familie and friends contact	Stay active in the community	Stay informed	Sort things out without help	Feeling of being equal to all	Opportunity to learn something new
People to talk with	1.000	.477	.180	.336	.014	.146	.182	.026	.059
Friends	.477	1.000	.117	.363	.206	.233	.195	.115	.049
A way to pass time	.180	.117	1.000	.109	.171	.243	-.070	.239	.217
Family and friends contact	.336	.363	.109	1.000	.207	.196	.382	.138	.102
Stay active in the community	.014	.206	.171	.207	1.000	.324	.251	.100	.206
Stay informed	.146	.233	.243	.196	.324	1.000	.255	.052	.244
Sort things out without help	.182	.195	-.070	.382	.251	.255	1.000	.110	.117
Feeling of being equal to all	.026	.115	.239	.138	.100	.052	.110	1.000	.172
Opportunity to learn something new	.059	.049	.217	.102	.206	.244	.117	.172	1.000

Table 5. KMO index and Bartlett's test

Kaiser-Meyer-Olkin Measure of Sampling Adequacy		.668
Bartlett's Test of Sphericity	Approx. Chi-Square	427.840
	df	36
	Sig.	.000

Summarizing the characteristics of our sample, we noted that most are female, aged between 65 and 80 years, married, with higher education and a number of offspring between 1 and 4 individuals.

They are mostly individuals who are actively involved in an organization, especially with regard to senior academy and partisan oriented associations.

We will make now an inferential analysis that allowed us to present the following results for the factor constituent items – Innovation from ICT use.

Examining the Table 3 we can verify that there is no item with averages or standard deviations neither too high nor too low, which means that data are average variability.

Through Table 4 we can find that this factor also present high enough numbers for the correlations so that we can use the method.

Through the analysis of Table 5 it appears that the value of KMO is 0.668, which leads us to conclude that the matrix is suitable to carry out the method.

As we see in Table 6 all values of the commonalities presented by the items that make up the factor analysis are greater than 0.5.

As can be seen in Table 7 will be extracted five components that explain 75% of the total variance.

The Varimax rotation performed allow us to do some groups: in the first dimension the communication with the primary network, in the second dimension the citizenship, in the third dimension the autonomy, in the fourth the inclusion and in the fifth dimension the innovation. So, we will define the first dimension as dimension 1 - Communication with the primary network, the second as Dimension 2 – citizenship, the third as dimension 3 – autonomy, the fourth as dimension 4 – inclusion and the fifth as dimension 5 – innovation (see Table 8).

Table 6. Commonalities for the items constituting the factor analysis

	Initial	Extraction
People to talk with	1.000	.782
Friends	1.000	.659
A way to pass time	1.000	.744
Family and friends contact	1.000	.597
Stay active in the community	1.000	.754
Stay informed	1.000	.638
Sort things out without help	1.000	.744
Feeling of being equal to all	1.000	.896
Opportunity to learn something new	1.000	.905

Next, we will use the dimensions created by the Principal Component Analysis and we will make a correlation between these and the variables that characterize the social support theory.

The aim of this correlation is to analyze the senior's social network, studying the relationship between the variables of the various dimensions presented with the characteristics of the senior's networks.

The Table 9 analysis makes us conclude that the variable "communication with the primary network" is related to the informal support. We can say that informal support is incremented by the forms of communication. It also correlates with the "citizenship" dimension, which suggest that the informal support increases as the citizenship and social participation also increases. This last dimension ("citizenship") is also correlated with the formal support, increasing in direct proportion.

With this analysis we can't conclude that the size of the network presented by the subject of the sample increases with the possible increase of the ICT-mediated communication, although

Table 7. Total variance explained by components factor analysis

Itens	Initial Eigenvalues			Extraction Sums of Squared Loadings			Rotation Sums of Squared Loadings		
	Total	% of Variance	Cumulative %	Total	% of Variance	Cumulative %	Total	% of Variance	Cumulative %
1	2.494	27.707	27.707	2.494	27.707	27.707	1.793	19.925	19.925
2	1.347	14.967	42.674	1.347	14.967	42.674	1.478	16.418	36.343
3	1.133	12.585	55.259	1.133	12.585	55.259	1.218	13.538	49.882
4	.957	10.633	65.892	.957	10.633	65.892	1.145	12.726	62.608
5	.790	8.774	74.666	.790	8.774	74.666	1.085	12.059	74.666
6	.677	7.523	82.190						
7	.641	7.125	89.315						
8	.540	5.998	95.312						
9	.422	4.688	100.000						

Table 8. Components rotation with Varimax

	Component				
	1	2	3	4	5
People to talk with	.870				
Friends	.765				
A way to pass time	.546		.477		
Family and friends contact		.843			
Stay active in the community		.697			
Stay informed			.790		
Sort things out without help			-.573		
Feeling of being equal to all				.941	
Opportunity to learn something new					.934

Table 9. Pearson correlation coefficient between the dimensions and the variables describing the social support

		Network size	Network density	Informal support	Formal support
Communication with the primary network	ρ	-.208**	.006	.158**	-.031
Citizenship	ρ	.029	.079	.123*	.190**
Autonomy	ρ	.019	-.092	.060	.023
Inclusion	ρ	-.158**	.054	.025	.089
Innovation	ρ	-.104	.017	-.031	.059

we can see that the same network will become denser with this type of communication. Moreover, it appears that the informal support (provided mainly by primary network) is closely related to ICT-mediated communication. Citizenship is an important factor with regard to the support provided by network elements, which leads us to believe that an individual who submits an active citizenship and effective social participation have a better chance of effective social support.

Final Considerations

Regarding the relationship between Internet use and seniors social-cultural capital, the results showed a close link between the use of the Internet, the network size, the network density and the network diversity, which is consistent with what Wellman defends when he says that the Internet helps to establish new social relationships, which may be continued off-line, creating bridges between the online and offline, therefore promoting greater social interaction. Eric also argues that the Internet can serve to expand existing patterns of contact and civic involvement.

As for the perceived support, it also increases with the increasing use of the Internet as well as reciprocal support among network members. Again, it is noted that, as advocated by Katz, Haythornthwaire & Wellman, people who use the Internet more frequently are more involved in their real communities. Melani Lewin also argues in her study, the importance of the Internet to maintain contact with senior and the surrounding society and the consequent support found in this way. According to the author, speaking of seniors is to speak of losses; these losses can be offset by the use of these tools. These will provide senior fellowship and distraction, increasing their social networks.

Thus, according to what was argued by the authors, we can say that seniors who presents an Internet use with those who are near and even for those who are far away physically, using the virtual space as an enhanced of the physical space, note the benefits of social support provided online, because it can be more accessible and visible and given any time, they tend to be more active citizens with an effective social participation, with the possibility of increase their social-cultural capital.

Authors such as Area Manuel Moreira argue that the use of ICT is contributing to an effective increase in the quality of life of seniors, as well as in their training for citizenship. Melanie Lewin has also the same opinion when she says that the use of computers has made the seniors regain the respect of their loved ones by increasing their citizen participation.

Farah, Arantes, Batista et al. all reiterate the importance of ICT to fill the "vacuum" left by the inherent reduction of the personal network of seniors citizens, and because they are powerful tools of social and cultural inclusion of older people. According to the authors, the creation of new relations is one of the possibilities presented by this tool that may provide greater increase of the individual networks. Moreover, by allowing the senior is in real time, informed, and inserted in the world and participating, this tool can, transform their effective and active participation and to be an important way of strengthening their social capital.

FUTURE RESEARCH DIRECTIONS

We could not finish, however, without leaving some suggestions for future research. Thus, we suggest that someone could try to carry out a longitudinal study, which allows the measurement of real changes in personal networks of seniors produced by ICT, starting by examining their networks prior to the introduction of ICT in their lives and after some time using them. As a statistical method, we suggest the use of structural equations in order to conduct a more accurate profile of the ICT senior user and its relation to the increase of the social-cultural capital.

CONCLUSION

There is a potential for the problems faced by humanity are somewhat modified from the use of new technologies and that, even among those who are critical, it is recognized. What is false, however, is to transform this potential as if it was reality itself. It is necessary to recognize that technological advances and, especially, their possible benefits, are still far from most of the population.

The Internet has some features that make it unique as a means of communication and information: it works in a system based on communication networks which, in theory, has no boundaries or barriers in their use. This technology helps the horizontality and the interactivity, that is, in principle, on the Internet are all "equal" and can exchange ideas and information instantly and without limits of geography and time, which becomes an asset especially for that group of people with special needs such as the elderly.

ICT are and must be, therefore, presented to the elders as a form of social integration which results in a more concrete way to reduce the isolation that this population is usually doomed, to a mental stimulation and a consequent promotion of welfare of this group and an easier alternative, though not completely replace, the communication process and their traditional ways. Elderly people often use the Internet in search of information on various issues, e.g. related to health, and still use the e-mail, already considered the most popular tool of the Internet, to communicate with family near and far. The belief that welcomes more fans, now, among the Portuguese seniors is that the use of these tools improves all areas of daily life.

However, several positions were taken on relation of the benefits or harm that involves the use of ICT for the networks and consequently for the production of capital. The author of this chapter is consistent with the position that the use of ICT as a mean of social relations does not replace face-to-face relationships, rather complements them and increases them, producing a greater civic involvement and a promotion of capital.

Also in the case of seniors, we can say that ICTs open up new horizons of participation and social inclusion that would otherwise be barred from this group. In fact, social networks of older people are usually composed of primary relationships, predominantly to the family relationships quadrant and which personal contact is of extreme importance. We perceive, however, that more and more individuals of this group are seeking closer ties resorting to the use of ICT as a mean of more regular and frequent contact.

REFERENCES

Adler, R. (2002). *The age wave meets the technology wave: Broadband and older americans*. Thousand Oaks, CA: Senior Net.

Bautista García-Vera, A. (2001). Desigualdades sociales, nuevas tecnologías y política educativa. In Area Moreira, M. (Ed.), *Educar en la sociedad de la información*. Bilbao, Spain: Desclée de Brower.

BECTA. (2001). *The 'digital divide': A discussion paper*. BECTA.

BT. (2004). *The digital divide in 2025*. BT.

Farah, R. M., & Arantes, R. P. (2010). *Novas tecnologias no envelhecimento*..

Fox, S. (2001). *pewInternet*. Retrieved from www.pewInternet.org

Moreira, M. A. (1998). *Desigualdades, educación y nuevas tecnologias*. Quaderns Digitals.

People, N. C. (n.d.). *ICT and older people in Ireland: Evidence from a study by the national council on ageing and older people*. Dublin, Ireland: Author.

Small, G. (2009). *El cerebro digital*. Barcelona, Spain: Ediciones Urano.

Sum, S. M. (2008). *Internet technology and social capital: how the Internet affects seniors' social capital and wellbeing*. Sydney, Australia: University of Sydney.

Watch, S. (2002). *Older people and information society technology: A comparative analysis of the current situation in the European Union and of future trends*. Academic Press.

ADDITIONAL READING

Alarcão, M., & Sousa, L. (2007). Rede social pessoal: Do conceito à avaliação. *Psychologica*, 353–376.

Antunes, M., Mealha, C., & Mealha, O. (2001). *Tecnologias da informação e comunicação na reconfiguração das redes de relação dos sujeitos*. Aveiro, Portugal: Universidade de Aveiro.

Castells, M. (2004). *A galáxia internet: Reflexões sobre internet, negócios e sociedade*. Lisboa, Portugal: Fundação Calouste Gulbenkian.

Castells, M. (2005). *A sociedade em rede*. Lisboa, Portugal: Fundação Calouste Gulbenkian.

Castells, M. (2007). *A era da informação: Economia, sociedade e cultura*. Lisboa, Portugal: Fundação Calouste Gulbenkian.

Correia, S. (2007). *Capital social e comunidade cívica, o círculo virtuoso da cidadania*. Lisboa, Portugal: Instituto Superior de Ciências Sociais e Políticas.

Durston, J. (2000). Qué es el capital social comunitario?. *Serie Políticas Sociales, 38*.

Ferlander, S. (2003). *The internet, social capital and local community*. Stirling, UK: University of Stirling Department of Psychology.

Foley, M., & Edwards, B. (1998). The paradox of civil society. *Journal of Democracy*, 38–52.

Government, D. F. (2008). *Online social networks - Research report*. London: Government.

Grupta, S. (2007). Developing the commitment to virtual community: The balanced effects of cognition and affect. *Information Resources Management Journal*, 28–43. doi:10.4018/irmj.2007010103.

Guadalupe, S. (2009). *Intervenção em rede: Serviço social, sistémica e redes de suporte social*. Coimbra, Portugal: Imprensa da Universidade de Coimbra.

Hampton, K. N. (1999). Netville on-line and off-line. *American Behavior Scientist, 43*(3).

Hofstade, G. (1980). *Culture's consequences: Internacional differences in work related values*. Newbury Park, CA: Sage Publications.

Inglehart, R. (1997). *Modernization and postmodernization — Cultural, economic and political change in 43 societies*. Princeton, NJ: Princeton University.

Karavidas, M., Lim, N. K., & Katsikas, S. L. (2005). The effects of computers on older adult users. *Computers in Human Behavior, 21*(5), 697–711. doi:10.1016/j.chb.2004.03.012.

Katz, J. E., & Rice, R. E. (2006). *Consecuencias sociales del uso de internet*. Editorial UOC.

Kauchakje, S., Penna, M. C., Frey, K., & Duarte, F. (2006). *Redes socio-técnicas y participación ciudadana: Propuestas conceptuales y analíticas para el uso de las TICs*. REDES.

Méndez, R. M. (2004). *Cibersociedad*. Retrieved Agosto 24, 2008, from http://www.cibersociedad.net

People, N. C. (n.d.). *ICT and older people in Ireland: Evidence from a study by the national council on ageing and older people*. Dublin, Ireland: Author.

Putnam, R. D. (1996). Who killed civic America?. *Prospect*, 66-72.

Raposo, R., & Mealha, Ó. (2005). *Tecnologias de apoio: um instrumento para a igualização das oportunidades de comunicar na sociedade de informação. Rumos da Sociedade da Comunicação* (pp. 393–401). Lisboa, Portugal: Nova Vega.

Seeman, T. E., & Berkman, L. F. (1988). Structural characteristics of social networks and their relationship with social support in the elderly: Who provides support? *Social Science & Medicine*, 737–749. doi:10.1016/0277-9536(88)90065-2 PMID:3358145.

KEY TERMS AND DEFINITIONS

Citizen: Person how participates actively in the society.

Information Age: Ability of individuals to transfer information freely, and to have instant access to information that would have been difficult or impossible to find previously.

Personal Network: A set of human contacts known to an individual, with whom that individual would expect to interact at intervals to support a given set of activities.

Senior: Elderly person.

Social Network: A social structure made up of a set of actors, such as individuals or organizations, and the dyadic ties between these actors.

Sociocultural Capital: The expected collective benefits derived from the preferential treatment and cooperation between individuals and groups.

Virtual Community: A social network of individuals who interact through specific media, potentially crossing geographical and political boundaries in order to pursue mutual interests or goals.

Chapter 20
Impact of 2.0 on Contemporary Marketing

Dora Simões
University of Aveiro, Portugal

Sandra Filipe
University of Aveiro, Portugal

ABSTRACT

Contemporary marketing recognizes the scope and complexities of marketing activities. It is a multidimensional and a dynamic concept, known as holistic marketing, that asks and allows for the support systems in order to permanently connect to the parties, to create value and long-term relationships among all. In this context, this chapter presents a wide review about conceptualization of relationship marketing and its evolution and integration within the broader concept of contemporary marketing. It highlights that the development of a program for implementing and managing a successful Customer Relationship Management (CRM) system is an essential part of a strategic contemporary marketing plan. Additionally, it is imperative to assess it to better demonstrate its success or failure. The metrics to do this are also revisited in this chapter. Still, the emerging capabilities of CRM systems using Internet technologies are putting tremendous challenges on organizations and their human resources. Reference is made to some social media tools that can be a cheap and useful support in marketing strategies.

INTRODUCTION

At the beginning of the third millennium, the process of market interaction requests from marketing the creation of expectations that should be seized and overcome, generating intrinsic values with all stakeholders, focusing on long-term relationships with them and strongly increasing ethical, environmental, and legal and social responsibilities to society as a whole. According to Kotler and Keller (2009) contemporary marketing is a Holistic Marketing that incorporates an Integrated Marketing, an Internal Marketing, a Relationship Marketing, and a Performance Marketing.

DOI: 10.4018/978-1-4666-4373-4.ch020

This chapter, placed within this new approach of Holistic Marketing, based his study on the concept of relationship marketing and assesses the contribution that Customer Relationship Management (CRM) system and the social media have on contemporary marketing. A brief review of the evolution of the marketing concept stresses that after the mass marketing focused on product (the concern was to sell one product to as many customers as possible), became the marketing of segments (requires the identification of categories of customers to create profiles based mainly in demographic elements). But liberalization of markets and competition easily lead to the conclusion that this is not enough. The new era assumes that marketing should be customer oriented (rather than the product) and requires customer identification at other levels. In addition, it is crucial to keep a study on customer behaviour over time, and consequently go adjusting the form of interaction with the mutual goal for retaining valuable customers the longest time possible, and thereby increase profit and reduce the cost with each customer. The concept of relationship marketing emerges. But for this to be possible technology plays an increasingly vital role, so relationship marketing concept is associated with CRM systems, as evidenced by some references in the literature about the concepts. On the other hand, the emerging capabilities of CRM systems enabling both reading and writing in online collaborative environments are putting tremendous challenges on organizations and their human resources. It is therefore important that agents involved be able to recognize it, a priori, as a philosophy and a strategy that must be understood and accepted, to be assumed. Additionally, the social media are in general huge data objects embodying complex knowledge concerning customer opinions, tastes and preferences as well as possible connections between single markets. Knowing, recognizing and understanding the related concepts, the technologies that can be used for automation and the performance indicators that can best demonstrate its achievement or failure is imperative.

The chapter begins with a background around the theme. After that, a state-of-the-art will be presented about the concepts of relationship marketing under the big umbrella of contemporary marketing. Its integration on this holistic approach and the intertwining of these concepts will be also explained based on pragmatics of theory and practice. The following section presents an overview around de CRM systems and their application. Under the perspective of the technology support, an architecture covering the organizational levels (operational, analytical and collaborative) is presented. Relevance will be made on the use of Internet technologies and collaborative platforms, namely on social media. The triumph or failure of a program of this nature will be analyzed in next section, where several performance indicators are presented to assess the degree of implementation of the program, either on the implementation level as on the outcomes level. Some critical success factors are also appointed. Finally, future research directions and conclusions are indicated.

BACKGROUND

Marketing is derived from "market" which refers to a group of sellers and buyers that cooperate to exchange goods and services. Contemporary marketing should be conceived as a complex multidimensional concept designated by Kotler and Keller (2009) as Holistic Marketing: an (1) Integrated Marketing Concept (integration of all components of the marketing-mix); (2) Internal Marketing (marketing as business perspective in all departments of the organization); (3) Relationship marketing (develop a strategic and long term vision for the organization with all its stakeholders); and (4) Performance Marketing (financial accountability and social responsibility marketing).

During the last decade of the twentieth century relationship marketing "was probably the major trend in marketing and certainly the major (and arguably the most controversial) talking point in business management" (Egan, 2011, p. 16). According to Gummesson (1987) the relationship marketing approach of the 90s emerges as opposed to transactional marketing approach from previous years and is based on: (1) the relationship (marketing orientation to creating, maintaining and developing relationships with customers), (2) the interactivity of the parties (strong process of communication between vendors and customers to create mutual value and delivery), and (3) and long-term (requiring a long timeline for the creation, maintenance and development of relationship). Gummesson (2008, p. 7) also upholds that "CRM is the values and strategies of Relationship Marketing – with special emphasis on the relationship between a customer and a supplier – turned into practical application and dependent on both human action and information technology."

On the other hand, society is facing an explosion of Web 2.0. The term Web 2.0 generated a new attitude towards the Web: there was a change in the role of the Internet user, from a mere passive spectator to global producer of content, using tools such as blogs, wikis, online social networks, virtual communities. The Web 2.0 is not just a technology access and unlimited supply of information, but it is also a social technology, where thousands and millions of individuals and social actors interact, creating new dimensions of social reactions and new forms of social organization (Peixoto, 2010).

CONCEPTUALIZATION

In his book originally published in 1973, Drucker argued against the receptivity of some authors "There is only one valid definition of business purpose: to create a customer... the customer is a foundation of a business and keeps it in existence... because it is the purpose to create a customer, any business organization has two—and only two—basic functions: marketing and innovation... marketing is the distinguishing, the unique function of the business" Drucker (2007, p. 61). Despite nearly four decades of existence, Drucker's idea still stands. According to Gummesson (2008, p. 14) marketing "is a culture, an organizational function and a set of processes for creating, communicating, and delivering value with customers and for interacting in networks of relationships in ways that benefit the organization, its customers and other stakeholders". This definition is imbued with the concept of relationship marketing.

In recent years, academic literature and marketing professionals have been putting a notorious emphasis over the concept of relationship marketing (Cristopher, Payne & Ballantine, 1994). These were driven by the new environment characterized by highly intense competition, high concern for quality, excess production capacity and strong technological development (Berry, 1995; Sheth & Parvatiyar, 1995). According to Nevin (1995, p. 327) the concept of relationship marketing has been used to reflect four different perspectives: (1) assumes a promotional approach and emphasizes that relationship marketing will direct the flow of promotional monies toward targeted customers; (2) focuses on individual customers and building a close relationship with individual customers or treating each customer as a segment of one; (3) concerned about keeping or retaining customers by using a variety of customers bonding techniques and staying in touch with the customer after the sale is made; (4) takes a more strategic perspective by putting the customer first and shifting the role of marketing from manipulating the customer (telling and selling) to genuine customer involvement (communicating and sharing the knowledge). We believe that the CRM and the social media must be an important role in all of the perspectives.

Contemporary Marketing

During the past decades, marketing has strengthened its role within organizations, although the understanding of marketing has undergone profound changes. Kotler *et al.* (2008) proposes six alternative concepts which organizations design and carry out their marketing strategies. One philosophy—production concept—assumes that consumers are primarily interested in product availability and low prices, and that managers should focus on achieving high production efficiency and mass distribution. A second approach—product concept—stresses the idea that consumers will favour products that offer quality, performance, or innovation, and that managers should concentrate on making superior products and improving them over time. A third view—selling concept—argues that consumers and businesses, if left alone, will ordinarily not buy enough of the selling company's products, and that managers should therefore undertake an aggressive selling and promotion effort. A fourth philosophy—marketing concept—holds that the key to achieving its organizational goals consists of the company being more effective than competitors in creating, delivering, and communicating customer value to its selected target customers. The fifth perspective—societal marketing orientation—assumes that the organization seeks considering consumer's needs, the organization's requirements, and consumer's and society's long term interests. Finally, the sixth philosophy—sustainable marketing concept—focuses on the requirement that the organizations should satisfy the needs of their customers without compromising the ability of future generations to satisfy their own needs.

It is commonly accepted that the trend is for these different approaches to be taken sequentially over time. At present, the focus of marketing is much broader; it is evident in the concern to meet the immediate and future needs of all stakeholders; it requires that managers should make good marketing decisions to determine the needs, desires and interests of target market and provide superior value to customers, so that the welfare of all stakeholders and society is maintained and improved in the future.

In the same way, American Marketing Association (AMA) has been renewing the concept of marketing. The definition of marketing, proposed and accepted by the AMA in 1985, assumed that marketing is "the process of planning and executing the conception, pricing, promotion and distribution of ideas, goods and services to create exchanges that satisfy individual and organizational objectives" (AMA, 1985). In 2007, the AMA redefined marketing as "the activity, set of institutions, and processes for creating, communicating, delivering, and exchanging offerings that have value for customers, clients, partners and society at large" (AMA, 2007).

Confronting the definition of marketing proposed by the AMA in 1985 with the redefinition of 2007, there is a clear renewal of the content of the marketing concept or marketing in key variables, both in the extent of its purpose. The AMA definition of marketing (1985) based his philosophy on the management of exchanges satisfying the needs and desires of the consumer as a means to achieve organizational objectives. It reinforces the key variables of the marketing-mix or model of 4 P's in a more operational aspect (Boss, 2011) and reflects a transactional marketing approach, still oriented to the product and for the transaction and less to the customer and the relationship. This conceptualization has prevailed for years as an unchanging concept of marketing. However, some studies have begun to criticize the transactional approach, reporting that this can only be applied to certain types of organizations and markets (Grönroos, 1994; Gummesson, 1987), and other studies highlighted the weakness and failure of the approach of the marketing mix to achieve a true market orientation (Constantinides, 2006; Cristopher et al., 1994; Harker, 1999).

The new definition of the AMA places marketing as providing long-term value rather than narrowly as an exchange of money (short-term) for the benefit of the shareholder of the organization. Harker and Egan (2006) refer that the definition of marketing reflects a change in marketing approach that supports somehow the definition of relationship marketing. The 2007 definition also has an expansion of the traditional view, and highlighted the value that is passed to all the various public (not limited only to customers) and points to a set of special challenges that social marketers face (Andreasen, Lee, & Rothschild, 2008).

In fact, the trends and forces that define the 21st century mean that organizations who want to be successful in the market must adopt new beliefs and practices in the exercise of their business. Thus, contemporary marketing should be conceived as a complex multidimensional concept designated by Kotler and Keller (2009) as Holistic Marketing. Based on the theory of holism which holds that the whole has priority over the sum of individual parts, all marketing is important and requires the development and implementation of programs, processes and activities with the recognition of their breadth and interdependencies of its effects long-term. Holistic marketing incorporates the following concepts (Kotler & Keller, 2009):

- **Integrated Marketing:** Ensuring an integration of all components of the marketing-mix tools—product, price, place, and promotion—in a coordinated and interdependent way.
- **Internal Marketing:** Adopting the marketing as business perspective by everyone in all departments of the organization.
- **Relationship Marketing:** Developing a strategic and long term vision for the organization with all its stakeholders (customers, employees, suppliers, distributors, investors, etc.).
- **Performance Marketing:** Understanding the returns to the business from marketing activities and programs, as well as addressing broader concerns and their legal, ethical, social and environmental effects.

In short, marketing integrates all of the marketing mix variables in a coordinated and interdependent manner; it is a complex set of activities carried out throughout the organization and not just one department; it should develop a long-term strategy to all stakeholders; it should care for a more financially and socially responsibility. Without neglecting the importance of the four concepts listed above, the focus of our study requires a detailed review of the literature of relationship marketing.

Relationship Marketing

The term relationship marketing was first introduced by Berry in 1983, stating that the relationship marketing is to attract, maintain and enhance relationships with customers (Berry, 1995). Despite this, there is some consensus that the original conceptual background of this new approach is the contribution that arises from two main lines of research developed by the Nordic School of Services and Industrial Marketing and Purchasing Group (IMP). This long-term perspective was clearly recognized in the services marketing (Grönroos, 1980) and industrial marketing (Jackson, 1985).

Of the various criticisms and reflections developed it was found that the analysis of industrial and service markets demanded a different perspective from the analysis of consumer markets. It begins to be recognized a new reality oriented for value creation, which results in the development of personalized marketing to meet the needs of consumers (Filipe & Barbosa, 2012). The emergence of the relationship marketing is therefore interpreted as a paradigm shift required for all marketing situations, not just restricted to services marketing and industrial marketing.

In the academic community, relationship marketing is presented as a new paradigm, focusing on the construction of stable and lasting relationships with its customers, in contrast to the traditional approach to promote oriented transactions (Grönroos, 1994, 1997, 2006; Gummesson, 1987, 1997, 1998).

From a business perspective, the organizations felt the need to satisfy, retain and engage their customers through an orientation towards long-term relationships. The major indicator of strategic positioning becomes the customer base at the expense of market share, being the crucial capacity owned by the organization to provide a set of relationships based in trust. Table 1 summarizes the key definitions of relationship marketing.

The definitions presented go in the same direction, i.e., enhancing marketing on the relationship with the customer in order to extend this period, and supporting it on mutual benefits. However, if first definitions focus on the relationships with customers, the most recent definitions focus on the relationships with all business partnerships. Webster (1992, p. 1) refers in his work "the new organization forms (for example strategic partnerships and networks) requires of marketing a managing strategic partnerships and positioning the firm between vendors and customers in the value chain with the aim of delivering superior value to consumers... some subtle changes in the concept and practise of marketing have been fundamentally reshaping the field". In the same way, Berling (1993) argues that in the 21st century, the traditional separation of sellers, suppliers, intermediates and customers does not already

Table 1. Key definitions of relationship marketing

Authors	Definitions
Grönroos (1990, p. 5)	"...is to establish, maintain, enhance and commercialize customer relationships (often but not necessarily always long term relationships) so that the objectives of the parties are met. This is done by a mutual exchange and fulfilment of promises."
Shani and Chalasani (1992, p. 34)	"An integrated effort to identify, maintain and build up a network with individual consumers and to continuously strengthen the network for mutual benefit of both sides, through interactive, individualized and value-added contacts over a long period of time."
Payne (1994, p. 29)	"The basis of the relationship marketing philosophy is that the attraction of new customers is merely the first step in the marketing process. The key is retaining that customer. Marketing should not begin and end with clinching the deal – it must also concern itself with keeping, and improving, the relationship with the customer."
Gummesson (1994, pp. 12,16)	"View marketing as relationships, networks and interaction." "The relationships can also be viewed as a series of concentric circles or even 'bodies', ranging from the nano relationship to the market relationships and the mega relationships."
Morgan and Hunt (1994, p. 22)	"All marketing activities directed toward establishing, developing, and maintaining successful relational exchanges."
Berry (1995, p. 236)	"...the attraction of new customers should be viewed only as an intermediate step in the marketing process. Solidifying the relationship, transforming indifferent customers into loyal ones, and serving customers clients also should be considered as marketing."
Peterson (1995, p. 278)	If relationship is "a logical affiliation, association, or connection between two entities that benefits both of them, then relationship marketing must refer to marketing relationship."
Sheth and Parvatiyar (1995, p. 1)	As an orientation "that seeks to develop close interactions with selected customers, suppliers and competitors for value creation through cooperative and collaborative efforts."
Nevin (1995, p. 329)	"The broadened definition marketing emphasized relational as opposed to discrete exchange. Relational exchange refers to a class of general control mechanisms often assigned the label of trust, norms, relationships, networks or a bilateral power system."

exist, so it requires trust for organizations to work together for a long period of time.

For Berry (2002) the traditional marketing activities, which rely on attracting customers, are only a subset of relationship marketing activities which are also part of all activities aimed at maintaining and strengthening the exchange with the other party over time. Relationship marketing is more recently cited as the philosophical foundation of CRM. Berry (2002, p. 73) defined it as "a philosophy, not just a strategy, a way of thinking about customers, marketing and value creation, not just a set of techniques, tools, and tactics". The goal of relationship marketing, according to Sheth and Parvatiyar (2002), is to increase the customer's commitment to the organization by offering the best value on an on-going basis at a low cost, and this is achieved inside the organization and through partnerships with suppliers and even competitors. The measure of success is the growth of the share of customer's business and its profitability (Sheth & Parvatiyar, 2002, p. 10). Payne *et al.* (1997) suggest that it is important to recognize that relationships must be built with a number of important groups in order to build and sustain real customer value. In this work Payne *et al.* (2005) named the "Six Markets Model": internal markets, referral markets, influence markets, employee markets, supplier markets and customer markets. Successful organizations tend to have good relationships with critical individuals and groups relevant to their markets.

Moreover, Kotler *et al.* (2008, p. 12) hold that the ultimate outcome of relationship marketing is a unique organizational asset called marketing network. They assume that relationship marketing aims at building mutually satisfying long-term relationships with four key constituents (customers, employees, marketing partners and members of the financial community) and require an understanding of their needs, goals, desires, capabilities and resources.

Solutions and Recommendations

Given the above we can say:

Contemporary marketing is a cross-activity for everyone in the long term.

Firstly, contemporary marketing is a cross-activity. Marketing is not a function of a restricted group or department of an organization, but an activity conducted by organizations and individuals. Marketing is an action word, something that organizations (including both formal marketing departments and others in organizations), as well as individuals (for example, entrepreneurs and consumers), engage in or do. Moreover, marketing operates through a set of institutions and processes, which recognizes that the institutions (market research firms, manufacturers, wholesalers, retailers) and marketing systems (distribution channels) are an important part of marketing.

Secondly, contemporary marketing is for everyone. Marketing must create, communicate, deliver and exchange market offerings that have value for customers, clients, marketers and. Thus, marketing is not limited to create, communicate, deliver value to its customers and/or clients, but to create, communicate, deliver value to everyone (including marketers).

Finally, marketing is an approach in the long term. The aggregated nature of marketing acknowledges the importance of creating market offerings and interactions that have value to organization and all partners, in the present and in the long term. Marketing should emphasize relationships between the organization and its markets more strongly. The role of marketing experienced a rapid changing in the developing global environment. The managements have to take the knowledge that relationships, business networks and interaction with customers and other partners are, at moment, critical key factors in business development.

THE CRM AND WEB 2.0 IN THE RELATIONSHIP MARKETING

In 1987 Grace Hopper said, "Life was simple before World War II. After that, we had systems" This is a good sentence to introduce this journey by the complexity of CRM systems (English acronym that stands for "Customer Relationship Management") and its intertwining with contemporary marketing. Beginning by the concept of a system as a "coherent set of interdependent components that exists for some purpose, has some stability, and can be usefully viewed as a whole" (Beynon-Davies, 2002, p. 4), we have to emerge on information system (computerized) concept, since it is what CRM systems are. In its essence, an Information System (IS) aims to support human activity system (on a social level) and it's supported by information technology (on a technical level), and should therefore be understood/perceived as a sociotechnical system (Simões & Soares, 2003).

In this context, it is also important to emphasize, according to these authors, that the implementation of a CRM system is a program and not a project. This view is based on the fact that a program refers to a set of activities planned for a given period of time, but that also provides for an inspection in time. Yet when it comes to a project, we refer to a plan to perform an act that has a well-defined time (Simões, 2010). Also, Dyché (2002) refers to implementing a CRM system as a program, explaining that this is a complex set of goals that are institutionalized and carried out, involving multiple projects. Some projects to be included in a program of implementing a CRM system are, for example, integration of multiple systems (legacy), improvement of data quality, business process reengineering, organizational culture change, training of users, or customer segmentation (Buttle, 2008).

The implementation of a CRM system involves a complex and long program, so deconstructing it into manageable pieces (projects) seems to be the wisest option. This idea is also based on the principles of process engineering, which were first applied to the transformation of organizations from the industrial to the information age, through models, methods, and tools (Osterle, 1995). To control this complexity, the author suggests the division into several levels, such as, strategy (decisions made to develop a long course to be done), process (connection between the strategic decisions and the systems and information technologies, including planning, sequencing, and delivering of the activities and tasks of information management), information systems (supporting the execution of the processes, including the collection, storage and dissemination of information) and change (sociocultural dimensions of transformation process), that is consistent with what was recently suggested particularly by Bueren, Schierholz *et al.* (2004) and Buttle (2008).

Paul Greenberg (2010) presents a definition of traditional CRM as "a philosophy and a business strategy supported by a system and a technology designed to improve human interactions in a business environment" (p. 30). Nevertheless, this definition seems to resemble more to the concept of relationship marketing, since, as we shall see, the concept of CRM has emerged to represent the technological support (automation) from the activities of the customer relationship management on the relationship marketing conceptualization. So, we can say that the theory and practice of CRM are based on two landmarks (Damacena & Pedron, 2004):

- **Conceptual:** The literature of relational marketing.
- **Technological:** The literature oriented to information technology, involving automation of sales, of marketing, and of service to customer, as well as, decision support based on data warehousing technology e all the techniques associated, as data mining and online analytical processing. Here

are also included all the collaborative tools which support operation and analyze activities.

In this context, the following sections present a state-of-art about the CRM concept on perspective of systems management and an architecture proposal of CRM system for practical application.

Customer Relationship Management

Although the concept of "Customer Relationship Management" has arisen associated with the implementation and put into practice the philosophy of "Relationship marketing," in some literature there is still the use of these two concepts interchangeably. However, considering the dates we find that the references to the concept of CRM are all recent. Despite the definition of "Relationship Marketing," the definitions given for CRM are far from a consensus. Essentially, it is difficult to tell whether it is a strategy, a process, a technology, and some people still refer to it as a philosophy.

Recently, Paul Greenberg in his book *CRM at the Speed of Light* (Greenberg, 2010, p. 34) explains all these ambiguities, i.e., CRM is (or should be) all that, a philosophy, a strategy that encompasses a set of processes and that is supported by technology. From his definition of traditional CRM, quoted above, Greenberg develops a social CRM concept, as: "a philosophy and a business strategy, supported by a technology platform, business rules, processes, and social characteristics, designed to engage the customer in a collaborative conversation in order to provide mutually beneficial value in a trusted and transparent business environment. It's the organization's response to the customer's ownership of the conversation."

The following authors also have the same opinion, i.e., CRM is a strategy supported on technology. Attending to their definitions of CRM on their books:

CRM is the core business strategy that integrates internal processes and functions, and external networks, to create and deliver value to targeted customers at a profit. It is grounded on high-quality customer data and enabled by IT (Buttle, 2008, p. 34).

CRM is a strategic approach concerned with creating improved shareholder value through the development of appropriate relationships with key customers and customer segments. CRM unites the potential of IT and relationship marketing strategies to deliver profitable, long term relationships. Importantly, CRM provides enhanced opportunities to use data and information both to understand customers and implement relationship marketing strategies better. This requires a cross-functional integration of people, operations, processes and marketing capabilities that is enabled through information, technology and applications (Payne, 2005, pp. 22-23).

CRM is the practice of analyzing and utilizing marketing databases and leveraging communication technologies to determine corporate practices and methods that will maximize the lifetime value[1] of each individual customer to the firm (Kumar & Reinartz, 2006, p. 5).

It is a consensus that successful organizations in an emerging economy of virtual/online networks and information will be those able to identify, enhance, create, and evolve their knowledge assets. The online social networks could be a good tool to do it. This idea was already sustained by Gerbert, Geib *et al.* (2003) by claiming that to build good relationships with customers is necessary to serve each customer according to their preferences, which require management of customer information (Davenport, Harris & Kohli, 2001). It can be stated that the assumption of a corporate strategy for managing the customer relationships should be based on the information[2], in order to enhance their retention and subsequent maintenance of these relationships for long time periods.

Along with the management of customer information should always be present the formation of relationships, whose ultimate goal of quality is the generation and sustain of confidence. This state is the ultimate result that is expected from the formation of a successful relationship, going through other buildings, such as symmetry, equity, dependence/uncertainty, satisfaction, and commitment (Britton and Rose in Peppers and Rogers (2004)).

All of these conceptualizations are also implied in the work of Zablah, Bellenger *et al.* (2004) and allow us to conclude that management of the knowledge[3] and of the interactions[4] are the main sub-processes of the CRM process. Information technology is a key prerequisite in these processes. Still, in the opinion of these authors, we can distinguish, and simultaneously relate CRM and Relationship marketing as follows:

CRM is a strategically driven process, related to the "production" of an ideal mix of customer relationships, while the Relationship Marketing focuses only on the tasks necessary to build and sustain relational exchanges.

Technology Support

The concept of CRM has been influenced by various concepts of information systems, focusing on different areas of application (Gebert, Geib, Kolbe & Brenner, 2003). From the technological point of view, CRM involves capturing customer data across the organization, consolidating all the data captured internally and externally in a central database, analyzing the consolidated data, distributing the results of this analysis among the various points of contact with the customer, and using this information to interact with the customer through any point of contact with the organization. In strategic terms, we can say that CRM systems support three distinct areas (Buttle, 2008; Chan, 2005; Dyché, 2002; Meta Group, 2001; Payne, 2005; Peppers & Rogers, 2004):

- **Operational:** Involves the automation of business processes that support customer interaction.
- **Analytical:** Involves the collection, organization, storage, analysis, interpretation and use of data created at the operational level to achieve value for customers and the organization.
- **Collaborative:** Involves the use of collaborative services and infrastructure to enhance the interaction between the organization and its multiple channels (external customers – organization – internal customers).

The integration of these three areas is essential in premise of obtaining a valid CRM system. This integration involves the applications at level of back-office, front-office e mobile-office (see Figure 1). At the back-office level, Enterprise Resource Planning (ERP) and Supply Chain Management (SCM) essentially aim to improve the efficiency of internal processes related to production and finance, using information from customers and from other sources (databases) to reduce costs. At the front-office level, Customer Service Automation (CSA), Marketing Automation (MA) and Sales Force Automation (SFA) aim to improve the external efficiency of the processes related to sales, marketing, and service to customer, using information from customers and from other sources to increase profits (Dyché, 2002; Payne, 2005). The mobile-office level refers to the use of wireless technologies for delivering data to customers, suppliers and business partners. At this level, Field Force Automation (FFA) aims to increase the efficiency of activities of sales and after-sales service (Dyché, 2002). Supply

Figure 1. Organizational levels of CRM (adapted from Meta Group, 2001)

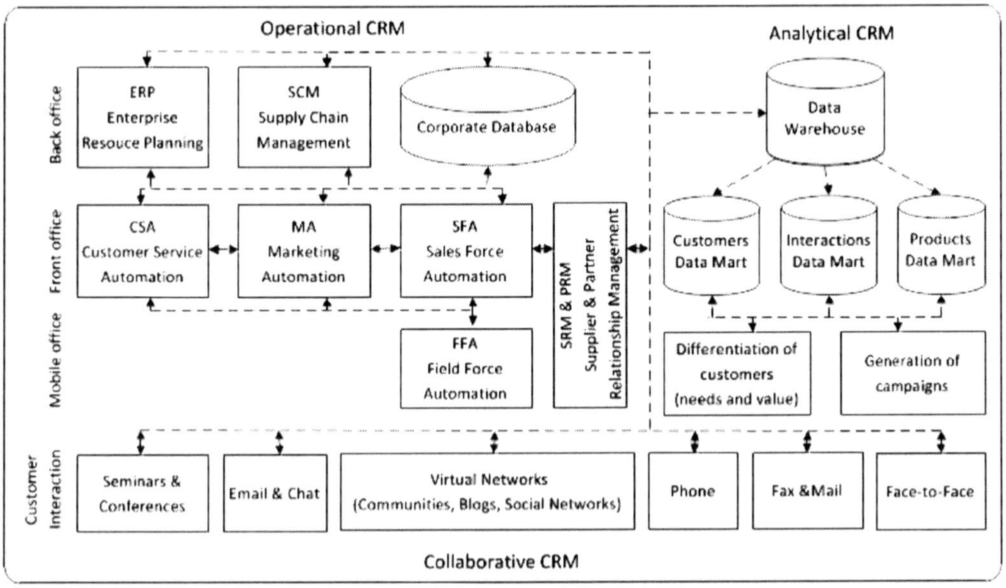

Relationship Management (SRM) and Partner Relationship Management (PRM) involve applications on front-office and mobile-office levels.

But essentially, we can distinguish two main components of information technology supporting the management of customer relationships (Payne, 2005):

- The data repository (database and data warehouse) that allows the organization to collect a set of information about customers which, used with a set of analytical tools, allows developing a better understanding of customers in terms of past, and predict their future behavior. Concerning the implementation of a data warehouse system, the work of Simões (2010) presents a comprehensive conceptual framework.
- A set of applications (CSA, SFA, and FFA, and MA) enabling value-added interactions with customers, often through different channels in order to know and answer to their needs.

Applications should enable organizations to perform certain key functions, including those presented in Table 2 (Doyle, 2002; Iriana & Buttle, 2005).

As mentioned earlier, for the main sub-processes of a CRM system, the objectives in terms of technology should support the business processes that are described below. At the knowledge management level, Bueren, Schierholz *et al.* (2004) indicate as the main business processes and respective goals related to CRM, the following:

- **Campaign Management:** Planning, execution, control and monitoring of management activities. Its central objective is to generate valid opportunities.
- **Opportunities Management:** Consolidation, qualification, and prioritizing of contacts of potential customers. Its central objective is to support the staff of offers management (sales) with one qualified list of potential customers (valuable).
- **Offers Management:** Making sales. Its central objective is to create and deliver individual offerings.

Table 2. Functions those CRM applications should leverage

Level	Functions
Operational	• Increase the efficiency of customer service (reducing cost and time spent). • Increase the efficiency of marketing. • Increase the efficiency of sales force.
Analytical	• Modeling and analysis of customer characteristics. • Forecast customer behavior. • Management and customization of communication with customers. • Optimization of trinomial products-customers-channels. • Determining the value of customers.
Collaborative	• Increase the efficiency and effectiveness of customer interaction. • Increase the effectiveness in obtaining customer information. • Increasing uptime in response to customer requests.

- **Contracts Management:** Creation and maintenance of contracts for supply of products and services. Its central objective is to support the processes of offers and services management.
- **Complaints Management:** Reception, processing, and communication of complaints. The main objectives are, in short-term, improving the customer satisfaction, and in medium/long-term, designing one process of continuous improvement.
- **Services Management:** Planning, implementation, and control measures for forecasting services (for example, maintenance, repair, and support activities in the aftermarket).

At the interaction management level, the same authors report the business processes of interaction and channel management. Thus:

- **Interaction Management:** Design and selection of channels based on communication technologies such as Interactive Voice Response (IVR), to find an optimal channel mix. Its central objective is to increase the quality and value of interactions, and simultaneously reduce the interaction costs shifting customers to cheaper channels.
- **Channel Management:** Configuration and synchronization of different communication channels. Its main objective is to define organizational responsibilities for each channel, to avoid conflicts and ensure a consistent flow of information through different channels.

Today it should be stressed that we cannot dissociate the concept of eCRM system from CRM system, since the use of electronic commerce tools or electronic channels in CRM, where are included the online social networks, is increasingly imperative. Thus, we have Web-based CRM systems.

Social Media

According to Greenberg (2010) social CRM is "designed to engage the customer in a collaborative conversation in order to provide mutually beneficial value in a trusted and transparent business environment" (p. 121). But, the customers are different, belonging to different segments of market. Assuming that, how to involve the customer in this collaboration? What tools to use?

There are some tools, usually designed as social media that could give a significant contribute. But what tool should one choose? What is the best or most appropriate? Some help could come from its understanding about its meaning and application (Evans & McKee, 2010). Some of the most used tools and those that seem to have more relevance in the context of Customer Relationship Management are blogs, wikis and podcasts. We could use these tools in interactions with customers – maybe in some sales, marketing, and customer service applications. Nevertheless, these tools have to be used as enablers, not as drivers. Thus (Greenberg, 2010):

- Blog "is a running account of events or thoughts or ideas that can be authored by one person or sometimes multiple people" (p. 127). In context of CRM, blogs could be the sites to customers collaborate with ideas and a form to link and collaborate with business partners and sale channels.
- Podcast "is an audio file that uses RSS (Really Simple Syndication) to distribute the broadcast to subscribers or allow them to download it to computers or portable music devices" (p. 129). In context of CRM, podcasts could be a powerful learning tools, for example, to explain the use of a feature of a product, could support efforts of marketing focused around of mindshare and leadership, and can also be helpful in training of employees.
- Wiki (corporate) "is a wiki (collection of Web pages designed to enable anyone who access it to contribute or modify content, using a simplified markup language) used in an organizational context, especially to enhance internal knowledge sharing" (pp. 130,131). In context of CRM, corporate wikis can be used for projects management or marketing purposes, enabling collaboration between customers and employees and for consequence innovation; but also can constitute a good repository for dynamic knowledge base.

Another resource being increasingly used for marketing purposes are the online social networks. Boyd & Ellison (2008, p. 211) define them as "Web-based services that allow individuals to (1) construct a public or semi-public profile within a bounded system, (2) articulate a list of other users with whom they share a connection, and (3) view and traverse their list of connections and those made by others within the system". In this context, the organizations can capture data from the customers (members). And with adequate tools, they can answer to concerns, fears, disclaimers, or tastes from the customers. One more time, there are diverse models that will be adopted according the purpose (see Greenberg (2010) for a deeper understanding around those models). The use of these tools for CRM purposes means that the involvement of customers is not only important, it is vital to improve the customer commitment, and in consequence increase the rates of acquisition and retention. All the tools cited before perform an important role in this strategy. Firstly, have a purpose, then choose the tools that fulfill this purpose.

It is important to highlight that in order to manage an online social network and others forms of community, it is necessary to have a clear understanding of its purpose and interest, ensure a good manager or group of managers, identify and work with the leaders, practice moderation by exception, answer to negative situation immediately, encourage the members to collaborate, valorize members continually, do not reward only activities related to sales, and in essence be proactive.

Solutions and Recommendations

Bearing in mind what was previously said, we can extract some main insights like that technology is an essential support on CRM system, but it is never the guarantee of success. Before thinking about the technology, the organization must develop a sustainable strategic plan. This plan will allows support and address all the steps and activities. We don't forget that the implementation of a CRM system is a program that will last the life of the organization. Obviously, the business will evolve, the interests could diverge, and if the organization spent time on defining a strategic plan that serves the current interests with vision on the future, any change will be more efficiently implemented. This plan will contemplate viability analyses in all perspective levels, i.e., economic, technological (hardware and software), human, technical, training, procedural, etc.

In technological terms, focus can be placed on the use of social media. Mainly small and medium organizations can achieve substantial savings when adopt some social media tool to improve the customer relationship, but special attention should be placed on responsiveness to customer requests and on the quality of the media. Never forget, that the social media and online social networks would be used as an enabler, never as a driver.

ASSESSMENT

Whilst the implementation of CRM systems is essentially based on two pillars, on one hand the definition of the conceptual model (relationship marketing) with the requirements' specification, and secondly the choice or development of technological infrastructure (information technology) that meets the specified requirements, including automation of organizational areas like marketing, sales and service, but also data analysis and information obtained with a view of greater efficiency in decision making. It is also recognized that the evaluation of range obtained with its implementation should not be neglected. Only then can we know whether or not the objectives are achieved, and then progress in function of the greater or lesser success.

The objectives of implementing a CRM system can be diverse, but in general terms and in most cases they are based on reducing the costs at the same time that the customers are retained. The performance indicator (KPI – Key Performance Indicator) can be obtained through some of the following metrics (Buttle, 2008):

- **In Operational Level:** Greater sales force productivity, lower service costs, higher share-of-purchases and increased customer satisfaction.
- **In Analytical Level:** Lower customer acquisition costs, increased productivity of marketing campaigns and higher rate of sales to cross-sell and up-sell.
- **In Collaborative Level:** Greater customization of products and more quickly response to the customer.

Nevertheless, it is important to assess the performance on two-pronged, namely on implementation level, i.e., rates of customers identified and differentiated, and improvement on interactions and customization of products and services. And of course on outcomes level, i.e., increase of revenues and/or decrease of costs.

Implementation Indicators

The construction of a CRM system with the potential for success must begin with the identification, and continue with the differentiation of customers (value and loyalty) (Kim, Jung, Suh, & Hwang, 2006). The real value gives indicators of financial point of view, and the potential value gives indicators on opportunities to cross-sell and/or up-sell. The loyalty estimates durability of the two previous values (real and potential).

This idea is well founded by renowned experts Peppers e Rogers (2004) through their model of customer relationship management—IDIC—Identification, Differentiation, Interaction, and Customization. These authors emphasize the importance of assessing, at each stage, the implementation degree of the program. Table 3 indicates a few metrics to assess the extent of implementation of the CRM concept.

The values resulting from the application of these metrics will be good indicators of the performance of the organization on implementation of the program aiming to improve the relationships with their customers.

Table 3. Metrics to assess the implementation degree of IDIC model (source: based on work of Peppers & Rogers, 2004)

Phases		Metrics
Identification		• % of customer base with Unique Customer Identifier. • % of customers identified in all the main channels of contact. • Ability to identify customers relocated / lost (yes or no). • % of customers with email addresses collected. • % of customers with mobile phone number collected.
Differentiation	Value	• Model LTV (Lifetime Value) in action (yes or no). • Ability to group customers by value. • % of customers assigned to the series of value MGCs (Most Growable Customers), MVCs (Most Valuable Customers) and BZs (Below Zeros). • % of customers with LTV measured. • % of customers who continue to be measured by the number of sales.
	Needs	• Ability to group customers by needs (yes or no). • Identified the gateways based on the needs for the main points of contact (yes or no). • Used golden questions to identify different needs (yes or no). • % of customers assigned to clusters of needs.
Interaction		• % of customers with data about needs collected. • % of customers who provided feedback on the service last year. • *Golden Questions* defined (yes or no). • Average cost per interaction. • Critical customer data available for each communication channel (yes or no). • The last interaction with the customer available at every communication channel (yes or no).
Customization		• % of customers who purchased personalized products last year. • % of product lines that are mass customization. • Savings per customer in mass customization and make-to-order. • % of customers receiving personalized communication. • % of customers with customized web pages. • % of customers with complementary services.

Outcomes Indicators

The benefits for business will obviously be associated with an adequate or inadequate change of organizational processes. Silva and Gardesani (2005) consider that outcome indicators from implementation of a CRM system can be obtained from four types of variables: acquiring new customers, win back customers, winning customer loyalty and sales by cross-sell and up-sell. Potential benefits should then be reflected by the evidences showed in Figure 2 (Dyché, 2002; Dyché & Levy, 2006; Kim et al., 2006; Peppers & Rogers, 2004; Silva & Gardesani, 2005; Zablah et al., 2004).

Figure 2. Potential benefits from implementation of a CRM system

Factors that are most often associated with failure of a program to implement a CRM system are usually related to the lack of creating a business strategy, with the inability to integrate the new system with legacy systems, or the lack of an analytical approach to CRM (Chan, 2005).

Solutions and Recommendations

The implementation of a new system or any change in an existing system should always include in its plan the objectives, in terms of system implementation (execution) and in terms of expected benefits (tangible and intangible) with the action of the new system. Consequently, after a running time of the new system (or modification of the former), it is essential to make its assessment. Only then, can we check whether or not the objectives are being achieved.

Attention should be given to the fact that on the one hand, there is the question of evaluation from the standpoint of implementation, i.e., ability to perform the activities and tasks expected. On the other hand, there should follow an evaluation of the gains achieved with its implementation and action.

FUTURE RESEARCH DIRECTIONS

Organizations have three basic types of resources: physical, human and organizational. To achieve and maintain competitive advantage in the market in which they operate, they need to reorganize and exploit these resources to work seamlessly. This not only allows to develop knowledge about customers and potential customers (market intelligence), but also to adapt their behavior to customers and potential customers based in this intelligence (use knowledge to influence the interactions) (Chan, 2005; Zablah *et al.*, 2004). This requires a comprehensive integrated change at level of processes, culture and organizational structure, information, and technology.

In summation we can say that market intelligence is generated through a process of effective implementation of knowledge management, and that resulting intelligence is used to build the portfolio of profit maximization of customer relationships, allowing the organizations to select the right customers, prioritize relationships and effectively manage the interactions. The customer intelligence facilitates the optimization of interactions with customers, facilitating their retention and, simultaneously, promoting an optimal mix of products offered to the right customers, at the right time, and through the appropriate channels (Chan, 2005).

An intelligent organization, and particularly, that has an (online) network-based structure is then an organization that continually expands, revises, renews, and refreshes their knowledge in its diverse forms (tacit, implicit and explicit) (Bandyo-Padhyay, 2002; Nonaka and Konno, 1998). It is therefore an organization facilitator of sharing, between all agents, of ideas, skills, tasks and responsibilities, including participation in decision-making process (Osarenkhoe, 2006). This is a vision that attempts to integrate the two main directions of knowledge management on Web 2.0: epistemological (content and skills) and ontological (composition and collaboration) (Bueren *et al.*, 2004; Gebert *et al.*, 2003). And it is in consensus with the definition of Greenberg (2010) of Social CRM, when he said that leverage social media, social networking, and social metadata to support new relationships structures and new processes as control of the relationship shifts from vendor-to-customer-to-community. Epistemological models can only estimate the value of knowledge based on their inner qualities, and thus independent of the context in which it is used, at their value in the business environment is limited. The ontological models based on the understanding that the characteristics of knowledge are defined through their relationships with the universe of discourse constructed, and therefore take into account the concern with the recognition and acceptance of common terminology of organizational knowledge.

More specifically, the dimensions commonly used by ontological models include both, the process dimension (characteristics of knowledge during their life cycle) and the agent dimension (characteristics of knowledge during its flow between individual versus group). Therefore, process-oriented models analyze the relationships and environmental variables that influence the processes of development, dissemination, modeling, and use of knowledge, and agent-oriented models analyze the variables that facilitate or limit the flow of knowledge in online networks/communities (Simões, Ferreira, & Soares, 2007; Simões & Soares, 2007). Overall, ontological models analyze the links between knowledge and its environment and can assess the knowledge in a specific business context. Obviously, this is an important area of research that needs continuity; we still lack research studies and it is essential to take advantage of shared knowledge within online social networks.

Another area in need of research development is that of the identification and differentiation of customers both in consumer markets (Business-to-Consumer) and in organizational markets (Business-to-Business). In consumer markets, this can be determined by demographics[5] or psychographics[6], such as age, sex, marital status, or lifestyle. As to business markets, segmentation criteria include data such as industry, firm size, etc. (Osarenkhoe, 2006; Payne, 2005). So far research has found, the longer the relationship between an organization and a customer, the lower the cost of serving that customer. This observation is justified due to the effects of learning. Loyal customers buy more, are less sensitive to prices of products and services, and offer new and positive references. But, it is necessary to know better the needs of the customers to better serve them and, consequently, they will be more satisfied and confidents about the relationship.

CONCLUSION

During the last decade of the twentieth century, Relationship marketing "was probably the major trend in marketing and certainly the major (and arguably the most controversial) talking point in business management" (Egan, 2011, p. 16). Contemporary marketing is facing new challenges and opportunities. In order to positively harness these opportunities and minimize the impact of threats have to follow market trends. Thus, marketing should be truly holistic, the main architect of business strategy, treat the customer as a personalized individual, and build their brands through performance, an electronic marketing with good information and communication systems.

In this sense, marketers need a new set of skills and competencies in areas such: customer relationship and CRM systems, marketing database and data mining, social media, and so on. A growing number of today's organizations are also shading separate offers, services, and messages to individual customers, based on information about past transaction, demographic, psychographics, and media and distribution preferences. Focusing on their most profitable customers, products and channels, these organizations hopes to achieve profitable growth by building high customer loyalty.

The Web 2.0 became visible between 2007 and 2008 in more developed countries. There is a new social dynamic, the shift towards Internet as a platform and understanding of their rules for success on that new platform. This provides a communication channel interaction and involvement of users with simplicity and transparency, available at a click. Organizations give it more attention now than ever, want to be present, because they recognize that their customers are connected to the network, but at the same time, fear it, because an image built over time can fall apart in real time.

This is the reason by this chapter ask for attention on the risks, if certain precautions are not taken. So, one more time reinforce the importance of the redesign of business processes and user training as key factors for success of a program of implementation of a CRM system (Pedron & Caldeira, 2005). Important influences are also the importance of a responsible management and a collaborative vision that contains guidance on the relationships, coupled with a concern and action for the involvement of the agents from the beginning of the program (Osarenkhoe, 2006).

In this chapter, after the state of the art around the concept of Relationship Marketing and its integration on contemporary marketing umbrella, it was presented architecture of organizational levels of CRM system including Internet applications. The main functions that CRM applications should support were also presented. Still that all that is implemented has to be assessed. Only this way we can understand if an action was successful or not. It was presented some metrics to analyze the degree of implementation of a CRM program and the outcomes (tangible and intangible) achieved with the use of the system.

REFERENCES

AMA. (1985). AMA board aproves new marketing definition. *American Marketing Association News, 19*(5).

AMA. (2007). *Definition of marketing*. Washington, DC: American Marketing Association.

Andreasen, A., Lee, N., & Rothschild, M. (2008). Further thoughts on the 2007 AMA definition of marketing and its implications for social marketing. *Social Marketing Quarterly, 14*(2), 101–104. doi:10.1080/15245000802103575.

Bandyo-Padhyay, N. (2002). *E-commerce: Context, concepts and consequences*. New York: McGraw-Hill.

Berling, R. J. (1993). The emerging approach to business strategy: Building a relationship advantage. *Business Horizons, 36*(4), 16. doi:10.1016/S0007-6813(05)80115-6.

Berry, L. L. (1995). Relationship marketing of services - Growing interest, emerging perspectives. *Journal of the Academy of Marketing Science, 23*(4), 236–245. doi:10.1177/009207039502300402.

Berry, L. L. (2002). Relationship marketing of services - Perspectives from 1983 and 2000. *Journal of Relationship Marketing, 1*(1), 59–77. doi:10.1300/J366v01n01_05.

Beynon-Davies, P. (2002). *Information systems: An introduction to informatics in organizations*. New York: Palgrave.

Boss, J. (2011). Les nouveaux visages du marketing. *Revue Française du Marketing,* (231), 61-74.

Boyd, D. M., & Ellison, N. B. (2008). Social network sites: Definition, history, and scholarship. *Journal of Computer-Mediated Communication, 13*, 210–230. doi:10.1111/j.1083-6101.2007.00393.x.

Bueren, A., Schierholz, R., Kolbe, L., & Brenner, W. (2004). *Customer knowledge management - Improving performance of customer relationship management with knowledge management.* Paper presented at the 37th Hawaii International Conference on System Sciences. Hawaii, HI.

Buttle, F. (2008). *Customer relationship management* (2nd ed.). Boston: Butterworth-Heinemann.

Chan, J. O. (2005). Toward a unified view of customer relationship management. *Journal of American Academy of Business*.

Constantinides, E. (2006). The marketing mix revisited: Towards the 21st century marketing. *Journal of Marketing Management, 22*(3-4), 407–438. doi:10.1362/026725706776861190.

Cristopher, M., Payne, A., & Ballantine, D. (1994). *Relationship marketing*. Boston: Butterworth-Heinemann, Ltd..

Damacena, C., & Pedron, C. D. (2004). *Estratégia de CRM: O desafio da implantação*. Paper presented at the Congresso Anual de Tecnologia de Informação (CATI 2004). Aviero, Portugal.

Davenport, T. H., Harris, J. G., & Kohli, A. K. (2001). How do they know their customers so well? *MIT Sloan Management Review, 42*(2), 63–73.

Doyle, S. (2002). Software review: Communication optimisation - The new mantra of database marketing: Fad or fact? *Journal of Database Marketing, 9*(2), 185–191. doi:10.1057/palgrave.jdm.3240074.

Drucker, P. (2007). *Management - Tasks, responsabilities and practices*. New Brunswick, NJ: Transaction Publishers.

Dyché, J. (2002). *The CRM handbook: A business guide to customer relationship management*. Reading, MA: Addison-Wesley Pearson Education.

Dyché, J., & Levy, E. (2006). *Customer data integration: Reaching a single version of the truth*. Hoboken, NJ: John Wiley & Sons, Inc..

Egan, J. (2011). *Relationship marketing* (4th ed.). Harlow, MA: Pearson Educational Limited.

Evans, D., & McKee, J. (2010). *Social media marketing: The next generation of business engagement*. New York: John Wiley & Sons, Inc..

Filipe, S., & Barbosa, M. (2012). The relationship markeitng under the perception of the client in the context of higher educaton: An exploratory study. *International Business and Economics Review, 3*.

Gebert, H., Geib, M., Kolbe, L., & Brenner, W. (2003). Knowledge-enabled customer relationship management: Integrating customer relationship management and knowledge management concepts. *Journal of Knowledge Management, 7*(5), 107–123. doi:10.1108/13673270310505421.

Greenberg, P. (2010). *CRM at the speed of light: Social CRM strategies, tools, and techniques for engaging your customers* (4th ed.). New York: The McGraw-Hill Companies.

Grönroos, C. (1980). Designing a long range marketing strategy for services. *Long Range Planning, 13*(2), 36–42. doi:10.1016/0024-6301(80)90030-8.

Grönroos, C. (1994). From marketing mix to relationship marketing: Towards a paradigm shift in marketing. *Management Decision, 32*(2), 4–20. doi:10.1108/00251749410054774.

Grönroos, C. (1997). Keynote paper: From marketing mix to relationship marketing - Towards a paradigm shift in marketing. *Management Decision, 35*(4), 322. doi:10.1108/00251749710169729.

Grönroos, C. (2006). On defining marketing: finding a new roadmap for marketing. *Marketing Theory, 6*(4), 395–417. doi:10.1177/1470593106069930.

Gummesson, E. (1987). The new marketing - Developing long-term interactive relationships. *Long Range Planning, 20*(4), 10–20. doi:10.1016/0024-6301(87)90151-8.

Gummesson, E. (1997). Relationship marketing as a paradigm shift: Some conclusions from the 30R approach. *Management Decision, 35*(4), 267. doi:10.1108/00251749710169648.

Gummesson, E. (1998). Implementation requires a relationship marketing paradigm. *Journal of the Academy of Marketing Science, 26*(3), 242–249. doi:10.1177/0092070398263006.

Gummesson, E. (2008). *Total relationship marketing* (3rd ed.). Oxford, UK: Butterworth-Heinemann.

Harker, M. J. (1999). Relationship marketing defined? An examination of current relationship marketing definitions. *Marketing Intelligence & Planning, 17*(1), 13–20. doi:10.1108/02634509910253768.

Harker, M. J., & Egan, J. (2006). The past, present and future of relationship marketing. *Journal of Marketing Management, 22*(1-2), 215–242. doi:10.1362/026725706776022326.

Iriana, R., & Buttle, F. (2005). *Strategic, operational and analytical customer relationship management: Attributes and measures (No. MGSM WP 2005-1)*. Macquarie Graduate School of Management.

Jackson, B. (1985). Building customer relationships that last: How close can industrial markets get to their customers - And for how long? *Harvard Business Review, 63*, 120.

Kim, S.-Y., Jung, T.-S., Suh, E.-H., & Hwang, H.-S. (2006). Customer segmentation and strategy development based on customer lifetime value: A case study. *Expert Systems with Applications, 31*, 101–107. doi:10.1016/j.eswa.2005.09.004.

Kotler, P., Armstrong, G., Wong, V., & Sauders, J. (2008). *Principles of marketing* (5th ed.). London: Prentice Hall.

Kotler, P., & Keller, K. L. (2009). *Marketing management* (13th ed.). Upper Saddle River, NJ: Pearson Education International.

Kumar, V., & Reinartz, W. J. (2006). *Customer relationship management: A databased approach*. New York: Wiley.

Meta Group. (2001). *Integration: Critical issues for implementation of CRM solutions*. Stanford, CA: Meta Group Inc..

Nevin, J. R. (1995). Relationship marketing and distribution channels: Exploring fundamental issues. *Journal of the Academy of Marketing Science, 23*(4), 327–334. doi:10.1177/009207039502300413.

Nonaka, I., & Konno, N. (1998). The concept of ba: Building a foundation for knowledge creation. *California Management Review, 40*(3), 40–55. doi:10.2307/41165942.

Osarenkhoe, A. (2006). Customer-centric strategy: A longitudinal study of implementation of a customer relationship management solution. *International Journal of Technology Marketing, 1*(2), 115–144.

Osterle, H. (1995). *Business in the information age: Heading for new processes*. Berlin: Springer.

Payne, A. (2005). *Handbook of CRM: Achieving excellence through customer managemen*. Boston: Butterworth-Heinemann.

Payne, A., Ballantyne, D., & Christopher, M. (2005). A stakeholder approach to relationship marketing strategy: The development and use of the six markets model. *European Journal of Marketing, 39*(7/8), 855–871. doi:10.1108/03090560510601806.

Payne, A., Christopher, M., Clark, M., & Peck, H. (1997). *Relationship marketing for competitive advantage*. Oxford, UK: Butterworth-Heinemann.

Pedron, C. D., & Caldeira, M. (2005). *Objectivos da adopção do CRM: Um estudo de caso em uma empresa brasileira de telecomunicações*. Paper presented at the 6ª Conferência da Associação Portuguesa de Sistemas de Informação. Aviero, Portugal.

Peixoto, S. (2010). *Web trends - 10 cases made in web 2.0. Gaia*. Comunicarte Publishing.

Peppers, D., & Rogers, M. (2004). *Managing customer relationships: A strategic framework*. Hoboken, NJ: John Wiley & Sons, Inc..

Sheth, J. N., & Parvatiyar, A. (1995). Relationship marketing in consumer markets: Antecedents and consequences. *Journal of the Academy of Marketing Science*, *23*(4), 255–271. doi:10.1177/009207039502300405.

Sheth, J. N., & Parvatiyar, A. (2002). Evolving relationship marketing into a discipline. *Journal of Relationship Marketing*, *1*(1), 3–16. doi:10.1300/J366v01n01_02.

Silva, A., & Gardesani, R. (2005). *Impactos do CRM no relacionamento da empresa com clientes*. Paper presented at the Congresso Anual de Tecnologia da Informação. Aviero, Portugal.

Simões, D. (2010). *Enterprise data warehouses: A conceptual framework for a successful implementation*. Paper presented at the Canadian Council for Small Business & Entrepreneurship Annual Conference (CCSBE 2010). Calgary, Canada.

Simões, D., Ferreira, H., & Soares, A. L. (2007). *Ontology engineering in virtual breeding environments*. Paper presented at the 8th IFIP Working Conference on Virtual Enterprises (PRO-VE'07). New York, NY.

Simões, D., & Soares, A. L. (2003). *Redes organizacionais e desenvolvimento de sistemas de informação*. Paper presented at the 4ª Conferência da Associação Portuguesa de Sistemas de Informação (CAPSI'03). Porto, Portugal.

Simões, D., & Soares, A. L. (2007). Knowledge communities and inter-organizational networks. In Putnik, G. D., & Cunha, M. M. (Eds.), *Encyclopedia of Networked and Virtual Organizations*. Hershey, PA: Information Science Reference.

Webster, F. E. Jr. (1992). The changing role of marketing in the corporation. *Journal of Marketing*, *56*(4), 1–17. doi:10.2307/1251983.

Zablah, A. R., Bellenger, D. N., & Johnston, W. J. (2004). An evaluation of divergent perspectives on customer relationship management: Towards a common understanding of an emerging phenomenon. *Industrial Marketing Management*, *33*, 475–489. doi:10.1016/j.indmarman.2004.01.006.

ADDITIONAL READING

Boyd, D. M., & Ellison, N. B. (2008). Social network sites: Definition, history, and scholarship. *Journal of Computer-Mediated Communication*, *13*, 210–230. doi:10.1111/j.1083-6101.2007.00393.x.

Buttle, F. (2008). *Customer relationship management* (2nd ed.). Boston: Butterworth-Heinemann.

Dyché, J. (2002). *The CRM handbook: A business guide to customer relationship management*. Reading, MA: Addison-Wesley Pearson Education.

Egan, J. (2011). *Relationship marketing* (4th ed.). Harlow, MA: Pearson Educational Limited.

Evans, D., & McKee, J. (2010). *Social media marketing: The next generation of business engagement*. New York: John Wiley & Sons, Inc..

Greenberg, P. (2010). *CRM at the speed of light: Social CRM strategies, tools, and techniques for engaging your customers* (4th ed.). New York: The McGraw-Hill Companies.

Gummesson, E. (2008). *Total relationship marketing* (3rd ed.). Oxford, UK: Butterworth-Heinemann.

Kotler, P., & Keller, K. L. (2009). *Marketing management* (13th ed.). Upper Saddle River, NJ: Pearson Education International.

Payne, A. (2005). *Handbook of CRM: Achieving excellence through customer management*. Boston: Butterworth-Heinemann.

Payne, A., Christopher, M., Clark, M., & Peck, H. (1997). *Relationship marketing for competitive advantage*. Oxford, UK: Butterworth-Heinemann.

Peppers, D., & Rogers, M. (2004). *Managing customer relationships: A strategic framework*. Hoboken, NJ: John Wiley & Sons, Inc..

KEY TERMS AND DEFINITIONS

Contemporary Marketing: Holistic vision that enhances that all marketing is important and requires the development and implementation of programs, processes, and activities with the recognition of their breadth and interdependencies of its effects long-term.

CRM System: Information system incorporating a set of subsystems to support the diverse activities of Customer Relationship Management.

Customer Relationship Management: Strategic business process implemented in organization to keep an ideal mix of customer relationships.

Information System: Set of interdependent components (hardware, software, telecommunication networks, databases, human resources, and procedures) that captures, processes, stores and disseminates information to meet some organizational goal.

Online Social Network: Web-based service that allows individuals to construct a public or semi-public profile within a bounded system, articulate a list of other users with whom they share a connection, and view and traverse their list of connections and those made by others within the system.

Relationship Marketing: Part of marketing strategy focused on the tasks necessary to build, develop and maintain long-term relationships with key stakeholders.

Social Media: Set of tools based on Internet technologies, as for example, blogs, podcasts, wikis and online social networks.

ENDNOTES

1 Life Time Value (LTV) is a multi-period evaluation of a customer's value to the firm (Kumar & Reinartz, 2006, p. 313).

2 According to Stair and Reynolds (2008), the information is the outcome from the process of applying knowledge on the data.

3 Organizational process focused in the creation, storage, retrieval, and application of knowledge (Alavi & Leidner, 2001).

4 Organizational process that focuses on exchange of benefits (products and services for money), exchange of information (communications planned or not), social exchange (interpersonal), and / or any combination of the three (Zablah, Bellenger, et al., 2004).

5 Measurable characteristics of a market or a population in terms of number of persons, territorial density, sex, age, race, marital status, education, occupation, etc. (http://www.portaldomarketing.com.br).

6 Characteristics that show the lifestyle and attitude of consumers (http://www.portaldomarketing.com.br).

Chapter 21
Comparative Analysis of Acceptance Factors for SAP and Microsoft Dynamics NAV ERP Solutions in their Maturity Use Phase:
Enterprise 2.0 Issues

Simona Sternad
University of Maribor, Slovenia

Samo Bobek
University of Maribor, Slovenia

ABSTRACT

Enterprise Resource Planning (ERP) systems have been implemented in numerous organizations over the last decade. However, research indicates that successful implementation of ERP solutions does not necessarily lead to successful ERP usage. ERP systems benefit organizations only to the extent that users accept and utilize them frequently and extensively. To improve the efficiency and effectiveness of ERP systems in the operation phase, organizations need to research the factors that impact user satisfaction. In this area, the Technological Acceptance Model (TAM) proposed by Davis (1989) has been widely used as it can enhance understanding of the influences that increase the efficiency and effectiveness of ERP system use. Regardless of ERP complexity and ERP implementation failure, very few studies have been conducted to examine technology acceptance, especially when dealing with autonomous ERP users and including more external factors, which can influence users' acceptance of ERP system. Because ERP solutions are implemented by different methodologies and some are more present at large organizations than at small and mid-sized organizations, the authors research and compare the importance of external factors of two global solutions—namely, SAP and Microsoft Dynamics NAV—regarding user acceptance. The chapter contributes to the body of knowledge in this specific area.

DOI: 10.4018/978-1-4666-4373-4.ch021

INTRODUCTION

Enterprise Resource Planning (ERP) solutions can be viewed as (1) a set of packaged application software modules, with an integrated architecture, that can be used by organizations as their primary engine for integrating data, processes, and IT in real time across internal and external value chains; (2) deep knowledge of business practices that vendors have accumulated and stored from implementations in a wide range of client organizations and that can exert considerable influence on the design of processes within new client organizations; and (3) a generic 'semi-finished' product with tables and parameters that client organizations and their implementation partners must configure, customize, and integrate with other computer-based IS to meet their business needs (Seddon, Shanks, & Willcocks, 2003). These systems are "Web enabled," meaning they work using Web clients; this makes them accessible to all of the organization's employees, clients, partners, and vendors at anytime and from anyplace, thereby promoting the business units' effectiveness (Motiwalla & Thompson, 2009). The ERP solution's goal is to make information flow be both dynamic and immediate, thereby increasing the usefulness and value of the information. In addition, an ERP system acts as central repository eliminating data redundancy and adding flexibility. In summary, ERP systems are the mission-critical IS in today's business organizations and solve the critical problem of integrating information from various sources both inside and outside the organization's environment to make it available in real time to all employees and partners of the organization.

ERP system adoption typically follows three lifecycle phases: selection, implementation, and operation, the latter of which can be divided into a stabilization stage and a routine stage. Most literature on ERP solutions is focused on either evaluating the appropriateness of the ERP system vis-à-vis software, vendors, or consultants or identifying Critical Successful Factors (CSF) affecting ERP selection and implementation (Yu, 2005); less effort has been given to identifying potential post-implementation impact (Gattiker & Goodhue, 2005).

ERP systems benefit organizations only to the extent that users accept and utilize them frequently and extensively. To improve the efficiency and effectiveness of ERP systems in the operation phase, organizations need to research the factors that impact user satisfaction. In this area, the Technological Acceptance Model (TAM) is widely used for explaining behavioral intent and usage; it can enhance understanding of the influences that increase the efficiency and effectiveness of ERP system use (Shih & Huang, 2009). Several researchers have applied TAM to examine ERP system use (e.g., Calisir, Gumussoy, & Bayram, 2009; Lee, Lee, Olson, & Chung, 2010; Shih & Huang, 2009; Sun, Bhattacherjee, & Ma, 2009; Youngberg, Olsen, & Hauser, 2009), but few researchers have examined multiple external factors that influence intention to use an ERP system or ERP system usage in the stabilization stage. Although a small number of external factors have failed to illuminate user opinions about specific systems (Agarwal & Prasad, 1999; Lu, Chun-Sheng, Liu, & Yao, 2003; Sun et al., 2009), most studies address only a small number of external factors.

The goal of this paper is to explore a large number of external factors that potentially influence attitudes and behavior related to ERP use in the operation phase of the ERP lifecycle and to investigate the importance of these factors for different ERP solutions (i.e., SAP solution and Microsoft Dynamics NAV solution). Because of the large sample size required to apply TAM to multiple individual variables, we combine external factors into three groups: personal characteristics and information literacy (PCIL); System and Technological Characteristics (STC); and organizational-process characteristics (OPL). To test these factors, we collected survey data from 15 organizations where a SAP system has been implemented and 29 organizations where Microsoft Dynamics NAV has been implemented. An

ERP system has been in operation for several years, and we employed Partial Least Squares (PLS) to analyze the data. The rest of this paper is organized as follows: lifecycle of ERP solutions, literature review, ERP acceptance model, methodology, results and analysis, discussion, and conclusion.

ERP SOLUTIONS LIFECYCLE

Ross, Vitale, and Willcocks (2003) identified five stages ERP solutions lifecycle: (1) design, (2) implementation, (3) stabilization, (4) continuous improvement, and (5) transformation. In the ERP design stage, organizations make two important design decisions: one about process change and another about process standardization. In the implementation stage, organizations carefully plan implementation, deploying implementation teams to train users on the new system and, to some extent, on new processes. Most found that "going live" tended to be highly disruptive as the new system tended to be linked to new processes. However, it was not possible to implement the new system and the new processes separately because they were highly interdependent. Consequently, "going live" introduced major organizational changes. In most cases, managers involved with implementations have found they had underestimated the extent to which individuals would be affected. A period of stabilization often immediately follows implementation, during which time the organization attempts to clean up its processes and data and adjust to the new environment. The typical stabilization period for an initial implementation is 4 to 12 months. For this stage, it is usual that an initial performance dip occurs, although the intensity and length of organizations' performance dips vary. Following stabilization, organizations enter a stage in which they add functionality through new modules. During this stage, organizations are focused primarily on continuous improvement, but they are also starting to engage in process redesign to implement new structures and roles to leverage the system. The transformation stage involves changing organizational boundaries, particularly with regard to systems, which means the extension of the ERP into customer and supplier systems.

Given the high number of failed ERP implementation projects, ERP vendors have developed their own methodologies that best fit their packages. Many different vendor-driven methodologies or approaches use the traditional ERP development lifecycle or rapid ERP lifecycle. Because of the leading market shares of SAP and Microsoft Dynamics packages, we also examine their respective methodologies.

Two methodologies are used to implement SAP projects: conventional and accelerated SAP (ASAP). The conventional methodology, better known as the SAP Procedure Model, has been widely used to implement SAP solutions (Khan, 2002). This methodology requires a very detailed analysis of the existing systems, current functionality, and business processes. As a result, organizations are often driven in mirroring existing systems instead of adopting those of the SAP solution. Today, this methodology is still preferred by very large organizations. On the basis of this finding, SAP introduced the ASAP implementation methodology in 1996 (Miller, 1998). The ASAP roadmap consists of five phases: project preparation, business blueprint, realization, final preparation, and go-live and support. Phase I, project preparation, consists of organizational readiness and preparation for the project. Phase II, business blueprint, deals with the scope, which is narrowed to fit the industry-specific processes to reflect the future vision of a business. Phase III, realization, means that the business blueprint becomes a reality. During this phase, the system is configured and tested. This is achieved through simulation, validation, unit and integration testing, data conversions and preparation of interfaces, enhancements, and reports. In phase IV, final preparation, system refinement, preparation of a go-live plan, end-user training, knowledge transfer, system administration, data migration, and final testing and fine-tuning have to be performed (Khan, 2002). In the last phase, go-live and support, final checks are made before and after taking-off, and procedures and measurements are developed to review the benefits on an ongoing basis.

Microsoft has also developed its own methodology for implementing Microsoft Dynamics ERP packages, called Microsoft Dynamics Sure Step (Shankar & Bellefroid, 2011). The methodology entails a phased approach including diagnostics, analysis, design, development, deployment, and operation. The diagnostics phase deals with gathering information in order to prepare an adequate proposal for the customer. During the analysis phase, functional requirements are documented and agreed upon. The design phase includes the design of both the overall solution configuration and the design of specific customizations and integrations needed to cover business requirements identified during the previous phase. The development phase includes the actual development of customizations, integrations, and data migration processes that are established through design specifications. This phase is followed by the deployment phase, including all activities related to final system and load testing, training of end users, and the actual cut-over to the new production environment. The main goal of the operations phase is the transition into ongoing support; final project- and software-related documentation is also prepared. Although the diagnostic phase is a pre-implementation phase, the analysis through operation phases represent the five phases of an implementation project. The operation phase encompasses post-implementation activities in that it extends the project lifecycle beyond the implementation into the operational phase.

We concluded that ERP researchers as well as ERP vendors expose different numbers of phases of the ERP lifecycle, which can generally be divided into three phases: selection, implementation, and operational phase. Much of the success of ERP implementation lies in operational phase of the ERP lifecycle (Bradford, 2008; Motiwalla & Thompson, 2009), which consists of the stabilization stage and the routine stage. In the stabilization stage, ERP systems go through a post-implementation breaking-in period in which performance may not be typical of the long-term effects an organization might experience (Gattiker & Goodhue, 2005). After the stabilization stage, companies enter the routine stage, in which they have to put more effort into people and process improvements (Bradford, 2008). In the routine stage, users accept the system and the usage becomes a regular day-to-day activity. It often takes many months or even years for experienced users to get comfortable with the ERP system because early in an ERP system's life, these users tend to resist using it for their work. However, at some point in the ERP system's life, users begin to see the advantages of the ERP system and they carefully begin to explore its functions, gradually reaching success. This shows that the ERP users have accepted the system and are putting it to extended use. In the routine stage, ERP systems might be implemented successfully from a technical perspective, but success depends on ERP users' attitudes toward and actual use of the system (Boudreau, 2002; Kwahk & Lee, 2008). To improve the efficiency and effectiveness of ERP systems in the operation phase, organizations need to research the factors that impact user satisfaction. In this area, TAM, proposed by Davis (1989), has been widely used to explain behavioral intent and usage; it can enhance understanding influences that increase the efficiency and effectiveness of ERP system use (Shih & Huang, 2009).

LITERATURE REVIEW

Technological Acceptance Model (TAM)

Several theoretical models have been used to investigate the determinants of acceptance and use of new Information Technology (IT), such as the Theory of Reasoned Action (TRA; Fishbein & Ajzen, 1975), the Theory of Planned Behavior (TPB; Ajzen, 1991), and the theory of technology acceptance model (TAM; Davis, Bagozzi, &

Warshaw, 1989). Compared to competing models, TAM is believed to be more parsimonious, predicative, and robust (Liu & Ma, 2006; Lu et al., 2003; Venkatesh & Davis, 2000); as such, among the theoretical models, it is most widely used by IS/IT researchers (Amoako-Gyampah & Salam, 2004; Davis, 1989; Davis et al., 1989; Lee et al., 2010). The key purpose of TAM is to provide a basis for tracing the impact of external factors on internal beliefs, attitudes, and intentions (Davis et al., 1989). TAM posits that two beliefs—namely, Perceived Usefulness (PU) and perceived ease of use (PEOU)—are of primary relevance for computer acceptance behavior (Davis et al., 1989). PU is defined as the "degree to which a person believes that using a particular system would enhance his or her job performance" (Davis, 1989, p. 320). PEOU, in contrast, refers to "the degree to which a person believes that using a particular system would be free of effort" (Davis, 1989, p. 320). The two central hypotheses in TAM state that PU and PEOU positively influence an individual's attitude toward using a new technology (AT), which in turn influences his or her behavioral intention (BI) to use it. Finally, intention is positively related to Actual Use (AU). TAM also predicts that PEOU influences PU, as Davis et al. (1989, p. 987) explained that "effort saved due to improved perceived ease of use may be redeployed, enabling a person to accomplish more work for the same effort." The original TAM is well established and tested; furthermore, a variety of extensions regarding external factors by examining the antecedents of PU and PEOU have been developed, such as TAM 2 proposed by Venkatesh and Davis (2000), model of the determinants of PEOU by Venkatesh (1998), and TAM 3 developed by Venaktesh and Bala (2008).

TAM and ERP Systems

One of the commonly cited reasons for the lack of sophisticated use of ERP systems is the lack of user acceptance. A literature review of past ERP studies regarding TAM indicates that few studies have investigated ERP user acceptance and usage. The review shows that a small number of studies have been published, and all of them expose small numbers of determinants (external factors) that could influence ERP acceptance and usage in different phases of the ERP lifecycle (Table 1).

As several studies (e.g., Nah, Tan, & Teh, 2004) have revealed, a common reason for ERP failures can be attributed to users' reluctance and unwillingness to adopt and use the implemented ERP system. A better understanding of factors leading to ERP users' acceptance of ERP systems is necessary to facilitate successful ERP usage. In this paper, we are interested in identifying factors leading users to extended usage of ERP systems. Thus, the goal of our research is to expand basic TAM with more generic contextual factors and to examine their influence on PU and PEOU for different ERP solutions (i.e., SAP solution and NAV solution).

ERP ACCEPTANCE MODEL

To examine ERP users' use of ERP systems, we need to extend the TAM model. Synthesizing prior research on TAM and on ERP systems, a research model has been developed (Figure 1). The grey area within the dotted line denotes the original TAM. Because our research is focused on current usage of ERP system in the routine stage, there is no need to examine the BI; thus, BI was dropped from the proposed research model. According to Davis (1989) and Davis et al. (1989), PEOU influences PU while PU and PEOU influence AT using the system.

In case of ERP implementations, other cognitive considerations besides PU and PEOU may become relevant (Nah et al., 2004). In the ERP context, organizations have to adopt business processes of an implemented ERP system. Although one of the major benefits of ERP systems is that they offer organizations the solution with

Table 1.ERP literature regarding TAM

Reference	Focus	Phase—ERP System Lifecycle
Nah et al. (2004)	They tested the impact of four cognitive constructors (PU, PEOU, perceived compatibility and perceived fit) on AT toward using ERP system and symbolic adoption.	Post-implementation (stabilization phase)
Amoako-Gyampah & Salam (2004)	Their study evaluated the impact of one belief construct (shared beliefs in the benefits of a technology) and two technology success factors (training and communications) on PU and PEOU in one global organization.	Implementation
Shivers-Blackwell & Charles (2006)	They researched student readiness for change (through gender, computer self-efficacy, and perceived benefits of ERP) on BI regarding the ERP implementation.	Implementation
Bradley & Lee (2007)	They used a case study to investigate the relationship between training satisfaction and the perceptions of PEOU, the perceptions of PU, and effectiveness and efficiency in implementing an ERP system at a mid-sized university.	Implementation
Hsieh & Wang (2007)	They researched the impact of PU and PEOU on extended use.	Post-implementation (routine stage)
Kwahk & Lee (2008)	They examined the formation of readiness for change (enhanced by two factors: organizational commitment and perceived personal competence) and its effect on the perceived technological value of an ERP system leading to its use.	Post-implementation (stabilization stage)
Bueno & Salmeron (2008)	They tested the influence of the critical success factors (top management support, communication, cooperation, training and technological complexity) on ERP implementation.	Implementation
Uzoka et al. (2008)	They researched the selection of ERP by organizations using impact of system quality, information quality, service quality, and support quality as key determinants of the cognitive response as well as which ERP system to purchase/use.	Selection
Sun et al. (2009)	They included the role of ERP's perceived work compatibility in users' ERP usage intention, usage, and performance in work settings.	Post-implementation (routine stage)
Shih & Huang (2009)	Their study attempted to explain BI and AU through incorporated additional behavioral constructs: top management support, computer self-efficacy, and computer anxiety.	Post-implementation (routine stage)
Calisir et al. (2009)	They examined factors (subjective norms, compatibility, gender, experience, and education level) that affect users' BI to use ERP system based on potential ERP users at one manufacturing organization.	Implementation
Youngberg et al. (2009)	They researched the impact of PEOU, result demonstrability, and subjective norm on PU and impact of it on usage behavior.	Post-implementation (stabilization stage)
Lee et al. (2010)	They examined factor organizational support (formal and informal) on original TAM factors.	Post-implementation

the best business practices, it is not necessary that this be the best option for ERP users. Inherent business rules behind the processes give them little choice but to follow strict business processes of ERP system, unlike the old systems, which allowed them to carry out many different process variations. Thus, organizations deploy ERP systems to facilitate organizational work rather than to match users' personal preferences or habits. Based on this understanding, we view Work Compatibility (WC) strictly as the fit of ERP system to organizational work and not to personal preferences or work habits. WC, like PU and PEOU, is more of a perceptual construct as it is the perception of fit between IT and work that motivates employees to use the system, irrespective of the actual extent of fit (Sun et al., 2009). WC refers to the degree to which ERP

Figure 1. Research model

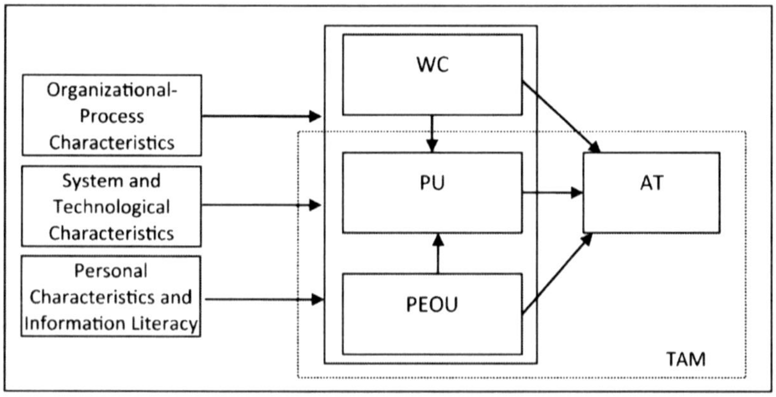

users can do most of their tasks in the ERP system. WC influences PU, thereby demonstrating the importance of incorporating WC into models of IT usage as explained in Sun et al. (2009) and Scott and Walczak (2009). In a context of ERP usage, it is expected that—with regard to the relationship between WC and PU—the more work compatible the ERP system is, the more useful it is for ERP users. We also presume that WC has a strong direct effect on AT, not just an indirect effect through PU; if ERP users believe that the ERP system is more work compatible with their daily tasks, they will have a more positive attitude toward using that system.

Research efforts have been devoted to extend to the theory by examining the antecedents of PU and PEOU. As noted by Venkatesh and Davis (2000), a better understanding of these factors would enable us to design effective organizational interventions that might lead to increased user acceptance and use of new IT systems. Although TAM is a model applicable to a variety of technologies, the constructs of TAM need to be extended by incorporating additional factors (Calisir et al., 2009). Schwarz (2003) identified antecedents to cognitive factors (PEOU and PU), classifying the factors into three groups: individual variables (such as computer experience, self-efficacy, and prior experiences), organizational influences (such as management and external support and perceived resources), and technology characteristics (such as accessibility of the medium and interface type). Meanwhile, Venkatesh and Bala (2008) identified four types of determinants of PU and PEOU: individual differences, system characteristics, social influences, and facilitating conditions. In the context of ERP systems, we use prior research to define three groups of external factors (Table 2): Personal Characteristics and Information Literacy (PCIL), System and Technological Characteristics (STC), and Organizational-Process Characteristics (OPC).

METHODOLOGY

Sample and Procedure

Our sample consists of companies that have used SAP or Microsoft Dynamics NAV solutions for more than one year, meaning they can be considered to have ERP systems in the routine stage. A total of 122 companies received the initial e-mail, which explained the purpose of the study and asked the organizations to verify if they matched our selection criteria. Forty-four organizations agreed to participate in the survey and were asked to distribute the survey questionnaire to their ERP users (15 organizations with implemented SAP solution and 29 organizations with implemented

Table 2. External factors mentioned by authors

	External Factors	Authors	Description
Personal Characteristics and Information Literacy (PCIL)	Experience with computer	Davis et al., 1998; Venkatesh et al., 2003; Thompson et al., 2006; Venkatesh & Bala, 2008; Calisir et al., 2009.	Experience with computer has been found to be an important factor for the acceptance of a technology (Calisir et al., 2009).
	Computer self-efficiency	Venkatesh & Davis, 2000; Venkatesh et al., 2003; Thompson et al., 2006; Shivers-Blackwell & Charles, 2006; Venkatesh & Bala, 2008; Shih & Huaug, 2009.	Computer self-efficiency is defined as the degree to which an individual believes that he or she has the ability to perform a specific task/job using the computer (Shih & Huang, 2009; Venkatesh & Bala, 2008).
	Personal innovativeness toward IT	Agarwal & Prasad, 1999; Yi et al., 2006; Thompson et al., 2006.	Personal innovativeness toward IT represents the degree to which an individual is willing to try out new IT (Agarwal & Prasad, 1999).
	Computer anxiety	Venkatesh et al., 2003; Liu & Ma, 2006; Venkatesh & Bala, 2008; Shih & Huang, 2009.	Computer anxiety represents the degree of an individual's apprehension, or even fear, when he or she is faced with the possibility of using computers (Venkatesh et al., 2003).
System and Technological Characteristics (STC)	ERP data quality	Venkatesh, 1998; Venkatesh & Davis, 2000; Gattiker & Goodhue, 2005; Kositnurit et al., 2006; Iansiti, 2007.	Without accurate and relevant data, an organization is severely constrained in the coordination and task efficiency benefits it can achieve from its ERP system (Gattiker & Goodhue, 2005).
	ERP system functionality	Musaji, 2003; Somers et al., 2003; Lu et al., 2003; Kositnurit et al., 2006; Iansiti, 2007.	System functions are used to measure the rapid response, stability, easy usage, and flexibility of the system.
	ERP system performance	Boudreau, 2002; Musaji, 2003; Venkatesh et al., 2003; Somers et al., 2003; Kositnurit et al., 2006; Lu & Ma, 2006; Iansiti, 2007.	ERP system performance refers to the degree to which a person believes that a system is reliable and responsive during the normal course of operations (Liu & Ma, 2006).
	User manuals (help)	Kelley, 2001; Boudreau, 2002; Musaji, 2002; Kositnurit et al., 2006; Bradford, 2008.	The degree to which an individual views inadequate user manuals as the reason for his or her unsuccessful ERP performance (Kelley, 2001).
Organizational-Process Characteristics (OPC)	Social influence	Venkatesh, 1998; Venkatesh et al., 2003; Bradford, 2008; Calisir et al., 2009.	Social influence joins two factors: subjective norm and social factors. Subjective norm is defined as a person's perception that most people who are important to him/her think that he/she should or should not perform the behavior in question (Venkatesh, 1998). Social factors are individual's internalization of the reference group's subjective culture and specific interpersonal agreements that the individual has made with others in specific social situations (Venkatesh et al., 2003).
	Fit with business processes	Amoako-Gyampah & Salam, 2004; Nah et al., 2004; Bradley & Lee 2007; Bradford, 2008.	Fit with business processes from an end-user's perspective is the degree to which the ERP system is perceived by a user to meet his/her organization's needs (Nah et al., 2004).
	ERP training and education	Amonko-Gyampah & Salam, 2004; Bradley & Lee, 2007; Bueno & Salmeron, 2008.	ERP training and education is defined as the degree to which a user thinks that he or she received enough formal and informal training after ERP implementation.
	ERP support	Boudreau, 2002; Lee et al., 2010.	We define ERP support as the degree to which an individual views adequate ERP support as the reason for his or her successful ERP usage.
	ERP communication	Kelley, 2001; Musaji, 2003; Boudreau, 2002; Amonko-Gyampah & Salam, 2004; Bueno & Salmeron, 2008.	ERP communication problems refer to the lack of communication regarding the ERP applications and their modifications (Kelley, 2001).

NAV solution). All respondents were required to use an ERP system in their daily work. Ultimately, 293 (192 SAP and 101 NAV) questionnaires were properly completed by respondents and used for the current analysis.

Measures

The constructs of the proposed model are Perceived Usefulness (PU), Perceived Ease Of Use (PEOU), Work Compatibility (WC), and attitude toward ERP use (AT) for basic TAM of ERP systems influenced by the external variable constructs. Previous TAM-based research has primarily investigated small numbers of external factors that influence user acceptance and usage. In the context of ERP systems, more external factors can influence users' acceptance and extended usage. Thus, the conceptualization of higher-order factors (in our case, second-order factors), in which more external factors have to be jointly included, have to be investigated if we want to extend the understanding of user behavior in ERP settings. The constructs of external variables are distributed among three second-level constructs: Personal Characteristics and Information Literacy (PCIL), System and Technological Characteristics (STC), and Organizational-Process Characteristics (OPC). PCIL includes experience with computer, computer self-efficiency, personal innovativeness toward IT and computer anxiety. STC includes ERP data quality, ERP system functionality, ERP system performance and user manuals (help). OPC includes social influence, fit with business processes, training and education on ERP, ERP support and ERP communication. Our model includes 17 first-order factors and 3 second-order factors. All factor items were measured on a 7-point Likert scale, ranging from "strongly disagree" to "strongly agree," taken from relevant prior research and adapted to relate to the context of ERP usage. In addition, demographic information was collected.

The instrument was developed in multiple stages, as suggested by Straub (1989). First, based on an extensive literature review, the initial instrument was developed. The research instrument was discussed with more experts of ERP systems. Based on the problems identified by the respondents, minor improvements to the questionnaire were made. Although all items had been validated by past research, the adopted instrument was examined to ensure content, construct validity, and reliability within the ERP context. As Amoako-Gyampah and Salam (2004) pointed out, instrument validation or re-validation is necessary because the validity of the instrument may not have been persistent across different technologies and user groups. The instrument was pilot tested with a group of 30 NAV users in one organization, and the instrument's reliability was evaluated; the Cronbach's alpha values ranged from 0.58 to 0.91, indicating a satisfactory level of reliability exceeding value 0.5 (Hinton, Brownlow, McMurray, & Cozens, 2004). As part of the pre-test comments and suggestions, questionnaire items' wording has also been taken into account. Based on the results of the pilot testing, revisions and additions were made to the instrument. Pilot participants were included in the main data gathering effort since they were part of the population of interest. Final scales and items are listed in Appendix A.

Model Estimation

Hierarchical models using latent variables can be estimated using Structural Equation Modeling (SEM). For many researchers, SEM is equivalent to carrying out Covariance-Based SEM (CB-SEM) analyses using software such as Amos, EQS, and LISREL (Hair, Ringle, & Sarstedt, 2011). However, in the last few years, another unique and very useful approach—Partial Least Squares SEM (PLS-SEM)—has become popular among researchers (e.g., Henseler, Ringle, & Sinkovics, 2009). PLS has several major strengths (Chin,

1998): It is a predicative technique suitable for situations with less theory development; it places minimal demands on measurement scales; it avoids factor indeterminacy problems and inadmissible solutions; it avoids identification problems of recursive models; it makes no assumptions about the data; it requires no specific distributions for measured variables; it assumes the errors are uncorrelated; it works well with small samples; and it is better suited for analyzing complex relationships and models.

Models that include second-order factors consist of higher-order factors modeled as causally impacting a number of first-order factors (i.e., standard factors with measured indicators; Chin, 1998). Therefore, these second-order factors are not directly connected to any measurement items. A higher-order factor can thus be created by specifying a latent variable that represents all the manifest variables of the underlying lower-order factors. The method of repeated indicators known as the hierarchical component model suggested by Wold (1989) is the easiest to implement. The second-order factor is directly measured by observed variables for all the first-order factors measured with reflective indicators. Although this approach repeats the number of manifest variables used, the model can be estimated using the standard PLS algorithm (Henseler et al., 2009; Tenenhaus, Vinzi, Chatelin, & Lauro, 2005).

Based on these benefits, we decided to use the PLS approach. The empirical data were analyzed in two stages involving a PLS technique using Smart PLS 2.0 M3 (Ringle & Will, 2005). In the first stage, all measurement scales were examined for their psychometric properties; the second stage focused on hypothesis testing and analysis. In analyzing the data, we followed the guidelines specified in Tenenhaus et al. (2005), Henseler et al. (2009), and Hair et al. (2011), which are presented in Table 3.

RESULTS AND ANALYSIS

Descriptive Statistics

A total of 293 questionnaires (101 NAV and 192 SAP) were properly filled by respondents from 29 organizations with the NAV solution and 15 organizations with the SAP solution; these responses were used for the current analysis. Survey respondents represented different groups of industries, including IT and telecommunications (44.0%), manufacturing (35.2%), professional, scientific and technical activities (10.2%), wholesale and retail trade (4.1%), and others (6.5%). Respondents were 51.5% male (47 NAV and 104 SAP) and 48.5% female (63 NAV and 79 SAP). Most (67.2%) had high school education or more; 53.6% (157) identified themselves as workers (experts and other employees), 31.7% (93) as low management (e.g., manager of group or organization unit), 12.6% (37) as middle management (e.g., CIO), and 2% (6) as corporate government and/or top management. The average number of total working years was 15.4 (min = 1, max = 43, SD = 10.2) and average number of working years in their current workplaces was 7.6 (min = 1, max = 37, SD =7.4).

The average respondent had used an ERP system for 4.7 years (*NAV* = 3.16 years and *SAP* = 5.56 years), with a minimum of 1 year and a maximum of 10 years for the NAV solution compared to a maximum of 18 years for the SAP solution. Respondents estimated their intensity of NAV/SAP usage via the following statement: "I would rate the intensity of my job-related NAV/SAP system use to be…." on a 7-point Likert scale, ranging from "not important" to "very important." The average value was 5 (*NAV* = 5.23 and *SAP* = 4.79), indicating a somewhat greater importance than average. Most respondents selected 6 (i.e., much greater importance). Furthermore, respondents estimated their frequency of NAV/SAP use via three statements proposed by Schwarz (2003), also on a 7-point Likert scale. Responses to these

Table 3. Rules for model evaluation

Measurement Model	
Measure	**Measure Evaluation**
Internal consistency reliability	Cronbach's alpha (α) should be higher than 0.70 (0.60 is considered acceptable). Composite reliability (CR) should be higher than 0.70 (0.60 is considered acceptable).
Indicator reliability	Indicator loadings should be significant and exceed 0.70.
Convergent validity	The average variance extracted (AVE) for each construct should exceed 0.50 (Fornell & Larcker, 1981).
Discriminant validity	The square root of AVE for each construct should exceed the bivariate correlations between that construct and all other constructs (Fornell & Larcker, 1981) An indicator's loadings should be higher than all of its cross loadings.
Structural Model	
R2	*R2* values of 0.75, 0.50, or 0.25 for endogenous latent variables in the structural model can be described as substantial, moderate, or weak, respectively (Chin, 1998).
Coefficients' significance	The relationships testing results are based on bootstrapping to test the statistical significance of each path coefficient using *t*-tests, as recommended by Chin (1998). The minimum number of bootstrap samples is 5,000 and the number of cases should be equal to the number of observations in the original sample. Critical *t*-values for a two-tailed test are 1.65 (significance level = 10%), 1.96 (significance level = 5%), and 2.58 (significance level = 1%) (Hair et al., 2011).
Predictive relevance	The blindfolding approach proposed by Wold (1982) has been followed to calculate the cv-communality and cv-redundancy indexes. The cv-communality index (*H2*) measures the global quality of the measurement model, if they are positive for all blocks of variables (Guenzi et al., 2009). Where the cv-redundancy index (i.e., Stone-Geisser's *Q2*) measures the global quality of the structural model. The model has predicative relevance if *Q2*>0 (Guenzi et al., 2009).
GoF	An important part of model evaluation is the examination of fit indexes reflecting the predictive power of estimated inner and outer model relationships, which can be measured by evaluating goodness-of-fit (GoF) coefficient (Guenzi et al., 2009; Tenenhaus et al., 2005). The general criterion for evaluating GoF is to calculate the geometric mean of the average communality and the average *R2* of endogenous variables (Tenenhaus et al., 2005).
f2	Effect size (*f2*) can be viewed as a gauge for whether a predictor latent variable has a weak, medium, or large effect at the structural level (Hensler et al., 2009). *f2* measures impact of independent variables on depended variables and can have a non-significant, small (0.02), medium (0.15), or large (0.35) effect on the dependent variable at the structural level (Henseler et al., 2009).

questions are presented in Table 4. For all three statements, the average value for the NAV solution is near 5, which represents an important degree of use, while the average value for the SAP solution is a little below 4, which represents a moderate degree of use.

Table 4. Degree of use

In a Typical One-Month Period, What is the Likelihood of You …	Average NAVa	Average SAPa
… using most of features of the ERP solution?	4.51	3.71
… using more features than other users of the ERP solutions?	4.82	3.86
… using more obscure aspects of the ERP solutions?	4.62	3.78

aScale 1-7, 'not important' to 'very important'.

Enterprise Resource Model for NAV Solution

Not all external factors met the assessment requirements of the measurement model, and we excluded these from further analysis. These external factors are experience with computer and computer anxiety from PCIL group, ERP system functionality from STC group and ERP support, ERP communications, and ERP training and education from OPC group. The final version of the model is presented here.

We examined two measures of reliability: Cronbach's alpha (α) and Composite Reliability (CR). As shown in Table 5, each of our 32 scales had a Cronbach's alpha exceeding 0.60 and CR exceeding 0.80, thereby ensuring adequate reliability for our measurement scales. Table 5 also lists item factor loadings, all of which were significant at $p < 0.01$ and were higher than the

Table 5. Psychometric properties of the instrument for NAV (n = 101)

Construct	Indicators	Item Mean	Item S.D.	Factor Loadings	α	CR	AVE
Personal innovativeness toward IT	pcil_pi1	5.35	1.37	0.89	0.86	0.92	0.79
	pcil_pi2	4.59	1.68	0.85			
	pcil_pi3	5.03	1.65	0.92			
Computer self-efficiency	pcil_cse1	5.29	1.13	0.90	0.64	0.84	0.73
	pcil_cse2	5.84	1.22	0.81			
Data quality	stc_dq1	5.60	0.84	0.78	0.89	0.91	0.64
	stc_dq2	5.54	1.12	0.81			
	stc_dq3	4.91	1.27	0.83			
	stc_dq4	5.49	1.03	0.87			
	stc_dq5	5.13	1.19	0.83			
	stc_dq6	5.30	1.30	0.69			
System performance	stc_sp4	5.68	0.94	0.80	0.80	0.88	0.71
	stc_sp5	5.63	1.17	0.85			
	stc_sp6	5.35	1.13	0.88			
User manuals	stc_um1	5.18	1.15	0.91	0.66	0.85	0.74
	stc_um2	5.06	1.21	0.80			
Business processes fit	opc_bpf1	5.80	0.99	0.88	0.80	0.87	0.64
	opc_bpf2	5.77	0.93	0.89			
	opc_bpf3	5.55	0.98	0.82			
Social influence	opc_si3	6.23	0.92	0.91	0.80	0.91	0.83
	opc_si4	6.24	0.82	0.92			
PU	u1	5.73	1.09	0.90	0.95	0.97	0.88
	u2	5.69	0.99	0.95			
	u3	5.73	1.03	0.97			
	u4	5.71	1.10	0.94			
PEOU	eou1	5.57	1.09	0.93	0.84	0.93	0.86
	eou2	5.23	1.23	0.93			
WC	wc1	5.04	1.35	0.88	0.88	0.92	0.80
	wc2	5.39	1.17	0.94			
	wc3	5.43	1.20	0.86			
AT	at1	5.98	1.03	0.96	0.93	0.97	0.94
	at2	5.86	1.00	0.97			

Table 6. Intercorrelations of the latent variables a

	1	2	3	4	5	6	7	8	9	10	11
1. Personal innovativeness toward IT	0.89										
2. Computer self-efficiency	0.29	0.85									
3. ERP data quality	0.28	0.15	0.80								
4. ERP system performance	0.34	0.06	0.66	0.84							
5. User manuals (help)	0.05	0.05	0.57	0.49	0.86						
6. Business processes fit	0.31	0.14	0.55	0.54	0.32	0.88					
7. Social influence	0.10	0.16	0.16	0.30	0.13	0.33	0.91				
8. PU	0.23	0.00	0.39	0.61	0.18	0.55	0.46	0.94			
9. PEOU	0.30	-0.11	0.53	0.60	0.42	0.40	0.23	0.62	0.93		
10. WC	0.31	0.02	0.63	0.65	0.32	0.67	0.25	0.74	0.65	0.90	
11. AT	0.24	0.05	0.48	0.60	0.22	0.60	0.37	0.80	0.64	0.81	0.97

a Square root of *AVE* on diagonal.

recommended 0.70; all values' AVE also exceeded 0.50, which satisfies Fornell and Larcker's (1981) assessment criteria for convergent validity. Table 8 indicates the α, CR, and AVE of the measures in the second-order model, demonstrating that CRs exceeding 0.80 and AVE exceeds 0.50, thereby providing evidence for reliable measurements.

The inter-construct correlation matrix (Table 6) shows that the principal diagonal elements (square root AVE) exceed non-diagonal elements in the same row or column (bivariate correlations), demonstrating that the discriminate validity of all scales is also adequate. Overall, these measurement results are satisfactory and suggest that it is appropriate to proceed with the evaluation of the structural model.

Table 7. Parameter estimation of the PLS model using the bootstrap method and effect size for NAV

Dependent Variable	Independent Variable	Standardized Path Coefficient	*t*-Values	*f2*
WC	OPC	0.38	6.37**	0.22
	STC	0.46	6.79**	0.33
PU	OPC	0.26	2.91**	0.18
	WC	0.41	3.13**	0.32
	PEOU	0.25	2.37*	0.11
PEOU	PCIL	0.03	0.29	0.00
	SCT	0.61	8.04**	0.55
AT	WC	0.44	4.67**	0.27
	PU	0.41	3.70**	0.27
	PEOU	0.10	1.09	0.00

Notes: $**p<0.01$, $*p<0.05$.

The next step in the analysis was to examine the path significance and magnitude of each of our relationship effects and the overall explanatory power of the proposed model. Results of bootstrapping are shown in Table 7 and Figure 2. PEOU has a positive and significant effect on PU ($\beta = 0.25, p<0.01$) and non-significant effect on AT ($\beta = 0.10, p>0.05$). PU has a strong positive effect on AT ($\beta = 0.41, p<0.01$). WC has a strong and significant positive effect on PU ($\beta = 0.41, p<0.01$). WC also has a strong significant positive effect on AT ($\beta = 0.44, p<0.01$).

As Table 8 and Figure 2 demonstrate, the loadings of the first-order factors on the second-order factors exceed 0.60 and second-order factors have a significant positive effect on WC, PU, and/or PEOU. PCIL does not have a significant effect on PEOU ($\beta = 0.03, p>0.05$). STC has a strong positive effect on PEOU ($\beta = 0.61, p<0.01$) and a somewhat less strong effect on WC ($\beta = 0.46,$

Figure 2. Results of structural model analysis of NAV solution a

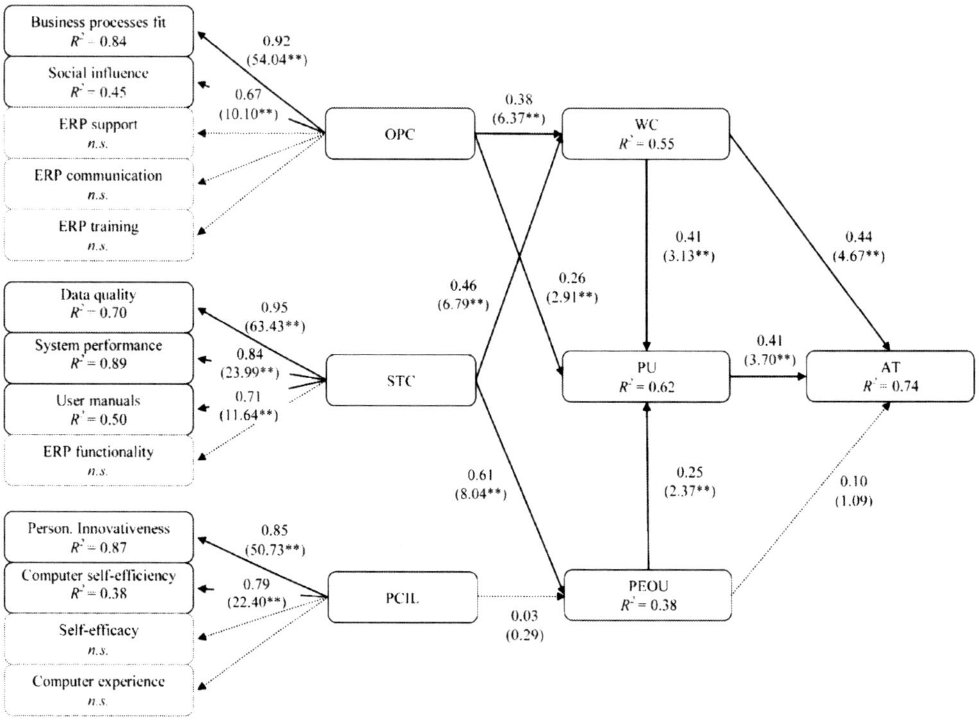

Table 8. Path coefficients' external variables in second-order model for NAV

First-Order External Factors	**PCIL** α **= 0.75** *CR* **= 0.84** *AVE* **= 0.52**	**OPC** α **= 0.90** *CR* **= 0.92** *AVE* **= 0.52**	**STC** α **= 0.79** *CR* **= 0.85** *AVE* **= 0.55**
Personal innovativeness toward IT	0.93 (t = 52.98)		
Computer self-efficiency	0.62 (t = 5.34)		
Business process fit		0.92 (t = 54.04)	
Social influence		0.67 (t = 10.10)	
ERP data quality			0.95 (t = 63.43)
ERP system performance			0.84 (t = 23.99)
ERP user manuals (help)			0.71 (t = 11.64)

$p<0.01$). OPC has a strong positive effect on WC ($\beta = 0.38, p<0.01$) and on PU ($\beta = 0.26, p<0.01$). Furthermore, we checked all other relationships between PCIL, STC, and OPC on PEOU, PU, and WC, but none were significant.

In our model, the average *f2* is 0.23, which represents medium effect predictor latent variables at the structural level (Table 7). The structural model demonstrates predictive power as the variance explained (*R2*) in key endogenous constructs is 0.55 for WC, 0.62 for PU, 0.38 for PEOU, and 0.74 for AT. All *R2* can be described as "moderate" (Chin, 1998). The findings indicate that our model explains a large part of the variance in the endogenous variables, with an average *R2* of 0.57. Communality and redundancy coefficients are also presented in Table 9. They can be used in essentially the same way as the *R2* as they reflect the relative amount of explained variance for latent and manifest variables. According to the results in Table 9, GoF is 0.61, which can be

Table 9. Explained variance (R2), communality, redundancy, and blindfolding results of cv-communality (H2) and cv-redundancy (Q2) for NAV

	R2	Communality	Redundancy	cv-Communality *(H2)*	cv-Redundancy *(Q2)*
OPC		0.55		0.39	0.39
STC		0.52		0.42	0.42
PCIL		0.52		0.28	0.28
PU	0.62	0.88	0.30	0.63	0.43
PEOU	0.38	0.86	0.25	0.79	0.55
WC	0.55	0.80	0.35	0.51	0.34
AT	0.74	0.94	0.30	0.59	0.54
Average	0.57	0.64 a	0.30	0.52	0.42

a Computed as a weighted average of the different communalities with the weights being the number of manifest variables per each construct (Tenenhaus et al., 2005).

considered satisfactory (Tenenhaus et al., 2005), and the measurement model (average *H2* is 0.52) shows a little better quality than the structural one (average *Q2* is 0.39).

Enterprise Resource Model for SAP Solution

Because not all of the external factors (i.e., computer self-efficacy and experience with computer from PCIL group, ERP functionality from STC group, and ERP support, ERP communications, and ERP training and education from OPC group) met assessment requirements of the measurement model for the SAP solution, we excluded them from further analysis. The final version of the model is presented. As shown in Table 10, each of our 11 scales had a Cronbach's alpha exceeding 0.70 and CR exceeding 0.8, ensuring adequate reliability for our measurement scales. Table 10 also lists item factor loadings, all of which were significant at $p < 0.01$ and were higher than the recommended level of 0.70; in addition, all AVE values exceeded 0.50. The remainder of our measurement scales shows strong evidence for convergent validity. In Table 13, the CR and AVE of the measures in the second-order model are included, which provides evidence for reliable measurements.

Table 11 shows the inter-construct correlation matrix, in which the principal diagonal elements (square root AVE) exceed non-diagonal elements in the same row or column (bivariate correlations), demonstrating that the discriminate validity of all scales is also adequate. Overall, these measurement results are satisfactory and suggest that it is appropriate to proceed with the evaluation of the structural model.

The next step in the analysis was to examine the path significance and magnitude of each of our hypothesized effects and the overall explanatory power of the proposed model for SAP. Results of this analysis are shown in Figure 3 and Table 12. In our model, average *f2* is 0.18, which represents medium-effect predictor latent variables at the structural level, with no insignificant impact of independent variables on dependent variables.

As Table 13 indicates, the loadings of the first-order factors on the second-order factors exceed 0.7 and second-order factors have a significant positive effect on PU, PEOU, and WC. PCIL has no significant effect on PEOU (β = 0.10, p>0.05), STC has a strong positive effect on PEOU (β = 0.62, p<0.01) and on WC (β = 0.40, p<0.01), and OPC has a strong positive effect on PU (β = 0.27. p<0.01) and on WC (β = 0.41, p<0.01).

Table 10. Psychometric properties of the instrument for SAP (n = 192)

Construct	Indicators	Item Mean	Item S.D.	Loadings	*α*	*CR*	*AVE*
Personal innovativeness toward IT	pcil_pi1	5.40	1.35	0.86	0.85	0.91	0.77
	pcil_pi2	4.57	1.68	0.86			
	pcil_pi3	5.14	1.59	0.92			
Computer anxiety	pcil_ca1a	1.57	1.00	0.87	0.76	0.87	0.69
	pcil_ca2a	1.42	0.95	0.87			
	pcil_ca3	6.37	1.00	0.73			
Data quality	stc_dq1	5.41	1.03	0.82	0.91	0.93	0.69
	stc_dq2	5.43	1.25	0.85			
	stc_dq3	4.90	1.41	0.82			
	stc_dq4	5.41	1.24	0.88			
	stc_dq5	4.96	1.44	0.85			
	stc_dq6	5.21	1.35	0.74			
System performance	stc_sp1	5.14	1.43	0.79	0.86	0.90	0.64
	stc_sp2	5.14	1.50	0.72			
	stc_sp3	5.45	1.23	0.87			
	stc_sp4	5.33	1.35	0.73			
	stc_sp5	5.23	1.30	0.88			
User manuals	stc_um1	5.00	1.51	0.88	0.84	0.91	0.76
	stc_um2	5.00	1.59	0.84			
	stc_um3	4.54	1.61	0.90			
Business processes fit	opc_bpf1	5.61	1.27	0.91	0.91	0.94	0.84
	opc_bpf2	5.56	1.28	0.89			
	opc_bpf3	5.39	1.29	0.89			
Social influence	opc_si1	5.94	1.16	0.76	0.84	0.90	0.68
	opc_si2	6.01	1.03	0.79			
	opc_si3	5.98	1.15	0.88			
	opc_si4	6.03	1.09	0.87			
PU	pu1	5.51	1.32	0.91	0.96	0.97	0.89
	pu2	5.44	1.32	0.96			
	pu3	5.49	1.33	0.97			
	pu4	5.40	1.40	0.93			
PEOU	peou1	5.25	1.34	0.94	0.85	0.93	0.87
	peou2	4.90	1.41	0.93			
WC	wc1	4.73	1.46	0.92	0.91	0.94	0.84
	wc2	4.65	1.64	0.89			
	wc3	4.95	1.50	0.95			
AT	at1	5.93	1.18	0.94	0.90	0.95	0.90
	at2	5.68	1.32	0.96			

a Items have been inverted before processing of statistical data in SmartPLS.

Table 11. Intercorrelations of the latent variables

	1	2	3	4	5	6	7	8	9	10	11
1. Personal innovativeness toward IT	0.87										
2. Computer anxiety	0.43	0.85									
3. ERP data quality	0.10	0.16	0.84								
4. ERP system performance	0.05	0.19	0.65	0.82							
5. User manuals (help)	0.15	0.17	0.52	0.49	0.89						
6. Business processes fit	0.14	0.20	0.72	0.57	0.46	0.84					
7. Social influence	0.06	0.17	0.26	0.25	0.31	0.49	0.84				
8. PU	0.16	0.17	0.58	0.57	0.35	0.67	0.41	0.94			
9. PEOU	0.15	0.21	0.55	0.57	0.50	0.51	0.18	0.62	0.93		
10. WC	0.07	0.07	0.64	0.56	0.40	0.73	0.36	0.73	0.58	0.92	
11. AT	0.06	0.15	0.53	0.53	0.36	0.56	0.30	0.73	0.58	0.67	0.95

The variance explained (*R2*) in key endogenous constructs is 0.63 for PU, 0.42 for PEOU, 0.53 for WC, and 0.59 for AT. These findings demonstrate that our model explains a large part of the variance in the endogenous variables, with an average *R2* of 0.54. Communality and redundancy coefficients are also presented in Table 14 and can be used in the same way as the *R2* as they reflect the rela-

Figure 3. Results of structural model analysis for SAP a

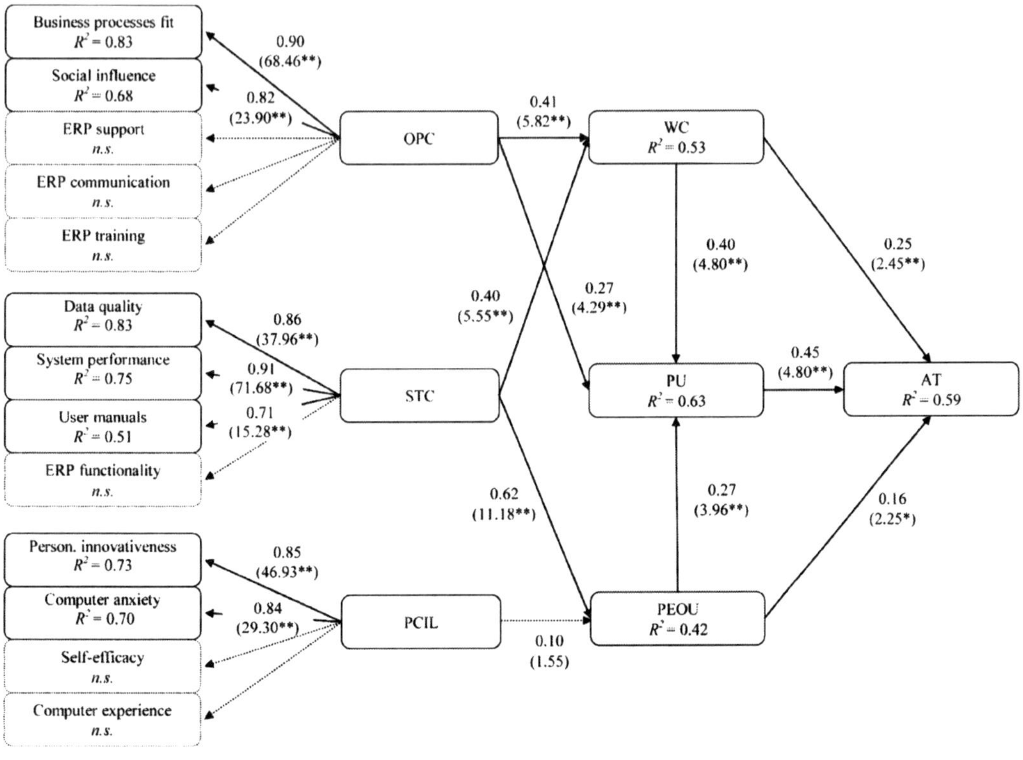

Table 12. Parameter estimation of the PLS model using the bootstrap method and effect size for SAP

Dependent Variable	Independent Variable	Standardized Path Coefficient	*t*-Values	*f2*
WC	OPC	0.41	5.82**	0.21
	STC	0.40	5.55**	0.19
PU	OPC	0.27	4.29**	0.11
	WC	0.40	4.80**	0.19
	PEOU	0.27	3.96*	0.11
PEOU	PCIL	0.10	1.55	0.02
	SCT	0.62	11.18**	0.64
AT	WC	0.25	2.45*	0.07
	PU	0.45	4.80**	0.22
	PEOU	0.27	3.96	0.05

Notes: $**p<0.01$, $*p<0.05$.

tive amount of explained variance for latent and manifest variables. GoF is 0.58, which can be considered satisfactory (according to the results in Table 14); the measurement model ($H2 = 0.66$) shows a little better quality than the structural one ($Q2 = 0.46$).

Table 13. Path coefficients' external variables in second-order model for SAP

First Order External Factors	PCIL $\alpha = 0.79$ $CR = 0.85$ $AVE = 0.49$	STC $\alpha = 0.92$ $CR = 0.93$ $AVE = 0.50$	OPC $\alpha = 0.86$ $CR = 0.89$ $AVE = 0.54$
Personal innovativeness toward IT	0.85 (t = 43.20)		
Computer anxiety	0.74 (t = 14.65)		
Business process fit		0.83 (t = 37.3)	
Social influence		0.72 (t = 15.05)	
ERP data quality			0.90 (t = 67.96)
ERP system performance			0.85 (t = 38.18)
ERP user manuals (help)			0.69 (t = 16.78)

RESULTS AND ANALYSIS

From Figures 2 and 3, it can first be noted that the PEOU has a positive direct influence on the PU for both solutions, which supports the findings of prior research concerning PEOU's influence on PU (Amoako-Gyampah & Salam, 2004; Bueno & Salmeron, 2008; Calisir et al., 2009; Hsieh & Wang, 2007; Lee et al., 2010; Sun et al., 2009; Youngberg et al., 2009). The findings that PEOU does not have a significant influence on AT for NAV solutions and a weak significant influence on AT for SAP solutions concur with results from other researchers, where some authors (i.e., Bueno & Salmeron, 2008; Nah et al., 2004) found an influence of PEOU on AT whereas others (i.e. Amoako-Gyampah & Salam 2004; Calisir et al., 2009; Shivers-Blackwell & Charles, 2006) did not. PU serves as a predictor of AT, although PEOU appears to be more important during the first phases, becoming less important over time (Davis et al., 1989; Nah et al., 2004; Pijpers & Montford, 2006; Simon & Paper, 2007). In particular, the current study shows that PU serves as a mediating role that enhances the positive effect of PEOU on AT of the ERP users in the organization. Third, the results indicate the influence of PU on AT (Amoako-Gyampah & Salam, 2004; Bueno & Salmeron, 2008; Calisir et al., 2009; Nah et al., 2004; Shivers-Blackwell & Charles, 2006).

Perceptual construct WC was presented as the degree to which an ERP user can do most of his or her tasks in an ERP system. In our research, WC influences PU, which supports prior findings (Scott & Walczak, 2009; Sun et al., 2009). Moreover, WC directly and indirectly (through PU) influences AT; if ERP users can do most of their tasks in ERP systems, they have a better attitude toward using ERP solutions.

The aim of our research was to expose and research which factors influence the NAV/SAP usage in the operation phase. Based on the analytical results, this study has found that it is possible to observe more external factors through the second-order factors. Research shows that PCIL

Table 14. Explained variance (R2), communality, redundancy and blindfolding results of cv-communality (H2) and cv-redundancy (Q2) for SAP

	R2	Communality	Redundancy	cv-Communality *(H2)*	cv-Redundancy *(Q2)*
OPC		0.52		0.52	0.52
STC		0.51		0.45	0.45
PCIL		0.53		0.34	0.34
PU	0.63	0.89	0.25	0.86	0.55
PEOU	0.42	0.87	0.35	0.84	0.36
WC	0.53	0.84	0.31	0.80	0.45
AT	0.59	0.90	0.41	0.82	0.52
Average	0.54	0.62a	0.33	0.66	0.46

a Computed as a weighted average of the different communalities, with the weights being the number of manifest variables per each construct (Tenenhaus et al., 2005).

does not have a significant effect on PEOU. STC has a strong positive effect on PEOU and on WC. Meanwhile, OPC has a strong positive effect on both PU and WC. Furthermore, we verified all other relationships among PCIL, STC, and OPC on PEOU, PU, and WC for both solutions; none of the relationships were significant.

In addition, analytical results of the model reveal that, among the four factors within PCIL (i.e., experience with a computer, computer self-efficiency, personal innovativeness toward IT, and computer anxiety), only personal innovativeness toward IT and computer anxiety for the SAP solution and personal innovativeness toward IT and computer self-efficiency for the NAV solution, appeared to be important. These factors appear to be important during implementation (Calisir et al., 2009; Davis et al., 1998; Shih & Huang, 2009; Shivers-Blackwell & Charles, 2006; Thompson, Compeau, & Higgins, 2006; Venkatesh et al., 2003; Venkatesh & Bala, 2008), but according to our research in the routine stage, they become less important. This is consistent with the arguments of Venkatesh and Davis (2000) and Thomson et al. (2006), who suggested that—through experience—ease-of-use perceptions become more rooted in specific features of the software and less influenced by general personal traits.

This study also demonstrated that STC factors (data quality, system performance, and user manuals) are significant in determining PEOU and WC, while the ERP functionality has not been found to be a statistically significant factor of STC. Quality of data has been cited as an important factor in successful ERP implementation (Gattiker & CFPIM, 2002; Ngai, Law, & Wat, 2007). Our research shows that, for NAV users, data quality is the most important external factor of STC; for SAP users, system performance is more important. Existing literature provides evidence in support of our findings—namely, that for ERP users it is important to acquire authentic and accurate data at the moment they need the information (Gattiker & Goodhue, 2005; Kositanuri, Nqwenyama, & Osei-Bryson, 2006; Venkatesh, 1998; Venkatesh & Davis, 2000). System performance is concerned with the performance characteristics of the ERP system, including reliability, flexibility, and response time, and is an important CSF in the operation phase (Bobek & Sternad, 2010). It was found to be an important factor of STC in the routine stage. Our study also demonstrated that complete and up-to-date user manuals (help) are an important STC factor in the routine stage.

The third group of researched external factors focused on factors included in OPC. Our results indicate that business process fit and social influence through OPC factor significantly influence PU and WC. The impact of OPC on PU supports the findings of prior studies (Venkatesh & Bala, 2008; Venkatesh & Davis, 2000). Furthermore, statistical analysis revealed that the business process fit is the most contributing factor in the OPC group. Bancroft, Seip, and Sprengel (2001) as well as Somers and Nelson (2004) pointed out that business process reengineering plays a particularly crucial role in the early stages of implementation; it is moderately important in the acceptance stage, and tends to be less important once the technology becomes part of the routine stage. Our study confirms previous studies in which the authors argued that business process fit and reengineering are a continuous process included in the post-implementation phase (Bradford, 2008; Welti, 1999). The social influence factor can be described with the CSF factors of top management support and sponsorship, which were critical in all phases of the ERP lifecycle. Nearly all of the research included top management support and involvement of CSF for successful ERP implementation, and their inclusion is needed throughout the implementation project (Bobek & Sternad, 2010; Gattiker & CFPIM, 2002; Somers & Nelson, 2004; Umble, Haft, & Umble, 2002). Sponsorship plays a critical role in the acceptance of technology; sponsors are usually at the senior management level, so they have the authority to make substantial organizational changes (Akkermans & Helden, 2002; Ngai et al., 2007). Despite the fact that ERP support (Bobek & Sternad, 2010; Lee et al., 2010), communication (Al-Mashari, Al-Mudimigh, & Zairi, 2003; Bobek & Sternad, 2010; Somers & Nelson, 2004), and training and education (Akkermans & Helden, 2002; Al-Mashari et al., 2003; Bancroft et al., 2001; Bobek & Sternad, 2010; Boudreau, 2002; Bradford & Florin, 2003; Motiwalla & Thompson, 2009; Umble et al., 2002) are often mentioned in CSF, they were not found to be statistically significant in our study.

The aim of each organization that has implemented ERP system should be for ERP users to use their ERP solution extensively. Through the researched model, we propose that organizations put more effort into the identified external factors that impact the second-order factors on ERP acceptance and usage. For more detail interventions in each organization, further research (including interviews with ERP users) should be conducted.

CONCLUSION

The most important contributions of the ERP systems are that they significantly reduce the time required to complete business processes and help organizations share information (Lee et al., 2010), and that organizations usually offer a better work environment for their employees as they are given a more efficient system with which to work. In the routine stage, ERP systems could be implemented successfully from a technical perspective, but success may depend on ERP users being willing to use the delivered system (Boudreau, 2002; Kwahk & Lee, 2008).

Studies on TAM regarding ERP systems tend to focus on the selection and implementation phase whereas studies focused on the post-implementation phase are scarce and have only been published very recently (i.e., since 2009: Lee et al., 2010; Shin & Huang, 2009; Sun et al., 2009). The majority of studies consider a limited number of factors that influence the acceptance and use of ERP systems. The aim of our paper was to examine acceptance factors for ERP solutions and research their importance for different solutions (NAV and SAP solutions). We included WC in TAM and extended the number of observed factors that influence user acceptance and use in the routine (mature) stage. Due to the need to observe a large number of external factors, the concept of second-order factors was used, which—when taken together with the use of the PLS approach to test our model—allowed us to use a small sample size. TAM was used because it is the most widely used and empirically tested model for explaining actual use of IS (Amoako-Gyampah & Salam, 2004; Davis, 1989; Davis et al., 1989; Lee et al., 2010), despite our research being focused on external factors and their influence on the actual use of ERP system based on the published research about this issue in the paper.

This research improved the understanding of how the influence of several external factors can increase the degree of attitude of ERP users toward the ERP system in the routine stage by incorporating three groups of external factors: personal characteristics and information literacy (PCIL), system and technological characteristics (STC), and organizational-process characteristics (OPC). PCIL includes personal innovativeness toward IT, computer anxiety, computer self-efficacy, and computer experience. Data quality, system performance, user manuals, and ERP functionality are included in STC. Business processes fit, social influence, ERP support, ERP communication, and ERP training are included in OPC. PCIL, STC, and OPC have been mentioned in several studies published within the context of external factors research in the field of IS acceptance (some of these authors eventually related their research to TAM, but not all). The research shows that PCIL is not important concerning the use of ERP systems in routine (mature) stage, despite the fact that it was mentioned in some other studies not related to ERP systems (Venkatesh et al., 2003; Venkatesh & Bala, 2008). STC and OPC are somewhat equally important, but they impact different variables of TAM related to ERP use for both researched solutions. STC external factors—namely, data quality, system performance, and user manuals—are significant in determining PEOU and WC, whereas business process fit and social influence through OPC have significant influence on the PU and WC.

This research has the potential for a practical application in the degree of ERP system usage. By confirming external factors, organizations should take into consideration exposed and researched factors if they want to improve the degree of ERP system usage.

REFERENCES

Agarwal, R., & Prasad, J. (1999). Are individual differences germane to the acceptance of new information technologies. *Decision Sciences*, *30*(2), 361–391. doi:10.1111/j.1540-5915.1999.tb01614.x.

Ajzen, I. (1991). The theory of planned behavior. *Organizational Behavior and Human Decision Processes*, *50*, 179–211. doi:10.1016/0749-5978(91)90020-T.

Akkermans, H., & Helder, K. (2002). Vicious and virtuous cycles in ERP implementation: A case study of interrelations between CSF. *European Journal of Information Systems*, *2*, 35–46. doi:10.1057/palgrave.ejis.3000418.

Al-Mashari, M., Al-Mudimigh, A., & Zairi, M. (2003). Enterprise resource planning: Taxonomy of critical factors. *European Journal of Operational Research*, *146*(2), 352–364. doi:10.1016/S0377-2217(02)00554-4.

Amoako-Gyampah, K., & Salam, A. F. (2004). An extension of the technology acceptance model in an ERP implementation environment. *Information & Management*, *41*, 731–745. doi:10.1016/j.im.2003.08.010.

Bancroft, N., Seip, H., & Sprengel, A. (2001). *Implementing SAP R/3* (2nd ed.). Greenwich, CT: Manning Publications Co..

Bobek, S., & Sternad, S. (2010). Management of ERP solutions. In Vaish, A. (Ed.), *Recent advances in management and information security* (pp. 31–47). New Delhi: Shree Publishers & Distributors.

Boudreau, M. C. (2002). Learning to use ERP technology: A causal model. In *Proceedings of the 36th Hawaii International Conference on System Sciences*. Retrieved July 7, 2008, from http://csdl2.computer.org/comp/proceedings/hicss/2003/1874/08/187480235b.pdf

Bradford, M. (2008). *Modern ERP—Select, implement & use today's advanced business systems*. Raleigh, NC: North Carolina State University, College of Management.

Bradford, M., & Florin, J. (2003). Examining the role of innovation diffusion factors on the implementation success of enterprise resource planning systems. *International Journal of Accounting Information Systems*, *4*(3), 205–225. doi:10.1016/S1467-0895(03)00026-5.

Bradley, J., & Lee, C. C. (2007). ERP training and user satisfaction: A case study. *International Journal of Enterprise Information Systems*, *3*(4), 33–55. doi:10.4018/jeis.2007100103.

Bueno, S., & Salmeron, J. L. (2008). TAM-based success modelling in ERP. *Interacting with Computers*, *20*(6), 515–523. doi:10.1016/j.intcom.2008.08.003.

Calisir, F., Gumussoy, C. A., & Bayram, A. (2009). Predicting the behavioural intention to use enterprise resource planning systems—An exploratory extension of the technology acceptance model. *Management Research News*, *32*(7), 597–613. doi:10.1108/01409170910965215.

Chin, W. W. (1998). Issues and opinions on structural equation modelling. *Management Information Systems Quarterly*, *22*, 7–16.

Davis, F. D. (1989). Perceived usefulness, perceived ease of use, and user acceptance of information technology. *Management Information Systems Quarterly*, *13*(3), 319–340. doi:10.2307/249008.

Davis, F. D., Bagozzi, R. P., & Warshaw, P. R. (1989). User acceptance of computer technology: A comparison of two theoretical models. *Management Science*, *35*(8), 982–1003. doi:10.1287/mnsc.35.8.982.

Fishbein, M., & Ajzen, I. (1975). *Belief, attitude, intention, and behavior: An introduction to theory and research*. Reading, MA: Addison-Wesley Reading.

Fornell, C., & Larcker, D. F. (1981). Evaluating structural equation models with unobservable variables and measurement errors. *JMR, Journal of Marketing Research*, *18*, 39–50. doi:10.2307/3151312.

Gattiker, T. F., & CFPIM. (2002). Anatomy of an ERP implementation gone awry. *Production and Inventory Management Journal*, *43*, 96–105.

Gattiker, T. F., & Goodhue, D. L. (2005). What happens after ERP implementation: Understanding the impact of interdependence and differentiation on plant-level outcomes. *Management Information Systems Quarterly*, *29*(3), 559–585.

Guenzi, P., Georges, L., & Pardo, C. (2009). The impact of strategic account managers' behaviors on relational outcomes: An empirical study. *Industrial Marketing Management*, *38*, 300–311. doi:10.1016/j.indmarman.2007.09.011.

Hair, J. F., Ringle, C. M., & Sarstedt, M. (2011). PLS-SEM: Indeed a silver bullet. *Journal of Marketing Theory and Practice*, *19*(2), 139–151. doi:10.2753/MTP1069-6679190202.

Henseler, J., Ringle, C. M., & Sinkovics, R. (2009). The use of partial least squares path modelling in international marketing. *Advances in International Marketing*, *20*, 277–319. doi:10.1108/S1474-7979(2009)0000020014.

Hinton, P. R., Brownlow, C., McMurray, I., & Cozens, B. (2004). *SPSS explained*. London: Routledge Taylor & Francis Group.

Hsieh, J. J. P. A., & Wang, W. (2007). Explaining employees' extended use of complex information systems. *European Journal of Information Systems*, *16*(3), 216–227. doi:10.1057/palgrave.ejis.3000663.

Insiti, M. (2007). ERP end-users business productivity: A field study of SAP & Microsoft. *Keystone Strategy Research 2007*. Retrieved June 12, 2010, from http://download.microsoft.com

Kelley, H. (2001). *Attributional analysis of computer self-efficacy*. (Unpublished doctoral dissertation). Richard Ivey School of Business, London, UK.

Khan, A. (2002). *Implementing SAP with an ASAP methodology focus*. San Jose, CA: Writers Club Press.

Kositanuri, B., Nqwenyama, O., & Osei-Bryson, K. M. (2006). An exploration of factors that impact individual performance in an ERP environment: An analysis using multiple analytical techniques. *European Journal of Information Systems*, *15*, 556–568. doi:10.1057/palgrave.ejis.3000654.

Kwahk, K. Y., & Lee, J. N. (2008). The role of readiness for change in ERP implementation: Theoretical bases and empirical validation. *Information & Management*, *45*(7), 474–481. doi:10.1016/j.im.2008.07.002.

Langenwalter, G. (2000). *Enterprise resources planning and beyond: Integrating your entire organization*. Boca Raton, FL: St. Lucie Press.

Lee, D. H., Lee, S. M., Olson, D. L., & Chung, S. H. (2010). The effect of organizational support on ERP implementation. *Industrial Management & Data Systems*, *110*(1-2), 269–283. doi:10.1108/02635571011020340.

Liu, L., & Ma, Q. (2006). Perceived system performance: A test of an extended technology acceptance model. *Journal of Organizational and End User Computing*, *18*(3), 1–24.

Lu, J., Chun-Sheng, Y., Liu, C., & Yao, J. E. (2003). Technology acceptance model for wireless Internet. *Internet Research: Electronic Networking Applications and Policy*, *13*(3), 206–222. doi:10.1108/10662240310478222.

Miller, S. S. (1998). *ASAP—Implementation at the speed of business*. New York: McGraw-Hill.

Motiwalla, L. F., & Thompson, J. (2009). *Enterprise systems for management*. Upper Saddle River, NJ: Pearson Education, Inc..

Musaji, Y. F. (2003). *Integrated auditing of ERP systems*. New York: John Wiley & Sons, Inc..

Nah, F. F., Tan, X., & Teh, S. H. (2004). An empirical investigation on end-users' acceptance of enterprise systems. *Information Resources Management Journal*, *17*(3), 32–53. doi:10.4018/irmj.2004070103.

Ngai, E. W. T., Law, C. C. H., & Wat, F. K. T. (2007). Examining the critical success factors in the adoption of enterprise resource planning. *Computers in Industry*, *59*, 548–564. doi:10.1016/j.compind.2007.12.001.

Pijpers, G. G. M., & Montfort, K. (2006). An investigation of factors that influence senior executives to accept innovations in information technology. *International Journal of Management*, *23*(1), 11–23.

Ringle, C. M., & Will, A. (2005). *SmartPLS 2.0 (M3)*. Retrieved June 1, 2009, from http://www.smartpls.de

Ross, J. W., Vitale, M. R., & Willcocks, L. P. (2003). The continuing ERP revolution: Sustainable lessons, new modes of delivery. In Shanks, G., Seddon, P. B., & Willcocks, L. P. (Eds.), *Second-wave enterprise resource planning systems—Implementing for effectiveness* (pp. 102–132). Cambridge, UK: Cambridge University Press. doi:10.1017/CBO9780511815072.005.

Schwarz, A. (2003). *Defining information technology acceptance: A human-centred, management-oriented perspective.* (Unpublished doctoral dissertation). University of Houston, Houston, TX.

Scott, J. E., & Walczak, S. (2009). Cognitive engagement with a multimedia ERP training tool: Assessing computer self-efficacy and technology acceptance. *Information & Management*, *46*(4), 221–232. doi:10.1016/j.im.2008.10.003.

Seddon, P., Shanks, G., & Willcocks, L. P. (2003). Introduction: ERP—The quiet revolution? In Shanks, G., Seddon, P. B., & Willcocks, L. P. (Eds.), *Second-wave enterprise resource planning systems—Implementing for effectiveness* (pp. 1–19). Cambridge, UK: Cambridge University Press. doi:10.1017/CBO97805118815072.001.

Shankar, C., & Bellefroid, V. (2011). *Microsoft dynamics sure step 2010: The smart guide to the successful delivery of Microsoft dynamics business solutions*. Birmingham, UK: Packt Publishing.

Shih, Y. Y., & Huang, S. S. (2009). The actual usage of ERP systems: An extended technology acceptance perspective. *Journal of Research and Practice in Information Technology*, *41*(3), 263–276.

Shivers-Blackwell, S. L., & Charles, A. C. (2006). Ready, set, go: Examining student readiness to use ERP technology. *Journal of Management Development*, *25*(8), 795–805. doi:10.1108/02621710610684268.

Simon, S. J., & Paper, D. (2007). User acceptance of voice recognition technology: An empirical extension of the technology acceptance model. *Journal of Organizational and End User Computing*, *19*(1), 24–50. doi:10.4018/joeuc.2007010102.

Somers, M. T., Nelson, K., & Karimi, J. (2003). Confirmatory factor analysis of the end-user computing satisfaction instrument: Replication within an ERP domain. *Decision Sciences*, *34*(3), 595–621. doi:10.1111/j.1540-5414.2003.02428.x.

Somers, T. M., & Neslon, K. G. (2004). A taxonomy of players and activities across the ERP project life cycle. *Information & Management*, *41*(3), 257–278. doi:10.1016/S0378-7206(03)00023-5.

Straub, D. (1989). Validating instruments in MIS research. *Management Information Systems Quarterly*, *13*(2), 147–169. doi:10.2307/248922.

Sun, Y., Bhattacherjee, A., & Ma, Q. (2009). Extending technology usage to work settings: The role of perceived work compatibility in ERP implementation. *Information & Management*, *46*, 351–356. doi:10.1016/j.im.2009.06.003.

Tenenhaus, M., Vinzi, V. E., Chatelin, Y. M., & Lauro, C. (2005). PLS path modelling. *Computational Statistics & Data Analysis*, *48*, 159–205. doi:10.1016/j.csda.2004.03.005.

Thompson, R., Compeau, D., & Higgins, C. (2006). Intentions to use information technologies: An integrative model. *Journal of Organizational and End User Computing*, *18*(3), 25–46. doi:10.4018/joeuc.2006070102.

Umble, E. J., Haft, R. R., & Umble, M. M. (2002). Enterprise resource planning: Implementation procedures and CSF. *European Journal of Operational Research*, *146*(2), 241–257. doi:10.1016/S0377-2217(02)00547-7.

Uzoka, F. M. E., Abiola, R. O., & Nyangeresi, R. (2008). Influence of product and organizational constructs on ERP acquisition using an extended technology acceptance model. *International Journal of Enterprise Information Systems*, *4*(2), 67–83. doi:10.4018/jeis.2008040105.

Venkatesh, V. (1998). *User acceptance of information technology: A unified view.* (Unpublished doctoral dissertation). University of Minnesota, Minneapolis, MN.

Venkatesh, V., & Bala, H. (2008). Technology acceptance model 3 and a research agenda on interventions. *Decision Sciences*, *39*(2), 273–315. doi:10.1111/j.1540-5915.2008.00192.x.

Venkatesh, V., & Davis, F. D. (2000). A theoretical extension of the technology acceptance model: Four longitudinal field studies. *Management Science*, *46*(2), 186–205. doi:10.1287/mnsc.46.2.186.11926.

Venkatesh, V., Morris, M. G., Davis, G. B., & Davis, F. D. (2003). User acceptance of information technology: Toward a unified view. *Management Information Systems Quarterly*, *27*(3), 425–479.

Welti, N. (1999). *Successful SAP R/3 implementation—Practical management of ERP project*. Boston: Addison-Wesley Longman Publishing Co..

Wold, H. (1982). Soft modelling: The basic design and some extensions. *Systems Under Indirect Observations,* 1–52.

Yi, Y. M., Fiedler, K. D., & Park, J. S. (2006). Understanding the role of individual innovativeness in the acceptance of IT-based innovativeness: Comparative analyses of models and measures. *Decision Sciences*, *37*(3), 393–426. doi:10.1111/j.1540-5414.2006.00132.x.

Youngberg, E., Olsen, D., & Hauser, K. (2009). Determinants of professionally autonomous end user acceptance in an enterprise resource planning system environment. *International Journal of Information Management*, *29*, 138–144. doi:10.1016/j.ijinfomgt.2008.06.001.

Yu, C. S. (2005). Causes influencing the effectiveness of the post-implementation ERP system. *Industrial Management & Data Systems*, *105*(1/2), 115–132. doi:10.1108/02635570510575225.

KEY TERMS AND DEFINITIONS

Enterprise Resource Planning (ERP): Systems are modular solutions based on principles of best practices that integrate activities across functional departments, from product planning to parts purchasing, inventory control, product distribution, and order tracking. They usually include application modules for the finance, accounting, and human resource aspects of a business.

Organizational-Process Characteristics (OPC): Capture various social processes, mechanisms, and support organizations that guide individuals to facilitate the use of an ERP system.

Partial Least Squares (PLS): Approach is one of the structural equation modeling (SEM) applications that can be used for situations with less theory development and a smaller sample size; it is better suited for analyzing complex relationships and models.

Perceived Ease of Use (PEOU): Refers to the degree to which a person believes that using a particular system would be free of effort.

Perceived Usefulness (PU): Refers to the degree to which a person believes that using a particular system would enhance his or her job performance.

Personal Characteristics and Information Literacy (PCIL): Includes personality characteristics that can influence individuals' perceptions of IS acceptance and usage.

System and Technological Characteristics (STC): Are silent features of ERP systems that can help individuals develop favorable/unfavorable perceptions regarding IT/IS.

Technological Acceptance Model (TAM): Is the most widely used model for explaining the behavioral intention and actual usage of IT/IS proposed by Davis (1989).

Work Compatibility (WC): Is the degree to which an ERP user can do most tasks in the ERP system.

APPENDIX: QUESTIONNAIRE ITEMS

(Likert scale: 1 = strongly disagree, 2 = disagree, 3 = somewhat disagree, 4 = neutral, 5 = somewhat agree, 6 = agree, 7 = strongly agree)

Table 15. Measurement scales

Variable	Source	Scale	Measurement items
Personal innovativeness	Yi et al., 2006; Thompson, 2006.	pcil_pi1	If I hear about new IT, I would look for ways to experiment with it.
		pcil_pi2	Among my peers I am usually the first to try out new IT.
		pcil_pi3	I like to experiment with new IT.
Computer anxiety	Venkatesh, 1989; Venkatesh et al., 2003.	pcil_ca1a	Working with a computer makes me nervous.
		pcil_ca2a	I get a sinking feeling when I think of trying to use a computer.
		pcil_ca3	I feel comfortable working with a computer.
Computer self-efficacy	Venkatesh et al., 2003; Thompson, 2006.	Pcil_cse1	I could complete the job using any program if I had only the software manuals and/or the built-in help for assistance.
		Pcil_cse1	I could complete the job using any program if I could call someone for help if I got stuck.
ERP data quality (content)	Gattiker & Goodhue, 2005; Venkatesh, 1998; Kositanuri et al., 2006.	Stc_dq1	The ERP system provides the precise information I need.
		Stc_dq2	The information contents provided by the ERP system meet my needs.
		Stc_dq3	The ERP system provides reports that seem to be exactly what I need.
		Stc_dq4	The ERP system provides sufficient information for my needs.
		Stc_dq5	The ERP system provides the complete features I need.
		Stc_dq6	I am satisfied with the speed of interacting with the system.
ERP system performance	Venktesh et al., 2003; Kositanuri et al., 2006; Liu & Ma, 2006.	stc_sp1	It is fast to search for data in the ERP system.
		stc_sp2	The ERP system loads quickly.
		stc_sp3	I was able to retrieve data quickly.
		stc_sp4	It is fast to create a new record in this system.
		stc_sp5	It is fast to use this ERP system.
User manuals (help)	Kelley, 2001.	stc_um1	The content and index of the user manuals are useful.
		stc_um2	The user manuals are current (up to date).
		stc_um3	The user manuals are complete.
ERP functionality	Kositanuri et al., 2006.	stc_fu1	It is easy to detect possible errors in the ERP system.
		stc_fu2	It is easy to correct errors that happen in the ERP system.
		stc_fu3	It is easy to change the output format.
ERP business processes fit	Amoako-Gyampah & Salam, 2004; Nah et al., 2004.	opc_bpf1	The ERP solution fits well with my business needs.
		opc_bpf2	The ERP solution fits well with the business needs of my department.
		opc_bpf3	All in all, the ERP system is satisfactory in meeting my needs.

continued on following page

Table 15. Continued

Variable	Source	Scale	Measurement items
Social influence	Venkatesh et al., 2003; Venkatesh, 1998.	opc_si1	My supervisor is very supportive of the use of the ERP system for my job.
		opc_si2	In general, the organization has supported the use of the ERP system.
		opc_si3	People who influence my behavior think that I should use the ERP system.
		opc_si4	People who are important to me think that I should use the ERP system.
ERP support	Kelley, 2001.	opc_su1	I do not know who to phone for support for this application.
		opc_su2	The support people talk in terms that I do not understand.
		opc_su3	I ask other users for help with this application rather than the support staff.
ERP communication	Kelley, 2001.	opc_cu1	The ERP team does not inform me about the current situation of the ERP solution.
		opc_cu2	The ERP team does not explain how application modifications will impact my job.
ERP training	Amoako-Gyampah & Salam, 2004; Kositanuri et al., 2006; Kelley, 2001.	opc_tr1	I have received additional formal training for ERP since the conclusion of the initial training.
		opc_tr1	I have received informal training (e.g., a half hour of support from a peer or training officer) for ERP.
PU	Davis, 1989; Venkatesh & Davis, 1996.	us1	Using the ERP solution in my job enables me to accomplish tasks more quickly.
		us2	Using the ERP solution improves my job performance.
		us3	Using the ERP solution enhances my effectiveness on the job.
		us4	Using the ERP solution makes it easier to do my job.
PEOU	Davis, 1989; Venkatesh & Davis, 1996.	eou1	My interaction with the ERP solution is clear and understandable.
		eou2	I find the ERP solution easy to use.
WC	Nah et al., 2004; Yi et al., 2006.	wc1	Using the ERP system is compatible with all aspects of my work.
		wc2	Using the ERP system fits well with the way I like to work.
		wc3	Using the ERP system fits with my work style.
AT	Venkatesh et al., 2003; Nah et al., 2004; Amoako-Gyampah & Salam, 2004.	1.1.1 at1	1.1.2 Using the ERP system is a good idea.
		at2	I like the idea of using the ERP system to perform my job.

Chapter 22
Attributes of Innovation Leaders

Fawzy Soliman
University of Technology Sydney, Australia

ABSTRACT

Many innovative companies pass through a number of transformation stages. The transformation is considered a chain of activities that begins with information that leads to knowledge, then into learning before it can finally be used for innovation. The chapter shows that transformational leadership is a key factor for moving the organisation from being information-based into knowledge-based and then into a learning organisation and an innovative company. The six important characteristics of the transformational leaders for the transformation are shown to be courage to switch off or terminate projects, rewarding performing staff, ability to appropriately time release of products to the market, ability to release products to the market within budget, and ability to inspire and be a role model for other staff. The chapter also shows that there are fourteen transformational leadership attributes that may be considered less critical than the above-mentioned six characteristics. Those non-critical characteristics include: degree of passion for the job, attracting talent, ability to build teams, coaching subordinates, communicating at all levels, driving projects successfully, enabling project-supporting environments, advising others managers, advocating for improvement, encouraging self-goal setting, ability of self rehearsal, ability of self reinforcement, ability of self-observation, and ability of self-expectation.

INTRODUCTION

Undoubtedly, the rise of globalisation in 1980s has led to many changes in business environments, and in particular, to the concept of competitive advantages. The significance of competitive advantages to business success has been highlighted by the use of the well recognised Porter five forces model of 1980 (Porter, 1980). The Porter model has been shown by number of authors in recent times, to be inadequate for business competitiveness in the 21st century (Soliman, 2011a, 2011b). For example the Porter model does not propose innovation and creativity as pre-requisites for

DOI: 10.4018/978-1-4666-4373-4.ch022

winning modern competition. The Porter model also does not recognise the concept of learning organisation as a source of competitive advantage.

It should be noted that the 1990s Senge's model (Senge, 1990) specified five disciplines of learning organisation as a central theme of any learning organisation model. The Senge's model was in fact a response to the many concerns aired by a number of authors such as Stata (1989) who suggested that "the rate at which individuals and organisations learn may become the only sustainable competitive advantage".

Further response to the rapid changes to business environments was made by Nonaka (1991) who introduced models of knowledge management which added further dimensions to the competitive advantage debate and prompted further studies on organisational competitive advantages. In this regards, a number of authors have pointed out to the significance of the role of knowledge management and learning techniques as important key competitive advantage tools that have not been fully researched (Nonaka and Takeuchi, 1995; Zack, 1999; Nonaka et al, 2000; Soliman and Spooner, 2000; Soliman and Youssef, 2003; Soliman, 2009, 2010, 2011a, 2011b, 2011c).

Further work by López et. al. (2006) and Senge (1990) suggest that some organisational failures may be due to lack of appropriate management of organisational learning which in turn leads to unsatisfactory management of organisational knowledge. These concerns have led to the formulation of the view that traditional competitive advantages may be overridden by a new set of key competitive advantages such knowledge management, learning and creativity (Christensen, 2007 and Maqsood, et. al., 2007). Furthermore, Maqsood, et. al. (2007) pointed out that satisfactory management of knowledge and learning activities not only a prerequisite for innovations but also the link between knowledge, learning and innovation and that knowledge management should be considered a key organisational activities. This view was supported by Garvin et. al. (2008) who noted that one of the main aspects of dynamic and continuously evolving organisations is that the organisation must be truly a learning organisation. (Rebelo and Gomes, 2008; Kalkan 2008, Mehrez 2010, Soliman 2010, 2011a, 2011b and 2011c).

This means that transforming organisations from the traditional information based form, into knowledge-oriented organisations requires strategies designed to utilize knowledge that foster learning at later stages. Such strategies need to engage managerial staff in order to facilitate the implementation of the appropriate knowledge management programs. In other words such significant transformation into knowledge based organisation should be carefully executed so that the transformation does not hinder the organisation's efforts in delivering goods or services in accordance with the organisations strategic plans.

TRANSFORMATION FROM INFORMATION-BASED ORGANISATION TO KNOWLEDGE-BASED ORGANISATION

The significance of knowledge management and its impact on modern enterprises have been enhanced by Nonaka's (1991) work on knowledge management. The Nonaka's work sparked a number of research activities about the modern corporation's power and its intellectual or intangible capabilities. A significant finding of some of these research activities is highlighted by the introduction of the definition of "knowledge-based intangibles" by Quinn (1992) who proposed that the value of most products and services may be dependent on such as technical know-how, product design, marketing presentation, understanding customers, personal creativity and innovation. Quinn findings have led many enterprises to consider collective knowledge as a key competitive tool from which innovation can emerge. Further work by Quinn et al (1996) resulted in identifying knowledge management as key value adding activities. Their statement "Three quarters of an organisation's added value is attributed to the possession of specific knowledge" points to the significant role of knowledge in the management of modern enterprises.

Furthermore, Clark and Soliman (1997) identified that the commercial emergence of knowledge-based information technology represents a tremendous opportunity to enhance an organisation's effectiveness. However, the findings of Clark and Soliman (1997) elaborate that the introduction of knowledge-based systems is a difficult task, which requires team effort and support throughout the enterprise including the transformational leader.

The full benefits from knowledge management programs have been identified by Although Eginton (1998) and Sbarcea (1998) as "benefits that are obtainable only when the knowledge management strategies are appropriately aligned with the organisation strategies". The work by Eginton and Sbarcea did not recognise that alignment of knowledge management programs with organisational strategy is a necessary pre-requisite before the full benefits from knowledge management programs can be realised. Furthermore, the work by Soliman et al (1999) described the knowledge management chain "as a number of decisions that need to be made at each stage in the chain requiring creation, capturing, accessing and using knowledge. In other words, each time a complex decision is made by the transformational leader, input from various teams and groups across the enterprise would be required warranting the use of knowledge-based systems". Further work by Hansen et al. (1999) pointed to the need for the enterprise to identify the most suitable knowledge management program that would best assist the organisation in achieving its strategic objectives.

Further attention to the link between knowledge and strategy was due to the work of Soliman and Spooner (2000) who argued that ensuring the alignment between knowledge and strategy is a complex and difficult task that the knowledge leader must address. Soliman and Spooner also concluded that one of the necessary success factors for a knowledge management program is the interaction between a knowledge management effort and the organisational culture. Soliman and Spooner (2000) also provided a list of seven attributes/characteristics of a leader in charge of transforming an organisation from information based into a knowledge driven one. These attributes include: knowledge focused, knowledge visible, knowledge defined, knowledge seeker, knowledge culture, knowledge assessor and knowledge exemplified.

However, in reality the organisation needs to consider whether to create a separate leadership role to develop and drive the process planning implementation of a knowledge management program. This is usually a difficult task for organisations given that the challenge is to find a leader with characteristics such as interpersonal skills, visionary leadership, business acumen, strategic thinking skills, ability to withstand ambiguity and uncertainty and teamwork, Soliman and Spooner (2000). Furthermore, Soliman and Spooner (2000) have added "in addition to the above roles, the leader should also drive the knowledge management process by avoiding recruitment of staff with poor managerial skills, inappropriate management philosophy, lack of control and low motivation. Further work by Soliman and Youssef (2003) pointed to knowledge as "a facilitator of creative practices that helps a company compete".

From the above discussion, it is clear that knowledge has become the new strategic imperative of organisations, and leaders in charge of knowledge management programs must ensure that the opportunities which are likely to result from transforming an organisation from information based into a knowledge driven organisation, actually take place.

Therefore, since the transfer into knowledge based is regarded as critical to the competitive position of the organisation, then the organisation must act to facilitate the transfer to knowledge based with the engagement of an appropriate transformational leader. This is the view proposed by Soliman (2010, 2011a) who argued that one of the aims of leadership is to facilitate the transfer into knowledge based and then into learning organisation.

TRANSFORMATION FROM KNOWLEDGE-BASED INTO A LEARNING ORGANISATION

Often, the concepts of organisational learning and learning organisation have been used interchangeably to refer to learning in organisations (Ortenblad 2001; Rebelo and Gomes 2008; Sun and Scott 2003). However, in terms of their similarities, such as the similarity between the double loop learning of organisational learning and the discipline of mental model in a learning organisation, it should be noted that the two concepts are quite different (Al-Qawabah, 2012). However, a clear distinction between the two concepts was provided by Sun and Scott (2003). According to Al-Qawabah (2012) it is possible to view the distinction as similar to the distinction between concepts such as: descriptive versus prescriptive; process versus new form of organisation; naturally occurring versus not naturally occurring; obtainable and necessary versus ideal State and domain of academics versus domain of practitioners:

Cavaleri et al. (2005) suggested that knowledge management initiatives must facilitate the transformation into learning organisation. Cavaleri et al. (2005) further added that such transformation should improve capabilities and would ultimately improve the organisation's competitive advantages.

It should be noted that organisational learning is a process that involves interactions among individuals and decision makers. Learning has been a very well-known and heavily studied subject. However, some authors have begun to study learning at the individual level of analysis in the organisational context. Garvin (1993) defined a learning organisation as "an organisation skilled at creating, acquiring and transferring knowledge, and at modifying its behaviour to reflect new knowledge and insights". Garvin's work shows that a learning organisation can be measured and manifested through series of activities. In more recent times, Ortenbald (2004) proposes an integrated model for a learning organisation that includes organisational learning, learning on-the job, a climate of learning and an organisational structure that is flexible and organic. Chang and Lee (2007) further explained that a learning organisation covers individual, grouping and organisational learning with the simultaneous proceeding effort for organisational and individual learning.

According to Senge (1990) and Rebelo and Gomes (2008), senior management must realise that the way in which an organisation learns is a key parameter to its effectiveness and potential to develop and grow. Rebelo and Gomes (2008) further added that "the popularity of learning organisations and organisational learning are due to the fact that learning is an important source of competitive advantages". It should be noted that Kumar and Idris (2006) found that team learning, embedded system and provision of leadership possess strong relationship with knowledge performance.

The origin of the concept of learning can be traced back to March and Olsen (1975) who were the first to link the efforts of the individual to organisational learning. On the other hand, Argyris and Schön (1978) were the first to propose models that facilitate organisational learning. Indeed the work of Argyris and Schön (1978) in identifying single-loop and double-loop learning has presented basis for further work that has led to the evolution of the concept of Learning Organisation proposed by Senge (1990). In this regards Kim (1993), proposed a single comprehensive model based on the integration of the Argyris and Schön and March and Olsen models which further enhances the application of the Senge (1990) model.

The concept of organisational learning was further enhanced by the work of Nonaka and Takeuchi (1995) who proposed a link between knowledge and learning. Further attention to the concept was made by Flood (1999) who discussed a link between the Senge model and the origins of the theory traced back to Argyris and Schön (1978). It should be noted that Amabile (1988) pointed out that "in order to build environments that support innovation the organisation must clearly demonstrate that creativity and innovation are valued by focusing communication within the organisation on the excitement and potential of the ideas being generated and the work being accomplished". In more recent time Bontis et. Al. (2002) empirically tested a model of organisational learning that is based on knowledge flow across the organisation. In other words, organisational qualities such as leadership, organisational motivation, resources, and innovation management practices may greatly influence individuals an organisation's overall innovation.

Although most managers now recognize the relationship between efficiency and profitability and that customers' demand is indeed dynamic and require continuous learning and complex analysis based on assumptions, uncertainty and trial and error. This thinking implies that standard learning tools may fall short of achieving desired organisational outcomes. For example, staff learning and competencies may ultimately lead to organisational innovation needed for sustainable performance. It is therefore, the role of the transformational leader is to ensure that learning and creativity would constitute essential foundation for innovation.

TRANSFORMATION FROM LEARNING ORGANISATION INTO INNOVATIVE ORGANISATION

Innovation may be defined as the act of propagating an idea and transforming it into a new product, service, or business model that can be useful to customers. There are two important segments of innovation; namely, product innovation and process innovation. It should be noted that innovation can also be pursued radically (i.e., sudden change of modus operandi) and incrementally (i.e., incremental with step-by-step improvement). It should be noted that Woodman et al. (1993) proposed that "organisational characteristics have an impact on the creative process and situation, resulting in the creative products or processes." This implies that, managing innovation could involve developing strategies, and processes that facilitate the transformation of ideas to final product or service.

Amabile (1996) proposed that "innovation requires an ongoing investment in leadership skills needed to support innovation" Amabile (1996) also suggested that to enhance and maintain creativity "the organisation need to establish stimulating, supportive, and positively challenging environments". This view was further enhanced by Egbu et al. (2001) who consider innovation as the new pre-requisite for competitive advantage.

In more recent times, Bel (2010) has identified innovation leadership as the most important driver of innovation. Bel stated "without great innovation leaders, there is no innovation" and has further added "A good innovation leader is characterized by the ability to excel on the apparently conflicting skills of creativity and discipline". Innovation leaders could be characterized by strong ability to recognize opportunities and to develop them, and by a set of attributes, skills and abilities, which makes them more suitable than others. Some of the leader attributes are: inspiring, driving, enabling, and advising. Other innovation leaders may exert the following attributes: Advocating, Rewarding, Managing linkages, and Supporting.

Further attributes of leaders were identified by Soliman (2011a) as: communicates with vision, energizing, accelerating innovation processes to innovate, committing employees to innovation and enabling employees to be innovative. These characteristics correspond to what is known as charismatic and strategic leadership.

Given that innovation involves risks (sometimes high risks) and uncertainty, then it follows that the innovation leader should also be one who handles risks successfully. Leaders in innovation do not necessarily avoid risks but carefully approach risks to navigate through and concurrently further learning. In addition to those attributes, innovation leaders share common leadership skills and abilities such as coaching, motivating, and rewarding.

According to Soliman (2011a), the subject of leadership has been widely researched but yet little has been published about the role of leaders in transforming organisations from knowledge based into learning and then into innovative organisations. The primary role of leadership should be to create a climate for innovation.

ATTRIBUTES OF THE INNOVATION LEADER

In current business environments, three leadership's types are frequently mentioned; namely transformational and transactional leadership (Bass and Avolio, 1990, cited in Chang and Lee 2007; Howell and Avolio, 1993), charismatic-visionary leadership (Yuki and Howell, 1999) and team leadership (Steckle and Fondas, 1995). The purpose of this study is to deal with transformational leadership with respect to transformation from knowledge based into learning and then into innovative organisations. Leaders who assist their organisations to learn can then build a workforce that possesses integrative competencies necessary for innovation process (Bennet, 2006).

Transformational leadership was originally proposed by Bass (1985). However later authors developed further transformational leadership theories (Burns, 1978; Conger and Kanungo, 1987; House, 1977; Sashkin, 1988; Bass, 1990). As such leadership theories have led to research on transformational leadership, which has expanded the range of leadership characteristics being examined, but still ignore transformational leadership with respect to transformation from knowledge based into learning and then into innovative organisation. For instance, Senge (1990) has identified several roles for leaders in a learning organisation and proposed that leadership must have the capability to affect others in a learning organisation. However, the leadership characteristics that create, capture, transfer, and mobilize knowledge before it can be used for innovation have still not been thoroughly researched.

Furthermore, Bass and Avolio (1994) proposed that transformational leadership usually emphasizes long-term and vision-based motivational activities. However little research has been conducted on the potential for a transformational leader to positively impact organisational creativity and its transformation from knowledge based into learning and then into innovation (Soliman, 2011a). A number of authors such Howell and Avolio (1993), Yammarino et al. (1993), Gardner and Avolio (1998), Jung et al. (2003) and Soliman (2011a) pointed out that the increase in the popularity of transformational leadership is due to its ability to motivate people, as compared with other leadership styles. This view was confirmed by the work of Bass and Avolio (1994) who characterized transformational leadership as being composed of four unique but interrelated behavioural components: inspirational motivation (articulating an appealing and/or evocative vision), intellectual stimulation (promoting creativity and innovation), idealized influence (charismatic role modelling), and individualized consideration (coaching and mentoring).

In more recent times Soliman (2011a) presented a quantitative approach and developed a questionnaire based on Politis (2001) work to evaluate leadership attributes. The results show that there are at least 22 factors or dimensions of leadership. Soliman (2011a) summarized the innovation dimension as: (1) acceptance of risks; (2) degree of passion for the job; (3) willingness to act proactively; (4) courage to switch off or terminate projects; (5) attracting talent; (6) ability to building teams; (7) coaching subordinates; (8) rewarding performing staff; (9) communicating at all levels; (10) inspiring and role model for other staff; (11) driving projects successfully; (12) enabling project supporting environments; (13) advising others managers; (14) advocating for improvement; (15) encouraging self-goal setting; (16) ability of appropriate timing to release products to the market; (17) ability to release products to the market within budget; (18) ability of self-rehearsal; (19) ability of self-reinforcement; (20) ability of self-observation; (21) ability of self-expectation; and (22) ability of self-criticism.

Soliman (2011a) summarized the results of three groups of managers who were asked to assess degrees of importance of leadership attributes associated with each of the above 22 factors. The result of the Soliman (2011a) analysis is shown in the following plot (Figure 1). Confirmatory factor analysis using SPSS factor analysis was employed and SPSS "Scree" plot was generated to explore the distinct break between the steep slope of the large factors and the gradual trailing of the rest. The factors that have eigenvalues greater than 1 are considered significant while all other factors (with eigenvalues less than 1) are considered insignificant and should be disregarded in assessing the leadership characteristics of the innovation leaders. Soliman (2011a) presented four critical innovation leadership characteristics that are critical (with eigenvalues greater than 1) to innovation projects. The four critical leadership characteristics are found to be: (1) acceptance of risks; (2) degree of passion for the job; (3) willingness to act proactively; (4) courage to switch off or terminate projects. It is found that acceptance of risks is the most critical followed by degree of passion for the innovation. However, it should be noted that the other 18 innovation leadership characteristics are important to the success of the innovation project.

Figure 1. Scree plot of innovation leadership characteristics (after Soliman, 2011a)

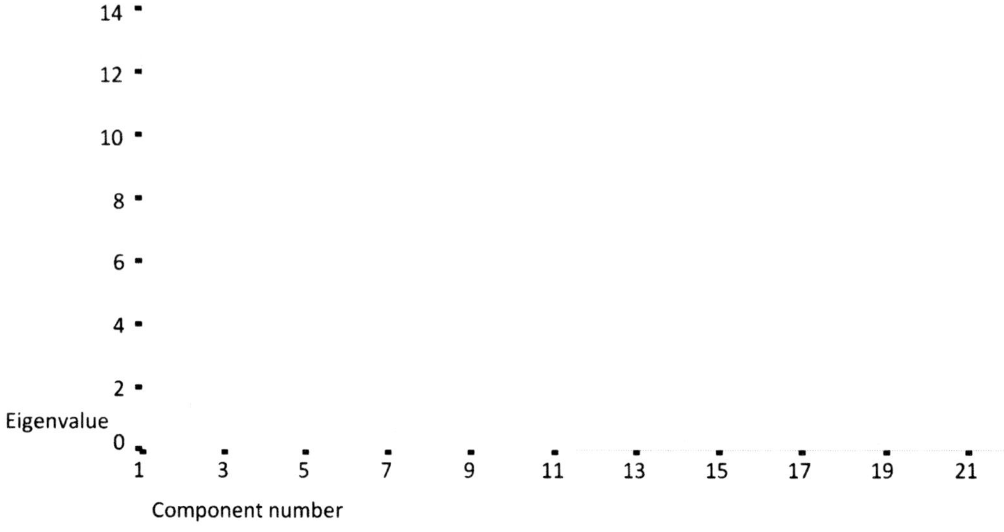

From the above Scree diagram, the three most critical factors for the three groups are acceptance of risks, willingness to act proactively and courage to switch off or terminate projects. All other 18 factors with eigenvalues less than 1 are considered less critical less but essential Characteristics.

CONCLUSION

From the above discussion, it is possible to describe innovation activities as a chain of activities that begins with information that leads to knowledge, then into learning before it can finally be used for innovation.

The above discussion also proposes that transformational leadership could facilitate moving the organisation from being information based into knowledge based then into learning organisation and into innovative company. Soliman (2011a) has shown that the six important characteristics of the transformational leaders may be courage to switch off or terminate projects, rewarding performing staff, ability to appropriately time release of products to the market, ability to release products to the market within budget and ability to inspire and be a role model for other staff. Soliman (2011a) also found that there are other fourteen transformational leadership characteristics that may be considered less critical. Those non-critical characteristics include: degree of passion for the job, attracting talent, ability to build teams, coaching subordinates, communicating at all levels, driving projects successfully, enabling project supporting environments, advising others managers, advocating for improvement, encouraging self-goal setting, ability of self rehearsal, ability of self reinforcement, ability of self-observation, and ability of self-expectation.

This discussion above demonstrates that shifting from information based into knowledge based then into organisational learning to become an innovative business could require a unique level of transformation leadership. In that regard, the above discussion also demonstrates that organisations need to create, capture, transfer, and mobilize knowledge before it can be used be used for innovation. However, it is necessary that organisations acknowledge the challenges facing transformational leadership.

REFERENCES

Al-Qawabah, M. (2012). *Assessing transformational leadership components as drivers in learning organisations*. (Doctor of Philosophy Dissertation). University of Technology, Sydney, Australia.

Amabile, T. M. (1988). A model of creativity and innovation in organisations. *Research in Organizational Behavior*, *19*, 123–167.

Amabile, T. M. (1996). *Creativity in context*. Boulder, CO: Westview Press.

Argyris, C., & Schön, D. A. (1978). *Organisational learning: A theory of action perspective*. Philippines: Addison-Wesley Publishing Co..

Bass, B. M. (1985). *Leadership and performance beyond expectations*. New York: Free Press.

Bass, B. M. (1990). *Bass and Stogdill's handbook of leadership: Theory, research, and applications* (3rd ed.). New York: Free Press.

Bass, B. M., & Avolio, B. J. (1990). *Transformational leadership development: Manual for the multifactor leadership questionnaire*. Palo Alto, CA: Consulting Psychologists Press.

Bass, B. M., & Avolio, B. J. (1994). *Improving organisational effectiveness through transformational leadership*. Thousand Oaks, CA: Sage Publications.

Bel, R. (2010). *Leadership and innovation: Learning from the best*. Retrieved frm www.interscience.wiley.com

Bennet, A. (2006). The learning organisation portfolio. *The Journal of information and Knowledge Management Systems, 36*(1).

Bontis, N., Crossan, M., & Hulland, J. (2002). Managing an organisational learning system by aligning stocks and flows. *Journal of Management Studies, 39*(4), 437–469. doi:10.1111/1467-6486.t01-1-00299.

Burns, J. M. (1978). *Leadership*. New York: Harper and Row.

Cavaleri, S., Seivert, S., & Lee, W. L. (2005). *Knowledge leadership: The art and science of the knowledge-based organisation*. Alexandria, VA: KMCI Press.

Chang, S. C., & Lee, M. S. (2007). A study on relationship among leadership, organisational culture, the operation of learning organisation and employees' job satisfaction. *The Learning Organization, 14*(2), 155–185. doi:10.1108/09696470710727014.

Christensen, P. H. (2007). Knowledge sharing: Moving away from the obsession with best practices. *Journal of Knowledge Management, 11*(1), 36–47. doi:10.1108/13673270710728222.

Clark, J., & Soliman, F. (1997). Application of scoring method for measuring the value of knowledge based systems to key employees. *Journal of Systems and Information Technology, 1*(2), 23–40. doi:10.1108/13287269780000736.

Conger, J. A., & Kanungo, R. N. (1987). Toward a behavioural theory of charismatic leadership in organisational settings. *Academy of Management Review, 12*, 637–647.

Egbu, C., Botterill, K., & Bates, M. (2001). The influence of knowledge management and intellectual capital on organisational innovations. In *Proceedings of ARCOM Seventeenth Annual Conference*, (pp. 547-555). ARCOM.

Eginton, K. (1998). Knowledge management – Law firms can do it too! *Australian Law Librarian, 6*, 247–255.

Flood, R. L. (2009). *Rethinking the fifth discipline: Learning within the unknowable*. London: Routledge.

Gardner, W. L., & Avolio, B. A. (1998). The charismatic relationship: A dramaturgical perspective. *Academy of Management Review, 23*, 32–58.

Garvin, D. A. (1993). Building a learning organisation. *Harvard Business Review, 71*, 78.

Garvin, D. A., Edmondson, A. C., & Gino, F. (2008). Is yours a learning organisation? *Harvard Business Review, 86*(3), 109.

Hansen, M. T., Nohria, N., & Tierney, T. (1999, March-April). What's your strategy for managing knowledge? *Harvard Business Review*, 106–116.

House, R. J. (1977). A 1976 theory of charismatic leadership. In Hunt, J. G., & Larsons, L. L. (Eds.), *Leadership: The cutting edge* (pp. 189–207). Carbondale, IL: Southern Illinois University Press.

Howell, J. M., & Avolio, B. J. (1993). Transformational leadership, transactional leadership, locus of control, and support for innovation: Key predictors of consolidated-business-unit performance. *The Journal of Applied Psychology, 78*(6), 891–911. doi:10.1037/0021-9010.78.6.891.

Jung, D. I., Chow, C., & Wu, A. (2003). The role of transformational leadership in enhancing organisational innovation: Hypotheses and some preliminary findings. *The Leadership Quarterly, 14*, 525–544. doi:10.1016/S1048-9843(03)00050-X.

Kalkan, V. D. (2008). An overall view of knowledge management challenges for global business. *Business Process Management Journal*, *14*(3), 390–400. doi:10.1108/14637150810876689.

Kim, D. H. (1993). The link between individual and organisational learning. *Sloan Management Review*, *35*(1), 37–50.

Kumar, N., & Idris, K. (2006). An examination of educational institutions' knowledge performance: Analysis, implications and outlines for future research. *The Learning Organization*, *13*(1), 96–116. doi:10.1108/09696470610639158.

López, S. P., Montes Peón, J. M., & Ordás, C. J. V. (2006). Human resources management as a determining factor in organisational learning. *Management Learning*, (37): 215–239. doi:10.1177/1350507606063443.

Maqsood, T., Walker, D., & Finegan, A. (2007). Extending the knowledge advantage: Creating learning chains. *The Learning Organization*, *14*(2), 123–141. doi:10.1108/09696470710726998.

March, J. G., & Olsen, J. P. (1975). The uncertainty of the past, organisational ambiguous learning. *European Journal of Political Research*, *3*, 147–171. doi:10.1111/j.1475-6765.1975.tb00521.x.

Mehrez, A. (2010). *The role of quality gaps in assessing the performance of management programs*. (Ph.D. thesis). University of Newcastle, Newcastle, Australia.

Nonaka, I. (1991). The knowledge creating company. *Harvard Business Review*, *69*(6), 96–104.

Nonaka, I., & Takeuchi, H. (1995). *The knowledge creating company: How Japanese companies create the dynamics of innovation*. New York: Oxford University Press.

Nonaka, I., Toyama, R., & Konno, N. (2000). SECI, ba and leadership: A unified model of dynamic knowledge creation. *Long Range Planning*, *33*, 5–34. doi:10.1016/S0024-6301(99)00115-6.

Ortenbald, A. (2004). The learning organisation: Towards an integrated model. *The Learning Organization*, *11*(2/3), 129. doi:10.1108/09696470410521592.

Politis, J. D. (2001). *The relationship between self-management leader behaviour, self-leadership worker behaviour and job-related attitudes and perceptions*. (PhD dissertation). University of Technology, Sydney, Australia.

Porter, M. (1980). *Competitive strategy*. New York: Free Press.

Quinn, J. B. (1992). *Intelligent enterprise: A knowledge and service based paradigm for industry*. New York: The Free Press.

Quinn, J. B., Anderson, P. Y., & Filkenstein, S. (1996, March-April). Managing professional intellect: Making the most of the best. *Harvard Business Review*, 71–80.

Rebelo, T. M., & Gomes, A. D. (2008). Organisational learning and the learning organisation. *The Learning Organization*, *15*(4), 294–308. doi:10.1108/09696470810879556.

Sashkin, M. (1988). The visionary leader. In Conger, J. A., & Kanungo, R. N. (Eds.), *Charismatic leadership: The elusive factor in organisational effectiveness*. San Francisco, CA: Jossey-Bass.

Sbarcea, K. (1998, March 6). Know what, know how, know why: Implementing a knowledge management system – The Phillips Fox experience. *Australian Law Librarian*, 4-8.

Senge, P. M. (1990). *The fifth discipline: The art and practice of the learning organisation*. New York: Doubleday.

Soliman, F. (2009). Modelling the appraisal of quality management programs. *The Employment Relations Record*, *9*(2), 73–83.

Soliman, F. (2010). Role of human resources management as a CoP match-maker. *The International Employment Relations Review*, *16*(1), 69–81.

Soliman, F. (2011a). Could one transformational leader convert the organisation from knowledge based into learning organisation, then into innovation? *Journal of Modern Accounting and Auditing*, *7*(12), 1352–1361.

Soliman, F. (2011b). Globalisation as driver for transforming organisations from knowledge to learning and then to innovation. In Srivastava, R., Pandy, T., Kumar, N., & Singhal, R. (Eds.), *Business Competitiveness in the 21st Century* (pp. 42–52). New Delhi: MacMillan Publishers India Ltd..

Soliman, F. (2011c). Modelling the role of HRM in the innovation chain. *The Employment Relations Record*, *11*(2), 1–20.

Soliman, F., Innes, C., & Spooner, K. (1999). Managing the human resources' knowledge. In *Proceedings of the Seventh Annual Conference of the International Employment Relations Association*, (pp. 497-510). Christchurch, New Zealand: Lincoln University.

Soliman, F., & Spooner, K. (2000). Strategies for implementing knowledge management: Role of human resources management. *Journal of Knowledge Management*, *4*(4), 337–345. doi:10.1108/13673270010379894.

Soliman, F., & Youssef, M. (2003). The role of critical information in enterprise knowledge management. *Industrial Management & Data Systems*, *103*(7), 484–490. doi:10.1108/02635570310489188.

Stata, R. (1989). Organisational learning-the key to management innovation. *Sloan Management Review*, *30*(3), 63–74.

Steckle, N., & Fondas, N. (1995). Building team leader effectiveness: A diagnostic tool. *Organizational Dynamics*, *23*(3), 20. doi:10.1016/0090-2616(95)90023-3.

Sun, P. Y. T., & Scott, J. L. (2003). Exploring the divide-organisational learning and learning organisation. *The Learning Organization*, *10*(4), 202–215. doi:10.1108/09696470310476972.

Woodman, R. W., Sawyer, J. E., & Griffin, R. W. (1993). Toward a theory of organisational creativity. *Academy of Management Review*, *18*, 293–321.

Yammarino, F. J., Spangler, W. D., & Bass, B. M. (1993). Transformational leadership and performance: A longitudinal investigation. *The Leadership Quarterly*, *4*, 81–102. doi:10.1016/1048-9843(93)90005-E.

Yuki, G., & Howell, J. M. (1999). Organisational and contextual influences on the emergence and effectiveness of charismatic leadership. *The Leadership Quarterly*, *10*(2), 257–283. doi:10.1016/S1048-9843(99)00014-4.

Zack, M. H. (1999). Developing a knowledge strategy. *California Management Review*, *41*(3), 125–145. doi:10.2307/41166000.

Section 3
Applications and Solutions

Chapter 23
The Portuguese School of Macao, China: A Traditional/Web 2.0 Assessment Facing Different Learning Styles

Zelia Baptista
University of Saint Joseph, China

João Negreiros
University of Saint Joseph, China

ABSTRACT

Technology is fundamental to the youth culture of today and high schools need to integrate it into live classes. This research hopes to provide a better understanding of the present learner styles and the technology impact towards enhancing and enriching the conventional learning process. Hence, the central focus of this writing is based on the four Index Learner Styles (Active VS Reflective, Sensing VS Intuitive, Visual VS Verbal, Sequential VS Global) of Felder and Soloman (1993, 2011) and on the teaching strategies impact that integrates technology (online lessons, blending learning topics, and collaboration software use) as a vehicle in the differentiation of the traditional learning curriculum. The field of experiment is the Portuguese language subject of the 8th grade students at the Portuguese School of Macau, China. One online survey and four tests (two for each class) are carried out to check whether the e-Learning perspective will benefit student learning in this new surrounded generation of mobile devices. Still, the main purpose relies on the learning style identification of high school scholars and to raise awareness of those personal characteristics to facilitate future development on personal learning strategies. Some other related topics are also highlighted such as Web 1.0 to Web 4.0 evolution and learning distance topics.

DOI: 10.4018/978-1-4666-4373-4.ch023

1. INTRODUCTION

The Net changes everything (Ellison, 1999). This means new mass Internet media of news and entertainment channels, synchronous tools of video/audio teleconferencing, autonomous agents and database assisted learning. According to Rosen (2006), in every 10 years comes a new twist: The 70's brought mainframes, the personal computer came on the 80s, the 90s created the WWW while the first decade of the 21st century ends up on the Web 2.0. Following the same line, the 2011-2020 time-period will bring the Web 3.0. According to Dawley (2007), Web 1.0 was just for reading and sending e-mails. With Web 2.0, it gave the users the free choice to interact or collaborate with each other in a social media dialogue as creators of user-generated content (prosumer) in a virtual community (social networking, blogs, wikis, or video-sharing sites). Under this e-Learning context, WebCT©, Blackboard© and Moodle© already allows content creation, online file exchange and messaging system, multi-channel communication, whiteboards, on-line testing and grading book.

By definition, a learning object is a digital and Web-based resource that can be used and re-used to support knowledge acquiring, such as the introductory programming subject of the London Metropolitan University (www.londonmet.ac.uk/ltri/learningobjects/) where the present code seeks to engage with the learner through attractive use of visualisation. Certainly, this may turn out a quite useful tool for the computer programming teaching.

However, one of the biggest disadvantages of asynchronous courses is related to the high dropout rate. Moore and Kearsley (2005) found that 30% to 50% of students left courses in the recent past. On the other hand, due to the high maintenance costs of universities, for Peter Drucker (1998), they are becoming unsustainable without improvements in terms of digital content and quality of education. The introduction of courses online will achieve them with only a fraction of the cost (Drucker 1998). Michael Zastrocky, in a survey conducted in March 2008 on the factors motivation for e-Learning platforms, found that students who were enrolled on online courses rated with four on a one-to-five scale. In 2009, students from the University of Hong Kong had access to a variety of study materials (which explores Wikis, blogs, and social networks) with frequently updated and reflection subjects throughout the semester participation. In the end, three other conclusions where drew by Churchill (2009): 79% of students felt that they learned quite a lot during the course; 83% of students enjoy the use of blogs to facilitate and contribute to the learning process; 92% of the students confirmed that due to blogs, the professor become more supportive than traditional courses.

According to a survey conducted by Becta (2008), 74% of two thousand and six hundred students from a universe of twenty-seven schools, had accounts in social networks. As well, professors prefer email (asynchronous) while students prefer to use Instant Messenger (synchronous). Moreover, in a data sample of one hundred and eighty students, another research conducted by Webster University in order to assess the advantages experienced of online courses, Tamashiro (2002) obtained the following advantages/disadvantages results given by Table 1.

Certainly, for workers within school courses, a hybrid structure could be an asset for these students, reducing the time presence within the classroom. Another characteristic of Web 2.0 is not requiring too much learning time to use with the available tools. Of course, the daily use of MP3, iPod's, computer games and tablets contributes to this trend. In addition, researchers found that collaborative learning helps students to retain information better than working individually (Johnson & Johnson 1986) because active participation is the component that contributes most to the learning effective (Ferdig, 2007). According to Brown and Adler (2008), within social learning, the students can ask questions to clarify dubious or confused topics easily, may learn from

Table 1. Pros and cons of online courses

Rank	Advantages of Online Learning	Disadvantages of Online Learning
1	Flexibility of time to work at own pace	Lack face-to-face with instructor or students
2	Save time on travel to/ from campus; parking hassles	Fear of technical problems
3	Freedom: accessible any time, from anywhere	Requires too much self-discipline, self-motivation and time management
4	More resources available for the course and easy access to course materials	Computer literacy and typing skills
5	Learn new technologies	Communication, directions or discussions are unclear or more difficult
6	Instructor more accessible	Lack of immediate feedback
7	More comfortable to work at home or place of my choice	Too many distractions and interruptions
8	Allow more time to think before answering questions	Lack of classroom atmosphere

the questions raised by other colleagues on issues not understood and can read the answers provided by other students. Most importantly, it allows students to take the place of the traditional teacher because the best way to learn something is, after acquired learning, teaching to others.

Inescapably, the Web 2.0 as also its evils. Gloria Gadsden, a professor of sociology at East Stroudsburg University of Pennsylvania, was escorted off the campus because of jokes she had made on her Facebook page about wanting to kill students: "Had a good day today, didn't want to kill even one student.:-) Now Friday was a different story..." (Miller, 2010). As well, it has also its benefits. Seton Hill University, a liberal-arts institution in Pennsylvania with more than 2,100 students, announced a program on Tuesday that offers an iPad to every full-time student (Laster, 2010). In the middle, a peculiar situation rises. Mark James, a visiting lecturer at the University of West Florida, declared his summer course in English literature technology-free by skipping the PowerPoint slides and YouTube videos he usually shows and he asked students to silence their cellphones and close their laptops (Young, 2012). "The students seemed more involved in the discussion than when I allowed them to go online. They were more attentive, and we were able to go into a little more depth."

The semantic 3.0 Web will try to connect meanings of words, with the purpose of giving an interpretation of the Internet content so that both are perceptible to the computer and for the users. It is, then, expected that the search engine results are listed in account not only the keywords but also the meaning of those keywords. In fact, AJAX (Asynchronous Javascript and XML) is already an integrated component of it. For Spivak (2007), Web 4.0 announces the arrival of cloud operating systems that runs in any browser by containing appealing features such as automatic files synchronization between our personal laptop and the online one, sharing files access from a smart-phone and run any Web software, avoiding any fastidious local installation and maintenance. Yet, no strategies or future directions are presented by any author concerning education teaching issues in the long run.

This article is divided into six sections, including already the present introduction. Second section reviews the Index Learning Style framework where learners are segmented into four major axes. The third section incorporate other views on online learning while the following section introduces and describes statistically the two student's population used in this work field. Section five addresses the major breakdown analysis of the quizzes results under the education and learner's styles view. The last section highlights the core conclusion of this chapter.

2. THE INDEX LEARNING STYLE (ILS)

The North Carolina State University ILS questionnaire (www.engr.ncsu.edu/learningstyles/ilsWeb.html) allows you to fill up forty-four questions in a two choice option answer (see Figure 1) in order to quantify what kind of learner are you in a four scale (-11 to +11) framework: Active VS Reflective, Sensing VS Intuitive, Visual VS Verbal and Sequential VS Global. Bear in mind that ILS is not a measure of intelligence (Felder & Soloman, 1993, 2011). Primarily, the ILS tries to provide an indication of an individual's learning preferences and the preference profile of a group of students. In other words, the student's learning style profile hints of possible strengths and possible tendencies or habits that might lead to the difficulty explanation in academic settings. Keep in mind that this outline does not reflect student's suitability or unsuitability for a particular subject, discipline, or profession.

As well, a learning style preference also does not serve as an excuse for a bad grade on the student's last chemistry test (Felder & Soloman, 1993, 2011). According to these authors, the distinctions among these four vertices learners are as follows:

- **Active VS Reflective:** Active tend to retain and understand information best by doing something active with it ("let's try it out and see how it works") such as discussing or applying it or explaining it to others. Reflective learners prefer to think about it quietly first ("let's think it through first"). As expected, the first ones tend to enjoy

Figure 1. Home page of ILS questionnaire

Index of Learning Styles Questionnaire

Barbara A. Soloman
First-Year College
North Carolina State University
Raleigh, North Carolina 27695

Richard M. Felder
Department of Chemical Engineering
North Carolina State University
Raleigh, NC 27695-7905

Directions

Please provide us with your full name. Your name will be printed on the information that is returned to you.

Full Name

For each of the 44 questions below select either "a" or "b" to indicate your answer. Please choose only one answer for each question. If both "a" and "b" seem to apply to you, choose the one that applies more frequently. When you are finished selecting answers to each question please select the submit button at the end of the form.

1. I understand something better after I
   - **(a)** try it out.
   - **(b)** think it through.

group work more than reflective learners, who prefer working alone.

- **Sensing VS Intuitive:** Sensing tend to enjoy learning facts while Intuitive learners often prefer discovering possibilities and relationships, that is, sensors often like solving problems by well-established methods and dislike complications and surprises. On the other hand, Intuitive individuals like innovation and dislike repetition. Sensors tend to be patient with details and good at memorizing facts and doing hands-on (laboratory) work while the second ones may be better at grasping new concepts and are often more comfortable with abstractions and mathematical formulations. Therefore, sensors tend to be more practical and careful than Intuitive persons who tend to work faster and to be more innovative. Sensors don't like modules that have no apparent connection to the real world while Intuitive ones don't like "plug-and-chug" courses that involve a lot of memorization and routine calculations.
- **Visual VS Verbal:** Visual learners remember best what they see: pictures, diagrams, flow charts, time lines, films, and demonstrations. Verbal learners get more out of words: written and spoken explanations. In most college classes, very little Visual information is presented. Instead, students mainly listen to lectures and read material written on chalkboards and in textbooks and handouts. Unfortunately, most people are Visual learners, which mean that most students do not get nearly as much as they would if more visual presentation were used in class.
- **Sequential VS Global:** Sequential learners tend to gain understanding in linear steps, with each step following logically from the previous one. Global learners tend to learn in large jumps, absorbing material almost randomly without seeing connections and then suddenly "getting it". That is, Sequential learners tend to follow logical stepwise paths in finding solutions whilst global learners may be able to solve complex problems quickly or put things together in novel ways once they have grasped the big picture. Oddly, they may have difficulty in explaining how they did it.

3. THE TEACHING UNDER THE WEB 2.0

Under the educational environment, Web 2.0 may contribute to the enrichment of teaching methods, diversifying them with new procedures, encouraging participation, development, and individual/cooperative work. Teachers and school staff now have a great challenge and responsibility within the Web 2.0, playing the engine role of this knowledge society and not the other way around, walking away from society. The blogs allow the teacher to set matters in that students can participate actively, they can be used as a general work guideline and they allow the links creation to reference materials. The podcast can be used in language audio classes. The wiki allows anyone to create an editable WWW space by all students in a collaborative context. Goowy©, for instance, is an online software that integrates email, calendar, file cabinet, contacts, games and notepad which can be used as the student e-book. Google Page Creator© and Google Docs© are also be very helpful in any educational setting. The Popfly© is a service to develop mashups, gadgets, Web pages and other applications. Wikipedia© itself can be considered a content manager thus encouraging search, location and creation of knowledge in a distributed collaborative environment. Definitely, the adoption of a complete school classroom with a proactive student's participation allows the subjects to be more focused in class, leading to a higher level of knowledge and resulting in better school outcomes.

The use of a collaborative learning portal such as Moodle© (used in the Portuguese School of Macau - EPM), rather than the tools being used individually, is that a single Web application are able to manage all collaborative tools, avoiding the wide spread of software. Moodle© allows the teacher to provide statistical tools such as time use of the platform by the students, number and quality of interventions or even the use of data filters to search specific information.

For all these reasons, Moodle© is considered a Content Management System (CMS) devoted to pedagogical agents, which enables cross-border education and where teachers and students can interact from their homes. As expected, it can also be used in international academic organizations by allowing the share of teaching resources online with a user-friendly interface. Its installation and configuration are easy and it is free of costs. Moodle is© multilingual, supporting over forty languages.

Theoretically, this platform could be used in both models of learning: (1) Model-face, where the platform is used to promote collaboration within student's activities but closely related to the subjects taught in the classroom face; (2) Mixture model, where it can replace part of the class face. For both models, some activities of the Moodle© learning portal that can be developed, among others, are: (a) Realization of glossaries of a particular discipline; (b) Use of forums for subject discussion; (c) Highlight of a daily topic (technology, research paper, article, newspapers), leading students to discuss these issues more frequently; (d) Creation of a set of questions for Internet research; (e) Online quizzes but limited in time.

Santos (2010), for instance, presents appealing conclusions on his questionnaire study for the secondary hi-school level (from 9th to 12th grade) in the Northern region of Portugal: (1) Students from eleventh grade are the most common users of CMS tools; (2) Technical professional schools only follow the traditional class model where the professor is the center of the world; (3) Only Moodle© (97%) and e-Socrates© (3%) are setup within the surveyed institutions; (4) 75% of the educators hold, at least, one year of experience on online lessons; (5) Peculiarly, 41% of the CMS access time by both professors and scholars are outside of the class; (6) New technologies, history and philosophy are the most demanding subjects of these collaborative software; (7) 80% of the students agree on the major communication facility with instructors by using CMS tools; (8) None of the students complained about the graphical user interface of Moodle©; (9) 63% of the lecturers versus 30% of the pupils believe that CMS help on the improvement of the lowest grades; (10) 49% of the students feels more motivated to school learning with the presence of online digital content; (11) 91% of the lecturers use the forum functionality as the main e-Learning capability; (12) 68% of the actual educators believe that in the near future, the learning process will be based on the Internet; (13) The mixture model (2/3 of the total time in class and the remaining 1/3 online) would be benefic for 69% of the inquire professors.

Among the various research methodologies, to extract results from two quizzes outcomes (the first one without any Moodle© support) versus the nature of EPM students becomes the initial goal. It is known that the use of rankings and other statistical measurements never allow the assessment the teaching-learning process in a global perspective by not measuring socio-economic-geographical factors. Yet, it can evaluate certain student's characteristics and contribute, somehow, to the evaluation of e-Learning, in general, and CMS tools, in particular.

4. THE PORTUGUESE HIGH-SCHOOL OF MACAU

Located in the heart of Macau, the Portuguese High School of Macau (EPM) is not an international school. Portuguese is its main language and it follows Portugal's educational system. With a total of students of four hundred and seventy, the school currently has more than ten non-Portuguese students from different countries such as the Philippines, Thailand, Ukraine and the UK, but all of them have already picked up Portuguese as a communicating language with their classmates. As expected, the core students are coming from the Portuguese or Macanese local community.

The undergoing study is based on the eight-year grade students (with an average age close to 14/15 years old) for the Portuguese language subject. The goal is to find patterns, outliers, sequences, consequences and trends based on the results of two written exams (taken in October and November 2010, respectively) of two different classes (8A with 24 students and 8B with 25 students) but classified according to the Index of Learning Style of each student (the ILS questionnaire was taken two weeks before the first quiz). Tables 2 and 3 show the variability outcome between the teacher's opinion and the ILS questionnaire result.

The last axis of this structure concerns the teaching method confrontation between the traditional teacher-centered method (paper books, grammar seminars, resolution of exercises in the blackboard, oral presentation) versus the e-Learning student-centered tutoring (Moodle© platform use, student-led and group activities, self-awareness), the extreme learning postures. Unsurprisingly, the raw outcomes from both quizzes may be found in the six appendices of this writing in a tabular form, according to three different factors: (a) learning style; (b) student's type; (c) individual ILS student result (see Figures 2-4).

Descriptive statistics are used to describe the basic data features of a study by providing simple summarization about the samples. Together with simple graphics analysis, they form the basis of virtually every data quantitative analysis (Healey & Prus, 2009). The sample mean is the most commonly used method of describing central tendency. To compute the average relies by add up all the values and divide by the number of values. On the other hand, dispersion refers to the spread of the values around the central tendency.

Table 2. Categorization variability of the 8a students based on the ILS questionnaire web site and the professor own judgement. It can be said the teacher knows his students pretty well.

Class 8A	Number of Students According to Professor's Expectation	Number of Students According to Students' ILS Questionnaire Results
Active	8	11
Passive	16	13
Sensitive	18	18
Intuitive	6	6
Visual	17	15
Verbal	7	9
Sequential	21	20
Global	3	4

Table 3. Categorization variability of the 8b students based on the ILS questionnaire web site and the professor own judgement. Analogous to the previous class, it can also be said that the results match in a good way.

Class 8B	Number of Students According to Professor's Expectation	Number of Students According to Students' ILS Questionnaire Results
Active	8	6
Passive	17	19
Sensitive	20	18
Intuitive	5	7
Visual	17	18
Verbal	8	7
Sequential	22	23
Global	3	2

The standard deviation is the most accurate estimate of dispersion because it presents a good resistance to outliers, a trend that is not followed by the maximum and minimum parameters. A

Figure 2. Student's classification of class 8a (top) and 8b (bottom) according to the ILS structure. It can be concluded both classes hold a similar behaviour concerning the eight learning styles. Moreover, the majority of students are passive, sensitive, visual, and sequential.

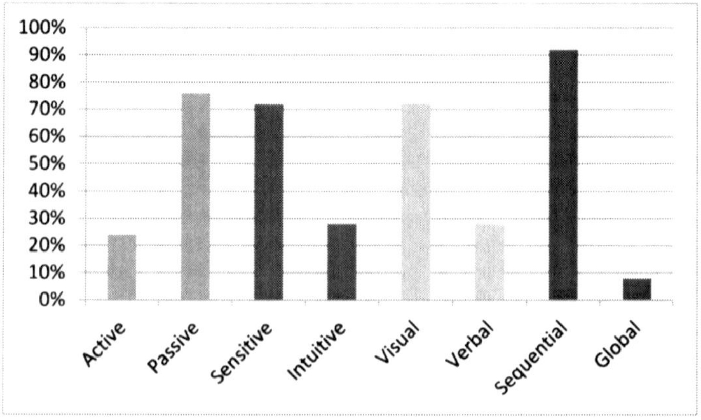

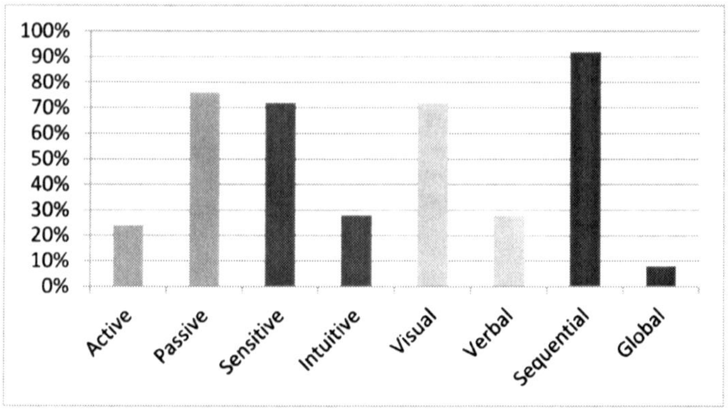

high kurtosis distribution (leptokurtic) means a sharper peak (value greater than zero) while a low kurtosis (mesokurtic) has a more rounded and low peak (negative value). A distribution is considered skewed if one of its tails is longer than the other. Henceforth, a positive skew means that it has a long tail in the positive direction while a negative one presents a long tail for the left. As expected, a symmetric distribution has no skew. The histogram is a graphical representation, showing a visual impression of the data distribution.

5. HUMAN DATA MINING

It is crucial to stress that the present analysis should not be generalized as a standard rule to other environments and teaching subjects. This qualitative approach to both quantitative quizzes results only try to highlight some hints by the present authors for further confirmations/refutations and developments/experiments with other settings.

With regard Appendix A, some interesting patterns can be found resulting from the intersection of the ILS and the teaching method approach for both classes: (a) If Active learners of class 8a are not affected by new technologies, this factor creates a major positive/negative impact for class 8b. Unfortunately, this behavior cannot be explain by the present data (a global class interview should be taken in order to explain this conduct); (b) A meaningful improvement for Passive and Visual lowest grade students with e-Learning technologies for both classes; (c) Small positive

Figure 3. Descriptive statistics of class 8a for both tests. Notice that there are no major changes in the overall grades distributions of both tests. The same conclusion can be taken from the descriptive statistics parameters.

Descriptive Statistics

	N	Minimum	Maximum	Mean	Std.	Skewness	Kurtosis
	Statistic	Statistic	Statistic	Statistic	Statistic	Statistic	Statistic
Test12	24	.37	.89	.5858	.16610	.578	-.848
Test22	24	.32	.89	.5867	.17026	.427	-.781

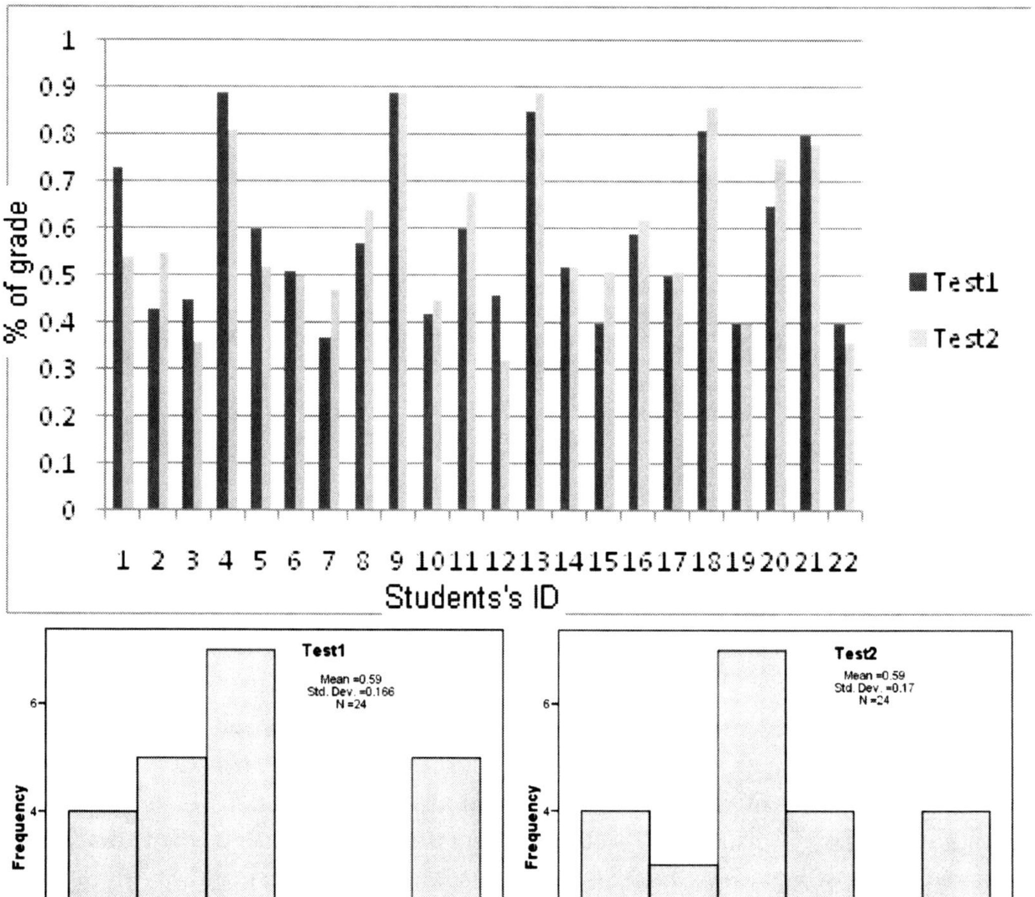

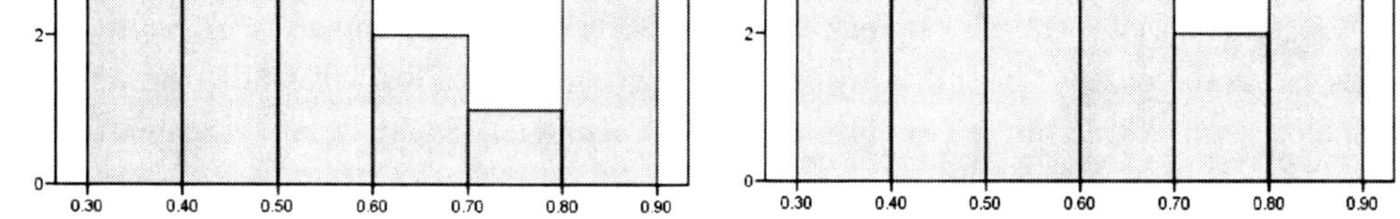

and negative variations on the final grades for Sensitive and Intuitive students for class 8a, a trend not complete followed by class 8b; (d) Class 8a exhibits less quiz results variability then class 8b for Verbal students; (e) Analogous to (a) and (d) items, Sequential learners of class 8b suffer a major positive impact of Web technologies, particular with the highest marks; (f) Global students seems not to be quite sensitive to virtual classes.

Based on the characteristics of the twenty-four students (class 8a), eleven subgroups were setup (check Appendix B) although 61% of them fall

Figure 4. Descriptive statistics of class 8b for both tests. It is clear an overall improvement of the second test average grade while the reasons for this dissimilar impact of the virtual learning in both classes are still unknown.

Descriptive Statistics

	N	Minimum	Maximum	Mean	Std.	Skewness	Kurtosis
	Statistic	Statistic	Statistic	Statistic	Statistic	Statistic	Statistic
Test1	25	.38	.97	.6008	.12990	.945	1.369
Test2	25	.33	.96	.6472	.15399	.289	.005

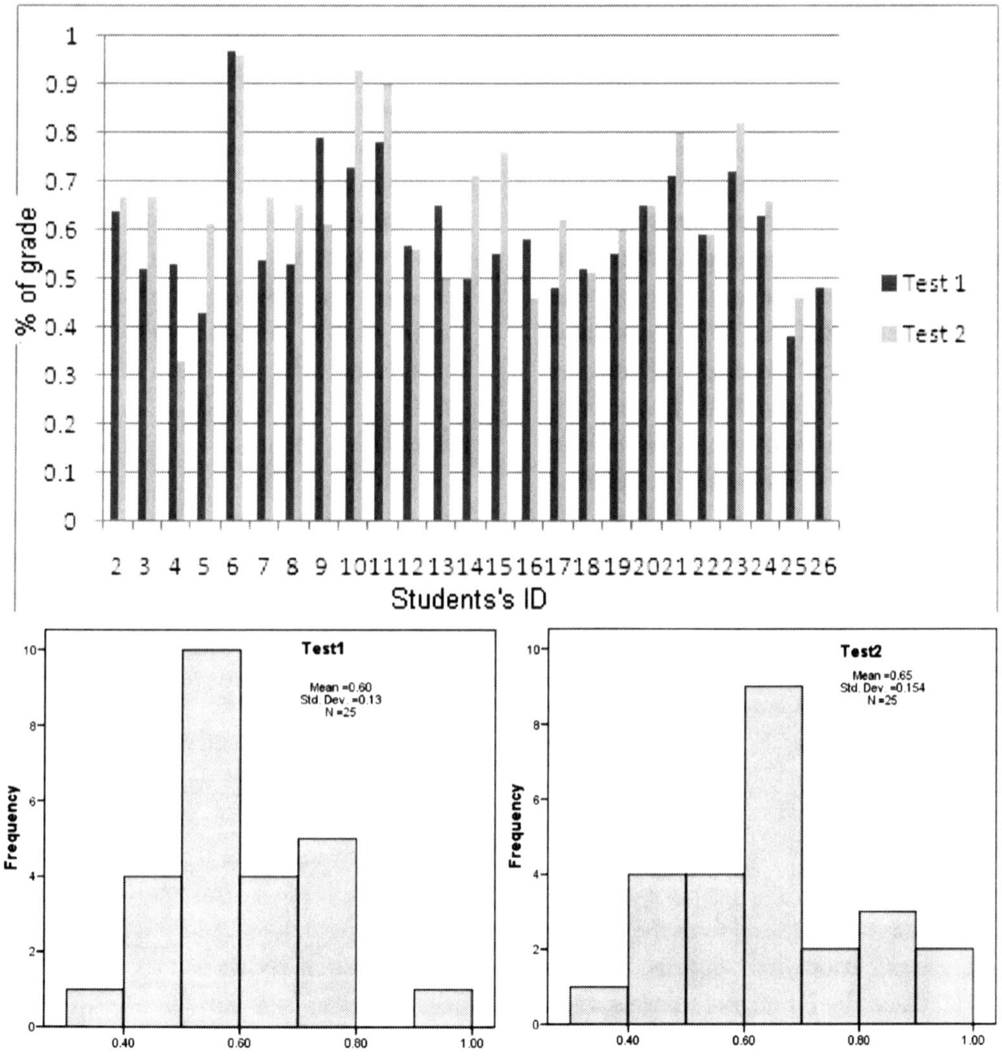

in the Sensitive/Sequential category. Only four students are considered Global. The major online learning impact is visible into four main subsets: Active/Sensitive/Verbal/Sequential and Active/ Sensitive/ Visual/Global with a negative effect while Active/Intuitive/Visual/Sequential and Passive/Intuitive/Visual/Sequential presents a positive stimulation into the final grades. According to class 8B (see Appendix E), the strongest positive outliers due to technological factors inclusion was an Active/Intuitive/Verbal/Sequential (from 73% to 93%) and Active/Intuitive/Visual/Sequential (from 72% to 82%) learners.

In a more in depth view, Appendix C illustrates that the eight best grades (class 8a) do not hold a specific rule concerning their own features whilst the last eight worst are all Sequential and predominantly Sensitive/Visual. Peculiarly, 50% of the lowest marks worsen with the introduction of digital contents, leading to the conclusion that weak learners require a close supervision of a tutor. The introduction of Internet based training only improved four results of the eight top students. Still, in a global context, it can be stated that the introduction of an e-Learning platform plus teacher tutoring helps on the achieving of better marks for 70% (class 8a) and 72% (class 8b) of the students. The overall average rate for class 8a and class 8b was 7% and 12%, respectively. For class 8a, the major four grades suffered an increase from 10% to 12% (Passive/Sequential) while class 8b reports an increase between 18% and 21% (Sequential). Another inner association between both classes can also be found: the lowest grades are predominantly Sequential/Visual/Sensitive students, average students are mainly Sequential while the best students do not show any Visual/Verbal pattern.

6. CONCLUSION

Several key issues can be raised from the Internet impact on general education such as: (a) Can teachers be replaced by intelligent machines? (b) How to handle inbuilt resistance and skepticism among faculty and institutions to virtual learning environments? (c) By giving teachers the opportunity to construct their own meaning from online sessions, does this mean less power to them? (d) What kinds of materials are well suited for Web teaching? (e) Can virtual learning always increase success rates? (f) How to score automatically student´s essays? (g) What are the differences of digital contents author's copyrights facing the traditional one? (h) How to discourage plagiarism among students? (i) If the Active learner prefers high instructor presence as the Passive style favors low instructor attendance then how to handle this issue in a practical way?

It is quite hard to judge all these education themes raised by the advent of the Internet but it is even harder to take physical laws for human matters. From this study, besides the hints given in the previous section, the best three added rules that can be taken from this research are: (a) Lower grading students achieve the same or better overall results in the presence of Web based learning, no matter what kind of student style is it; (b) Proportionally, the grades of the Memory subsection are, in general, greater than the Reasoning one. Unexpectedly (or not), the grades in the Memory subsection preserve or decrease, in general, with the inclusion of virtual environments. In reverse, both classes stress improvements on the Reasoning subsection with Internet access resources. (c) It can be stated that there is a direct relationship of the partial grades between the Reasoning and the Memory sections for any type of scholars.

ACKNOWLEDGMENT

The authors would like to express our gratitude to all the students of the 8th grade of EPM (Escola Portuguesa de Macau) for following all our instructions and participating in this study by using all the provided materials and answering the former questionnaires and quizzes necessary to pursue this research. To all of them, thank you very much. As well, the present authors would like to offer our sincerest gratitude to FDCT (The Science and Technology Development Fund) of Macao, China, for supporting this research through the project number 060/2010/A.

REFERENCES

Anderson, L. (2004). *E-learning at Augsburg college*. Retrieved April 2011 from http://www.augsburg.edu/eteam/report.pdf

Becta. (2008). *Harnessing technology: Next generation learning 2008-14: A summary*. Retrieved April 2011 from http://www.becta.org.uk

Brown, J., & Adler, R. (2008). *Minds of fire: Open education, the long tail and learning 2.0*. Retrieved May 2011 from http://net.educause.edu/ir/library/pdf/ ERM0811.pdf

Churchill, D. (2009). Educational applications of web 2.0: Using blogs to support teaching and learning. *British Journal of Educational Technology*, *40*(1), 179–183. doi:10.1111/j.1467-8535.2008.00865.x.

Dawley, H. (2007). *Coming at you and real soon, web 3.0*. Retrieved January 2011 from http://www.medialifemagazine.com/artman2/publish/New_media_23/Coming_at_you_and_real_soon_Web_3_0.asp

Ellison, L. (1999). *The internet changes everything and the CEO of Oracle is living proof*. Retrieved June 2011 from http://money.cnn.com/magazines/fortune/fortune_archive/1999/05/24/260276/index.htm

Felder, R. (1993). Reaching the second tier: learning and teaching styles in college science education. *Journal of College Science Teaching*, *23*(5), 286–290.

Felder, R., & Soloman, B. (2011). *Learning styles and strategies*. Retrieved February 2011 from http://csu.edu/unity/lockers/users/f/felder/public/ILSdir/styles.htm

Healey, J., & Prus, S. (2009). *Statistics: A tool for social research* (First Canadian Edition). Cengage Learning.

Laster, J. (2010). Seton Hill to offer iPads to full-time students. *The Chronic of Higher Education*. Retrieved February 2012 from chronicle.com/blogs/wiredcampus/seton-hill-to-offer-ipads-to-full-time-students/22153

Miller, M. (2012). *East Stroudsburg University suspends professor for Facebook posts*. Retrieved February 2012 from chronicle.com/blogs/wiredcampus/east-stroudsburg-u-suspends-professor-for-facebook-posts/21498

Moore, M., & Kearsley, G. (2005). *Distance education: A systems view* (2nd ed.). Belmont, CA: Wadsworth Publishing Company.

Rosen, A. (2006). *Technology trends: E-learning 2.0 learning solutions*. Retrieved March 2011 from http://www.readygo.com/e-learning-2.0.pdf

Santos, A. (2010). *Robust and adaptable platforms of dynamic educational environment content: Contribution to the Portuguese education success in the secondary level*. (Unpublished master dissertation). Open University, Aviero, Portugal.

Spivack, N. (2007). *How the WebOS evolves?* Retrieved February 2011 from http://novaspivack.typepad.com/ nova_spivacks_Weblog/2007/02/steps_towards_a.html

Tamashiro, R. (2002). *Pros and cons of online learning: Conflicting perceptions among teacher education students*. Retrieved January 2011 from http://www.hiceducation.org/edu_proceedings/Roy Tamashiro.pdf

Young, J. (2012). *College 2.0: Teachers without technologies strikes back*. Retrieved February 2012 from chronicle.com/article/College-20-Teachers-Without/123891/

KEY TERMS AND DEFINITIONS

E-Learning: Is the learning process created by interaction with digitally delivered content, services and support. This includes On-Demand e-learning, Live On-Line e-learning,-Learning Objects, On-Line Coaching, Knowledge Bases, Simulation Based Learning and Blended Learning.

Learning Styles: Are various approaches or ways of learning. They involve educating methods, particular to an individual that are presumed to allow that individual to learn best. Everyone has a mix of learning styles and there is no right mix. As expected, anyone can develop ability in less dominant styles, as well as further develop styles that you already use well.

Moodle: Is a Course Management System (CMS), also known as a Learning Management System (LMS), or a Virtual Learning Environment (VLE). It is a free Web application that educators can use to create effective online learning sites.

Qualitative Research: Is a method of inquiry employed in many different academic disciplines, particularly in the social sciences. In the conventional view, qualitative methods produce information only on the particular cases studied while general conclusions are only propositions (informed assertions).

Quantitative Research: Refers to the systematic empirical investigation of social phenomena via statistical: mathematical or computational techniques. The objective of quantitative research is to develop and employ mathematical models, theories and/or hypotheses pertaining to phenomena. The process of measurement is central to quantitative research because it provides the fundamental connection between empirical observation and mathematical expression of quantitative relationships.

The Index of Learning Styles: Is an on-line instrument used to assess preferences on four dimensions (active/reflective, sensing/intuitive, visual/verbal, and sequential/ global) of a learning style model formulated by Richard M. Felder and Linda K. Silverman.

Web 2.0: Is the term given to describe a second generation of the WWW that is focused on the ability for people to collaborate and share information online. It refers to the transition from static HTML Web pages to a more dynamic Web and based on Web applications to users. Other improved functionality of Web 2.0 includes open communication with an emphasis on Web-based communities of users and more open sharing of information.

APPENDIX A

Table 4. Quiz results of the Portuguese language subject according to the learning styles (8th Grade, Class A, 24 Students)

Learning Style (ILS)		Quiz 1: Traditional Learning (Final grade interval – Number and % of students)	Quiz 2: Technological Learning (Final grade interval – Number and % of students)
Active	10 students (41.7%)	20-49(%) - 2 students = 20%	20-49(%) - 2 students = 20%
		50-55(%) - 1 student = 10%	50-55(%) - 2 students = 20%
		56-74(%) - 4 students = 40%	56-74(%) - 3 students = 30%
		75-89(%) - 3 students = 30%	75-89(%) - 3 students = 30%
		90-100(%) - 0 students = 0%	90-100(%) - 0 students = 0%
Passive	14 students (58.3%)	20-49(%) - 6 students = 42.8%	20-49(%) - 4 students = 28.6%
		50-55(%) - 2 students = 14.2%	50-55(%) - 6 students = 42.8%
		56-74(%) - 4 students = 28.6%	56-74(%) - 1 students = 7.1%
		75-89(%) - 2 students = 14.2%	75-89(%) - 3 students = 21.4%
		90-100(%) - 0 students = 0%	90-100(%)- 0 students =0%
Sensitive	17 students (70.9%)	20-49(%) - 7 students = 41.2%	20-49(%) - 6 students = 35.2%
		50-55(%) - 2 students = 11.6%	50-55(%) - 6 students = 35.2%
		56-74(%) - 5 students = 29.4%	56-74(%) - 1 students = 5.8%
		75-89(%) - 3 students = 17.6%	75-89(%) - 4 students = 23.5%
		90-100(%) - 0 students = 0%	90-100(%) - 0 students = 0%
Intuitive	7 students (29.1%)	20-49(%) - 1 student = 14.3%	20-49(%) - 0 students = 0%
		50-55(%) - 1 students = 14.3%	50-55(%) - 2 students = 28.6%
		56-74(%) - 3 students = 42.9%	56-74(%) - 3 students =42.9%
		75-89(%) - 2 students = 28.6%	75-89(%) - 2 students = 28.6%
		90-100(%) - 0 students = 0%	90-100(%) - 0 students = 0%
Visual	15 students (62.5%)	20-49(%) - 6 students = 40%	20-49(%) - 4 students = 26.6%
		50-55(%) - 0 students = 0%	50-55(%) - 5 students = 33.3%
		56-74(%) - 6 students = 40%	56-74(%) - 3 students = 20%
		75-89(%) - 3 students = 20%	75-89(%) - 3 students = 20%
		90-100(%) - 0 students = 0%	90-100(%) - 0 students = 0%
Verbal	9 students (37.5%)	20-49(%) - 2 students = 22.2%	20-49(%) - 2 students = 22.2%
		50-55(%) - 3 students = 33.3%	50-55(%) - 3 students = 33.3%
		56-74(%) - 2 students = 22.2%	56-74(%) - 1 students =11.1%
		75-89(%) - 2 students = 22.2%	75-89(%) - 3 students = 33.3%
		90-100(%) - 0 students = 0%	90-100(%) - 0 students = 0%
Sequential	20 students (83.3%)	20-49(%) - 8 students = 40%	20-49(%) - 6 students = 30%
		50-55(%) - 3 students = 15%	50-55(%) - 7 students = 35%
		56-74(%) - 6 students = 30%	56-74(%) - 3 students = 15%
		75-89(%) - 3 students = 15%	75-89(%) - 4 students = 20%
		90-100(%) - 0 students = 0%	90-100(%) - 0 students = 0%

continued on following page

Table 4. Continued

Learning Style (ILS)		Quiz 1: Traditional Learning (Final grade interval – Number and % of students)	Quiz 2: Technological Learning (Final grade interval – Number and % of students)
Global	4 students (16.7%)	20-49(%) - 0 students = 0%	20-49(%) - 0 students = 0%
		50-55(%) - 0 students = 0%	50-55(%) - 1 students = 25%
		56-74(%) - 2 students = 50%	56-74(%) - 1 students = 25%
		75-89(%) - 2 students = 50%	75-89(%) - 2 students = 50%
		90-100(%) - 0 students = 0%	90-100(%) - 0 students = 0%

APPENDIX B

Table 5. Quiz results of the Portuguese language subject according to the student's type (8th Grade, Class A, 24 Students)

Type of Student		Quiz 1: Traditional Learning			Quiz 2: Technological Learning		
		Reasoning (80%)	Memory Capability (20%)	Total (100%)	Reasoning (80%)	Memory Capability (20%)	Total (100%)
Passive	8 Students =33.3%	38.8%	14.9%	53.7%	40.8%	11.5%	52.3%
Sensitive	ID Student: 1.4.5.6.7.9.18.24						
Visual							
Sequential							
Passive	3 Students =12.5%	39.5%	14.8%	54.3%	40.8%	12.6%	53.4%
Sensitive	ID Student: 14.16.22						
Verbal							
Sequential							
Active	3 Students =12.5%	57.7%	17.3%	75%	45.6%	14%	59.6%
Sensitive	ID Student: 8.11.21						
Verbal							
Sequential							
Active	2 Students =8.3%	54%	16.5%	70.5%	61.2%	15.5%	76.7%
Intuitive	ID Student: 13.20						
Visual							
Global							
Active	2 Students =8.3%	58%	17%	75%	60.7%	15.7%	76.4%
Intuitive	ID Student: 2.15						
Verbal							
Sequential							

continued on following page

Table 5. Continued

Type of Student		Quiz 1: Traditional Learning			Quiz 2: Technological Learning		
		Reasoning (80%)	Memory Capability (20%)	Total (100%)	Reasoning (80%)	Memory Capability (20%)	Total (100%)
Active	1 Student =4.2%	41.5%	15.5%	57%	46.5%	17.3%	64%
Intuitive	ID Student: 10						
Visual							
Sequential							
Active	1 Students =4.2%	29%	13%	42%	31%	13.6%	45%
Sensitive	ID Student: 12						
Visual							
Sequential							
Passive	1 Students =4.2%	27.5%	12.5%	40%	38.5%	12%	51%
Intuitive	ID Student: 17						
Visual							
Sequential							
Passive	1 Students =4.2%	63.5%	16.5%	80%	59.5%	18.2%	78%
Sensitive	ID Student: 23						
Visual							
Global							
Passive	1 Students =4.2%	35%	15%	50%	38%	12.8%	51%
Intuitive	ID Student: 19						
Verbal							
Sequential							
Active	1 Students =4.2%	56%	17%	73%	42%	12%	54%
Sensitive	ID Student: 3						
Visual							
Global							

APPENDIX C

Table 6. Quiz results of the Portuguese language subject according to each student (8th Grade, Class A, 24 Students)

Student ID	ILS	Quiz 1: Traditional Learning	Quiz 2: Technological Learning
1	Passive/Sensitive/Visual/ Sequential	Reasoning (41.5%) + Memory (15.5%) = 57%	Reasoning (37.5%) + Memory (13.5%) = 51%
2	Active/ Intuitive / Verbal/ Sequential	Reasoning (48.5%) + Memory (16.5%) = 65%	Reasoning (50.5%) + Memory (13.5%) = 64%
3	Active/Sensitive/Visual/ global	Reasoning (56%) + Memory (17%) = 73%	Reasoning (42%) + Memory (12%) = 54%
4	Passive/Sensitive/Visual/ Sequential	Reasoning (28.5%) + Memory (14.5%) = 43%	Reasoning (46%) + Memory (9%) = 55%
5	Passive/Sensitive/Visual/ Sequential	Reasoning (30%) + Memory (15%) = 45%	Reasoning (28%) + Memory (8%) = 36%
6	Passive/Sensitive/Visual/ Sequential	Reasoning (70.5%) + Memory (18.5%) = 89%	Reasoning (63%) + Memory (18%) = 81%
7	Passive/Sensitive/Visual/ Sequential	Reasoning (47%) + Memory (13%) = 60%	Reasoning (40%) + Memory (12%) = 52%
8	Active/Sensitive/Verbal/ Sequential	Reasoning (34%) + Memory (17%) = 51%	Reasoning (35.5%) + Memory (14.5%) = 50%
9	Passive/Sensitive/Visual/ Sequential	Reasoning (22.5%) + Memory (14.5%) = 37%	Reasoning (34.5%) + Memory (12%) = 47%
10	Active/Intuitive/Visual/ Sequential	Reasoning (41.5%) + Memory (15.5%) = 57%	Reasoning (46.5%) + Memory (17.3%) = 64%
11	Active/Sensitive/Verbal/ Sequential	Reasoning (71.5%) + Memory (17.5%) = 89%	Reasoning (72%) + Memory (17%) = 89%
12	Active/Sensitive/Visual/ Sequential	Reasoning (29%) + Memory (13%) = 42%	Reasoning (31%) + Memory (13.6%) = 45%
13	Active/Intuitive/Visual/ Global	Reasoning (44%) + Memory (16%) = 60%	Reasoning (54%) + Memory (13.5%) = 68%
14	Passive/Sensitive/Verbal/ Sequential	Reasoning (32.5%) + Memory (13.5%) = 46%	Reasoning (23.5%) + Memory (9.5%) = 32%
15	Active/ Intuitive /Verbal/ Sequential	Reasoning (67.5%) + Memory (17.5%) = 85%	Reasoning (71%) + Memory (18%) = 89%
16	Passive/Sensitive/Verbal/ Sequential	Reasoning (37.5%) + Memory (14.5%) = 52%	Reasoning (39.5%) + Memory (12.8%) = 52%
17	Passive/Intuitive/Visual/ Sequential	Reasoning (27.5%) + Memory (12.5%) = 40%	Reasoning (38.5%) + Memory (12%) = 51%
18	Passive/Sensitive/Visual/ Sequential	Reasoning (45.5%) + Memory (13.5%) = 59%	Reasoning (49%) + Memory (13%) = 62%
19	Passive/Intuitive/Verbal/ Sequential	Reasoning (35%) + Memory (15%) = 50%	Reasoning (38%) + Memory (12.8%) = 51%
20	Active /Intuitive/Visual/ Global	Reasoning (64%) + Memory (17%) = 81%	Reasoning (68.5%) + Memory (17.5%) = 86%
21	Active/Sensitive /Verbal/ Sequential	Reasoning(27.5%)+Memory (12.5%) = 40%	Reasoning (29.5%) + Memory (10.5%) = 40%
22	Passive/Sensitive/Verbal/Sequential	Reasoning (48.5%) + Memory (16.5%) = 65%	Reasoning (59.5%) + Memory (15.5%) = 75%
23	Passive/Sensitive /Visual/ Global	Reasoning (63.5%) + Memory (16.5%) = 80%	Reasoning (59.5%) + Memory (18.2%) = 78%
24	Passive/Sensitive/Visual/ Sequential	Reasoning (25%) + Memory (15%) = 40%	Reasoning (29%) + Memory (7%) = 36%

APPENDIX D

Table 7. Quiz results of the Portuguese language subject according to the learning styles (8th Grade, Class A, 24 Students)

Learning Style (ILS)		Quiz 1: Traditional Learning (Final grade interval – Number and % of students)	Quiz 2: Technological Learning (Final grade interval – Number and % of students)
Active	6 students (24%)	20-49(%) - 0 students = 0%	20-49(%) - 2 students = 33.3%
		50-55(%) - 2 students = 33.3%	50-55(%) - 0 students = 0%
		56-74(%) - 4 students = 66.6%	56-74(%) - 1 students = 16.6%
		75-89(%) - 0 students = 0%	75-89(%) - 2 students = 33.3%
		90-100(%) - 0 students = 0%	90-100(%) - 1 students = 16.6%
Passive	19 students (76%)	20-49(%) - 4 students = 21%	20-49(%) - 2 students = 10.5%
		50-55(%) - 6 students = 31.6%	50-55(%) - 2 students = 10.5%
		56-74(%) - 6 students = 31.6%	56-74(%) - 13 students = 68.4%
		75-89(%) - 2 students = 10.5%	75-89(%) - 1 students = 5.3%
		90-100(%) - 1 student = 5.7%	90-100(%) - 1 student = 5.3%
Sensitive	18 students (72%)	20-49(%) - 3 students = 16.7%	20-49(%) - 4 students = 22.2%
		50-55(%) - 7 students = 38.9%	50-55(%) - 1 students = 5.6%
		56-74(%) - 6 students = 33.3%	56-74(%) - 10 students = 55.5%
		75-89(%) - 2 students = 11.1%	75-89(%) - 2 students = 11.1%
		90-100(%) - 0 students = 0%	90-100(%) - 1 students = 5.6%
Intuitive	7 students (28%)	20-49(%) - 1 student = 14.3%	20-49(%) - 0 students = 0%
		50-55(%) - 1 students = 14.3%	50-55(%) - 1 students = 14.3%
		56-74(%) - 4 students = 57.1%	56-74(%) - 3 students = 42.8%
		75-89(%) - 0 students = 0%	75-89(%) - 1 students = 14.3%
		90-100(%) - 1 student = 14.3%	90-100(%) - 2 students = 28.6%
Visual	16 students (64%)	20-49(%) - 2 students = 12.5%	20-49(%) - 4 students = 25%
		50-55(%) - 7 students = 43.7%	50-55(%) - 1 students = 6.3%
		56-74(%) - 6 students = 37.5%	56-74(%) - 8 students = 50%
		75-89(%) - 1 students = 6.3%	75-89(%) - 3 students = 18.7%
		90-100(%) - 0 students = 0%	90-100(%) - 0 students = 0%
Verbal	9 students (36%)	20-49(%) - 2 students = 22.2%	20-49(%) - 0 students = 0%
		50-55(%) - 1 student = 11.1%	50-55(%) - 1 student = 11.1%
		56-74(%) - 4 students = 44.4%	56-74(%) - 5 students = 55.6%
		75-89(%) - 1 student = 11.1%	75-89(%) - 0 students = 0%
		90-100(%) - 1 student = 11.1%	90-100(%) – 3 students = 33.3%
Sequential	23 students (92%)	20-49(%) - 4 students = 17.4%	20-49(%) - 4 students = 17.4%
		50-55(%) - 8 students = 34.8%	50-55(%) - 1 students = 4.3%
		56-74(%) - 8 students = 34.8%	56-74(%) - 12 students = 52.2%
		75-89(%) - 2 students = 8.6%	75-89(%) - 3 students = 13.05%
		90-100(%) - 1 student = 4.3%	90-100(%) - 3 students = 13.05%

continued on following page

Table 7. Continued

Learning Style (ILS)		Quiz 1: Traditional Learning (Final grade interval – Number and % of students)	Quiz 2: Technological Learning (Final grade interval – Number and % of students)
Global	2 students (8%)	20-49(%) - 0 students = 0%	20-49(%) - 0 students = 0%
		50-55(%) - 1 student = 50%	50-55(%) - 1 student = 50%
		56-74(%) - 1 student = 50%	56-74(%) - 1 student = 50%
		75-89(%) - 0 students = 0%	75-89(%) - 0 students = 0%
		90-100(%) - 0 students = 0%	90-100(%) - 0 students = 0%

APPENDIX E

Table 8. Quiz results of the Portuguese language subject according to the student's type (8th Grade, Class A, 24 Students)

Type of Student		Quiz 1: Traditional Learning			Quiz 2: Technological Learning		
		Reasoning (80%)	Memory Capability (20%)	Total (100%)	Reasoning (80%)	Memory Capability (20%)	Total (100%)
Passive Sensitive Visual Sequential	9 students=36% ID Student: 3.7.9.14.19.21.22.25.26	41.6%	15.7%	57.3%	47.8%	14.2%	62%
Passive Sensitive Verbal Sequential	4 students=16% ID Student: 5.8.11.13	43.8%	16%	54.8%	50.5%	15.8%	63.3%
Active Sensitive Visual Sequential	4 students=16% ID Student: 4.12.15.16	43.8%	16%	59.8%	40.5%	12.7%	53.2%
Passive Intuitive Verbal Sequential	3 students=12% ID Student: 6.17.24	54.5%	18%	72.5%	60%	14.6%	74.6%
Passive Sensitive Verbal Global	1 student=4% ID Student: 2	48%	16%	64%	52%	15%	67%

continued on following page

Table 8. Continued

Type of Student		Quiz 1: Traditional Learning			Quiz 2: Technological Learning		
		Reasoning (80%)	**Memory Capability (20%)**	**Total (100%)**	**Reasoning (80%)**	**Memory Capability (20%)**	**Total (100%)**
Passive Intuitive Visual Global	1 student=4% ID Student: 18	37%	15%	52%	37%	14%	51%
Passive Intuitive Visual Sequential	1 student= 4% ID Student: 20	50%	15%	65%	55%	10%	65%
Active Intuitive Visual Sequential	1 student=4% ID Student: 23	56%	16%	72%	64%	18%	82%
Active Intuitive Verbal Sequential	1 student=4% ID Student: 10	54%	19%	73%	74%	19%	93%

APPENDIX F

Table 9. Quiz results of the Portuguese language subject according to each student (8th Grade, Class A, 24 Students)

Student ID	ILS	Quiz 1: Traditional Learning	Quiz 2: Technological Learning
2	passive/sensitive/verbal/global	reasoning (48%) + memory (16%)	reasoning (52%) + memory (15%)
		Total = **64%**	Total = **67%**
3	passive/sensitive/visual/sequential	reasoning (35%) + memory (17%)	reasoning (50%) + memory (17%)
		Total = **52%**	Total = **67%**
4	activo/sensitive/visual/sequential	reasoning (38%) + memory (15%)	reasoning (24%) + memory (9%)
		Total = **53%**	Total = **33%**
5	passive/sensitive/verbal/sequential	reasoning (27%) + memory (16%)	reasoning (45%) + memory (16%)
		Total = **43%**	Total = **61%**
6	passive/intuitive/verbal/sequential	reasoning (77%) + memory (20%)	reasoning (78%) + memory (18%)
		Total = **97%**	Total = **96%**
7	passive/sensitive/visual/sequential	reasoning (48%) + memory (16%)	reasoning (53%) + memory (14%)
		Total = **54%**	Total = **67%**
8	passive/sensitive/verbal/sequential	reasoning (37%) + memory (16%)	reasoning (49%) + memory (16%)
		Total = **53%**	Total = **65%**
9	passive/sensitive/visual/sequential	reasoning (62%) + memory (17%)	reasoning (47%) + memory (14%)
		Total = **79%**	Total = **61%**
10	activo/ intuitive/ verbal/ sequential	reasoning (54%) + memory (19%)	reasoning (74%) + memory (19%)
		Total = **73%**	Total = **93%**
11	passive/sensitive/verbal/sequential	reasoning (62%) + memory (16%)	reasoning (72%) + memory (18%)
		Total = **78%**	Total = **90%**
12	activo/sensitive/visual/sequential	reasoning (41%) + memory (16%)	reasoning (45%) + memory (13%)
		Total = **57%**	Total = **56%**
13	passive/sensitive/verbal/sequential	reasoning (49%) + memory (16%)	reasoning (37%) + memory (13%)
		Total = **65%**	Total = **50%**
14	passive/sensitive/visual/sequential	reasoning (34%) + memory (16%)	reasoning (56%) + memory (15%)
		Total = **50%**	Total = **71%**
15	activo/sensitive/visual/sequential	reasoning (41%) + memory (14%)	reasoning (60%) + memory (16%)
		Total = **55%**	Total = **76%**
16	activo/sensitive/visual/sequential	reasoning (41%) + memory (17%)	reasoning (33%) + memory (13%)
		Total = **58%**	Total = **46%**
17	passive/intuitive/verbal/sequential	reasoning (32%) + memory (16%)	reasoning (49%) + memory (13%)
		Total = **48%**	Total = **62%**
18	passive/intuitive/visual/global	reasoning (37%) + memory (15%)	reasoning (37%) + memory (14%)
		Total = **52%**	Total = **51%**

continued on following page

Table 9. Continued

Student ID	ILS	Quiz 1: Traditional Learning	Quiz 2: Technological Learning
19	passive/sensitive/visual/sequential	reasoning (40%) + memory (15%)	reasoning (45%) + memory (15%)
		Total = **55%**	Total = **60%**
20	passive/intuitive/visual/sequential	reasoning (50%) + memory (15%)	reasoning (55%) + memory (10%)
		Total = **65%**	Total = **65%**
21	passive/sensitive/visual/sequential	reasoning (56%) + memory (15%)	reasoning (62%) + memory (18%)
		Total = **71%**	Total = **80%**
22	passive/sensitive/visual/sequential	reasoning (44%) + memory (15%)	reasoning (49%) + memory (10%)
		Total = **59%**	Total = **59%**
23	activo/intuitive/visual/sequential	reasoning (56%) + memory (16%)	reasoning (64%) + memory (18%)
		Total = **72%**	Total = **82%**
24	passive/intuitive/verbal/sequential	reasoning (46%) + memory (17%)	reasoning (53%) + memory (13%)
		Total = **63%**	Total = **66%**
25	passive/sensitive/visual/sequential	reasoning (23%) + memory (15%)	reasoning (32%) + memory (14%)
		Total = **38%**	Total = **46%**
26	passive/sensitive/visual/sequential	reasoning (33%) + memory (15%)	reasoning (37%) + memory (11%)
		Total = **48%**	Total = **48%**

Chapter 24
Visibility of the Airport Sector: Web 2.0 and Social Communication Networks

Arturo Haro de Rosario
University of Almería, Spain

Carmen Caba Pérez
University of Almería, Spain

María del Mar Sánchez Cañadas
University of Almería, Spain

ABSTRACT

The aim of this chapter is to analyse the use of social communication media and Web 2.0 tools at airports to determine whether these technologies are being used as a means of raising the airports' visibility, enhancing their level of e-participation and improving corporate dialogue. In addition, the authors seek to determine which variables influence the use and development of these tools. The results obtained reveal a moderate use of Web 2.0 tools by airports, with the most noteworthy finding being their presence in social networks and the use of the latter as channels through which to increase e-participation.

INTRODUCTION

In recent years, advances in Information and Communication Technologies (ICTs) have brought about a transformation of society that has affected companies' organisation and management (Bonsón, Escobar, and Flores, 2006; Serrano, Fuertes, and Gutiérrez, 2007). Thus, applications based on Web 2.0 are changing relationships between society and business. This situation means that customers are making increasing use of the Internet as a tool to express their experiences with organisations, and that potential consumers make purchasing decisions, for products or services, on the basis of the information found on the Internet.

In this sense, let us refer to the phenomenon of transparency, which is gaining increasing importance in society due to the constantly increas-

DOI: 10.4018/978-1-4666-4373-4.ch024

ing demand for information. Numerous studies have shown that information is ever more highly valued within the community (Oyelere, Laswad and Fisher, 2003; Petersen and Plenborg, 2006; Birt et al., 2006; Lim, Matolcsy and Chow, 2007). The transparency of an organization depends on the degree or extent to which it explains itself to its stakeholders, and so the two phenomena, the development of new technologies and that of transparency, are closely linked today. Let us also refer to a concept that is rising fast in public view, namely e-participation. Generically, this includes the processes that facilitate and enhance the direct involvement in decision-making and in the generation of alternatives by those affected by such decisions, through the use of participatory channels based on ICTs, such as Web 2.0 or social networks.

As an evolution of Web 1.0, O'Reilly (2005) coined the concept of Web 2.0, based on the use of new technologies such as RSS channels, podcasting, mashups (combining existing applications), folksonomies (social indexing), widgets (mini Web applications) and resource-sharing environments (to store and share data online). And it is on this technological base that the social media have been developed, these being applications that offer services to online user communities, such as blogs, social bookmarking, wikis, multimedia sharing applications or social networks. All of these instruments facilitate collaboration, joint learning and the rapid exchange of information among users.

Any organisation can greatly improve its corporate Website by incorporating Web 2.0 services and technologies (Jiang, Raghupathi and Raghupathi, 2009), thus creating relationships with stakeholders who, with traditional means of communication, had previously been inaccessible or invisible (Hearn, Foth and Gray, 2009).

In this respect, the term "Enterprise 2.0" was introduced by McAfee in 2006, such term referring to the use of Web 2.0 applications in a business context. Enterprise 2.0 illustrates how a correct implementation of Web 2.0 and its tools not only aids the socialisation among organizations but also improves the resolution of problems, the leveraging of experience, the generation of ideas and the knowledge of the public opinion (McAfee, 2009).

Along the same line, Mackeviciute y Iacubiţchi (2010) suggest that Enterprise has a direct impact to key aspects such as communication, collaboration, cooperation and innovation activities. Likewise, diverse authors argue for the benefits of Web 2.0 in all types of business (Benkler, 2006; Bonsón, Escobar y Flores, 2008; Constanzo, 2009; Hwang, Altman, y Kim, 2009; IDC, 2008; Kupp y Anderson, 2007). Due to the enormous use of the Web 2.0 tools, the formulation of metrics to determine the impact of such tools and level of use has been initiated (Herget and Mader, 2009).

As a result of these changes, the Internet is no longer just another channel of communication, but has become a key factor for companies that pursue a higher degree of transparency and accountability; it enables information of all kinds to be offered as soon as the user requests it (Larrán and Giner, 2002), and at the same time facilitates interaction via different mechanisms of participation. However, although social technologies have generated a high degree of interconnectivity among users, allowing them to exchange all kinds of opinions and experiences (Vazquez, Saldaña and Celaya, 2009) many organizations continue to rely on communication and positioning strategies that ignore the advantages provided by participation in the blogosphere, by Wikipedia, by the publication of podcasts or videos, through Twitter conversations or by creating profiles on social networks like Facebook, MySpace or Xing.

We are thus faced with social change, in which a firm's positioning and its digital reputation on the Internet will play a key role in the knowledge society of the 21st century. Accordingly, the organisations that are most active and innovative in their communication policies will be most likely to triumph. However, we must take into account that the concept of business dialogue and the use of Web 2.0 to promote e-participation are still at an early stage (Bonsón et al., 2011).

Let us now examine the airport sector, in particular. The development of aviation has been accompanied by widespread ignorance of the mechanisms governing the operation of airports, aircraft and airspace. According to Jordá (2008), this situation, combined with the headline-making nature of accidents, the problems of saturation of the major airports (with endemic delays and queues) and noise problems in their vicinity, all lead to society having a very negative view of the sector. The main criticisms aimed at airports concern their large-scale consumption of land, water and energy, the negative impact on biodiversity, problems of waste discharge, the disposal of hazardous substances, and noise and air pollution.

In this context, Web 2.0 offers the airport sector a way to improve its transparency and reputation. Web 2.0 services include new channels of communication, grounded upon freedom of expression, the free flow of information and diversity of opinion. These tools can be used by airports to listen to their customers and potential customers and to exchange information and comments with them. Thus, airports have the means to improve the currently unfavourable opinion held of them by society.

In the airport sector, the recent implementation of Web 2.0 to a number of new terms such as Aviation 2.0, Airlines 2.0, Flight 2.0 or enclosedly Stewardess 2.0 has given rise. As Lambercy (2010) indicates, Web 2.0 gives a new dimension to the word community and, according to the aviation sector; Web 2.0 imply both the development of new platforms as Connectingpilots and social specific networks as myTransponder.

In keeping with this, Serusi (2011) suggests a number of reasons that justify the importance of providing customer service via social networks, not only as an attractive option for customers but also to airlines. Among them there are the elimination of waiting calls, the possibility of having a complaints and suggestions box open to the public, the ability to understand the common customers issues, the rapid supply of information, etc.. In short, the sensitive, interactive and opened nature of the social networks helps customers to feel more comfortable, expressing better their opinions, and also to the improvement of companies in their services and image.

Due to the importance of Web 2.0 in the sector, Aviation Leadership Summit 2010 in Singapore (one of the greater fairs where experiences of industry leaders are exchanged) considered that, to build the system of aviation of the future and also, to maintain the attraction of the industry, Aviation 2.0 is needed.

This paper has the following main objectives: 1) to analyse the use of Web 2.0 tools and social communication media at airports to determine whether these technologies are being used as a means of increasing the level of e-participation and of improving corporate dialogue; and 2) to study the factors accounting for the level of use and development of these tools. As a study sample, we examined the 50 airports rated by passengers as the world's most important, according to a survey carried out in 2010 by Airports Council International.

With these goals in mind, this paper is structured as follows. After this introduction, the following section outlines the tools available in Web 2.0 and social communication media. In the next section, the study per se is presented, and we describe the methodology used, the scope of the study and the results analysis performed. This is followed by possible lines for future research, and a discussion of the main conclusions drawn. Finally, we provide bibliographic references, some recommended reading and the study's key words.

TOOLS USED IN WEB 2.0 AND SOCIAL COMMUNICATION MEDIA

In general, media coverage of Web 2.0 focuses on commonly-used applications and services, such as blogs, video sharing, social networks and podcasting; in short, a more socially connected Web in which people can both contribute and consume (Anderson, 2007). However, a clear distinction should be made between the tools of Web 2.0 and those of social communication media, which are the result of applying Web 2.0 technology in an online social environment.

For Elia, Margherita and Taurino (2009) the paradigm of the evolution of Web 2.0, together with the rise of social networks and virtual communities, provides an opportunity to create "spaces" where people learn together and share their experiences.

Although in technological terms there has been no great breakthrough in the development of Web 2.0 services, since they are mainly based on technologies and open standards that have been in use since Web 1.0, the latter have been improved, and this progress has led to the creation of Web 2.0 (Anderson, 2007). The following Web 2.0 tools are especially important:

- **RSS (Really Simple Syndication):** Used to transmit frequent updates to users who have subscribed to the content source. The format makes it possible to distribute content without a browser, using software designed to read these RSS feeds, although a browser can also be used to view RSS feeds. The latest versions of the major browsers can read RSS without additional software. RSS feeds are part of the family of XML formats which were developed specifically for all types of Websites that are updated frequently. By this means, information can be shared and used on other Websites or programs. This form of information provision is usually known as Web retransmission or syndication.
- **Podcasting:** The distribution of audio files, usually in mp3 format, via a system of RSS syndication by which users can subscribe and use a program that downloads the podcast content for subsequent listening. It is not necessary to be a subscriber to download.
- **Vodcasting:** The concept is similar to that of podcasting, but instead of having only audio it also includes video. Vodcasting, also known as videocasting, applies the concept of blogging to video content. Vodcasting is actually an acronym, where "vod" stands for "video on demand".
- **Widgets:** Small applications or programs, usually presented in small files or folders, which are executed by a widget engine. Intended basically to provide easy access to frequently used functions and to provide visual information. However, widgets are limited only by the designer's imagination, and can interact with all types of information services distributed on the Internet. Thus, they can be colourful on-screen clocks, notepads, calculators, calendars, diaries, games, windows with weather information for your city, etc. Widgets also allow many kinds of interaction with a Website, such as the extension to a business application, providing real-time information on the current status of the business (e.g., continuous updating of stock market prices). A common feature of widgets is that they are distributed free of charge via the Internet.
- **Facilities to Share, Tag and Classify Information:** Applications that allow a user to share information in a Website with other users. Similarly, social bookmarking is used to store, sort and share content through social networks.

- **Mashup:** An application that uses and combines data from one or more sources to create new services. The term implies quick and easy integration, using data sources to produce enriched results that were not the reason for which the original data were created. The main features of a mashup are combination, visualization and aggregation. For an application to be considered a mashup it is imperative that existing data can be transformed into others. The best known examples of mashup applications are those based on the use of Google maps.
- **Data Embedding Systems:** The inclusion of content on a Website created by a third party in order to form a composite content. Often confused with mashups. For example, an application that allows users to embed YouTube videos on a Website is not a mashup, because a mashup must access external information and process these data in order to increase their value to the user.
- **Webcast:** A live Internet transmission, similar to that offered by a television or radio station. Webcast applications allow a user to connect to the server through which the Webcast is distributed. Initially, Webcasts were not interactive, and so the customer only watched the action without being able to change anything, but there are now Webcasts that allow users to interact by sending in comments.

The *Web 2.0 tools* mentioned above are present in almost all social communication media, among which the following are the best known:

- **Blogs:** Regularly updated Websites that chronologically compile texts or articles by one or more authors, the most recent appearing first, where the author retains the freedom to publish whatever he/she sees fit. Typically, in each blog item, readers can add comments and the author can answer them, and so a dialogue may be established. However, this is merely an option, depending entirely on the blogger's decision, because blogs can be designed in which not all Internet users—or perhaps none of them—are allowed to participate by adding comments.
- **Wiki:** A Website whose pages can be edited by multiple users, through the Web browser. Users can create, modify or delete a shared text. Wikis have unique titles, and so if a wiki title is written between double square brackets ([[...]]) in another wiki, this word becomes a link to the wiki page. The most significant and best known application to date is that of collective encyclopaedias, chief among which is Wikipedia. Currently, most wikis keep a record of changes in order to easily return to a previous state and to identify which user makes each change; this greatly facilitates the maintenance of the site and helps counteract malicious users.
- **Media Sharing Platforms:** Based on Web 2.0 applications to share, tag and classify information, these platforms not only enable users to share presentations (Slideshare), photos (Flickr), documents (Docstoc), and videos (YouTube), but also allow them to be rated, ordered and discussed with other users.
- **Social Networks:** Web sites that offer services and communication features enabling users of the network to keep in touch. These networks are based on special software that incorporates many individual features: blogs, wikis, forums, chat, messaging, etc., within a single interface, and which provides connectivity between all the users of the network. Social networking sites typically allow interconnection, so that a user who has one account on Twitter and another on Facebook can connect them; thus, a

message posted on Twitter will also appear on Facebook. Regarding types of social network, they include those for general use or for social purposes, such as Facebook or MySpace, and others for professional use, like LinkedIn or XING, and yet others that are more specific, for example Delicious, a management service for social bookmarking (folksonomy) via the Web.

- **Twitter:** A microblogging platform based on 140-character messages; this is not considered a social network, but as a communication tool. Twitter allows users to send small-sized, plain text messages called tweets, which are shown in the user's home page. Users can subscribe to the tweets of other users (known as following) and subscribers are called "followers." By default, messages are public, but they can also be distributed privately, visible only to followers.

VISIBILITY OF THE AIRPORT SECTOR: EMPIRICAL STUDY

Methodology

Our analysis of the visibility of airports is divided into two phases. Initially, we conducted a descriptive study of the use of Web 2.0 tools and social media by the airports in question. Then, in the second phase, we analysed the factors underlying the greater or lesser development of these technologies in the sector.

For the analysis of airports' use of Web 2.0 applications, we examined the official Website of each airport, in search of the following items: 1) Blogs, 2) Podcasts, 3) Vodcasts, 4) RSS, 5) Widgets, 6) Mashups, 7) Webcasts, 8) Link to the official YouTube channel, 9) Link to the official Twitter account, 10) Link to the official Facebook page. Items are rated on a dichotomous scale: if the item is available, it is scored with a 1, otherwise, with a 0.

In our study of social media, each one was measured in terms of specific different items, such as the number of groups, the number of followers or the number of visits. The communication media analysed were Twitter, Facebook, YouTube and Google blogs (we also reviewed LinkedIn and Flickr, but these are not included in the results because no such use was found). For Twitter, the following items were examined: 1) Existence of an official Twitter account; 2) Number of followers; 3) Number of tweets; 4) Number of lists. In Facebook, we examined: 1) Existence of an official Facebook page; 2) Number of pages-groups of which the airport is a follower; 3) Number of followers; 4) Number of visits; 5) Number of people talking about the airport. In YouTube, we examined the following: 1) Existence of an official channel on YouTube; 2) Number of subscribers; 3) Number of conversations. Finally, in Google Blogs, following the methodology used by Bonsón et al. (2011) for European local authorities, we examined the number of blogs indexed when a search was made for the official name of the airport in Google blogs.

The second stage of the analysis is that of explanation. In order to analyse the influence of independent factors on the development of these technologies at airports, we need first to quantify the level of use of these applications. For this purpose, each airport was classified according to an index of visibility (IV) consisting of the 10 items used previously in analysing the official Website. The IV of each airport was calculated as the ratio of the sum of the items available (scored with a 1) and the total number of items (10). This Web analysis included items related to the presence of the airport on YouTube, Twitter and Facebook, and so the IV is based on both the analysis of the official Website and on the presence of each airport in the most important social communication media.

Table 1. Explanatory factors

Factor	Measurement Parameter	Expected Relation
Size	No. of passengers, annually, in 2010	Positive
Turnover (T/OVER)	Turnover in Euros, in 2010	Positive
Age	No. of years' functioning	Positive
Debt	Ratio: External debt / Total debt (2010)	Positive
Internet penetration (INT/P)	Level of Internet penetration in the country where the airport is located (www.internetworldstats.com)	Positive
Social network penetration (SNT/P)	Level of social network penetration in the country where the airport is located (http://globalwebindex.net/)	Positive

Having defined the dependent variable (IV), taking into account prior research on transparency, visibility, Websites and social networks (Bertot, Jaeger and Grimes, 2010; Bonsón, Escobar and Martin, 2002; Bonsón and Flores, 2011; Celaya et al., 2009; Ettredge, Richardson and Scholz, 2001 and 2002; Oyelere, Laswad and Fisher, 2003), we selected the factors that may promote the development of Web 2.0 tools and social communication media at airports. These were tested using a multiple regression model. The explanatory factors considered are summarised in Table 1, showing the units of measurement used and the expected relationships with the IV.

Scope of the Study

The study sample comprised the 50 airports rated most important in the world, according to passengers, in the 2010 Airports Council International (ACI) survey. The ACI was founded in 1991 by global airport operators as the first global partnership to represent their common interests and to promote cooperation in the air transport industry.

Table 2. Geographical distribution

Continent	%
America	42%
Europe	20%
Asia	32%
Oceania	6%
Africa	0%

The data used for our empirical analysis are drawn from the annual report for 2010 on the corporate Website of each airport.

With respect to the geographical regions of the airports examined, we note that nearly 75% are in America or Asia (Table 2).

Regarding the age of these airports, on average they have been operating for 59.14 years since their inauguration. However, the data contain a standard deviation of 22.99 years. This high dispersion is due to the fact that the sample is composed of airports of widely varying ages, ranging from the early twentieth century to the turn of the millennium (see Table 3).

Analysis of the Results

As shown in Table 4, the airports make a moderate use of *Web 2.0 tools* and social communication

Table 3. Age distribution

AGE (Years)	%
0 - 10	0.00%
10 - 20	13.89%
20 - 30	0.00%
30 - 40	8.33%
40 - 50	11.11%
50 - 60	5.56%
60 - 70	27.78%
70 - 80	11.11%
80 - 90	22.22%
90 - 100	0.00%

platforms. Just over half of the Webs analysed contain widgets and mashups, making these the most commonly used tools. In second place come RSS feeds and vodcasts, which are used by 26% of the sample. Let us also note that only 8 airports use podcasts, while none have a blog or any system for live transmissions via the Internet. This situation has a negative impact on the *visibility* result, since 2 of the 10 items examined are not used by any of the airports, and a third, by very few. Finally, note that no more than 7 items are used by any single airport, and that 16% of the airports do not use any.

Of the social communication media, Twitter is most commonly used by the airports (56%) followed closely by Facebook, with half of the sample also having an official page on this social network. Thirdly, 30% have an official channel on YouTube in which users have access to all videos posted by the airport, and can publish comments on them. As stated in the Methodology section, we also searched for other platforms such as LinkedIn, Flickr and any other that might have a link on the airport's Website, but none were found.

Table 4. Utilisation of web 2.0 and social communication media

	Airports	
	N	%
Blogs	0	0%
Podcasts	8	16%
Vodcasts	13	26%
RSS channels	13	26%
Widgets	27	54%
Mashups	26	52%
Webcasts	0	0%
Link to the official YouTube channel	15	30%
Link to the official Twitter account	28	56%
Link to the official Facebook page	25	50%

Table 5 summarises the presence of the airports in the major social media communication platforms. As can be seen, this presence is considerable, with 62% of the airports having an official account in one or more of the three media selected; more than 50% are present on Facebook or Twitter, and 44% on both. In addition, there is a high average number of subscribers, especially on Facebook, with an average of 9,259 followers, and Twitter, with 6,325.

Other important items reflecting the significance of the airport sector in social media include the average number of tweets (2,064), the high average number of visits to Facebook (193,346) and the average number of blogs indexed obtained by searching for the official name of the airport in Google Blogs (198,747).

Finally let us must make special mention of the latest Facebook metric "n People Are Talking About This," launched in September 2011. This new indicator has quickly become the best

Table 5. Use of social communication media

	Social Communication Media	Media
Twitter	Official account in Twitter	(56%) 28
	Number of followers	6,325
	Number of tweets	2,064
	Number of lists	324
Facebook	Official page in Facebook	(50%) 25
	Number of page-groups followed by the airport	15
	Number of followers	9,259
	Number of visits	193,346
	Number of people talking about the airport	3,154
YouTube	Official channel in YouTube	(30%) 15
	Number of subscribers	148
	Number of conversations	16
Google Blogs	Number of blogs indexed in Google Blogs	198,747

Table 6. Pearson's correlation matrix

	IV	Size	T/Over	Age	Debt	INT/P	SNT/P
IV	1						
SIZE	-0.155	1					
T/OVER	0.082	-0.140	1				
AGE	0.229	-0.041	0.188	1			
DEBT	-0.088	-0.198	0.184	-0.004	1		
INT/P	0.347	-0.136	-0.056	0.344**	-0.067	1	
SNT/P	0.400**	-0.050	0.407**	-0.019	-0.118	-0.077	1

* The correlation is significant at the level of 0.10 (bilateral). **The correlation is significant at the level of 0.05 (bilateral). ***The correlation is significant at the level of 0.01 (bilateral).

reference of a page's level of interaction with the community. It counts the number of unique individuals that have generated diverse interactions with the page, which tells us how interesting it is for viewers and at what level it is connected with the community. The success of a page (previously calculated only by the number of followers) will now be measured as the "n People are talking about this" divided by the number of followers, with a value above 5% being considered a good one. In the case of airports, this ratio, compiled from average data, was 34.06%, which confirms the considerable importance of this sector in the social media analysed.

The second phase of this study was to examine the influence of certain independent variables in the use of Web 2.0 tools and social communication media by airports. To do this, we applied a multiple regression analysis; assuming that the variables under study presented a linear relationship, the statistical technique selected was that of Multiple Linear Regression. The critical value of Fisher's F statistic ($F = 3.672$, $Sig = 0.019$) confirmed the existence of a significant linear relation between the dependent variable and the set of independent variables.

After confirming compliance with the initial assumptions of the model (linearity, homoscedasticity, normality, independence and collinearity), the Pearson correlation matrix was created (Table 6). As can be seen, the matrix only shows two weak correlations, and so there are no problems of multicollinearity among the independent variables. The index of visibility only shows a weak correlation with the level of penetration of social networks. The absence of significant, strong correlations between the dependent variable and the independent ones gives us an idea of the regression results, which presumably will have a medium-low fit and few significant variables.

According to our analysis (see Table 7), the explanatory power of the resulting model, as measured by the adjusted R-squared value, is 43.30% and so the fit is moderate. As for the significance of the variables, only 3 of the 6 independent factors are significant.

In relation to the age of the airports, the results show there is a significant negative relationship between this factor (measured as the number of years the airport has been in operation) and the dependent variable (-2.023*). In other words, it is the newer airports that present the greater development of Web 2.0 applications and social platforms. This result is contrary to our initial hypothesis that this relationship would be positive. This finding may be due to modern airports' need to promote e-participation and corporate dialogue in order to consolidate themselves in the market.

In terms of Internet penetration, the analysis shows this to be positively related to the visibil-

Table 7. Results of regression analysis

MODEL	NON-STANDARDISED COEFFICIENTS		STANDARDISED COEFFICIENTS	T
	B	STANDARD ERROR	BETA	
(Constant)	13.100	7.357	-0.248	1.781
SIZE	-0.494	0.380	-0.223	-1.299
T/OVER	-0.068	0.059	-0.502	-1.159
AGE	-0.655	0.324	-0.221	-2.023*
DEBT	-0.466	0.430	0.739	-1.084
INT/P	2.341	0.735	0.595	3.184***
SNT/P	1.394	0.479		2.913**
R	R Squared	Adjusted R Squared	Standard Error of the Estimate	Durbin-Watson
0.771	0.595	0.433	0.491	2.401

* The correlation is significant at the level of 0.10 (bilateral). **The correlation is significant at the level of 0.05 (bilateral). ***The correlation is significant at the level of 0.01 (bilateral).

ity index, with a high level of significance ($p < 0.01$). Therefore, the higher the level of Internet penetration in the country where the airport is located, the greater the use of Web 2.0 tools and social communication media. The level of penetration of social networks is the third significant variable identified, and as in the case of Internet penetration, the relationship is positive (2.913**).

For the other independent variables analysed, there is insufficient evidence to suggest a significant relation with the level of use of Web 2.0 applications and social communication platforms by airports.

FUTURE LINES OF RESEARCH

Although Web 2.0 is still at an early stage, some researchers are beginning to examine the possibilities of Web 3.0. According to Cerf (2007), with the advent of software that is both more powerful and, at the same time, easy to use, production processes to generate online content will become more sophisticated. Furthermore, the development of programs that allow the visualisation of documents in 3D (Floating World) has opened up the possibility of making a reality of the concept of a three-dimensional social networking system. Possible negative effects might include problems with intellectual property protection. Moreover, the overload of available information could create anxiety and stress situations within society.

The development of personal digital catalogues (collections of music, photos, videos, books, etc.) is another important trend. These collections will reflect the uploader's personality and their contents can be shared and exchanged (Beagrie, 2005; Borgman, 2003). Furthermore, it is likely that individuals will want to manipulate the contents of these catalogues and files (cutting, pasting, copying, and editing) and thus carry out a process of innovation (Borgman, 2003).

In short, changes in the way we relate to others are becoming increasingly evident. Shadbolt (2006) defines the "structure within which people connect" as the set of new technologies and the formation of new social communities in which information is shared and collective efforts undertaken. Accordingly, the social aspects of this interconnection are becoming ever more significant and in the long term will represent an incredibly important transformation in social relations.

Finally, as an extension to this study, an analysis could be made of time series data to determine whether there is any trend toward an improved use of social media and Web 2.0 tools. In addition, the sample used in this study could be enlarged to include smaller airports, which would provide more representative results.

CONCLUSION

Airports are interested in ICT and the information required by society, concretely, in the demand on accessibility, networking, socialization and globalization of the sector. Having been successful the implementation of Web 2.0 tools in other organizations, airports must also take advantage of the benefits of these new technologies.

Moreover, as experts point out, the situation is critical and to ensure the sustainability and profitability of this volatile business, new business models in the aviation industry must be adopted. Regarding to this, the creation of new and the improvement of intangible assets (such as those derived from social networks) are the main challenge.

According to the results of our study, although the use by airports of Web 2.0 tools is only moderate, their presence in social networks and the use of the latter for increasing e-participation is more widespread.

Good visibility for a Website indicates that it is perceived as important by users. This provides it with an advantage over competitors and ensures a significant and sustained flow of new visitors. However, the airport sector in general does not seem to be aware these benefits, and our analysis shows that much remains to be done in the use of Web 2.0 by airports.

Moreover, it seems unlikely that, at least for the moment, Web 2.0 applications will generate any significant revolution in relations between airports and society. To all appearances, airports have taken a relatively minor step in the use of ICTs as a means of providing information and services to the general public, but they have not achieved a significant advance in improving corporate dialogue.

As for social communication media, with the popularity of social networking, online forums and blogs, many companies have rushed to create a Facebook page and open a Twitter account, but this is by no means sufficient. It is not merely a question of creating a presence and a reputation, it is also necessary to manage an online presence using a well-considered social media strategy, to make the airport visible to potential customers or in the environment in which it is to be promoted. Our results show that airports have recognised the benefits of social platforms as regards increasing their visibility, and 62% of airports now have an official account with one or more of the three media selected, and the items and ratios reflecting the interest and relevance of social networks testify to this.

Airports that are not present in social networks face a double handicap: in the first place, they are less aware of their users' opinions, and so may miss out on an important source of information; secondly, even if an airport has no official page on a social network, people do speak about airports, and so opportunities to participate in conversations about themselves are being lost – and these opportunities could be utilised to improve the currently unfavourable opinion of this sector among many sectors of society.

Finally, regarding the factors that influence the use of social communication media and Web 2.0 tools at airports, our regression analysis shows that it is the most modern airports located in geographic areas with a strong Internet penetration and presence of social networking where these applications are most highly developed.

REFERENCES

Anderson, P. (2007). What is web 2.0? Ideas, technologies and implications for education. *JISC Technology and Standards Watch*, 2-64.

Beagrie, N. (2005). Plenty of room at the bottom? Personal digital libraries and collections. *D-Lib Magazine, 11*(6). Retrieved October 22, 2011, from http://www.dlib.org/dlib/june05/beagrie/06beagrie.html

Benkler, Y. (2006). *The wealth of networks - How social production transforms markets and freedom*. New Haven, CT: Yale University Press.

Bertot, J. C., Jaeger, P. T., & Grimes, J. M. (2010). Using ICTs to create a culture of transparency: E-government and social media as openness and anti-corruption tools for societies. *Government Information Quarterly, 27*(3), 264–271. doi:10.1016/j.giq.2010.03.001.

Birt, J. L., Bilson, C. M., Smith, T., & Whaley, R. E. (2006). Ownership, competition, and financial disclosure. *Australian Journal of Management, 31*(2), 235–263. doi:10.1177/031289620603100204.

Bonsón, E., Escobar, T., & Flores, F. (2006). Online transparency of the banking sector. *Online Information Review, 30*(6), 714–730. doi:10.1108/14684520610716180.

Bonsón, E., Escobar, T., & Flores, F. (2008). Navigation quality as a key value for the web page of a financial entity. *Online Information Review, 32*(5), 623–634. doi:10.1108/14684520810914007.

Bonsón, E., Escobar, T., & Martín, M. P. (2002). La mejora del sistema de información contable mediante la integración de tecnologías emergentes. *Revista de Contabilidad, 3*(6), 21–48.

Bonsón, E., & Flores, F. (2011). Social media and corporate dialogue: The response of the global financial institutions. *Online Information Review, 35*(1), 34–49. doi:10.1108/14684521111113579.

Bonsón, E., Torres, L., Royo, S., & Flores, F. (2011). *Local e-government 2.0: Social media and corporate transparency in municipalities*. Paper presented at XVI Congreso AECA. Granada, Spain.

Borgman, C. (2003). Personal digital libraries: Creating individual spaces for innovation. *NSF/JISC Post Digital Library Futures Workshop*. Retrieved October 22, 2011, from http://www.sis.pitt.edu/~dlwkshop/paper_borgman.html

Celaya, J., Vázquez, J. A., Saldaña, I., & García, Y. (2009). *Visibilidad de las ciudades en la web 2.0*. Grupo BPMO.

Cerf, V. (2007). An information avalanche. *IEEE Computer, 40*(1).

Constanzo, H. (2009). Web 2.0: A simple concept, a complex solution. *Bank Technology News, 22*(3), 24.

Elia, G., Margherita, A., & Taurino, C. (2009). Enhancing managerial competencies through a wiki-learning space. *International Journal of Continuing Engineering Education and Life-long Learning, 19*(2-3), 166–178. doi:10.1504/IJCEELL.2009.025025.

Ettredge, M., Richardson, V., & Scholz, S. (2001). The presentation of financial information at corporate web sites. *International Journal of Accounting Information Systems, 2*, 149–168. doi:10.1016/S1467-0895(00)00017-8.

Ettredge, M., Richardson, V., & Scholz, S. (2002). Dissemination of information for investors at corporate web sites. *Journal of Accounting and Public Policy, 21*, 357–389. doi:10.1016/S0278-4254(02)00066-2.

Hearn, G., Foth, M., & Gray, H. (2009). Applications and implementations of new media in corporate communications: An action research approach. *Corporate Communications, 14*(1), 49–61. doi:10.1108/13563280910931072.

Herget, J., & Mader, I. (2009). Social software in external corporate communications - A conceptional approach towards measuring, assessment and optimization of web 2.0 activity. *Information-Wissenschaft und Praxis, 60*(4), 233–240.

Hwang, J., Altman, J., & Kim, K. (2009). The structural evolution of the web 2.0 service network. *Online Information Review, 33*(6), 1040–1057. doi:10.1108/14684520911010990.

International Data Corporation (IDC). (2008). The hyperconnected: Here they come! A global look at the exploding 'culture of connectivity' and its impact on the enterprise. *Framingham USA/ MA*. Retrieved February 9, 2012, from www.nortel.com/hyperconnectivity/idc/hyperconnectivity_idc.pdf

Jiang, Y., Raghupathi, V., & Raghupathi, W. (2009). Content and design of corporate governance web sites. *Information Systems Management, 26*(1), 13–27. doi:10.1080/10580530802384704.

Jordá, C. (2008). Impacto ambiental del transporte aéreo y de las infraestructuras aeroportuarias. *Ingeniería y Territorio, 83*, 26–33.

Kupp, M., & Anderson, J. (2007). Zopa: Web 2.0 meets retail banking. *Business Strategy Review, 18*(3), 15–17. doi:10.1111/j.1467-8616.2007.00478.x.

Lambercy, V. (2010). Preaching for aviation 2.0. *PlasticPilot*. Retrieved February 9, 2012, from http://www.plasticpilot.net/blog/2010/11/14/preaching-for-aviation-2-0/

Larrán, M., & Giner, B. (2002). The use of the internet for corporate reporting by Spanish companies. *The International Journal of Digital Accounting Research, 2*(1), 53–82.

Lim, S., Matolcsy, Z., & Chow, D. (2007). The association between board composition and different types of voluntary disclosure. *European Accounting Review, 16*, 555–583. doi:10.1080/09638180701507155.

Mackeviciute, A., & Iacubiţchi, S. (2010). *The impact of enterprise 2.0 tools on innovation processes: The case study of incentive at IBS*. (Master Thesis). Jönköping International Business School, Jönköping, Sweden.

McAfee, A. P. (2006). Enterprise 2.0: The dawn of emergent collaboration. *MIT Sloan Management Review, 47*(3), 20–28.

McAfee, A. P. (2009). *Enterprise 2.0: New collaborative tools for your organization's toughest challenges*. Boston: Harvard Business Press.

O'Reilly, T. (2005). What is web 2.0: Design patterns and business models for the next generation of software. *O'Reilly*. Retrieved October 22, 2011, from http://oreilly.com/Web2/archive/what-is-Web-20.html

Oyelere, P., Laswad, F., & Fisher, R. (2003). Determinants of internet financial reporting by New Zealand companies. *Journal of International Financial. Management and Accounting, 14*(1), 26–63.

Petersen, C., & Plenborg, T. (2006). Voluntary disclosure and information asymmetry in Denmark. *Journal of International Accounting, Auditing & Taxation, 15*, 127–149. doi:10.1016/j.intaccaudtax.2006.08.004.

Serrano, C., Fuertes, , & Gutiérrez, B. (2007). Online reporting by banks: A structural modelling approach. *Online Information Review, 31*(3), 310–332. doi:10.1108/14684520710764096.

Serusi, M. (2011). Customer service 2.0: Top 10 airlines and airports performing customer service through social media. *SimpliFlying*. Retrieved February 9, 2012, from http://simpliflying.com/2011/customer-service-2-0-top-10-airlines-and-airports- performing-customer-service-through-social-media/

Shadbolt, N. (2006). *Problemas sociales, eticos y legales: ¿Cómo afecta el aumento al acceso al conocimiento a nuestra sociedad?* Paper presented at Memories for Life: The Future of our Pasts. London, UK.

Vázquez, J. A., Saldaña, I., & Celaya, J. (2009). La visibilidad de los museos en la web 2.0. *Portal Cultural Dosdoce.com*. Retrieved October 17, 2011, from http://www.dosdoce.com/articulo/estudios/3071/la-visibilidad-de-los-museos-en-la-Web-2-0/

ADDITIONAL READING

Aced, C., Benítez, M., Arqués, N., Llodrà, B., & Sanagustín, E. (2009a). Visibilidad y viralidad. In *Visibilidad: Cómo gestionar la reputación en internet* (pp. 83–102). Barcelona, Spain: Gestión.

Aced, C., Benítez, M., Arqués, N., Llodrà, B., & Sanagustín, E. (2009b). Las redes sociales. In *Visibilidad: Cómo gestionar la reputación en internet* (pp. 65–81). Barcelona, Spain: Gestión.

Allen, M., & Long, J. (2004). Domesticating the internet: Content regulation, virtual nation-building and the family. In Goggin, G. (Ed.), *Virtual Nation: The Internet in Australia* (pp. 229–240). Sydney, Australia: UNSW Press.

Bonsón, E. (2011). Web 2.0 y medios sociales: Un nuevo modelo de comunicación corporativa. *Andalucía Innova*, *14*, 60–61.

Bonsón, E., Escobar, T., & Flores, F. (2009). Social media, del reporting digital al diálogo corporativo. *Revista de la Asociación Española de Contabilidad y Administración de Empresas*, *88*, 7–9.

Boyd, D. M., & Ellison, N. B. (2007). Social network sites: Definition, history, and scholarship. *Computer-Mediated Communication*, *13*(1), 11.

Brown, M. (2003). Technology diffusion and the 'knowledge barrier': The dilemma of stakeholder participation. *Public Performance and Management Review*, *26*(4), 345–359. doi:10.1177/1530957603026004003.

Casacuberta, D., & Gutiérrez-Rubí, A. (2010). E-participación: de cómo las nuevas tecnologías están transformando la participación ciudadana. *Razón y palabra, 73*. Retrieved October 22, 2011, from http://www.razonypalabra.org.mx/N/N73/MonotematicoN73/12-M73Casacuberta-Gutierrez.pdf

Chu, H., & Xu, C. (2009). Web 2.0 and its dimensions in the scholarly world. *Scientometrics*, *80*(3), 717–729. doi:10.1007/s11192-008-2103-y.

Giones, A., & Serrat, M. (2010). La gestión de la identidad digital: Una nueva habilidad informacional y digital. *BiD: Textos Universitaris de Biblioteconomia i Documentació, 24*. Retrieved October 22, 2011, from http://www.ub.edu/bid/24/giones2.htm

Hart, J., Ridly, C., Taher, F., Sas, C., & Dix, A. (2008). *Exploring the Facebook experience: A new approach to usability*. Paper presented at NordiCHI Conference. Lund, Sweden.

La Porte, T. M., Demchak, C. C., & De Jong, M. (2002). Democracy and bureaucracy in the age of the web: Empirical findings and theoretical speculations. *Administration & Society*, *34*(4), 411–446. doi:10.1177/0095399702034004004.

Livingston, J. A. (2005). How valuable is a good reputation? A sample selection model of internet auctions. *The Review of Economics and Statistics*, *87*, 453–465. doi:10.1162/0034653054638391.

Livingstone, S. (2004). Media literacy and the challenge of new information and communication technologies. *Communication Review*, *7*, 3–14. doi:10.1080/10714420490280152.

Melitski, J. (2003). Capacity and e-government performance: An analysis based on early adopters of internet technologies in New Jersey. *Public Performance and Management Review*, *26*(4), 376–390. doi:10.1177/1530957603026004005.

Mislove, A., Marcon, M., Gummadi, K. P., Druschel, P., & Bhattacharjee, B. (2007). *Measurement and analysis of online social networks*. Paper presented at 7th ACM SIGCOMM conference on Internet Measurement. San Diego, CA.

Murphy, J., & Moulaison, H. (2009). *Social networking literacy for librarians: Exploring considerations and engaging participation*. Paper presented at ACRL 14th National Conference Pushing the Edge: Explore, Engage, Extend. Seattle, WA.

O'Reilly, T. (2006). Web 3.0? Maybe when we get there. *O'Reilly Radar.* Retrieved October 22, 2011, from http://radar.oreilly.com/archives/2006/11/Web_30_maybe_wh.html

OECD. (2007). *Participative web and user-created content*. Paris: OECD.

Solove, D. J. (2007). Rumor and reputation in a digital world. In Solove, D. J. (Ed.), *The future of reputation: Gossip, rumor, and privacy on the internet* (pp. 17–102). New Haven, CT: Yale University Press.

Tindall, D. B., & Wellman, B. (2001). Canada as social structure: Social network analysis and Canadian sociology. *Canadian Journal of Sociology*, *26*(3), 265–308. doi:10.2307/3341889.

Tredinnick, L. (2006). Web 2.0 and business: A pointer to the intranets of the future? *Business Information Review*, *23*, 228–234. doi:10.1177/0266382106072239.

Trkman, M., & Trkman, P. (2009). A wiki as intranet: A critical analysis using the Delone and McLean model. *Online Information Review*, *33*(6), 1087–1102. doi:10.1108/14684520911011025.

Zacijek, M. (2007). *Web 2.0: Hype or happiness?* Paper presented at 2007 International Cross-Disciplinary Conference on Web Accessibility (W4A). Banff, Canada.

Zhao, S., Grasmuck, S., & Martin, J. (2008). Identity construction on Facebook: Digital empowerment in anchored relationships. *Computers in Human Behavior*, *24*, 1816–1836. doi:10.1016/j.chb.2008.02.012.

KEY WORDS AND DEFINITIONS

Corporate Dialogue: This concept is based on the idea that companies may eliminate the barriers posed by paper-based formats, through the use of Web 2.0 capabilities. Thus, they can provide information that is much more detailed and useful to stakeholders, and also, through the use of new platforms, enable the effective participation of external users.

E-participation: Encompasses the processes that facilitate and enhance direct involvement in decision-making and in the generation of alternatives through the use of participatory channels that use ICTs, such as Web 2.0 and social networks.

Digital Identity: Generically, a virtual representation enabling the user to interact in cyberspace, to project a personality and to describe a personal or professional trajectory, in order to learn and share information, such as news, Websites, hobbies, opinions, etc. The host of technological platforms now available on the Internet are the best showcase for companies to identify the main features of their clients, who meet in virtual communities, with well defined profiles, where they interact and freely express their tastes, experiences and problems. Participating, getting closer and talking to the customer: these are benefits made available by technology and which should be exploited. Nevertheless, companies should be aware that in these platforms where exchange and sharing take place, there are people, not brands or organizations, interacting and therefore a company's digital identity must project a personality.

Social Communication Media: Are online platforms where content is created by users themselves using Web 2.0 technologies that facilitate the editing, publication and exchange of information. Social media can take many different forms, including Internet forums, personality blogs, social blogs, wikis, podcasts, photos and videos. Examples of social media include Wikipedia (reference), Facebook (social networking), Last.fm (personal music), YouTube (video sharing), Second Life (virtual reality), Flickr (photo sharing) and Twitter (microblogging and social networks). Many of these services may in turn be integrated into social networks as aggregation platforms.

Transparency: This term refers, in the business field, to opening up the information flow within organisations. Thus, information becomes accessible to everyone, enabling review, analysis and the detection of possible anomalies. Transparency includes issues such as the publication of audited accounts and budgets, financial statistics, trade and currency information, among others. Ultimately, transparency is the transmission of certainty and confidence, with information being freely available without obstacles or burdensome requirements, in a form that is understandable, which includes all relevant elements, which can be relied upon and which is of high quality.

Visibility: In the business world and in reference to ICTs, this concept suggests that all the online activity generated by a company constitutes its visibility. This may be self-constructed from blog posts, Twitter messages or comments to videos or photos, among other possibilities, but can also be the result of referrals or comments from third parties. The impact of an organisation's visibility in the digital world is measurable, for example, by the number of contacts it has, by the number of times content is replicated (the replication of a blog entry, comments on a video, etc.) or by analysing the number of links to it. In short, a company generates online visibility by absorbing information, processing it and sharing it, always provided this is useful to and appreciated by other users.

Web 2.0: Is a concept that refers to the social phenomenon arising from the development of diverse Internet applications. The term draws a distinction between the early days of the Web (where the user was basically a passive subject who received information or who published it, but without many possibilities existing to generate interaction) and the revolution that led to the rise of blogs, social networks and other tools. Web 2.0, therefore, consists of content-publishing platforms, the social networking services known as wikis, and photo, audio or video hosting sites. The essence of these tools is the ability they provide for users to interact or to provide additional content.

Chapter 25
Online Social Networks: Recommendation Diffusion and Co-Consumption Influence

Ana Torres
University of Porto, Portugal

Francisco Vitorino Martins
University of Porto, Portugal

ABSTRACT

The chapter is conceptual, based on analysis and synthesis of social network theory and e-consumer literature. Despite a broad spectrum of disciplines that investigate social networks and the interest of marketing practitioners in the consequences of social networks, there are still areas open for research into networked-consumer behavior in marketing. Based on previous theoretical and empirical research, this study examines and discusses the influence of social network structure and ties in matched dyads, recommendation diffusion, social contagion and co-consumption influence, and individual motivations to spread market information. The chapter proposes a theory of matched dyadic ties in close networks of connections as a proxy for information about the potential market that is difficult and expensive for businesses to measure or access directly.

INTRODUCTION

Social networks are an interesting phenomenon, which are gaining business and researchers' attention for their potential for market information and attraction. Customer´s virtual collaboration is, therefore, emerging as organizations embrace new e-business processes to take advantage of electronic communication technologies. In such turbulent times, with marketing pressure for more efficient targeting of resources, marketers are rediscovering the importance of social contagion, facilitating brand communities and social network sites for customer "voice." Many factors underlie this interest including the ability of brand communities or social networks to influence members'

DOI: 10.4018/978-1-4666-4373-4.ch025

perceptions and actions, often through frequent social interactions, to rapidly disseminate information, to learn consumer evaluations about new offerings, to speed up market product novelty and so forth; and to maximize opportunities to engage and collaborate with highly loyal customers. One way to create linkages to external resources, as a proxy to market (e.g. customer referrals), is through personal electronic communication networks. In the present-day competitive and often hostile marketing environment, many researchers believe social multiplication of marketing efforts gained from social networks is both cost effective and powerful (Balasubramanian & Mahajan, 2001; Cole, 2007; Varian, 2002). Electronic networks create enormous potential for interaction that would be impossible or too costly through traditional media. In such interconnected times, individuals and consumers have an increasing power of information diffusion and influential behavior in social networks. Despite the attraction of online social networks for "viral marketing" however, such practices are more associated with spreading online content anonymously (Ho & Dempsey, 2010). What we do not know is which consumer is "influential" and plays an important role in engaging in collaborative recommendation diffusion through online network communication: customer participation, ties and intensity of use of online networks. Thus, identifying the best customers to give network referrals, not only involves customer potential diffusion and influence, but also dispositional behavior.

Whereas e-businesses look for appropriate responses for virtual collaborative recommendation diffusion and how to target those people with the highest network value, we should also ask what drives consumers to engage in collaborative action, sharing market information, offering personal opinions and giving free and voluntary market recommendation through their network of connections, and who is influential in engaging others in joint consumer action. Despite the power of online social networks for information diffusion and social contagion (Cole, 2007; Rezabakhsh, Bornemann, Hansen, & Schrader, 2006), however, less research has focused on the traits and abilities of consumers who are best-suited to the process: How and when do network patterns matter? How does network structure affect individuals' behaviors? What kind of social networks are relevant for which types of marketing decisions?

Which consumer has the highest potential for recommendation diffusion and contagion? Which motivations drive consumer to share and spread market information?

This chapter discusses these questions by reviewing theoretical and empirical studies on social network analysis and e-consumer behavior. The primary purpose of this chapter is to bring together apparently disparate and yet interconnected strands of research and present an integrated theoretical framework of virtual recommendation diffusion and influence on co-consumption. Building on the central prediction of the "better match" theory in economics (Castilla, 2005; Simon & Warner, 1992); the question here is whether individual similarities and close ties in small networks, i.e. match dyads, help to determine better-matched recommendations and also to determine whether better recommendation diffusion helps to explain co-shopping influence. The secondary objective of this chapter is to stimulate more research in these under-explored areas.

This chapter is organized as follows. The first section presents a theoretical background on social network analysis providing readers with primary and relevant concepts to describe some network properties, such as structure and ties i.e. the position of actors within them. It also presents a general discussion of the benefits that social networks can provide both to consumers and organizations, a topic which generally goes under the label "social capital". The following section discusses the influence of the strength of network ties and matched dyads on online recommendation diffusion, social contagion and consumption influence. Then it discusses individual motivations to spread market information. Lastly, it offers new research directions in identifying under-researched areas of networked-consumer, presents managerial recommendations and research conclusion. Finally, it provides key terms definitions (terms which appear in-text in italic characters) and additional reading section.

SOCIAL NETWORKS: TIES AND STRUCTURE

Social network theory defines "social network as a set of discrete social entities (called nodes) and the collection of ties between them." The entities or nodes in a social network are often called actors. They can be individuals, organizations or other collective social units. Actors are linked to one another by social ties. Ties which are also often referred to as relations or relationships, might include formal or informal relations (Van Den Bulte & Wuyts, 2007). Social philosophers and political scientists use "social capital" (e.g. those aspects of social structure that can be used by actors to realize their interests) to refer to the norms of *reciprocity* and trustworthiness that arise from social networks (Putnam, 2000), or simply the informal norms that promote cooperation (Fukuyama, 1995). The core idea of social capital is simply that some networks (e.g. network structure and position) confer more advantages to actors other.

An alternative conception of social networks– and one that is more useful to marketing – has been developed by sociologists. They focus on individual actor-level and on the network features providing advantages or other membership benefits (Coleman, 1990). These benefits include: (1) access to information and other resources, (2) improved coordination through higher trust, (3) control over the flow of information and resources, and (4) status which allows value appropriation (Burt, 1992; Lin, 2001; Portes, 1998). How do social networks provide such benefits? Theory and research point to the resources of direct contacts (Lin, 2001), the number of ties (Ball, Eckel, Grossman, & Zame, 2001), the strength of ties (Krackhardt, 1992), closure or local clustering (Coleman, 1990, 1998; Granovetter, 1992), and "bridging structural holes" (Burt, 1992) as the relevant features. There follows a discussion of each one of these features.

Number and Strength of Ties

The number of ties i.e. the number of links or connections between two actors in a network represents limited value. From a network point of view, access to a diversity of resources typically requires being connected to a diversity of actors, in other words, being positioned at the intersection of several social circles rather than only within a single cohesive subgroup (Van Den Bulte & Wuyts, 2007). Such positions also tend to be associated with high closeness and betweenness centrality; simply having many ties (e.g. *degree centrality*) is not enough. Having more ties allows an actor to put smaller demands on each *alter* when some alters are not able or willing to provide resources. In fact empirical evidence indicates that the value of alters' social capital lies in the resources they control directly and in the indirect access they provide to other resources (Ball, Eckel, Grossman, & Zame, 2001).

Independently of the larger structure in which the tie is embedded, tie strength is a combination of two metrics: tie intensity or activity (in terms of frequency of contact) and tie valence (in terms of the affective, supportive, or cooperative character of the tie). High frequency ties increase the opportunities to communicate needs and to assess others' available resources. High frequency is particularly useful when resource transfers are complex and require a lot of tailoring or back-and-forth coordination. High frequency combined with strong ties (and long duration) may also be associated with the presence of a shared language, status and a deep knowledge of each other's routines, which can further boost the ability to transfer specific and unique information that match other peers' needs (Krackhardt, 1992).

Moreover, long-standing ties multiplied by frequency are likely to increase actors' confidence in reciprocation when other actors request or receive support. In addition, it increases the likelihood of any favor being reciprocated in the future, providing opportunities to build positive valence: advice, for example, can be repaid by respect or gratitude.

Overall, tie strength provides two kinds of benefits. First, it improves access to alters' resources through a triple route of opportunity, ability, and motivation. Second, it helps the coordination of activities between two parties through richer information transfer and through higher expectations that acts of cooperation will be reciprocated (Chan & Li, 2010).

It is important to note here that the long-term nature of ties has, in and of itself, only limited power to activate support through benevolent and trustworthy information transfer. As we discuss later, what matters is the ability, opportunity, and motivation to share resources.

Furthermore, the aspects of tie strength we discuss here map relatively well into the large literature on trust in marketing, where trust is defined as an attribution of ability (i.e., presence of resources and ability to transfer), honesty (intention to honor an implicit or explicit promise of reciprocation) and benevolence (willingness to support even without expectation of reciprocation).

Similarly, high interaction frequency enhances the ability to transfer resources; tie frequency and duration provide experience with the *alter* and hence information about likely intentions and future behavior. Finally, positive tie valence increases the motivation to treat others benevolently, or even in an altruistic manner.

The Strength of Weak Ties Paradox

As we discuss above, strong ties have many benefits and hence are a major form of social capital. Yet, "The Strength of Weak Ties" (Granovetter, 1973, 1982) is one of the most famous paradox theories involving social networks. In his research, Granovetter concludes that among the social mechanisms through which people find employment weak ties are more valuable than strong ties when it comes to job leads. This was a paradox, and hence interesting, and Granovetter suggested the following explanation: people we know intimately and see often (strong ties) all tend to know each other well (*transitivity*, i.e. if the presence of a tie between A and B and between B and C also implies the presence of a tie between A and C). As a consequence, they tend to share the same limited information (closure, i.e. the density among those with whom one has a tie) and are less able to offer new information on job leads. On the other hand, people we know only casually (weak ties) are less likely to know each other (lower transitivity and closure) and are more likely to have new information on job leads.

Granovetter argues "Weak ties provide people with access to information and resources beyond those available in their own social circles; but strong ties have greater motivation to be of assistance and are typically more available" (1982, p. 113). Thus, it is consistent with the early discussion of social capital and the benefits of strong ties.

To consider the value of strong ties, a study of social networks in China (Bian, 1997) shows that people might share valuable and scarce information only with those with whom they have a close relationship. In fact the study's findings contrast with those of Granovetter (1973, 1982) in the sense that jobs were acquired through strong ties more frequently than through weak ties. In short, (1) only *bridging* weak ties are of special value to individuals and (2) weak ties suffer from a low-motivation problem. Thus, this low-motivation problem of weak ties diminishes their value as an information advantage and in some cases, even in the search for "cheap" information.

However, in the "small world" experiments most chains did not reach their target because people were either not able or not willing to make the requested connections. For example, in a recent study, participants were informed that their task was to help relay an email message to their allocated target by passing the message to a social acquaintance whom they considered 'closer' than themselves to the target (Dodds, Muhamad, & Watts, 2003). There was clear evidence that people use homophily (i.e. the tendency for actors to connect with other actors who are similar rather than dissimilar to them) as the basis to decide who to forward the email to: men passed messages more frequently to men (57%) and women to other women (61%). Additionally, the acquaintance's geographical proximity to the target and similarity of occupation were among the most common reasons for selecting a particular acquaintance to be a recipient. However, only 384 out of 24,163 chains started reached their target. According the authors, the noncompletion rate (94.8%) suggests that people were clearly not using their networks effectively. Participants who did not forward their message claimed that they could not think of an appropriate recipient, suggesting that lack of interest or incentive, not difficulty, was the main reason for chain termination. Here again, the low-motivation problem of weak ties demonstrates their lack of value even for disclosure of "cheap information". In short, using weak ties may improve one's ability to reach farther into the network, but won't necessarily help one to mobilize the actor and his or her resources. In contrast, strong ties lead to cooperative expectation based on the greater ability, opportunity, and motivation that stem from experience and affect within the dyad, independently of the larger structure in which the tie is embedded (Van Den Bulte & Wuyts, 2007). Therefore, strong ties are more valuable in a network than weak ties, keeping everything else constant.

Network Density

Network density (i.e., the proportion of possible ties in a network that are actually present) also referred to as "closure" or "local clustering", is thought to foster identification with the group, which makes it easier to mobilize support and resources because the presence of common third parties supports the emergence of cooperation (Portes & Sensenbrenner, 1993). Hence, actors with a densely knit network may be better able to motivate their contacts to make their resources available when called upon. Closure may also affect the ability to transfer resources. Specifically, greater social closure may lead to greater cognitive cohesion characterized by shared language, codes, and stories among the members of a subgroup, which in turn can boost the ability to transfer resources, especially complex knowledge (Nahapiet & Ghoshal, 1998).

Strong ties tend to be associated with closure (via *transitivity*) and both strong ties and closure facilitate trust and cooperation through benevolence (Van Den Bulte & Wuyts, 2007). As a result, tie strength is associated with particularized trust: the trustor expects the trustee to reciprocate, based on prior experience, positive valence, and possibly also *multiplexity* (i.e. the presence of multiple kinds of ties between two actors) of their *dyadic* tie. *Closure*, in contrast, is associated with generalized and enforceable trust. For example, in organizational networks, such as associations or affiliations, the trustor expects the trustee to reciprocate because of the penalties enforced by common alters in case of nonreciprocation and other malfeasance. Thus, closure leads to cooperative expectation based on enforcement mechanisms that are only effective in closed network structures but do not require any prior history or positive affect between the two parties for cooperation to emerge. On the other hand, network closure leads to high redundancy among an actor's alters: when everyone is connected to everyone, no one has unique information. So closure does not provide any actor with an information advantage but keeps everyone at parity. Hence, from a business perspective, network closure actually reduces the opportunities to locate valuable resources to transfer innovative information.

Bridging Structural Holes

In contrast, spanning *structural holes*, that is, the ability to be connected to many poorly interconnected actors, provides an actor with an important information advantage: more varied bits of information are received sooner than the average network member receives them (Burt, 1992). In addition, such a brokerage position creates opportunities to control information flow and transfer of resources between these otherwise unconnected parts of the network.

In conclusion, the rationale of structural holes for bridge position is quite different from closure. Whereas closure provides value creation through cooperation benefits, the emphasis of the "structural holes" argument lies in value appropriation through superior information and control.

In the following section, we go on to discuss how network structure affects social influence and contagion among consumers.

NETWORKED CONSUMER: MATCHED DYADIC TIES, RECOMMENDATION DIFFUSION AND CO-CONSUMPTION INFLUENCE

In this section, theory and empirical evidence is used to critically frame the effect of inter-customer networks on influence of customer behavior. Most evidence comes from the sphere of innovation diffusion, i.e., how consumers spread market information and how new products get adopted and gain market acceptance. There is less evidence about the effects of social networks on influence to purchase together existing products, and with regard to *co-shopping* influence (relevant for understanding the leverage of network externalities), we are not aware of any rigorous quantitative evidence. Each of these areas is discussed in turn.

Our review of the relevant knowledge on customer networks makes it possible to identify several social network issues that managers must think about. As to the connection between social network structure and ties and customer behavior, we discuss the area of speed to market new product diffusion, customer motivation to cooperate, sharing knowledge and market information and co-consumption influence through *social contagion.* Social contagion is a phenomenon describing that actors are influenced in their behavior through exposure to other actor's knowledge, attitude, or behavior. Imitation is the most common form of social contagion and is relevant for new product adoption.

Taking an economic value approach, we first discuss the network externalities effects, how network ties, intensity and reciprocity relate to individual potential information diffusion and social contagion i.e. co-consumption or co-shopping. We next turn to customer motivations to engage in collaborative recommendation diffusion, and conclude with a brief discussion of managerial implications and relevant insights to future research.

Network Externalities

Different theories of the economic leverage of networks among consumers describe different "causal mechanisms" of social influence in the recipient perspective. Such external causes, i.e. network externalities, or complementary network effects, occur when the benefits of use, and hence of adoption, increase with the number of prior adoptions. However, these effects are from a recipient perspective. Our view stresses network externalities for both consumers and business markets.

For business, there are different reasons why networks matter. Among the most relevant, theory posits that social network externalities potentially impact firm value. This network effect is crucial for firm's market share and profitability, especially for consumer goods where competition is higher.

For example, complementary issues are typically more pronounced in product categories with competing technological standards. Researchers find that product categories with competing standards exhibit patterns of new product diffusion that are more consistent with social contagion than is the case with other products (Van den Bulte & Stremersch, 2004). Another example is the success of electronic commerce, which strongly benefits from the existence of network externalities effect: a product's value increases, due to scale effect, when more consumers join the network, even for marginal products (Varian, 2002).

Moreover, social network externalities potentially impact firm value through increasing online interaction. Theoretically, the exponential increase in customers' communications should decrease firms' efforts and investments in attracting new customers e.g. advertising, promotions, and market data gathering (Balasubramanian & Mahajan, 2001). Networks will erode the effectiveness of traditional marketing. The relevance of networks for branding efforts, connecting brand and retailers to consumers, new product development and innovation diffusion will be a challenged by e-marketing. Thus, the role of social networks as a new "customer" media represents a great challenge for e-marketing investment in customer alliances for new product recommendation and attraction of new customers.

In relation to consumers' benefits, peer information diffusion provides the value of trusted and unbiased market information and search cost reduction (Gefen, Benbasat, & Pavlou, 2008). People may update their beliefs about the costs and benefits of adopting the new product after discussing it with previous adopters. This additional information may lead to an upward or downward revision of beliefs or it may simply confirm different beliefs, thus reducing uncertainty about the product. Different disciplines focus on slightly different facets of this process, but all agree on the basic idea of belief updating through social contagion (also called social learning). Examples are Bayesian updating through social learning under risk aversion in economics and decision science (Chatterjee & Eliashberg, 1990; Roberts & Urban, 1988).

Belief updating through social contagion is particularly important to adoption in certain situations. The first are situations where potential adopters view the product as complex with difficult-to-understand links between features and benefits. The second are situations where communication channels have little source credibility and as consumers are risk averse, this is an issue nowadays among consumers and Internet retailers (Gefen, et al., 2008). The third type of situation where belief updating through contagion is likely to be important are cases where the product's performance or utility varies across actors, so the potential adopters want to know not simply whether the product is "good in general" but "good for folks like us". Here, feedback from actors like oneself can be critical. B2C marketers have long capitalized on references from satisfied customers to achieve additional sales. As Van den Bulte and Wuyts (2007) state, "Individual consumers may want to know what other people like themselves - rather than some expert in a white lab coat - think about the product" (p. 40).

Network Structure and Social Contagion: Which E-Customer is Influential?

Social contagion theory (Coleman, Katz, & Menzel, 1966; Weber, 1968 [1921]) posits that actors are influenced in their behavior through exposure to other actors' knowledge, attitude or behavior. This influenced or imitation behavior acts as a type of belief updating and is a source of credibility concerning retailer endorsement, new product or complex products adoption, as discussed above. Leading researchers have long studied how innovations diffuse through populations of individuals, households, and organizations (Rogers, 2003). Sociologists have offered the important insight that innovation diffusion may be driven by social contagion,' i.e., "actors' adoption behavior is a function of their exposure to other actors' knowledge, attitude, or behavior concerning the innovation. Within an online purchasing setting, it is claimed that more experienced and pioneering e-consumers act as a basis of trust, and reduce the risk perception of complex products or product innovation adoption for emergent e-consumers. In addition, social contagion behavior works as a social learning process for less experienced e-consumers in their purchasing decision. Thus, we propose that the role of leading e-consumers is crucial to advise and influence the network. However, this raises several issues: Why does such contagion occur? How prevalent is it? How does the network structure affect that process? Which motivations drive individuals to spread market information and give product recommendation? How can marketers take advantage of contagion? We elaborate on each below.

The Role of "Small Worlds" and "Match Dyads"

Social networks are turning to close or small worlds (e.g. network of friends or relatives on Facebook) which are likely to have more strong ties and influential behavior. Small worlds' properties are observed in many human and inter-firm networks. To illustrate, the Facebook experience is an example of Web communities where members are clustered in groups of friends (e.g. sub-networks) but linkages exist between these groups. According (Bagozzi & Dholakia, 2006), in these small groups individuals are strongly influential because relational ties are structured on social interaction with a small group of friends, often also beyond the online social interactions. These small groups are strongly sociocentric (e.g. strong identification with the group), and tend to be egalitarian collectivities horizontally organized by friendship ties having similar group-referent values (e.g. social enhancement).

Based on this empirical evidence, we suggest that online social networks of influence provide the structural route for social interactions and reciprocating behaviors which encourages virtual recommendation diffusion and co-shopping response. The rationale behind this proposition is supported by social network literature (discussed in the first section), which refers to the fact that the "small worlds" are structured on strong ties and close social bonds and that "match dyads" are more exposed to social contagion. Networks of this kind have received little attention, yet they appear to have an enormous potential for information diffusion and social influence (Watts, 1999).

To understand this relationship, we first discuss network size influence on recommendation behavior and co-shopping influence. Research provides evidence that smaller networks (those with fewer than 50 members "everybody knows everybody else") are characterized by strong relational ties, rather than weak ties, which result in stronger and multifaceted interpersonal relationships between consumers influencing sharing behavior "I am willing to share personal information and experiences with close friends, not with anonymous people (Algesheimer, Dholakia, & Herrmann, 2005); strong feelings of social identity, shared history, individuals have similar needs, shared interests and consumption tendencies "other Network members and I have close friendship ties and share the same objectives and interests" (Bagozzi & Dholakia, 2006; Dholakia, Bagozzi, & Pearo, 2004). Small world contact networks are structures with startlingly efficient process performance, are premised on the existence of shortcuts, are a potential structural basis of reliable flows of information, influence, material like a simple model of disease transmission (Friedkin, 2011).

When these networks of relations form a closed network, individuals' asymmetries are pooled and information transmission is faster (Lippert & Spagnolo, 2008). In this network of interpersonal influence, actors are structurally equivalent i.e. the social positions and opinions of actors and any dissimilarity is reduced by the social influence process, and structurally equivalent actors (e.g. match dyad) will adopt an innovation at approximately the same time (Friedkin & Johnsen, 1997). Based on previous research and "better match" theory (Simon & Warner, 1992) we propose, that "match dyads," i.e. social bonds and strong ties in close network of connections, enhance the likelihood of "better matched" recommendations, based on individuals' similarities, shared needs and previous awareness of consumption behavior tendencies, which in turn are more likely to positively influence co-consumption.

Online Network Interactivity: Speed to Market Information

What underpins information network theory is the maximization of information diffusion. According to the fundamental concepts of Network theory, firstly, it is only a network when it transfers information. Thus, individuals in networks should be motivated to "exchange information". Otherwise, they have no value for the company. Secondly, it is only a network if an actor (e.g. individual consumer, company) has a relational tie (e.g. friendship, transaction), and can advise the network (e.g. influential behavior).

The extensive use of online communication channels, such as social networks, blogs, chats, information diffusion is increasing exponentially. On average an individual has 25 friends on his or her online network and a connector (e.g. hub) has 150 connections (Wasko & Faraj, 2005). According to social network literature, "hubs" are individuals with large numbers of social ties with an important influential role. Because of their large exposure on the network, innovative and e-leading "hubs" speed up the information diffusion process and follower "hubs" increase the market size. Thus, a "broker" has an important position in knowledge access and transfer to the network.

We assume these increasing electronic communications provide a base for linking resources and speed information diffusion to potential market. Besides, forwarding online content requires low effort, as it can be either directly attached to electronic communication channels like emails/instant messaging or be stored on specific URLs, which are shown in the body of electronic communications (Ho & Dempsey, 2010).

Moreover, individuals communicate extensively with one another in cyberspace (e.g. through email, social network sites and other forms of interactive communications), and also often have offline social relationships. This relational capital provides a base for enduring ties (Cole, 2007) and requires intensive interaction and close social bonds, which is crucial for social exchange and influence in establishing a basis for trustworthy recommendation for economic exchange (Balasubramanian & Mahajan, 2001).

Researchers agree that interactivity is a key Internet feature, which facilitates reciprocal peer-to-peer interactions (Chan & Li, 2010). Furthermore, we also suggest the strong effect of social bonds in close networks encourages individuals to interact reciprocally, which also encourages resource sharing, voluntary collaboration, and cooperation, which are critical for recommendation diffusion and co-shopping influence. In line with this rationale, Chan and Li (2010) find that the strength of social bonds that consumers established in the community positively influences the consumers' reciprocating behaviors, which in turn induce co-shopping intentions. This finding gives support to our rationale, since these dyadic, network-based interactions, which are reciprocal rather than generalized, provide the structural route for virtual recommendation diffusion. For example, researchers have noted that higher participation levels lead to higher levels of involvement in the brand communities (Algesheimer, et al., 2005). These findings imply that individual levels of interactions in social networks will contribute to sharing market information and recommendation diffusion in the network. In our view, this "e-linking value" is supported by "match dyads" in close networks, where people who connect more to others are likely to sustain their contributions to the network through reciprocal interactions sharing and speed market information. Thus, it is our belief that leading e-consumers, high in online network communications (e.g. use of several networks and intensity of use), have great potential for market information diffusion. In addition, the level of intensity of network-based peer-to-peer interaction is likely to positively impact the strength of recommendation behavior which in turn is more likely to positively influence others co-shopping (e.g. peers' joint consumption actions).

Recommendation Diffusion and Reciprocity

Social interaction and reciprocating behaviors in electronic networks provide the structural route for virtual recommendation diffusion and co-shopping response. The rationale behind this premise is that consumers seek the advice of other to solve consumption-related problems and they forward online content giving opinions and suggestions about purchase opportunities (Ho & Dempsey, 2010). We suggest that the Internet shopper, like market mavens (Price, Feick, & Guskey, 1995) has the knowledge of best sites to shop, product novelty or promotions to recommend to their acquaintances and network peers with similar consumption needs. Meanwhile, members reciprocate the support they receive by those valuable matched resources. Research provides evidence that social interaction, including reciprocating behaviors, reflects processes of receiving and giving various resources. The helper who provides resources, such as information or social support, receives reciprocal expressions of gratitude, and admiration or recognition from the person(s) helped. Moreover, reciprocity as a collective behavior, pertains to the value dimension of reciprocity, a generalized moral norm that states people should reciprocate by repaying those who provide direct help (Hars & Qu, 2002). In this context, resource exchange theory (Foa, 1971) posits that individuals share information as a valuable resource and that social systems facilitate the exchange of various types of resources by matching available resources with needs. However, whether or not a resource exchange occurs depends on the appropriateness of the environment and the exchangers' capability and motivation to give and receive. In this sense, as we discussed above, Internet facilities of Web 2.0, such as interactivity, rich media and communication tools of higher addressability (e.g. email, blogs, message boards on social networks) allow consumers to interact and allow convenient and efficient resource exchanges. These features reflect the central components that help generate efficient, useful and rich information resources for consumers in matched needs and thus motivate them to engage in reciprocal interaction. However, the impact of consumers' reciprocal interaction on consumption behavior remains largely absent from research, but reciprocity should provide community members with a stable and safe social context (Wikström, Carlell, & Frostling-Henningsson, 2002) in which they exchange resources and shop together.

Co-Consumption Influence

In this study, we define co-consumption or co-shopping influence as a response to the influence of matched recommendations on other peers' joint consumption actions. In our conceptualization, co-shopping "influence" is a sustained feedback mechanism in the reciprocal interactions of network peers leading to "better matched" recommendation influence in joint consumption action. We note here that such joint action may not necessarily be contemporaneous; members can perform their respective parts at different times. Few researchers have conceptually examined the co-shopping construct in depth. In general, the findings of such studies are quite mixed. For example, Dholakia, Bagozzi, & Pearo (2004) describe the co-shopping phenomenon as "we-intentions, defined as a commitment of an individual to engage in joint action and involves an implicit or explicit agreement between the participants to engage in that joint action" (p. 247). Chan & Li (2010) found that co-shopping intentions are more related to motivations and benefits of community group-based consumption behavior, e.g. "Let's buy this product together to get bigger discounts" (p. 1037). Other researchers found that co-shopping was more likely to be a phenomenon of teenagers shopping with friends, related to peer influence and to the enjoyment of shopping with pals (Mangleburg, Doney, & Bristol, 2004).

By extending "better match" theory, in our view co-consumption influence is a response or feedback mechanism of the influence of matched recommendations on joint purchase action. This feedback is supported by social interactions and dyadic reciprocating behaviors.

Another aspect of virtual recommendation that has not been investigated relates to expectations that an individual's collective efforts will be reciprocated in the form of a co-shopping response which enhances ongoing recommendations. Broadly speaking we suggest the role of reciprocating behavior as a response of co-shopping influence 1) is a substantiation of "better matched" recommendations and 2) a self-reinforcing mechanism ensuring ongoing recommendations. The rationale behind this proposition is that prior research indicates the role of reciprocity may be relevant to ensure ongoing contributions to electronic networks. When there is a strong norm of reciprocity in the collective, individuals trust that their knowledge contribution efforts will be reciprocated by peer recognition, thereby rewarding individual efforts as future returns to maintain ongoing contributions (Hars & Qu, 2002; Wasko & Faraj, 2005). Accordingly, social exchange theory considers all interactions as exchanges of rewards and that the valuation of rewards is varied because people reflect their own preferences, e.g. which arise from the feeling of being rewarded simply by being in a relationship (Blau, 1964). Moreover, feedback always has a positive effect on individual behavior: it shows that people who receive expressions of gratitude and recognition from other peers are more motivated to engage in ongoing recommendations. Hence, in our point of view co-consumption influence providing feedback of "better matched" recommendations is a self-reinforcing mechanism as it encourages the referral to expend additional effort and ongoing recommendations.

Consumer Motivation: Why Should I "Share"?

There exist some unobserved individual characteristics that lead to higher information sharing and recommendation level. This assumption is consistent with sociological and psychological theories which posit that what drives people to share market information is a combination of intrinsic and extrinsic individual motivations. Here we discuss two individual dimensions that prior research indicates may be relevant to explain market information sharing and recommendation diffusion in social networks of connections: "voluntary collaboration" and "incentive seeking". We expand upon each of these dimensions below.

Voluntary Collaboration

First, consider the customers' reasons to give free and voluntary market information and personal recommendations. By voluntary collaboration we mean what induces people to engage in spontaneous sharing behavior to give free and voluntary market or product recommendation among their network of connections. The construct receives theoretical support both from previous research on market helping behavior (Price, et al., 1995) and group-based consumer interactions (Dholakia, et al., 2004; Hars & Qu, 2002; Wasko & Faraj, 2005) and altruism literature on arousal of "match dyad" empathy and reciprocity.

Extensive research provides evidence to illustrate that what drives consumers to engage in voluntary collaboration, concerns both individual's altruistic characteristics (Hars & Qu, 2002; Ho & Dempsey, 2010) and helping market behavior (Price, et al., 1995) which is defined as acts performed by individuals in the marketplace that benefit others in their purchases and consumption (e.g. giving free and voluntary market information, answering others' questions, influencing peer consumers, helping them make good purchase decisions, and even validating their past decisions and behavior). As some researchers (Nelson & Otnes, 2005) note in their netnography study, online social connections initiate helping behaviors and feelings of moral obligation to help, which sustain commitments to the community. For example, Hars & Qu (2002) measure altruism as "I don't care about money", "Recognition from others is my greatest reward", "Community members should help each other out", or "I deeply enjoy helping others—even if I have to make sacrifices" (p. 38) to explain motivations to engage in virtual collaboration in open source online communities.

Moreover, the relationship with altruism and the sharing of market information appears particularly salient in close networks: the role of empathic emotions and caring responses gained from strong relational ties boost altruistic motivations. This rationale is also supported by social exchange theory which posits all interactions as exchanges of rewards and distinguishes between extrinsic and intrinsic rewards that arise from the feeling of being rewarded simply by being in a relationship, the valuation of which differs as people reflect their own preferences (Blau, 1964). On the basis of prior research we suggest the greater the consumers' level of altruism the more likely they are to engage in spontaneous sharing behavior to give free and voluntary market or product recommendation into the network of connections with matched needs.

Incentive Seeking

Another motivational dimension relates to external rewards or incentives that consumers receive from firms to give referrals. The emergence of the incentive motive suggests that consumers use brands to obtain rewards and incentives in exchange for their collaboration. In certain cases, brand communities and e.tail sites tend to provide monetary and nonmonetary incentives such as sales promotions, community events, contests, sweepstakes, and coupons as rewards for member's participation and recommendation diffusion. This suggests that consumers are already aware of the fact that a number of e.retailers offer a variety of promotions and future rewards. They may therefore join such communities mainly for reasons associated with the incentives offered there. Evidence of this belief is provided by few empirical studies that find monetary compensations and future rewards e.g. "I receive some form of explicit compensation, salary, contract for participating in the project", "Participating in the project makes me more marketable" are a more significant predictor of sharing knowledge with community than intrinsic or altruistic motivations (Hars & Qu, 2002; Sung, Kim, Kwon, & Moon, 2010). An explanation for this behavioral motivation is that a surprisingly large number of participants were paid for their open-source efforts which in some way poisoned the voluntary collaboration engagement.

These findings suggest that such monetary incentives play a significant role in motivating consumers who are less altruistic and less motivated to process and share market information for free in large networks. In certain cases, while members of small networks may hope their recommendation behavior is interpreted by the sender as altruistic, what they are really seeking is some sort of incentive. Furthermore, in some cases e-retailers offer such monetary incentives on the base of referral effectiveness, i.e. on the basis of new customers' first purchases. From a marketing standpoint, by rewarding individual efforts and ensuring ongoing recommendations, managers do more than simply generate positive word-of-mouth among consumers, which in turn can reinforce the consumer-brand relationship but also drive customers to engage in more purchase-related behaviors and co-consumption influence. These possibilities imply that such monetary incentives may play a significant role in motivating consumers to engage in ongoing recommendations on the network on a regular basis. This process is consistent with social exchange theory, in the sense that "incentive seeking" helps explain when members choose to participate and contribute in a manner that maximizes their total social-interaction utility. Therefore, we suggest both voluntary collaboration and incentive should have a positive impact on recommendation intentions and behavior. However, these relationships lack stronger empirical evidence and market returns of recommendation behavior under customer incentive have also been neglected by researchers.

Solutions and Recommendations

Overall network structure can have a strong effect on the extent and speed of a diffusion process. This insight has important implications for new product diffusion and viral marketing. From a managerial point of view, however, the important question is: How can marketers exploit the network to speed up the acceptance or adoption of new products? Rogers (2003) has suggested five different product characteristics associated with diffusion speed in which hurdles or thresholds can be low or high. Based on Roger's framework we suggest a few mixed solutions to spread product innovation. For example, when all consumers have low acceptance or adoption thresholds, local clustering is bad for marketing efforts. But when consumers have various acceptance or adoption thresholds, a mixture of dense clusters interconnected by some bridging ties is optimal: local clustering will "wear out" the highly resistant customers, while the bridges will help spread the disease among the clusters (provided that the nodes linking the clusters to each other have very low thresholds so that the disease can gain a foothold in a previously untouched cluster simply by one contact with an infected node from a different cluster).

Let us now apply this reasoning to a marketing context. To spread awareness of a brand or a company name, it is necessary to overcome an attention hurdle, but nothing else. Similarly, a product that is cheap but provides major benefits to the customer and is low-risk as well will not be associated with high hurdle.

In such cases, a standard media campaign or a straightforward buzz marketing campaign that spreads a simple message and ignores the network structure will be sufficient to create the awareness that is needed to overcome the adoption threshold.

Conversely, when the message is more complex or induces fear or the product has a high price, unclear benefits, or there is some risk involved, the adoption threshold will vary across people depending on their income, their experience with similar products, and their risk aversion. In such cases, simple buzz marketing will not work as people will want input from several other sources, preferably from people they truly trust. Also, structural equivalence of ties in close networks may foster group identification and trust among members. In such a scenario, local clustering, which is inefficient for simple innovations with uniformly low adoption thresholds, becomes an asset in the marketing effort (Van Den Bulte & Wuyts, 2007). This reasoning sustains the argument of the strength of direct ties as a source of trusted and unbiased information.

There is also a problem of over-embeddedness when considering network structure variables (e.g. centrality, closure, or density) and ignoring actors' traits, attitudes, and motivations. For managers, the million dollar question is: Which tie is most relevant for which social contagion driver? An obvious approach is to identify the best-connected actors and motivate them to talk about the product, so that adoption occurs as quickly as possible.

Based on discussion of the preceding section, we stress that close networks of acquaintances, characterized by strong relational ties, rather than weak ties, due to a shared history and social identity and individuals' shared needs are more suited to influence others' consumption tendencies. Therefore, this networked consumer like a "matchmaker" will provide better matched connections that lead to "better matched recommendation" diffusion which are more likely to influence co-shopping. In this sense, they provide e-business with "better matched" resources as a prime tool to attract new customers more efficiently and speed to market product novelty or business information that will leverage the economic value of the social network of influence. From a marketing standpoint these networked-based social interactions are crucial to disseminate and speed to market product recommendation, to target viral and influential consumers, creating an effective customer referral program and benefit from network externalities. Such benefits imply that social contagion gained from online social networks is both cost effective and powerful, which leverages their economic value for potential market attraction (Balasubramanian & Mahajan, 2001).

This insight provides specific guidance to managers on actions they can take: targeting networked e-influential' customers to develop efficient customer referral programs and "crowdsourcing" strategy. Firms should use "better matched" resources as a prime "tool" for capturing new customers to create an entire referral chain, showing the importance of using the best customers as a valuable asset, as an alternative to resource based view.

Besides, for firms there is a lot of interest in increasing market share by targeting and making marketing alliances with those most likely to influence others. Linking bridges with unconnected individuals, through customer networks, joining people by similarity, capturing resources from different networks in a constructive fashion: in brief, looking for synergy and combinational customer needs and preferences. These matched dyads synergies introduce customers as an information resource and a co-developer of firm value-creation.

FUTURE RESEARCH DIRECTIONS

As a conceptual study, this chapter is limited to literature and prior empirical research. It offers the benefit of new research directions for e-business in identifying under-researched areas of e-consumer behavior in a marketing context.

One way to make progress on this subject is to directly examine the relationship between personal networks, recommendation behavior, and co-shopping influence via customer referrals as indicators of preexisting matched social connections.

To the best of our knowledge, no other study has sought to determine whether customer recommendation made through online social contacts are better matched than those made through other channels. What is more, no study has focused specifically on the performance implications of customer virtual recommendation diffusion on future sales or co-shopping influence by using current customers' online connections.

It is clear that consumer incentives to provide referrals are emerging as a current practice among e-retailers. However, the relationship between customer recommendation and co-shopping influence lack stronger empirical evidence, and market returns of recommendation behavior under customer incentive have also been neglected by researchers. As a result, we encourage further research on this topic.

Another future research opportunity is within the domain of crowdsourcing, exploring Internet network externalities, creating a customer-base for new market attraction and social sales. Besides, there is a lot of interest in increasing market share by targeting those most likely to influence others. However, it remains a relevant and unexplored issue to target e-leading customers most likely to influence and attract others using network grouping influence.

This insight suggests that social network analysis requires new approaches regarding the impacts on social behavior and on capturing individual idiosyncrasies and demographics which leverage their economic value to organizations. For example, we suggest examining consumers' status quo bias on social network engagement and social cooperation.

CONCLUSION

Our review of social network theory provides relevant knowledge on social network properties to aid in the understanding of how different network structure and ties have distinct effects on social capital. Both social network theory and consumer behavior studies suggest social capital is more complex and richer than simply reaching out one's acquaintances. Linking a significant body of literature regarding online social networks and consumer traits, motivations and influence behavior, here we make some concluding comments.

We conclude that the existence of "strong ties" in close network of connections increases the recommendation accuracy and influential behavior. While using dense networks may improve one's ability to reach farther into the network, however it can also be restrictive. In dense network individuals have "weak ties" lacking in social cohesion, which could be restrictive in their influential or contagion power. Conversely, cohesion and structural equivalence of ties in close networks may foster group identification and trust among members. Thus, "strong ties" facilitate the transfer of information (e.g. complex and tacit knowledge) which requires intensive interaction (e.g. ability to transfer) and positive valence (e.g. a good understanding and willingness to transfer).

In addition, "strong ties" multiplied by intensive online network interactivity provide the structural route for speed to market information diffusion and reciprocating behaviors, which encourages virtual recommendation diffusion and co-shopping response. Because individuals are increasingly using online communications to share experiences, it is our belief that social exposure of lead e-users creates synergy for referral behavior. We conclude that heavy Internet users such as individuals participating in online networks, highly experienced e-consumers, influential lead users and consumers with high disposition to recommend are more likely to engage in the process of development a "collaborative network recommendation system" to appeal to mainstream emergent e-consumers. Just as a "broker" in a network has an important position in knowledge access and transfer, we believe that real-world leading e-consumers are a source of unbiased information most likely to influence others in the network. In short, one of the conclusions of this study is that leading e-consumers who are highly online network connected, influential, and high in recommendation motivations could be profiled as potential "net-promoters" to engage in the process of network recommendation diffusion.

As a result, this study contributes to a new research stream on networked customers to better understand e-consumer traits, behavioral intentions, and potential influence so they could be effectively profiled as a "match-net-promoter" to be involved in the collaborative recommendation process in the network, turning dyadic-into-triadic relationships. By extending better match theory in economics, this study contributes theoretically to propose that "match dyads" in close networks of connections provide high-quality valuable information that will improve the match between the product and the potential customer. Under this assumption, these "matched" online social connections, act as a proxy for information about aspects of the potential market that are difficult and expensive to measure or observe directly, such as customer needs.

Both these networked consumer characteristics and behaviors are not only relevant from a measurement imperative in the sense of being unobservable, but also managerially significant in the sense that they provide specific guidance to managers on targeting more effective referral customers.

ACKNOWLEDGMENT

Research for this study was supported by PhD grant from the Portuguese Science Foundation.

REFERENCES

Algesheimer, R., Dholakia, U. M., & Herrmann, A. (2005). The social influence of brand community: Evidence from european car clubs. *Journal of Marketing*, *69*(3), 19–34. doi:10.1509/jmkg.69.3.19.66363.

Bagozzi, R. P., & Dholakia, U. M. (2006). Antecedents and purchase consequences of customer participation in small group brand communities. *International Journal of Research in Marketing*, *23*(1), 45–61. doi:10.1016/j.ijresmar.2006.01.005.

Balasubramanian, S., & Mahajan, V. (2001). The economic leverage of the virtual community. *International Journal of Electronic Commerce*, *5*(3), 103–138.

Ball, S., Eckel, C., Grossman, P. J., & Zame, W. (2001). Status in markets. *The Quarterly Journal of Economics*, *116*(1), 161–188. doi:10.1162/003355301556374.

Bian, Y. (1997). Bringing strong ties back In Indirect ties, network bridges, and job searches in China. *American Sociological Review*, *62*(3), 366–385. doi:10.2307/2657311.

Blau, P. M. (1964). *Exchange and power in social life*. New York, NY: Wiley.

Burt, R. S. (1992). *Structural holes: The social structure of competition*. Cambridge, MA: Harvard University Press.

Castilla, E. J. (2005). Social networks and employee performance in a call center. *American Journal of Sociology*, *110*(5), 1243–1283.

Chan, K. W., & Li, S. Y. (2010). Understanding consumer-to-consumer interactions in virtual communities: The salience of reciprocity. *Journal of Business Research*, *63*(9-10), 1033–1040. doi:10.1016/j.jbusres.2008.08.009.

Chatterjee, R., & Eliashberg, J. (1990). The innovation diffusion process in a heterogeneous population: A micromodeling approach. *Management Science*, *36*, 1057–1079. doi:10.1287/mnsc.36.9.1057.

Cole, M. (2007). The networked consumer: A critical review and assessment. *Journal of Customer Behaviour*, *6*(1), 5–18. doi:10.1362/147539207X198347.

Coleman, J. S. (1990). *Foundations of social theory*. Cambridge, MA: Harvard University Press.

Coleman, J. S. (1998). Social capital in the creation of human capital. *American Journal of Sociology*, *94*(Supplement), S95–S120. doi:10.1086/228943.

Coleman, J. S., Katz, E., & Menzel, H. (1966). *Medical innovation: A diffusion study*. Indianapolis, IN: The Boobs-Merrill Company.

Dholakia, U. M., Bagozzi, R. P., & Pearo, L. K. (2004). A social influence model of consumer participation in network- and small-group-based virtual communities. *International Journal of Research in Marketing*, *21*(3), 241–263. doi:10.1016/j.ijresmar.2003.12.004.

Dodds, P. S., Muhamad, R., & Watts, D. J. (2003). An experimental study of search in global social networks. *Science*, *301*, 827–829. doi:10.1126/science.1081058.

Foa, U. G. (1971). Interpersonal and economic resources. *Science*, *29*, 345–351. doi:10.1126/science.171.3969.345.

Friedkin, N. E. (2011). Spine segments in small world networks. *Social Networks*, *33*(1), 88–97. doi:10.1016/j.socnet.2010.11.004.

Friedkin, N. E., & Johnsen, E. C. (1997). Social positions in influence networks. *Social Networks*, *19*(3), 209–222. doi:10.1016/S0378-8733(96)00298-5.

Fukuyama, F. (1995). *Trust: The social virtues and the creation of prosperity*. New York, NY: Free Press.

Gefen, D., Benbasat, I., & Pavlou, P. A. (2008). A research agenda for trust in online environments. *Journal of Management Information Systems*, *24*(4), 275–286. doi:10.2753/MIS0742-1222240411.

Granovetter, M. S. (1973). The strength of weak ties. *American Journal of Sociology*, *83*, 1420–1443. doi:10.1086/226707.

Granovetter, M. S. (1982). The strength of weak ties: A network theory revisited. In Marsden, P. V., & Lin, N. (Eds.), *Social structure and network analysis* (pp. 105–130). Beverly Hills, CA: Sage Publications.

Granovetter, M. S. (1992). Problems of explanation in economic sociology. In Nohria, N., & Eccles, R. G. (Eds.), *Networks and organizations: Structure, form, and action* (pp. 25–56). Boston, MA: Harvard Business School Press.

Hars, A., & Qu, S. (2002). Working for free? Motivations for participating in open-source projects. *International Journal of Electronic Commerce*, *6*(3), 25.

Ho, J. Y. C., & Dempsey, M. (2010). Viral marketing: Motivations to forward online content. *Journal of Business Research*, *63*(9-10), 1000–1006. doi:10.1016/j.jbusres.2008.08.010.

Krackhardt, D. (1992). The strength of strong ties: The importance of philos in organizations. In Nohria, N., & Eccles, R. G. (Eds.), *Networks and organizations: Structure, form, and action* (pp. 216–239). Boston, MA: Harvard Business School Press.

Lin, N. (2001). *Social capital: A theory of social structure and action*. Cambridge, UK: Cambridge University Press. doi:10.1017/CBO9780511815447.

Lippert, S., & Spagnolo, G. (2008). Internet peering as a network of relations. *Telecommunications Policy*, *32*(1), 33–49. doi:10.1016/j.telpol.2007.11.004.

Mangleburg, T. F., Doney, P. M., & Bristol, T. (2004). Shopping with friends and teens' susceptibility to peer influence. *Journal of Retailing*, *80*(2), 101–116. doi:10.1016/j.jretai.2004.04.005.

Nahapiet, J., & Ghoshal, S. (1998). Social capital, intellectual capital, and the organizational advantage. *Academy of Management Review*, *23*(2), 242–266.

Nelson, M. R., & Otnes, C. C. (2005). Exploring cross-cultural ambivalence: A netnography of intercultural wedding message boards. *Journal of Business Research*, *58*(1), 89–95. doi:10.1016/S0148-2963(02)00477-0.

Portes, A. (1998). Social capital: Its origins and applications in modern sociology. *Annual Review of Sociology*, *22*, 1–24. doi:10.1146/annurev.soc.24.1.1.

Portes, A., & Sensenbrenner, J. (1993). Embeddedness and immigration: Notes on the social determinants of economic action. *American Journal of Sociology*, *98*(6), 1320–1350. doi:10.1086/230191.

Price, L. L., Feick, L. F., & Guskey, A. (1995). Everyday market helping behavior. *Journal of Public Policy & Marketing*, *14*(2), 255–266.

Putnam, R. D. (2000). *Bowling alone: The collapse and revival of american community*. New York, NY: Simon & Schuster. doi:10.1145/358916.361990.

Rezabakhsh, B., Bornemann, D., Hansen, U., & Schrader, U. (2006). Consumer power: A comparison of the old economy and the Internet economy. *Journal of Consumer Policy*, *29*(1), 3–36. doi:10.1007/s10603-005-3307-7.

Roberts, J. H., & Urban, G. L. (1988). Modeling multiattribute utility, risk and belief dynamics for new consumer durable brand choice. *Management Science*, *34*, 167–185. doi:10.1287/mnsc.34.2.167.

Rogers, E. M. (2003). *Diffusion of innovations* (5th ed.). New York, NY: The Free Press.

Simon, C. J., & Warner, J. T. (1992). Matchmaker, matchmaker: The effect of old boy networks on job match quality, earnings, and tenure. *Journal of Labor Economics*, *10*(3), 306–330. doi:10.1086/298289.

Sung, Y., Kim, Y., Kwon, O., & Moon, J. (2010). An explorative study of korean consumer participation in virtual brand communities in social network sites. *Journal of Global Marketing*, *23*(5), 430–445. doi:10.1080/08911762.2010.521115.

Van den Bulte, C., & Stremersch, S. (2004). Social contagion and income heterogeneity in new product diffusion: A meta-analytic test. *Marketing Science*, *23*(4), 530–544. doi:10.1287/mksc.1040.0054.

Van Den Bulte, C., & Wuyts, S. (2007). *Social networks and marketing*. Cambridge, MA: Marketing Science Institute.

Varian, H. R. (2002). Market structure in the network age. In Brynjolfsson, E., & Kahin, B. (Eds.), *Understanding the digital economy: Data, tools, and research*. Cambridge, MA: MIT Press.

Wasko, M. M., & Faraj, S. (2005). Why should I share? Examining social capital and knowledge contribution in electronic networks of practice. *Management Information Systems Quarterly*, *29*(1), 35–57.

Watts, D. J. (1999). Networks, dynamics, and the small-world phenomenon. *American Journal of Sociology*, *105*, 493–527. doi:10.1086/210318.

Weber, M. (1968). *Economy and society*. Totowa, NJ: Bedminster Press.

Wikström, S., Carlell, C., & Frostling-Henningsson, M. (2002). From real world to mirror world representation. *Journal of Business Research*, *55*(8), 647–654. doi:10.1016/S0148-2963(00)00205-8.

ADDITIONAL READING

Bechky, B. A. (2003). Sharing meaning across occupational communities: the transformation of knowledge on a production floor. *Organization Science, 14*, 312–330. doi:10.1287/orsc.14.3.312.15162.

Borgatti, S. P., & Everett, M. G. (1999). Models of core/periphery structures. *Social Networks, 21*, 375–395. doi:10.1016/S0378-8733(99)00019-2.

Borgatti, S. P., & Foster, P. C. (2003). The network paradigm in organizational research: A review and typology. *Journal of Management, 29*(6), 991–1013.

Breiger, R. L. (2004). The analysis of social networks. In Hardy, M., & Bryman, A. (Eds.), *Handbook of data analysis* (pp. 505–526). London: Sage. doi:10.4135/9781848608184.n22.

Burt, R. S. (2004). Structural holes and good ideas. *American Journal of Sociology, 110*, 349–399. doi:10.1086/421787.

Childers, T. L., & Rao, A. R. (1992). The influence of familiar and peer-based reference groups on consumer decisions. *The Journal of Consumer Research, 19*(2), 198–211. doi:10.1086/209296.

de Nooy, W., Mrvar, A., & Batagelj, V. (2005). *Exploratory social network analysis with Pajek*. Cambridge, UK: Cambridge University Press. doi:10.1017/CBO9780511806452.

DiMaggio, P., & Louch, H. (1998). Socially embedded consumer transactions: For what kinds of purchases do people most often use networks? *American Sociological Review, 63*(5), 619–637. doi:10.2307/2657331.

Freeman, L. C. (2004). *The development of social network analysis: A study in the sociology of science*. London: Empirical Press.

Golbeck, J. (2009). *Computing with social trust*. Berlin: Springer. doi:10.1007/978-1-84800-356-9.

Hansen, M. (1999). The search-transfer problem: The role of weak ties in sharing knowledge across organization subunits. *Administrative Science Quarterly, 44*, 82–111. doi:10.2307/2667032.

Hossain, L., & Fazio, D. (2009). The social networks of collaborative process. *The Journal of High Technology Management Research, 20*(2), 119–130. doi:10.1016/j.hitech.2009.10.001.

Hummon, N. P. (2000). Utility and dynamic social networks. *Social Networks, 22*(3), 221–249. doi:10.1016/S0378-8733(00)00024-1.

Iacobucci, D. (1989). Modeling multivariate sequential dyadic interactions. *Social Networks, 11*(4), 315–362. doi:10.1016/0378-8733(89)90011-7.

Keller, E., & Berry, J. (2003). *The influentials: One american in ten tells the other nine how to vote, where to eat, and what to buy*. New York, NY: Free Press.

Perry-Smith, J. E. (2006). Social yet creative: The role of social relationships in facilitating individual creativity. *Academy of Management Journal, 49*, 85–101. doi:10.5465/AMJ.2006.20785503.

Reagans, R., & McEvily, B. (2003). Network structure and knowledge transfer: The effects of cohesion and range. *Administrative Science Quarterly, 48*(2), 240–267. doi:10.2307/3556658.

Scott, J. (2000). *Social network analysis: A handbook*. London: Sage.

Tortoriello, M., & Krackhardt, D. (2010). Activating cross-boundary knowledge: Simmelian ties and the generation of innovation. *Academy of Management Journal, 53*(1), 167–181. doi:10.5465/AMJ.2010.48037420.

Wasserman, S., & Kathreen, F. (1994). *Social network analysis: Methods and applications*. Cambridge, UK: Cambridge University Press. doi:10.1017/CBO9780511815478.

Watts, D. J. (2003). *Six degrees: The science of a connected age*. New York, NY: W. W. Norton & Company.

Watts, D. J. (2004). The 'new' science of networks. *Annual Review of Sociology*, *30*, 243–270. doi:10.1146/annurev.soc.30.020404.104342.

Weimann, G. (1994). *The influentials: People who influence people*. Albany, NY: State University of New York Press.

Yikuan, L., & O'Connor, G. C. (2003). New product launch strategy for network effects products. *Journal of the Academy of Marketing Science*, *31*(3), 241–255. doi:10.1177/0092070303031003003.

KEY TERMS AND DEFINITIONS

Alter: An actor to whom a focal actor is connected; a neighbor to the focal actor in an egocentric network.

Co-Shopping: When individuals join consumption action and such joint action may not necessarily be contemporaneous; individuals can perform their respective parts at different times.

Degree Centrality: Number of direct ties an actor has.

Density: The proportion of possible ties in a network that is actually present.

Dyad: A pair of nodes and the (possible) tie(s) between them.

Reciprocity: A tie between A and B is reciprocal, if it is bi-directional, i.e., if the tie is directed and symmetric (a flow occurs front A to B. and front B to A). A reciprocal tie is also called symmetric.

Structural Hole: If a tie that uniquely connects two parts of the network that, without it, would be unconnected, actors involved in such a tie are said to "fill" or "bridge" a structural hole.

Transitivity: A relation is transitive if the presence of a tie between A and B and between B and C also implies the presence of a tie between A and C.

Virtual Community: Social aggregations that emerge from the net when enough people carry on those public discussions long enough, with sufficient human feelings, to form Webs of personal relationships in cyberspace.

Web 2.0: A term coined by media consultant Tim O'Reilly to describe trends in the Internet. An important aspect of Web 2.0 is interactivity, in other words, technology which allows Website visitors to modify the content of the Websites by posting messages and articles, publishing photos and so on. Before there was Web 1.0 where Website visitors could only read content published by the authors.

Chapter 26
The Evolving Value of eTourism for Suppliers and Visitors

João V. Estêvão
Polytechnic Institute of Guarda, Portugal

Maria João Carneiro
University of Aveiro, Portugal & Governance, Competitiveness and Public Policies (GOVCOPP) Research Unit, Portugal

Leonor Teixeira
University of Aveiro, Portugal & Institute of Electronics and Telematics Engineering of Aveiro (IEETA), Portugal

ABSTRACT

The tourism industry is known to have an extensive use of the Internet, both on the supply and on the demand side. The steady and fast emergence of the Internet has dramatically changed the business processes within the sector, forcing suppliers and intermediaries to adapt to a scenario in which visitors have multiple and more flexible choices regarding the search, planning, booking, and purchase of tourism services and products. This chapter explores the main impacts and trends that the dynamic use of the Internet within the tourism sector—the so-called eTourism—has originated in each of the sector's main stakeholders, including suppliers, intermediaries, destination management organizations, and tourists.

INTRODUCTION

The emergence of the Internet has completely transformed the global economy, namely the relations among suppliers and between them and their customers, optimizing management, Business-to-Business (B2B) cooperation and production practices (Castells, 2001). Nowadays, Information and Communication Technologies (ICTs) continue to have a profound effect on the economies and societies where they are used (Ho, Kauffman, & Liang, 2007).

Regarding the evolution of the Internet in terms of its users, the worldwide growth was exponential. Hence, according to the *Internet World Stats* (2011), while by the end of the year 2000 there were

DOI: 10.4018/978-1-4666-4373-4.ch026

only 360.985.492 Internet users, the most recent data, concerning the year 2011, point to about two billion Internet users worldwide. Surely, the Internet penetration rate is very different between nations and continents. Thus, while in 2001, in North America the Internet penetration reached 78.3% of the population, the highest in the world, Africa only reached 11.4% in the same year. It is estimated that by the end of 2011, the world average penetration rate will be around 30.2%. In the US alone, the online market in terms of the value of commercial transactions rose up from a market share of only 20% in 2003 to 33% in 2009, representing a total of 91 billion dollars in *eCommerce* transactions (JupiterResearch, 2011).

According to Öörni (2004), electronic markets substantially benefit from ICTs such as the Internet, since product information can be disseminated with a higher speed, quantity and quality. Due to the nature of the tourism sector, which is highly intangible and also demands suppliers to promote their products to potential customers at a global scale, tourism was, undoubtedly, one of those sectors which were more dramatically transformed by the advent of the Internet (World Tourism Organization Business Council, 1999). In fact, according to Werther and Klein (2000), tourism is perceived as a leading sector and even as a driver of Business-to-Consumer (B2C) *eCommerce*.

The advent of the Internet opened a whole new range of possibilities but also created challenges to individual tourism suppliers and to destinations as a whole. According to Buhalis (2003) the Internet brought some key innovations, such as "melting" down geographical barriers in both B2B and B2C perspectives, which enhanced the capacity of tourism suppliers to act at a global level with much less financial costs, and also allowed tourists to become more informed, autonomous and demanding.

However, given that tourism is a multidisciplinary sector composed by many different actors ranging from national airlines to family-managed restaurants, there is a considerable gap regarding the use of the Internet among the various tourism subsectors. Egger and Buhalis (2008) state that even in the same subsector there might be considerable differences in the level of Internet usage and *eReadiness*.

In such a volatile scenario, it is not easy for the academia and for the strategic players within the sector to keep up with new trends in terms of *eTourism*. However, perhaps more than ever, to gain competitiveness, it is essential to analyze how Internet affects and will affect the tourism industry in the future.

In this context this chapter aims to: a) analyze the way Internet has transformed the tourism sector as a whole as well as different subsectors is particular; b) identify which challenges and competitive advantages *eTourism* brings to tourism suppliers and intermediaries; c) analyze new trends of *eTourism* that empower consumers, such as Travel 2.0.

BACKGROUND

Regarding the conceptual framework required to analyze the ideas conveyed in this chapter, it was considered adequate to start by approaching the concept of tourism system and, in a second moment, to illustrate the role of *eTourism* as an enhancer of tourism's Supply Chain Management (SCM).

The Concept of Tourism System

According to the World Tourism Organization (2001), the nature of the tourism sector is inherently defined by a complex variety of interrelations established between the diverse actors. These interactions should be considered, under a systematic approach, as an ensemble of interdependent stakeholders evolving dynamically. Also, in order to better understand and analyze the wide and complex range of interrelations within the tourism industry, it is necessary to provide a theoretical framework in order to study the tourism sector.

One of the first researchers to approach tourism as a functional system was Gunn (1972), suggesting that "when a state, province or country contemplates improvement and expansion of tourism development, it has to consider tourism in its totality, not just a few parts" (Gunn, 1972: p. 11). The author argues that although it is obvious that every part involved in tourism must prove to be successful, "equally important is how they interrelate" (Gunn, 1972: 11), recognizing both the relevance of integration among various stakeholders and the poor connectivity patterns between them usually observed at the destination level. However, also according to Gunn (1972), it is often difficult to realize how the different tourism stakeholders may/should interrelate in order to maximize benefits deriving from tourism. Consequently, the author suggests a functional tourism system, understood as a broad perspective of how tourism works in order to effectively coordinate and integrate tourism stakeholders through functional planning processes. Therefore, Gunn's (1972) tourism system is divided in two sides – the market side and the supply side. In the first one Gunn identifies one component: tourists – including their behavioral patterns and their ability to travel. On the supply side Gunn (1972) identifies four components: information/promotion; transportation; attractions, and; services. Before, during and even after their travel experiences, tourists should be given the possibility to use each one of these components. Thus, at the destination level, suppliers must coordinate efforts and establish a value chain that can add value to each supplier's services and satisfy tourists' expectations.

Another important author in the study of tourism systems is Leiper. Although recognizing the need to understand tourism dynamics through systems' theory, Leiper (1990) considers that Gunn's model incurs in the failure to explicitly recognize the interactions between the components of the tourism system and the environment, and argues that, in the perspective of systems' theory, tourism should be seen as an open system. The author's model suggests that the tourism system encompasses three main tourism components – the geographical element, the tourism sector, and the tourists.

As geographical elements Leiper (1990) points out the traveller-generating region, the tourist destination region and the transit route region. The traveller-generating region is where tourists come from. It is the market of origin, which is stimulated to travel by both pull and push factors. Leiper (1990) considers the transit route region not only the route tourists use for traveling from generating regions to destinations, but also the routes they undertake while leaving one visited place to reach another one. Finally, the tourist destination, one of the most relevant components of the tourism system, is the main pull factor affecting tourist's motivation to travel and is where most suppliers of tourism and non-tourism services are located and where the tourists can fulfill their temporary goals of travel and go through a memorable tourism experience. As outlined by the author, destinations should provide visitors with varied attractions consciously aimed at alluring pre-determined types of tourists. To do so, the development of planning and management strategies is particularly relevant and requires some kind of leading entity (usually belonging totally or partially to the public sector) acting as a catalyst of the pursued planning objectives.

The second element of Leiper's system is the tourism sector (also addressed as tourism industry by some authors), which is the set of businesses and organizations that help to promote the tourism product. According to Leiper (1990) various actors of the tourism system may be located in the previously mentioned geographical elements. In the traveler-generating region, tourists can find travel agents and tour operators. The destination region is where most of the tourism businesses available to tourists can be found, such as attractions, the hospitality industry, activities and ancillary services. In the route region, one can find, for example, many transportation companies.

The third element of Leiper's tourism system is the tourist demand. The author considers that tourism is a complete and comprehensive system in which tourists play an important role and, as such, should not be viewed in a somewhat narrow perspective as passive consumers of services (Leiper, 1990). Although, on the one hand, tourism often increases tourists' knowledge, provides pleasant escapes from stressful modern living and fosters multiculturalism, such as outlined by Przeclawski (1990), on the other hand, tourists can help to improve the tourism environment, to enhance the images of the destinations, to push the tourism industry forward and, consequently, to maximize the whole tourism system.

Hall (2000), whose focus on tourism planning takes him to emphasize the spectrum of relationships established among destinations' stakeholders, defines a system "as an assemblage or combination of things or parts forming a complex or unitary role" (p. 50). According to Leiper (1990) a system "can be defined as a set of elements interacting with one another". Although recognizing that systems' analysis is an abstract construction rather than the reality itself, Hall (2000) recognizes that "we all have our ideas, models or theories about how the world or people operate. These are our abstractions which we use to understand the world, explain what is happening, and act accordingly in various situations" (Hall, 2000: p. 49).

A rather similar approach to Leiper's tourism system is proposed by Hall (2000), which argues that different types of systems' models have been used in tourism studies, according to the interest of the analysis. As an example, the author considers that the three main basic elements that should be identified in a system designed to analyze tourism at a geographical level are the generating region, the transit region and the destination region (Hall, 2000). However, a systems' model, focused on a geographical level, is unlikely to be the most appropriate in a more economical and commercially-oriented perspective because it will tend to privilege a land use approach highlighting issues such as environmental sustainability or tourism impacts rather than economical ones (Getz, 1987). To demonstrate that the elements of a tourism system are not (should no) be static and should change according to the perspective of analysis, Hall (2000) quotes the rather untypical and commercially oriented Mill and Morrison's tourism system that incorporates four elements that differ from the previously discussed model: market, travel, destination and marketing. According to Mill and Morrison (1998) the tourism functional system is like a spider's Web – touch one part of it and the reverberations will be felt throughout.

According to Cunha (2001) the tourism sector can be considered a system because it consists on an ensemble of elements that establishes interdependent connections among themselves. These connections have spatial and functional natures that include source, transit and destination regions. Cunha (2001) stresses the need to approach tourism as a functional system at all levels (academic, political, and economical, among others). Analyzing tourism as a functional system is crucial as it is not enough to know and describe each of the actors of the system but rather to understand the interdependencies among them and how a certain actor affects others (MacIntosh, & Goeldner, 1986).

Leiper suggests that systems "where the elements, and the system as a whole, are also interacting with environments" are considered open systems (Leiper, 1990, p. 546). As Cunha (2001) argues, open systems are those influenced by externalities where one can observe a continuous flow of inputs and outputs. Leiper (1993) suggests that tourism systems are very open systems because, besides the interaction that exists among its components, it also interacts with multiple diverse environments. Also according to the same author, the tourist demand is the main responsible for the emergence of tourism systems, as it assumes the main role in generating businesses, transit routes and destinations. Consequently, Leiper (1990) argues that it is a fallacy to define the tourism supply, in itself, as a system, as it is originated and molded by tourists. From the moment tourists "set out, places assume the roles of generating regions, transit routes and destinations. When they begin using services in tourist markets, the service-based component of the industry begin producing" (1990, pp. 547-548).

The previously noticeable variety of perspectives that different authors use to analyze the tourism system demonstrates the diversity of priorities of research in the area of tourism and leisure. In fact, while some investigators tend to privilege a perhaps more pragmatic analysis of the tourism system focused on the tourism product *ready to sell* to the demand, others tend to prioritize the components that, in a first instance, make a destination more or less cohesive and sustainable, focusing the analysis on the nature and variety of components inside the destination.

In order to exist and keep competitive, a tourist destination must possess a set of components capable of meeting the demand's needs and requirements (Cooper, Fletcher, Gilbert, & Wanhill, 1998). Again, authors with dissimilar perspectives and research interests identified different types of tourism destination components. Cooper *et al.*'s (1998) understanding of the components in tourism is subordinated to the destination and its internal competitiveness and sustainability. The main components of destinations proposed by Cooper *et al.* (1998) are: attractions, comprising natural and artificial resources and events; amenities, which include accommodation, food and beverage and retailing and other services; access, namely the set of transports and accessibilities to/from and within destinations; and ancillary services, usually non-profitable services, such as tourism information offices, often developed by public or public-private bodies, such as Destination Management Organizations (DMOs).

When facing the need to select one the most appropriate approaches to classify the components of tourism destinations on which to base the present research, and that could be used in the analysis of the dynamic relationship between the Internet and the tourism industry, it seemed that Cooper *et al.*'s approach would be the most adequate one to adopt. The present chapter will not analyze the role and advantages of *eTourism* to the first component outlined by Cooper *et al.* (1998)—attractions—as it will focus on specific services within the tourism sector, namely amenities (hotel industry), access (transportation) and ancillary services (Destination Management Organizations). To these destination-based services it was considered adequate to add a fourth subsector on which *eTourism* has been playing a major role: tourism intermediaries.

Regarding the competitiveness of destinations in general and of suppliers in particular, it is paramount to establish an effective supply chain management (Zhang, Son, & Huang, 2009). As will be discussed in the next subsection, *eTourism* has an indispensable role to play in this process.

eTourism as an Enhancer of Tourism's Supply Chain Management

Nowadays, individual businesses no longer compete as isolated bodies but rather as supply chains (Lambert, & Cooper, 2000). Thus, companies should not only focus on their intra-organizational business functions (e.g. management and administration, human resources, finance and accounts), but also on their inter-organizational business functions, such as supply chain management (SCM) (Lee, & Lan, 2007). Supply chains consist of the alignment of firms that bring products or services to the market, demanding the establishment of a network of organizations involved, through linkages, in processes and activities that produce value to the consumer (Christopher, 1992, Lambert, Stock, & Ellram, 1998, Mentzer, De Witt, Min, Nix, Smith, & Zacharia, 2001). However, the simple fact that supply chains exist does not mean that they are properly managed or even managed at all (Mentzer *et al.*, 2001).

In order to remain effective and competitive, supply chains require SCM, which demand ongoing and systematic management efforts from the organizations within the supply chain (Lambert, & Cooper, 2000). According to Chou, Tan and Yen (2004), SCM can be seen as both a managerial philosophy and as a set of managerial processes. Regarding the first, which Mentzer *et al.* (2001) referred to as Supply Chain Orientation, SCM adopts a systems' approach considering the supply chain as a single body rather than a set of fragmented entities in which each firm directly and indirectly affects the results of the other supply chain members (Ellram and Cooper, 1990). As a set of managerial processes, SCM allows the management of relationships, information and materials across enterprises, delivering enhanced customer service and economic value to consumers (Chou *et al.*, 2006).

The tourism industry is no exception as it must create and maintain effective supply chains linking individual businesses to their target market(s). Regarding supply chain management within the tourism industry, studies are still very limited (Zhang *et al.*, 2009). Official tourism bodies, usually designated as DMOs, are often responsible for planning and executing marketing programs to serve the strategic goals of the respective regions or countries (Douglas, & Mills, 2004). Destination supply chain management is a challenging process for DMOs due to the destinations' many independent suppliers and service providers, often dispersed and fragmented (Uysal, Chen, & Williams, 2000). Additionally, adversary relations are often the norm within tourism destinations (Zhang *et al.*, 2009). Thus, DMOs should not only engage in promotional initiatives of their offerings, as they often do, but also play the leading role regarding the destination development process and the coordination among all destination stakeholders, including in fostering adequate supply chains for their destinations (Buhalis, 2000, Hall, 2000, Page, & Hall, 2003).

Web-marketing is likely to be nowadays' most relevant and impacting vehicle of destination marketing due to its growing importance and because of its effectiveness and efficiency in terms of global presence, communication and of the possibilities of generating interaction flows within destination stakeholders (Presenza, Sheehan, & Ritchie, 2005).

CHALLENGES AND ADVANTAGES FOSTERED BY ETOURISM TO DIFFERENT TOURISM STAKEHOLDERS

The presence of the Internet in the travel and hospitality is growing at a fast pace. Over two-thirds of travel and hospitality firms consider their Websites as important competitive tools and 60% of them believe that the Internet is essential to acquire new customers (Baloglu, & Pekcan, 2006).

As previously referred, the present section aims at describing and exploring the main challenges and advantages that *eTourism* has been fostering within the following stakeholders of the tourism activity: transportation, hotel industry, intermediaries and DMOs.

The advantages that the Internet can bring to each of the different tourism suppliers are intimately related to the types of contents and functionalities that they implement on their own Web applications. Li and Wang's (2010) evaluation of Chinese destination Websites proposes an assessment model of contents and functionalities contemplating five dimensions, one of them being purely technical—Technical Merit Dimension—and the other four more related to specific contents and functionalities available to users, namely information, communication, relationship and transaction dimensions. Excluding the technical merit dimension, the other four dimensions pro-

Figure 1. Advantages of eTourism to the transportation and hotel industries, intermediaries, and DMOs Sources: Based on Aksu & Tarkan, 2002; Anckar, 2008; Andersson, 2008; Baloglu & Pekcan, 2006; Blum, n.d.; Fallon, 2003; Buhalis, 2003; Casielles, Martín, & Vázquez, 2004; Chu, 2001; Chung & Law, 2003; Egger & Buhalis, 2008; Egger & Wörndl, n.d.; Gilbert, Powell-Perry, & Widijoso, 1999; Ham, Kim, & Jeong, 2004; Kaldis & Kaldis, 2008; Law & Leung, 2000; Law & Hsu, 2005; Li & Wang, 2010; Lubbe, 2008; Murphy, n.d.; Forrest, n.d.; Wotring & Bryman, 1996; Nalazek, 2008; Sigala, 2002; SITA, 2007; The European e-Business Market Watch, 2006; Wei, n.d.; Ruys, n.d.; van Hoof & Combrink, 2001; Zafiropoulos, n.d.; Vrana & Paschaloudis, 2006.

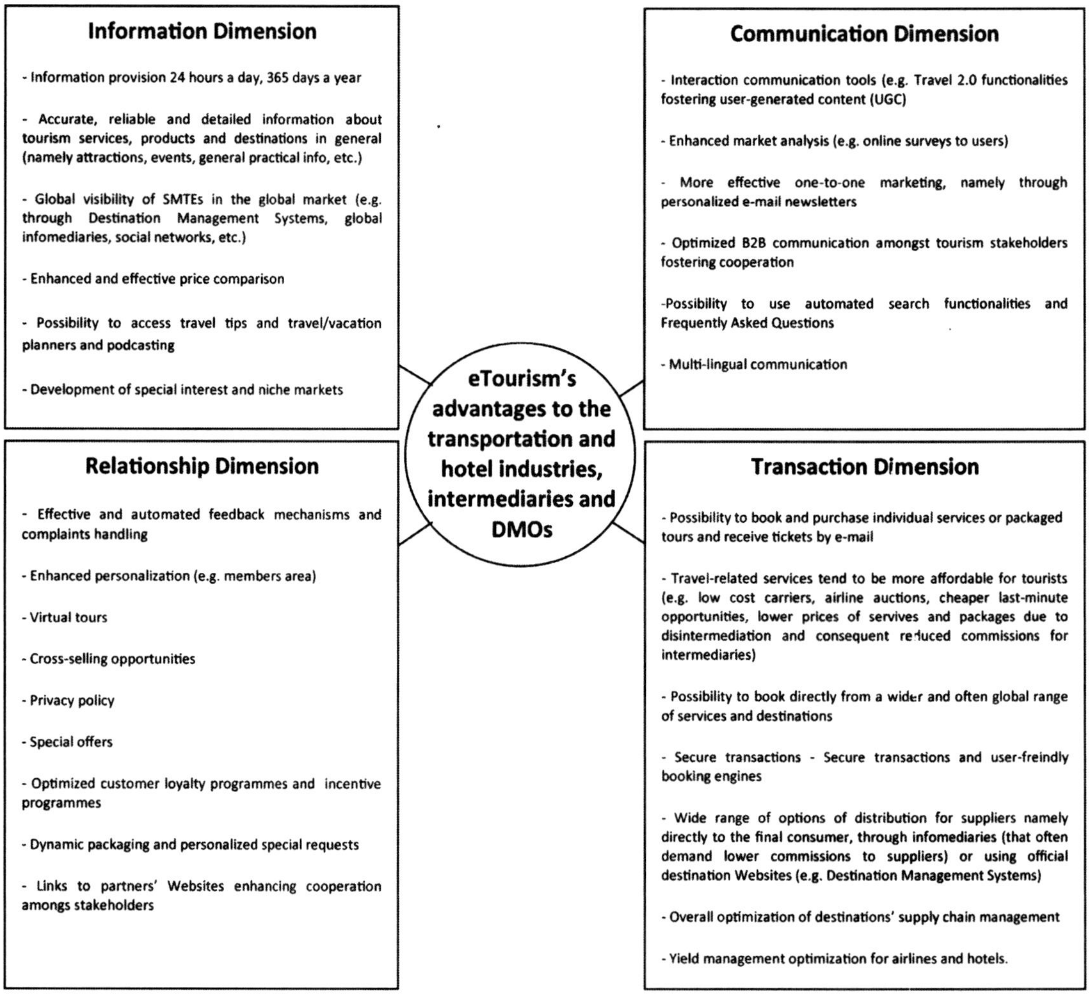

posed by Li and Wang (2010) seem appropriate to serve as a basis to illustrate some of the most important advantages that the Internet can bring to the previously referred tourism stakeholders. Figure 1 illustrates the potential advantages of *eTourism* to those same stakeholders in general, related to each of the four dimensions proposed by Li and Wang (2010).

Transportation

Although linkages to outside of the destination are essential to bring tourists to a certain destination, it is also crucial to ensure mobility to tourists inside the destination and to integrate transportation and corresponding infrastructure (such as cycle ways) in the overall tourism experience. Cooper *et al.*

(1998) highlight the importance of having a creative approach to transportation at the destination as it can help diversify and maximize the tourist experience. As innovative examples of transportation inside a destination, the authors include scenic drives; park and ride schemes; shuttle buses for walkers; cycle ways; explorer buses. The creative integration of certain means of transportation in the destination's tourist experience is often linked to its particular features in terms of mobility. For instance, some of the major tourism attractions of certain destinations are the traditional means of transportation of their communities that were often maintained and improved mainly to optimize tourist experiences. Some examples of this are the tramways of Lisbon or San Francisco which are a tourism landmark for both cities and the scenic railway heritage routes that, in terms of promotion, are often the aggregator element of complex and diverse tourism experiences in rural areas.

Regarding transport infrastructure, Page (1999) suggests that the development of tourism requires that same infrastructure in order to facilitate the free movement of tourist traffic. However, despite its relevance, the author highlights the fact that most studies on tourism transports have traditionally overlooked transport infrastructure by focusing on mobile forms of travel, such as rail travel, air travel and car-based trips.

Although considering the importance of providing safe and comfortable means of transportation along with planning and maintaining adequate connection infrastructures such as roads and railways, Leiper (1999) argues that terminal facilities, such as ports, airports and railway stations, which provide the context in which the tourist embarks in the mode of transport, ensuring a smooth interaction between the supply and the demand, is particularly important for the sector.

In its approach to one of the most important elements of the access component—the transportation—the World Tourism Organization (Organización Mundial del Turismo, 1998) suggests that the development of tourism has always been intimately connected with the development of transportation. This is due to the fact that tourism demands "the means to reach the destination as well as the means tourists use to move at the destination" (Burkart and Medlick, 1981, as quoted by Organización Mundial del Turismo, 1998: p. 109).

Regarding the importance of transportation to the tourism sector, Holloway (2002) argues that it has been one of the most relevant prerequisites behind the arise of tourism as an industry, The author stresses that the two main factors that determine the accessibility of destinations are price – that is highly influenced by the costs of transportations to tourists - and the time it takes to travel from origin markets to destinations. Holloway (2002) especially emphasizes the role of the aviation industry in the fast global spreading of source markets and destinations around the world.

According to Egger and Buhalis (2008), the airline industry is still dominated by senior carriers and a considerable number of smaller airlines. The aviation sector is considered one of the most sophisticated and digitalized industries as it depends on highly technological stakeholders, such as airport infrastructures or aircraft manufacturers.

According to Davidson (2002), the deregulation of the air space, first in the USA (1978) and followed by Europe (1987 to 1997) fostered competition between airlines and demanded a more cost-efficient management from airlines. Deregulation led to a structural change in the market, increased productivity, improved customer service and lower prices (Holloway, 2002).

The Global Distribution Systems (GDSs), namely *Galileo*, *Amadeus*, *Worldspan* and *Sabre* were traditional the most prominent distribution channel for airlines, as they allowed any travel agent to book and sell tickets from most carriers (Egger, & Buhalis, 2008). According to Egger and Buhalis (2008) "they were effectively developed as travel supermarkets in the pre-Internet era and their primary objective were to connect travel agencies with airlines" (p. 264).

Although GDSs are still an important part of the distribution strategy of airlines, being the most important link between airlines and intermediaries, the Internet has been diminishing their relevance since it allows airlines to sell their own tickets without the need of third-party intermediaries. A good example of this fact is the emergence of the low cost airlines, which sell almost every seat in their inventory directly through the Internet. According to the 2006 European Commission *e-Business W@tch* (2006), in 2005, *Ryanair*, the Irish biggest low cost airline in the world, sold around 95% of their tickets directly to the final clients through the Internet.

According to Klein, Könhe and Öörni (2004), the first subsector within tourism that better grasped and took advantage of the Internet was the airline industry, mostly due to its already strong technological nature. The authors suggest that airline tickets seem especially appropriate for online distribution since they can be easily reproduced and distributed online. Hence, the fact that low cost carriers have enormously grown from the mid-90s is especially due to the possibility, given by the Internet, to sell their tickets directly to the general public without the need for intermediation from travel agencies. Airlines have increased the direct sale of their tickets through e-ticketing in order to save commission and other marketing costs, since the latter amount to up to 30% of the price of a ticket (Buhalis, 2003). According to Egger and Buhalis (2008), "while before the turn of the millennium it was practically impossible to buy tickets via the Internet, today, in at least the business models of the low-cost carriers, it is the only way for customers, both B2C and B2B, to obtain tickets" (p. 264). Additionally, according to the results of 2007 Annual Airline ICT Trends Survey, around 90% of the airlines currently use their Websites as a distribution channel (SITA, 2007).

It is becoming ever clearer that ICTs and the Internet in particular will become more and more indispensable to the operational and strategic dimensions of airlines. According to Buhalis (2003), the Internet will heavily support successful airlines not only regarding the marketing mix of airlines, as it will also determine their strategic thinking and will become more critical to their operations and strategy of airlines. It can therefore be foreseen that ICTs will not only establish all elements of the marketing mix of airlines in the future, but they will also determine their strategic directions, partnerships and even ownership (Egger, & Buhalis, 2008).

Regarding its turnover, the car hire subsector is the second most important within the transportation sector. Large companies, such as Avis and Hertz, have long implemented ICT systems contemplating the Web, aiming to manage their extensive and disperse inventory and support their relationship with their customers, namely through direct online marketing. More recently, car hire companies have also been using the Internet to optimize their synergies with airlines, empowering customers to use their airline loyalty programs' bonus points to rent a car from a partner company (Egger, & Buhalis, 2008).

Concerning the railway subsector, only a minority of travelers tend to purchase train tickets though the Internet, with the exception of long distance travels and fast trains such as TGV. However, this tendency is gradually changing as there has been a recent increase in the number of online platforms developed by the railway industry. According to Egger and Buhalis (2008), *Bahn.de*, the German Railways Website is a good example of this shifting trend, as it is not only one of the most visited travel portals in Europe but also allows dynamic travel planning and e-ticketing of train and bus transportation, also through mobile devices.

Hotel Industry

Accommodation provided by the hotel subsector is crucial within the tourism industry. According to Mill and Morrison (1998), accommodations can range from hotel chains to camping sites and homes of friends and relatives. In terms of its economic weight, the same authors outline that lodging represent between one-fifth and one-fourth of the total expenditures of tourists. For the tourist demand, hotels are the physical and psychological basis of their tourist experiences.

The hotel industry is overwhelmingly diverse, namely in terms of the size and capacity of properties and types of management. Especially in regions where the hotel sector has a longer tradition, such as Europe, small, family-managed hotels coexist alongside larger multinational hotel chains adopting more systematic and, often, professional approaches to hotel management. Although the diversity in terms of types of hotel firms enriches the range of hospitality options of a certain destination, it also favors a digital gap within the same subsector, diminishing the capacity of the whole range of hotel businesses to have the same degree of *eReadiness* and, thus, effectively cooperate via the Web.

Despite this diversity, according to Go and Pine (1995), the hotel subsector has been experiencing a global trend towards hotel chain affiliation. In fact, Kotler *et al.* (2003) suggest that the modern hotel industry is dominated by chains, managed in a highly competitive environment and using aggressive marketing strategies. In an empirical study conducted by Yeung and Law (2004) aimed at comparing the usability levels between the Websites of hotel chains with those of independent hotels in Hong Kong, the authors demonstrated that the usability performance of hotels chains' Websites was significantly better than that of independent properties (Yeung, & Law, 2004).

Already in 1998, Mutch suggested that although smaller hotel firms could significantly gain benefits from Information Technologies (IT), perhaps even more than hotel chains, the effective use of IT, especially of the Internet, by this type of hotel firms, still remained scarce.

In fact, in comparison with the airline industry, the hotel industry as a whole was relatively slow to start using ICTs (Egger, & Buhalis, 2008), especially due to the, predominance, in this subsector, of Small and Medium-Sized Enterprises (SMEs) with lower levels of IT knowledge and less economical possibilities to invest in ICTs (Buhalis, 2003). However, larger hotel chains, such as the Intercontinental Group, have rapidly taken advantage of the Internet in innovative ways, such as in creating networks linking internal Property Management Systems (PMS) with online intermediaries allowing real-time reservations from travel portals operating at a global scale (O'Connor, 2008).

Despite the fact that the hotel industry was the least automated subsector within tourism, the fast growth of the Internet led to a gradual adoption of the Internet as an operational and strategic tool for hotels. Nowadays, according to Mathies and Weiermair (2003), ICTs, including the Internet, are used in four main areas of the internal operations of a hotel as well as in other four dimensions of the relationship of the hotel with their customers. Regarding the internal operations, ICTs are more widely used to manage the business infrastructure (Property Management Systems; Yield Management Systems allowing hotels fast real-time price changes and a more effective pricing policy instantaneously available to all users through the hotel's Website; CRM systems, among others); in human resource management (personnel information systems); information (consulting and information systems) and procurement (eProcurement). Regarding the B2C and C2B dimensions, Mathies and Weiermair (2003) outline the role of ICTs in distribution, namely through the adoption of e-Commerce, and of more appealing marketing practices, such as the widely implementation of more captivating functionalities allowing users to engage in virtual visits and enriched media (such as videos or panoramic photos) of the hotels.

Intermediaries

The tourism industry is considerably heterogeneous in terms of the quantity and diversity of players, which are usually geographically dispersed and have scarce levels of cohesion. Additionally, although there is currently a tendency towards concentration within the sector (e.g. vertical integration), small and medium-sized tourism enterprises are still predominant. Thus, destinations as a whole and, especially, individual suppliers often suffer from lack of visibility in the global market, justifying the need for intermediaries who can "bring together" different services, assembling multi-service products and promoting and selling them abroad (Buhalis, 1999).

In the pre-Internet era intermediaries within the tourism sector were traditionally divided in two main types of companies: tour operators and travel agencies. As will be discussed later, these actors still exist but now have to face fierce competition from new types of intermediaries, namely infomediaries (Law, Leung, & Wong, 2004). Tour operators can be considered aggregators, since they produce a new product by combining basic services or components. Travel agents, on the other hand, can be seen as information brokers, giving consumer relevant information and booking facilities (Werthner & Klein, 1999).

However, their relevance for tourism destinations goes far beyond distribution. In fact, although researchers such as Baloglu and Mangaloglu (2001) recognize the importance of travel agencies and tour operators in developing, promoting, and distributing destination packaged tours, they often have the ability and the power to decisively influence the imagery of destinations and, in some cases, of countries as a whole. This is especially common in regions and countries with scarce resources or strategies in terms of tourism development and promotion, which almost totally rely on the promotional effort of exogenous intermediaries to build a destination image.

Perhaps the tourism service suppliers that suffered the deepest changes through the advent of the Internet were tourism intermediaries. According to some researchers "the accessibility of online travel Websites reduces the importance of travel agencies and might ultimately result in travelers bypassing travel agencies altogether" (Law *et al.*, 2004, p. 101) which may lead to a scenario in which "traditional distribution channels will be replaced by electronic distribution channels" (Law, *et al.*, 2004, p. 106). However, the simplistic logic suggesting that the Internet would, in itself, guarantee direct interaction between suppliers and visitors, thus turning tourism intermediaries obsolete (Gellman, 1996), proved to be wrong (Gomis, 2005). In fact, although the Internet originated processes of disintermediation, in which individual companies were able to relate directly to their final customers, it is also true that the Internet gave origin to processes of reintermediation since it fostered the emergence of a new kind of online, global intermediaries capable of promoting and selling their own tourism packages to an also global audience without the need for local retailers (Buhalis, 2003). Since, on one hand, this relatively recent generation of intermediaries sell virtually the whole range of tourism services of most tourism destinations and, on the other hand, they developed new and innovative tools allowing a more participatory role of tourists in their travels' planning and booking processes, they empowered tourists, by allowing them, for instance, to build their own personalized packages (dynamic packaging), to compare prices of different service providers and even to consult or insert comments, ratings and media files available to all users (Web 2.0).

It seems evident that having an official Website helped SMEs such as independent hotels to improve their brandbuilding and their Customer Relationship Management (CRM) initiatives. However, being most of the tourism sector worldwide composed by SMEs, the fact that a small company developed an independent Website would not assure, by itself, global visibility and the possibility of avoiding the costly intermediation of tour operators. Another factor against Small and Medium Tourism Enterprises (SMTEs) in terms of Internet use is the fact that the Internet has, inherently, an enormous dispersion of information and the tendency of the demand is to search for Websites that, somehow, aggregate that huge amount of data. As a result, shortly after the emergence of the Internet, the first online tour operators appeared and, in many cases, overcame more traditional offline intermediaries (Gomis, 2005).

So, at a first glance, the emergence of the Internet did not, in itself, solved the problem of SMTEs to distribute their offerings, only replacing offline intermediaries by online ones, such as *Expedia*, *Bookings.com* or *Lastminute*, three of the biggest and fastest growing intermediaries worldwide, that operate at a global scale, selling a global range of destinations to an also global demand, meaning that they often have more power over destinations' suppliers than the previous offline tour operators (Park, & Gretzel, 2006).

Destination Management Organizations

In recent years, the entities usually responsible for the development of tourism destinations as a whole, often designated as DMOs, have also been developing Web-based platforms, in most cases limited to an official Website used for promoting the destination. However, a shorter number of DMOs have been able to establish and successfully develop destination Web-based networks linking suppliers, usually designated as Destination Management Systems (DMSs). These systems empower official destination Web platforms to go beyond the basic task of promoting their destinations, also allowing them to sell their offerings to prospective tourists (Dwyer, Edwards, Mistilis, Roman, & Scott, 2009; Pollock, 1995). By integrating the concepts of virtual reality in DMSs, DMOs can make the destination more accessible and may promote the destination in a more creative way (Guttentag, 2010). Additionally, since tourists are becoming active mobile technology users while visiting a destination, one can find in several countries a significant number of regional or local destinations that have or are developing new Web-based tourism mobile services used to assist visitors on route and enrich their experiences (Martin, Alzua, & Lamsfus, 2011).

In terms of the relevance of the Internet in promoting and distributing accurate and up-to-date information and services of a certain destination, visitors are becoming more sophisticated and demanding. They are seeking online platforms that allow them to search for information about a destination, plan an individual experience and make the corresponding reservations, often using a single Web application. However, most of these applications are privately owned and managed, such as *Expedia.com* or *Lastminute.com*. Publicly owned and managed Web applications of this kind, such as DMS still remain rarely implemented by official, public tourism organizations (Buhalis, 2000).

Among the most frequently mentioned advantages of DMSs for both destinations' suppliers and visitors, (Buhalis, 2003; Buhalis, & Spada, 2000; Egger, & Buhalis, 2008; World Tourism Organization, 2001) regarding intra-destination development one can outline, on one hand enhanced visibility of Small and Medium Sized Tourism Enterprises (SMTEs) in the global market diminishing their dependency on external intermediaries and, consequently, allowing them to reach higher revenues. In this context, according to Cooper (2006: 57), "clearly, small- and medium-sized enterprises can benefit from entering into alliances, clusters, or franchises to achieve mutually beneficial objectives or work through intermediaries such as tourist boards" in order to gain visibility. As Buhalis suggests (2003), the contribution of DMSs "to strategic management and marketing is demonstrated by their ability to integrate all stakeholders at destinations and also to reach a global market at a fairly affordable cost" (p. 283). Regarding the role of ITCs and, particularly, of DMSs in this process, Dwyer *et al.* (2009) suggest that "smaller players can benefit from technology as the Internet makes it possible for marketing activity to be undertaken on a more level playing field whereby small businesses can connect directly to consumers and to compete for market share on an even footing with larger firms." As a result of empirical evidence derived from a series of workshops comprising a range of Australian tourism stakeholders, the authors suggest that "smaller tourism providers need to form partnerships with Internet providers and online intermediaries to help them communicate their message via database marketing and information technology" (p. 73) such as DMSs.

Another major advantage of DMSs is the fact that they foster coordinated promotion and distribution of the whole destination leading to a higher cohesion among various stakeholders that share the same marketing and *eCommerce* platform. In fact, when analyzing the utility of information elements available in destination portals, Teichmann and Zins (2008) consider that "the more features the Website incorporates the more it can meet the needs of consumers at different information consumption stages" (p. 209). DMSs not only provide information about various elements of the destination as they also allow reservations. They also give members (usually, destination-based companies) access to privileged information and tools usually available for DMS affiliate members (image bank, destination's facts and figures, legal documentation).

However, the existence of high levels of cooperation among stakeholders is often considered a prerequisite to create and maintain DMSs. According to Ndou and Petti (2007) in destinations with low levels of cohesion, where there are low levels of coordination among stakeholders, DMSs can be seen as the means, rather than the end of a destination management policy. This means that the attempt to establish any kind of Web-based destination management should be preceded by a change in the management process aimed at establishing the necessary cultural, organizational and technological conditions for any further steps regarding the strengthening of destination's competitiveness. Thus, any attempt to create a destination-wide Web-based system should focus on the preliminary issue of establishing bonds of cooperation and spreading the message of the importance of choosing and pursuing a shared model for the integral and participated development of the tourism destination. Thus, even at the lower levels of its development, Web-based platforms can help reshape destinations, enhancing B2B information flows and cooperation among various stakeholders (Sigala, & Marianidis, 2010).

At a macro-economic level, DMSs can help entire countries diversifying their supply and its territorial distribution, and also communicating with a more autonomous and mature demand that does not look for package tours from traditional intermediaries. DMSs also contribute for a higher cohesion inside the destination and, consequently, to a more coordinated promotion of the destination. Secondly, as previously discussed, they provide small and medium-sized tourism enterprises, usually marginal in the global market, a direct and effective presence/distribution through the destination portals provided by DMSs, diminishing their dependence on intermediaries (Buhalis, 2000; Ndou, & Petti, 2007).

TRAVEL 2.0 AS A WEB-BASED TOOL EMPOWERING VISITORS

Ever since the advent of the World Wide Web, an increasing number of travelers have been using the Internet for travel planning (Ye, Law, Gu, & Chen, 2011). However, until recently, most Websites were built under a Web 1.0 perspective, in which the vast majority of users were only able to act as consumers of content (Cormode & Kirshnamouthy, 2008). More recently, the advent of Web

2.0 introduced a different and original philosophy allowing any user to become a content creator, thus democratizing online content creation (Cormode & Kirshnamouthy, 2008).

Regarding the definition of Web 2.0, Egger (2010) suggests that, although this is still an unclear and relatively vague concept, which has lead to harsh criticism of the concept itself, Web 2.0 is a "collective expression comprising both the technical but above all the social and societal advances in the Internet" (Egger, 2010: p. 126).

Concerning the role of Web 2.0 in fostering coordination amongst organizations, Lee and Lan (2007) argue that with Web 2.0, the traditional knowledge management based on central information repositories has shifted into a more interactive conversational approach. This approach emphasizes the integration and collaboration of knowledge creation amongst stakeholders (Lee, & Lan, 2007). According to the authors, the most important advantage of Web 2.0 is that is fosters cooperation and creates new opportunities for dynamic knowledge and inter-organizational collective intelligence. Besides, Web 2.0 also presents clear collaborative advantages since novice users, with limited Web skills, are able to contribute with their expertise to the virtual communities.

Sigala (2011) was one of the various authors who made a conceptual approach to the concept of Web 2.0 defining it as a set of tools of "mass collaboration as they enable and empower Internet users to actively and simultaneously collaborate with others for producing, consuming and diffusing Internet-based information and applications" (p. 608). Also according to Sigala (2011), Web 2.0 gave origin to two major features—User-Generated Content (UGC) and social networks—which have dramatically transformed the way users search, distribute, share and create information. Thus, UGC or CGM (consumer-generated media) is a result of Web 2.0, which is a new form of word-of-mouth that serve informational needs by offering non-commercial, detailed, experimental, and up-to-date information with an access beyond the boundaries of one's immediate social circle" (Yoo & Gretzel, 2011, p. 610). The main Web 2.0 applications that empower UGC are online communities and discussion forums, blogs, online reviews, and podcasting (namely video and photo sharing) as well as wikis (Gray, Thompson, Clerehan, Sheard, & Hamilton, 2008).

Regarding the recent development of UGC there is evidence that its development and sharing, made possible by Web 2.0 applications, is continuously increasing (Casaló, Flavián, & Guinalíu, 2011; Parra-Lopéz, Bulchand-Gidumal, Gutiérrez-Taño, & Díaz-Armas, 2011; Sigala, 2008; Yoo & Gretzel, 2008). In some countries, such as the US, a substantial majority of consumers search for fellow consumers' product reviews online and most of these reported that they had a more decisive role on their decision-making processes than reviews posted by professionals (Casaló *et al.*, 2011).

Nowadays, Web 2.0 is changing the way that consumers engage with information presented via the Internet (Del Chiappa, 2011) and is having major implications in the way companies relate to their publics such as: the opportunity to exchange, systematize and evaluate information via users (collective intelligence); the possibility to obtain feedback and record users behavior in order to systematically adapt and enhance offerings (perpetual beta); among others (Egger, 2010).

Currently, the "interactive Web" made possible by Web 2.0 has a major role in the tourism industry and is particularly suited to the sector, especially due to the intense interaction and communication levels inherent to travel and tourism (Egger, 2010). Being information the "lifeblood" of the tourism industry, the use and spread of Web 2.0 have an extensive impact on both tourism suppliers and visitors (Sigala, 2011).

The relevance of the Web 2.0 in tourism justified the adoption of the expression Travel 2.0 to designate Web 2.0 used within the tourism industry. Regarding the advantages that Web 2.0 and consequent UGC might bring to tourism businesses, Ye *et al.* (2011) empirically demonstrated that there is a close cause-effect relationship between the use of Web 2.0 by hotels and their online sales of rooms. In their analysis, the authors demonstrated that a 10% increase in the ratings of user reviews could boost their online bookings (Ye *et al.*, 2011). Although commercially Websites adopting Web 2.0 are rapidly emerging within the tourism industry, they are mostly developed by individual businesses or tourism intermediaries (Casaló *et al.*, 2011). The use of Web 2.0 by destinations and respective official Web applications yet seems to be only starting while it is still a virtually unexplored area in terms of research.

Regarding the role of Web 2.0 and resulting UGC in official destination Websites in a B2C perspective, Yoo, Lee, Gretzel and Fesenmaier (2009) study the trustworthiness of travel related UGC, argued that official tourism bureau Websites would greatly benefit from supporting a venue for UGC contents because they proved to me more trustworthy when featuring in official bureaus Websites. However, there is evidence that regional and national tourism bureaus scarcely adopt UGC applications in their Websites (Estêvão, Carneiro, & Teixeira, 2011).

Concerning the potential benefits of the Web 2.0 applications for destinations in a B2B perspective, the implementation of Web 2.0 by official destination bureaus also allows suppliers themselves to share and spread information through the destination's extranet that can prove to be useful in supporting DMOs' role aimed at maximizing interaction flows among internal destination suppliers and can be valuable in enhancing the pivotal role of DMOs towards a more collaborative destination management (Sigala & Marianidis, 2010).

Most studies encompassing Web 2.0 in tourism tend to focus on the demand's trust and behavior towards the UGC it originates (Casaló *et al.*, 2011; Del Chiappa, 2011; Yoo & Gretzel, 2011; Yoo *et al.*, 2009) or rather explore the advantages they bring to visitors and to particular businesses or subsectors within the tourism industry (Sigala, 2011; Ye *et al.*, 2011). However, the analysis of the implementation of these applications by destination Websites, namely DMSs, yet seems to remain relatively unexplored in the literature. Although there is a gap in the literature in this scope, there is evidence that both advanced destination Web applications—such as DMS—and the Web 2.0 paradigm, share the goal of fostering a more direct, close and flexible relationship between destinations and respective publics.

On the other hand, private actors such as infomediaries (e.g. *Tripadvisor* or *Holidaycheck*), have a more homogeneous use of commercially-oriented Web 2.0 tools, focusing of consumers' ratings and reviews of concrete products. Travel portals such as *TripAdvisor*, the most visited travel-related Website in the world, are inherently Travel 2.0 Web applications and are among the fastest growing Websites globally. Regarding the comparative level of adoption of Travel 2.0 from different types of suppliers, it seems pertinent to refer an empirical study conducted by Schegg, Liebrich, Scaglione and Ahmad (2008), having the Swiss tourism system as a case study. The main results of this study demonstrated that the types of companies more committed to the implementation of Travel 2.0 tools were multinational hotel chains and international tour operators whereas the subsectors with a lower adoption of these tools were cable car companies, small and medium-sized Swiss hotels and local retail travel agencies (Schegg *et al.*, 2008). The same authors highlight that these trends seem to be not only a characteristic of the Swiss tourism system but can be extrapolated to the global setting.

FUTURE RESEARCH DIRECTIONS

Although the present paper focused on the advantages of the Internet for the supply side rather than for the demand, it seems clear that *eTourism* is empowering tourists to a greater extent. In fact, particularly due to the advent of the Internet and of the many options provided to tourists, they are becoming more demanding in terms of tourism services, they are asking for more specific and "niche" offers, they are getting more mobile and critical, but less loyal to specific destinations and services (Werthner & Klein, 2000). Simultaneously, another trend in terms of the demand is that, although more demanding and sophisticated, it is becoming more sensitive to pricing as it is now able to quickly and comfortably compare prices, especially through aggregator Websites. Also, the fact that visitors tend to engage more and more often in short-breaks, thus leading them to decide later which destinations to visit and which services to purchase means that there is a "decreased time span between searching, planning and booking a specific travel. All these trends are both cause and consequence of the development of *eTourism* in most, if not every, subsector of the travel and hospitality sector (Werthner, & Klein, 2000).

However, the existing gap in terms of *eReadiness* from different stakeholders often does not allow tourists to plan and book an integral tourism travel online. Thus, it seems pertinent to suggest that future research in *eTourism* focused on the development of strategies that can fill the existing gap between the digitalization levels of various suppliers at the destination level. In other words, highlighting the destination's *eTourism* strategies rather than only focusing on individual businesses seems to be a pertinent and necessary line of investigation.

Additionally, it is suggested that future research regarding Travel 2.0 addresses more intensively the reasons and solutions for the scarce use of Web 2.0 from specific subsectors within the tourism industry. The recognition of UGC as a valuable and trustworthy instrument for prospective tourists demands a more homogeneous and harmonious use of Travel 2.0 from all tourism suppliers and from destinations as a whole.

CONCLUSION

In order to gain and maintain competitive, entire destinations and individual suppliers should be able to implement effective, multichannel *eTourism* strategies and practices allowing them to cope with the new trends regarding the tourism demand. The simple fact that a DMO or supplier has Internet access and implements a Website is no longer, in itself, criteria for success.

As seen in the case of destinations' *eTourism* strategies, DMOs should be able to consider the Internet as not only an electronic promotional and informational brochure of the destination but should, most importantly, act as a network linking all suppliers and fostering interaction flows among these and connecting them, in bulk, with the demand markets. Thus, advanced destination Websites are not only informational and promotional tools but also relational and transactional platforms responsible for higher revenues to local suppliers as they often bypass the need for intermediation (Bédard, & Louillet, 2008). Besides, the development of official destination Web applications specialized in special interest tourism products, such as heritage cultural tourism, foster the diversification of the range of tourism products and correspondent demands' motivations (Baggio, 2008).

As previously discussed, different tourism subsectors have dissimilar approaches to the Internet, originating a gap in terms of the intensity and depth of eBusiness practices from various suppliers. As demonstrated earlier, the aviation subsector has long been in the forefront of IT usage and innovation and *eTourism* is not an exception. In fact, a clear evidence of the impact of the Internet in the aviation industry was that it originated a new type of airline—the low-cost—whose main success criteria is the direct eTicketing with no need for intermediation, forcing the previously existing carriers to go online or go out of business.

Due to the geographical dispersion of the hotel business and of the fact that most of the accommodation units are still SMEs, the Internet gives them the opportunity to directly relate to the final consumer through the hotel's own Website or by the use of social networks (disintermediation). On the other hand, smaller hotels will not gain immediate visibility abroad just by implementing an attractive and functional Website. Thus, the Internet provides them the chance to establish partnerships with new infomediaries, such as *bookings.com*, which often require lower commissions than traditional offline intermediaries (reintermediation).

Regarding tourism intermediation, the ending of the middleman within the tourism system which was often prophesized in the early stages of the Internet era could not be more wrong. In fact, online-based intermediaries—the infomediaries—are among today's fastest growing tourism firms, which were capable of spreading their offerings globally outperforming most of the traditionally offline-based intermediaries. Companies which did not simply exist only a few years ago, such as *lastminute.com*, *expedia.com*, *tripadvisor.com* or *bookings.com*, just to name a few, are now competing and often threatening the traditional dominance of tour operators that have been in business for decades, much before the advent of the Internet. Another noteworthy regarding trend is that some of the so-called vertical portals, such as *golf.com*, which did not have any relation to the tourism sector and were only aimed at globally bonding people sharing the same interests online, are now implementing their own tourism-related engines. Taking advantage of the visibility of their Website amongst golfers globally, *golf.com*'s managers decided to develop a tourism-related search, planning and booking engine promoting and selling golf destinations and associated services, already menacing the predominance of traditional golf–related tour operators (Egger & Buhalis, 2008).

Lastly, an irrefutable evidence of the empowerment that Internet gives to tourists is the fact that the Web 2.0 in tourism is developing at a faster pace and depth than in most other sectors, enhancing viral marketing and the electronic-word-of-mouth (eWOM). Web 2.0 tools, which foster UGC, allow tourists to "give their reasons on the Web" (De Ascaniis, & Morasso, 2011: 125). The specific current advent of Travel 2.0, is dramatically changing not only the way tourism firms develop their Websites in terms of their philosophy and specific functionalities in order to empower UGC, as it is also encouraging entire destinations to change their promotional messages and tourism themes based on the viral marketing originated by UGC-specific Websites, such as tripadvisor.com. Such is the case of Lugano, one of the most prominent Swiss tourism destinations, which totally reimaged its marketing efforts and changed its tourism themes and slogans as a result of a systematic analysis of Lugano-related contents that tourists inserted in Travel 2.0 Websites (De Ascaniis, & Morasso, S. G., 2011). Additionally, as previously demonstrated, the past fears that Web 2.0 and UGC might not be a trustworthy source of information were dissipated by researchers, who demonstrated its high levels of trustworthiness amongst prospective visitors. However, although Travel 2.0 tools inaugurated a new era in the relationship between suppliers and the demand, with clear benefits for both sides, there is also a gap in terms of the implementation of such tools by different types of tourism stakeholders. Thus, while online intermediaries tend to be one of the businesses that most intensively implemented Web 2.0 functionalities, even taking into account all sectors of the economy, other tourism subsectors, such as independent hospitality providers or even official destination Websites yet do not seem to have grasped the potential of Travel 2.0 and, in general, have scarcely given voice to past or potential tourists thought UGC.

REFERENCES

Aksu, A. A., & Tarcan, E. (2002). The internet and five-star hotels: A case study from the Antalya region in Turkey. *International Journal of Contemporary Hospitality Management*, *14*(2), 94–97. doi:10.1108/09596110210419282.

Anckar, B. (2008). Omena hotels: Technology towards operational efficiency. In Egger, R., & Buhalis, D. (Eds.), *eTourism: case studies* (pp. 37–47). Oxford, UK: Butterworth Heinemann - Elsevier.

Andersson, S. (2008). Finnair: Innovating interactivity. In Egger, R., & Buhalis, D. (Eds.), *eTourism: Case studies* (pp. 293–303). Oxford, UK: Butterworth Heinemann - Elsevier.

Baggio, R. (2008). Province of Rimini: Communicating with the customer. In Egger, R., & Buhalis, D. (Eds.), *eTourism: Case studies* (pp. 213–223). Oxford, UK: Butterworth Heinemann - Elsevier.

Baloglu, S., & Mangaloglu, M. (2001). Tourism destination images of Turkey, Egypt, Greece, and Italy as perceived by US-based tour operators and travel agents. *Tourism Management*, *22*, 1–9. doi:10.1016/S0261-5177(00)00030-3.

Baloglu, S., & Pekcan, Y. A. (2006). The website design and Internet site marketing practices of upscale and luxury hotels in Turkey. *Tourism Management*, *27*, 171–176. doi:10.1016/j.tourman.2004.07.003.

Bédard, F., & Louillet, M. C. (2008). BonjourQuebec.com: A vision, a strategy, a brand. In *R. Egger & D. Buhalis (2008). eTourism: Cases studies* (pp. 200–212). Oxford, UK: Ed. Butterworth Heinemann – Elsevier.

Blum, V., & Fallon, J. (2002). Welsh visitor attraction web sites: Multipurpose tools or technological tokenism? *Information Technology & Tourism*, *4*, 191–201. doi:10.3727/109830501108750985.

Buhalis, D. (1999). Limits of tourism development in peripheral destinations: problems and challenges. *Tourism Management*, *20*, 183–185.

Buhalis, D. (2000). Marketing the competitive destination of the future. *Tourism Management*, *21*, 97–116. doi:10.1016/S0261-5177(99)00095-3.

Buhalis, D. (2003). *eTourism: Information technologies for strategic tourism management*. Harlow, MA: Pearson Higher Education.

Buhalis, D., & Spada, A. (2000). DMS: Criteria for success – An exploratory research. *Information Technology and Tourism*, *3*(1), 41–58.

Casaló, L. V., Flavián, C., & Guinalíu, M. (2011). Understanding the intention to follow the advice obtained in an online travel community. *Computers in Human Behavior*, *27*, 622–633. doi:10.1016/j.chb.2010.04.013.

Casielles, R. V., Martín, A. M., & Vázquez, A. S. (2004). Cómo usan Internet las líneas aéreas para desarrollar relaciones estables con los clientes. *Universia Business Review*, *2*(2), 34–47.

Castells, M. (2001). *A galáxia Internet – Reflexões sobre internet, negócios e sociedade*. Lisbon, Portugal: Ed. Fundação Calouste Gulbenkian.

Chou, D. C., Tan, X., & Yen, D. (2004). Web technology and supply chain management. *Information Management & Computer Security*, *12*(4), 338–349. doi:10.1108/09685220410553550.

Chu, R. (2001). What online Hong Kong travelers look for on airline/travel websites? *International Journal of Hospitality Management*, *20*(1), 95–100. doi:10.1016/S0278-4319(00)00046-3.

Chung, T., & Law, R. (2003). Developing a performance indicator for hotel websites. *Hospital Management*, *22*, 119–125. doi:10.1016/S0278-4319(02)00076-2.

Cooper, C., Fletcher, J., Gilbert, D., & Wanhill, S. (1998). *Tourism: Principles and practice*. London: Prentice Hall.

Cormode, G., & Krishnamurthy, B. (2008). Key differences between web 1.0 and web 2.0. *First Monday*, *13*(6). doi:10.5210/fm.v13i6.2125.

Cunha, L. (2001). *Introdução ao turismo*. Lisbon, Portugal: Ed. Verbo.

Davidson, R. (2002). Distribution channel analysis for business travel. In Buhalis, D., & Eric, L. (Eds.), *Tourism distribution channels: Practices, issues and transformations* (pp. 73–86). New York: Continuum.

De Ascaniis, S., & Morasso, S. G. (2011). When tourists give their reasons on the web: The argumentative significance of tourism related UGC. In Law, R., Fuchs, M., & Ricci, F. (Eds.), *Information and Communication Technologies in Tourism 2011* (pp. 125–138). New York: Springer. doi:10.1007/978-3-7091-0503-0_11.

Del Chiappa, G. (2011). Trustworthiness of web 2.0 applications and their influence on tourist behavior: An empirical investigation in Italy. In Law, R., Fuchs, M., & Ricci, F. (Eds.), *Information and Communication Technologies in Tourism 2011* (pp. 331–342). New York: Springer. doi:10.1007/978-3-7091-0503-0_27.

Douglas, A., & Mills, J. E. (2004). Staying afloat in the tropics: Applying a structural equation model approach to evaluating national tourism organization websites in the Caribbean. *Journal of Travel & Tourism Marketing*, *17*(2/3), 269–293. doi:10.1300/J073v17n02_20.

Dwyer, L., Edwards, D., Mistilis, N., Roman, C., & Scott, N. (2009). Destination and enterprise management for a tourism future. *Tourism Management*, *30*(1), 63–74. doi:10.1016/j.tourman.2008.04.002.

e-Business W@tch. (2006). *ICT and e-business in the tourism industry*. Retrieved from http://www.ebusiness-watch.org/resources/tourism/SR08-2006 Tourism.pdf

Egger, R. (2010). Theorizing web 2.0 phenomena in tourism: A sociological signpost. *Information Technology & Tourism*, *12*, 125–137. doi:10.3727/109830510X12887971002666.

Egger, R., & Buhalis, D. (2008). *eTourism: Case studies*. Oxford, UK: Ed. Butterworth Heinemann.

Egger, R., & Wörndl, L. (2008). Hotel Sallerhof: Innovations in interaction. In Egger, R., & Buhalis, D. (Eds.), *eTourism: Case studies* (pp. 56–64). Oxford, UK: Butterworth Heinemann - Elsevier.

Estêvão, J. P., Carneiro, M. J., & Teixeira, L. (2011). Destination management systems: Improving the tourism experience by empowering visitors. In *Proceedings of the 4th Advances in Tourism Marketing Conference*. ATMC.

Gellman, R. (1996). Disintermediation and the internet. *Government Information Quarterly*, *1*, 1–8. doi:10.1016/S0740-624X(96)90002-7.

Getz, D. (1987). Tourism planning and research: Traditions, models and futures. In *Proceedings of the Australian Travel Workshop* (pp. 407-448). Bunbury, Australia: Australian Travel Workshop.

Gilbert, D. C., Powell-Perry, J., & Widijoso, S. (1999). Approaches by hotels to the use of the Internet as a relationship marketing tool. *Journal of Marketing Practice: Applied Marketing Science*, *5*(1), 21–38. doi:10.1108/EUM0000000004549.

Gomis, J. M. (2005). *Tourism, distribution and IT: Strategic approach to the effects of a new paradigm on intermediation*. (Doctoral Thesis). Universitat de Barcelona, Barcelona, Spain.

Gray, K., Thompson, C., Clerehan, R., Sheard, J., & Hamilton, M. (2011). Web 2.0 authorship: Issues of referencing and citation for academic integrity. *The Internet and Higher Education*, 112–118.

Gunn, C. (1972). *Vacationscape: Designing tourist regions*. Austin, TX: University of Texas.

Guttentag, D. A. (2010). Virtual reality: Applications and implications for tourism. *Tourism Management, 31*(5), 637–651. doi:10.1016/j.tourman.2009.07.003.

Hall, C. M. (2000). *Tourism planning: Policies, processes and relationships*. Harlow, MA: Pearson Education.

Ham, S., Kim, W. G., & Jeong, S. (2004). Effect of information technology on performance in upscale hotels. *International Journal of Hospitality Management, 24*, 281–294. doi:10.1016/j.ijhm.2004.06.010.

Ho, S., Kauffman, R. J., & Liang, T. (2007). A growth theory perspective on B2C e-commerce growth in Europe: An exploratory study. *Electronic Commerce Research and Applications, 6*, 237–259. doi:10.1016/j.elerap.2006.06.003.

Holloway, J. C. (2002). *The business of tourism* (6th ed.). London: Prentice Hall.

Internet World Stats. (2011). *Internet users in the world*. Retrieved from http://www.Internetworldstats.com/stats.htm

JupiterResearch. (2011). *Jupiter research report 2006-2011*. Retrieved from www.jupiterresearch.com

Kaldis, K., & Kaldis, E. (2008). Emmantina and Palmira beach hotels: Distribution for independent hotels. In Egger, R., & Buhalis, D. (Eds.), *eTourism: Case studies* (pp. 65–73). Oxford: Butterworth Heinemann - Elsevier.

Klein, S., Köhne, F., & Öörni, A. (2004). Barriers to online booking of scheduled airline tickets. *Journal of Travel & Tourism Marketing, 17*(2/3), 27–29. doi:10.1300/J073v17n02_03.

Kotler, P., Bowen, J. T., & Makens, J. C. (2003). *Marketing for hospitality and tourism* (3rd ed.). Upper Saddle River, NJ: Pearson Prentice Hall.

Lambert, D. M., & Cooper, M. C. (2000). Issues in supply chain management. *Industrial Marketing Management, 29*, 65–83. doi:10.1016/S0019-8501(99)00113-3.

Lambert, D. M., Stock, J. R., & Ellram, L. M. (1998). *Fundamentals of logistics management*. Burr Ridge, IL: Irwin/McGraw-Hill.

Law, R., & Hsu, C. H. C. (2005). Customers' perceptions on the importance of hotel web site dimensions and attributes. *International Journal of Contemporary Hospitality Management, 17*(6), 493–503. doi:10.1108/09596110510612130.

Law, R., Leung, K., & Wong, R. J. (2004). The impact of the Internet on travel agencies. *International Journal of Contemporary Hospitality Management, 16*(2), 100–107. doi:10.1108/09596110410519982.

Law, R., & Leung, R. (2000). A study of airlines' online reservation services on the Internet. *Journal of Travel Research, 39*, 202–211. doi:10.1177/004728750003900210.

Lee, M. R., & Lan, Y. (2007). From web 2.0 to conversational knowledge management: Towards collaborative intelligence. *Journal of Entrepreneurship Research, 2*(2), 47–62.

Leiper, N. (1990). *Tourism systems: An interdisciplinary perspective*. Palmerston North, New Zealand: Massey University Printery.

Leung, H., Lee, A., & Law, R. (2011). Adopting web 2.0 technologies on chain and independent hotel websites: A case tudy of hotels in Hong Kong. In Law, R., Fuchs, M., & Ricci, F. (Eds.), *Information and Communication Technologies in Tourism 2011* (pp. 331–342). New York: Springer. doi:10.1007/978-3-7091-0503-0_19.

Li, X., & Wang, Y. (2010). Evaluating the effectiveness of destination marketing organisations' websites: Evidence from China. *International Journal of Tourism Research, 12*, 536–549.

Lubbe, B. (2008). Kulula.com: Low-cost carrier and ICTs. In Egger, R., & Buhalis, D. (Eds.), *eTourism: Case studies* (pp. 282–292). Oxford, UK: Butterworth Heinemann – Elsevier.

MacIntosh, R. W., & Goeldner, C. R. (1986). *Tourism principles, practices, philosophies*. New York: John Wiley & Sons INC.

Martin, D., Alzua, A., & Lamsfus (2011). A contextual geofencing mobile tourisdm service. In R. Law, M. Fuchs, & F. Ricci (Eds.), *Information and Communication Technologies in Tourism 2011* (pp. 331-342). New York: Springer.

Mathies, C., & Weiermair, K. (2003). *Technological change in the accommodation industry - Enhancing and constraining factors of the IT adaptation*. Paper presented at the Biennal Conference: Leisure, Change and Diversity. Sydney, Australia.

Mentzer, J. T., De Witt, W., Keebler, J. S., Min, S., Nix, N. W., Smith, C. D., & Zacharia, Z. G. (2001). Defining supply chain management. *Journal of Business Logistics, 22*(2), 1–25. doi:10.1002/j.2158-1592.2001.tb00001.x.

Mill, R. C., & Morrison, A. M. (1998). *The tourism system: An introductory text* (3rd ed.). Dubuque, IA: Kendall/Hunt.

Murphy, J., Forrest, E. J., Wotring, C. E., & Bryman, R. A. (1996, June). Hotel management and marketing on the internet. *The Cornell Hotel and Restaurant Administration Quarterly*, 70–82. doi:10.1177/001088049603700322.

Mutch, A. (1998). Using information technology. In Thomas, R. (Ed.), *The management of small tourism and hospitality firms* (pp. 92–206). London: Cassell.

Nazalek, M. (2008). Orbis on line: Internet distribution strategies for a regional hotel group. In Egger, R., & Buhalis, D. (Eds.), *eTourism: Case studies* (pp. 74–82). Oxford, UK: Butterworth Heinemann - Elsevier.

Ndou, V., & Petti, C. (2007). DMS business models design and destination configurations: Choice and implementation issues. *Information Technology and Tourism, 9*, 3–14. doi:10.3727/109830507779637602.

O'Connor, P. (2008). InterContinental hotel group: Dealing with online intermediaries. In Egger, R., & Buhalis, D. (Eds.), *eTourism: Case studies* (pp. 15–22). Oxford, UK: Butterworth Heinemann - Elsevier.

Öörni, A. (2004). Consumer objectives and the amount of search in electronic travel and tourism markets. *Journal of Travel & Tourism Marketing, 17*(2/3), 3–14. doi:10.1300/J073v17n02_01.

Organización Mundial del Turismo. (1998). *Introducción al turismo*. Madrid, Spain: Organización Mundial del Turismo.

Page, S. J. (1999). *Transport and tourism*. Harlow, MA: Addison Wesley Longman.

Page, S. J., & Hall, C. M. (2003). *Managing urban tourism*. Harlow, MA: Prentice Hall.

Park, Y., & Gretzel, U. (2006). Evaluation of emerging technologies in tourism: The case of travel search engines. In Hitz, M., Sigala, M., & Murphy, J. (Eds.), *Information and communication technologies in tourism 2006* (pp. 371–382). Vienna, Austria: Springer Verlag. doi:10.1007/3-211-32710-X_51.

Parra-López, E., Bulchand-Gidumal, J., Gutierrez-Taño, D., & Díaz-Armas, R. (2011). Intentions to use social media in organizing and taking vacation trips. *Computers in Human Behavior, 27*, 640–654. doi:10.1016/j.chb.2010.05.022.

Pollock, A. (1995). The impact of information technology on destination marketing. *EU Travel and Tourism Analyst*, *3*, 66–83.

Presenza, A., Sheehan, L., & Ritchie, B. J. (2005). Towards a model of the roles and activities of destination management organizations. *Journal of Hospitality, Tourism and Leisure Science*.

Przeclawski, K. (1990). *Le tourisme et le monde de l'unité dans la pluralité. Cahiers du Tourisme (139, Série C)*. Aix-en-Provence: Centre des Hautes Etudes Touristiques.

Schegg, R., Liebrich, A., Scaglione, M., & Ahmad, S. F. S. (2008). An exploratory field study of web 2.0 in tourism. In O'Connor, P., Höpken, W., & Gretzel, U. (Eds.), *Information and Communication Technologies in Tourism 2008* (pp. 209–219). New York: Springer. doi:10.1007/978-3-211-77280-5_14.

Sigala, M. (2002). Modelling e-marketing strategies: Internet presence and exploitation of Greek hotels. *Journal of Travel & Tourism Marketing*, *11*(2), 83–103.

Sigala, M. (2008). Web 2.0, social marketing strategies and distribution channels for city destinations: Enhancing the participatory role of travelers and exploiting their collective intelligence. In Gascó-Hernández, M., & Torres-Coronas, T. (Eds.), *Information Communications Technologies and City Marketing*. Hershey, PA: Information Science Publishing.

Sigala, M. (2011). Preface – Special issue on web 2.0 in travel and tourism: Empowering and changing the role of travelers. *Computers in Human Behavior*, *27*, 607–608. doi:10.1016/j.chb.2010.04.005.

Sigala, M., & Marianidis, D. (2010). DMOs, e-democracy and collaborative destination management: An implementation framework. In Gretzel, U., Law, R., & Fuchs, M. (Eds.), *Information and Communication Technologies in Tourism 2010* (pp. 235–246). New York: Springer. doi:10.1007/978-3-211-99407-8_20.

SITA. (2007). *Airline ICT trends survey 2007 executive summary*. Retrieved from http://www.sita.aero/NR/rdonlyres/2C464901-6574-4AA0-B4E317199B9B8D45/0/AirlineIT07Booklet.pdf

Teichmann, K., & Zins, A. (2008). Information elements on DMO-Web sites: Alternative approaches for measuring perceived utility. In O'Connor, P., Höpken, W., & Gretzel, U. (Eds.), *Information and Communication Technologies in Tourism 2008* (pp. 209–219). New York: Springer. doi:10.1007/978-3-211-77280-5_19.

Uysal, M., Chen, J. S., & Williams, D. R. (2000). Increasing state market share through a regional positioning. *Tourism Management*, *21*, 89–96. doi:10.1016/S0261-5177(99)00082-5.

Wei, S., Ruys, F., van Hoof, H. B., & Combrink, T. (2001). Uses of the internet in the global hotel industry. *Journal of Business Research*, *54*, 235–241. doi:10.1016/S0148-2963(00)00117-X.

Werthner, H., & Klein, S. (1999). *Information technology and tourism – A challenging relationship*. New York: Springer Verlag. doi:10.1007/978-3-7091-6363-4.

Werthner, H., & Klein, S. (2000). ICT and the changing landscape of global tourism distribution. *EM-Electronic Markets*, *9*(4), 256–262.

World Tourism Organization. (2001). *E-business for tourism – Practical guidelines for tourism destinations and businesses*. Madrid, Spain: World Tourism Organization.

World Tourism Organization Business Council. (1999). Introduction. In *Marketing tourism destinations online: Strategies for the information age*. Madrid, Spain: World Tourism Organization.

Ye, Q., Law, R., Gu, B., & Chen, W. (2011). The influence of user-generated content on traveler behavior: An empirical investigation on the effects of e-word-of-mouth to hotel online bookings. *Computers in Human Behavior*, *27*, 634–639. doi:10.1016/j.chb.2010.04.014.

Yeung, T. A., & Law, R. (2004). Extending the modified heuristic usability evaluation technique to chain and independent hotel websites. *Hospital Management*, *23*, 307–313. doi:10.1016/j.ijhm.2003.03.001.

Yoo, K. H., & Gretzel, U. (2008). Understanding differences between online travel review writers and non-writers. In T. Hara (Ed.), *Proceedings of the 13th Annual Graduate Education and Student Research* (pp. 21-29). Orlando, FL: GESR.

Yoo, K. H., & Gretzel, U. (2010). Antecedents and impacts of trust in travel-related consumer-generated media. *Information Technology and Tourism*, *12*, 139–152. doi:10.3727/109830510X12887971002701.

Yoo, K. H., Lee, Y., Gretzel, U., & Fesenmaier, D. R. (2009). Trust in travel-related consumer generated media. In Höpken, W., Gretzel, U., & Law, R. (Eds.), *Information and Communication Technologies in Tourism 2009* (pp. 49–59). New York: Springer. doi:10.1007/978-3-211-93971-0_5.

Zafiropoulos, C., Vrana, V., & Paschaloudis, D. (2006). The Internet practices of hotel companies: An analysis from Greece. *International Journal of Contemporary Hospitality Management*, *18*(2), 156–163. doi:10.1108/09596110610646709.

Zhang, X., Song, M., & Huang, G. Q. (2009). Tourism supply chain management: A new research agenda. *Tourism Management*, *30*, 345–358. doi:10.1016/j.tourman.2008.12.010.

ADDITIONAL READING

Alamdari, F., & Mason, K. (2006). The future of airline distribution. *Journal of Air Transport Management*, *12*(3), 122–134. doi:10.1016/j.jairtraman.2005.11.005.

Alford, P., & Clarke, S. (2009). Information technology and tourism a theoretical critique. *Technovation*, *29*(9), 580–587. doi:10.1016/j.technovation.2009.05.006.

Anderson, S. (2003). *Online hotel sales and third parties: A review and analysis.* Retrieved from http://www.hsmai.org/docs/online_hotel_sales_and_3rd_parties.pdf

Andriole, S. (2010). Business impact of web 2.0 technologies. *Communications of the ACM*, *53*(12), 67–79. doi:10.1145/1859204.1859225.

Birkinshaw, J. (2009, Summer). Using web 2.0 to create management 2.0. *Business Strategy Review*, 21-23.

Bohley, K. (2010). Web 2.0: What is it and is it for me? *American Journal of Business Education*, *3*(7), 7–9.

Buhalis, D. (2004). eAirlines: Strategic and tactical use of ICTs in the airline industry. *Information & Management*, *41*(7), 805–825. doi:10.1016/j.im.2003.08.015.

Buhalis, D., & Licata, M. C. (2002). The future eTourism intermediaries. *Tourism Management*, *23*, 207–220. doi:10.1016/S0261-5177(01)00085-1.

Carroll, B., & Siguaw, J. (2003, August). The evolution of electronic distribution. *The Cornell Hotel and Restaurant Administration Quarterly*, 38–47. doi:10.1016/S0010-8804(03)90257-6.

Carroll, D. (2006). Travel communities present online players with opportunities. *Travel Weekly*, 6-7.

Cerami, E. (2002). *Web services essentials*. Sebastopol, CA: O'Reilly Media.

Chircu, A., & Kauffman, R. (2000). Reintermediation strategies in business-to-business electronic commerce. *International Journal of Electronic Commerce*, *4*, 7–42.

Curbera, F., Duftler, M., Khalaf, R., Nagy, W., Mukhi, N., & Weerawarana, S. (2002). Unraveling the web services. *Internet Computing*, *6*(2), 86–93. doi:10.1109/4236.991449.

Estis Green, C. (2005). *De-mystifying distribution: Building a distribution strategy one channel at a time*. McLean, VA: Hospitality Sales & Distribution Association International.

Faché, W. (2001). New entrants in travel and tourism intermediation and the future of destination management systems. In Kreilkamp, E., Pechlaner, H., & Steinecke, A. (Eds.), *Gemachter oder gelebter Tourismus? Destinationsmanagement und Tourismuspolitik* (pp. 41–56). Vienna, Austria: Linde Verlag.

Friedman, T. (2006). *The world is flat*. New York, NY: Farrar, Straus and Giroux.

Iverson, W. (2004). *Real world web services*. Sebastopol, CA: O'Reilly Media.

Iyer, B., Freedman, J., Gaynor, M., & Wyner, G. (2003). Web services: Enabling dynamic business networks. *Communications of the Association for Information Systems*, *11*, 525–554.

Jarach, O. (2002). The digitalisation of market relationships in the airline industry: The impact and prospects of eBusiness. *Journal of Air Transport Management*, *8*(2), 115–120. doi:10.1016/S0969-6997(01)00039-4.

Leonard, C. (2006, January 29). Enterprise in rental car driver's seat. *Associated Press*.

Lim, B., & Wen, H. J. (2003). Web services: An analysis of the technology, its benefits, and implementation difficulties. *Information Systems Management*, *20*(2), 49–57. doi:10.1201/1078/43204.20.2.20030301/41470.8.

Martini, U. (2001). Information and communication technologies as competitive drives for new destination management concepts. In Kreilkamp, E., Pechlaner, H., & Steinecke, A. (Eds.), *Gemachter oder gelebter Tourismus? Destinationsmanagement und Tourismuspolitik* (pp. 141–172). Vienna, Austria: Linde Verlag.

Morrison, A., & Harrison, A. (1998). From corner shop to electronic shopping mall? *Progress in Tourism and Hospitality Research*, *4*, 349–356. doi:10.1002/(SICI)1099-1603(199812)4:4<349::AID-PTH165>3.0.CO;2-M.

O'Connor, P. (2004). *Using computers in hospitality*. London: Thomson.

O'Connor, P., & Frew, A. J. (2002). The future of hotel electronic distribution: Expert and industry perspectives. *The Cornell Hotel and Restaurant Administration Quarterly*, *43*(3), 33–45.

O'Connor, P., & Piccoli, G. (2003). Marketing using global distribution systems revisited. *Cornell Hotel Administration Quarterly*, *44*(5 & 6), 105–114.

O'Toole, K. (2003, August). ICT trends survey. *Airline Business*, 40-47.

Palmer, A., & McCole, P. (2000). The role of electronic commerce in creating virtual destination marketing organizations. *International Journal of Contemporary Hospitality Management*, *12*(3), 198–204. doi:10.1108/09596110010320760.

Parks-Smith, S. (2004). *British airways – Customer enabled BA*. Paper presented at the Europe Travel Distribution Summit, Eye for Travel. London, UK.

Poon, A. (1993). *Tourism, technology and competitive strategies*. Wallingford: CAB International.

Porter, M. (2001). Strategy and the Internet. *Harvard Business Review*, *103D*, 63–78. PMID:11246925.

Rappa, M. (2004). The utility business model and the future of computing services. *IBM Systems Journal*, *43*(1), 32–42. Retrieved from http://www.research.ibm.com/journal/sj/431/rappa.pdf doi:10.1147/sj.431.0032.

Roy, J., & Ramanujan, A. (2001). Understanding web services. *ICT Professional*, *3*(6), 69–73. doi:10.1109/6294.977775.

Shapiro, C., & Varian, H. R. (1998). *Information rules: A strategic guide to the network economy*. Boston, MA: Harvard Business School Press.

Sheldon, P. (1997). *Information technologies for tourism*. Oxford, UK: CAB.

Shona, Z., Chenc, F., & Chang, Y. (2003). Airline e-commerce: The revolution in ticketing channels. *Journal of Air Transport Management*, *9*(5), 325–331. doi:10.1016/S0969-6997(03)00040-1.

Tesone, D. V. (2006). *Hospitality information systems and e-commerce*. Hoboken, NJ: John Wiley & Sons.

Travel Research Bureau. (2004). *Travel distribution report*. Retrieved from content.groople.com/PressReleases/tdr-vol12-p124-125.pdf

World Tourism Organization. (1991). *Tourism to the year 2000: Qualitative aspects affecting global growth*. Madrid, Spain: World Tourism Organization.

Ye, Q., Law, R., & Gu, B. (2009). The impact of online user reviews on online room sales. *International Journal of Hospitality Management*, *28*, 180–182. doi:10.1016/j.ijhm.2008.06.011.

KEY TERMS AND DEFINITIONS

Destination Management Organization (DMO): Public or public-private entity whose aim is to foster, plan and coordinate the tourism development of a destination as a whole.

Destination Management System (DMS): Official destination Web application aimed at fostering B2B cohesion levels within destination-based stakeholders, providing tourist a one-stop-only platform in which it is possible to search, plan, book and purchase individual services or packaged tours.

eReadiness: The level of preparation and competences that a single person, an organization or a society possesses in terms of a specific type of ICT usage.

eTourism: The set of digitization of procedures in the tourism sector, including both the tactical and strategic adoption of ICT applications, such as the World Wide Web.

Global Distribution System (GDS): Centrally managed global computerized reservation network used by travel agents, tour operators and online travel portals in order to book airline tickets, hotels rooms or car rentals, among other tourism and travel related services.

Supply Chain Management (SCM): Set of managerial philosophies and processes which effectively align firms through the establishment of linkages between organizations aiming at bringing products and services to the market capable of producing added value to the consumer.

Tourism Infomediaries: The recently emerged generation of online-based intermediaries within the tourism industry.

Travel 2.0: The whole array of Web 2.0 tools specifically used within the tourism and travel industry.

User-Generated-Content (UGC): The possibility that Websites' Web 2.0 functionalities give to Internet users to insert contents—under the form of text, ratings, podcasting, among others—that will later be available to other users.

Web 2.0: Set of tools of mass collaboration enabling and empowering Internet users to actively and simultaneously interact with their peers for producing, consuming and diffusing Internet-based information and applications. Web 2.0 fosters both UGC and social media.

Chapter 27
Organizational Learning and Web 2.0 Technologies:
Improving the Planning and Organization of a Software Development Process

Neide Santos
State University of Rio de Janeiro, Brazil

ABSTRACT

The knowledge era redefines companies' scenarios and workers' profiles, requiring models and tools for Knowledge Management (KM) and Organizational Learning (OL) to respond to external demands. The growth of the Internet and the emergence of Web 2.0 created the conditions for Enterprise 2.0. This chapter analyzes Web 2.0 usefulness in the workplace and presents a software application for KM and OL that aims to support the software development process in software houses. The conclusion discusses controversial issues related to collaboration and competitive markets and presents some reasons for the apparent negative reaction of companies to adopt systems based on social networks.

INTRODUCTION

In the knowledge era, the new corporative scenario is redefining the profile of workers. This perspective requires professionals who are able, at same time, to learn in non-conventional ways and to work collaboratively to engender innovative solutions. In this scenario, models and tools for Organizational Learning (OL) can be useful as OL deals with the ways an organization learns and adapts to respond to external demands. In organizations that learn, people continually expand their capacity to create results using new forms of thinking and free collective aspiration. OL has emerged from the belief that design and intensive knowledge-based organizations' competitiveness depends on its commitment with the workers long term learning processes foundations (Senge, 1990).

DOI: 10.4018/978-1-4666-4373-4.ch027

The challenge is to manage the exchange of knowledge among individuals and promote learning. In software development projects, such as in other domains, the knowledge built by the team is usually valuable and can be useful for similar projects in the future. There, people can learn, consulting and analyzing previous projects and benefiting from the team knowledge and background in similar projects. It happens that this knowledge with information concerning the decision-making at different stages of development often gets lost because it is not properly stored. Moreover, it is actually the result of collective learning about the internal work processes themselves and ways of working. How do you solve this problem? Organizations should learn from their experiences, record the lessons learned and share the knowledge internally. Knowledge should be institutionalized and thus become common property rather than be restricted to a few key people and lost when they leave the organization. Thus, it is necessary to have easy to use systems to support the processes of OL and Knowledge Management (KM).

On the other hand, the expansion of the Internet in business and commercial contexts has led to the emergence of advanced technologies that have allowed the Web to become a forum for information exchange and collaboration. This set of new technologies are referred to as Web 2.0, whose characteristics are users as co-developers, more lightweight applications, greater ease of use, flexible and accessible uses and culturally acceptable technologies. As a result, Web 2.0 tools are increasingly being proposed to support training programs via distance education and KM. McAfee (2006) argues that Web 2.0 technology is now popular and effective for generating, sharing and refining information. The need to manage business knowledge and the popularity of Web 2.0 have created positive conditions for the emergence of so-called Enterprise 2.0 or Enterprise Social Software. Enterprise 2.0 is the business use of Web 2.0 to enable business processes by improving collaboration via the use of social media tools. McAffe (2006) describes Enterprise 2.0 as the use of emergent social software platforms within companies, or between companies and their partners or customers. Enterprise 2.0 focuses on the platforms that companies can sell or buy to reveal best practice and production, resulting from the knowledge built by their employees. It brings together social software to be used in commercial contexts and includes the changing social network for corporate intranets, with a variety of tools and features.

Given this context, this chapter aims to broadly analyze the usefulness of Web 2.0 technologies in the workplace argue its possibilities of use and productivity. Our specific goal is to present a software application for KM and OL that aims to support the software development process in software houses. The application allows the storage of all employee interactions (emails, wiki), involved in a project or in several projects, and project documents (diagrams, code, software tests, meeting minutes, and so on), generated throughout the development process. In order to do this firstly the chapter discusses OL, KM, Web 2.0 and Enterprise 2.0, it then presents the developed system. In addition, the work offers a discussion on KM evaluation to identify companies' possible reactions to the adoption of Web 2.0 technologies-based KM systems. Finally, conclusions and future works are presented.

ORGANIZATIONAL LEARNING, KNOWLEDGE MANAGEMENT, AND WEB 2.0: BRIEF OVERVIEW

In the field of our study, there are many related concepts involved: organizational learning, knowledge management, Web 2.0, and Enterprise 2.0 proposal. In the following sections, we discuss these concepts as they provide our rationale. .

Organizational Learning

Theoretical and practical organizational learning has emerged from the belief that the competitiveness of an organization depends on its commitment to learning processes of the workers. Over time organizations face adverse and varied challenges, such as new technologies, changes in the market, and new competitors. The mutable surroundings require fast and innovative answers, and to cope with this companies need to continually acquire knowledge. The effort to survive and grow as an organization depends on its ability to take advantage of collective learning available inside the organization about its own processes and ways of action. Organizational learning can be defined as the processes that seek to create, acquire and transfer knowledge and modify the behavior of people to reflect new knowledge and insight. (Senge, 1990). Through continuous learning, the organization exercises its power and intelligence to respond to its internal environment (objectives, goals, results) and external environment (strategy). "Organizations learn that people continually expand their capacity to create the results that they really want, where new and expansive ways of thinking are encouraged, where collective aspiration is free, and where people are constantly learning to learn collectively" (Senge, 1990).

The conditions for the achievement of organizational learning are now more favorable than ever. A growing number of organizations are clarifying and improving their processes, and advances in technology collaboration focused on knowledge and learning are more mature and available on the Internet, such as that occurring in communities of practice. As part of an organization, knowledge can be grouped into two types: external and internal (formal and informal). External knowledge, obtained through studies and training, is described in official documents in different formats and can be accessed by work teams. In these documents standardized literature in the area of the business can be found, which serves as the basis for consultation and the setting of internal formats of the organization. Structured internal knowledge is also available through various artifacts and is produced internally according to the projects and standards adopted by the company. Informal internal knowledge is represented by information generated from meetings at work (for example, meetings, discussions, decision-making processes of project) or even informal meetings, where ideas are generated and insights happen. The problem observed in many organizations is that most of these types of knowledge, particularly the informal type, is not registered and therefore can not be recovered and reused in other projects or similar situations. Tacit knowledge, which is known by only some individuals, does not always become explicit knowledge for the public domain (Nonaka and Takeushi, 1999). Thus, the evolution of knowledge in the organization does not happen, i.e. the company does not learn from their experience.

Generally people do not have the availability or the motivation to spend their time providing information for the possible use of unknown people in the future. Therefore, the process of converting informal knowledge into formal knowledge must be integrated into work processes (Ives et al., 1998). Thus, what is the best way to capture and represent informal knowledge. The experience accumulated by teams, how they do their work, the practices applied, that is, know-how and know why – the tacit knowledge from past projects often get lost over time. Even the information contained in official documents is not easy to retrieve. Several computational tools have been proposed, including commercial products and research projects to support knowledge management and organizational learning.

The area of research in Computer Supported Cooperative Learning (CSCL) offers some initiatives to support organizational learning with a focus on traditional concepts of continuous learning (life-long learning) and learn by doing. These approaches seem promising as a solution to the problem of integrating the provision of information and learning in the workplace. The availability of online instruction via e-learning activities today is an important prerequisite for the success of communities of learners that can generate knowledge repository, which can configure the organizational memory. Its purpose is to ensure that the desired knowledge can be recovered at the right time and place for those who need it. This knowledge base consists of both formal and structured data (explicit knowledge), as well as informal and non-represented (tacit knowledge). Ontology[1] could organize and structure the stored material facilitating its recovery through search associated with the performed activities.

The organizational memory of a cooperative process includes aspects such as the elements involved, capture, storage and retrieval. All these aspects are interdependent. The elements are the objects related to the activity that you want to save, such as dialogues, discussions and documents, regardless of format. They need to be captured in any way during the process. The capture can be performed automatically (the system captures the information transparently to the user), semi-automatically (part of the information is automatically captured and the other not) and / or manually (the user must tell the system what elements and moments are to be captured).

However, these solutions still do not provide satisfactory answers for most of the questions raised. Many authors propose models to facilitate the understanding of organizational learning. (e.g. Argirys, 1993). To understand the theoretical foundations of organizational learning, one has to understand the learning process itself. You can understand it from the Vygotsky's Sociocultural Theory (1978). This theory suggests that social interaction leads to continuous step-by-step changes in people's thought and behavior that can vary greatly from culture to culture. Basically Vygotsky suggests that knowledge building depends on interaction with people and the tools that the culture provides to help form their own view of the world. An important way in learning development is related to cultural tools passed to others through collaborative learning, which involves a group of peers who strive to understand each other and work together to learn a specific skill. From Vygotsky's point of view, learning is a collective process that occurs primarily within the group and is then internalized by each individual. An interesting question is how to adapt the epistemological theory of Vygotsky, which was developed to explain the emergence of knowledge in human beings for their use in organizations. One possible solution is the use of collaborative systems which are systems designed specifically to support the work group and collaborative learning. However, a critical point in the use of collaborative systems to support OL strategies is how to reconcile collective learning and individual learning.

Organizational learning has strong relationship with the processes of knowledge management.

Knowledge Management

Knowledge Management (KM) comprises the activities of identification, acquisition, development, dissemination, use and maintenance of organizational knowledge in a systematic way (Abecker et al., 1998; Markkula, 1999). It requires the deployment of services that enable the creation and widespread use of knowledge. The creation of knowledge requires collecting information, evaluating if the information is relevant for the organization, packaging, and distributing information to places where it is useful. In KM, more than in OL area, tacit knowledge and formal knowledge are key concepts. Moreover, if the process of eliciting the knowledge from an individual is difficult, the capturing of group knowledge is more complex. The challenge here is to know how to manage the exchange of knowledge among individuals and promote learning. Ccurrently the main way of transferring and disseminating external and formal knowledge in organizations is by means of training programs. The training given is often poorly adjusted to the specific needs of the organization and ends up not being helpful for organizational learning. Furthermore, the organization can learn about itself, using data and information obtained from its past experiences in problem solving, decision-making processes and other internal experiences (Kouwenhoven, 1998; Giaever, 1999). The role of mechanisms for KM is to collect this body of experience and make it available to everyone within the organization, promoting OL widely.

Combined with the early development of collaborative technologies, KM technologies expanded in the mid-1990s. Subsequent KM efforts leveraged meaningful technologies for search and retrieval and the development of online learning tools for communities of practice (Capozzi, 2007). Knowledge management systems can thus be categorized as falling into one or more of the following groups: groupware, document management systems, expert systems, semantic networks, relational and object oriented databases, simulation tools (Gupta & Sushil, 2004). Gallupe (2001) also mentions some tools to support knowledge management systems. They range from a simple Intranet to the sophisticated expert systems, which store expert knowledge in the form of rules or cases to then provide this knowledge to novice employees or other experts. Linking these two extremes are for example groupware and intelligent agents. Groupware uses software and hardware to allow workgroups to communicate and collaborate. It usually possesses features that help groups to perform tasks such as generating ideas in order to create new knowledge, supporting negotiation and consensus. Intelligent agents can filter the knowledge that user really needs. Agents can be particularly important in situations that require the intensive use of knowledge and situations in which the sources of expertise need to be monitored because of constant updates and additions for example.

More recently, the development of social computing tools have led to the emergence of unstructured and self-managing approaches for the transfer, capture and creation of knowledge, including the development of new forms of communities. However, most of these are still based on text and code, and thus represent the transfer of knowledge. These tools face challenges in distilling meaningful re-usable knowledge and ensuring that their content is transmissible through diverse channels (Andrus, 2005).

There are few KM systems with specialized support, such as specialized commercial portals, conversation-based systems, and knowledge communities-based tools. Perhaps the low availability of specific KM systems and the emergence of Web 2.0 have given rise to an emerging trend of KM called Enterprise 2.0 (McAfee, 2006). The fast growth of business Internet, among other factors, has enabled the development of new advanced technologies, making the Web a forum for information exchange and collaboration. This set of new technologies led to the term Web 2.0.

Web 2.0

In many scenarios, collaboration and the broad exchange of ideas and information are key points. This is not different in work scenarios. The Web is a great repository of technical information, tools, software, Web services, specifications, standards, and pieces of code. However, in the current Web, Web 1.0, given the lack of hierarchy and categorization, the location of Web resources is a critical aspect. To deal with this problem at least two solutions have been implemented: Web 2.0 and the Semantic Web[2].

A set of tools and features has led to the emergence and consolidation of social networks – the central idea of Web 2.0. Web 2.0 aims to promote collaboration and knowledge sharing in a collective and decentralized way, offering participants the freedom to use, and re-edit content (O'Reilly, 2005). Its tools enable an environment, which encourages collaborative work by providing richer and more dynamic communication.

The term Web 2.0 is being used to describe the second generation of the World Wide Web with a view to making the online environment more dynamic and interactive where users can collaborate to organize and publish content using lightweight applications (Wikis, Blogs, Forums). In addition, Web 2.0 applications are more flexible, accessible and culturally acceptable. There are a range of applications that comprise the Web 2.0 paradigm: software for social networking (Blogs, Orkut) applications for collaborative editing (Blogs, Wikis, Podcasts, Google Docs), for on-line communication (Skype, Google Talk), for access to videos (YouTube, Google videos) and for social bookmarking (Del.icio.us), among others. This range of tools can be classified into two categories:

- The first category includes applications that can only exist on the Internet and whose effectiveness increases with the number of registered users, such as: Google Docs & Spreadsheets, Wikipedia, del.icio.us, YouTube, Skype, eBay, Hi5, and so on.
- The second category includes applications that can work offline, but which can also bring great benefits if they are online, Picasa Photos, Google Maps, Mapquest, iTunes, etc..

Current Web 2.0 tools, and others that are emerging, are increasingly being used to support training and knowledge management processes and distance education activities. In the workplace – our focus in this work, Web 2.0 can facilitate task management and the day-to-day routine of employees, enabling companies and people to share information, resources and to support work groups developing the same project. As a result, companies can save on travel expenses as employees, distributed in various locations, can collaborate and can integrate new employees, regardless of their location into the same project without the need to change the course of the project.

Since its beginnings, Web 2.0 has changed. O'Reilly and Battelle (2009) state in the paper "Web Squared: Web 2.0 Five Years On" that Web 2.0 have expanded this original idea of "the network as platform." Now, the Web "technologies, its business models, and perhaps most importantly, its philosophies of openness, collective intelligence, and transparency" have led to a new level by engaging in finding solutions to real world problems. For these authors, all sectors of society are being modified by Web 2.0 technologies, or will be modified in the very near future.

From the business potential of Web 2.0, Enterprise 2.0 has appeared to oxygenate the debate on knowledge management area.

Enterprise 2.0

For McAfee (2006), current information technology focusing on communication and knowledge management falls into two categories:

- The first one contains channels of communication such as email and instant messaging systems, where information can be created and distributed to every employee, but the degree of commonality of this information is low. Even if the e-mail is for all employees on the same server, it is only visible to people who are participating in the ongoing discussion.
- The second category includes platforms such as intranets, corporate Websites and information portals. In this case, the content is generated by a small group, but it is highly visible and available.

According to McAfee (2006), knowledge management systems have tried to use both approaches, but they have failed to elicit tacit knowledge, best practices and to extract relevant information from employees to put in databases. The author believes that Web 2.0 can Web 2.0 can play an important role in KM. Enterprise 2.0 or

Enterprise Social Software is the use of Web 2.0 technologies within an organization to enable or streamline business processes while enhancing collaboration – connecting people through the use of social media tools. Enterprise 2.0 social software for use in commercial contexts includes social networks for corporate intranets, with tools and features: hypertext and unstructured search tools, wikis, microblogging, blogs and Weblogs for storytelling and sharing personal knowledge and experiences, the social bookmarking company to identify and build knowledge organizational planning software for collaborative planning and management based on partnership, stock ideas to generate ideas, social networking tools, mushups for viewing, among others. Today's crowded enterprise social Web technology—Enterprise 2.0—landscape ranges from complete platforms to 'social software' suites to hosted communities to point solution blogs, wikis, and on to the various free public Internet services (Marks and Patel, 2010).

The first wave of Enterprise 2.0, mainly relating to how to combine open platforms, has increased interoperability, broad collaboration and communication with security and efficient management. After the initial euphoria accompanying Enterprise 2.0, its central concepts have tended to consolidate and its use has also tended to increase in companies of different sizes. For Marks and Patel (2010), "the next wave of solutions emanating from Enterprise 2.0 collaborative design will drive large-scale workplace performance as well as discrete process performance to improve relationships between employees, customers and partners. This will result in moving from closed linear processes to a more consciously collaborative design, but one that's cognizant of the necessary controls and governance between teams and at the edge."

For Bughin (2008), a global survey of the pattern of Enterprise 2.0 diffusion and its likely expected benefits suggests that adoption is relatively at par with—if not faster than—other IT-based technologies. He observes that it is a global phenomenon, and is not only spreading inside but also outside the boundaries of the typical enterprise. Adoption would be related to competitive advantages expected with Web 2.0. On the other hand, the competitive advantage does not emerge from Web 2.0 technologies, but the adoption of new business paradigms, but taking advantage of the contributions of the group of business and social networks in corporate (Burghin, 2008)

However, there is an ongoing debate as to whether Enterprise 2.0 is just a fad that does not bring anything new or useful, as understood by Davenport (2008), or be, in fact, the future of knowledge management as McAfee believes (2006). In any case, the ability of social networks to help organizations capture tacit knowledge has been discussed in different forums, but the difficulty of its use and distribution still lies in its ability to extract meaningful and reusable knowledge content captured in tools such as blogs, wikis, among other tools of Web 2.0 (Boateng, Mbarika, and Thomas, 2010).

Given this scenario, the following section presents the use of Web 2.0 tools for knowledge management / organizational learning to support the organization of corporate software projects.

PROPOSAL FOR A WEB 2.0 APPLICATION TO SUPPORT THE PLANNING AND ORGANIZATION OF SOFTWARE PROJECTS

We have developed an application to support software development work teams – software house employees, using Web 2.0 technologies and aiming to support OL and KM activities. A software house is a company whose primary products are software. There are many different kinds of software houses, but often they are small, focusing on delivering custom software solutions for companies of the same business (mobile phones, example) and for particular geographical regions. A software house normally has three technical teams: (a) Project manager who manages software development projects; (b) Software designers/ programmers who create the technical specification and write the software; and, (c) Software testers who are responsible for the whole process of software quality.

In many software houses, the team is young and the members have a college degree in Computer Science, but they often lack experience in developing real computer systems. Given the costs involved in Km system acquisition, we can assume that these companies do not invest, or invest very little, in systems for knowledge management. However, in this type of company, Web 2.0 based organizational learning and knowledge management would be efficient strategies for storing and disseminating past experiences and successful solutions as Web 2.0 technologies are widely used by young people in their personal and professional daily routines. It would be interesting therefore to develop an application for knowledge management, following the central idea of the Enterprise 2.0 movement, based on Web 2.0 tools.

Considering the software houses specificity, we developed a software application bringing together some Web 2.0 tools in a Web interface to support employees of the same company in planning and organizing software projects. The application allows the storage of all interactions among software house employees involved in a project. The interactions range from its creation by the Project Manager to the last test done before delivery to the customer, including questions, suggestions, reports of meetings and training courses that have occurred during the development process. It works primary as a channel of communication and exchange of information among the project participants and as a mechanism for group memory.

Web 2.0-Based System for Promoting OL and KM Activities

To achieve its purpose, the system was developed following the classic cycle of software development, composed of requirements analysis, design, implementation, testing, and maintenance. First of all, the functional requirements were identified. They are:

- Allow the group manager to register new projects
- Allow project information changes, if the group manager gives permission
- Allow all those involved have access to all processes, except confidential processes
- Provide tools to facilitate the information flow
- Provide tools and routines to optimize the processes of interaction among participants
- Allow people involved in the project to receive related messages
- Allow all users to edit the wiki project.

Users, Functionality, and Features

The system has five kinds of users:

- System administrator who provides access and ensures system safety
- Project manager who registers new projects and displays past projects
- Software specification team
- Software coding team and,
- Software testing team.

The system offers the following functionalities:

- Register new projects
- Offer access to all projects for which the user has permission
- Make changes to existing projects
- Allow interaction among users

- Allow the receipt of messages related to the project
- Allow the receiving of project updates
- Include messages in the project
- Include videos in the project, and
- Permit the user to edit the wiki project

The system has the following features:

- Each employee has "locals" (tabs), the Web interface in the software project which he/she is allocated.
- The Project Manager creates new projects in the system as well the related wiki with a brief description about the project.
- The wiki can be edited later by other employees involved in the project, so as to detail the software development (specification, implementation, testing, etc).
- Each project has related posts to allow the various project phases to be explained, i.e. employees at each stage of development can ask questions about the previous phases or the ongoing phase, without losing relevant information. In a project day-by-day with strict schedules, the answers and questions end up getting lost in e-mails and they cannot be updated in the project documents.
- Each employee can send messages to another specific employee or to the team stating that updates have been made to the wiki, or even posting his/her current task that day, among other things.
- Meetings, explanations, or training courses related to the project are recorded by staff in audio or video and these resources are posted on the tab of the related project.
- The specifications, tests and all control documents, such as checklists that are used by the company, continue to exist and are attached to the post to report the closing of a certain stage.
- All users can visualize projects already finished in separate tabs as well as those under development, in which each user is allocated, and all related messages, also in separate tabs.
- In each tab, there is the wiki project; the related posts separated by topic; the videos; and, the files that are sent to the client, as part of the documentation.
- Users have permission to create a new post, add a new video, attach a new file, add data to the wiki and send instant messages to other users, but only the project manager has permission to create a new project, delete posts and wiki, and edit videos that he/she considers inappropriate.

The central idea underlying the system is that software house employees over time shape themselves into a community of practice. Communities of practice are groups of people who get together regarding a sense of responsibility in the work process in progress, the common interests in learning and mainly in practical applications of the learned contents. The community is not a pool of people defined by certain characteristics, but people who learn, build and "make" the KM (Wenger and Snyder, 2001). To create the communities, the resources needed are spaces for conversation, an adjustable desktop, and management of multiple views on relevant information sources.

Design and Implementation

The system data model is shown in Figure 1.

The data dictionary contains the following data with respective descriptions:

- USERS: models the users data
- USERS_PROFILE: Models the user profile
- ENGAGEMENT: Models the extra properties data from Wiki table.
- PROJECT: Models the project data.

- PROJECT_PROFILE: Models the extra properties data from PROJECT table.
- BLOG_POSTS: Models the posts data
- BLOG_POSTS_FILE: Models of the data files attached to posts.
- BLOG_POSTS_PROFILE: Models the extra properties data from BLOG_POSTS table.
- BLOG_POSTS_TAGS: Models data from HTML tags allowed inside posts.
- MESSAGE: Models message data
- RECIPIENTS: Models the user data that receives the message
- WIKI: Models the wiki data
- WIKI_PROFILE: Models the extra properties data from Wiki table.
- WIKI_VERSION: models of different versions of wiki editions.

The system was developed using PHP language, Apache server and MySQL, and was tailored for a typical small software house. The prototype is ready to be used and tested in a small software house, but the evaluation of KM systems is an open point. What should be evaluated? In following subsection, a brief discussion of evaluation systems for KM will be offered.

Figure 1. System data model

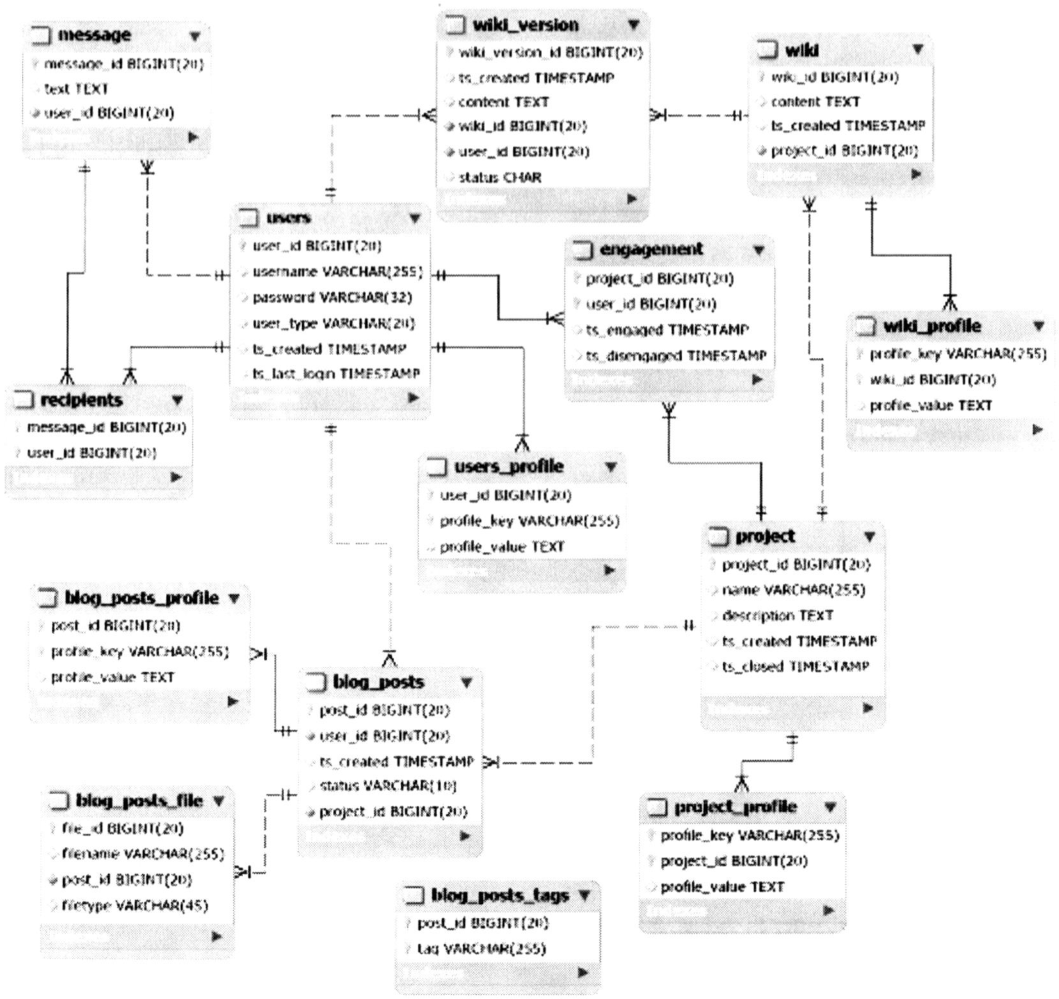

KM Evaluation

The core components of any system oriented to build and share knowledge is a mix of many aspects such as people, work process, context, culture, and stimulus. According to Santoro, Borges and Santos (2006), context and culture influence the objective of KM. Stimulus for sharing information and knowledge is related to the ways the work process is established. It embodies activity (the tasks carried out by the groups involved the cooperative process of work); evaluation (the mechanisms that allow the manager to observe throughout the entire process whether or not the goals are being reached by individual and group outcomes); group memory (storage of the all the data that is related to the activity development); awareness (information to guarantee that people understand the process itself and how the participants interact in the environment); roles (the responsibilities that can be assumed by the members of the group); and, coordination (the management of the process). KM evaluation should consider the main features of a KMS, such as the purpose, context, users, and tools. The issue is how to assess these dimensions?

It seems there are few methods for systematic evaluations of KM. Analyzing methods for similar systems evaluation – groupware, we find difficulties. Pinelli and Gutwin (2000) conducted a survey and concluded that there is no consensus on how to conduct evaluations in groupware. The authors analyzed the main types of assessment that have been conducted in this area and concluded that the evaluation process takes one of these approaches: naturalistic (with field experiments or case studies) and controlled (with laboratory experiments or exploratory studies). Twidale, Randall, and Bentley (1994) observed that in most situations in which cooperative systems were evaluated, exploratory studies or case studies with qualitative and informal assessments were adopted. The results can hardly be generalized, however, the experiences allow reflection on the area. The same seems to occur with KM.

Another difficulty to be faced in the evaluation of KM activities is to isolate and control the involved variables. There are at least two possibilities for KM evaluation: to evaluate the KM system or the KM process, i.e. the results obtained in terms of transforming tacit knowledge into explicit knowledge. To evaluate the system, criteria such as Cost, Functionality (Document Management, Collaboration, Communication, Measurement, workflow management) and scalability can be adopted. We can also evaluate the KM system in terms of usability, utility and productivity. Here the question is how to define the criteria and metrics to be used. Another issue is when to perform the evaluation of the actions of KM as it seems to be necessary to wait 2 to 3 years after the implementation of KM strategies to obtain results. It is also necessary to define what you want to know about the acquisition of formal knowledge, as knowledge may be accessed at three stages at least: before, during, or after KM-related activities. Hence what do we want to evaluate: the KM product or the KM process over time?

Given the complexity of KM evaluation, we chose to evaluate the tool itself. For this evaluation, we planned a case study to evaluate the usability, usefulness and productivity of the system in a software house. The usability testing approach basically tests the user interface. The scenario is a group of users working on typical tasks using the system. In the usability testing approach, we planned to use the question-asking protocol. This approach provides the users with the product to be tested and a set of tasks to perform, asking them to perform the tasks using the product, and explaining what they are thinking about while working with the product's interface. We also ask them direct questions about the product; for example, "How would you post a message in the tab?" Their responses will be expressed either in terms of the product being tested or in other products from their past experience and will provide insights into their mental model of the product. We also planned to use structured interviewing, where evaluators formulate questions about the product based on the issues of interest. Then we interview representative users to ask them these questions in order to gather information. Structured interviewing has a specific, predetermined agenda with specific questions to guide and direct the interview. However, the case study was not conducted in accordance with the pre-defined conditions, because we did not obtain agreement from the board of the software house. We explained to the board that we were doing academic work, the system was freeware and that the testing system would require little time, not delaying the tasks of the company. Despite this, we did not obtain permission to test the system

We believe, in general, that the company reacted negatively to adopting a new working environment. It can also reveal that they do not trust the reliability and privacy of social networking tools-based system, even if the application server is stored in the company intranet. This inhibits voluntary participation and as a consequence employees are not motivated to adopt innovations spontaneously without some kind of reward. However, in informal conversations with a small group of employees, we explained the system scenario of use. They found the system interesting and helpful, and understood that it could be of great help for organizational learning and for KM activities.

CONCLUSION

The conclusions we offer as endpoints of our chapter are of two natures: the first is some bottlenecks in Enterprise 2.0. Today's society presents more and more complex problems that require interdisciplinary solutions which are increasingly knowledge-intensive and less dependent on raw materials. We are immersed in a so-called knowledge society, where terms such as collective intelligence and distributed intelligence have become familiar, and where it is expected that human-machine and machine machines work together toward a common goal. But now we live in an age of paradoxes: it is expected that there is broad collaboration and fierce competitiveness at the same time. Web 2.0 collaborative technologies promise new business models, philosophies of openness, collective intelligence, and transparency in social and economic processes. On the other hand, corporations increasingly want to ensure captive markets, using proprietary solutions in their closed source software. Companies' low adherence to standards proposed by some international consortiums (W3C, OGC, and so on) is evident, with the result that the dream of database interoperability and successful solution reuse are still distant targets. However, Enterprise 2.0, and proposal based on the promises of Web 2.0 technologies, seems to have wide acceptance by companies to solve their problems of KM and OL, as point out Bughin (2008).

Even if the promise of Web 2.0 and Enterprise 2.0 is fulfilled, many problems remain open: how to promote collaboration in very competitive markets; how to integrate Web 2.0 tools with traditional enterprise software; how to aggregate organization inner data with external data; how to represent knowledge adequately; how to manage Communities of practice; how to organize them efficiently so that they do not become unstructured Facebooks; how to foster organizational memory, and finally, how to organize the storage of documents so that this memory is easily recovered. Many of these open issues can be addressed with the use of domain ontology. Ontology can be a viable solution to organize Communities of practice, offering categories for storing documents of organizational memory, and eventually to support the integration of heterogeneous platforms.

The second endpoint of this chapter is directly related to our proposed Web 2.0 system. We have developed a simple system, tailored to the needs of a small software house, respecting some basic principles of Web 2.0: its application is more lightweight and has greater ease of use and flexibility, and is quite familiar to end users. The system offers each employee "locals" (tabs) in the interface where he/she can follow the development of the software design, posting messages and adding nodes to created wiki. In addition, meetings, explanations, or training courses related to the each project are recorded by staff in audio or video and posted on the corresponding tab, for use by all employees. Our initial expectation was that the system would be able to promote collaboration and exchange of information, so that over time it can perform some KM tasks (mainly transforming tacit knowledge into formal knowledge represented in the wiki nodes) and support OL informal activities by information sharing and visualization of process of software development phases. For the reasons given, we could not test the system's usability and we believe that the main reason for negative response relates to the lack of trust in the reliability and privacy of social networking tools-based system.

However, the research development was an excellent opportunity for experimentation and for free exposure of ideas and concepts. In its short existence, Web 2.0 has transformed the face of the Web. It will be interesting to see how Enterprise 2.0, based on similar principles to those of Web 2.0, will change the face of KM activities within companies. The expectation of the community of KM and OL practitioners and researchers is to see the next waves of Enterprise 2.0, in the hope that they are towards the democratization of knowledge.

REFERENCES

Abecker, A., & Decker, S. (1998). Organizational memory: Knowledge acquisition, integration and retrieval issues. In *Proceedings of XPS-99* (LNAI), (vol. 1570, pp. 113-124). Berlin: Springer.

Andrus, D. (2005). The wiki and the blog: Toward a complex adaptive intelligence community. *Studies in Intelligence, 49*(3).

Argyris, C. (1993). Education for leading-learning. *Organizational Dynamics, 21*(3), 5–17. doi:10.1016/0090-2616(93)90067-B.

Boateng, R., Mbarika, V., & Thomas, C. (2010). When web 2.0 becomes an organizational learning tool: Evaluating web 2.0 tools. *Development and Learning in Organizations, 24*(3), 17–20. doi:10.1108/14777281011037254.

Bughin, J. (2008). The rise of enterprise 2.0. *Journal of Direct. Data and Digital Marketing Practice, 9*(3), 251–259. doi:10.1057/palgrave.dddmp.4350100.

Capozzi, M. (2007). Knowledge management architectures beyond technology. *First Monday, 12*(6). doi:10.5210/fm.v12i6.1871.

Davenport, T. (2008). Enterprise 2.0: The new, new knowledge management? *Harvard Business Review.*

Gallupe, B. (2001). Knowledge management systems: Surveying the landscape. *International Journal of Management Reviews, 3*(1), 61–77. doi:10.1111/1468-2370.00054.

Giaever, H. (1999). Collecting, storing and utilizing information about improvement opportunities: A discussion of the non-technological barriers to success. In *Proceedings of the 11th International Conference on Software Engineering & Knowledge Engineering*, (pp. 200-202). Kaiserslautern, Germany: IEEE.

Gruber, T. (2008). Ontology. In Liu, L., & Ozsu, M. (Eds.), *Encyclopedia of Database Systems.* Berlin: Springer-Verlag.

Gupta, J., & Sushil, S. (2004). *Creating knowledge based organizations.* Hershey, PA: Idea Group Publishing.

Ives, B., & Gersting, A. (1998, February/March). Implementing knowledge management – Lessons learned. *Knowledge Management*.

Kouwenhoven, T. (1998). Reengineering for learning. *SIGGROUP Bulletin*, *19*(1), 39–45.

Markkula, M. (1999). Knowledge management in software engineering projects. In *Proceedings of the 11th International Conference on Software Engineering & Knowledge Engineering*, (pp. 20-27). Kaiserslautern, Germany: IEEE.

Marks, O., & Patel, S. (2010). *Accelerating business performance*. Retrieved from http:/// www.e2conf.com/downloads/whitepapers/ent2-10_TWwhitepaper.pdf

McAfee, A. (2006). Enterprise 2.0: The dawn of emergent collaboration. *Sloan Management Review*.

Nielsen, J. (1993). *Usability engineering*. Academic Press.

Nonaka, I., & Takeushi, H. (1991). The knowledge creating company. *Harvard Business Review*.

O'Reilly, T. (2005). *What is web 2.0: Design patterns and business models for the next generation of software*. Retrieved from http://oreilly.com/ Web2/archive/what-is-Web-20.html

O'Reilly, T., & Battelle. (2009). Web squared: Web 2.0 five years on. *Web 2.0 Summit*. Retrieved from http://assets.en.oreilly.com/1/event/28/ Web2009_Websquared-whitepaper.pdf

Pinelle, D., & Gutwin, C. (2000). A review of groupware evaluations. In *Proceedings of 9th IEEE WETICE 2000 - Workshop on Enabling Technologies: Infrastructures for Collaborative Enterprises*. WETICE.

Santoro, F. M., Borges, M. R. S., & Santos, N. (2006). Patterns for designing planning mechanisms. *International Journal of Computer Applications in Technology*, *25*(2/3), 102–115. doi:10.1504/IJCAT.2006.009066.

Senge, P. (1990). *The fifth discipline: The art and practice of the learning organization*. New York: Doubleday.

Shum, S. B., Motta, E., & Domingue, J. (2000). ScholOnto: An ontologybased digital library server for research documents and discourse. *International Journal on Digital Libraries*, *3*(3), 237–248. doi:10.1007/s007990000034.

Twidale, M., Randall, D., & Bentley, R. (1994). Situated evaluation for cooperative systems. In *Proceedings of Computer-Supported Cooperative Work Conference – CSCW'94*. Chapel Hill, NC: CSCW.

Vygotsky, L. S. (1978). *Mind in society: The development of higher psychological processes*. Cambridge, MA: Harvard University Press.

ADDITIONAL READING

Araujo, R. M., & Brézillon, P. (2005). Reinforcing shared context to improve collaboration. *Revue d'Intelligence Artificielle*, *19*(3), 537–556. doi:10.3166/ria.19.537-556.

Baldauf, M., Dusstdar, S., & Rosenberg, F. (2007). A survey on context-aware systems. *International Journal of Ad Hoc and Ubiquitous Computing*, *2*(4), 63–277. doi:10.1504/IJAHUC.2007.014070.

Bosua, R., & Scheepers, R. (2002). Towards web support for tacit knowledge exchanges. In *Proceedings of the Information Systems Research Seminar in Scandinavia (IRIS25)*. Bautahøj, Denmark: IRIS.

Brézillon, P. (2002). Making context explicit in communicating objects. In Kintzig, C., Poulain, G., Privat, G., & Favennec, P.-N. (Eds.), *Communicating Objects*. Hermes Science Ed.

Brézillon, P., & Pomerol, J. C. (2001). Modeling and using context for system development: Lessons from experiences. *Journal of Decision Systems*, *10*, 265–288. doi:10.3166/jds.10.265-288.

Capuano, N., Gaeta, M., Orciuoli, F., & Ritrovato, P. (2010). Semantic web fostering enterprise 2.0. In *Proceedings of the IV International Conference on Complex, Intelligent and Software Intensive Systems (CISIS 2010)*. CISIS.

Chen, H., Finin, T., & Joshirry, A. (2004). An ontology for context-aware pervasive computing enviroments. *The Knowledge Engineering Review*, *18*(3), 197–207. doi:10.1017/S0269888904000025.

Choli, I., Jung, J., & Song, M. (2004). An integrated framework for process knowledge management. *International Journal of Innovation and Learning*, *1*(4), 399–408. doi:10.1504/IJIL.2004.005500.

Christopoulou, E., Goumopoulos, C., & Kameas, A. (2005). An ontology-based context management and reasoning process for ubicomp applications. In *Proceedings of the 2005 Joint Conference on Smart Objects and Ambient Intelligence*, (pp. 265-270). ACM/IEEE.

Conklin, E. J. (1992). Capturing organizational memory. In *Proceedings of Groupware'92*. San Mateo, CA: Morgan Kaufmann.

Davenport, T. H., & Prusak, L. (1998). *Working knowledge: How organizations manage what they know*. Boston: Harvard Business School Press.

Dey, A. K., Salber, D., & Abowd, G. D. (2001). A conceptual framework and a toolkit for supporting the rapid prototyping of context-aware applications. *Human-Computer Interaction Journal*, *16*(2-4), 97–166. doi:10.1207/S15327051HCI16234_02.

Gu, T., Pung, H. K., & Zhang, D. Q. (2005). A service-oriented middleware for building context-aware services. *Elsevier Journal of Network and Computer Application*, *28*(1), 1–18. doi:10.1016/j.jnca.2004.06.002.

Hildret, P., Kimble, C., & Wright, P. (2000). Communities of practice in the distributed international environment. *Journal of Knowledge Management*, *4*(1), 27–38. doi:10.1108/13673270010315920.

Korpipaa, P., Mantyjarvi, J., & Kela, J. et al. (2003). Managing context information in mobile devices. *IEEE Pervasive Computing / IEEE Computer Society [and] IEEE Communications Society*, *2*(3), 42–51. doi:10.1109/MPRV.2003.1228526.

Kuhn, O., & Abecker, A. (1997). Corporate memories for knowledge management in industrial practice: Prospects and challenges. *Journal of Universal Computer Science*, *3*(8), 929–954.

Lai, J., & Fan, Y. (2002). Workflow and knowledge management: Approaching an integration. In *Proceedings of the 1st International Conference on Engineering and Deployment of Cooperative Information Systems* (LNCS), (Vol. 2480, pp. 16-29). Berlin: Springer-Verlag.

Mahé, S., & Rieu, C. (1998). A pull approach to knowledge management. In *Proceedings of the 2nd International Conference on Practical Aspects of Knowledge management (PAKM98)*. PAKM.

Malhorta, Y. (1998). *Knowledge management for the new world of business*. Retrieved from http://www.brint.com/km/whatis.htm

Maurer, F., & Holz, H. (1999). Process oriented knowledge management for learning software organizations. In *Proceedings of the 12th Knowledge Acquisition Workshop (KAW'99).* Banff, Canada: KAW.

McBurney, P., & Parsons, S. (2004). Locutions for argumentation in agent interaction protocols. In *Proceedings of the Third International Joint Conference on Autonomous Agents and Multiagent Systems*. ACM/IEEE.

Nonaka, I., Toyama, R., & Hirata, T. (2008). *Managing flow: A process theory of the knowledge-based firm*. New York: Palgrave Macmillan.

Nunes, V. T., Santoro, F. M., & Borges, M. (2006). Context in knowledge intensive collaborative work. In *Proceedings of the 10th International Conference on CSCW in Design* (vol. 2, pp. 793-798). CSCW.

Nunes, V. T., Santoro, F. M., & Borges, M. (2007). Capturing context about group design process. In *Proceedings of the 11th International Conference on CSCW in Design, 2007.* CSCW.

O'Leary, D. E. (1998). Enterprise knowledge management. *IEEE Computer Systems, 13*(2), 54–61. doi:10.1109/2.660190.

Perret, R., Borges, M. R. S., & Santoro, F. M. (2004). Applying group storytelling in knowledge management. In *Proceedings of CRIWG 2004.* San Carlos, Costa Rica: CRIWG.

Santoro, F., Borges, M. R. S., & Santos, N. (2003). Learning through collaborative projects: The architecture of an environment. *International Journal of Computer Applications in Technology, 16*(2/3), 127–141. doi:10.1504/IJCAT.2003.000320.

Santoro, F. M., Borges, M. R. S., & Santos, N. (2003). Experimental findings with cooperative writing within a project-based environment. InLlamas-Nistal, , Fernández-Iglesias, , & Anido-Rifón, (Eds.), *Computers and Education: Towards a Lifelong Learning Society*. Holland: IEEE.

Santoro, F. M., Borges, M. R. S., & Santos, N. (2004a). Evaluation of collaborative learning processes. *Advanced Technology For Learning, 1*(1), 164–173.

Santoro, F. M., Borges, M. R. S., & Santos, N. (2004b). Planning the collaboration process: One-way to make it happen. In *Proceedings of CSCWD 2004*. Xiamen, China: CSCWD.

Santoro, F. M., Guerrero, L. G., Zapata, S., Borges, M., & Santos, N. (2004). Evaluating collaboration in CSCL application domain within the CSCW lab. In *Proceedings of the 8th International Conference on Computer Supported Cooperative Work in Design*. CSCWD.

Schmohl, R., & Baumgarten, U. (2008). Context-aware computing: A survey preparing a generalized approach. In *Proceedings of the International MultiConference of Engineers and Computer Scientists 2008.* IMECS.

Schneckenberg, D. (2009). Web 2.0 and the empowerment of the knowledge worker. *Journal of Knowledge Management, 13*(6), 12. doi:10.1108/13673270910997150.

Steels, L. (1993). Corporate knowledge management. In *Proceedings of ISMICK'93 Conference.* ISMICK.

Strang, T., & Linnhoff-Popien, L. (2004). Context modeling survey. In *Proceedings of the First International Workshop on Advanced Context Modelling, Reasoning and Management Nottingham, 6th International Conference on Ubiquitous Computing*. IEEE.

Van Der Aalst, W. M. P., et al. (2003). Business process management: A survey. In *Proceedings of the 1st International Conference on Business Process Management.* Berlin, Germany: IEEE.

Wang, X., Zhang, D. Q., Gu, T., et al. (2004). Ontology based context modeling and reasoning using OWL. In *Proceedings of the Workshop on Context Modeling and Reasoning at IEEE International Conference on Pervasive Computing and Communication.* Orlando, FL: IEEE.

Wenger, E., McDermott, R., & Synder, R. (2002). *Cultivating communities of practice: A guide to managing knowledge – Seven principles for cultivating communities of practice.* Boston: Harvard Business School Press.

KEY TERMS AND DEFINITIONS

Collaboration: A working practice where individuals work together towards a common purpose to achieve common benefit.

Communities of Practice: Groups of people who get together regarding sense of responsibility in the work process in progress, the common interests in learning and mainly in practical applications of the learned contents.

Enterprise 2.0: Also known as Enterprise Social Software; it is the use of Web 2.0 technologies within an organization to enable or streamline business processes while enhancing collaboration - connecting people through the use of social media tools.

Group Memory: Also known as organizational memory or group memory; the accumulated body of data, information, and knowledge created in the course of organization processes.

Groupware: Technology designed to facilitate and provide support to the work of groups. It may be used to communicate, cooperate, coordinate, solve problems, compete, or negotiate.

Knowledge Management: Activities of identification, acquisition, development, dissemination, use and maintenance of organizational knowledge in a systematic way.

Organizational Learning: The processes that seek to create, acquire and transfer knowledge and modify people behavior within company in order to reflect new knowledge and insight.

Software Development: Process of developing software by successive phases in an methodical way, such as: software requirements analysis, detailed specification, software design, programming, testing and maintenance.

Web 2.0: Term coined by O'Reilly (2004) to define a set of technologies and tools to promote collaboration and knowledge sharing in a collective and decentralized way. Its tools enable an environment for encouraging collaborative work by providing a richer and more dynamic communication.

ENDNOTES

1 Ontology specifies a shared understanding of a domain of interest and contains a set of concepts, together with its definitions and interrelationships, and possibly encodes a logical layer for inference and reasoning. The role of ontology is to reflect a community's consensus on a useful way to conceptualize a particular domain.

2 Semantic Web is not a separate Web but an extension of the current one in which information is given well-defined meaning, better enabling computer and people to work in cooperation.

Chapter 28
Valuing Learning Objects Shared in an Online Community

Jacqueline Guzmán
Universidad de la República, Uruguay

Regina Motz
Universidad de la República, Uruguay

Alberto Rodrigues da Silva
Instituto Superior Técnico, Portugal

ABSTRACT

In this chapter, the authors analyze and discuss how the activity inside a social network impacts on the value of a Learning Object (LO) used in a collaborative e-learning platform. Recent works propose metrics for measuring LO reusability based on a variety of approaches. In this work, they combine and extend these approaches in order to design a valuation strategy which helps to identify the usage of LOs inside a social network. Their proposal is to identify the factors that are relevant for the valuation of a LO and determine which of them can be computed automatically from its context of usage, the level of success of its authors and its metadata. The authors' analysis was performed on a particular social network called LOP (LO Poll) system, which strongly motivates the creation and collaborative valuation of LOs. They present preliminary conclusions obtained from an experiment performed in order to analyze the feasibility of the proposal.

INTRODUCTION

For some years now, all of us have started giving more and more importance to the community-society in the information systems. But today, not only does the community consume a technological product, but it has also become part of the product-system. Systems nowadays model the community and its behavior as they learn from the society. Thus, the main idea of enterprise 2.0 is to consider the social software as the element that allows for the creation of new knowledge without being limited to administrating the existing one.

DOI: 10.4018/978-1-4666-4373-4.ch028

The technology-community link is more important and deep when using technology to support education, since technology plays here a dual role of learning and teaching. On one hand, the e-learning systems must know-infer-learn the behavior and preferences of users (e.g. teachers, students); and on the other hand, they should be the support of the e-learning process. The system learns from the community so as to teach them in the best way.

As we have seen, the value of the knowledge produced in social networks is recognized as a key issue in any organization (Dalkir, 2011; Barão & Rodrigues da Silva, 2011). Moreover, this is extremely relevant in the context of e-learning communities where collaboration and quality of resources is of ultimate importance.

The wide variety of resources used in learning contexts are called Learning Objects (LO) Widley (2001), i.e. pieces of pedagogical information that can be reused. Usually these LOs are stored in repositories of LO, such as MERLOT[1], ARIADNE[2], eLERA[3], Connexions[4], Agrega[5], which coincide on the need to create valuable reusable LOs.

In reference to giving value to a LO, we ask ourselves "What is the value of something?" The axiological definition of value according to Frondizi (1992) is related to the value of a socio-personal interpretation according to reality and needs. Therefore, opinions about the LO coming from the community of authors, the community of users and the community of reviewers must be taken into account.

Ochoa (2011) presents a comparative study of LO repositories that show that LO reusability is bigger in repositories in which users are part of a community. Besides this, there exists no standardization about how the activity inside a social network impacts the value of the LOs.

This proposal aims at identifying the factors which are relevant for the valuation of a LO and determine which of these factors can be computed automatically from the LO's context of usage, the level of success of its authors and its metadata. We perform our analysis on a particular social network called LOP (Learning Objects Pull) system (Dinis & Rodrigues da Silva, 2007, 2009), which motivates the creation and collaborative valuation of LOs. We consider the necessity to prove that the community is important in a measurable way, in the same way that Enterprise 2.0 does in reference to the business performance. Therefore, our proposal measures the value that the LOP's community gives to the learning objects of the LOP.

We present preliminary conclusions obtained from an experiment performed to analyze the feasibility of the proposal.

RELATED WORK

This section presents an overview of several works which focuses on diverse issues related to the problem of measuring the LO's quality in terms of reusability.

Factors Related to the Reusability

Sanz, Dodero and Sanchez-Alonso (2009) proposed a model to evaluate the reusability of LOs which is based on the main following factors:

- **Cohesion:** Is directly proportional to the semantic density, and is inversely proportional to the amount of: relations, aggregations, concepts and objectives covered.
- **Coupling:** Is defined by the information given by the relation category of LOM. More relations mean more coupling.
- **Size and Complexity:** Represent a degree of granularity of a LO (e.g. resource, lesson, course) and are directly proportional to the size, duration and typical learning time of the object.
- **Portability:** Has a technical and educational aspect. The first one is based on the format of the LO, the requirements of the hardware and software, and the criteria defined in the proposal to assign each of these a value. The educational aspect of a LO's portability is

based on the following metadata: context, typical age range, language, and classification.

These factors agree with fields' LOM metadata, and are considered according to their importance. The proposal was tested using a set of eLera's objects, and compared with LORI's evaluations.

In summary, this work is based on: (1) defining the factors that determined the LO's reusability; (2) establishing the mapping between these factors and the metadata LOM; (3) specifying the guidelines to qualify each factor.

Further work of Sanz (2010) proposes an automatic process to measure the reusability of a LO from the metrics of the following factors: cohesion, portability and size. The work defines a unique metric which is a combination of the previous metrics weighted according to their importance. In addition, the proposal considers a possible interdependence between the criteria. The validation of the proposal was made through the comparison of the results performed with the Merlot's and eLera's evaluations.

In addition, Sanz proposes improving the previous metric with the opinions of users, experts and empirical data such as amount of access, amount of users, and the like.

Work conducted by Meyer, Hannappel, Rensing, and Steinmetz (2007) considers the pedagogical granularity as the most important factor in reference to the reusability. This kind of granularity has been called information's granularity and it is determined by the didactic functions that an LO may have. A LO may have several pieces of information which have varied didactic functions types (e.g. overview, theorem, example, test). These functions are obtained from ontologies Meder (1999).

The research's goal was to classify the objects' information in different didactic functions which are defined in the Meder's ontologies Meder (1999). The function types are: receptive knowledge types (facts, overview, etc.) and interactive assessments (multiple choice tests, assignment tests). Particularly, they wanted to test multimedia features in the classification process. Therefore, they considered the following features in the classification task: Length of the text according to the amount of words, number of javascript functions, keywords in the page headlines, HTML code containing lists, forms, input elements, choice elements, interaction elements and embedded flash animations.

They constructed a set of objects' information from different sources and multiple authors. Then, these objects were manually classified by reviewers. Four algorithms were used to classify these objects (Bayes, SVM, JRip, C4.5), and the results were compared with the human-made classifications. The experimentation was made several times considering: different levels of details, multi-label classifications, all features and then selected features. Finally, they introduced the possibility of analyzing the position of the objects' information as a relevant factor to consider, besides analyzing the style of speech as a way to identify some didactic functions.

In summary, this work proposes to annotate the objects' information according to didactic functions and to consider these functions as a measure of the LO's granularity which is related to the LO's reusability. The correctness of the proposal is based on measuring how close the result is as compared to human evaluation, a fact which is stated in most related works.

Many metrics are based in the LO's metadata, but are these metadata good enough? In this sense, Ochoa & Duval (2006) proposed measuring the quality of the metadata through metrics calculated automatically. Their work is based in LOM metadata and in the following parameters:

- **Completeness:** Is measured considering that each field of metadata has an importance and a value which will be 1 if the field has information; otherwise, it will be 0.
- **Accuracy:** Is based in semantic distances and content analysis. This comparison between the metadata's information and the docu-

ment's information can be made sometimes by algorithms and others by persons.

- **Provenance:** Depends on the reputation of: the metadata register, the metadata producer, the community, or those who use the metadata.
- **Conformance of Expectations:** Evaluates whether the amount of information is enough to describe the LO. The metrics proposed measure the amount of unique information given by each field of metadata. Although there are other aspects related with the conformance, they are covered by others metrics, for instance the completeness of the information.
- **Logical Consistency and Coherence:** Are based on the consistency rules suggested by LOM about its fields. For example, LOM establishes that if the field *structure* has the value *'atomic'*, then the field *aggregation level* should be *1*.
- **Timeless:** Represents the age and the frequency of use of the metadata.
- **Accessibility:** Represents the difficulty to find and understand the information.

In order to carry out the experimentation they had to generate LOM from ARIADNE's repository (mostly manually) and from OpenCourseWare documents (automatically).

Environment Elements and Community Behavior

Some works propose metrics which are based on: the mapping between characteristics and preferences of the environment elements (e.g., situations, users, courses and so on), and the analysis of the users' behavior patterns. The knowledge about the preferences of the community in the past helps to predict the users' needs or preferences in the present.

Ochoa and Duval (2008) proposed several metrics used to rank objects in search problems. These metrics can be automatically calculated and they are based on: similarity measurements, frequency of use, and the references between elements (courses, objects and users). These measurements required a historical register of: the users' behavior, object's metadata (LOM), and information about the context. The proposed metrics are related to the quality of relevant dimensions Duval (2005):

- **Basic Topical:** Has to do with the number of times that the objects were selected in queries which are similar to the current query. The similarity is calculated comparing the terms of the queries.
- **Course-Similarity Topical:** Is based on the fact that the objects are used in courses. The proposal considers the level of similarity between the existing courses and the course in which the selected object will be used. Then, these degrees of similarity will be used to sort the output objects according to the courses to which the objects belong.
- **Internal Topical:** Considers the object's references that are the amount of courses in which the object was used. Rank Web page's algorithms are applied on LO, considering the LO references instead of page links.
- **Basic Personal Ranking:** Uses LO metadata which correspond to previous user selections as the users' preferences.
- **User-Similarity Personal:** These metrics are similar to Course-Similar Topical Relevance's metric, but the similarity is applied to the users. The similarity between two users is given by the amount of objects that they have in common
- **Basic Situational:** Compares the descriptions of the activities that the learner should be able to do with the LO's metadata (fields such as descriptions, keywords, and so on). This comparison is made to find the objects which are closer to the objectives. The similarities were calculated according to the terms' importance and to the semantic distances

- **Context Similarity Situational:** Proposes that LOs are ranked according to the level of similarity between them and the courses LOs where the evaluating LO are to be used.The similarity is determined by a vector of the frequency of the values of the LO metadata.

In summary, this work relies on the need of a historical record of the users' behavior, and on the analysis of this record to find similarities (between objects, courses, users and queries). The metadata LOM was used. They propose to measure the similarity in different ways: (1) number of relations between elements; (2) semantic comparison between terms and/or values of metadata; (3) number of repetitions of the values of the fields.

Another research, by Yen, Shih, Chao, and Jin (2010), defined a metric to rank LOs. Each object has a value determined by three factors: the time windows in which the object was used, the feedback given by the user (the object was successful or not for the user), and the object download called references (self references and other references have different weight). The importance of the object is made up by its value and the weighted average of the similar objects. This similarity is calculated based on the following LOM metadata: title, language, keyword and coverage of the general category, learning resource type, Intended End User Role, Typical Age Range, Difficulty, and Typical Learning Time of the educational category. The level of similarity is determined by the amount of fields with equal value.

Users Valuing and LO's Characteristic Quality

The research by Cechinel, Sánchez-Alonso, Sicilia, and Velazquez Amador (2011) proposed three models to automatic valuing of MERLOT's resources. These models are based in the LO's subject (the disciplines of Science, Technology, Mathematics, and Statistics) and materials' type in a pedagogical sense (Simulation and Tutorial). All material are the same type in a technological sense, they are Web pages. The features measured (metrics) were intrinsic characteristics of the Web page material, such as: link measures (number of different type of links), text measures (number of words), graphic measures (images, scripts, applets) and site architecture measures (pages: size, number) .The LO were classified in good or not-good according to the following algorithms: J48, Simple Cart, PART, Multilayer Perceptron, and Bayesian Network. Then, classification results were compared to the evaluation given by peer-reviewers as a way to test the metrics.

This work identifies some features as appropriate to classify LOs as good or not-good material. The features are about material which must be in particular disciplines, type of material and type of format.

The research by Blumenstock (2008) proposed the count of words as a measure of the quality for English articles in Wikipedia. The author came up with 1554 articles selected after a cleaner task, which were used for training and for testing. He compared the results with some other techniques of classification and got good results that supported the proposal. This proposal is simple, clear to understand and easy to measure.

In addition, even today, the experts-based evaluations are considered the best approach, so the majority of proposals tend to be validated this way. Besides, many proposals required human intervention during some of their process.

The proposal by Cechinel and Sánchez-Alonso (2011) is strongly based in the valuing given by different kind or users. They consider the ranking given by experts in specific topics and the ranking given by the repository's users (the community) as well. This research compares both rankings to obtain the similarities about the material's quality. This analysis searches the best way to use both strategies in the determination of the quality. The experts and users-based rankings are made according to the following dimensions: quality of the content, the ease of use, and the potential of effectiveness as a learning tool.

In general terms, the problem of the human intervention is the time (and consequently cost) required to value the LOs. This is the reason why we need to complement these approaches with automatic mechanisms.

Table 1 shows a comparative analysis of the proposals referred in this section.

ASPECTS OF GIVING AN INITIAL VALUE TO A LEARNING OBJECT

The issue of giving a value to a LO implies establishing which factors are relevant according with a criteria of application and determining how they can be measured. Although the relevant factors might vary according to different realities, there is a consensus in considering the reusability of LOs as one of the most important ones. Other factors worth considering are: portability, granularity, cohesion, coupling, complexity, adaptability, among others. Many of these factors are interrelated, and all of them affect the reusability. However, in order to determine which factors are relevant, we need to consider the purposes for which we want to give a value to the LO. The value of a LO can be used to solve a variety of problems according to the existing realities: (1) organize the objects in order of importance (ranking problem); (2) search the most adequate object according to user needs (search problem); (3) integrate the LO with others

Table 1. Comparative analysis of related work

Research's Type	Research's Ref	Main Ideas/Porposed
Factors related to the Reusability	J. Sanz Rodriguez, J. M. Dodero and S. Sanchez-Alonso (2009)	Reusability = Factors = Cohesion, Coupling, Size and Complexity, Portability, Difficulty of Compression Mapping Factors with LOM's fields Guidelines to qualify Factors
	J. Sanz Rodriguez (2010)	End metric = F (Cohesion, Size and Portability) F = Agregations + Integral Chiquet (x interdependece) Test = comparison with experts evaluations
	M. Meyer, A. Hannappel, C. Rensing, R. Steinmetz (2007)	Reusability = Granularity Granularity = didactic functions
	X. Ochoa, E. Duval (2006)	Metadata's Quality (LOM) = Factors Factors = completeness, accuracy, provenance, logical consistency and coherence, timeliness, and accessibility
Environment Elements and Community Behavior	X. Ochoa, E. Duval (2008)	History of the users' behavior Used metadata LOM Similarity concepts (objects, courses, users and queries) ≠ ways
	N. Y. Yen, T. K. Shih, L. R. Chao, and Q. Jin (2010)	History register of the user's behavior Used metadata LOM Similarity concept (comparison of the object's metadata)
User's valuing and LO's characteristics-Quality	C. Cechinel, S. Sánchez-Alonso, M. Sicilia, C. Velazquez Amador (2011)	Identify features classify the LO as good or not-good material Material = disciplines (math, ...), type (tutorial, ...), format (web pages)
	Joshua E. Blumenstock (2008)	Quality = Feature = count of word Material = English article, format (Wikipedia)
	C. Cechinel, S. Sánchez-Alonso (2011)	The rankings of experts and users Dimensions to rank: quality of the content, the ease of use, and the potential of effectiveness as a learning tool Compares both to obtain the similarities about the material's quality

(integrate problem); (4) relate it to a suitable price or cost (business problem); and so on.

Another aspect to be considered to determine the relevant factors is the environment in which the LO is used. For example, the LO may be in connection with other elements such as: social communities (e.g. students, teachers, reviewers), courses in which the LO was used or could be used, and the topics that the LcO covers. These connections might be more or less relevant according to the specific reality and the expected use of the LO. For example, in the online community scenario, the reputation and activity of their members is a very important factor to be considered (Iriberri & Leroy, 2009).

The impact of the relevant factors can be calculated in function of the LO's metadata. We understand by metadata all the information that is used to describe the object, not only social features but also structural ones. Standard metadata seeks to determine which information should be known about the object. For instance, LOM establishes a series of information groups that correspond to different kinds of LO's information: general, life cycle, meta metadata, technical, educational, rights, relation, annotation, and classification. Another metadata standard is Dublin Core, defined originally to be used in libraries, but currently used in other domains, such as describing Web resources. Dublin Core defines the minimum set of metadata necessary to describe resources such as: title, author, copyright. In general, applications use some of the metadata standard but extend or specialize them with specific metadata profiles. The use of standards is important because it adds value in terms of interoperability and reusability. In addition, it may reflect some characteristics of the LO that cannot be drawn from the analysis of the object itself.

Another important aspect to consider in the problem of valuing a LO, is valuing each of the factors identified as relevant from a technological perspective but also from a socio-pedagogical one. These factors are determined by LO's metadata; therefore, these metadata must be also composed by technological and pedagogical features. Moreover, another perspective to be considered for the LO analysis is the LO's structure, content and environment. For example, Figure 1 shows a diagram of the analysis of the complexity factor, which is analyzed by examining the structural, content and environment features through a technological and socio-pedagogical point of view. Following Sanz (2010), the features are grouped in two categories: Structural and Content, but considering our analysis of relevance we also added the Environment grouping category. The size and format are some features from the Structural group whereas words and pages belong to the Content. Some features may be considered in both perspectives simultaneously. As shown in Figure 1, the duration factor, i.e. the time that the user needs in order to hear or view the material, is considered as a technological feature (depending on the hardware device that supports the user's experience) but it is also considered as a pedagogical feature (depending on the level of concentration required by the topic).Technological

Figure 1. Analysis framework for the LO's complexity factor

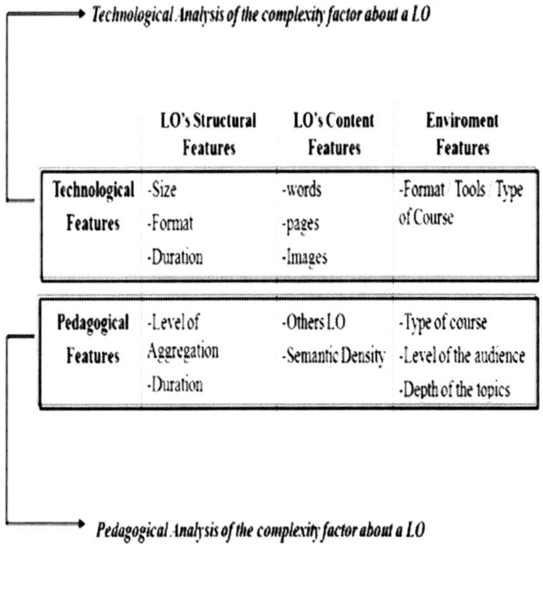

and Pedagogical classifications are presented in the works of Sanz, Dodero. & Sanchez-Alonso (2009), Sanz (2010) among others.

When analyzing the complexity factor in relation to the Environment, the following features are identified: the level of the audience for which the LO is designed (e.g. courses, students), the depth of the topics it deals with (e.g. basic, medium or advanced), and the type of courses in which the object can be used (e.g. online, classroom, or semi-presenciales courses). Some of these features can be also analyzed either from the technological or pedagogical point of view.

In summary, to measure the value of LOs in an application we need to establish: what the relevant factors are (such as complexity, portability or granularity), what the point of view from which we would like to analyzed them is (structural content, environment, technological, educational, or any combination of these); which the needed metadata to describe these factors are and whether they follow some standard (e.g., Dublin Core, LOM); how the metadata values are loaded (automatically or manually); and, finally, how the factors are measured.

THE LOP System

The Learning Objects Pool (LOP) System is a collaborative Web-based application that supports user communities as part of the teaching and learning process (Dinis & Rodrigues da Silva, 2007, 2009). Technically the LOP system is a LO repository that promotes the active collaboration of its users, both in submission of LOs, as well as in the submission of relevant information that will contribute to its understanding. The system distinguishes and rewards users who contribute the most in the creation of quality LOs. In addition, LOP also compensates the end-users active and regular collaboration through a credit-based system that calculates the level of users' collaboration. This mechanism also updates the LO value according to its popularity, similar to the stock exchange metaphor, where the LO value raises or falls depending on the number of acquisitions which represent the LO's popularity.

The LOP system currently provides a good stability in terms of usability and functionality, and has been instantiated for different usage scenarios, namely the BOA-GPI and the VemAprender.net instances. The BOA-GPI[6] is supporting the "IT Project Management" course at IST (Technical University of Lisbon), supporting several generations of students and faculties assigned to this course. The VemAprender.net[7] is an open and public-access instance, for everyone interested in sharing or reusing LOs, particularly targeted to students and teachers at K-12 education levels. (There is also the "BOA4OpenCommunity"[8] just for simple demonstration and evaluation purposes.) In the context of this research we have used the data available from the VemAprender.net instance.

Teachers, students and administrators work collaboratively in this LOP community (the VemAprender.net platform) sharing and reusing LOs to support the teaching-learning process. This LOP repository not only has the LOs, but also an important set of information—LO's metadata—that describe them, such as topics, type of resource, description, language; in addition to registers of the users and information on activities (e.g. submitter, comments, suggestions).

The LOP system aims at achieving LOs excellence through an open and competitive environment. This platform allows the centralized gathering of LOs besides their reuse in different courses. LOs have an associated value and the users can download them if they have enough credits. Users increase their own credits by doing different activities such as creating and sharing LOs or commenting, rating, describing instructions or good practices related the LOs or even by writing suggestions for new LOs.

Currently, when a user submits a LO to the repository he first has to upload the LO and its metadata and he has to specify an initial value to that object. Then, optionally, a reviewer can evaluate the object being able to comment and give recommendations to the author and/or negotiate with him the initial value of the object. Finally, the LO becomes available to the community members who might download it. The value of the object varies periodically, increasing or decreasing, according to the number of downloads carried out. Figure 2 shows the LO submission workflow.

The LO can have more than one author. Part of the information that the submitter should introduce is related to the LO's authors, their percentage of involvement, and which the responsible author should be (the LO responsible is the only one who is enabled to change some information about the object such as its metadata).

Additionally, the LOP system should keep track of other information to better categorize and organize LOs such as groups, level of audience and size of the object among others. This information is encoded in different types of metadata, called intrinsic or manual metadata. The metadata that LOP system employs to describe its objects are made up by 39 fields, some required and most of them optional, which extend the Dublin Core Standard[9].

The LOP allows for LOs to be described by the following metadata groups:

- **General Information Group:** The main information which is required in most fields. In this group of metadata we can find the following information:
    - **Submitter:** Corresponds to the information about the author who submits the LO. Each LO has to have at least one author. If the LO has more than one author, authors and level of participation in the development of the LO should be assigned in the Authoring metadata group.
    - **Group and Level of Audience:** This information describes the object's profile from a pedagogical perspective. On one hand, the Group corresponding to the context where the LO may be used. This information is specified by the submitter. Each user of the LOP system is associated to groups for which he is able to publish, consult and download LOs. Moreover, if the object can be used in more than

Figure 2. LO submission workfow (Dinis & Rodrigues da Silva, 2009)

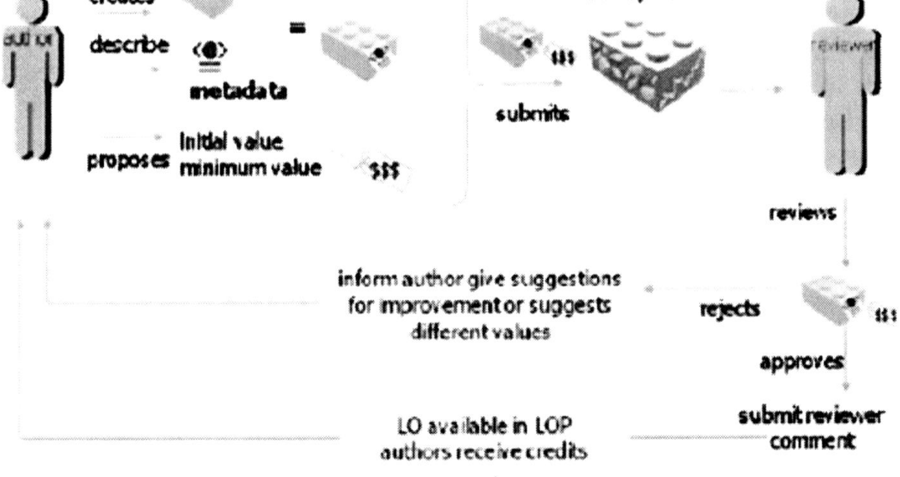

one group, the detail can be stated in the Topic. On the other hand, Level of audience indicates whether the LO is designed for students in basic, intermediate or advanced levels.
  - **Title, Description, Keywords, Language, Date of creation and Format:** This information depict the features of the LO itself. Though some of these metadata could be uploaded automatically analyzing the object's content file, the information is currently uploaded manually by the object's submitter.
  - **Initial and Minimum Value of the Object:** This metadata indicates the initial and minimum value of the LO according to the criteria of his author.
- **Topic Group:** Permits to indicate the topics that best describe the LO; each group has its specific hierarchy of topics.
- **Authoring Group:** Is the information about the users that participate in the authoring of the object.
- **Collaborators Group:** Is information regarding people who in spite of not being users of the system or authors of the objects, have collaborated somehow in its design or production.
- **Relationship Group:** Is the information that states relationships between the LO and others LOs in the repository; several types of relationship are supported, such as: part-of, version-of, addition, or generalization-of.
- **Types Group:** Is about the type of material from a pedagogical perspective, for instance: exercise, simulation, example, and others.
- **Images Group:** Includes images associated to the LO, those images that appear in the content of the objet itself as well as other suggestive images.
- **Other Information:** This group contains other information such as author's rights, editorials, instructional methods, coverage or the source of the object.

The proposal discussed in this paper aims at using the information specified by the submitter, as well as information extracted automatically from the object, to suggest the initial value for the corresponding LO.

THE INITIAL VALUE OF A LEARNING OBJECT IN THE LOP SYSTEM

Based on the related work and the characteristics of the LOP systems we identify the following main factors which determine the LO's capacity of reusability: granularity, complexity, portability, completeness and provenance of metadata.

- **Granularity:** We understand the granularity as the number of topics covered by the LO. We consider the criteria used in (Meyer, Hannappel, Rensing & Steinmetz, 2007): "Producing large units (e.g. whole courses) provides the best usability in the first place, but decreases the probability that this large unit be re-used in another context".
- **Complexity:** We consider the complexity of a LO as the difficulty to understand the LO. In this sense, we believe that the more information the LO has, then the more understandable the LO is. In this work, we associate the measure of the complexity to the measure of the amount of information according to pages/slice, words, paragraphs, images and formulas that the LO contains. However, the relation between complexity and amount of information depends on the type of file of the LO and the context of its use.

- **Portability:** In terms of reusability the capacity of carrying an object from one context to another (courses, platforms, and users) is very important and it is necessary to analyze the pedagogical and technological features of the object to measure these capacities. From the technological point of view the format of the object must be considered. Some optional metadata should be taken into account but we don't use optional features in the proposal. From the pedagogical point of view the granularity and the complexity determine the portability. And we consider the context for which the author creates the object is given by the group features of LOP.
- **Completeness:** Is based on the amount of optional metadata of the LO filled by the user. The relevance that we assign to this factor is in order to encourage authors to load the optional metadata.
- **Provenance:** Like Duval (2006) and Stack Overflow community[10] we consider the source's reputation as a relevant factor. In the LOP system the optional metadata is provided by the authors; consequently, we measure the authors' reputation.

Figure 3. Assessment process of LOP objects

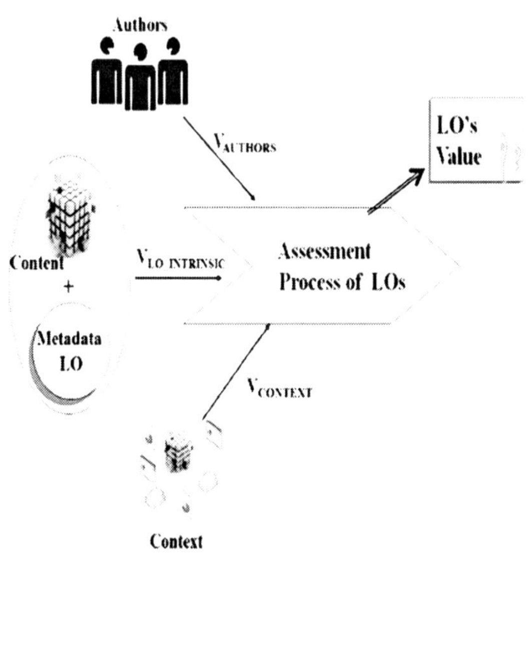

These factors are measured through the properties of LOs (structural and content features), users and context. Therefore, our proposal consists of determining the value of a LO in terms of the following elements: Authors, Context, the content of the LO, the LO's Metadata and the LO itself (Figure 3).

The proposal follows the simplicity principle. The aim of the functions proposed to calculate the LO's value is to be simple to understand, implement and process.

We determine the initial value of a LO taking into account: the value of the author, the value of the context, and the value given by the intrinsic characteristics of the object. We propose that the value of the LO can be calculated as the sum of the values of the elements mentioned above (in order of importance) as shown in Equation 1:

$$\mathbf{V}_{\mathbf{LO}} = \alpha_{\mathbf{A}}\mathbf{V}_{\mathbf{AUTHORS}} + \beta_{\mathbf{C}}\mathbf{V}_{\mathbf{CONTEXT}} + \mu_{\mathbf{LO}}\mathbf{V}_{\mathbf{LO\_INTRINSIC}}$$
$$\text{t.q. } 0 <= \alpha_A, \beta_C, \mu_{LO} <= 1 \qquad \alpha_A + \beta_C + \mu_{LO} = 1 \tag{1}$$

where:

$V_{AUTHORS}$ represents the reputation value of the LO's authors which is associated not only with their profile but also in relationship with their level of participation in authoring tasks and with the level of success obtained.

$V_{CONTEXT}$ represents the importance of the context of usage and the pedagogical granularity of the LO. The first is defined by groups and subjects in which the LO can be used, and the second is the level of LO's specialization

$V_{LO\_INTRINSIC}$ represents the values of the intrinsic properties of the LO. Some of those metadata can be automatically extracted which determines the LO's portability, and other metadata are optional and are related with the completeness factor

The relevance assigned to the $V_{AUTHORS}$, $V_{CONTEXT}$ or $V_{LO\_INTRINSIC}$ in the calculation of the initial value of the LO is specified by the constants α_A, β_C, μ_{LO}. In our scenario of LOP system, we propose to give the most importance to the intrinsic characteristics of the object because of the mechanisms of loading used, then the characteristics of the authors, and last the context. In the following subsections we present our proposal of formulas to calculate the values of Authors, Context and Intrinsic Metadata; $V_{AUTHORS}$, $V_{CONTEXT}$ and $V_{LO\_INTRINSIC}$ respectively.

The Authors

Similarly to the way StackOverflow uses the concept of reputation, the LOP System encourages the users to create reusable LOs. Therefore, we consider measuring the reputation in relation with the users' participations (authoring task). We propose measuring the value of an author not only by the level of activity of the author, but also considering the level of acceptance of his LOs among users of the community (success), and the profile of the author (e.g. student, teacher,). Therefore we consider the V_{AUTHOR} as a function of the initial value of the author's type plus the amount of LOs published by the author in the repository (N_{LO_PUB}) and the value of success of his/her LOs (distinguished by LOs download at least once and those which present a good success of downloads: $N_{DOWNLOAD} + V_{LO\_DWN}$. This is depicted in Equation 2:

$$V_{AUTHOR} = V_{AUTHOR\_TYPE} + N_{LO\_PUB} + N_{DOWNLOAD} + V_{LO\_DWN} \tag{2}$$

The value of the author V_{AUTHOR_TYPE} is initialized with a fixed value depending on the author type configurated by the system administrator. In the beginning, the importance of the author's group and the LO's topics encourage the community to download the object, but only the author's profile is measured The LOP system has four type of authors: students, teachers, students' representatives (e.g. parents), and others. The teacher is the most valuable type.

The level of activity of the authors (N_{LO_PUB}) influence directly in the value of the author because of LOP system strategy to motivate the participation of the members of the community to produce LOs.

The success of the author is measured through the number of downloads of his/her LOs. Each download is added to the author's value ($N_{DOWNLOAD}$) and this value is increased with the average of the LO's value that have had a special success (V_{LO_DWN}), this is, those LOs which have been downloaded at least a minimum number of times, for example the 10% of the number of members of the community.

$$\begin{aligned} V_{LO\_DWN} &= [\Sigma_{i:1..n} V_{LO}(O_i)] / N_{LO\_PUB} \\ \text{t.q.} \quad & N_{DOWNLOAD}(oi) > k, \\ & k = 10\% \text{ N} - \text{members} \end{aligned} \tag{2.1}$$

Finally, the value of a LO as compared to the value of its authors ($V_{AUTHORS}$) is the average of the authors' values (V_{AUTHOR}) affected by the percentage of participation that each author has in the authorship.

The Context

In LOP system, when the LO is uploaded to the repository the author can indicate the Groups and the Topics in which she/he considers it is most appropriate to use the LO. Even though the groups have topics, the author should indicate the specific topics covered by the LO (selected topics).

The Group and the Selected Topics determine the profile of the context in which the LO can be used, therefore the proposal considers the group's value and the selected topics' value in the valuation of the context.

As mentioned above, we consider that a fine granular LO is more valuable than general ones. This is because the greater the amount of topics covered by an object, the less portable and reusable this object is. Then, we consider that the number of topics covered by the object is a measure of the LO's reusability and we propose the following formula to calculate the value of the context of a given LO:

$$\mathbf{V}_{\mathbf{CONTEXT}} = \alpha_{\mathrm{G}} * \mathbf{V}_{\mathbf{GROUP}} + \beta_{\mathrm{T}} * \mathbf{V}_{\mathbf{TOPICS}}$$
$$\text{where } 0 <= \alpha_{\mathrm{G}} < \beta_{\mathrm{T}} <= 1 \qquad \alpha_{\mathrm{G}} + \beta_{\mathrm{T}} = 1 \tag{3}$$

The initial value of the groups and topics are configurated by the system administrator according to the application. But for the topics we propose the Equation (3.1) because LOs with only one topic are the most specialized object. Then, they have the highest level of reusability and they are the most valuable. When the LO has different topics, we propose that the value of the topic corresponds to the less valuable topic in relation with the total amount of selected topics for the LO.

$$\begin{aligned} V_{\mathrm{TOPICS}} &= V_{\mathrm{SELTOPIC}} && \text{one topic selected} \\ &= V_{\mathrm{SELTOPIC\_MIN}} / \mathrm{N\_Topics} && >1 \text{ topic selected} \end{aligned} \tag{3.1}$$

Although the proposal allows for a different weight to the group and the topics (α_G, β_T), we consider that the information given by the topics is more important because it refers to the knowledge transmitted by the LO. Moreover, the value of the group is general information about the context of the LO that depends on the application, i.e. a large number of members in the group may be considered more or less valuable.

LO Content and Metadata

The proposal aims at estimating the value of the intrinsic characteristics of the LO ($V_{LO\_INTINSIC}$) described by metadata. Some metadata can be obtained automatically (V_{LO_AM}), while others are given manually by the author (V_{LO_MM}). Then we propose to calculate the value of the intrinsic characteristics of the LO as follows:

$$\mathbf{V}_{\mathbf{LO\_INTRINSIC}} = \alpha_{\mathbf{MM}} * \mathbf{V}_{\mathbf{LO\_MM}} + \beta_{\mathbf{MA}} * \mathbf{V}_{\mathbf{LO\_AM}}$$
$$\text{where } 0 <= \alpha_{\mathrm{MM}} < \beta_{\mathrm{MA}} <= 1 \qquad \alpha_{\mathrm{MM}} + \beta_{\mathrm{MA}} = 1 \tag{4}$$

The proposal gives different importance to manual metadata and automatic metadata (α_{MM}, β_{MA}) according to how they are obtained. The automatic extraction is a reliable mechanism; therefore, we consider that the information automatically obtained is more valuable than the information given by the submitter ($\beta_{MA} > \alpha_{MM}$). In the next sections we describe: how to calculate the value of a LO given by manual and automatic metadata, the LO's features considered; the criteria used to assess the metadata that the user must sign in; and the criteria used to assess the metadata automatically obtained.

Automatically Extracted Metadata

Automatically extracted metadata corresponds to characteristics of the LO such as: format, size, number of pages, date of creation, and others. However, deciding which part of these metadata is relevant for each LO depends on the application and on the type of the LO, i.e. if we consider a presentation LO we would take into account the number of slides, rather than its size. On the other hand, if we consider a video LO it would be of interest the duration of the LO, rather than its number of pages. In this work we focus on text and presentation files.

We consider the format of a LO file as the level of technical portability of the object, in the sense of the actual degree of diffusion (knowledge and use) of the type of file. For example, a PDF file is managed by almost all PCs, while the DOCX file is a commercial format and not all PCs can read this kind of file; consequently, PDF is a more portable format than DOCX. Thus, the proposal in order to value this feature (format feature) is to assign values to the different MIME format. The actual values for each format may be established by the administrator of the system at configuration time.

Another issue about the LO content is the amount of information that the LO possesses. The amount of information can be seen as a measure of how in detail the issues have been covered. In this sense, the more the information the object has, the more valuable it is, this is because it may be less complex to understand its content. Consequently, it may be easier to use it in a variety of contexts, a fact that makes it more pedagogically portable and reusable. In our context, *words* are atomic elements that contain some information, and *paragraphs* may be considered more relevant than words since it is expected that each paragraph transmit an idea or a unit of knowledge. The same applies to *images* and *formulas*, since we can assume that they transmit an idea. Therefore, within these considerations, in order to value the properties of a LO that we can obtain automatically we distinguish between the content and the format of the LO and the content between information and ideas.

$$V_{OA-AM} = V_{Content} + V_{Format} \quad (4.1)$$

$$V_{Content} = V_{Info} \, / \, N_{PageORSlices} \quad (4.1.1)$$

$$V_{Info} = V_{OneInfo} * N_{Words} + V_{OneIdea} * \left(N_{Paragraphs} + N_{Images} + N_{Formula}\right)$$
$$\text{where } 1 <= V_{OneInfo} < V_{OneIdea} \quad (4.1.2)$$

The values for information and idea ($\mathbf{V}_{OneInfo} \mathbf{V}_{OneIdea}$) must be configured by the administrator of the system according to the specific application.

Manual Acquired Metadata

There are some LO's properties which are very difficult to be automatically extracted, for example, the pedagogical objective of the LO, the appropriate audience to use the LO, and so on. Most of this information must be given by a person who knows the LO, we call this information Manual Metadata. This section presents the manual metadata used by the LOP system and how they participate in our valuation of a LO.

Optional metadata completeness is an important aspect because they reflect the concern of the author to describe well her/his LO. And giving value to this factor motivates the author to provide this information. Table 2 shows the LOP's groups of metadata and indicates the names of the factors where they are used in order to value the LO.

In order to calculate the intrinsic value of the LO, we consider the level of completeness achieved by the author in the description of manual metadata for each group ($V_{\%M\_TOPICS}$, $V_{\%M\_AUTH}$, e tc.).

$$V_{OAIntMM} = V_{\%M\_Topics} + V_{\%M\_Auth} + V_{\%M\_Imgs} + V_{\%M\_Types} + V_{\%M\_Colab} + V_{\%M\_Rel} + V_{\%M\_Others} \quad (4.2)$$

The following experiment section details the completeness values suggested for each of group and the criteria used to assign them.

EXPERIMENTATION: VALUATION PROCESS OF LOP OBJECTS

A preliminary test was implemented to the metrics proposed to value the LO's LOP. This test was made to show the feasibility of the metrics and to identify the conditions in which a completed test must be done. A completed test must be carried out in order to compare the results with human experts

Table 2. Classification of metadata groups

Metadata Group	Description	Required Optional	Group's value
General Information	Keywords, description, title, group, submissor, creation date, format mime, language, level of audience, and so on.	Requiered	--
Topics	Topics of the LO	Optional	V_{*,M_Topics}
Authoring	Authors and their degree of participations	Optional	V_{*,M_Auth}
Images	Images, give an complementation information	Optional	V_{*,M_Imgs}
Types	LO's type, e.g. exercise, example, simulations, and so on	Optional	V_{*,M_Type}
Collaborators	Collaborators that aren't BOA's users	Optional	V_{*,M_Colab}
Relations	Relation with others LO, such as: is part of, is version of, is referenced by, and son on.	Optional	V_{*,M_Rel}
Others Information	Information about coverage, copy rights, method of instruction, publisher, and others.	Optional	V_{*,M_Others}

valuation, and with the success of the object in LOP over the time. The proposal is based on the value and the weight of some elements and features, the criteria to configure these values are described in this section. In addition, the experimentation and its results are described too.

Configuration of the Criteria's Values

The Table 3 specifies the criteria, conditions and suggested values to assign the weights required by the Equations 1, 3 and 4.

Because of Equations 2,3 and 4.2 the value of the following elements and features must be configured, they are: authors' type (V_{AUTHOR_TYPE}), groups (V_{GROUP}), topics (V_{TOPIC}), the value given to different file types (V_{Format}), and the value of each optional metadata groups (V_{M_TOPICS}, V_{M_AUTH}, V_{M_IMGS}, V_{M_TYPES}, V_{M_COLAB}, V_{M_RELS}, V_{M_OTHERS}).

The value, by default, of an author that does not have LO in LOP yet is according to the type of authors. The value of a teacher set to 4, to a student is 3, to teaching's responsible is 2, and to others is 1.

The criteria used to assign the groups and topics' value was: if there are no references about the group or topic then its value must be 1 (default value), if there are some references then the value must be 2, but if there are several references the value suggested is 3. These values will be assigned

Table 3. Weigh's configurations

Criteria	Conditions	Suggested Values
LO's intrinsic features are more important than the reputation's authors Context's importance is the less relevant	$1 > \mu_{LO} > \alpha_A > \beta_C > 0$ and $\mu_{LO} + \alpha_A + \beta_C = 1$	$\mu_{LO} = 0.5$ $\alpha_A = 0.3$ $\beta_C = 0.2$
Topics are more important than Groups	$1 > \beta_T > \alpha_G > 0$ and $\alpha_G + \beta_T = 1$	$\alpha_G = 0.4$ $\beta_T = 0.6$
Automatic metadata is more important than manual ones	$0 <= \alpha_{MM} < \beta_{MA} <= 1$ and $\alpha_{MM} + \beta_{MA} = 1$	$\alpha_{MM} = 0.4$ $\beta_{MA} = 0.6$

by the person who loads the new group/topic. The value assigned in each group of optional metadata was: 40 to the groups that are more important in the calculus process which are V_{M_TOPCIS}, V_{M_AUTH}; 30 to V_{M_TYPES} and V_{M_RELS}; and the least important groups with the value of 20 to V_{M_IMGS}, V_{M_COLAB} and V_{M_OTHERS}. The end values will be a percentage of these values according to the degree of completeness (normalized). Regarding the elements that can be identified in the content of the file, the proposal is to consider the word as the atomic piece of information ($V_{OneInfo}$) and its value will be 2, and consider one image or paragraph or formula as one basic idea to transmit ($V_{OneIdea}$), the value of one idea will be 3.

To value the type of file (V_{Format}) the criterion defined is that the not generalized/diffused format must be valued 1, the diffused format which is not free/open must be valued 2, and the diffused and free format must be valued 3. In our case we tested with DOC, PPT and PDF format because they are the most used in the LOP system, for which we used 2, 2 and 3 values respectively.

Experimentation

We performed an experiment within VemAprender.net instance of LOP System (Dinis P., Rodrigues da Silva A., 2007) which had: 7 groups, 53 authors, 163 LOs. This preliminary experiment aimed at detecting problems in the data used, the limitations of the platforms and metadata, and to identify the indicators which needed to be modified to produce a great impact on the evaluation metrics of the LO.

In the following section, we analyze each of the considered indicators.

Authoring

We simplified the experiment assuming one author by object. The value of reputation of each author was calculated according to the Equation 2. Therefore we used the values of the author's type and the LO; we used the amount of objects by author, the amount of downloads by author, and the amount of downloads by object. The results were analyzed with the purpose of verifying the existence of a relation between the calculated values and the behavior that the community has had. We analyzed the authors of the most successful LOs (and also the least successful ones) with the best (and worthy) authors according with the proposed formulas. None of the worth LOs had been authored by one of the best authors, and the same situation occurred with the best LO respect to the worth authors.

The analysis was made over general terms because the calculations used initial LO values assigned by the author, consequently these values don't have a unique and objective criterion. Therefore the set of authors and LOs considered were filtered. The authors which don't have at least three download over their objects were removed. Two authors were removed because they have objects which were initialized with very low or high value compared with the rest of the object initial values. Some authors had low rate because they were in LOP recently. These cases were identified by a human analysis. LOP had 53 authors and finally only 15 authors were used in the experimentation.

We run the experiment with 15 authors selected using the previous criteria, each with their respective values of authorship (range of values between 107 and 263), and value of success (the amount of downloads on their LOs). These authors are classified in three intervals: great success, medium and insufficient success. The process obtained 5 authors in each category. None of the authors of recognized success was rated negatively nor was any author misclassified as insufficient success. Furthermore, the analysis of the cases assessed as medium by the process shows that this result depends on the initial value assigned by the author of the LO. This initial value is observed to be very different among the various members of the community; therefore, a possible way to deal with this deviation is assigned reviewers with a uniform view of the community or automatically produce a valuation based on intrinsic LO's metadata.

LO Metadata

As it has been analyzed in previous sections, there are a great amount of LO's features specified by metadata that are relevant factors in the valuation of an LO. Some values of these metadata can be automatically extracted, while others must be given by the author his/herself.

Regarding the first group of metadata, we propose a metric that represents their impact in the LO's value which is depicted by Equation 4.1. In the next paragraphs we use this formula to evaluate the LO's value inside our experiment.

Step1: The LOs were grouped according to the files type PDF (15 LOs), DOC (4 LOs), and PPT (29 LOs). The LO were categorized according to two criteria: the level of success (high, medium, low), and the value of the LO (high, medium, low).

- We analyzed the LO categorized simultaneously as 'most successful and less valuable', and as 'less successful and most valuable'. The objective is to find the reasons of the inconsistency.
- We analyzed the LO categorized as 'half successful and half valuable'. The objective is to identify the characteristic of the general behaviors

Step2: The most successful LO are analyzed. We compare their level of success with the amount of: images, formulas, pages, paragraph and words that its files have.

Step3: The LOs with similar levels of success but with different types of file are compared.

The early results show the need to have values given by some mechanisms which are reliable and more independent of the environment factors such as context and authors. We could compare the calculation values with values given by experts. In this preliminary test the LO's success (amount of downloads) was used in some analysis. Although the LO success gives an idea about the value given by the LOP community, this success is strongly influenced by environment factors such as authors, times, and context. For example, we find many objects with low values and high level of success because of the authors' reputation; while other objects had high values and low level of success because of their availability time in the platform. Other erratic indicators appears when the metric to valuing the LO is based in some metadata that is not possible to be extracted for the specific LO's format.

In order to refine the corpus of the experiment each erratic LO was eliminated and other LOs that fall into the same situation where added to repeat the test and identify common factors in the general case.

The optional metadata gives pedagogical information that cannot be obtained if it is not through the author. Therefore, it allows for evaluation of pedagogical aspects of the object which are relevant, but on a first stage our objective is to motivate the author to load this information. This is the reason why on this proposal the completeness of the metadata loaded by the author will be considered as a priority. Measuring the quality of the information given by the author and the value that each of these data gives to the object is out of the reach of this research. Therefore, the metrics proposed (Equation 4.2) measure the level of completeness (the amount of fields filled by the author). An important aspect of this kind of information is the identification of the necessity to add metadata to the LOP system.

Context

The metrics to measure the value of a LO's context is given by the Equation 3. These values are calculated considering the configured values given to the groups and topics, and the amount of topics covered by the LO. However, in our scenario we find that most of the LOP's LOs had the group of the author by default, and did not have topics information. Another unexpected problem that appeared in the experiment was the difference between the level of specificity of the LO's topics. Some LOs have only one topic e.g. " Introduction to TICs," while others had various topics with different level of generality, for example 'informatics,' 'TICs,' 'programming.' This kind of difference affects the metrics because the proposal considers the amount of topics selected by the author.

Preliminary Results

These preliminary results led us to determine conditions to the next complete experimentation; and let us identify possible extensions to the platform and metadata that would improve the results. They are:

1. The complete test must have a set of LOs with an expert evaluation to compare the calculated values with these evaluations.
2. The preliminary test verified that the authors' reputations may determine the value of the intrinsic features of the LO. Therefore, one conclusion is that in the complete test we would isolate the author's reputation to evaluate the other factors. Therefore, we suggest that the LOs should be submitted by one unknown author.
3. We identify some problems related to the age of the LO and the authors. A LO can have few downloads because it is a new LO and not because of its quality. The analog situation occurs with the authors old in LOP. Therefore, we suggest to submit the set of LOs to the experimentation at the same time by a new LOP user/author.
4. Regarding the context value results, we observe that the capture of the topics' information doesn't have clear criteria on how to fill it. As our proposal measures how specific the LO is according to the topics, then the calculation value is affected. Therefore, the platform must be clear about the criteria to capture this metadata. One possible solution may be to use taxonomy of the topics group presented as a tree to the user, who must select the topics.
5. The test carried out verifies that one of the most important elements in the re-use of the object is the community. Therefore, it is an added value to know and consider who re-used the LO.
   Consequently, the registration of the filiations of the users that make downloads could improve the estimation of the LO's value and the authors' value.
6. By adding the pedagogical objective of the LO, the measure of granularity and portability from the educational point of view could be improved. For example, one possibility is to describe them through verbs associated with Bloom's Taxonomy (Anderson & Krathwohl, 2001).
7. Finally, we have to consider some limitations that the extractor of metadata tools may have. Tools used to extract the metadata used in the valuing process could affect the conclusion to which we arrived.

FUTURE RESEARCH DIRECTIONS

Modern systems learn from the community in order to give assistance to the community in the best way. On one hand the e-learning system must know-infer-learn the behavior and preferences of users (teachers, students, etc.), and on the other hand, they should be the support of the e-learning process. In this sense, we find different types of activities which are developed today: connection repositories, hybrid collaborative recommender systems based in the user's opinion and in the analysis of the community behavior, and the possibility to integrate the produced data in order to produce knowledge as it is performed in the linked data approach.

CONCLUSION

Research on measuring the LO's quality according to the reuse has been presented and factors which are related to the reusability and their relation with LOM have been described. We have stressed the needs of the metadata. Research which measures the reusability based on the type and topics of the material has been explored. The importance of the community in the e-learning systems and in the metrics to measure the success of a LO was presented, not only as mentioned by recent research but also in our proposal. The problem of valuing a LO was analyzed from different points of view: technological, socio-pedagogical, structural and content. The LOP systems were described and the problem of giving an initial value to their LOs was analyzed, moreover, a solution was proposed and tested.

The main contributions of this work are the following:

- It is confirmed that LOs are as important as the community itself. This means that the user is important both as an individual and as part of a group. In our case, the experiments show that the object's success is strongly determined by the author's reputation.
- We define and discuss an automatic process to calculate the initial value of LOs, based on explicit but also implicit LO's features.
- We also propose an automatic process to measure the implicit/ intrinsic features of a LO.
- We show that although the calculation process of the LO's value can be automatic, the experts' opinion and the community's opinions affect directly the valuing of those LOs. These opinions and feedback should be also considered at the initial stage but also periodically to allow updating the value of such as LOs and authors.
- We also propose a framework of metrics that has into consideration motivational strategies to promote the users' participation in the community.

ACKNOWLEDGMENT

This project is carried out with the support of the SOLITE-CYTED and LACCIR_R1210LAC007

REFERENCES

Anderson, L.W., & Krathwohl (Ed.). (2001). *A taxonomy for learning, teaching and assessing: A revision of Bloom's taxonomy of educational objectives*. New York: Longman.

Barão, A., & Rodrigues da Silva, A. (2011). A model to evaluate the relational capital of organizations (SNARE-RCO). In *Proceedings of Conference of Enterprise Information Systems* (Centeris'2011). Springer-Verlag.

Blumenstock, J. E. (2008). Size matters: Word count as a measure of quality on Wikipedia. In *Proceeding of the 17th International Conference on World Wide Web*. IEEE.

Cechinel, C., & Sánchez-Alonso, S. (2011). *Analyzing associations between the different ratings dimensions of the MERLOT repository*. Interdisciplinary Journal of E-Learning and Learning Objects.

Cechinel & Sicilia. (2011). Evaluating models for automated quality assessment of learning objects inside repositories. In *Proceedings of Laclo2011*. Laclo.

Dalkir, K. (2011). *Knowledge management in theory and practice* (2nd ed.). Cambridge, MA: The MIT Press.

Dinis, P., & Rodrigues da Silva, A. (2007). Design experiences with the learning objects board system. In *Proceedings of the 40th of Hawaii International Conference on System Sciences*. IEEE.

Dinis, P., & Rodrigues da Silva, A. (2009). Application scenarios for the learning objects pool. *Journal of Universal Computer Science, 15*(7), 1455–1471.

Duval, E. (2005). LearnRank: The real quality measure for learning materials. In Policy and Innovation in Education-Quality Criteria. European Schooet.

Frondizi, R. (Ed.). (1992). *Qué son los valores? Introduccion a la axiología* (3rd ed.). Breviarios del Fondo de Cultura Económica.

Iriberri, A., & Leroy, G. (2009). A lifecycle perspective on online community success. *ACM Computing Surveys, 41*(2). doi:10.1145/1459352.1459356.

Meder. (1999) Didaktische ontologien: Globalisierung und wissensorganisation: Neue aspekkte fur wissen. *Wissenschaft und Informationsysteme,* 401-416.

Meyer, M., Hannappel, A., Rensing, C., & Steinmetz, R. (2007). Automatic classificaion of didactic functions of e-learning resources. In *Proceedings of 15th International Conference on Multimedia* (pp. 513-516). Augsburg, Germany: ACM.

Neil, Y., Shih, Chao, & Jin. (2010). Ranking metrics and search guidance for learning object repository. *IEEE Transactions on Learning Technologies, 3,* 250-264.

Ochoa, X. (2011). Intercambio social y recomendación de material educativo. *Tutorial LACLO 2011*. Retrieved from www.slideshare.net/xaoch

Ochoa, X., & Duval, E. (2006). Quality metrics for learning object metada. In *Proceedings of World Conference on Educational Multimedia, Hypermedia and Telecommunications 2006* (pp. 1004-1011). IEEE.

Ochoa, X., & Duval, E. (2008). Relevance ranking metrics for learning objects. *IEEE Transactions on Learning Technologies, 1*(1), 34–48. doi:10.1109/TLT.2008.1.

Sanz, J., Dodero, J. M., & Sanchez-Alonso, S. (2009). A preliminary analysis of software engineering metrics-based criteria for the evaluation of learning objects reusability. *International Journal of Emerging Technologies in Learning, 4.*

Sanz Rodriguez, J. (2010). *Evaluación apriorística de la reusabilidad de los objetos de aprendizaje.* Retrieved from http://dbspace.uah.es/dbspace/handle/10017/8715

Wiley, D. (2001). Peer-to-peer and learning objects: The new potential for collaborative constructivist learning online. [ICALT.]. *Proceedings of ICALT, 2001*, 494–498.

ADDITIONAL READING

Ching-Chieh & Lee. (2007). Learning objects reusability and retrieval through ontological sharing: A hybrid unsupervised data mining approach. *IEEE International Conference on Advanced Learning Technologies*, (pp. 548 – 550). IEEE.

Cuadrado-Gallego, J. (2005). Adapting software engineering reusability metrics to Learning Object. *RED Revista de Educación a Distancia, Monográfico IV.- Diseño, Evaluación y Descripción de Contenidos Educativos Reutilizables (III). Julio 2005*. Retrieved from http://revistas.um.es/red/issue/view/2551

Erla Mariela Morales Morgado. (2010). *Gestión del conocimiento en sistemas e-learning, basado en objetos de aprendizaje, cualitativa y pedagógicamente definidos. Ediciones Universidad de Salamanca*. España.

Kurilovas, E., & Dagiene, V. (2009). Learning objects and virtual learning environments technical evaluation criteria. *Electronic Journal of e-Learning, 2*(7), 127 – 136.

Kurilovas, E., & Dagiene, V. (2010). Multiple criteria evaluation of quality and optimisation of e-learning system components. *ECEL, 8*(2), 141–150.

Kurilovas, E., & Dagiene, V. (2011). Multiple criteria evaluation of quality and optimisation of e-learning system components. *ECEL, 9*(1), 39–51.

Margaritopoulos, T., Margaritopoulos, M., Mavridis, I., & Manitsaris, A. (2009). A fine-grained metric system for the completeness of metadata. In *Proceedings of Metadata and Semantic Research, Communications in Computer and Information Science*. Springer. doi:10.1007/978-3-642-04590-5_8.

Ochoa, X. (2011). Modeling the macro-behavior of learning object repositories. *Interdisciplinary Journal of E-Learning and Learning Objects, 7*, 25–35.

Orthmann, M., Friedrich, M., Kirschenmann, U., Niemann, K., Scheffel, M., & Schmitz, H. ... Wolpers M. (2011). Usage-based clustering of learning objects for recommendation. In *Proceedings of the IEEE International Conference on Advanced Learning Technologies*, (pp. 553 – 557). IEEE.

Sánchez, S., & Sicilia, M. A. (2004). On the semantics of aggregation and generalization in learning object contracts. In *Proceedings of the 4th IEEE International Conference on Advanced Learning Technologies – ICALT 2004*. IEEE.

Sicilia, M. A., García, E., Sánchez, S., & Rodriguez, E. (2004). Describing learning object types in ontological structures: Towards specialized pedagogical selection. In *Proceedings of ED-MEDIA 2004 – World Conference on Educational Multimedia, Hypermedia and Telecommunications*. ED-MEDIA.

Zapata, A., Menendez, V., & Prieto, M. (2009). Discovering learning objects usability characteristics. In *Proceedings of the Ninth International Conference on Intelligent Systems Design and Applications 2009, ISDA*, (pp. 1126-1130). ISDA.

KEY TERMS AND DEFINITIONS

DC: Metadata standard to describe resources.

E-Learning: Systems which give support to the teach task.

LO: Resource, material used to teach.

LOM: Metadata standard to describe learning objects.

Metric: Measure of something.

Ranking: Relevance value.

Reusability: The capacity of adapting to be used in different ways.

Value: Quantification of the importance.

ENDNOTES

1 http://www.merlot.org
2 http://www.ariadne-es.org/
3 http://wwww.elera.net
4 http://www.cnx.org
5 http://proyectoagrega.es
6 http://isg.inesc-id.pt/BOA-GPI
7 http://vemaprender.net
8 http://isg.inesc-id.pt/BOA
9 http://www.dublincore.org/
10 http://stackoverflow.com/

Chapter 29
A Framework Proposal to Assess the LARG Index of a Supply Chain in a Fuzzy Context

Paulo Fazendeiro
Instituto de Telecomunicações, Portugal

Susana G. Azevedo
University of Beira Interior, Portugal

V. Cruz-Machado
Universidade Nova de Lisboa, Portugal

ABSTRACT

Bearing in mind the new Supply Chain Management (SCM) paradigms, it is important that supply chains be aware of the implementation level of the main practices associated to each SCM paradigm (Lean, Agile, Resilient, and Green, hereafter referred as LARG). The main objective of this chapter is to propose a framework, based on Enterprise 2.0 approach, for global supply chains to assess their LARG index in order to evaluate the leanness, agility, resilience, and greenness of their practices. Enterprise 2.0 technologies and Fuzzy Logic techniques are used as enablers to the proposed LARG evaluation model in the following assessment tasks: 1) determination of an adequate set of Lean, Agile, Resilient, and Green practices; 2) consensual definition of the relative weights of the considered practices; 3) adjustment of the evaluation policy to the particular supply chain; and 4) effective follow-up of the assessment results.

INTRODUCTION

A Supply Chain (SC) can be described as a chain that links various agents, from the customer to the supplier, through manufacturing and services so that the flow of materials, money and information can be effectively managed to meet the business requirements (Gunasekaran & Tirtiroglu, 2001). In present-day business there is the assumption that SCs compete instead of companies, while the success or failure of SCs is mainly determined in the marketplace. Supply Chain Management (SCM) is considered a strategic factor for in-

DOI: 10.4018/978-1-4666-4373-4.ch029

creasing organizational effectiveness and for the better attainment of organizational goals such as enhanced competitiveness, better customer service, and increased profitability.

The static connections between enterprises are typically insensitive to the changes in the business environment. Instead, flexible, agile, short, and dynamic connections that facilitate seamless information flow across different value chains are needed for dynamic business partnership formation to take place (Camarinha-Matos, 2002).

The research developed by the Association for Information and Image Management (AIIM) shows that most organizations look at Enterprise 2.0 as the application of Web 2.0 to the enterprise, next generation of enterprise content management technology, or as technology that enables people to collaborate and/or form online communities. According to Capuano et al. (2010) the term Enterprise 2.0 applies to the use of Web 2.0 technologies as a support for business activities within the organizations. These technologies are exploited to foster inter-persons collaboration, information exchange, and knowledge sharing and also to establish relationships to outside partners based on conversational modalities rather than on traditional business communication.

The Enterprise 2.0 is considered a strategic tool to improve Business-to-Business (B2B) interactions and communication capabilities for enterprise integration (Capuano et al., 2010). Enterprise integration is about connecting companies for particular business processes in the supply chain. Companies today no longer operate as isolated entities. Instead, they form supply chains with their suppliers, customers and partners.

The extent of B2B interactions and communications could be overwhelming between the various parties and services, especially in an adaptive environment where a lot of information needs to be exchanged. This requires higher capabilities of interaction and communication among businesses partners.

Bearing in mind the new SCM paradigms, it is important for supply chains to be aware of the implementation level of the main practices associated to each SCM paradigm (Lean, Agile, Resilient, and Green, hereafter referred as LARG).

The LARG assessment is a problem surrounded by a great deal of uncertainty resulting from the number of actors involved in the task and from the vagueness, imprecision and even incompleteness of some assessments. Fuzzy Logic as information processing science has given proofs of its adequacy to deal with problems defined in such imprecise and uncertain environments offering a range of tools and techniques which enable approximate inferences on (vague) linguistic terms and incomplete data in a very close agreement with the process of human reasoning (Zhou & Gan, 2008).

In this context, the main objective of this chapter is to propose a framework combining Enterprise 2.0 and fuzzy Logic approaches as a way to enable that global supply chains can assess their LARG index, that is, to get information about the leanness, agility, resilience and greenness of their practices.

BACKGROUND

Lean, Agile, Resilient, and Green Supply Chain Management Paradigms

The Lean approach is essentially focused on waste reduction as a means to increase actual value-added, in order to fulfill customer needs and maintain profitability (Womack et al., 1991). Disney et al. (1997) extended Lean to the SC context arguing that; Lean processes create value through the elimination of "waste" across the SC. To Parveen and Rao (2009) the Lean SC focus is on eliminating waste or non value-added processes or activities along the chain to achieve internal manufacturing efficiencies and set-up time reduction, enabling the economic production of small quantities and enhancing cost reduction, profitability and manufacturing flexibility.

Several authors have highlighted key Lean principles or practices such as: 1) respect for people (Treville & Antonakis, 2006); 2) customer relationship (Anand & Kodali, 2008); 3) quality management (Brown & Mitchell, 1991); 4) JIT (Just In Time) (Gurumurthy & Kodali, 2009); 5) pull production/flow (Brown & Mitchell, 1991; Anand & Kodali, 2008); 6) supplier relationships/ long-term business relationship (Gurumurthy & Kodali, 2009); and 7) mistake-proofing (Stewart & Grout, 2001). At the operational level, the Lean paradigm is implemented by using a number of techniques such as kanban, 5S, visual control, takt-time, Poke-yoke and SMED (Melton, 2005).

Since customer requirements are continuously changing it is more difficult to SCs attain their objectives, i.e. deliver the right product, in the right quantity, in the right condition, to the right place, at the right time, for the right cost. To overcome these conditions Hoek et al. (2001) suggest that SCs should be Agile to respond appropriately to market requirements and changes. That is, the SCs should be flexible and responsive in terms of their processes, networks and how they are integrated across other organisations. The Agile SCM is crucial since it intends to create the ability to respond rapidly and cost effectively to unpredictable changes in markets and increasing levels of environmental turbulence, both in terms of volume and variety (Agarwal et al., 2007; Christopher & Towill, 2001; Ismail & Sharifi, 2006).

Some of the main Agile practices in the SC context are: 1) to increase frequencies of new product introductions (Agarwal et al., 2007); 2) speed in improving customer service (Swafford et al., 2008); 3) centralized and collaborative planning (Agarwal et al., 2007); 4) use of IT to coordinate/ integrate activities in manufacturing (Swafford et al., 2008); 5) to use IT to coordinate/integrate activities in design and development (Swafford et al., 2008); 6) ability to change delivery times of supplier's orders (Swafford et al., 2008); 7) to use IT to coordinate/integrate activities in manufacturing (Lin et al., 2006); 8) to reduce development cycle times (Swafford et al., 2008); 9) and to increase frequencies of new product introductions (Agarwal et al., 2007).

Today's marketplace is also characterized by higher levels of turbulence and volatility. As a result, SCs are vulnerable to disruption and, in consequence, the risk to business continuity has increased (Azevedo et al. 2008). Whereas in the past the main objective in SC design was cost minimization or service optimization, the emphasis today has to be upon resilience (Tang, 2006). Resilient SCs may not be the lowest-cost, but they are more capable of coping with the uncertain business environment. Resilience is referred as the SC ability to cope with unexpected disturbances (Azevedo et al., 2010). The aim of resilience strategies is twofold (Haimes, 2006): 1) to recover to a desired state of the system that has been disturbed, within an acceptable time period and at an acceptable cost; and 2) to reduce the disturbance impact by changing the effectiveness level of a potential threat.

The ability to recover from a disturbance occurrence is related to the development of responsiveness capabilities through flexibility and redundancy (Rice & Caniato, 2003). A representative sample of the main Resilient practices in the SC context found in the literature is: 1) strategic stock (Tang, 2006); 2) lead time reduction (Christopher & Peck, 2004); 3) maintaining a dedicated transit fleet (Rice & Caniato, 2003); 4) flexible supply base/ flexible sourcing (Tang, 2006); 5) sourcing strategies to allow switching of suppliers (Rice & Caniato, 2003); 6) creating total SC visibility (Iakovou et al., 2007); 7) flexible transportation (Tang, 2006); 8) developing visibility to a clear view of downstream inventories and demand conditions (Christopher & Peck, 2004).

Green SCM has emerged as an organizational philosophy which allows to achieve corporate profit and market-share objectives by reducing environmental risks and impacts while improving the ecological efficiency of such organizations and their partners (Rao & Holt, 2005). Srivastava (2007) defined Green SCM as "integrating environmental thinking into SCM, including product design, material sourcing and selection, manufacturing processes, delivery of the final product to the consumers as well as end-of-life management of the product after its useful life."

According to Srivastava (2007), Green SCM can reduce the ecological impact of industrial activity without sacrificing quality, cost, reliability, performance or energy utilization efficiency; meeting environmental regulations to not only minimize ecological damage but also to ensure overall economic profit.

Some of the SC Green practices found in literature are: 1) environmental collaboration with suppliers (Holt & Ghobadian, 2009); 2) ISO 14001 certification (Gonzalez et al., 2008); 3) minimization of waste (Rao & Holt, 2005); 4) reverse logistics (Gonzalez et al., 2008); 5) environmental monitoring upon suppliers (Paulraj, 2009); 6) to reduce energy consumption (Zhu et al., 2008); 7) to reuse/recycling materials and packaging (Paulraj, 2009); 8) environmental collaboration with the customer (Hu &Hsu, 2006); 9) reverse logistics (Srivastava, 2007).

Fuzzy Logic Applied to Supply Chain Performance Measurement

Due to the limited capability of human mind and sensory organs to deal with complex information its decomposition into manageable chunks of information is essential. The aggregations of similar or nearby objects into information granules (class abstraction) as well as the encapsulation of functional commonalities are fundamental skills for a successful approach to the great majority of problems that we face every day. The fuzzy logic approach to information granulation relies on the notion of (fuzzy) set, opposite to the member of a classical set, to represent uncertain and imprecise knowledge.

A fuzzy set is characterized by a membership function that maps each point of the universe X to a number in the interval [0,1] (1 represents full degree of inclusion and 0 non-membership at all). For instance, consider the universe $X = R^+$ as the set of admissible ages for a human being. A feasible membership function for the set of ages "around 30 years old" is graphically represented in Figure 1. The fuzzy set can be perceived as a more expressive generalization of the conventional set.

In this setting, typically, an information granule is a fuzzy set and the process of information granulation consists in describing a crisp or fuzzy object as a collection of fuzzy granules (or eventually as relationships between them).

Figure 1. Fuzzy set around 30 years old

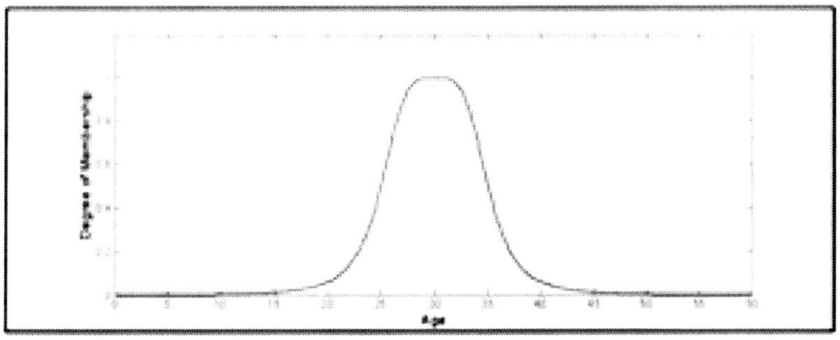

In the last few years there has been an increasing awareness on the fuzzy logic as a mean for measuring the supply chain performance due to its inherent capability to capture the uncertainty and ambiguity surrounding the supply chain performance measurement task (Lau et al., 2002; Ohdar and Ray, 2004; Ho et al., 2008). Consequently a number of fuzzy set theory applications in SC performance measurement (SCPM) have emerged. In this context, it is important to highlight the Olugu (2009) work where a good survey of recent studies in SCPM along with its main trends and challenges can be found. Also Chan & Qi (2003) introduced a measurement method applying fuzzy logic as a mean to aggregate cross organizational assessment of different measures of the SC by evaluators with different relative strengths of opinion (the weights of the measures also depend on the importance of each measure for each evaluator).

Chen et al. (2007) followed a similar approach, using a fuzzy analytical hierarchical process to combine qualitative and quantitative information and their relative weights. The approach was applied to the evaluation of third party logistics providers.

The related supplier-selection problem was tackled by Chen et al. (2006) considering the importance weights for various criteria as linguistic variables and using trapezoidal membership functions to represent the vagueness of the experts' linguistic assessments. Once again the usefulness of employing linguistic variables instead of numerical values in order to translate the decision-makers' expertise was emphasized.

To assess the agility of a SC (Pilevari et al., 2008) a Mamdani fuzzy inference system to aggregate the effects of the different agility factors is proposed. Later the same authors (Seyehoseini et al., 2010) applied a neuro fuzzy inference system as a way to optmize a first-order Sugeno type inference system in a way that could approximate the knowledge collected from experts.

The measurement of the sustainability of a SC was approached by Erol et al. (2011) with the proposal of fuzzy multi-criteria framework based on fuzzy entropy and fuzzy multi-attribute utility for determining the relative weights of each criterion.

COMPOSITE LARG INDEX CONSTRUCTION

The main objective of this section is to construct the composite LARG index to assess the leanness, agility, resilience and greenness of companies and corresponding SCs. Since the SC is composed by a set of *n* companies, each one with different levels of SCM practices implementation, the behaviour of all the SC will be affected by the aggregation of individual companies' behaviours.

So, in a first step it is necessary to compute the company behaviour according to each paradigm. The hierarchical relationships evolved in this assessment are illustrated in Figure 2.

Each indicator in Figure 2 intends to reflect the individual company behaviour in terms of its leanness, agility, resilience and leanness. These indicators are a representative parameter of Lean, Agile, Resilient and Green SCM practices implemented by each company. They are obtained by combining the information from a set of sub-indicators: (1) Lean practices (P_{L1}... P_{Li}); (2) Agile practices (P_{A1}... P_{Ai}); (3) resilient practices (P_{R1}... P_{Ri}) and (4) Green SC practices (P_{G1}... P_{Gi}). Each sub-indicator is assessed in a 5 points Likert scale where 1 means "practice not implemented" and 5 "practice totally implemented".

For each company a set of four indicators are proposed:

- **Lean Behaviour (B_L):** It represents a set of SCM practices implemented by the organization to maximize customer value while minimizing waste;
- **Agile Behaviour (B_A):** It reflects the company ability to respond rapidly and cost effectively to unpredictable changes;

Figure 2. Hierarchical relationships evolved in the company LARG behaviour assessment

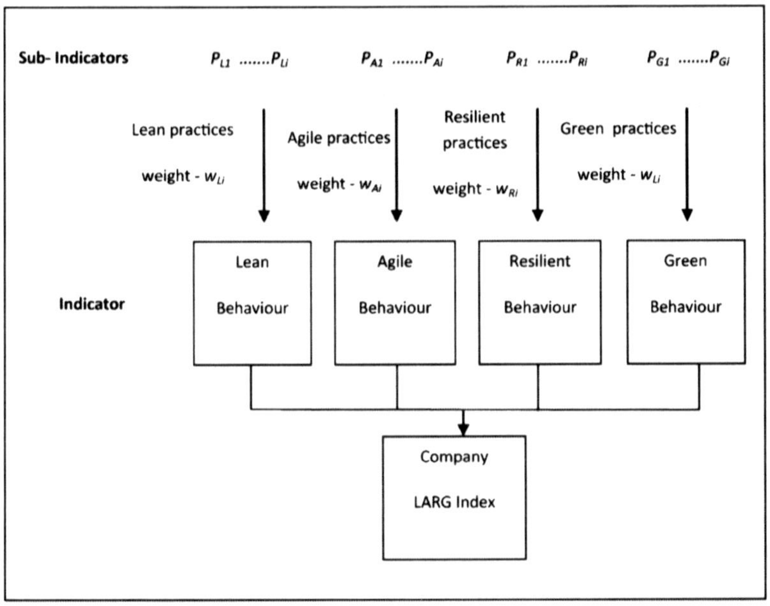

- **Resilient Behaviour (B_R):** Representing a set of SCM practices reflecting the company's ability to cope with unexpected disturbances.
- **Green Behaviour (B_G):** Representing the set of SCM practices to achieve corporate profit and market-share objectives by reducing environmental risks and impacts while improving the company ecological efficiency.

After computing the four behaviours and the corresponding LARG index for each company, then the same index is constructed but now for all the SC.

A methodology to assess the SC behaviour in terms of Lean, Agile, Resilient and Green paradigms is proposed considering the following: 1) a set of Lean, Agile, Resilient and Green practices deduced from the literature review on automotive SC; 2) the weight of the practices and paradigms are assessed by a set of experts in the focused paradigms and automotive industry using the Delphi method; and 3) the variables independency is assessed to allow a correctly interpretation of the proposed composite additive index, named LARG index.

LARG Practices Considered

In a first step, it is necessary to identify the set of practices Lean, Agile, Resilient and Green relevant for the companies belonging to the automotive SC. Using the literature review a set of practices was selected to assess the company indicators (Table 1).

Each practice of Table 1 is obtained in a 5-point Likert scale, which makes possible the individual company behaviour assessment in terms of the four SCM paradigms focused in this study.

Weighting Determination

A series of weighted SCM paradigms and corresponding practices was developed based on the Delphi approach. Each SCM paradigm and corresponding practices rating was measured using a score between 1 and 5, with 1 representing "nothing important" and 5 representing "extremely important."

Table 1. Indicators and sub-indicators for company behaviour assessment

Indicators	Sub- indicators
BL= Lean behaviour	PL1= Just in time (First tier supplier → Focal company)
	PL2= Supplier relationships/ long-term business relationship
	PL3= Just in time (Focal company)
	PL4 = Pull flow
	PL5= Total quality management
	PL6= Customer Relationships
	PL7= Just in time (Focal company → first tier customer)
BA = Agile behaviour	PA1= To Use IT to coordinate/integrate a ctivities in design and development
	PA2= Ability to change delivery times of supplier's order
	PA3= To Use IT to coordinate/integrate activities in manufacturing
	PA4= To reduce development cycle times
	PA5= Centralized and collaborative planning
	PA6= To increase frequencies of new product introductions
	PA7= To Speed in improving customer service
BR = Resilient behaviour	PR1= Sourcing strategies to allow switching of suppliers
	PR2= Flexible supply base/ flexible sourcing
	PR3= Strategic stock
	PR4= Lead time reduction
	PR5= Creating total supply chain visibility
	PR6= Flexible transportation
	PR7= Developing visibility to a clear view of downstream inventories and demand conditions
BG = Green behaviour	PG1= Environmental collaboration with suppliers
	PG2= Environmental monitoring upon suppliers
	PG3= ISO 14001 certification
	PG4= To reduce energy consumption
	PG5= To reuse/recycling materials and packaging
	PG6= Environmental collaboration with the customer
	PG7= Reverse logistics

The weighting for each set of variables, i.e. Lean, Agile, Resilient, Green paradigms importance, and also the four sets of SCM practices importance, was computed by using Equation 1 (Yeung et al., 2007):

$$w_z = \frac{M_z}{\sum_{g=1}^{n} M_g} \qquad (1)$$

where: wz represents the weighting of a particular variable z (it can be paradigm importance or a practice importance)

Mz represents the mean rating of a particular variable z

$$\sum_{g=1}^{n} M_g$$

represents the summation of mean rating of each set of variables.

Delphi Study

Delphi technique offers important advantages in situations where it is crucial to define areas of uncertainty or disagreement, as it is the case. It also makes possible to assess uncertainty in a quantitative manner. Therefore, it is appropriate to adopt the Delphi technique to obtain a series of weighted SCM paradigms and corresponding practices to assess the level of leanness, agility, resilience, and greenness of the automotive SC.

According to Linstone and Turoff (1975) the key steps in preparing a Delphi study are: (1) the definition of experts and their selection; (2) the number of rounds; and (3) the questionnaire structure in each study round. Generally, the number of rounds ranges from two to seven and the number of participants varies between three and fifteen (Rowe and Wright, 1999).

The success of the Delphi method depends largely on the careful selection of the panel members (Chan et al., 2001). As the information solicited requires in-depth knowledge and sound experience about, for one hand the automotive industry, and for the other the Lean, Agile, Resilient, and Green SCM paradigms, a purposive approach was adopted to select this group of experts (Chan et al., 2001). The following two criteria were considered in order to identify eligible participants for this part of the study: 1) having current/recent involvement in automotive industry research topics; 2) having a sound knowledge and understanding of Lean, Agile, Resilient, and Green SCM paradigms. In order to obtain the most valuable opinions, only academics/experts who met the two selection criteria were considered. A total of eleven academics/experts participated in this study.

Virtual (by email) interviews were launched with academics/experts in automotive research topics to verify the validity of the considered SCM practices and also to rank the four management paradigms according to their importance to the competitiveness of the automotive SC.

The Delphi method used in this research comprised two rounds. In the first round the respondents were asked to give their perception about the importance of each SCM paradigm to the automotive SC to be considered competitive, and also to register the importance of each suggested practice to the leanness, agility, resilience, and greenness of the automotive SC. In the second round respondents were provided with the consolidated results from Round 1 and were invited to reconsider their options to see if they would like to adjust their original choice.

The first round of Delphi questionnaire was sent to the group of panel members by e-mail in September 2011. The panel members constituted by academics/experts were informed that would be two rounds of questionnaires. In this first round the eleven academics/experts were asked to give their perception about the importance of Lean, Agile, Resilient, and Green paradigms and also the corresponding practices to the competitiveness of the automotive SC. Similar to the first round, the second round questionnaire was forwarded to the group of panel members (eleven academics/experts) by e-mail in the first week of October. In this round the results of first round were consolidated and presented to the experts. Then they were requested to reconsider whether they would like to change any of their original choices in the light of the consolidated results from the first round. All the eleven questionnaires were completed at the end of October 2011.

Using Equation 1 it was computed the weighting for each of the SCM paradigms and also Lean, Agile, Resilient, and Green practices (Table 2). Table 2 shows the relative importance of each SCM paradigm and corresponding practices by the 11 academics/experts. The order of importance of the SCM paradigms obtained from the academics/experts perception, after the two rounds, is the following one: the most important is Lean, followed by Resilient, Agile and Green. As can be seen from the Kendall's coefficient of concordance the consistency of the experts/academic rankings was improved after the Round 2. Also, among the seven practices associated to each SCM paradigm the rank of importance to a SC to be considered Lean, Agile, Resilient, and Green is presented in Table 2.

Analysis of Consistency after the Two Rounds

In order to obtain a measure of consistency of the 11 experts/academics responses, the Kendall's Coefficient of concordance (W) was applied. This coefficient is used to study the degree of association among rankings of several objects by several judges (Israel, 2009). This coefficient varies between "0" indicating no agreement between judges and "+1" indicating complete agreement among the judges on the ranking of various attributes. Using MegaStat application for

Table 2. Results of round 1 and round 2 of delphi questionnaire for the paradigms and practices importance

	\ Statistics Variables	First round			Second round		
		Mean rating	Rank	Weighting	Mean rating	Rank	Weighting
SCM paradigms	Lean	4.45	1	0.27	4.6	1	0.28
	Agile	4.36	3	0.26	4.2	3	0.26
	Resilient	4.45	1	0.27	4.5	2	0.27
	Green	3.36	3	0.20	3.1	4	0.19
	Number (n) Kendall's Coefficient of concordance (W) Level of significance	11 0.297 0.020			11 0.596 0.000		
Lean practices	Just in time (First tier supplier → Focal company)	4.55	2	0.15	4.5	2	0.15
	Supplier relationships/ long-term business relationship	4.00	6	0.13	4.1	4	0.14
	Just in time (Focal company)	4.82	1	0.16	4.9	1	0.17
	Pull flow	4.45	3	0.15	4.3	3	0.14
	Total quality management	4.36	4	0.14	4.3	3	0.14
	Customer Relationships	3.90	7	0.13	3.5	5	0.12
	Just in time (Focal company → first tier customer)	4.27	5	0.14	4.3	3	0.14
	Number (n) Kendall's Coefficient of concordance (W) Level of significance	11 0.237 0. 016			11 0.345 0.001		
Agile Practices	To Use IT to coordinate/integrate activities in design and development	4.09	4	0.15	4.0	3	0.15
	Ability to change delivery times of supplier's order	4.55	1	0.16	4.8	1	0.18
	To Use IT to coordinate/ integrate activities in manufacturing	4.09	4	0.15	3.8	5	0.14
	To reduce development cycle times	4.27	2	0.15	4.4	2	0.16
	Centralized and collaborative planning	4.18	3	0.15	3.9	4	0.14
	To increase frequencies of new product introductions	2.90	6	0.11	2.9	7	0.11
	To speed in improving customer service	3.55	5	0.13	3.3	6	0.12
	Number (n) Kendall's Coefficient of concordance (W) Level of significance	11 0.268 0.007			11 0.505 0.000		

continued on following page

Table 2. Continued

	\ Statistics Variables	First round			Second round		
		Mean rating	Rank	Weighting	Mean rating	Rank	Weighting
Resilient Practices	Sourcing strategies to allow switching of suppliers	4.36	1	0.17	4.5	2	0.15
	Flexible supply base/ flexible sourcing	4.27	2	0.16	4.6	1	0.16
	Strategic stock	3.82	4	0.15	4.1	5	0.14
	Lead time reduction	3.27	6	0.12	4.1	5	0.14
	Creating total supply chain visibility	3.55	5	0.13	4.3	3	0.15
	Flexible transportation	4.20	3	0.16	4.2	4	0.14
	Developing visibility to a clear view of downstream inventories and demand conditions	2.91	7	0.11	3.3	6	0.12
	Number (n) Kendall's Coefficient of concordance (W) Level of significance	11 0.151 0.126			11 0.309 0.0024		
Green Practices	Environmental collaboration with suppliers	4.27	4	0.14	4.2	3	0.15
	Environmental monitoring upon suppliers	3.45	7	0.12	2.9	7	0.10
	ISO 14001 certification	4.00	5	0.14	3.9	5	0.14
	To reduce energy consumption	4.73	2	0.16	4.9	1	0.17
	To reuse/recycling materials and packaging	4.82	1	0.16	4.8	2	0.17
	Environmental collaboration with the customer	3.91	6	0.13	3.7	6	0.13
	Reverse logistics	4.36	3	0.15	4.1	4	0.14
	Number (n) Kendall's Coefficient of concordance (W) Level of significance	11 0.446 0.000			11 0.663 0.000		
Note: For "Mean rating"= 1 nothing important and 5 = extremely important							

Excel, the Kendall's Coefficient of concordance was computed for each set of experts/academics responses related to the SCM paradigms and LARG practices importance.

Table 2 shows that Kendall's Coefficient of concordance for SCM paradigms and practices rankings were improved after the two rounds. Therefore, it can be concluded that after the second round of Delphi questionnaire there is a significant amount of agreement among respondents with the group of experts/academics.

LARG Composite Index

The proposed composite LARG index is composed by the weights determined through the two rounds of the Delphi questionnaire. As referred above the additive weighting method was selected as aggregation method for composite LARG Index. In order to test the assumption of a linear model was determined a correlation matrix for each set of variables. The correlation coefficient values range from "-1" to "+1". The value "-1" indicates a perfect negative relationship, a value

Table 3. Correlation matrix among the weighted paradigms

Correlation matrix	Lean	Agile	Resilient	Green
Lean	1.000			
Agile	.192	1.000		
Resilient	.236	.793**	1.000	
Green	-.234	-.045	-.392	1.000
Notes:** Correlation is significant at the 0.01 level (2-tailed) * Correlation significant at the 0.05 level (2-tailed)				

"+1" indicates a perfect positive relationship and "0" indicates no relationship at all (Israel, 2009). Table 3 contains the correlation matrix for the weighted paradigms and Table 4 the correlation matrix for the weighted practices.

Table 3 and Table 4 reveal that the variables are not highly correlated to each other at 5% significance level; more, the majority of them are even insignificantly correlated with each other. Therefore, it is valid to consider a linear additive weighting model in deriving the LARG Index.

After the weights computed and the linear model assumption verified it is now possible to suggest a LARG index to assess the level of leanness, agility, resilience, and greenness for the automotive SC through one composite indicator (Equation 2).

where:

n is the number of companies considered in a particular SC

(Pxi)j represents for company j, the level of implementation of practice i of paradigm x. A total of 7 practices (i = 1, ...,7) are considered to each paradigm. The implementation level for each practice is assessed in a 5 points Likert scale were 1 means "practice not implemented" and 5 "practice totally implemented

LARG index is a composite indicator constituted by a set of sub-indicators reflecting the SC behaviour in terms of Lean, Agile, Resilient, and Green paradigms. This composite indicator is computed to a specific SC, considering the level of implementation of the focused practices in the companies belonging to the SC. The LARG index goes from 1 (none paradigms put into practice in the SC companies) to 5 (all the paradigms are completely deployed in the SC companies).

THE FUZZY ENTERPRISE 2.0 ASSESSMENT APPROACH

The Supply Chain Management is progressively becoming Internet based. In a typical supply chain the generation of an activity at one end flows down the supply chain till it reaches the root from where the basic flow of material begins.

The data may be available over the complete supply chain and there may be a need to interpret it in different formats over the chain and at the same node over the time. There arises the necessity to integrate the information flow over the whole chain and across different platforms and utilities such that there is virtually no loss of data in transmission and conversion (Rajib et al., 2002).

The corporate world is increasingly feeling a need to get instantaneous access to business information status across the various SC' partners.

The Internet changes the way companies do business. The changes are permanent in the transaction from the industrial economy to the network economy (Short, 2002). The Internet facilitates companies to conduct business in the global village. The Web 2.0 changes the way enterprises and SC are managed, planned and controlled. Information and decisions related to business are integrated into the Web breaking the old paradigms of inter-organizational boundaries (Chou et al., 2004). So, a powerhouse of information is created through the integration of all these islands of information using the World Wide Web and providing access across any physical boundary (Rajib et al., 2002).

Table 4. Correlation matrix among the SCM weighted practices

Correlation matrix		PL1	PL2	PL3	PL4	PL5	PL6	PL7
Lean practices	PL1	1.000						
	PL2	.124	1.000					
	PL3	.346	.516	1.000				
	PL4	.638*	-.180	-.239	1.000			
	PL5	.404	.381	.140	.334	1.000		
	PL6	.134	.476	.175	.226	.502	1.000	
	PL7	.559	.528	.194	.463	.391	.695*	1.000
Correlation matrix		**PA1**	**PA2**	**PA3**	**PA4**	**PA5**	**PA6**	**PA7**
Agile practices	PA1	1.000						
	PA2	-.553	1.000					
	PA3	.298	-.120	1.000				
	PA4	.332	.267	.539	1.000			
	PA5	-.319	-.064	.346	-.346	1.000		
	PA6	-.237	.214	.115	.214	-.316	1.000	
	PA7	.000	-.143	.262	-.017	-.132	.710 *	1.000
Correlation matrix		**PR1**	**PR2**	**PR3**	**PR4**	**PR5**	**PR6**	**PR7**
Resilient practice	PR1	1.000						
	PR2	.812**	1.000					
	PR3	.620*	.564	1.000				
	PR4	-.255	-.152	.132	1.000			
	PR5	.368	.028	.507	.507	1.000		
	PR6	.793**	.720*	.772**	.131	.506	1.000	
	PR7	-.082	-.279	-.423	-.051	.283	-.318	1.000
Correlation matrix		**PG1**	**PG2**	**PG3**	**PG4**	**PG5**	**PG6**	**PG7**
Green practice	PG1	1.000						
	PG2	.292	1.000					
	PG3	.350	.426	1.000				
	PG4	.080	-.056	.363	1.000			
	PG5	.449	-.083	.243	.671*	1.000		
	PG6	.375	.354	.230	-.100	-.149	1.000	
	PG7	.449	.031	.689*	.671*	.542	.466	1.000
	Notes:** Correlation is significant at the 0.01 level (2-tailed) * Correlation significant at the 0.05 level (2-tailed)							

Knowing that the Internet and the World Wide Web are a reality to enterprises and also SC, the proposed LARG index is constructed over the Internet platform. This makes it easy to individual enterprise and corresponding partners to fill in the LARG index framework with their implementation level of the research practices associated to all the four paradigms (Lean, Agile, Resilient, and

Equation 2.

$$LARG_{SC} = 0.28 \times \frac{\sum_{i=1}^{n} \left(0.15 \times P_{L1_i} + 0.14 \times P_{L2_i} + 0.17 \times P_{L3_i} + 0.14 \times P_{L4_i} + 0.14 \times P_{L5_i} + 0.12 \times P_{L6_i} + 0.14 \times P_{L7_i}\right)}{n} +$$
$$0.26 \times \frac{\sum_{i=1}^{n} \left(0.15 \times P_{A1_i} + 0.18 \times P_{A2_i} + 0.14 \times P_{A3_i} + 0.16 \times P_{A4_i} + 0.14 \times P_{A5_i} + 0.11 \times P_{A6_i} + 0.12 \times P_{A7_i}\right)}{n} +$$
$$0.27 \times \frac{\sum_{i=1}^{n} \left(0.15 \times P_{R1_i} + 0.16 \times P_{R2_i} + 0.14 \times P_{R3_i} + 0.14 \times P_{R4_i} + 0.15 \times P_{R5_i} + 0.14 \times P_{R6_i} + 0.12 \times P_{R7_i}\right)}{n} +$$
$$0.19 \times \frac{\sum_{i=1}^{n} \left(0.15 \times P_{G1_i} + 0.10 \times P_{G2_i} + 0.14 \times P_{G3_i} + 0.17 \times P_{G4_i} + 0.17 \times P_{G5_i} + 0.13 \times P_{G6_i} + 0.14 \times P_{G7_i}\right)}{n}$$

Green) and to get automatically the individual and SC LARG index values.

In a nutshell we can say that Enterprise 2.0 is all about the interest of the organizations in embracing community cooperation in order to achieve a competitive edge (using blogs and wikis, social networking, rating systems, widgets and other so called Web 2.0 appliances). According to Capuano et al. (2010), the Enterprise 2.0 is an enabler to improve business-to-business (B2B) interactions and communication capabilities for enterprise integration. In the same way, as the Enterprise 2.0 is already a reality for companies and global SC, in this research the use of Web 2.0 is suggested as an important enabler to a better integration among supply chain partners in order to reach the LARG index to the supply chain.

Fuzzy Logic is an area of research especially well suited to tackle problems defined in uncertain and imprecise environments due to its inherent capability to deal and reason with (vague) linguistic terms and incomplete data. The LARG assessment is a multi-actor human-dependent task hence permeated by a great amount of uncertainty and imprecision. These characteristics are revealed in two main aspects: on the way evaluators issue their assessments and on the expression of multiple fuzzy preferences (as many as the selected evaluators).

The concept of linguistic variable (Zadeh, 1976) can play a critical role in this task. Informally, a linguistic variable is a granulated variable whose granular values are words or phrases represented by fuzzy sets (altogether with their connectives, modifiers and negation). These linguistic characterizations are, usually, less specific than the numeric ones, but in compensation are safer. Thus the linguistic variable can be viewed as a way to accomplish (lossy) compression of information. Moreover the linguistic variable provides a descriptive mean for complex or poorly understood systems and, more important, offers a bridge between linguistics and computation. As a matter of fact fuzzy numbers can even be used as a mean to combine linguistic expressions of performance and quantitative data.

Moreover Fuzzy Logic has been successfully applied in (group) decision making and consensus reaching processes, demonstrating that difficult problems and changes in the management environment can be more easily handled by bringing fuzzy logic into the practice of management (Carlsson et al., 2004).

In a synthetic way, the Fuzzy Logic is mainly about computing with words and consequent information granulation. In this section we will present our view on how a proper implementation of these two knowledge-processing solutions (Enterprise 2.0 and Fuzzy Logic) can foster the

Figure 3. LARG assessment procedure

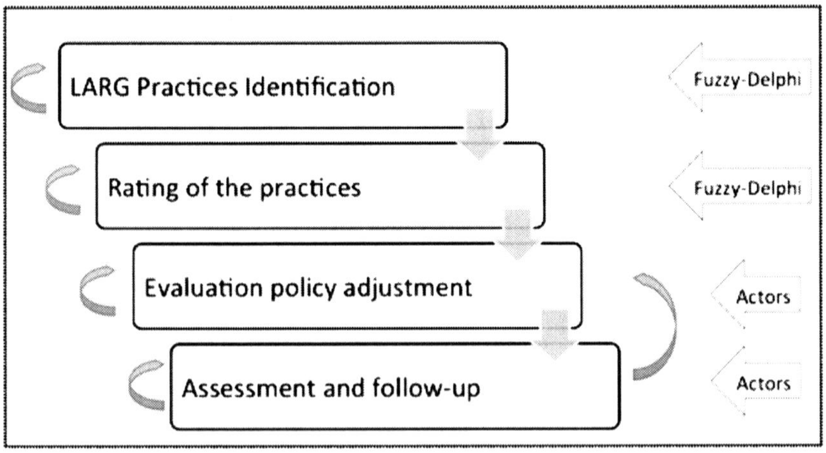

simple effective application of the LARG index to a given supply chain.

The establishment of this novel evaluation model into a new industry is an iterative and interactive procedure that comprises four different phases as depicted in Figure 3.

Enterprise 2.0 technologies and Fuzzy Logic techniques may have a preponderant role as enablers of a seamingless adaptation to this new evaluation model, in the following key processes:

1. The determination of an adequate set of Lean, Agile, Resilient, and Green practices;
2. The consensual definition of the relative weights of the considered practices;
3. The adjustment of the evaluation policy to the particular supply chain; and
4. The effective follow-up of the assessment results.

Identification of an Adequate Set of LARG Practices

The institutional management model is highly hierarchical and at the top of the hierarchy, there are enough experts with a brighter wide enough vision able to capture all the relevant aspects of the LARG practices. However, the dimension of the supply chain, the various sources of uncertainty and the specificities of the intervenient enterprises as well as their complex interrelationships make this a difficult task. Much of the organizational knowledge and expertise is scattered across the SC and even a single undifferentiated employee may contribute with the elicitation of an unforeseen key practice. Moreover a proper communication of the evaluation policies as well as the participation in their definition may promote the enthusiastic enrollment in their enforcement.

To build and enable this new collaborative infrastructure the managers can choose to have a wiki in their corporate intranet and encourage usage by putting up an initial wiki page with a set of practices based on the ones presented in the previous section. This common platform will likely allow the emergence of unsuspected collaborations between knowledge workers in different enterprises of the SC – in some cases sharing a common view on a particular set of practices, in others disagreeing or even fighting for opposite ones. The resulting group authorship, regardless of the intensity of the discussion or being moderated or not, has the advantage of being readable by anyone in the organization making the entire process of knowledge elicitation persistently visible. After a stabilization period it is expected that the ground rules for the assessment of the whole SC are assimilated and accepted as legitimate.

Rating of the LARG Practices

Once the first step concluded several methods for defining the set of weights for the SCM paradigms and corresponding practices can be devised. The corporate wiki page can be enriched with some sort of polling user interface through which visitors can cast their vote on each practice. This can be simply an extension of the numeric Delphi study (or a fuzzy-Delphi one) to a wider group of intervenients (some possibilities include experts and academics inside and outside organization with a mix of selected workers in key points of the SC).

The LARG index weight assessment can be seen as a Multi-Criteria Decision Making (MCDM) problem where the independent assumption between criteria does not hold. The Analytic Hierarchy Process (AHP) introduced by Saaty (Saaty, 1980) has successfully been applied to many practical MCDM problems. The basic assumption of the AHP is that the decision-making problem can be decomposed into a linear hierarchy, where the different levels are functionally independent, and the elements in each level are also independent. To overcome these limitations Saaty (1996) proposed Analytic Network Process (ANP) dealing with interrelationship among decision levels. The weights of criteria in the ANP are assessed indirectly from pair-wise comparison judgments. However in the present case, as in many others, it is relatively difficult for the decision makers provide exact numerical values for the comparison ratios. Regardless of their own occasional uncertainty about their level of preference, the complexity and uncertainty within the SC decision environment promotes a linguistic approach as a more effective way to express preferences when opposed to a numerical description. Thus Fuzzy Analysis Network Process (FANP) emerges as a system analysis method combining the principles of ANP while employing a linguistic representation of knowledge supported by fuzzy logic. Figure 4 depicts the resulting analysis model for the LARG index weight assessment problem.

Hence, the weight assessment can be done resourcing to a set of qualitative elements ordered by a complete pre-order. Without entering into much detail, the process starts with the evaluators conducting pairwise comparisons using linguistic data. Next, a fuzzy pairwise comparison matrix is synthesized through the expression of preferences as triangular fuzzy numbers. Finally, the inner dependency matrix of the criteria with respect to each criterion is calculated and the weight of each criterion is deduced. Notice that regardless the qualitative human-centric nature of the resulting rating system it does not preclude attaching precise numerical values to the practices. As a matter of fact fuzzy numbers can even be used as a mean to combine linguistic expressions of performance and quantitative data. For instance, to illustrate the context of fuzzy preference, a practice P1 could be classified as being 'just equal' to P2 or as being 'insignificantly', 'a little', 'mildly', 'much', 'very much' or 'definitely' more important than a practice P2. In this way decision makers may express their preference relations in linguistic labels that are easily implementable for solving group decision-making problems (Marimin et al., 1998). The linguistic labels are more appropriate for approximating preference values which are too complex to be represented using precise numerical values (Zadeh, 1976). This procedure is prone to provide a new insight on the order relations that exist between the practices of the SC promoting a voting system based on their relative pairwise comparison.

Adjustment of the Evaluation Policy

Information granules emerge at the conceptual level as a powerful mean to accomplish knowledge representation, information processing and structured thinking and problem solving (Yao, 2006). The materialization of the information granulation in the framework of fuzzy sets as pro-

Figure 4. LARG assessment analytic model

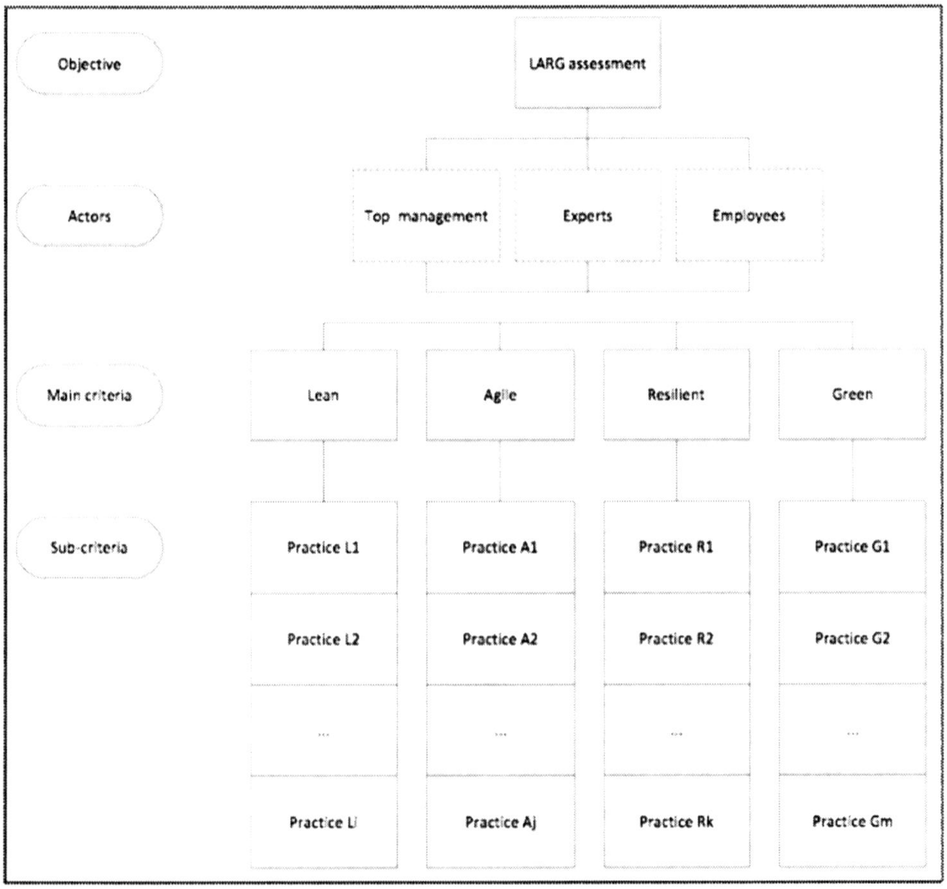

posed by Zadeh (Zadeh, 1997) presents appealing features regarding the human understandability of the produced granules. Furthermore the linguistic granules can be used as the point of departure for further meaningful refinements and support the modularization of the dataset reducing the computing power that would be necessary to reveal detailed relationships at a numeric level (Hirota & Pedrycz, 1999). Another way to take advantage of the semantics of fuzzy sets consists in constructing hierarchies of concepts through sound operators of generalization and specialization and also linguistic modifiers.

The LARG assessment policies can be operationalized by the use of Mamdani fuzzy inference systems due to its inherent comprehensibility and adequateness to capture the experts' knowledge in the form of rules with clear semantics (commonly referred to as IF-THEN rule-based form, closely related to the deductive way of linguistically expressing knowledge).

Mamdani type fuzzy model (also known as linguistic fuzzy model) is represented by linguistic rules with the following structure:

$Rule_i$: if X_1 is $A_{i,1}$ and ... and X_m is $A_{i,m}$ then Y is B_i, $i = 1,...,n$

where $Rule_i$ denotes the i-th rule, n is the number of rules and $X_1 \ldots X_m$ are the input linguistic variables and Y is the output variable. $A_{i,1}$ and B_i are the linguistic labels expressed as fuzzy sets with specific semantic meanings in the context of the system being modeled. For instance, each practice can be conceived as a linguistic variable whose degree of fulfillment is classified according to the

Figure 5. A fuzzy rulebase (compact form) encoding LARG evaluation policy

Agile/Resilient \ Lean/Green	VP	BA	A	AA	EX
VP	VP	BA	A	AA	AA
BA	VP	BA	A	AA	AA
A	VP	BA	A	AA	EX
AA	BA	BA	A	AA	EX
EX	BA	A	AA	EX	EX

following five linguistic terms: Very Poor (VP), Below Average (BA), Average (A), Above Average (AA) and Excellent (EX). Figure 5 presents a set of rules in compact form encoding a part of a hypothetical assessment policy.

Such rulebase encodes the evaluation policy at a higher abstraction level since it is hiding the individual practices while focusing on the LARG paradigms. Notice that the rulebase can be deduced from the above polling system, can be made publicly available in the corporate wiki and if the assessment policy slightly changes, for instance by deciding that it should be given higher merit to green aware practices, the rulebase is easily updated to reflect the new policy and is readily communicated in a clearly comprehensible way.

Assessment and Follow-Up

The LARG index assessment can be an effective tool to be used not only by strategic decision makers, who need comprehensive models to support their decisions aimed to the enrichment of the SC, but also by the individual echelons aiming at improving their added value in the SC. With this regard it is important that the entire evaluation be made simple, preferably in a familiar enough environment. Thus the corporate wiki can be enriched with an evaluator's reserved area having a Web widget allowing each evaluator to classify each practice using natural language. Once all the data gathered it would be the input to a linguistic fuzzy logic inference engine resulting in the LARG index assessment. Frequent assessment loops (or even a continuous one) should help improving the overall SC performance.

Also the practical adhesion of the SC's enterprises and employees to the LARG practices should be higher if they feel themselves as an integral part of the collective intelligence system that is being formed. To this aim it is essential that the individual chains be aware of the current status of the evaluation process and can maintain track of the previous evaluations conditions and results. This double purpose can be easily achieved through the deployment of an organizational Web widget providing access to the recorded assessments. Moreover its usefulness can be highly improved if complemented with a simulator of the evaluation process giving a greater feedback on the effective role of the SC partners, and his real impact on the LARG index of the organization.

FINAL REMARKS

The approach developed in this chapter is innovative. The scope used in this research cannot be found in literature. There are no works that focus simultaneously the LARG Index construction, the Fuzzy logic and the Delphi technique. Only the work of Azevedo et al (2011) focuses on LARG practices and proposes a set of management practices to help manufacturing SCs becoming simultaneously more lean, agile, resilient and green (LARG) and also to explore the relationships between these kinds of practices and SC's performance, however it uses a theoretical approach. There exists some researches that touch the topic of this chapter however focusing only one paradigm. For example, a Lean production index proposal can be found in Kojima and Kaplinsky (2004) however using statistical methods. A Green index is suggested by Lau (2011) employing the one-way analysis of variance (ANOVA) and Principal Component Analysis (PCA) in home electronic appliance industry in China and

Japan. The methodology proposed in this chapter using simultaneously the Delphi technique to attain weights and the Fuzzy logic to capture the uncertainty and ambiguity surrounding the level of implementation of the four focused paradigms is innovative in nature.

In order to operationalize the LARG index this chapter proposes a Web 2.0 numeric-linguistic interface based on fuzzy logic. The fuzzy formalism allows the translation of human knowledge expressed in a linguistic manner into a numeric format manageable by computers.

An issue of paramount importance is the comprehensibility of the resulting system. Comprehensibility refers to the ability of the model to express the behavior of the system in an easily understandable way (from the human stand-point). This is a property dependent on subjective factors as diverse and important as the structure of the model, the number of input variables, the number of fuzzy rules, the number of linguistic terms and the form of the fuzzy sets (Oliveira & Fazendeiro, 2003). This requirement usually lumps together criteria such as compactness, completeness, consistency and transparency (Zhou & Gan, 2008). It is expected that the decision-maker would feel a great deal of comfort by using an assessment system that provides a clear and quick explanation on how its decisions are being made so that he could validate them online and suggest alternatives when needed.

Another key issue is the number of actors that can contribute to the SC assessment: multiple enterprises, comprising sets of evaluators, each one having different perceptions (possibly vague, antagonic, ambiguous or even contradictory) of the fulfillment level of each one of the LARG practices. This chapter addresses this issue by proposing a Web-based voting system that has the ability to adapt and evolve (the LARG evaluation policy) according to the expression of multiple fuzzy preferences. This procedure is prone to provide a new insight on the order relations that exist between the practices of the SC promoting a voting system based on their relative pairwise comparison.

Arguably this platform, properly implemented in an Enterprise 2.0 context, will foster the emergence of unsuspected collaborations between knowledge workers in different enterprises of the SC. The resulting group authorship has the advantage of being readable by anyone in the organization making the entire process of knowledge elicitation persistently visible. Moreover, it is also clear that the assessment system will benefit from the introduction or modification of evaluation rules in a decision-maker friendly way, allowing the fast and flexible inclusion of new knowledge and expertise.

REFERENCES

Agarwal, A., Shankar, R., & Tiwari, M. (2007). Modeling agility of supply chain. *Industrial Marketing Management*, *36*(4), 443–457. doi:10.1016/j.indmarman.2005.12.004.

Anand, G., & Kodali, R. (2010). Development of a framework for implementation of lean manufacturing systems. *International Journal of Management Practice*, *4*(1), 95–116. doi:10.1504/IJMP.2010.029705.

Azevedo, S., Carvalho, H., Cruz-Machado, V., & Grilo, F. (2010). The influence of agile and resilient practices on supply chain performance: An innovative conceptual model proposal. In Blecker, Kersten, & Luthje (Eds.), Innovative Process Optimization Methods in Logistics: Emerging trends, concepts and technologies, (pp. 265-281). Berlin: Erich Schmidt Verlag GmbH & Co. KG.

Azevedo, S. G., Carvalho, H., & Cruz-Machado, V. (2011). A proposal of LARG supply chain management practices and a performance measurement system. *International Journal of e-Education, e-Business, e-. Management Learning*, *1*(1), 7–14.

Azevedo, S. G., Machado, V., Barroso, A., & Cruz-Machado, V. (2008). Supply chain vulnerability: Environment changes and dependencies. *International Journal of Logistics and Transport*, *1*, 41–55.

Barrett, R., & Maurice Salles, M. (2006). *Social choice with fuzzy preferences. Center for Research in Economics and Management (CREM), University of Rennes 1*. University of Caen and CNRS.

Brown, K., & Mitchell, T. (1991). A comparison of just-in-time and batch manufacturing: The role of performance obstacles. *Journal of the Academy of Management*, *34*(4), 906–917. doi:10.2307/256395.

Carlsson, C., Fedrizzi, M., & Fuller, R. (2004). *Fuzzy logic in management*. Berlin: Springer. doi:10.1007/978-1-4419-8977-2.

Chan, A., Yung, E., Lam, P., Tam, C., & Cheung, S. (2001). Application of delphi method in selection of procurement systems for construction. *Construction Management and Economics*, *19*(7), 699–718. doi:10.1080/01446190110066128.

Chan, F., & Qi, H. (2003). An innovative performance measurement method for supply chain management. *Supply Chain Management*, *8*(3), 209–223. doi:10.1108/13598540310484618.

Chen, C.-T., Lin, C.-T., & Huang, S.-F. (2006). A fuzzy approach for supplier evaluation and selection in supply chain management. *International Journal of Production Economics*, *102*, 289–301. doi:10.1016/j.ijpe.2005.03.009.

Chen, T., Sun, F., & Lu, Y. (2007). Research on TPL-oriented fuzzy integrated evaluation method for supply chain. In *Proceedings of the Sixth Wuhan International Conference on E-Business*. Wuhan.

Christopher, M., & Peck, H. (2004). Building the resilient supply chain. *The International Journal of Logistics Management*, *15*(2), 1–14. doi:10.1108/09574090410700275.

Christopher, M., & Towill, D. (2001). An integrated model for the design of agile supply chains. *International Journal of Physical Distribution & Logistics Management*, *31*(4), 235–246. doi:10.1108/09600030110394914.

Disney, S., Naim, M., & Towill, D. (1997). Dynamic simulation modeling for lean logistics. *International Journal of Physical Distribution & Logistics Management*, *27*(3/4), 174–196. doi:10.1108/09600039710170566.

Dubois, D., & Prade, H. (1987). The mean value of a fuzzy number. *Fuzzy Sets and Systems*, *24*, 279–300. doi:10.1016/0165-0114(87)90028-5.

Dubois, D., Prade, H., & Ughetto, L. (1999). Fuzzy logic, control engineering and artificial intelligence. InVerbruggen, , Zimmermann, , & Babuska, (Eds.), *Fuzzy Algorithms for Control*, (pp. 17-57). Dordrecht, The Netherlands: Kluwer Academic Publishers. doi:10.1007/978-94-011-4405-6_2.

Erol, I., Sencer, S., & Sari, R. (2011). A new fuzzy multi-criteria framework for measuring sustainability performance of a supply chain. *Ecological Economics*, *70*, 1088–1100. doi:10.1016/j.ecolecon.2011.01.001.

Gonzalez, P., Sarkis, J., & Adenso-Diaz, B. (2008). Environmental management system certification and its influence on corporate practices: Evidence from the automotive industry. *International Journal of Operations & Production Management*, *28*(11), 1021–1041. doi:10.1108/01443570810910179.

Gunasekaran, C., & Tirtiroglu, E. (2001). Performance measures and metrics in a supply chain environment. *International Journal of Operations & Production Management*, *21*(1/2), 71–87. doi:10.1108/01443570110358468.

Gurumurthy, A., & Kodali, R. (2009). Application of benchmarking for assessing the lean manufacturing implementation. *Benchmarking: An International Journal, 16*(2), 274–308. doi:10.1108/14635770910948268.

Haimes, Y. (2006). On the definition of vulnerabilities in measuring risks to infrastructures. *Risk Analysis: An Official Publication of the Society for Risk Analysis, 26*(2), 293–296. doi:10.1111/j.1539-6924.2006.00755.x PMID:16573621.

Hirota, K., & Pedrycz, W. (1999). Fuzzy computing for data mining. *Proceedings of the IEEE, 87*(9), 1575–1600. doi:10.1109/5.784240.

Ho, G., Lau, H., Chung, S., Fung, R., & Chan, T. (2008). Fuzzy rule sets for enhancing performance in a supply chain network. *Industrial Management + Data Systems, 108*(7), 947-972.

Hoek, V., Harrison, A., & Christopher, M. (2001). Measuring agile capabilities in the supply chain. *International Journal of Operations & Production Management, 21*(1/2), 126–148. doi:10.1108/01443570110358495.

Holt, D., & Ghobadian, A. (2009). An empirical study of green supply chain management practices amongst UK manufacturers. *Journal of Manufacturing Technology Management, 20*(7), 933–956. doi:10.1108/17410380910984212.

Hu, A., & Hsu, C. (2006). Empirical study in the critical factors of green supply chain management (GSCM), practice in the Taiwanese electrical and electronics industries. In *Proceeding of 2006 IEEE International Conference on Management of Innovation and Technology*. Singapore: IEEE.

Iakovou, E., Vlachos, D., & Xanthopoulos, A. (2007). An analytical methodological framework for the optimal design of resilient supply chains. *International Journal of Logistics Economics and Globalisation, 1*(1), 1–20. doi:10.1504/IJLEG.2007.014498.

Ismail, H. S., & Sharifi, H. (2006). A balanced approach to building agile supply chains. *International Journal of Physical Distribution & Logistics Management, 36*(6), 431–444. doi:10.1108/09600030610677384.

Israel, D. (2009). *Data analysis in business research: A step-by-step nonparametric approach*. Thousand Oaks, CA: Sage Publications Pvt. Ltd..

Kojima, S., & Kaplinsky, R. (2004). The use of a lean production index in explaining the transition to global competitiveness: The auto components sector in South Africa. *Technovation, 24*(3), 199–206. doi:10.1016/S0166-4972(03)00142-1.

Lau, H., Pang, W., & Wong, C. (2002). Methodology for monitoring supply chain performance: A fuzzy logic approach. *Journal of Enterprise Information Management, 15*(4), 271–280.

Lau, K. (2011). Benchmarking green logistics performance with a composite index. *Benchmarking, 18*(6), 873–896. doi:10.1108/14635771111180743.

Linstone, H. A., & Turoff, M. (Eds.). (1975). *The delphi method: Techniques and applications*. Reading, MA: Addison-Wesley.

Marimin, M., Hatono, I., & Tamura, H. (1998). Linguistic labels for expressing fuzzy preference relations in fuzzy group decision making. *IEEE Transactions on Systems, Man, and Cybernetics. Part B, Cybernetics, 28*(2), 205–218. doi:10.1109/3477.662760 PMID:18255937.

Ohdar, R., & Ray, P. (2004). Performance measurement and evaluation of suppliers in supply chain: An evolutionary fuzzy-based approach. *Journal of Manufacturing Technology Management, 15*(8), 723–734. doi:10.1108/17410380410565311.

Oliveira, J., & Fazendeiro, P. (2003). On the achievement of both accurate and interpretable fuzzy systems using data-driven design processes. In Casillas, J. et al. (Eds.), *Accuracy Improvements in Linguistic Fuzzy Modeling*. Physica-Verlag.

Olugu, E., & Wong, Y. (2009). Supply chain performance evaluation: Trends and challenges. *American Journal of Engineering and Applied Sciences*, *2*(1), 202–211. doi:10.3844/ajeas.2009.202.211.

Parveen, M., & Rao, T. (2009). An integrated approach to design and analysis of lean manufacturing system: A perspective of Lean supply chain. *International Journal of Services and Operations Management*, *5*(2), 175–208. doi:10.1504/IJSOM.2009.023232.

Paulraj, A. (2009). Environmental motivations: A classification scheme and its impact on environmental strategies and practices. *Business Strategy and the Environment*, *18*(7), 453–468. doi:10.1002/bse.612.

Pilevari, N., Hosseini, S., & Jassbi, J. (2008). Fuzzy logic supply chain agility assessment methodology. *IEEE International Conference on Industrial Engineering and Engineering Management*, 1113-1117.

Rajib, P., Tiwari, D., & Srivastava, G. (2002). Design and development of an integrated supply chain management system in an Internet environment. *Journal of Service Research*, *2*(1), 22–43.

Rao, P., & Holt, D. (2005). Do green supply chains lead to competitiveness and economic performance? *International Journal of Operations & Production Management*, *25*(9), 898–916. doi:10.1108/01443570510613956.

Rice, J., & Caniato, F. (2003). Building a secure and resilient supply network. *Supply Chain Management Review*, *7*(5), 22–31.

Rowe, G., & Wright, G. (1999). The delphi technique as a forecasting tool: Issues and analysis. *International Journal of Forecasting*, *15*(4), 353–375. doi:10.1016/S0169-2070(99)00018-7.

Saaty, T. L. (1980). *The analytic hierarchy process*. New York: McGraw Hill Publications.

Saaty, T. L. (1996). *Decision making with dependence and feedback: The analytic network process*. Pittsburgh, PA: RWS Publications.

Seyedhoseini, S., Jassbi, J., & Pilevari, N. (2010). Application of adaptive neuro fuzzy inference system in measurement of supply chain agility: Real case study of a manufacturing company. *African Journal of Business Management*, *4*(1), 83–96.

Srivastava, S. (2007). Green supply-chain management: A state-of-the-art literature review. *International Journal of Management Reviews*, *9*(1), 53–80. doi:10.1111/j.1468-2370.2007.00202.x.

Stewart, D., & Grout, J. (2001). The human side of mistake-proofing. *Production and Operations Management*, *10*(4), 440–459. doi:10.1111/j.1937-5956.2001.tb00086.x.

Swafford, P., Ghosh, S., & Murthy, N. (2008). Achieving supply chain agility through IT integration and flexibility. *International Journal of Production Economics*, *116*(2), 288–297. doi:10.1016/j.ijpe.2008.09.002.

Tang, C. S. (2006). Robust strategies for mitigating supply chain disruptions. *International Journal of Logistics: Research and Applications*, *9*(1), 33–45. doi:10.1080/13675560500405584.

Treville, S., & Antonakis, J. (2006). Could lean production job design, be intrinsically motivating? Contextual, configurational, and levels-of-analysis issues. *Journal of Operations Management*, *24*(2), 99–123. doi:10.1016/j.jom.2005.04.001.

Womack, J., Jones, D., & Roos, D. (1991). *The machine that change the world*. New York: HarperCollins Publishers.

Yao, Y. (2006). Three perspectives of granular computing. *Journal of Nanchang Institute of Technology*, *25*(2), 16–21.

Yeung, J., Chan, A., Chan, D., & Li, L. K. (2007). Development of a partnering performance index (PPI) for construction projects in Hong Kong: A Delphi study. *Construction Management and Economics*, *25*(12), 1219–1237. doi:10.1080/01446190701598673.

Zadeh, L. (1976). The concept of linguistic variable and its application to approximate reasoning. *Information Sciences*, *8*, 199–249, 301–357. doi:10.1016/0020-0255(75)90036-5.

Zadeh, L. (1997). Toward a theory of fuzzy information granulation and its centrality in human reasoning and fuzzy logic. *Fuzzy Sets and Systems*, *90*, 111–127. doi:10.1016/S0165-0114(97)00077-8.

Zhou, S.-M., & Gan, J. (2008). Low-level interpretability and high-level interpretability: A unified view of data-driven interpretable fuzzy system modelling. *Fuzzy Sets and Systems*, *159*, 3091–3131. doi:10.1016/j.fss.2008.05.016.

KEY TERMS AND DEFINITIONS

Agile: The agile paradigm intends to create the ability to respond rapidly and cost effectively to unpredictable changes in markets and increasing levels of environmental turbulence.

Fuzzy Analysis Network Process (FANP): System analysis method supported on the principles of Analytic Network Process while employing a linguistic fuzzy logic-based knowledge representation.

Fuzzy Logic: Branch of logic especially well suited to tackle problems defined in uncertain and imprecise environments due to its inherent capability to deal and reason with (vague) linguistic terms and incomplete data.

Green: The Green SCM has emerged as an organizational philosophy by which to achieve corporate profit and market-share objectives by reducing environmental risks and impacts while improving the ecological efficiency of such organizations and their partners.

LARG Index Construction: Approach to synthesize an index in order to assess the leanness, agility, resilience and greenness of companies and corresponding SCs.

Lean: The lean management paradigm, developed by Taiichi Ohno of the Toyota Motor Corporation in Japan, forms the basis for the Toyota Production System (TPS) with two main pillars: 'autonomation' and 'just-In-Time' (JIT) production. The lean paradigm has essentially focused on waste reduction as a means to increase actual value-added.

Resilient: Is referred as the SC ability to cope with unexpected disturbances. The goal of SC resilience analysis and management is to prevent the shifting to undesirable states.

Chapter 30
Objective-Oriented Modeling of Enterprises under the Service Paradigm

José C. Delgado
Technical University of Lisbon, Portugal

ABSTRACT

Current enterprise architecture frameworks are inherently committed to the process paradigm by separating the data and application architectures. The N-tier architectural style is a good match to those methods, since it is based on the same separation principle. However, the process paradigm does not satisfy the information hiding and low semantic gap principles heralded by the object-oriented paradigm. This chapter presents an enterprise architecture framework that emphasizes the motivations (stemming from the business), the ends (expectations, what the business needs to achieve), and the means (what is needed to accomplish the ends), as the basis for a method to develop architectures better prepared for changes, either due to maintenance, adaptation, or enterprise integration and interoperability. The main tenets are to refine the ends into goals and objectives, increasing the level of concreteness as much as possible before delving into the design, and to adopt the service paradigm, for which a tierless architectural style is a more suitable match.

INTRODUCTION

Thanks to computers and computer networks, the informational diameter of the world is getting smaller and smaller. It is increasingly easier for users to access information anywhere (powered by search engines such as Google) and to be interconnected to anyone on the planet, with social networking on the rise (according to the statistics presented in the media resources of Facebook's site, Facebook has surpassed the mark of 900 million active users in March 2012).

DOI: 10.4018/978-1-4666-4373-4.ch030

Enterprises are also more and more interconnected and interdependent. Success on the market implies agility and optimization of business processes, which in turn implies concentrating on core business activities and outsourcing the rest. Virtualization, down from physical devices up to whole enterprises, has been the key for dynamic adaptation that is the basis for competitiveness. Cloud computing (Shroff, 2010) is one of the latest manifestations of the ease with which enterprises can coexist and interlink with others in the same informational space.

All this connectivity is both a bonus and a curse, leading to what could be called *interaction sprawl*. If the cost of interconnecting enterprises lowers, it will be increasingly done, raising problems on the interoperability, integration and alignment sides of the issue.

SOA (Earl, 2007) has been heralded as a solution to conceive and structure enterprises in a distributed world, but in practice it has been used as an enterprise integration layer to interconnect basically centralized information systems, based on an N-tier architectural style and orchestration (processes). It is not a native solution to the enterprise integration problem. The enterprise architectures should be conceived as distributed systems themselves, right from their inception. If the Enterprise 2.0 wants to seamlessly blend and be integrated in the overall distributed enterprise fabric, with an architecture geared for the constant changes and adaptations that will inevitably occur, it must adopt the same underlying distribution and decoupling principles.

This chapter concentrates on two problems that, in our opinion, have significantly contributed to hamper the changeability and adaptability of many enterprise architectures:

- The mismatch between the essence of a business model and the organization and structuring paradigm used to describe it. What we usually call *the business* is in fact a choreography performed by a set of interacting entities, which exchange values (information, money, products, service transactions, and so on). This is valid both in the external context (environment) of an enterprise (customers, suppliers, competitors, regulators, and so on) and in its internal context (stakeholders, governance board, departments, units, applications, and so on). This is an actor oriented universe, for which the service paradigm (Earl, 2007) is a close match, but usually enterprise architectures have the process as the main paradigm to describe the business. For example, Winter and Fischer (2007) structure an enterprise architecture in five layers: business, process, integration, software and infrastructure. The proposal is to perform a paradigm shift, from processes to services and from architecture layers to a society of interacting, self-contained actors that implement services;
- In the method used to develop the architecture, adopting a specific organization and design without sufficiently detailing the business motivations and requirements, such as defining processes directly from generic goals (Markov and Kowalkiewicz, 2008). This gives little support for transitioning from the business layer to lower, more concrete architectural layers, places a burden on analysts and turns changes and adaptations of an enterprise architecture into a harder task. The proposal is to refine goals into objectives and subobjectives, staying on the declarative side as much as possible before delving into the prescriptive side of design.

BACKGROUND

Modeling before designing has always been an important tenet. Since the early days of the Zachman framework (Sowa & Zachman, 1992), we understand that enterprise architecture and its underlying principles (Greefhorst & Proper,

2011; Winter & Aier, 2011) are the cornerstones of enterprises themselves.

Today, several enterprise architecture frameworks exist, with Zachman framework and TOGAF (The Open Group, 2009) as the two most used among a wide set that includes (Minoli, 2008) the Department of Defense's Architectural Framework (DoDAF), the Extended Enterprise Architecture Framework (E2AF), the Federal Enterprise Architecture Framework (FEAF), the Treasury Enterprise Architecture Framework (TEAF) and the Integrated Architecture Framework (IAF).

TOGAF is gaining widespread acceptance as a *de facto* standard in the industry (Dietz & Hoogervorst, 2011), having influenced and been influenced by the ANSI/IEEE Standard 1471-2000 (Recommended Practice for Architectural Description), which has been superseded by ISO/IEC/IEEE 42010:2011 (Systems and software engineering – Architecture description) in 2011. This standard establishes a metamodel and a set of best practices for architectural description, including ontology and requirements for architecture frameworks and architecture description languages.

One of the relevant issues of the 42010:2011 standard, aligned with the terminology of TOGAF, is the distinction between a *view* (an abstraction of an architecture according to a set of concerns) and a *viewpoint*, the metamodel that describes how to build a given kind of views. Architectural dimensions (or axes), present in frameworks such as the Zachman framework and the one described in this chapter, bear a close relationship to viewpoints.

The service paradigm is now widely used in the enterprise architecture field, both in architecture modeling languages, such as ArchiMate (Lankhorst, Proper & Jonkers, 2009) and ARMOR (Quartel, Engelsman, Jonkers & van Sinderen, 2009), and frameworks such as SOMF (Bell, 2008).

Since this chapter focus on the early stages of architecture development, the BMM, or Business Motivation Model (Malik, 2009), is of particular importance and has, in fact, influenced the architecture framework presented in this chapter. Instead of organizing the architecture into layers, from business down to technology (Winter and Fischer, 2007), the BMM emphasizes the motivations (the reasons why an architecture should be the way it is), the ends (the expectations which should be satisfied) and the means (what should be done to achieve those ends). Each of these types of concerns is derived from the previous one, in a business driven way. Berkem (2008) establishes a bridge to the service oriented paradigm, by describing how to derive SOA specifications from BMM.

Classical development methods, such as the Rational Unified Process (Kruchten, 2004), concentrate on requirements and design, rather than motivations or expectations. Nevertheless, the area of Requirements Engineering is also relevant to the early stages of architecture development (Nuseibeh & Easterbrook, 2000; Cheng & Atlee, 2007; Saeki, 2010). In particular, Goal-Oriented Requirements Engineering (Regev & Wegmann, 2005) has a closer match to enterprise architectures (van Lamsweerde, 2001; Anwer & Ikram, 2006), because making the expectations (most commonly, goals) explicit is a crucial part of describing the business requirements in a declarative, non-prescriptive way (Gehlert, Bramsiepe &Pohl, 2008).

The most used frameworks in this domain are i* (Gordijn, Yu & van der Raadt, 2006) and KAOS (Dardenne, van Lamsweerde & Fickas, 1993;), dealing mostly with early and late requirements, and Tropos (Castro, Kolp & Mylopoulos, 2002; Fuxman *et al.*, 2004), encompassing a wider range of applicability, from requirements to architecture design.

THE LIFECYCLE OF A SYSTEM

Figure 1 depicts the typical lifecycle of the conception and animation of a system's architecture in several stages, used here in the enterprise

Figure 1. Typical lifecycle of a system, with different perspectives chained in changeability loops

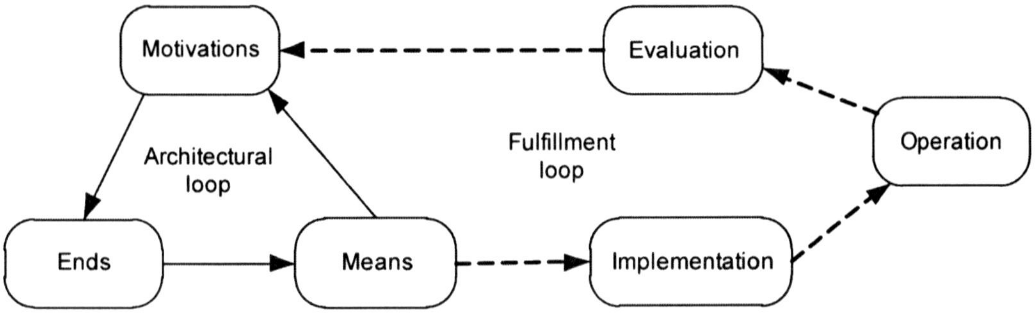

context. The word *system* is used instead of *enterprise* because the framework presented here can equally be applied to a group of enterprises, a single enterprise or a unit within an enterprise.

Each stage reflects a different perspective that is not independent of others, but rather occupies a specific position in a graph that is part of an overall method and includes loops to cater for changes and improvements.

The *architectural loop* is inspired by the Business Motivation Model (Malik, 2009) and laid around three main concepts:

- **Motivations:** Which emphasize the reasons behind the architectural decisions taken, in accordance with the business needs;
- **Ends:** Which express the desires and expectations of stakeholders (e.g., goals and objectives);
- **Means:** Which describe the mechanisms used to fulfill those expectations (e.g., actions).

The *fulfilment loop* in Figure 1 is based on classical development methods, such as the Rational Unified Process (Kruchten, 2004):

- The ends and the means of the architectural loop correspond roughly to the analysis and design stages of those methods;
- The *implementation* includes stages such as development, testing and deployment;
- The *operation* corresponds to animating (executing) the system;
- The *evaluation* measures KPIs (Key Performance Indicators) and assesses how well the system meets the expectations caused by the motivations.

This chapter focuses on the *architectural loop*, albeit bridging the means to the implementation. If needed (either due to imperfections in the various stages of the cycle or to changes in the motivations), the loop is repeated. In any case (at least conceptually), there should be no shortcuts to these loops:

- The method should always start at the motivations;
- The architectural loop should be iterated until a satisfactory and sufficiently detailed architecture is reached, before entering the fulfilment loop;
- The fulfilment loop should always return to the motivations, even if only to check that they have not changed.

This means that the method should be model driven. However, in many cases there are bad practices that should be avoided:

- The ends (the expectations) are mistaken for the motivations (the reasons behind them). In other words, the ends are used to justify the means but there is no true justification for the ends;

- The ends are specified at a very high level and used as mere guidelines to specify the means, with the ends abstracted later from the means for documentation purposes;
- The architectural loop is used only once, with evaluation looping directly through the implementation.

The *consistency*, *alignment* and *traceability* throughout these loops are fundamental. A stage *B* must be derived from the previous one *A* by adding further detail and turning abstract aspects into concrete ones, but maintaining *conformance* (Kim & Shen, 2007) to *A*. This means fulfilling at least all the requirements imposed on *A*, with the following characteristics:

- Decisions taken in *B* cannot be inconsistent with the decisions taken in *A*;
- The ontology, semantics and paradigm used in *B* should match those used in *A*, with the smallest semantic gap possible;
- Any constraints should be forward propagated and able to be traced back to the stage that took the decisions that originated them;

Note the explicit asymmetry. It is *B* that must ensue *A*, deriving from it, not the other way around. This means that stating what an architecture is cannot be done without laying down the expectations that led to it and these must in turn be justified by a rationale. This entails another conclusion: no architecture is complete without exercising the method that led to it.

The Zachman framework (Sowa & Zachman, 1992) strives to separate focus (*what*, *how*, *where*, *who*, *when*, *why*) from perspective (*planner*, *owner*, *designer*, *builder* and *subcontractor*), in a two-dimensional matrix arrangement in which each cell is meant to represent a unique abstraction (orthogonal to all others) over the system. However, it recognizes that each row must include the constraints from the row below (transitively), which roughly corresponds to the conformance concept referred to above, and the semantics of some of the focus words imply some sort of precedence. For instance, *why* should be used to justify which *what* to use, from several possible, and the *what* in turn imposes constraints on *how* to implement. The relative order of *where*, *who* and *when* is subject to a greater variability.

AN N-DIMENSONAL ARCHITECTURE FRAMEWORK

Not counting time (each stage takes time to complete), Figure 1 includes an implicit dimension, versions, because the architecture can be successively changed and improved, but even so it does not capture all the most important aspects. In particular, we need two additional axes:

- **Concerns:** The Zachman focus words (*what*, *how*, *where*, *who*, *when*, *why*) are generic but do not address the entire focus range. Other questions can be made, such as *whence* (where from), *whither* (where to), *how much* (quantitative assessment) and *how well* (qualitative assessment). It is important to be able to express the dynamics of the architecture, its quality (how good it is, quantitatively and qualitatively) and other stakeholders' concerns (financial, regulatory compliance, domain specific, and so on). TOGAF's (The Open Group, 2009) architecture principles fit in here. This axis can be organized into categories of concerns, from more qualitative to more quantitative;
- **Concreteness:** Each stage in Figure 1 can be seen at a very high, abstract level, or at a very detailed, concrete level. We have discretized this axis into four levels: *conceptual*, *strategic*, *tactical* and *operational*.

These designations are usually mixed with the perspective axis (embedded into the motivations, ends, means and implementation stages, respectively), but note that it corresponds to a specific instantiation of the method, in which tactical decisions are made only after the strategy has been laid out and detailed. In other words, the strategy is the motivation for the tactics. However, the motivation for the tactics should be a refinement of the motivation for the strategy and not a consequence of strategy design. We can have the implementation perspective at a conceptual level (ideas on how to do it) as well as the motivations perspective at an operational level (justification for the lowest level objectives). Perspectives and their level of concreteness are orthogonal concepts. The operational level is the bridge to system design.

The two dimensional lifecycle of Figure 1 (perspectives and versions) is in fact a projection of a four dimensional space, including all axes. Figure 2 depicts only three, by considering only one version. Other axes could be considered by promoting some relevant concerns to axes, such as maturity, security and regulatory compliance. In general, an architecture framework is N-dimensional but, for the sake of simplicity, several axes are collapsed into a value along some other, more relevant axis and dealt with in a qualitative fashion only.

The *concerns* axis is simplified, conveying only the perception that the concerns near the origin are more subjective and qualitative, whereas those at the other end are more objective and quantitative. The *perspectives* axis includes the stages of Figure 1, not shown for simplicity (motivations are near the origin).

The *concreteness* axis shows four levels, from conceptual, more fuzzy and abstract, down to operational, more detailed and concrete. Each level is a refinement of the level above it, by including decisions that turn some abstract aspects into concrete ones. Strategy and tactics are usually bound to the notion of course of action (Malik, 2009) and therefore it may seem strange that the motivations stage, for example, can be described at the strategic, tactic and even operational levels. However, as motivations are progressively detailed and made more concrete, they have to include some notion of approach. The strategical and tactical levels of the motivations stage, for instance, describe the

Figure 2. The pool metaphor: a 3-dimensional architecture framework

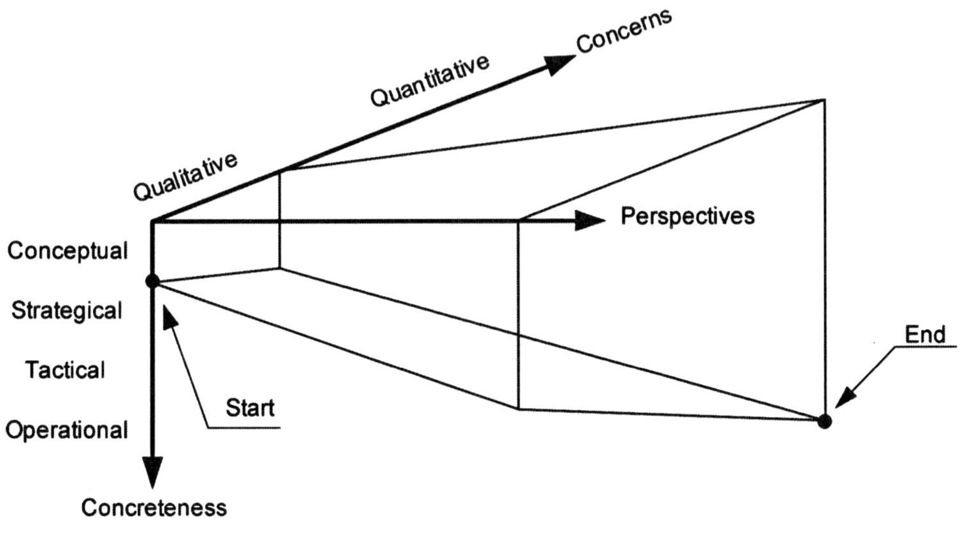

motivations for the strategy and tactics to use in subsequent stages.

In the same way, policies and rules appear in the Business Motivation Model (Malik, 2009) as directives in the course of action stemming from tactics and motivated by a SWOT-type assessment, which clearly should appear in the motivation stage and not afterwards, in the means stage.

In fact, we can look at each horizontal plane (parallel to the concerns-perspectives plane) as global descriptions of the system at increasingly depths of detail and concreteness. The top plane (*conceptual*) is a view that describes essentially the main concepts, ideas and features, both in the various perspectives (motivations, ends, means, and so on) and in stakeholder's concerns. The next plane (*strategical*) is a refinement of the previous one, with decisions that reflect a strategic approach by making it partially more concrete. The same happens in the two lower planes (*tactical* and *operational*), with increasingly level of refinement and detail. Each plane can lead to different lower planes, according to the decisions taken and approach followed.

These planes correspond roughly to the main rows of the Zachman framework (*planner*, *owner*, *designer* and *builder*). TOGAF also includes a level of detail dimension (and strategy as the top level), but with refinement essentially linked to structure, with the strategic level architecture decomposed into segment (business areas) and capability (business units) level architectural units. Aspect refinement in TOGAF is accomplished by considering different types of architectures, or domains (*business*, *data*, *application* and *technology*), which may have its justification in terms of current technology (namely, by separating data and applications, which assumes the process paradigm) but that in practice tend to act as architectural silos. The concreteness axis in Figure 2 supports both structural decomposition and aspect refinement.

Note that, in our framework, both the perspectives and concreteness axes reflect features of the method itself (nature of considerations and level of refinement) and not stakeholder's perspectives of the system (Zachman) nor architectural units, types or domains (TOGAF).

Vertical planes that are parallel to the concreteness-perspectives plane correspond to concern oriented views (for example, looking at everything from the security or compliance point of views). Vertical planes that are parallel to the concreteness-concerns plane correspond to considering every issue in each perspective (for example, the ends, namely goals and objectives, to achieve under the various concerns at various levels of detail).

Like most architectural frameworks (Minoli, 2008), ours is recursive (Greefhorst & Proper, 2011), in the sense that progression downwards the concreteness axis can be made by aspect refinement or structural decomposition. In the latter case, each subsystem can be modeled by the same framework. The architecture concept can thus refer to a set of interacting enterprises, an enterprise, a department, a business unit, and so on, down to the level of a small module in an application. It all depends on the granularity envisaged.

The method to develop the architecture can be pictured in Figure 2 as the path taken from the initial steps, near the origin and with very little detail (referred to as *start*), down to the last perspectives (operation, evaluation), quantitative concerns and full level of detail (referred to as *end*). Figure 2 looks like a *pool*, shallow and narrow near the origin (start), more abstract and less detailed, and deep and wide at the opposite point (end).

The surface of this pool reflects the executive view of the system, with everything at the conceptual level. The bottom of this pool corresponds to the concepts and/or modules that already exist and which the top plane must be mapped onto. Near the origin, the bottom maps onto large, high level, abstract concepts. Near the end, the bottom maps onto small, low level, concrete modules.

Any development method starts with a high level description of an entity that is decomposed and mapped onto already existing, lower level entities, usually in a mixed top-down and bottom-up approach. This corresponds to the functional and constructional views, respectively, identified by Hoogervorst (2004; 2009) in the context of enterprise architecture. This decomposition can be made in features (a specification becomes more detailed) or in structure (an entity is partitioned into several others, less complex).

In this example, the bottom of the pool is a surface, not necessarily a plane (since not all existing entities will have the same level of detail), but it usually leans toward the end to reflect the fact that the mapping is initially rather abstract but gets concrete and detailed at the end.

Several paths from start to end are possible, yielding several possible methods, such as:

- **Top Plane Downwards:** Consider all concerns in each stage of the perspective axis at the conceptual level and then repeat for each of the lower concreteness levels;
- **Front Plane Backwards:** Do the same for only one concern and then iterate over all concerns;
- **Left Plane Rightwards:** Consider all concerns and detail all levels for each perspective, then repeat for all perspectives;
- **Spiral Downwards:** Evolve the perspectives at the conceptual level and with qualitative concerns only, then repeat but now at the next lower concreteness level and including more concerns (towards the quantitative end), successively until the bottom;
- **Origin Outwards:** Evolve progressively from the origin, increasing the concreteness depth and the quantitative nature of concerns for each successive perspective.

The last one seems to be the most natural, since it builds detail in a sustainable fashion from all axes, instead of fully developing a partial view before backtracking and developing the rest. Due to complexity, architecture development methods are usually a mixture of these (for example, origin outwards with just a few key concerns and then repeat with more concerns).

THE FRONT PLANE

Figure 3 details the front plane of Figure 2. Concerns exhibit a greater variability (Kurpjuweit & Winter, 2009) and will not be detailed here. The implementation column also includes test

Figure 3. The front plane: perspectives and concreteness

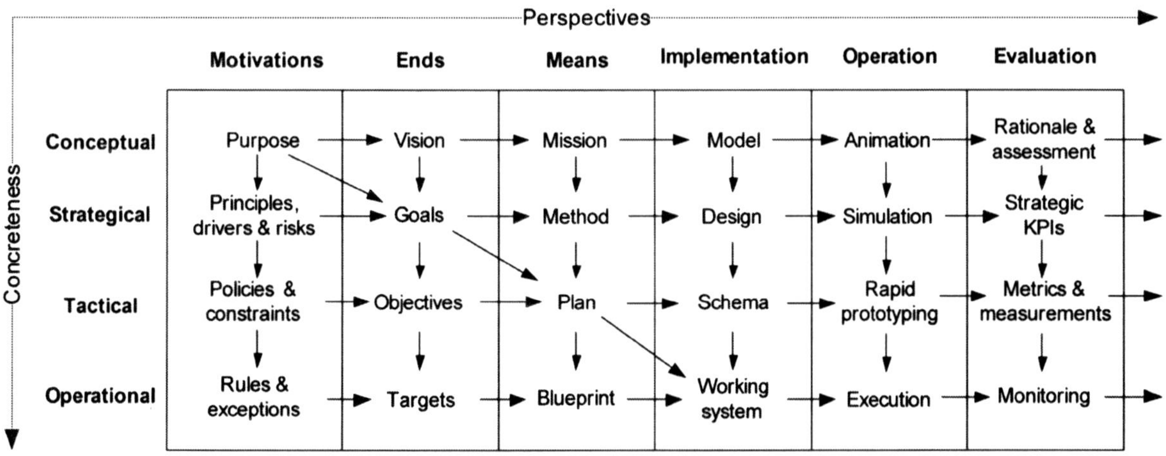

and deployment, but these details are ignored for simplicity, and only the outcome is represented.

This figure reflects the basic steps of the method in this plane and can be read as follows:

- Each column represents each perspective over the architecture, in increasingly level of concreteness from top to bottom (more detailed description below);
- Each row represents an iteration over all the perspectives, at a given level of concreteness. For example, at the conceptual level, *Purpose* is what justifies the existence of this architecture, *Vision* is what is expects to achieve, *Mission* is what it must accomplish to reach the vision, *Model* is an organization to carry out the mission, model *Animation* conceptually exercises the architecture, probably in a scenario based setup, and *Rationale & assessment* evaluates that animation and provides the top level insight on the adequacy of the model to accomplish the vision and honor the purpose. Lower rows refine and detail this pipeline of perspectives;
- Each cell represents one perspective at a given level of concreteness;
- The arrows represent possible transitions between cells;
- Only rightwards and downwards transitions are represented, but the evaluation perspective can loop leftwards to the motivations perspective, as indicated in Figure 1. Actually, any cell can make a leftwards transition to the first column or upwards to the first row, to allow some change to be performed. The important issue is to acknowledge that any cell must be derived from another that is either leftwards, upwards or both. Any other transition is a loop and must backtrack to the first column and/or row (to ensure forward consistency) and repeat the complete iteration;
- Transitions are not limited to vertical or horizontal moves, not even to adjacent cells, but that means leaping over intermediate steps and therefore greater effort and less support (from the development method) in performing the transition. Figure 3 exemplifies this by showing direct transitions from *Purpose* to *Goals*, *Goals* to *Plan* and *Plan* to the *Working system*. Usually, this corresponds to laying down goals and programming processes directly from them;
- An architecture development method (in this front plane) is the path taken from the *Purpose* cell down to the *Monitoring* cell, in which the architecture is being exercised in full detail. Incomplete paths can be useful for partial goals of the development method. For instance:
    - Traversing only the first row (conceptual level) is useful for producing executive level documentation and rationale;
    - Stopping at the *Means* column produces documentation, at a level of detail that depends on how low the traversal went;
    - Reaching the *Evaluation* column, but above *Monitoring*, can be used to partially exercise the architecture to draw conclusions, such as statistical simulation or user interface animation for rapid prototyping.

In a closer look, each column can be described as:

- **Motivations:** These are the result of contextual requirements and express the issues that must be dealt with to satisfy those requirements, acting as motivation and justification for the ensuing perspectives. At the top level, we have the *Purpose*, the starting point of any architecture development method, which reflects the essence and the reason for the existence of this architecture. The *Principles, drivers & risks* refine the *Purpose* by establishing not only the basic tenets that this architecture must obey but also the enablers and inhibitors that foster and limit the characteristics of the architecture (resulting probably from a SWOT analysis – *Strengths*, *Weaknesses*, *Opportunities* and *Threats*). The *Policies & constraints* perform a similar role, but at a lower level and greater detail, which in turn are refined into *Rules & exceptions* (special cases), at the *Operational* level. It is important to realize that polices and rules stem directly from the refinement of the motivations, instead of appearing only as part of the mission accomplishment (although they may be further refined in a subsequent iteration);

- **Ends:** These are the expectations established for the architecture and that are justified by the *Motivations*. At the top level, the *Vision* corresponds to the global scenario sought that fulfills the purpose. The vision is refined and decomposed into *Goals*, which express, usually in a qualitative way, a desired state or set of properties to achieve. Goals are in turn refined into *Objectives*, concrete enough to be declared SMART (*Specific*, *Measureable*, *Achievable*, *Realistic* and *Time framed*). *Targets* are lower level and simpler objectives, at the atomic level (which cannot be further decomposed) or close. Note that refinement along the *concreteness* axis can be accomplished by detailing features or by structural decomposition. In this case, a vision can entail several goals, each goal can be made concrete by several objectives and each objective can require several targets to be achieved;
- **Means:** These specify what needs to be done in order to meet the expectations. The *Mission* is the top level expression of the type of actions to carry out, the *Method* is a refinement of the mission by including the choice of an approach or paradigm, the *Plan* is a graph of steps that make the method concrete by choosing a set of techniques and the *Blueprint* is a set of actions that detail the plan by choosing a set of algorithms. The method here refers to the high level plan underlying a specific architecture and should not be mixed up with the architecture development method that we are describing;
- **Implementation:** This column specifies the tools, languages and procedures to provide an implementation of the means, by transforming them into workable representations. It is a simplification of what should include development, test and deployment, but for simplicity we consider only the resulting representations, disregarding what needs to be done to produce them and assuming that they are correct and in place to be worked upon. The *Model* is an overall representation of the architecture chosen to carry out the mission, expressed in some notation, such as UML. The *Design* details the model, structuring it into modules, or subsystems, and establishing their interactions. The *Schema* is the description of each module, usually as a black or grey box. The *Working system* makes this modules white, by providing additional details (such as data and code);
- **Operation:** This column exercises the system with this architecture, either to operate it in real conditions or just to get insight about its quality, in both functional (how well does it fulfill the motivations) and non-functional (how much does it comply with a set of fulfilment criteria) terms. At the conceptual level, we can only imagine what will happen by *Animation* of scenarios and use cases (nevertheless, important

to check global behavior). *Simulation* can abstract many details by using statistical models and still obtain meaningful insight into the behavior (in statistical terms). *Rapid prototyping* works with partial specifications (not statistical, but not fully implemented modules, either) and enables exercising some specific concerns (user interfaces, for instance). At the lower level, *Execution* corresponds to exercising the completely implemented system, under real conditions;

- **Evaluation:** This is the assessment of the operation, so that changes and improvements can be introduced, if deemed necessary to better fulfill the purpose in the *motivations* perspective. At the top level, *Rationale & assessment* perform reasoning over the scenario and use case animation. Simulation provides the inputs to *Strategic KPIs*, which can be checked against the *Principles, drivers & risks* in *Motivations*. *Metrics & measurements* can check how well and how much the *Policies & constraints* in *Motivations* are satisfied. *Monitoring* checks events and serves as the basis for all higher level evaluation procedures, assessing whether all *Rules & exceptions* in *Motivations* are deal with satisfactorily.

FROM PURPOSE TO WORKING SYSTEM

Assuming that we are aiming at developing the architecture and fully implementing the system, we need to take the path *Working system*, *Execution* and *Monitoring*. This corresponds to commissioning the system and typically is not achieved in the first iteration. Before that, we need to tackle the rightmost columns at higher levels, either during prototyping, product development and first trials.

We ignore the details of these activities, since we are concentrating on the first perspectives, and we concentrate on which paths we can take in Figure 3 from *Purpose* to *Working system*. Each path corresponds to one (pure) method but, since systems are structured and each subsystem needs to follow the full path, we can conceive a more flexible method that adjusts the path taken according to the characteristics of each subsystem.

Three radical paths exist in Figure 3:

- **Breadth-first:** Go along the conceptual level until the *Implementation* column is reached and then plunge until the *Working system*. This is the worst path. Initially all goes well, since we are evolving only with concepts, but when we want to detail we have no support from intermediate steps, so we need to decide everything on the spot and on the fly, without a guiding map. Actually, the way most systems are developed is even worse, since they are limited to the *Implementation* column (they start by layingt out a *Model*, without previous considerations);
- **Depth-first:** Work as much as possible at the *Motivations* column, successively detailing from Purpose down to *Rules & exceptions*, and then follow right at this detailed level until the *Working system*. This seems the best path, since everything is thoroughly justified, but crashes into complexity, loses sight of overall picture and takes the risk of deciding everything at high level, without taking into account possible implementation restrictions and limitations;
- **Straight line:** Traverse the front plane in a straight line (*Purpose*, *Goals*, *Plan* and *Working system*). This is a tradeoff between the previous two, evolving along the *perspectives* axis at the same time that concreteness is increased. It is better than the breadth-first path, because each con-

cretization level is based on information from the previous column, and it is better than the depth-first path because each perspective is based on information from the previous concretization level. In a word, it is *incremental*. However, the steps are rather long, deriving a plan directly from (high level) goals and producing a working system directly from a non-detailed plan. Nevertheless, it is commonly used: processes are typically programmed with goals in mind (checked afterwards), but without a sustained method to derive activities from goals.

Two other types of paths can be used:

- **Stairway:** Move only vertically or horizontally, to keep steps as small and incremental as possible. It is not mandatory to alternate vertical and horizontal steps, in a perfect stairway (more than one move in the same direction is possible), but in general terms it makes sense (corresponds to the straight line in which a diagonal step is replaced by two steps, one vertical e another horizontal, or vice-versa). A possible path would be *Purpose*, *Principles, drivers & risks*, *Goals*, *Objectives*, *Plan*, *Blueprint* and *Working system*. This way, and as an example, *Goals* would be refined into *Objectives* before deriving the *Plan*, which gives a better understanding of what needs to be done;
- **Multipath:** The stairway is fine but loses path opportunities. For example, going from *Goals* to *Plan* through *Objectives* does not take the *Method* into account. The idea of multipath is to take more than one path and combine the insight. For example, we can decompose *Goals* into *Objectives* taking into account that the *Plan* that will result from them must conform to the *Method* that has been adopted. Note that different plans can result by mapping objectives to a plan under different methods.

The conclusions to draw are essentially the following:

- Make transitions between adjacent cells only (this rules out diagonal transitions), to make small and sustained steps;
- At a first approach, always go depth-first, but only while complexity is manageable. Otherwise, go one step right. If iterations (versions) are considered, a subsequent iteration may be able to go deeper at a given column, due to the insight gained in previous iterations;
- Goals are a commonly used source to derive processes. Inasmuch as possible, refine them into objectives before delving into programming;
- Preferably use multipath, with alternative paths to a cell to combine all possible informations and better insight;
- When decomposing the system structurally, use a path that is adjusted to the nature of each subsystem. If it is complex, it is better to outsource details to simpler (sub) subsystems than insisting in making them explicit in that subsystem.

CHOOSING A PARADIGM: PROCESSES OR SERVICES?

The Zachman framework separates data (*what*) from function (*how*). TOGAF separates the data architecture from the application architecture. Other enterprise architecture frameworks (Minoli, 2008) do essentially the same. They are also recursive, in the sense that they can be applied to a large enterprise as well as to a small module in an application. In practice, however, granularity tends to be very high. The complexity of the entire set of considerations and rationale is enough to grant its applicability only to the entire enterprise or to reasonably sized units within an enterprise.

In this context, and by separating data from applications, these frameworks implicitly assume that:

- There is a shared data repository, with the existence of a canonical data model as typical architectural principle (Greefhorst & Proper, 2011);
- Applications read, process and update the data stored in this shared repository.

In doing so, there is an implicit choice of the process paradigm that is inherent to the frameworks themselves. This separation is also a good match to the N-tier architectural style (Figure 4), in which application logic (processes) is separated from the database. This is not merely a question of paradigm, but also a result of technological issues (such as database implementation and optimization). The presentation tier is also separated, but for different reasons (such as interface independence and security).

This centralization of data and its separation from applications is a classical, but unnecessary assumption (restriction) that has raised many problems in the area of EAI (Enterprise Architecture Integration), when business processes cross the boundaries of the architecture of an enterprise. Each tier is a functional silo.

The same can be said about the maintainability and adaptability of an enterprise's architecture, in which unintended effects of changes easily propagate throughout the shared data. It is hard to keep track of which data is used by or affects which processes and CRUD matrices do not scale well with complexity.

Another disadvantage of this paradigm is that the architecture development method has to deal with the semantic gap between the business, seen as a set of interacting entities, both inter- and intra-enterprise, and the data/application architecture level, which removes the boundaries of these entities instead of modeling them as they appear at the business level.

Object-oriented programming has long abandoned the shared data model of structured programming, by structuring the programs according to some principles that tend to limit the impact of a change (affecting fewer objects) and to increase the adaptability (allowing objects to be adapted, even without the source code), namely:

- **The Least Semantic Gap Principle:** The entities in the problem and solution spaces should have a one to one mapping, by modeling each problem entity with a solution

Figure 4. A typical N-tier system

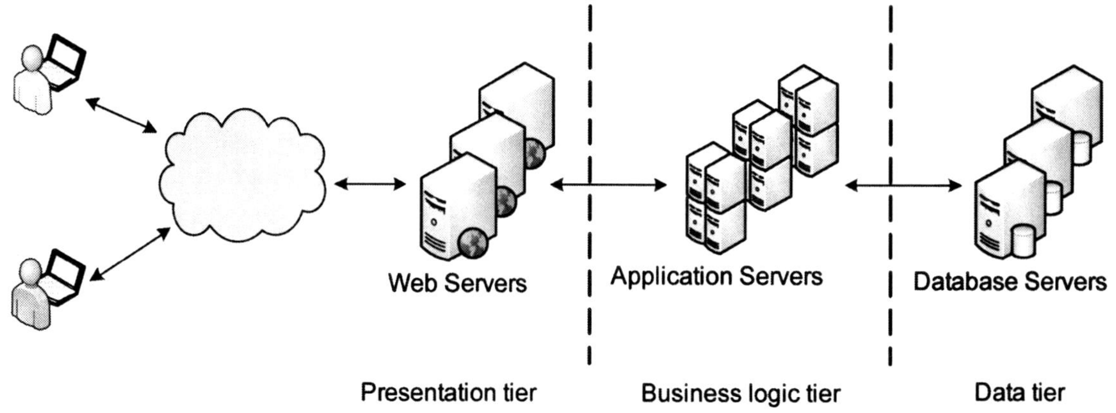

entity, with includes both state and related behavior;

- **The Information Hiding Principle:** which states that there must be a clear separation between interface (syntax and semantics) and its implementation (both code and data). This reduces the change propagation effect. A change in one object affects those that use it only if its interface is affected.

In a distributed, not necessarily restricted to software, context such as an enterprise or a group of enterprises, the *object* and its *interface* are replaced by the *resource* and the *service*, respectively. The goal is to benefit from the advantages heralded by object-oriented programming in the enterprise architecture context, without being restricted to software or to a centralized application.

Services and processes are dual of each other. Where there is a service, there is a process and vice-versa. The question is which paradigm is used first and foremost in modeling an enterprise's architecture, with the other derived from it. The relationship between resources, services and processes can be briefly described in the following way:

- A *resource* is anything of any nature (material, virtual, conceptual, noun, action, and so on) that embodies a meaningful, complete and discrete concept that makes sense by itself and can be distinguished from, although interact with, other resources. A resource can be an application, a small software module, a person, a truck, an enterprise, and so on;
- A resource can be atomic (an indivisible whole) or structured (recursively composed of other resources, its *components*, with respect to which it performs the role of *container*). Each component can only have one direct container (yielding a strong composition model, in a tree shaped resource structure);
- A *service* is a set of logically related operations of a resource. In other words, it is a *facet* of that resource that makes sense in terms of modeling of the envisaged system. A service is pure behavior (albeit the implementation of concrete operations may depend on state) that needs a resource (and eventually its components) to be implemented. In most cases, only one service will be defined for each resource, but in other cases, usually more complex, it makes sense to organize the full set of the resource's operations into several services;
- Resources interact by sending each other messages. A resource R_X that sends a message to a resource R_Y is in fact invoking a (or the) service of R_Y, as long as the operation which that message stimulates belongs to that service. This constitutes a *service transaction* between these two resources, in which the resources R_X and R_Y perform the role of *service consumer* and *service provider*, respectively. A service transaction can entail other service transactions, as part of the (chain) reaction to the message on part of the service provider. Note that a service should be defined in terms of reactions to messages (an external view) and not in terms of state transitions or activity flows (an internal view);
- A *process* is a graph of all service transactions that are allowed to occur, starting with a service transaction initiated at some resource R_X and ending with a final service transaction, which neither reacts back nor initiates new service transactions. The process corresponds to a use case of resource R_X and usually involves other resources as service transactions flow (including loops, eventually).

Resources entail structure, state and behavior. Services refer only to behavior, without implying a specific implementation. Processes are a view on the behavior sequencing and flow along services, which are implemented by resources. These are informal definitions, proposed in this chapter in a modeling context, but are part of a model inspired in real life, applicable not only to computer science but also to humans (themselves resources) and any other type of resources.

For physical resources, the strong composition model is the most adequate. No two resources can share the same physical space and any object is located inside another. Moving an object from one box to the other is actually a *migration*.

In terms of services, the *society metaphor* is the most familiar to us. Some resource (person or organization) executes an activity as a request of and on behalf of another. Actually, service transactions constitute the foundations of our society. Each resource, from the outside, constitutes a black box which we deal with only by indirect means (by sending it a message). Each person, organization, and so on, can offer a different service (usually called *role*).

Figure 5 depicts an example of such a model. R_X, R_Y, R_W and R_Z are resources. R_Y exemplifies resource structure. Its interior reveals three resources, of which one is also structured, with two resources inside (relationships omitted for simplicity).

S_X, S_Y, S_W and S_Z are services offered by R_X, R_Y, R_W and R_Z, respectively, and its operations are graphically represented by the trapezoid on the left side of each resource (only one is represented, but any combination of operations can be used to define a service). Structured resources, such as R_Y, can offer both behavior (in the form of services) and structure (in the form of internal resources accessible from its exterior).

The operations of a service are implemented by a resource by a set of actions, including sending a message to another service. In this example, an operation in S_X invokes S_Y, which in turn invokes S_W and S_Z. This flow of invocations of operations (and of the execution of individual actions within each operation) forms a process, exemplified by activities A_X, A_Y, A_W and A_Z, in Figure 5b.

We consider two main paradigm possibilities, although there are others, such as rule based (Vasilecas & Smaizys, 2010):

Figure 5. An example of resources, services, and processes: (a) resources with services; (b) process view as a flow of service invocations

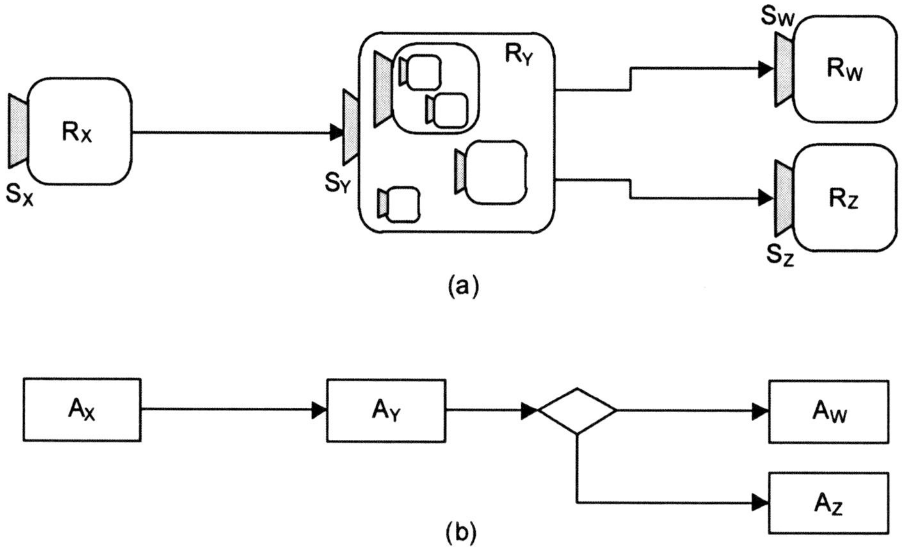

- **Processes Over Services:** This is the case of Figure 5b and consists of modeling the system's use cases by processes, spanning over all the services that it needs to invoke. Use cases tend to be system wide and processes can be very long. It should be noted that services are needed at least to provide system (platform) primitive functionality;
- **Services Over Processes:** This the case of Figure 5a, in which the model contemplates interacting entities, not system wide processes. Each entity sees only the interface of the other entities it interacts with (information hiding). There is a close mapping between business entities and model entities (small semantic gap). The execution of a service's operation can be seen as a process, which passes control to another process in the service that it happens to invoke.

At some point in the architecture development method, a choice must be made over whether to use processes or services at the top paradigm to model the course of action. With most frameworks, this is made right from the start, by using processes over services, albeit some parts of the methods are agnostic on this. In the framework of Figure 3, this decision can be deferred until the *Method* cell in the *Means* column. Up to that point, the method deals with motivations and goals (which establish dependencies but not any form of control flow). At that point, there is the flexibility of choosing processes over services or services over processes.

We clearly argue in favor of the services over processes (service, for short) paradigm, in which we recognize the following main advantages:

- **Lower Semantic Gap:** resulting from a much closer match between a set of interacting entities (which fundamentally is what any business is), a set of resources with their services. Any model will be easier to change if its abstractions match the entities it models. A sale, for example, will be the result of the cooperation of several entities (users, employees, information system, logistics, etc.). These entities are much closer to the service paradigm, since processes do not exist as real world entities. A small semantic gap reduces the maintainability and adaptability efforts. A small change in the system requirements translates to a small change in the system's architecture, due to that close match;
- **Information Hiding:** which limits the impact of changes and also contributes to increased changeability and adaptability. Processes are usually modeled after use cases (global uses of a system) and therefore tend to span across a large part of that system. Several processes will use the same service. A change in one service has potential impact in many processes. In contrast, services use the outsourcing mechanism and the information hiding principle. For example, consider that in Figure 5a resource R_X is a customer that invokes S_Y to place a purchase order. The implementation of this service, supported on R_Y, is partially outsourced to resources R_W and R_Z, by invoking their services, S_W and S_Z, but service S_Y knows nothing about them apart from their interface. In the same way, the customer R_X knows nothing of the implementation of S_Y, which can replace S_W and/or S_Z by other services without the knowledge of the customer, as long as the functionality of S_Y is maintained (a form of polymorphism). In contrast, this change would have impacted the corresponding process, laid out in Figure 5b. The conclusion is clear: don't use long processes; structure them into services instead.

In what modeling and change is concerned, the service paradigm is much better than the process paradigm, and the way to go to make enterprises agile (Uram & Stephenson, 2005).

FROM N-TIER TO TIERLESS

What is the impact of using services instead of processes as the main paradigm? We use the N-tier architectural style of Figure 4 to illustrate it. In modeling terms, in a classical N-tier architecture, each entity is spread throughout the various tiers, as depicted in Figure 6a. By changing to a service oriented paradigm, we are collapsing all the bits of each tier that pertain to a given entity into one resource, which becomes a first class citizen in a tierless society of interacting resources. Each of these resources includes (conceptually) its own independent database, holding the permanent data.

Regarding implementation, the resources that reside in the same server can map their conceptual databases onto the same DBMS, but with logically separate records (Ahmad & Bowman, 2011), as depicted in Figure 6b, which can be tables or objects, depending on the underlying model of the DBMS. Note that this has no impact on the service of each record, since the service is an interface at the entity level, not database access level.

This is a flexible arrangement (since data is logically partitioned and bound with the behavior that manages that data), which exploits the essential advantages of services referred to above in a distributed environment, either between enterprises or within the enterprise itself.

However, this raises two main problems:

- How to derive the specification of services in the context of the architecture development framework of Figure 3. This issue is dealt with in the next section;
- Users normally access the system by a browser and notifications usually involve e-mail. It should be apparent from Figure 6b that we introduced a huge change in the

Figure 6. Migration from an N-tier system (a) to a tierless, potentially distributed society of interacting resources (b)

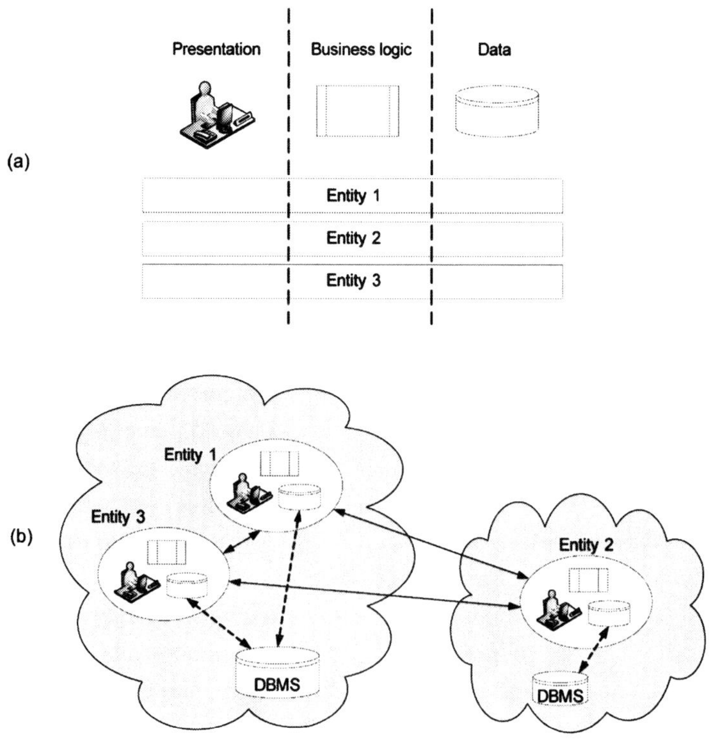

user interface. User roles became active and can contact each other directly. A user role is no longer a module in the business logic tier, with presentation on one side and a database on the other, but it is now a self-contained resource, with all the behavior and persistent data that it needs. It becomes a first class resource, supporting services. The browser is no longer sufficient because it must now also provide services (his roles) to their fellow resources (other users and computer applications). There are two main solutions for this:

- To maintain each of the entities as software modules, hosted in a server, but in which the interface resides remotely, in a browser. This is the equivalent of having a private N-tier architecture for each entity;
- To use a *browserver* (Delgado, 2012) composed of a browser and a local server working in tight cooperation, in a single package, running in the user's laptop (or other personal device). The advantages are
  - Privacy is tighter (sensitive information stays with the user);
  - Workflow interactivity is increased. If the user needs to be contacted to fill in some form or to setup a meeting, for example, his role will open up a window, without technological workarounds for the browser limitations, such as Comet (Crane & McCarthy, 2008);
  - Continuous presence (when the user is offline or his laptop is disconnected) can be maintained, by resorting to a reverse proxy.

THE IMPORTANCE OF OBJECTIVES

As the straight line path from *Purpose* to *Working system* in Figure 3 illustrates, a common development method consists of establishing business goals (typically KPIs and large granularity functionalities) and modeling processes that are implemented (generating BPEL from BPMN, for example), executed and checked for goal compliance. This is largely the work of analysts and modelers, receiving little support from the method.

To improve on this scenario, we make two basic proposals:

- To use services, instead of processes, as the main paradigm (discussed above);
- To refine goals into objectives first and derive the services from them (discussed in this section).

Vision, *Goal*, *Objective* and *Target*, the terms used in the *Ends* column of Figure 3, are types of expectations (desired accomplishments) that differ in their degree of concreteness. A vision is very high level and with almost no details, such as the *one PC in every desk* vision of Microsoft in the early days of personal computing. A target is something very concrete, such as issuing a receipt after payment. Goals and objectives lie in the between, with objectives concrete enough to be considered SMART (*Specific*, *Measurable*, *Achievable*, *Realistic* and *Time framed*).

The distinction between goals and objectives is not clear cut. In requirements engineering (Anwer & Ikram, 2006), the terminology is different (*soft goals* and *hard goals*, or goals for short), but the notion of different levels of concreteness is the same. A goal can be refined (made more concrete) into objectives by decomposing it into subgoals (goals on which it depends) recursively, until these subgoals are concrete enough to be considered objectives.

Figure 7. An example of a goal graph

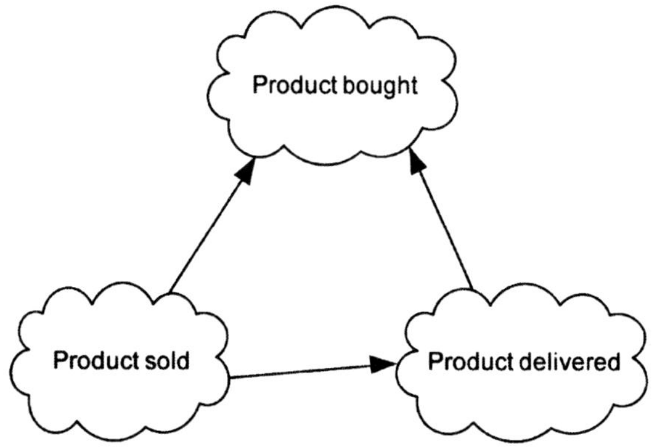

Consider a simple example in which a customer wants to buy a product, which requires some entity to sell it and another to deliver it. Three role types can easily be identified and a goal graph can be built, such as the one in Figure 7. In this example, each goal will be the responsibility of (owned by) a different entity. Arrows establish goal dependencies. Incoming arrows indicate the subgoals that need to be fulfilled so that the goal becomes fulfilled in turn. Dependency on subgoals can be AND (by default) or OR (example in Figure 8). The cloud notation reflects the fuzzy nature of goals.

In process based modeling, this would be considered a use case of the seller and a process would be drawn to implement it, starting with a customer request, including a payment transaction and ending by the delivery of the product. Other use cases (such as requesting a quotation) can be envisaged, each implemented by a process that encompasses all entities involved. The processes tend to be system wide, which makes them more prone to be affected by a change, wherever it needs to occur.

In Figure 3, this corresponds to deciding to use the process paradigm and to building a plan (a high level process) or even a blueprint (a detailed process) directly from the goals. However, and as argued above, a better method consists of deferring transtition to the *Means* column and staying in the *Ends* column a bit longer, refining the goals into objectives (without deciding on services or processes yet). This is equivalent of detailing a model before starting the implementation path.

Figure 8 illustrates such a refinement with an objective graph, considering two possibilities, buying at a (physical) store or online. For simplicity, many details are omitted (such as payment of the delivery). We assume that the product is small and delivery is needed only in the online store (the customer will carry the product in the physical store). The objectives enclosed by the rightmost cloud correspond to the refinement of the *Product delivered* goal and are the responsibility of the delivery company. Those enclosed by the cloud in the center refine the *Product sold* goal and are the responsibility of the company selling the product. The remaining objectives refine the *Product bought* goal and are the responsibility of the customer.

Note that:

- Identifying roles of actors (active and interacting entities) and assigning responsibility for objectives is not always clear cut or mutually exclusive. For example, the *Product payed* objectives are common to the customer and to the selling company (that is why they are shown partially in and out of the center cloud). This objective has to be further refined and decomposed into payment and receiving subobjectives, which can now be assigned to only one actor. The same happens with the *Purchase ordered* objective, which is a common objective to the customer and selling company, needing to be further refined into, for example, *Purchase order sent* and *Purchase order received*;
- The goal and objective graphs are not operational diagrams, expressing either activity or state transition. They merely express dependencies and what needs to be accomplished to achieve something at a higher level. The order, timing and policy (eager

Figure 8. An example of an objective graph. Clouds indicate clusters of objective responsibility

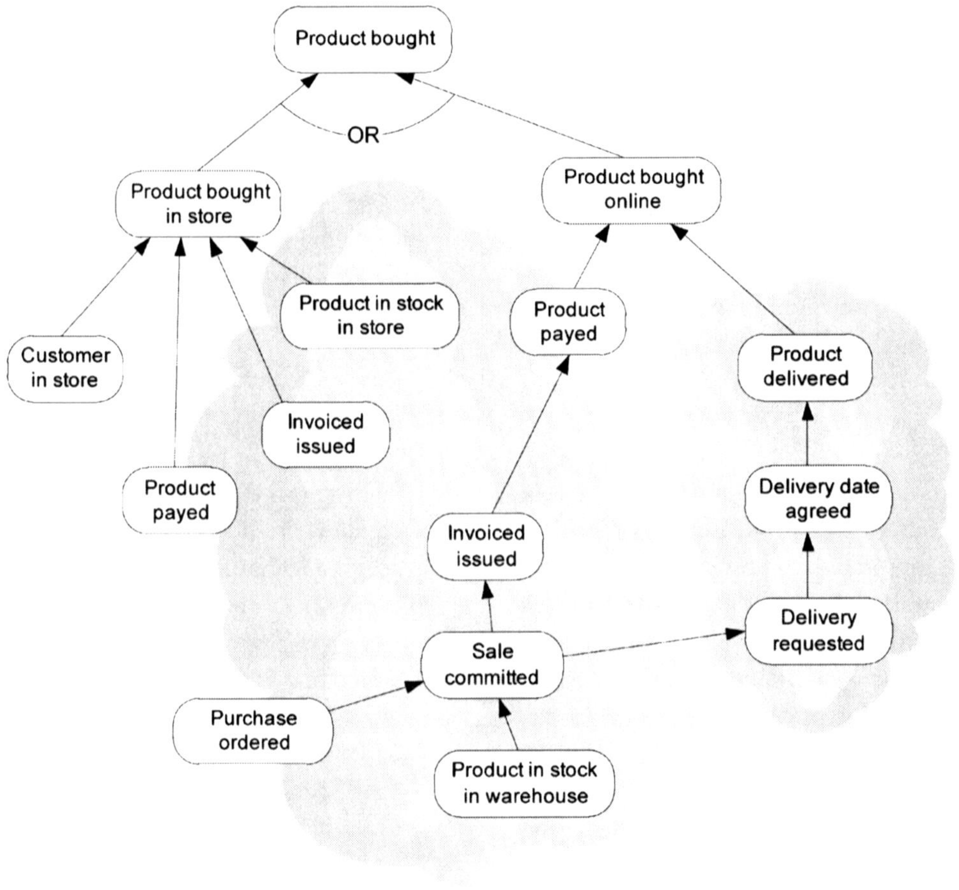

or lazy) of accomplishment are to be decided later.

The decomposition of goals into objectives, before deciding further aspects, not only allows to identify the intervening actors but also contributes to elaborate their plan and blueprint (Figure 3), namely in terms of the operations they need to support. Any objective must be refined until it can be mapped onto an operation, which will be defined in the actor that has the responsibility to fulfill that objective. In this particular example, from a simple inspection we conclude that we need at least the following operations:

- **Customer:**
  - Pay product;
  - Send purchase order;
  - Schedule a delivery date (interacting with delivery company);
  - Receive product;
  - Carry product;
- **Selling Company:**
  - Process purchase request;
  - Check stock;
  - Issue invoice;
  - Receive payment;
  - Request delivery;
  - Hand over product (to customer or delivery company);

- **Delivery Company:**
  - Receive delivery request;
  - Receive product to deliver;
  - Schedule a delivery date (interacting with customer);
  - Deliver product.

The interactions between actors (namely in purchasing, paying and delivering) express choreographies that have to be specified in detail. Now is the time, but not before, to decide if we are using the process or the service as the primary paradigm:

- With processes, we chain the activities resulting from the invocation of the various operations into a workflow, from the beginning until the end of the use case (in this case, purchase and delivery of a product);
- With services, we transform the objective of an operation into subobjectives and outsource them to the operations that implement them (in the same service or in another), not depending on their implementation (information hiding).

In the end, the set of elementary activities is very similar in both cases, but they differ in how they are organized. Services lead of a better structuring (with better information hiding and a lower semantic gap) that favors maintainability and adaptability.

FUTURE RESEARCH DIRECTIONS

Our main lines of research in the near future are the following:

- Refining the goals as much as possible before tackling design has great potential, but needs a graphical notation and editing tool to support it. There are several notations tools at the requirements level from the Requirements Engineering domain, such as those used with the Tropos (Fuxman *et al.*, 2004) and KAOS (Dardenne, van Lamsweerde & Fickas, 1993) frameworks, but that exibit limitations when increasing the detail and concreteness level, as well as establishing a bridging point to design. On the other hand, notations such as BPMN are committed to the process paradigm and do not allow reaping the benefits of the service paradigm. We are tackling this issue with an objective based notation and a graphical editor based on the Eclipse IDE;
- Technologies based on Web Services and BPEL (or RESTful applications, for that matter) are not adequate to implement the design stemming from the architecture development method described in this chapter. Web Services do not include code nor structure, introducing relevant limitations in the WS-* stack with respect to the support of the *Motivations* (namely policies) and *Means* (namely, structural decomposition of goals and objectives). BPEL, like BPMN, is committed to the process paradigm. RESTful applications are strong in structure but weak in the information hiding and semantic gap principles. We need a language and execution platform natively conceived for services. We are developing SIL (Service Implementation Language) for that purpose, based on the service paradigm, which has data interoperability based on structural compliance (Kokash & Arbab, 2009) and conformance (Kim & Shen, 2007), constituting a direct match for objectives and providing native support for policies.

CONCLUSION

Current enterprise architecture frameworks stratify architectures into layers (from business down to technology) and are inherently process based (by separating data, assumed to be shared in a database, from the behavior that manipulates it). This corresponds to having silos, both horizontally (layers) and vertically (tiers), which entail the well-known disadvantages in what changeability and adaptability are concerned.

Basic principles, such as low semantic gap (between problem and model entities) and information hiding, which we have learned to praise with object-oriented programming, have not reached the enterprise architecture world yet, given this separation of data and behavior.

In this chapter, we have argued that the service paradigm can support these principles, without loss of generality, simply by encapsulating data with the behavior that manages them and mapping these data logically onto a database but under information hiding. This corresponds to abandoning the classical N-tier architecture style in favor a society of interacting actors, each implementing one or more services.

To support this, we have presented a framework and architecture development method that, instead of being organized into horizontal layers, such as TOGAF or the Zachman frameworks, emphasizes business driven refinement (increasing level of detail and concreteness) and perspective derivation (what the architecture is and will do when exercised, the *means*, must be derived from business expectations, the *ends*, which in turn must be justified in business terms, the *motivations*).

Inspired by the Business Motivation Model, we have extended it with subsequent stages of architecture development, and argued that the transition from the expectations to the means should be done as late as possible (by refining and detailing as much as possible the expectations, from goals to much simpler objectives, which can then be seamlessly converted to operations of services). This entails a better support from the method and a smaller semantic gap between the business and the architecture, which has no horizontal layers (only refinement, but independently for each service). In turn, this reduces the effort involved in changes that result from maintenance or adaptations.

REFERENCES

Ahmad, M., & Bowman, I. (2011). Predicting system performance for multi-tenant database workloads. In *Proceedings of the Fourth International Workshop on Testing Database Systems* (pp. 6.1-6.6). ACM Press.

Anwer, S., & Ikram, N. (2006). Goal oriented requirement engineering: A critical study of techniques. In *Proceedings of the Software Engineering Conference* (pp. 121-130). IEEE Computer Society Press.

Bell, M. (2008). *Service-oriented modeling: Service analysis, design, and architecture*. New York: John Wiley & Sons.

Berkem, B. (2008). From the business motivation model (BMM) to service oriented architecture (SOA). *Journal of Object Technology*, *7*(8), 57–70. doi:10.5381/jot.2008.7.8.c6.

Castro, J., Kolp, M., & Mylopoulos, J. (2002). Towards requirements-driven information systems engineering: The Tropos project. *Information Systems*, *27*(6), 365–389. doi:10.1016/S0306-4379(02)00012-1.

Cheng, B., & Atlee, J. (2007). Research directions in requirements engineering. In *Proceedings of the Future of Software Engineering Symposium* (pp. 285-303). IEEE Computer Society Press.

Dardenne, A., van Lamsweerde, A., & Fickas, S. (1993). Goal-directed requirements acquisition. *Science of Computer Programming*, *20*(1-2), 3–50. doi:10.1016/0167-6423(93)90021-G.

Delgado, J. (2012). The user as a service. In Vidyarthi (Ed.), *Technologies and Protocols for the Future of Internet Design: Reinventing the Web* (pp. 37-59). Hershey, PA: Information Science Publishing. 10.4018/978-1-4666-0203-8.ch003

Dietz, J., & Hoogervorst, J. (2011). A critical investigation of TOGAF - Based on the enterprise engineering theory and practice. In Albani, Dietz, & Verelst, (Eds.), *Advances in Enterprise Engineering V* (pp. 76-90). Berlin: Springer-Verlag. doi:10.1007/978-3-642-21058-7_6.

Earl, T. (2007). *SOA: Principles of service design*. Upper Saddle River, NJ: Prentice Hall PTR.

Fuxman, A. et al. (2004). Specifying and analyzing early requirements in Tropos. *Requirements Engineering*, *9*(2), 132–150. doi:10.1007/s00766-004-0191-7.

Gehlert, A., Bramsiepe, N., & Pohl, K. (2008). Goal-driven alignment of services and business requirements. In *Proceedings of the International Workshop on Service-Oriented Computing Consequences for Engineering Requirements* (pp. 1-7). IEEE Computer Society Press.

Gordijn, J., Yu, E., & van der Raadt, B. (2006). e-Service design using i* and e3value modeling. *IEEE Software*, *23*(3), 26–33. doi:10.1109/MS.2006.71.

Greefhorst, D., & Proper, E. (2011). *Architecture principles: The cornerstones of enterprise architecture*. Berlin: Springer-Verlag. doi:10.1007/978-3-642-20279-7.

Hoogervorst, J. (2004). Enterprise architecture: Enabling integration, agility and change. *International Journal of Cooperative Information Systems*, *13*(3), 213–233. doi:10.1142/S021884300400095X.

Hoogervorst, J. (2009). *Enterprise governance and enterprise engineering*. Berlin: Springer-Verlag. doi:10.1007/978-3-540-92671-9.

Kim, D., & Shen, W. (2007). An approach to evaluating structural pattern conformance of UML models. In *Proceedings of the ACM Symposium on Applied Computing* (pp. 1404-1408). ACM Press.

Kokash, N., & Arbab, F. (2009). Formal behavioral modeling and compliance analysis for service-oriented systems. In Boer, F., Bonsangue, M., & Madelaine, E. (Eds.), *Formal Methods for Components and Objects (LNCS)* (*Vol. 5751*, pp. 21–41). Berlin: Springer-Verlag. doi:10.1007/978-3-642-04167-9_2.

Kruchten, P. (2004). *The rational unified process: An introduction*. Boston: Pearson Education Inc..

Kurpjuweit, S., & Winter, R. (2009). Concern-oriented business architecture engineering. In *Proceedings of the ACM Symposium on Applied Computing* (pp. 265-272). ACM Press.

Lankhorst, M., Proper, H., & Jonkers, H. (2009). The architecture of the archimate language. In Halpin, et al. (Eds.), *Enterprise, Business-Process and Information Systems Modeling* (pp. 367–380). Berlin: Springer-Verlag. doi:10.1007/978-3-642-01862-6_30.

Malik, N. (2009). Toward an enterprise business motivation model. *The Architecture Journal*, *19*, 10–16.

Markov, I., & Kowalkiewicz, M. (2008). Linking business goals to process models in semantic business process modeling. In *Proceedings of the International Enterprise Distributed Object Computing Conference* (pp. 332-338). IEEE Computer Society Press.

Minoli, D. (2008). *Enterprise architecture A to Z*. Boca Raton, FL: Auerbach Publications. doi:10.1201/9781420013702.

Nuseibeh, B., & Easterbrook, S. (2000). Requirements engineering: A roadmap. In *Proceedings of the Conference on The Future of Software Engineering* (pp. 35-46). ACM Press.

Quartel, D., Engelsman, W., Jonkers, H., & van Sinderen, M. (2009). A goal-oriented requirements modelling language for enterprise architecture. In *Proceedings of the International Conference on Enterprise Distributed Object Computing* (pp. 1-11). IEEE Press.

Regev, G., & Wegmann, A. (2005). Where do goals come from: The underlying principles of goal-oriented requirements engineering. In *Proceedings of the International Conference on Requirements Engineering* (pp. 353-362). IEEE Press.

Saeki, M. (2010). Semantic requirements engineering. In Nurcan, Salinesi, Souveyet, & Ralyté, (Eds.), *Intentional Perspectives on Information Systems Engineering* (pp. 67-82). Berlin: Springer-Verlag. doi:10.1007/978-3-642-12544-7_4.

Shroff, G. (2010). *Enterprise cloud computing: Technology, architecture, applications*. Cambridge, UK: Cambridge University Press. doi:10.1017/CBO9780511778476.

Sowa, J., & Zachman, J. (1992). Extending and formalizing the framework for information systems. *IBM Systems Journal, 31*(3), 590–616. doi:10.1147/sj.313.0590.

The Open Group. (2009). *TOGAF version 9 – The open group architecture framework (TOGAF)*. The Open Group.

Uram, M., & Stephenson, B. (2005). Services are the language and building blocks of an agile enterprise. In Pal, & Pantaleo, (Eds.), *The Agile Enterprise* (pp.49-86). New York, NY: Springer. doi:10.1007/0-387-25078-6_4.

van Lamsweerde, A. (2001). Goal-oriented requirements engineering- A guided tour. In *Proceedings of the International Symposium on Requirements Engineering* (pp. 249-262). IEEE Computer Society Press.

Vasilecas, O., & Smaizys, A. (2010). Business rule model integration into the model of transformation driven software development. In Grundspenkis, Kirikova, Manolopoulos, & Novickis, (Eds.), *Advances in Databases and Information Systems* (pp. 153-160). Berlin: Springer-Verlag. doi:10.1007/978-3-642-12082-4_20.

Winter, R., & Aier, S. (2011). How are enterprise architecture design principles used? In *Proceedings of the International Enterprise Distributed Object Computing Conference Workshops* (pp. 314-321). IEEE Computer Society Press

Winter, R., & Fischer, R. (2007). Essential layers, artifacts, and dependencies of enterprise architecture. *Journal of Enterprise Architecture, 3*(2), 7–18.

ADDITIONAL READING

Athanasopoulos, G., Tsalgatidou, A., & Pantazoglou, M. (2006). Interoperability among heterogeneous services. In *Proceedings of the International Conference on Services Computing* (pp. 174-181). IEEE Computer Society Press

Brocke, J., Schenk, B., & Sonnenberg, C. (2009). Organizational implications of implementing service oriented ERP systems: An analysis based on new institutional economics. In Abramowicz (Ed.), *12th International Conference Business Information Systems*, (pp. 252-263). Berlin, Germany: Springer-Verlag.

Chen, D., Doumeingts, G., & Vernadat, F. (2008). Architectures for enterprise integration and interoperability: Past, present and future. *Computers in Industry*, *59*, 647–659. doi:10.1016/j.compind.2007.12.016.

Crane, D., & McCarthy, P. (2008). *Comet and reverse ajax: The next-generation ajax 2.0*. Berkely, CA: Apress, Inc..

Delgado, J. (2012). Bridging provider-centric and user-centric social networks. In Cruz-Cunha, et al. (Eds.), *Handbook of Research on Business Social Networking: Organizational, Managerial, and Technological Dimensions* (pp. 63–83). Hershey, PA: IGI Global.

Dietz, J. (2006). *Enterprise ontology: Theory and methodology*. Berlin: Springer-Verlag. doi:10.1007/3-540-33149-2.

Dillon, T., Wu, C., & Chang, E. (2007). Reference architectural styles for service-oriented computing. In Li et al. (Eds.), *IFIP International Conference on Network and Parallel Computing* (LNCS), (vol. 4672, pp. 543–555). Berlin: Springer-Verlag.

Earl, T. (2005). *Service-oriented architecture: Concepts, technology and design*. Upper Saddle River, NJ: Pearson Education.

Earl, T. (2008). *Principles of service design*. Boston, MA: Pearson Education.

Fricke, E., & Schulz, A. (2005). Design for changeability (DfC): Principles to enable changes in systems throughout their entire lifecycle. *Systems Engineering*, *8*(4), 342–359. doi:10.1002/sys.20039.

Ganguly, A., Nilchiani, R., & Farr, J. (2009). Evaluating agility in corporate enterprises. *International Journal of Production Economics*, *118*(2), 410–423. doi:10.1016/j.ijpe.2008.12.009.

Gorton, I. (2006). *Essential software architecture*. Berlin: Springer-Verlag.

Havey, M. (2005). *Essential business process modeling*. Sebastopol, CA: O'Reilly.

Heckel, R., et al. (2008). Architectural transformations: From legacy to three-tier and services. *Software Evolution*, 139-170.

Juric, M., & Pant, K. (2008). *Business process driven SOA using BPMN and BPEL: From business process modeling to orchestration and service oriented architecture*. Birmingham, UK: Packt Publishing.

Kaindl, H., & Wagner, P. (2009). A unification of the essence of goal-oriented requirements engineering. In *Proceedings of the International Conference on Software Engineering Advances* (pp.45-50). IEEE Press.

Khadka, R. et al. (2011). Model-driven development of service compositions for enterprise interoperability. *Lecture Notes in Business Information Processing*, *76*, 177–190. doi:10.1007/978-3-642-19680-5_15.

Läufer, K., Baumgartner, G., & Russo, V. (2000). Safe structural conformance for java. *The Computer Journal*, *43*(6), 469–481. doi:10.1093/comjnl/43.6.469.

Levy, M., & Powell, P. (2005). *Strategies for growth in SMEs: The role of information systems*. Burlington, MA: Elsevier Butterworth-Heinemann.

Loutas, N., Peristeras, V., & Tarabanis, K. (2011). Towards a reference service model for the web of services. *Data & Knowledge Engineering*, *70*, 753–774. doi:10.1016/j.datak.2011.05.001.

Lovelock, C., & Wirtz, J. (2007). *Services marketing: People, technology, strategy*. Upper Saddle River, NJ: Pearson Prentice Hall.

Papazoglou, P., Traverso, P., Dustdar, S., & Leymann, F. (2008). Service-oriented computing: A research roadmap. *International Journal of Cooperative Information Systems*, *17*(2), 223–255. doi:10.1142/S0218843008001816.

Patten, K., Whitworth, B., Fjermestad, J., & Mahinda, E. (2005). Leading IT flexibility: Anticipation, agility and adaptability. In N. Romano (Ed.), *Proceedings of the 11th Americas Conference on Information Systems*. Red Hook, NY: Curran Associates, Inc.

Perepletchikov, M., Ryan, C., Frampton, K., & Tari, Z. (2007). Coupling metrics for predicting maintainability in service-oriented designs. In *Proceedings of Australian Software Engineering Conference* (pp. 329-340). IEEE Computer Society Press.

Ross, A., Rhodes, D., & Hastings, D. (2008). Defining changeability: Reconciling flexibility, adaptability, scalability, modifiability, and robustness for maintaining system lifecycle value. *Systems Engineering*, *11*(3), 246–262. doi:10.1002/sys.20098.

Schekkerman, J. (2006). *How to survive in the jungle of enterprise architecture frameworks*. Bloomington, IN: Trafford Publishing.

Spohrer, J., Vargo, S., Caswell, N., & Maglio, P. (2008). The service system is the basic abstraction of service science. In Sprague (Ed.), *Proceedings of the 41st Hawaii International Conference on System Sciences*. Big Island, HI: IEEE Computer Society.

van der Aalst, W. (1999). Process-oriented architectures for electronic commerce and interorganizational workflow. *Information Systems*, *24*(8), 639–671. doi:10.1016/S0306-4379(00)00003-X.

Xu, X., Zhu, L., Kannengiesser, U., & Liu, Y. (2010). An architectural style for process-intensive web information systems. [LNCS]. *Proceedings of the Web Information Systems Engineering*, *6488*, 534–547.

Xu, X., Zhu, L., Liu, Y., & Staples, M. (2008). Resource-oriented architecture for business processes. In *Proceedings of Software Engineering Conference* (pp. 395-402). IEEE Computer Society Press.

KEY TERMS AND DEFINITIONS

Conformance: Property between service *A* and another *B* (*A* conforms to *B*) that indicates that *A* implements all the features of *B* required to allow it to replace *B* in its role in some enterprise architecture.

Enterprise Architecture Framework: Set of guidelines, best pratices and tools to analyse, classify, structure and describe the architecture of an enterprise.

Enterprise Architecture Method: Set of steps to be taken to derive an enterprise architecture from an initial problem statement or from an already existing enterprise. This is usually used in conjunction with an enterprise architecture framework.

Goal: Description, usually in a qualitative and fuzzy way, of a desired state or set of properties to achieve.

Lifecycle: Set of stages which a system goes through, starting with a motivation to build it and ending with is destruction. Different versions of a system result from iterations of these stages, in which the system loops back to an earlier stage so that changes can be made.

Objective Graph: Decomposition of an overall objective into smaller objectives that must be satisfied, in OR or AND dependencies, to meet the satisfaction of the overall objective.

Objective: Description, usually in a concrete way, of a desired state or set of properties to achieve. This description must be concrete enough to be considered SMART (Specific, Measureable, Achievable, Realistic, and Time framed).

Process: A graph of all interactions that are allowed to occur in a set of services, starting with an external request and ending with a service which neither reacts back nor initiates new service interactions.

Resource: An entity of any nature (material, virtual, conceptual, noun, action, and so on) that embodies a meaningful, complete and discrete concept, which makes sense by itself and can be distinguished from, although interact with, other entities.

Service: A set of related functionalities that define a meaningful concept in a resource interaction context.

Chapter 31
Enterprise 2.0 in Engineering Curriculum

Andreas Ahrens
Wismar University of Applied Sciences, Germany

Olaf Bassus
Wismar University of Applied Sciences, Germany

Jeļena Zaščerinska
Centre for Education and Innovation Research, Latvia

ABSTRACT

Engineering education is facing a challenge to bring e-business closer to student engineers. Enterprise 2.0 application in engineering education advances engineering students' enterprise for the development of innovative products, processes, and services. The aim of the research is to analyze student engineers' Enterprise 2.0 application underpinning elaboration of pedagogical guidelines on student engineers' Enterprise 2.0 application in engineering curriculum. The meaning of key concepts of Enterprise 2.0 and engineering curriculum is studied. Moreover, the study indicates how the steps of the process are related following a logical chain: Enterprise 2.0 → engineering curriculum design → modelling Enterprise 2.0 application in engineering curriculum → empirical study within a multicultural environment. The present empirical research was conducted during the Baltic Summer School "Technical Informatics and Information Technology" in 2009, 2010, and 2011. The findings of the research allow drawing the conclusions that student engineers' Enterprise 2.0 application in engineering curriculum is efficient.

INTRODUCTION

Engineers succeed harder to find a job: engineer entering the service area has changed from working permanently at a large-scale enterprise to accepting project-related orders of large-scale enterprises by free engineers' office (Bassus, Wolfgramm, 2009, p. 38). Starting own business is a viable solution to overcome the unemployed or migrant status student engineers are exposed to.

Engineering curriculum is facing a challenge of Enterprise 2.0 application that brings e-business

DOI: 10.4018/978-1-4666-4373-4.ch031

closer to student engineers and advances their enterprise.

Aim of the research is to analyze student engineers' Enterprise 2.0 application underpinning elaboration of pedagogical guidelines on student engineers' Enterprise 2.0 application in engineering curriculum.

The remaining part of this paper is structured as follows: The introductory background section demonstrates the authors' position on the topic of the research. The following part of the chapter involves five sections. Section 1 introduces theoretical framework on Enterprise 2.0 in engineering education. Research design is revealed in Section 2. The associated results of the empirical study are presented and interpreted in Section 3. Findings of the empirical study are analyzed in Section 4 followed by issues, controversies and their solutions. Afterwards, pedagogical guidelines on student engineers' Enterprise 2.0 application in engineering curriculum are given. Finally, some concluding remarks and a short outlook on interesting topics for further work are elaborated.

BACKGROUND

The conceptual framework of the present research is based on the approach to enterprise considered in a broader social context than within business framework only (Oganisjana & Koke, 2008, p. 225). Therein, the term *enterprise* involves *entrepreneurship* as shown in Figure 1 (Zaščerinska, Ahrens, & Bassus, 2011, p. 475).

Figure 1. The relationship between enterprise and entrepreneurship

Enterprise is defined as an individual complex capability to identify, generate and realize new socially valuable opportunities in the personal, professional, cultural, economic and other contexts of the social life (Oganisjana & Koke, 2008, p. 225).

The methodological background of the present research is based on System-Constructivist Theory. System-Constructivist Theory and, consequently, System-Constructivist Approach to learning introduced by Reich (Reich, 2005) emphasize that human being's point of view depends on the subjective aspect:

- Everyone has his/her own system of external and internal perspectives that is a complex open system and
- Experience plays the central role in the knowledge construction process (Maslo, 2007, p. 39).

MAIN FOCUS OF THE CHAPTER

Theoretical Framework

The theoretical framework of the present contribution involves the meaning of the key concepts of *Enterprise 2.0* and *engineering curriculum design* studied.

Enterprise 2.0 Definition

The present research is based on a widely accepted conception of Enterprise 2.0 as use of Web technologies for enterprise (business) purposes (Bassus, Ahrens, & Zaščerinska, 2011, p. 376).

Typical Enterprise 2.0 includes corporate blogs, wikis, feeds, and podcasts (Vossen, 2009, p. 38) as shown in Figure 2.

Blogs are a common way to stay in touch with customers, to inform about new products and to receive immediate feedback; they can also be used internally in order to discuss specific topics among the staff of an enterprise, in particular if people are geographically distributed (Vossen, 2009, p. 38). Blogs allow a moderated interaction between participants, be it customers or colleagues, and a simple and efficient distribution of announcements, experiences, opinions, reports, or evaluations. A blog is useless without regular updates, a reasonable number of readers, continuous moderation, and good content. It is also a good idea for a company to treat independent bloggers just like regular journalists, since they might have a considerable readership. In order to stay up-to-date with a company blog, but also with other information an enterprise might publish, there are essentially two approaches: pull and push. The active or pull way is to read the information at my own liberty and pace; in the passive or push approach, the information will be delivered to me automatically.

A podcast is a particular form of feed consisting of audio or video material (Vossen, 2009, p. 38).

Wikis allow collaborative work on a common set of documents by many authors, and have been discovered as a new way of performing knowledge management in a learning organization.

Online networks bring a dimension to the Web that goes beyond simple links between pages; they add links between people, between communities (Vossen, 2009, p. 38) and between organizations.

A network on the Web is typically the result of employing some software that is intended to focus on building an online community and, consequently, organization for a specific purpose (Vossen, 2009, p. 38). Social networks connect people with common interests and may be as simple as a blog, or as complex as Facebook or MySpace for mostly private applications, as LinkedIn or Xing for professional applications, or as Twitter for both. Another impact is that a social network may open up novel sources of revenue, in particular through advertising. Finally, Vossen (Vossen, 2009, p. 38) underlines that technology enables functionality, which as a "byproduct" leads to data collections, and users have a new tendency to socialize over the Web, by exploiting that functionality and the technology.

Figure 2. Elements of Enterprise 2.0

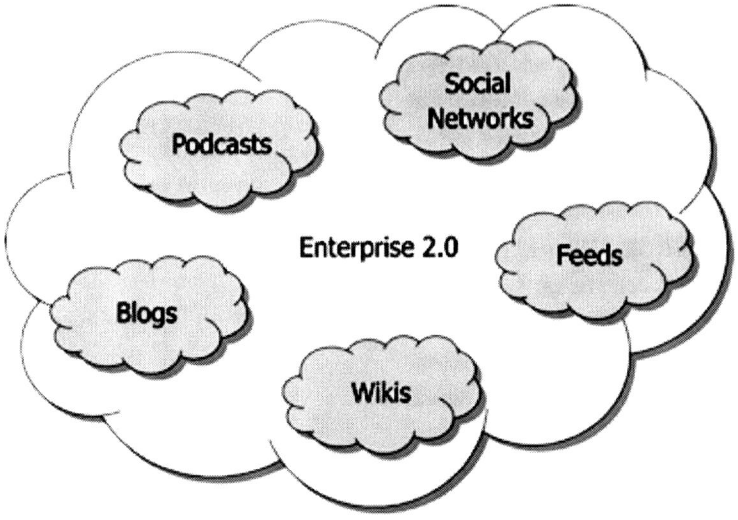

Figure 3. Curriculum components

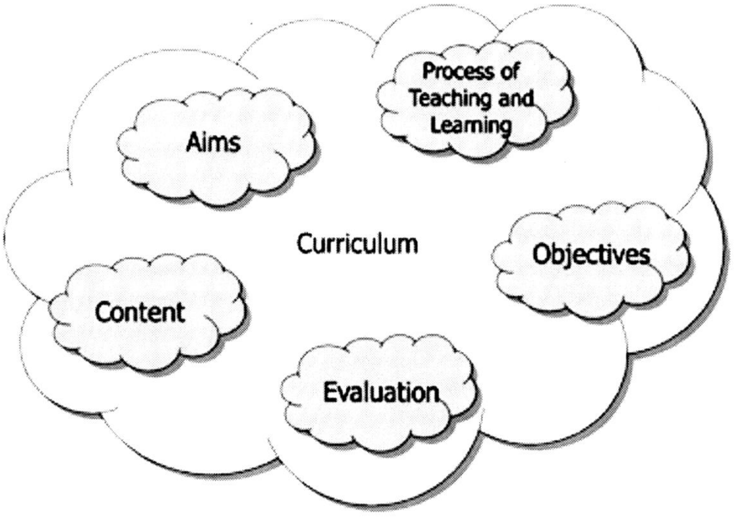

Engineering Curriculum Design

The search for an engineering curriculum design reveals the interaction of synonyms of the term *curriculum*, namely, *approach, plan* (often in Germany and Russia), *design*, *way of thinking,* as well as *strategy* and *programme* (Bassus, Zaščerinska, & Ahrens, 2011, p. 84).

The present contribution considers curriculum as a central, organizing stance (Portelli & Vilbert, 2002a, p. 39). Curriculum comprises the following components: aim, objectives, content, process of teaching and learning as well as evaluation as depicted in Figure 3.

Curriculum based on System-Constructivist Approach to learning centres on possibilities for the co-construction and co-production of enterprise innovation, rather than on enterprise innovation as simply manager transmitted or simply employee created (Portelli & Vilbert, 2002a, p. 39). Therein, curriculum is centred on the process design (Philippou, 2005, p. 357). Moreover, the curriculum paradigm changes from an input based teaching/learning process to an outcome based process (Bluma, 2008, p. 673). Hence, the curriculum demonstrates how the learning outcomes are to be achieved by determining the phases of the process of teaching and learning: from teaching in Phase 1 to learning in Phase 3 through peer-learning in Phase 2 as depicted in Figure 4. Consequently, the present curriculum is regarded as peer-centred.

The stages of engineering curriculum design include the following steps (Boev, et al., 2011, pp. 41-42):

Figure 4. Phases of the process of teaching and learning

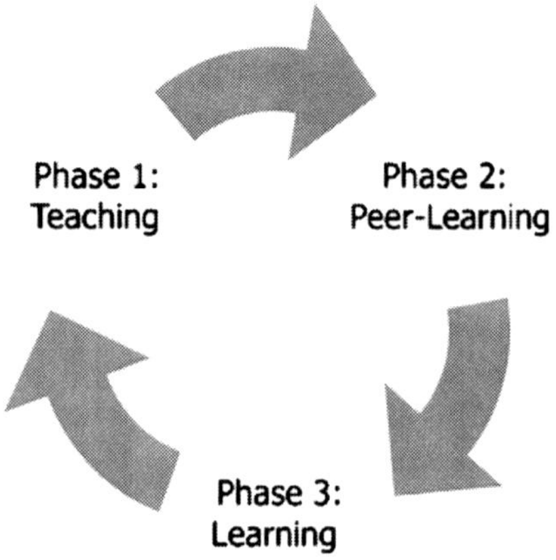

1. Curriculum conception (a brief description of the curriculum) that is aimed at identifying the curriculum constituencies and creation of the system ensuring the interaction with constituencies and studying of their needs.
2. Determination of curriculum educational objectives that are based on the needs of the constituencies. The curriculum objectives should be consistent with the mission of the institution to ensure its market competitiveness and demand of constituencies.
3. Definition of measurable curriculum learning outcomes, namely, knowledge, skills, and attitudes, which a student acquires during his study within the curriculum. The curriculum learning outcomes should correspond with the needs of the constituencies and ensure the achievement of the programme objectives by the graduates.
4. The curriculum design that demonstrates how the learning outcomes are to be achieved by defining the curriculum modules that ensure their achievement and by assigning European Credit Transfer and Accumulation System (ECTS) to learning outcomes. Each module has a number of learning outcomes that have their credit value depending on their contribution to achievement of programme outcomes. An educator responsible for a module must ensure development of its syllabus, teaching technologies, and supporting facilities aiming at achievement of module learning outcomes. Each module must have the assessment methods and tools for achievement of planned learning outcomes. The credits should not be assigned to a module if module does not include assessment of outcomes to be achieved. The notional learning time for a module is defined in accordance with its credit value.
5. Development of the assessment system for achievement of learning outcomes and curriculum objectives that should be done systematically and used for curriculum continuous improvement. The professional accreditation of curriculum by the accrediting agency is an important part of the assessment system of an institution.

Modelling Enterprise 2.0 Application in Engineering Curriculum

Theoretical analysis and empirical findings (Bassus, Zaščerinska, & Ahrens, 2011; Zaščerinska, Ahrens, & Bassus, 2011; Ahrens & Zaščerinska, 2011; Bassus, Ahrens, & Zaščerinska, 2011) allow modelling Enterprise 2.0 application in engineering curriculum as following:

1. Enterprise 2.0 application in engineering curriculum is conceptualized as promoting student engineers' self-confidence and capability to cope with their own problems in all spheres of life in a knowledgeable and enterprising way (Oganisjana & Koke, 2008, p. 225).
2. Educational objective of Enterprise 2.0 application in engineering curriculum is determined as to actively involve the student engineers in the life of Enterprise 2.0 (Portelli & Vilbert, 2002b, p. 15) by providing innovative opportunities and organizing student engineers' cognitive activity (Ahrens & Zaščerinska, 2011, p. 314).
3. Measurable learning outcomes are defined as
    a. Student engineers' knowledge of the Enterprise 2.0 concept,
    b. Student engineers' skills to use Enterprise 2.0 for their individual, organizational and professional purposes. It should be mentioned that by individual purposes private use of Enterprise 2.0 is meant: business functions are used within the family and friends. By organizational purposes use of Enterprise 2.0 between the colleagues is determined: business is made between the

participants within the enterprise. And by professional purposes Enterprise 2.0 is used for business with the partners of the enterprise (Zaščerinska, Ahrens, & Bassus, 2011, p. 478).

c. Student engineers' attitude towards participation in activities for their professional development such as education, in-service training and/or learning.

4. Enterprise 2.0 application is implemented in the Web 2.0 module of engineering curriculum (Ahrens & Zaščerinska, 2011, p. 316). The Web 2.0 module examines the advantages and problems of this technology such as architecture and management, protocol design, and programming, which makes new social communication forms possible. The Web 2.0 module does not reveal the concept of Enterprise 2.0. However, the Web 2.0 module comprises Enterprise 2.0 technologies (Ahrens & Zaščerinska, 2011, p. 316). The Web 2.0 module is assigned to 1 credit relevant to the European Credit Transfer System (ECTS). The teaching technology proceeds as following (Ahrens & Zaščerinska, 2011, p. 314-315):
   a. Phase 1 Teaching of Enterprise 2.0 application is aimed at a safe environment for all the students considering the essence of constructive social interaction and its organizational regulation. The present phase of Enterprise 2.0 application is organized in a frontal way involving the students to participate.
   b. Phase 2 Peer-Learning of Enterprise 2.0 application is designed for the students' analysis of an open professional problem situation and their search for a solution. The present phase of Enterprise 2.0 application involves the students to act in peers. A variety of teaching/learning activities with use of Enterprise 2.0 is provided by role plays, simulations, dialogues, prepared talks, discussions, and communication games and information-gap activities (Zaščerinska, 2009).
   c. Phase 3 Learning of Enterprise 2.0 application emphasizes the students' self-regulation with use of assessment of the process and self-evaluation of the results. The students present their self-evaluation by the end of each class.
5. The assessment system for achievement of learning outcomes and curriculum objectives comprises student engineers' self-evaluation, internal evaluation, and external evaluation (Hahele, 2005).

Research Design

The research design comprises the purpose and question, sample and methodology of the present empirical study to be considered.

Research Purpose and Question

The present empirical study was conducted during student engineers' Enterprise 2.0 application in the engineering curriculum of Baltic Summer School *Technical Informatics and Information Technology* to examine the efficiency of Enterprise 2.0 application in engineering curriculum. The research question is as follows: Has student engineers' Enterprise 2.0 application been efficient?

Sample of the Research

The present research conducted during the Baltic Summer School „Technical Informatics and Information Technology" in 2009, 2010 and 2011 involves 85 respondents, namely,

- 22 participants of Fifth Baltic Summer School, August 7-22, 2009, Tartu, Estonia,

- 28 participants of Sixth Baltic Summer School, August 13-28, 2010, Kaunas, Lithuania,
- 24 participants of Seventh Baltic Summer, August 12-27, 2011, Riga, Latvia,
- an educator of Baltic Summer School and
- 10 researchers in the field of educational research from different countries.

All the participants of Baltic Summer School *Technical Informatics and Information Technology* have got Bachelor or Master Degree in different fields of Computer Sciences and working experience in different fields related to computing and information technology.

The participants of Baltic Summer School *Technical Informatics and Information Technology* are with different cultural background and diverse educational approaches from different countries, namely, Latvia, Lithuania, Estonia, Russia, Belarus, Mongolia, Egypt, Germany, Pakistan, Indonesia, Great Britain, China, India, Nigeria, Romania and Mexico, etc. Hence, the sample is multicultural as the respondents with different cultural backgrounds and diverse educational approaches were chosen. Hence, the group's socio-cultural context (age, field of study and work, mother tongue, etc.) is heterogeneous.

Research Methodology

Interpretative research paradigm which corresponds to the nature of humanistic pedagogy (Lūka, 2008, p. 52) has been determined. Interpretative paradigm is characterized by the researchers' practical interest in the research question (Cohen, Manion, et al., 2003).

The qualitative evaluation research aimed at examining the efficiency of Enterprise 2.0 application has been used in the study (Kardoff, 2004, p. 137; Flick, 2004, p. 149).

Therein, efficiency involves quality and effectiveness as depicted in Figure 5 (Zaščerinska & Ahrens, 2011).

Figure 5. Elements of efficiency

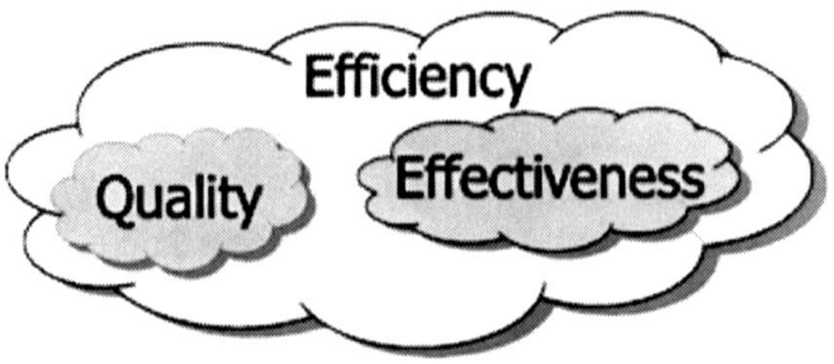

Quality of Enterprise 2.0 application is regarded as the improvement of student engineers' knowledge, skills and attitudes (Zaščerinska, 2011a, p. 125). In its turn, effectiveness is considered as the educator's contribution to the student engineers' knowledge, skills and attitudes in Enterprise 2.0 application (Zaščerinska, 2011a, p. 125-126).

Enterprise 2.0 application is efficient if the inputs (Enterprise 2.0 application) produce the maximum output (students' knowledge, skills and attitudes (Zaščerinska, 2010b, p. 3) (Commission of the European Communities, 2006, p. 2). Therein, students' knowledge, skills and attitudes are the outcome criterion of efficiency of Enterprise 2.0 application (Zaščerinska, 2010b, p. 3).

Figure 5 shows how the qualitative evaluation research proceeds (Zaščerinska, 2011a, p. 109)

- From the phase of exploration of the context analysis aimed at determining the present situation of Enterprise 2.0 application in promoting students' motivation and their readiness to implement the joint activity,
- Through the description of the practice that analyzes differences in levels of features researched and
- To the phase of generalization of the model that evaluates whether or not Enterprise 2.0 application is efficient for the development of students' knowledge, skills and attitudes (see Figure 6).

Figure 6. Phases of qualitative evaluation research

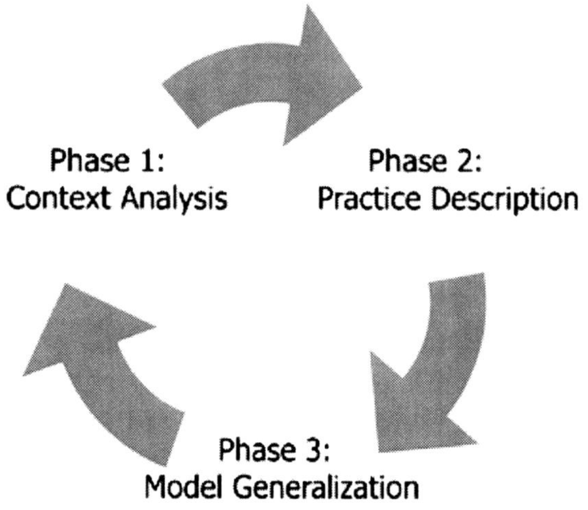

The qualitatively oriented research allows the construction of only few cases (Mayring, 2007, p. 1). Moreover, the cases themselves are not of interest, only the conclusions and transfers we can draw from this material (Mayring, 2007, p. 6).

Selecting the cases for the case study comprises use of information-oriented sampling, as opposed to random sampling (Flyvbjerg, 2006, p. 229). This is because an average case is often not the richest in information. In addition, it is often more important to clarify the deeper causes behind a given problem and its consequences than to describe the symptoms of the problem and how frequently they occur (Flyvbjerg, 2006, p. 229).

Educator Contribution to Engineering Students' Learning Outcomes

The present part of the empirical study reveals analysis of engineering students' learning outcomes in Enterprise 2.0 application within Baltic Summer School *Technical Informatics and Information Technology* in 2009, 2010, and 2011 through thorough analysis of two surveys of the student engineers' feedback regarding their needs before and after educators' contribution.

Pre-Survey

In 2009 analysis of the students' feedback regarding their needs in Enterprise 2.0 application in the pre—and post-survey was based on the following questionnaire:

- **Question 1:** Do you know the word Web 2.0?
- **Question 2:** Do you know the basic idea of Web 2.0?
- **Question 3:** Have you already used Web 2.0, namely, Facebook, Twitter, Wikipedia, etc.?
- **Question 4:** Do you think Web 2.0 requires a lot of profound knowledge, namely, math, physics, etc.?
- **Question 5:** Do you think Web 2.0 is useful for your individual needs?
- **Question 6:** Do you think Web 2.0 is useful for your organizational use?
- **Question 7:** Do you think Web 2.0 is useful for your professional use?

It should be mentioned that needs analysis of three levels, namely, individual, organizational and professional, serves as an indicator of Enterprise 2.0 application in engineering education (Zaščerinska, Ahrens, & Bassus, 2011, p. 482).

The evaluation scale of five levels for each question is given where "1" means "disagree" and low level of experience (knowledge, skills and attitudes (Zaščerinska, 2010a, p. 415) in Enterprise 2.0 application and "5" points out "agree" and high level of experience in Enterprise 2.0 application.

Analysis of the pre-survey, as depicted in Figure 7, carried out with 22 participants of Fifth Baltic Summer School, shows that the student engineers' Enterprise 2.0 application is heterogeneous as well as the student engineers do not know the possibilities offered by Web 2.0 properly.

In 2010 analysis of the students' feedback regarding their needs in Enterprise 2.0 application

Figure 7. PDF (probability density function) of the pre-survey on August 7, 2009

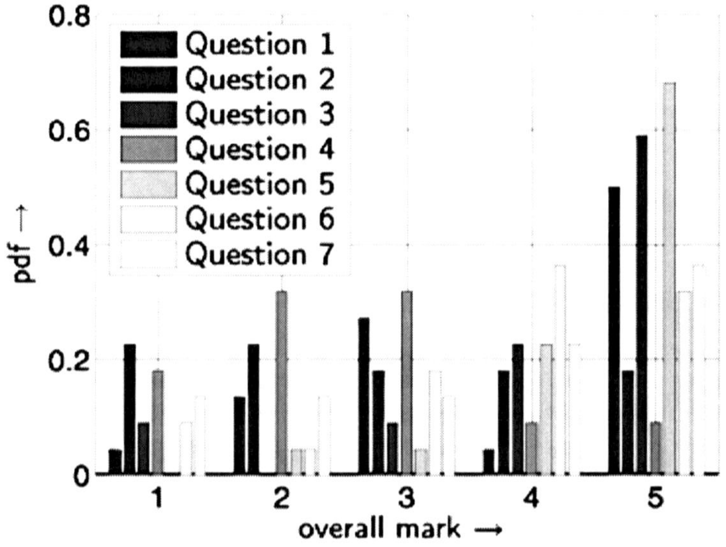

in the pre—and post-survey was based on the following questionnaire:

- **Question 1:** Do you know the concept of Enterprise 2.0?
- **Question 2:** Do you use Enterprise 2.0 for your individual purposes?
- **Question 3:** Do you use Enterprise 2.0 for your organizational purposes?
- **Question 4:** Do you use Enterprise 2.0 for your professional purposes?
- **Question 5:** Do you participate in activities for your professional development, namely, education, in-service training, and/or learning, in use of Enterprise 2.0?

The evaluation scale of five levels for each question is given where "1" means "disagree" and low level of experience in Enterprise 2.0 application and "5" points out "agree" and high level of Enterprise 2.0 application.

Results of the pre-survey reveal that the student engineers do not realize the possibilities offered by Enterprise 2.0 properly.

In 2011 analysis of the students' feedback regarding their needs in Enterprise 2.0 application in the pre—and post-survey was based on the following questionnaire:

- **Question 1:** Do you have your own business and/or enterprise? The evaluation scale of two levels for the question is given where "1" means "no" and "2" - "yes."
- **Question 2:** Do you plan to start your own business and/or enterprise? The evaluation scale of two levels for the question is given where "1" means "no" and "2" - "yes."
- **Question 3:** To which extent do modern business and enterprise employ Web technologies? The evaluation scale of five levels for the question is given where "0-20%" means a low level of experience in Enterprise 2.0 application and "80-100%" points out a high level of Enterprise 2.0 application.
- **Question 4:** Please, indicate at least 3 Web technologies used by business and / or enterprise for business applications (up to five). The evaluation scale of five levels for the question is pointed out. 1 point is given for each correct answer thereby "1" means a low level of experience in Enterprise

2.0 application and "5" – a high level of Enterprise 2.0 application.

Results of the pre-survey reveal that the student engineers do not realize the possibilities for business offered by Enterprise 2.0 properly:

- One engineering student has got his/her own business,
- 11 engineering students plan to start their own business and/or enterprise,
- Nine engineering students consider that modern business employs Web technologies to 40-60%, 10 student engineers – 60-80% and five engineering students – 80-100%.
- Four student engineers indicated no Web technologies used by business, two engineering students - one Web technology used by business, three engineering students – two Web technologies used by business, 14 student engineers – three Web technologies used by business and one engineering student – four Web technologies used by business.

This is a reason why a support system to contribute to students' learning outcomes in a multicultural study's context was elaborated. This support system differs from the one offered in the special module of Web 2.0 by other educators as the proposed support system proceeds in a certain sequence.

Educator Contribution

Baltic Summer School *Technical Informatics and Information Technology* has been held in the Baltic States since 2005. The goal of studies in the Baltic Summer School is to prepare the student for international Master and Ph.D. programs in Germany, further specialization in computer science and information technology or other related fields, and learning in a simulated environment.

The Baltic Summer School contains a special module on Web 2.0 where Enterprise 2.0 is part. The process of teaching and learning was implemented in a certain sequence as following:

Phase 1 *Teaching* of Enterprise 2.0 application: The *Preparing a Good Introduction to a Presentation* information-gap activity (Buckmaster, 2004, p. 1) was analyzed in details. The student engineers' ability to make presentations for academic purposes in English is one of the expected results in the Web 2.0 module. The *Preparing a Good Introduction to a Presentation* information-gap activity is aimed at specialized training in Enterprise 2.0 application. The preparatory phase of Enterprise 2.0 application includes e-mailing the student engineers the task. The *Preparing a Good Introduction to a Presentation* information-gap activity comprised the following procedure:

Stage 1 was aimed at asking the student engineers to read out the task and at discussing the task in the whole group. There were no difficulties to understand the task because the student engineers did similar exercises.

Stage 2 assumed the student engineers to implement the task individually and/or in peers. If necessary, they applied Enterprise 2.0: the Web 2.0 module was hold in a computer classroom with the Internet connection available. The student engineers shared the Enteprise 2.0 resources available with pleasure.

Stage 3 dealt with sharing the student engineers' experience in reordering and completing the sentences with the group's participants. The student engineers managed to complete the sentences without any difficulty. However, the sentence order was given by the student engineers in a variety of combinations.

Stage 4 was designed to compare the engineering student dicoveries with the findings of other students. All the student engineers were helpful and friendly during the present stage of the studies: if there was a difficulty to find an idea on reordering the sentences, expression or word, the student engineers could get the necessary assistance from the groupmates and the educator. The observation revealed that word order contained some difficulties for the particular student engineers.

Stage 5 was devoted to re-completing the task by each student in the classroom. It was carried out by the engineering students with an interest: the student engineers re-asked some questions.

Phase 2 *Peer-Learning* of Enterprise 2.0 application: The prepared talk on the topic of the student engineers' master thesis was analyzed in details. The prepared talk on the topic of the students' master thesis is aimed at specialized training in searching for information with Enterprise 2.0 application. The preparatory stage included

- E-mailing the student engineers the task to prepare a presentation in English on the topic of the students' master theses,
- Clarifying whether the engineering students are able to work with the PowerPoint programme,
- A class with the emphasis on making a successful presentation for academic purposes in English that involves discussion on the presentation aims, its structure, materials, its procedure, use of the PowerPoint programme.

The prepared talk on the topic of the engineering students' master theses comprised the following procedure:

Stage 1 was aimed at a student engineer's presentation to his/her groupmates about his/her master thesis with Enterprise 2.0 application and the PowerPoint programme. The student engineers assisted each other in the technical area of presenting with use of the PowerPoint programme if there were some problems with the technical equipment, namely,

- New version of the PowerPoint programme of the student's presentation was not suitable to the PowerPoint programme available in the computer classroom,
- Transferring the presentation from the students' flash to the desktop of the computer, etc.,
- Opening the presentation files saved in the programmes different from the programmes available in the classroom, and
- Re-connecting the projector from the classroom computer to a private computer, etc.

Stage 2 engaged the students to switch the roles of speakers and listeners and to repeat the activity.

Stage 3 was devoted to the discussion on the student engineers' presentations. The discussion revealed that the engineering students while futher practising a presentation would take into consideration

- Pronunciation of academic terminology: the engineering students know how to spell the term, however, they do not pay a lot of attention to its pronunciation,
- Time limit for academic presentation, namely, 10 minutes in the Web 2.0 module, whereas the students' presentations took 15-20 minutes,
- Slide limit for academic presentation: there were 10 slides set as a requirement whereas the engineering students prepared 12-25 slides to emphasize the significance of the content of their master theses,
- To put only key words or phrases on a slide, not the whole sentence or text,
- Non-verbal aspects of communication:
    - The engineering students' location and distance within the public zone while making a presentation whereas some of the presenting students were standing at a classroom's wall,
    - To vary the pace and pitch of his/her voice,
    - Irritating nervous habits such as running his/her fingers through his/her hair or clicking the fingers or a pen, etc,

  - Not to turn his/her back on the audience in order to read the text of the presentation from the screen on the wall,
  - Not to cross his/her arms and
  - To look into each other's eyes,
- To bring an answer to a question subsequently if there is no possibility to reply immediately: for example, the presentation took a longer time than it was suggested.

Phase 3 *Learning* of Enterprise 2.0 application: The student engineers presented their self-evaluation. Self-evaluation comprised three questions as following:

1. What is your attitude to the Enterprise 2.0 application today?
2. What have you learned in the Enterprise 2.0 application?
3. How can you apply this knowledge in your academic field?

The present phase of English studies for academic purposes was organized in an individual way.

The students revealed their willingness to share their experience obtained in the classroom by the end of each class. Moreover, the students emphasized the importance of the possibility (Ilyinska, 2004, p. 92-93, 95)

- To see things from different perspectives,
- To produce a new organisation of familiar components and
- To consider new ideas by making connections among the olds.

Phase 3 *Learning* of Enterprise 2.0 application identified the most successful teaching and learning methods as demonstrated in Table 1 in order to improve the engineering students' learning outcomes.

Table 1. Phases of Enterprise 2.0 application and their most successful teaching and learning methods

Phase	Most successful teaching and learning methods
Phase 1 Teaching Phase	communication games, information-gap activities
Phase 2 Peer-Learning Phase	Dialogue, role play, discussion, simulation: - conference and video-conference, - debate, - seminar and - project; prepared talk
Phase 3 Learning Phase	self-evaluation

Post-Survey

In 2009, analysis of the post-survey carried out in the Fifth Baltic Summer School on August 11, 2009 reveals that the participants' Enterprise 2.0 application has become homogeneous and the participants have put the emphasis on Enterprise 2.0 application for professional needs as shown in Figure 8.

In 2010, results of the post-survey demonstrate the positive changes in comparison with the pre-survey:

- The level of the participants' experience in terms of knowledge of the concept of Enterprise 2.0 has been enriched,
- The level of the participants' experience in Enterprise 2.0 application for individual needs, for organizational and professional needs increased and
- The level of the participants' experience in terms of participation in activities for professional development such as education, in-service training and/or learning has been improved.

Figure 8. PDF (probability density function) of the post-survey on August 11, 2009

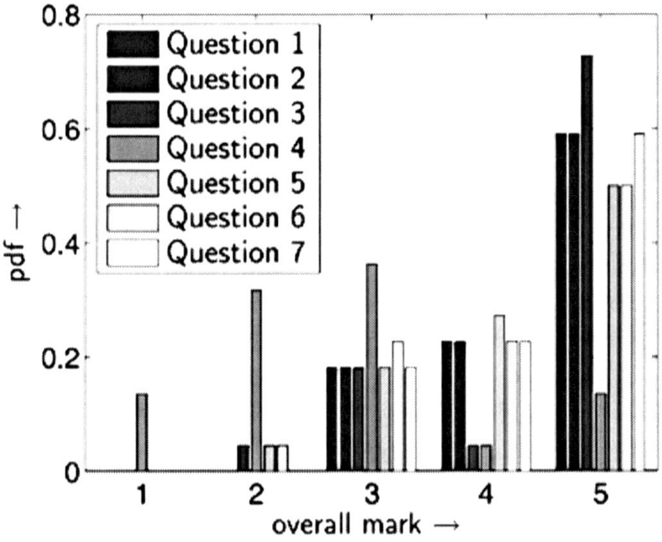

In 2011, results of the post-survey demonstrate the positive changes in comparison with the pre-survey:

- The number of engineering students who plan to start their own business increased from 11 to 16.
- The number of student engineers who considered that modern business employs Web technologies to 40-60% decreased from nine to five, 60-80% – decreased from 10 to nine and 80-100% – increased from five to 10 engineering students.
- The number of engineering students who indicated one or no Web technologies used by business decreased from six student engineers to five, two Web technologies used by business – decreased from three engineering student to one, three Web technologies used by business – increased from 14 student engineers to 15 and four Web technologies used by business – increased from one engineering student to three.
- The number of students who has got his/her own business remained steady – one engineering student.

Findings of the Research

The present part reveals analysis of the research results in Enterprise 2.0 application within Baltic Summer School *Technical Informatics and Information Technology* in 2009, 2010, and 2011 through thorough analysis of student engineers' self-evaluation, internal and external evaluation.

Analysis of Students' Self-Evaluation of the Research Results

In 2010, in order to find out how each student's learning outcomes changed after Enterprise 2.0 application, analysis of the engineering students' self-evaluation comprised the structured interviews of three questions, namely,

1. What is your attitude to the Enterprise 2.0 application today?
2. What have you learned in the Enterprise 2.0 application?
3. How can you apply this knowledge in your academic field?

The aim of the interviews was to reveal the engineering students' evaluation of Enterprise 2.0 application for the development of student engineers' learning outcomes.

Comparing the answers of those 28 engineering students in the sample, the structured interviews were focused on the engineering students' positive experience in Enterprise 2.0 application. For example, a student reveals the inter-relationship between the positive experience of social interaction and cognitive activity in Enterprise 2.0 application:

I feel this class to be very useful to me because I am improving my knowledge in Enterprise 2.0 application.

The student evaluates her own learning process:

I think I like the Web 2.0 module, because I begin to understand how to apply Enterprise 2.0.

The summarizing content analysis (Mayring, 2004, p. 269) of the structured interviews demonstrates that Enterprise 2.0 application promotes the development of students' learning outcomes. Moreover, Enterprise 2.0 application contributes to the safe and friendly teaching/learning environment for all the participants and provides opportunities of constructive social interaction and cognitive activity.

Analysis of Internal Evaluation of the Research Results

Internal evaluation involves engineering students and educators of the educational establishment. Analysis of the internal evaluation of the engineering students' learning outcomes comprised the data processing, analysis, interpretation, and analysis of the results of the pre-survey and post-survey of the student engineers.

In order to determine the developmental dynamics of each student's learning outcome in 2010, comparison of the pre-survey and post-survey results was carried out.

The *Mean* results of the descriptive statistics highlighted in Table 2 demonstrate that the level of the students' Enterprise 2.0 application has increased in the post-survey (3.28) in comparison with the pre-survey (1.68).

The comparison of the *Standard Deviation* results as shown in Table 3 reveals that the scores of the post-survey are spread wider than the scores in the pre-survey.

The results of *Mean* and *Standard Deviation* within the surveys of the students' feedback regarding their needs in Enterprise 2.0 reveal that most of answers are concentrated around Level 2 and 3. Thus, there is a possibility to increase the students' use of Enterprise 2.0 within Web 2.0 technologies.

In order to determine the developmental dynamics of each student's learning outcome in 2011,

Table 2. Mean analysis of the pre- and post-survey in 2010

Question	Pre-Survey	Post-Survey
1	1.86	3.25
2	1.75	3.44
3	1.54	3.33
4	1.57	3.16
5	1.68	3.21
mean	**1.68**	**3.28**

Table 3. Standard deviation analysis of the pre- and post-surveys in 2010

Question	Pre-Survey	Post-Survey
1	1.85	2.35
2	1.14	2.40
3	1.99	2.39
4	1.57	2.19
5	1.96	2.31
mean	**1.70**	**2.33**

Table 4. Mean analysis of the pre- and post-survey in 2011

Question	Pre-Survey	Post-Survey
1	1.04	1.04
2	1.46	1.66
3	3.83	4.21
4	2.25	2.66
mean	**2.15**	**2.39**

comparison of the pre-survey and post-survey results was carried out.

The *Mean* results of the descriptive statistics highlighted in Table 4 demonstrate that the level of the students' Enterprise 2.0 application has increased in the post-survey (2.39) in comparison with the pre-survey (2.15).

The results of *Mean* within the surveys of the students' feedback regarding their needs in Enterprise 2.0 reveal that most of answers are concentrated around Level 2. Thus, there is a possibility to increase the students' Enterprise 2.0 application within Web 2.0 technologies.

Hence, considering judgment to be part of the art of statistics (Gigenzer, 2004, p. 603), the conclusion has been drawn that Enterprise 2.0 application influenced the development of the engineering students' learning outcomes demonstrated by the difference between the levels of the student engineers' learning outcomes in the pre- and post-survey.

Analysis of External Evaluation of the Research Results

The external evaluation comprises 10 researchers from different countries. It should be mentioned that all the researchers participated in the external evaluation of the research results are professors in the fields connected with educational research.

The external evaluation of the research results comprised the non-structured interview of one question as following: What is the researcher's view on the present research on Enterprise 2.0 application for the development of engineering students' learning outcome? The aim of the non-structured interviews was to reveal the researchers' evaluation of Enterprise 2.0 application for the development of engineering students' learning outcome.

For example, a respondent considered the model of Enterprise 2.0 application for the development of engineering students' learning outcome to be a transformative methodology. The researcher stressed the following advantages of the model: focus of establishing a system, viewing the overall personality of the learner, the fact that educators can indeed change the typical classroom environment, the sequence of the implementation of the model, developing newer constructs that will truly help the student to internalize new material and the student having the "ability to create knowledge".

The summarizing content analysis (Mayring, 2004, p. 269) of the data reveals that the respondents evaluate Enterprise 2.0 application for the development of engineering students' learning outcome positively. Thus, the conclusion can be drawn that Enterprise 2.0 application enhances development of engineering students' learning outcome.

ISSUES, CONTROVERSIES, PROBLEMS

One of the Enterprise 2.0 issues is to consider the historical development of *Enterprise 2.0* and *Enterprise 2.0* in pedagogy.

Another point is the paradigm shift from socialization within Web 2.0 to peer contribution within Web 3.0 (Ahrens & Zaščerinska, 2011, p. 319) and growing need to quantify uncertainty with greater precision (Nadhan, 2008) that has already increased the significance in the Enterprise 2.0 institutionalization. However, Enterprise 2.0 is conceptualized but still not institutionalized (Nadhan, 2008).

SOLUTIONS AND RECOMMENDATIONS

Table 5 demonstrates that the study of *Enterprise 3.0* and *Enterprise 3.0* in pedagogy has not had a long story (Bassus, Ahrens, & Zaščerinska, 2011, p. 381).

Regarding the institutionalization of Enterprise 2.0, an attempt has led to the concept of Enterprise 3.0 defined as an agency based on the curriculum practice (Bassus, Zaščerinska, & Ahrens, 2011, p. 84).

FUTURE RESEARCH DIRECTIONS

Enterprise 3.0 demonstrates the technology of online networks to assemble and manage large communities with a common interest in peer contribution, where organisations and enterprises have made use of the potential of Web 3.0 with single solutions such as online networks. However, Enterprise 4.0 as shown in Table 5 will be derived from the full application of Web 4.0 concepts such as ambient intelligence, WebOS or Web operating system, artificial intelligence, rather than Web 3.0 point solutions (Bassus, Ahrens, & Zaščerinska, 2011, p. 381). This remains as an open point for the future. It should be mentioned that the concept of a Web operating system or WebOS is distinct from Internet operating systems. Web operating system or WebOS is independent of the traditional individual computer operating system.

Another direction of further research might include Enterprise 2.0 application in five phases (Zaščerinska, 2011b, p. 145):

- Teaching in Phase 1,
- Teaching with elements of peer-learning in Phase 2,
- Peer-learning in Phase 3,
- Peer-learning with elements of learning in Phase 4 and
- Learning in Phase 5.

CONCLUSION

The findings of the research allow drawing the conclusions that Enterprise 2.0 application is efficient for the enhancement of student engineers' learning outcomes.

Regarding quality assurance, it is evident that the student engineers' learning outcomes have been enriched. Therein, Enterprise 2.0 application has contributed to the development of the engineering students' learning outcomes.

Regarding effectiveness of the educator's contribution to the student engineers' learning outcomes, it is evident that the engineering students widened their experience in social interaction and cognitive activity with the Enterprise 2.0

Table 5. Enterprise 2.0 in pedagogy in different historical periods

Phase	Historical Period	Approach	Elements of Enterprise	Educational settings
1.	2000 - 2006	Enterprise 1.0 as socialization	Social software	Tasks with use of Enterprise 1.0
2.	2006 - up to now	Enterprise 2.0 as community	Social software and online networks	Teaching techniques with use of Enterprise 2.0
3.	2007 - up to now	Enterprise 3.0 as organization	Online networks	Practice of the Enterprise 3.0 curriculum
4.	2010 - up to now	Enterprise 4.0 as society	Ambient intelligence, WebOS or Web operating system, artificial intelligence	University Degree

application. The engineering students' attitude is positive. That shows that the studies influence the student engineers' learning outcomes.

Moreover, validity of the qualitative evaluation research has been provided by use of the mixed methods' approach to the data obtaining, processing, and analysis. Validity and reliability of the research results have been provided by involving other researchers into several stages of the conducted research. External validity has been revealed by international co-operation. Therein, the researchers' positive evaluation of Enterprise 2.0 application for the development of engineering students' learning outcomes validates the findings of the present research.

Thus it might be stressed that Enterprise 2.0 application is efficient if students' needs are met and a support system implemented in the phases of a certain sequence is designed that would secure their social experience in social interaction and cognitive activity.

The present research has *limitations*. The inter-connections between engineering students' learning outcomes, Enterprise 2.0 application, and the sequence of its implementation have been set. Another limitation is the empirical study conducted by involving educators and students at master level of one tertiary institution. Therein, the results of the study cannot be representative for the whole area. Nevertheless, the results of the research - definition of Enterprise 2.0, Enterprise 2.0 application and the qualitative evaluation research – may be used as a basis of the development of engineering students' learning outcomes at master level of other tertiary institutions.

The following pedagogical guidelines on Enterprise 2.0 application in engineering curricula are elaborated: Enterprise 2.0 application proceeds from Phase 1 *Teaching* aimed at determining the notion of constructive social interaction and its organizational regulation through Phase 2 *Peer-Learning* designed for the students' analysis of an open academic problem situation and their search for its solving that provide each student with the opportunity to construct his/her own social experience to Phase 3 *Learning* focused on the students' self-regulation with use of evaluation of the process and self-evaluation of the result.

REFERENCES

Ahrens, A., & Zaščerinska, J. (2011). Enterprise 3.0 in engineering education. In G. Noviks (Ed.), *Proceedings of the 15th International Student Scientific Practical Conference Human Environment. Technology* Rēzekne: Rēzeknes Augstskolas Izdevniecība.

Bassus, O., Ahrens, A., & Zaščerinska, J. (2011). Clustering for the development of engineering students' use of enterprise 3.0. In *Proceedings of the 4th International Conference of Engineering & Business Education and 1st SAFRI Journey to Excellence Conference* (pp. 373-383). Cape Town, South Africa: Cape Peninsula University of Technology.

Bassus, O., & Wolfgramm, K. (2009). The innovative entrepreneurship training program at Hochschule Wismar University of Technology, Business and Design. In Ahrens & Lange (Eds.), *First Asian Conference on e-Business and Telecommunications* (pp. 36-39). Berlin: Mensch & Buch.

Bassus, O., Zaščerinska, J., & Ahrens, A. (2011). From enterprise 2.0 to 3.0: Challenges in engineering and business education. In Bassus, , Ahrens, , & Lange, (Eds.), *Information and Communication Technologies in Engineering and Business* (pp. 79-96). Berlin, Germany: Mensch & Buch.

Bluma, D. (2008). Teacher education in the context of Bologna process. In Žogla, I. (Ed.), *Association for Teacher Education in Europe Spring University Conference Teacher of the 21st Century: Quality Education for Quality Teaching* (pp. 673–680). Riga, Latvia: University of Latvia.

Boev, O. V., Kriushova, A. A., Kulyukina, E. S., Surygin, A. S., Freeston, I., Heitmann, G., & Chuchalin, A. I. (2011). *Guidelines on engineering curriculum design aligned with the European qualification framework and European standards for quality assurance of engineering education.* Tomsk: TPU Publishing House.

Buckmaster, R. A. (2004). *English for specific purposes on-line course.* Retrieved March 15, 2005, from http://www.sisekaitse.ee/?id=831

Cohen, L., & Manion, L. et al. (2003). *Research methods in education.* London: Routledge/Falmer Taylor & Francis Group.

Commission of the European Communities. (2006). *Efficiency and equity in European education and training systems.* Retrieved December 3, 2011, from ec.europa.eu/education/policies/2010/doc/comm481_en.pdf

Flick, U. (2004). Design and process in qualitative research. In Flick, U., Von Kardoff, E., & Steine, I. (Eds.), *A Companion to Qualitative Research* (pp. 146–152). London: SAGE.

Flyvbjerg, B. (2006). Five misunderstandings about case-study research. *Qualitative Inquiry, 12*(2), 219–245. doi:10.1177/1077800405284363.

Gigerenzer, G. (2004). Mindless statistics. *Journal of Socio-Economics, 33*(5), 587–606. doi:10.1016/j.socec.2004.09.033.

Ilyinska, L. (2004). *English for science and technology: Course design, text analysis, research writing.* RTU Publishing House.

Kardoff, E. (2004). Qualitative evaluation research. In Flick, U., Von Kardoff, E., & Steinke, I. (Eds.), *A Companion to Qualitative Research* (pp. 137–142). London: SAGE.

Lūka, I. (2008). Development of students' ESP competence and educator's professional activity in tertiary level tourism studies. In Žogla, I. (Ed.), *Association for Teacher Education in Europe Spring University Conference Teacher of the 21st Century: Quality Education for Quality Teaching* (pp. 689–697). Riga, Latvia: University of Latvia.

Maslo, E. (2007). Transformative learning space for life-long foreign languages learning. In D. Cunningham, D. Markus, J. Valdmanis, et al. (Eds.), *International Nordic-Baltic Region Conference of FIPLV Innovations in Language Teaching and Learning in the Multicultural Context* (pp. 38-46). Rīga: SIA Izglītības Soļi.

Mayring, P. (2004). Qualitative content analysis. In Flick, , von Kardoff, , & Steinke, (Eds.), *A Companion to Qualitative Research* (pp. 266-269). London: SAGE.

Mayring, P. (2007). On generalization in qualitatively oriented research. *Forum Qualitative Sozial Forschung, 8*(3), 1–8.

Nadhan, E. G. (2008). *Forecast for the next generation enterprise 3.0.* Paper presented at the EDS Distinguished SE Open Group Enterprise Architecture Practitioners Conference. Chicago, IL.

Oganisjana, K., & Koke, T. (2008). Developing students' enterprise. In Maslo, Kiegelmann, & Huber (Ed.), Qualitative Psychology in the Changing Academic Context (pp. 218-233). Tübingen, Germany: Academic Press.

Philippou, S. (2005). The problem of the European dimension in education: A principled reconstruction of the Greek Cypriot curriculum. *European Educational Research Journal, 4*(4), 343–367. doi:10.2304/eerj.2005.4.4.2.

Portelli, J. P., & Vilbert, A. B. (2002a). A curriculum of life. *Education Canada, 42*(2), 36–39.

Portelli, J. P., & Vilbert, A. B. (2002b). Standards, equity, and the curriculum of life. *Analytic Teaching*, *22*(1), 4–19.

Reich, K. (2005). *Systemisch-konstruktivistische pädagogik*. Weinheim: Beltz.

Vossen, G. (2009). Web 2.0: A buzzword, a serious development, just fun, or what? In J. Filipe, D. A. Marca, B. Shishkov, M. van Sinderen (Eds.), *ICE-B 2009 - Proceedings of the International Conference on e-Business*, (pp. 33-40). Milan, Italy: INSTICC Press.

ZaščerinskaJ. (2009). Designing teaching/learning activities to promote e-learning. In AhrensLange (Eds.), First Asian Conference on e-Business and Telecommunications (pp. 22-35). Berlin, Germany: Mensch & Buch.

Zaščerinska, J. (2010a). Conditions, criteria, indicators and levels of forming communicative competence. In *Proceedings of International Scientifical Conference Society, Integration, Education of Rezekne Higher Education Institution*. Rēzekne, Latvia: Rēzeknes Augstskolas Izdevniecība.

Zaščerinska, J. (2010b). *Efficiency of English for academic purposes activity in student language education: developing the system of the external and internal perspectives*. Paper presented at the European Conference on Educational Research Education and Cultural Change. Helsinki, Finland. Retrieved December 3, 2011, from http://www.eera-ecer.eu/ecer-programmes/conference/ecer-2010/contribution/465-2/?no_cache=1&cHash=3b88f1a563

Zaščerinska, J. (2011a). Social dimension of web 3.0 in engineering education. In Bassus, , & Ahrens, , & Lange (Eds.), *Information and Communication Technologies in Engineering and Business* (pp. 101-130). Berlin, Germany: Mensch & Buch.

Zaščerinska, J. (2011b). How to teach content: Existing concepts and prospects for development. *Changing Education in a Changing Society, 1*, 134–149.

Zaščerinska, J., & Ahrens, A. (2011). *Components of languaging in tertiary studies*. Paper presented at the European Conference on Educational Research 2011 Urban Education. Berlin, Germany.

Zaščerinska, J., Ahrens, A., & Bassus, O. (2011). Enterprise 2.0 and 3.0 in education: Engineering and business students' view. In Cruz-Cunha, M. M., Putnik, G. D., Lopes, N., Gonçalves, P., & Miranda, E. (Eds.), *Business Social Networking: Organizational, Managerial, and Technological Dimensions* (pp. 472–494). Hershey, PA: IGI Global. doi:10.4018/978-1-61350-168-9.ch025.

KEY TERMS AND DEFINITIONS

Constituencies: Broad statements that describe what graduates are expected to attain within a few years of graduation.

Curriculum: A central, organizing stance (Portelli & Vilbert, 2002a, p. 39).

Effectiveness of Enterprise 2.0 Application: Educator's contribution to the student engineers' knowledge, skills and attitudes to Enterprise 2.0 application (Zaščerinska, 2011a, p. 125-126).

Enterprise 2.0: Use of Web technologies for enterprise (business) purposes.

Enterprise 3.0: An agency based on the curriculum practice (Bassus, Zaščerinska, & Ahrens, 2011, p. 84).

Experience: Knowledge, skills, and attitudes (Zaščerinska, 2010a, p. 415).

Learning Outcomes: Knowledge, skills, and attitudes.

Quality of Enterprise 2.0 Application: Improvement of students' knowledge, skills and attitudes (Zaščerinska, 2011a, p. 125).

Chapter 32
Brazilian Government's Training Network for Digital Inclusion:
Analysis of Strategies for Improving Interactivity

Silvana Rossy de Brito
Federal Rural University of Amazônia (UFRA), Brazil

Aleksandra do Socorro da Silva
Federal Rural University of Amazônia (UFRA), Brazil

Dalton Lopes Martins
University of Sao Paulo (USP), Brazil

Cláudio Alex Jorge da Rocha
Federal University of Pará (UFPA), Brazil & University of Amazônia (UNAMA), Brazil

João Crisóstomo Weyl Albuquerque Costa
Federal University of Pará (UFPA), Brazil

Carlos Renato Lisboa Francês
Federal University of Pará (UFPA), Brazil

ABSTRACT

This chapter summarizes several previous studies on the analysis of social networks and presents some challenges in monitoring and evaluating large-scale training programs that make use of social networks. The main objective is to understand the dynamics and identify how information is shared among the participating agents of the training program. In this regard, the authors present various algorithms that apply metrics to social network analysis to assess the evolution of networks throughout the training process, and specifically, to discuss the application of these metrics in the evaluation of large-scale training programs for digital inclusion.

INTRODUCTION

Evaluation and monitoring of large scale training programs requires different techniques, systems, and methods of analysis. For training programs that make extensive use of social networks, we emphasize approaches based on Social Network Analysis (SNA). SNA facilitates quantitative and qualitative analysis of social networks by describing the features of a network, either through numerical or visual representations.

The aim of this chapter is to present an application of SNA for the evaluation and monitoring of a training program for young people to act as

DOI: 10.4018/978-1-4666-4373-4.ch032

agents of digital inclusion in their role as monitors of telecenters, specifically, in the context of the Telecentros.BR program. One of the objectives of Telecentros.BR is to train monitors in different regions of the country so that they can play an important role as agents of digital inclusion. Moreover, the monitors are encouraged to embrace social networking to facilitate collaboration in solving simple problems in the daily routine of telecenters.

In light of this, the chapter has the following objectives: (1) the application of algorithms to measure the centrality and density of interactions in a real scenario with a consolidated social network; (2) improving the process of large scale training by incorporating the use of social networks.

The chapter is organized as follows.

- Background provides broad definitions and discussions of the topic by incorporating a literature review of the application of algorithms for visualization and measurement of large-scale social networks.
- Challenges in measuring and monitoring large-scale training programs based on social networks – This section reports the main difficulties in applying monitoring and evaluation methodologies in training programs required to use social networks on a large scale. Additionally, this section provides solutions and recommendations for dealing with the problems presented. To this end, we present an application scenario, the "The National Network of Training", which is a training program for monitors of telecenters covering all regions of Brazil . The scenario helps the reader to understand how social networks can support the daily tasks of monitors.
- Metrics to analyze the social networks of monitors, tutors and collaborators – presents metrics of centrality (for degree, closeness, and betweenness), average distance, and density of monitors in the network. The algorithms associated with these metrics are applied to networks of monitors, tutors and collaborators over ten months of training, in order to visualize and analyze the evolution of these indicators.
- Results and Discussion presents a discussion on the relevance of the indicators obtained from the metrics , to provide feedback for the promotion of strategies and monitoring of interactions between monitors and monitors and tutors. The discussion is centered on the possibility of incorporating metrics for network analysis in the construction of a methodology for monitoring and evaluating large scale training programs.

BACKGROUND

Social Network Analysis (SNA) involves the mapping and measurement of relationships and flows between people, groups, organizations, computers, or other information/knowledge processing entities (Krebs, 2000). It is an approach that originated in Sociology, Psychology, and Social Anthropology (Freeman, 1996), and deals with relational ties between actors that can be analyzed as individual units or collectively, for example, departments within an organization, public service agencies, nation-states on a continent or in the world (Wasserman & Faust, 1994). This research approach has developed rapidly over the past twenty years, principally in studies in sociology (Galaskiewicz & Wasserman, 1993; Wellman & Berkowitz, 1988), science (Ben-David & Collins, 1966; Mullins, 1972; Price, 1986), and communication science (Monge & Contractor, 2001; Rogers & Kincaid, 1981).

SNA represents an area of interest for researchers from several fields of knowledge, giving rise to various methods of analysis that are based on structures of networks constructed from the relations between social units. This interest in analyzing actors (e.g., individuals, organizations, Websites, computers, words or neurons) and their relationships, the mathematical foundation of which is based on graph theory, has resulted in several important discoveries being made about the emergent properties of these networks in terms of how they are established, evolve, and function. Taking advantage of the flexibility of the concept of an actor, SNA can be applied to studies in several areas, such as bibliometrics (Otte & Rousseau, 2002), infometrics (Wasserman & Faust, 1994), and communities of practice (Cullen & Morse, 2011; Salvetti & Srinivasan, 2005). According to different applications, the entities to be analyzed can be social actors (individuals, organizations, countries, etc.) (Wasserman & Faust, 1994), Web pages (Brin &Page, 2006; Page, Brin, Motwani, & Winograd, 1998), or documents, amongst others.

In SNA, attributes observed from the social actors (such as race or ethnic group of individuals, firms or nation-states) are understood in terms of patterns or structures of connections between units. The relational links between actors are the primary focus of the actors, while the attributes are the secondary focus (Wasserman & Faust, 1994).

The study of social networks and complex networks involves techniques and methods of analysis that can be applied in different contexts (e.g., friendship, research development, business relationships, or the relationship between words in a speech) to model the observed relationships between actors and clarify / explain the structure of a given network, recognizing that it is not possible to assess the social relations using levels of abstractions that do not consider the relationships. In other words, you need to think relationally, and see, on the one hand, the weight of the structures and social systems and on the other hand, the subjects and their processes of individual decisions.

Social Network

A social network consists of one or more finite sets of actors [and events] and all defined relationships between them (Wasserman & Faust, 1994). It should be understood that the classification of a social network adopted here is broad and may even include non-human actors. In this context, a social network is a set of nodes (people, organizations, or other social entities) connected by a set of relationships, such as affiliation, friendship, and information exchange (Wasserman & Faust, 1994).

Actors or Nodes

In SNA, an actor is a discrete unit of different types, more specifically a person, or a discrete set of people aggregated into a collective social unit, such as a subgroup, organization, or other group (Wasserman & Faust, 1994). For the authors, the concept of an actor is flexible enough to allow different levels of aggregation, making it suitable for different research problems, i.e., an actor can be an individual, a company, a public service agency, or a nation. The attributes of an actor are obtained from its own individual characteristics.

To Lemieux and Ouimet (2004), social actors were characterized more by their relationships than by their attributes (gender, age, social class). These relations have a variable density, i.e., the distance between two actors can be greater or smaller and some actors may occupy more central positions than others. This phenomenon has been explained by various researchers in terms of the existence of strong and weak ties and "structural holes" where the actors cannot communicate with each other except through a third actor.

Therefore, although the primary focus of SNA is on "relational ties," this does not mean that the attributes are analyzed, for example, by traditional statistical methods, because the values of attributes are collected. The set of attributes of a network is called the composition of the social network (Wasserman & Faust, 1994).

Ties or Links

A "relational tie," also referred to simply as a tie or linkage, is responsible for establishing the link between pairs of actors. Thus, the links between actors are channels for the transfer or flow of material and nonmaterial resources (Wasserman & Faust, 1994). The most common types of bonds are: friendship or respect; transaction and transfer of material resources, purchase and sale transactions, transfer of non-material resources, exchange of electronic (or other) data messages, association or affiliation, which occurs when actors participate in common events, studying migration and occupation, links between formal roles, such as the ties between a boss and subordinates in businesses; and biological relationships (Wasserman & Faust, 1994).

Sociological studies of social networks distinguish strong ties, absent ties, and weak ties (Granovetter, 1983). Granovetter's work alerted sociologists to the importance of weak ties, mainly as a result of their bridging function between parts of a social network that are not linked directly through strong ties. This gave rise to the concept of a bridge (Granovetter, 1983). An actor that acts as a bridge is responsible for the ties between two subgroups of a social network. In other words, the 'bridge agent' or 'bridge actor' is an individual strongly linked to a [sub] primary group that regularly interacts with one another [sub] group" (Grosser, 1991). For Granovetter (1983), the strength of a tie is a combination, probably linear, of the amount of time, emotional intensity, intimacy (mutual trust), and reciprocal services that characterize the tie.

Given a set of actors, a relation in a network defines the entire set of links satisfying the criteria of the relationship. Multi-relational networks are those in which there is more than one type of tie, and thus, more than one relationship (Wasserman & Faust, 1994). For the authors, relationships have two important properties that should be considered in research:

1. **Direction:** Relationships may be directional, i.e., if there is a transmitter and a receiver, or non-directional, if the relationship is reciprocal, as in the case of friendship, for example.
2. **Valuation:** Relationships may be dichotomous (implying the presence or absence thereof) or valued (consisting of discrete or continuous values). In the case of valued relationships, values can, for example, refer to the intensity of ties.

As examples of communication between actors (nodes), we list the following works:

- Communication between actors (nodes) to obtain beneficial information (Borgatti &, Croos, 2003; Granovetter, 1983; Lin, Cook, & Burt, 2001;Uzzi & Schwartz, 1993);
- Exchange of electronic messages between people (Wasserman & Faust, 1994);
- Formal relations of authority in an organization (Krackhardt, 1987, 2000; Krackhardt & Hanson, 1993; Molina, 1999);
- Analysis of business networks in clusters or local clusters (APL's) (Macías, 2002; Saxenian, 1994);
- Study of networks of small and medium enterprises (Rocha, 2003);
- Entrepreneurship and family networks (Lin, Fu, & Hsung, 2001);
- Networks between large firms and their suppliers (Carleial, 2001);
- Social network analysis as a method for analyzing interaction in collaborative online learning environments (Mazur, Doran,

&Doran, 2010; Rice Doran, Doran, & Mazur, 2011; Yu, Tian, Vogel, & Chi-Wai Kwok, 2010);
- Detection of online communities (Bouguessa, Wang, & Dumoulin, 2010; Cullen & Morse, 2011; Kleinberg, 1999; Newman & Girvan, 2003; Salvetti & Srinivasan, 2005); and
- Social Inclusiveness and e-governance (Becker, Bergener, Niehaves, & Räckers, 2008; Gaved & Mulholland, 2010; Matheus, Ribeiro, Vaz, & De Souza, 2010).

Types of Social Networks

With respect to actors, a social network can be classified as (Wasserman & Faust, 1994):

- A single mode network (one-mode), which represents the relationships between social entities of the same type, for example, who is a friend of whom, or who asks for advice for anyone that depends on whom; or
- A dual mode network (or two-mode network), which has two distinct sets of actors, with specific attributes for each set. Distinct sets of actors can be, for example, the people and government agencies, or students and teachers. In a dual mode network, one set of actors is usually the "sender" of the relationship, while the other is the "receiver" (Wasserman & Faust, 1994). From a two-mode network, one can obtain the associated one-mode networks using mathematical operations on the network.

There are also higher-mode networks that have more than two sets of actors, but the calculation methods used in SNA are generally not designed for such networks (Wasserman & Faust, 1994).

Social networks can deal with the following types of relationships (Wasserman & Faust, 1994):

- Dyad, which is the unit of analysis of the relationship between two actors. This is the lowest level of network analysis, which seeks to identify, for example, if the links are reciprocal and, in a multi-relational network, whether a specific set of multiple relationships tends to occur simultaneously (Wasserman & Faust, 1994).
- Triad, which is the unit of analysis of the relationship between a subset of three actors and the possible links between them. This type is related to studies of tautologies. Transitivity (or the lack thereof) of a relationship (if actor A likes B and B likes C, then A likes C) is a type of analysis using the concept of a trinity. Granovetter (1983), for example, assuming the premise of transitivity between actors with strong ties, showed why weak ties are of particular importance as bridges between parts of the network that are not tightly linked. The analysis of transitivity is the central theme in the analysis of the structural balance of a network, which is part of the balance theory (Wasserman & Faust, 1994).
- Group, which is a collection of dyads, triads, and groups with a finite number of actors. A subgroup is a subset of all possible actors and relations (sets of ties) among them (Wasserman & Faust, 1994). In terms of social networks, a clique is a subgroup in which each actor has ties with all others, but there can be any other actor outside the clique that has links with all actors in the clique. According to Houaiss and Villar (2001), a clique is a small group of people spontaneously structured within a larger group according to empathy and mutual interests and in which all members display only positive feelings towards each other. In view of networks, a clique is a complete subgraph.

Social networks can also be defined with respect to scope and by considering the data contained therein (Hanneman & Riddle, 2005). According to the scope, social networks can be classified (Hanneman & Riddle, 2005) as total (also known as sociocentric), egocentric, or open systems.

Metrics (Measures) in Social Network Analysis

In recent years, when confronted with the work of Wasserman and Faust (1994), research in SNA resulted in themes that promoted the emergence of different metrics . The set of metrics for SNA includes the following.

1. **Centrality:** One of the methods used to understand networks and their participants is to evaluate the location of the participants in the network, where measuring the network location implies finding the "centrality" of a node (Salvetti & Srinivasan, 2005). This measure helps to determine the importance or relevance of a node in the network. Three of the most popular measures of centrality are the degree, betweenness, and closeness (Wasserman & Faust, 1994). This measure also gives a rough indication of the social power of a node based on how well it is "connected" in the network. A central actor is one that is extensively involved in relationships with other actors, or is a transmitter or receiver. This involvement makes it more visible to others. There are four types of metrics for centrality (Wasserman & Faust, 1994):
   a. **Degree Centrality:** The centrality of a node in the network is related to the degree of the node. This metric focuses on the visibility of a node in the network. The most central node is the one with the highest degree, and as such, is in contact with the most other nodes. It occupies a central place in the network.
   b. **Closeness Centrality:** This metric is based on distance and focuses on how close an actor is in relation to other network actors. An actor is central if it can quickly interact with others. In the context of a communication network, for example, the central actors can be very productive in sharing information with the rest of the group because they have a fast way of communicating with the others. In this case, centrality is inversely related to distance. Thus, closeness is the inverse of the sum of the shortest distances between each individual and every other person in the network. The shortest path is also known as the "geodesic distance". Thus, the greater the distance is from one vertex to the rest of the network, the smaller is the closeness centrality; that is, the degree to which an individual is close to all other individuals in a network (directly or indirectly). The metric reflects the ability to access information through the "grapevine" of network members.
   c. **Betweenness Centrality (BC):** Interactions between two non-adjacent nodes depend on nodes that are located on the path between them. These intermediate nodes potentially have control over the interactions between two non-adjacent nodes. To have a high BC, a node must be on the path between several other nodes. BC is, in some sense, a measure of the influence that a node has over the flow of information through the network. Conceptually, nodes with high betweenness lie on a large number of non-redundant shortest paths be-

tween other nodes; they can therefore, be thought of as "bridges" or "boundary spanners". BC has been shown to increase exponentially with connectivity as a power law, and, therefore, is a computationally intense network measure (Salvetti & Srinivasan, 2005). Current algorithms for computing betweenness can deal efficiently with networks of up to several hundred nodes (Brandes, 2001). However, with the increasing interest in Web magnitude datasets, there is an increasing demand for efficient computation of centrality indices for networks with millions of nodes (Salvetti & Srinivasan, 2005).

   d. **Information Centrality:** Generalizes the notion of betweenness centrality in all walks between nodes, giving weights to edges depending on the length of each path. In this sense, information centrality is the inverse of the length of the path.

2. **Path Length:** The distance or path length is the length (number of edges) of the shortest path between two vertices. The average path length is the average of the distances between all pairs of nodes in the network. The length of the longest shortest path in a graph is called its diameter (Batagelj, 2009).
3. **Density:** This denotes the degree to which a respondent's ties know about one another or the proportion of ties among an individual's nominees. Network or global-level density is the proportion of ties in a network relative to the total number possible (sparse versus dense networks).

In addition to the metrics described above, Table 1 presents a summary of other relevant metrics discussed in the literature.

Research Methodology used in SNA

Data collection for SNA is carried out using methods commonly used in the social sciences (Borgatti, Mehra, Brass, & Labianca, 2009) such as questionnaires, interviews, observations, data files, controlled experiments, and diaries (Wasserman & Faust, 1994).

Visual Representation of Social Networks

Visual representation of social networks is important to understand the network data and convey the results of the analysis (Freeman, 2004). Many of the analytic software systems have modules for network visualization. Exploration of the data is done by displaying nodes and ties in various layouts, and attributing different colors, sizes and other advanced properties to nodes. Although visual representation of networks is a powerful method for conveying complex information, care should be taken in interpreting node and graph properties from visual displays alone, as they may misrepresent structural properties better captured through quantitative analyses (McGrath, Blythe, & Krackhardt, 1997).

Huisman and van Duijn (2003) analyzed 27 software packages, comparing the types of data, features, and support available for the different packages. Included in the analysis were UCINET, Pajek, NetMiner II, STRUCTURE, and MultiNet StOCNET.

Display types most commonly used in the literature are viewing time, which shows changes that occur in the social network at various time intervals (Santos & Souza, 2008) and multidimensional view, which combines multiple social networks seeking to understand how these different networks influence or are related to each other (Balieiro, Sousa, & Souza, 2008).

Table 1. Metrics (measures) in social network analysis

Metrics	Description
Bridge	An edge is said to be a bridge if deleting it would cause its endpoints to lie in different components of a graph (Grosser, 1991). Is a line such that the graph containing the line has fewer components than the subgraph that is obtained after the line is removed (Wasserman & Faust, 1994).
Local bridge	An edge is a local bridge if its endpoints share no common neighbors. Unlike a bridge, a local bridge is contained in a cycle (Wasserman & Faust, 1994).
Centralization	Centralization considers the indegree centrality scores of the most central points and those of all other points in the graph. It is the ratio of the actual sum of differences between the most central node and all others compared to the maximum possible sum of the differences. A centralized network will have many of its links dispersed around one or a few nodes, while a decentralized network is one in which there is little variation between the number of links each node possesses (Scott, 2000).
Clustering coefficient	Measures the extent to which two associates of a node are also associates themselves. The clustering coefficient is an indication of the "cliquishness" of a network (Shi, Zhu, & Lui, 2007).
Cohesion	The degree to which actors are connected directly to each other by cohesive bonds (Wasserman & Faust, 1994).
Structural cohesion	Structural cohesion is defined as the minimum number of actors who, if removed from a group, would disconnect the group (Moody & White, 2003).
Eigenvector centrality	Another popular measure of centrality is eigenvector centrality (Bonacich, 1972). It assigns relative scores to all nodes in the network based on the principle that connections to nodes having a high score contribute more to the score of the node in question.
Human interaction	Links in social networks are formed through human interactions. Scaling laws in human interaction activity (Rybski, Buldyrev, Havlin, Liljeros, & Makse, 2009).
Influential Spreaders	A method to identify influential spreaders (Kitsak *et al.*, 2010).
Prestige	In a directed graph prestige is the term used to describe a node's centrality. "Degree Prestige," "Proximity Prestige," and "Status Prestige" are measures of Prestige (Wasserman & Faust, 1994)
Radiality	Degree an individual's network reaches out into the network and provides novel information and influence (Wasserman & Faust, 1994).
Reach	The degree any member of a network can reach other members of the network (Wasserman & Faust, 1994).
Second order centrality	It assigns relative scores to all nodes in the network based on the observation that important nodes see a random walk (running on the network) "more regularly" than other nodes (Kermarrec, Le Merrer, Sericola, & Trédan, 2010).
Structural equivalence	Refers to the extent to which nodes have a common set of linkages to other nodes in the system. The nodes don't need to have any ties to each other to be structurally equivalent (Wasserman & Faust, 1994).
Structural hole	Static holes that can be strategically filled by connecting one or more links to link together other points. Linked to ideas of social capital: if you link to two people who are not linked you can control their communication (Andrews, 1995; Burt, 2004; Uzzi & Schwartz, 1993).

CHALLENGES IN MEASURING AND MONITORING LARGE SCALE TRAINING PROGRAMS BASED ON SOCIAL NETWORKS

Investment in large scale training programs to meet the challenges of social exclusion has been reported in several countries. To meet the Millennium Development Goals for digital inclusion, countries in Latin America have invested in public policies that promote universal access and facilitate the creation and use of community technology centers or telecenters, where public access to Information and Communication Technology (ICT) is available to less privileged communities at minimal cost. In Brazil, several initiatives under the auspices of different government institutions have been implemented to reduce the digital divide. Among these initiatives, we highlight the implementation of public or community centers (telecenters) for universal access to ICTs, through the concerted efforts of a large number of decentralized initiatives, such as Casa Brazil, the Points of Culture, Rural Telecenters, Telecenters for Communities of fishermen and people living along rivers, and other programs registered with the portal for digital inclusion programs of the Federal Government (http:// http://www.inclusaodigital.gov.br).

Successful local government initiatives and international experience have served as examples and inspiration for the dissemination of telecenters around the country, not only by the Federal Government, but also by local government and civil society organizations (Prado, Câmara, & Figueiredo, 2011). In this context, telecenters are public and community spaces that provide free public access to ICTs through Internet-connected computers available for multiple uses, including free navigation and assisted courses and other activities to promote local development in its various dimensions, created by both public and private nonprofit local entities.

However, despite recent efforts to consolidate public policy to minimize the digital divide, there are many challenges that the Brazilian Federal Government and third sector organizations are facing (Gomez, 2012; Mori & Assumpção, 2007); namely, broadband Internet access, funding for the maintenance of existing infrastructure (schools, telecenters), production of local content, qualified agents for digital inclusion in initiatives with adequate working conditions, mechanisms for participatory government programs and initiatives for digital inclusion, universal access to services at the local level, co-responsibility between the Federal, state and local governments, and development of budgetary and administrative capacity in local government. The extraordinary geographical dimensions of the Brazilian territory may justify the fact that many rural communities and rural people, and riparian areas under environmental protection remain isolated from the actions derived from the public policy of digital inclusion in the adopted country.

With the deployment of telecenters, the policy of digital inclusion in Brazil has taken a step forward, unveiling an attractive scenario for researchers to trace the evolution of telecenters in various countries, and examine the impact of access to ICT in social justice and in raising the Human Development Index (HDI):

- Brazil (Bossio, 2006; Madon, Reinhard, Roode, & Walsham, 2009; Mori & Assumpção, 2007; Sorj, 2003);
- Colombia (Amariles, Paz, Russell, & Johnson, 2006; Gomez & Baron, 2011; Montoya, 2007; Parkinson & Lauzon, 2008; Parkinson & Ramirez, 2006);
- Dominican Republic (Granqvist, 2005; Prado, 2009);
- Mexico (Robertson, 1998; Sandoval-Almaz, 2007);
- India (Kumar & Best, 2006; Pick & Gollakota, 2010);
- China (Zhang, 2008);
- Peru (Heeks & León, 2009); and
- South Africa (Parkinson, 2005).

However, despite the growing number of researchers evaluating both quantitatively and qualitatively the impact of the use of telecenters in communities, further study is needed to determine whether reducing the digital divide has had a positive impact on the prosperity of these communities, by reducing inequalities and improving the quality of the lives of people in the communities (Pather & Gomez, 2010).

Despite the challenges of infrastructure for the implementation and maintenance of these community spaces, we must recognize that one of the main challenges for the development of e-government and a digital city is participation by low income, older and technology-challenged citizens (Bailey & Ngwenyama, 2011). Furthermore, the characteristics of Web 2.0 are changing the way citizens interact and participate (Ramanathan, Ramnath, Singh, Xu, & Xu, 2011). On the other hand, participation in virtual communities and the interaction of community members offline using telecenters (Bailey & Ngwenyama, 2011) indicate that these communities can provide support for the delivery of electronic services for the development of digital cities and increased e-governance. It is against this backdrop that some progress has been made in the public policy of digital inclusion focused on placing qualified agents of digital inclusion directly in those communities with high rates of social exclusion.

Given these findings, proposals have been put forward for digital inclusion training based strongly on the characteristics of Web 2.0 and social networks as a way of enhancing the actions of these agents in their communities. In Brazil, the proposed digital inclusion training with greater geographical reach has been implemented through the auspices of the Telecentros.BR program (Decree n. 6991, 2009).

Telecentros.BR Program: Training Based on Social Networks of Monitors and their Communities

The Telecentros.BR program (Decree n. 6991, 2009) is an initiative of the Federal Government to support the implementation of new public centers and strengthen existing units in the country for the program. Community and public centers are spaces that provide public access to free ICTs with Internet-connected computers available for multiple uses, including free navigation and assisted courses and other activities to promote local development in its various dimensions, under the responsibility of a local entity, either a public or private nonprofit organization. Telecenters have monitors that, in addition to facilitating the use of ICTs as tools to leverage social change in the community, undergo training, offered by the National Training Network for Digital inclusion (http://www.telecentros.br.com).

The Telecentros.BR network includes the participation of five regional centers (one for each region of the country), two state centers (in the states of Sao Paulo and Ceará), and a national center, selected by the public notice. The regional centers are responsible for the training of monitors, tutors, and managers of telecenters. For the construction of a proposal consistent with the formation network, these organizations are in a learning community at the time while they are forming will be graduating from the process of collaborative networking. The guidelines that guide the actions of the training network are being constructed during the process of setting up this network.

Faced with the challenges of articulating different views (teaching strategies, cultures, social networking and structuring technological tools), the efforts of the different training centers require the use of technological resources that form several collaborative spaces, which is the target of this research. With the focus on the construction of collaboration between the different agents in the centers in the training network, this work explores the interactive aspects of network monitors and networks of centers to contribute to the discussion on indicators for evaluating large-scale training programs, as in the case of Telecentros.BR.

The overall objective of Telecentros.BR is to develop joint activities (between Federal Government agencies, states, municipalities, and civil society) that enable lifelong learning and continuous large-scale agents for digital inclusion (Department of Digital inclusion [DDI], 2011). Therefore, it is necessary to coordinate the various initiatives for digital inclusion in the country, and in this respect, the training centers work collaboratively to specify, design, and implement learning spaces, and procedures for conducting training and for the activation of social networks of monitors for telecenters. The specific objectives of the training network include (DDI, 2011):

1. Building an integrated agenda for training for digital inclusion at the national level, by optimizing efforts and resources in pursuit of these activities;
2. Promoting social and educational processes that support human social transformation through digital inclusion initiatives;
3. Developing participatory, cooperative and unified training processes, that respect and value the ethnic-racial and sexual balance in gender relations and intergenerational differences between urban and rural communities, and promote accessibility;
4. Promoting processes for collaboration and network activities.

One of the first activities of the Training Network was the establishment of Telecenters for the Training Course for Monitors and activation of social networks of agents working for social inclusion in communities. Thus, based on the collective proposals created through collaboration and negotiation between members of the centers, the project includes training of monitors to offer a 480 hour course, divided into two modules: 80 hours for introductory information and setting out the contents of the training and 400 hours with a specific focus on the development of community projects supported by the infrastructure of the telecenter.

During the course, to develop their community projects, the monitors undergo training in different thematic areas based on their interests and needs, without any pre-defined structure. The monitors have the support of tutors and tutor supervisors from the various regional centers.

The training must ensure that monitors can use ICTs as tools to leverage social change in the communities they serve. As such, monitors must achieve technical mastery of the tools and instruments related to ICTs, acting in unison, cooperatively and interactively with their peers, and work training, under conditions to recognize and act as an agent of social transformation in the community in which they operate.

Although the course has been developed over a network, using distance-learning methods and focusing on collaboration in online communities with the support of the Moodle platform (http://moodle.org) and social networks, face-to-face meetings also take place with the focus on experiential and practical community projects.

Challenges and Findings

The collaborative work of the centers, with a focus on training of monitors and the activation of social networks of monitors in their communities, has produced reflections that translate into challenges and findings:

- Monitors, while sharing knowledge, questions, expectations, outcomes and learning experiences, build social networks with other monitors and with their communities;
- Social networks of monitors can be activated, stimulated, and guided to function as an area of support and articulation of ideas aimed at improving technical solutions to common problems in the telecenters and the sharing of solutions;
- Social networks of monitors functioning as a space for the articulation of community projects and the search for solutions to day-to-day technical problems indicate that monitors and communities are making use of the telecenters;
- Monitors, tutors, and supervisors have different profiles (e.g., age, education, social networks, serving on community projects,

and other more specific features) dependent on regional particularities, which are not always observed and considered;

- Monitors discuss different topics, mainly through community projects, with the most diverse actors (not necessarily participants) of the training program. The topics under discussion motivate the review and development of new content based on the issues of greatest interest or motivation. Therefore, the Training Network must include services that promote self-regulation of the production of content based on the demands of communities, to improve the training process;
- The activation of social networks of monitors in the field creates relationships with learners of a common core of content and issues. From this perspective, the production of content and activities can help to stimulate interaction and increase the potential for network evolution in training;
- The proposed activities should start from a systemic perspective of reality, by identifying local issues of common interest, in view of the ownership of the telecenter community. They should look to considering the differences between urban and rural communities, respect and appreciation of ethnic-racial and sexual balance in gender relations, and intergenerational security and accessibility, among others (DDI, 2011).

To meet these challenges, the course offers training over a network, based on flexible, open and horizontal relations, involving monitors and agents of the centers. This is achieved through online communities, in which the actors create collective solutions to daily challenges and extend the activities contributing to the promotion of telecenter spaces and the feeling of belonging to a network of agents of digital inclusion.

The activation strategies of network monitors require investment in interactive resource use, places where, through the correct processes, information is contextualized and transformed to local realities. In this context, the joint work of the centers is faced with creating participatory learning environments, that are supportive, marked by warmth, the joy of living, care for others, and respect for differences, and based on cooperation (DDI, 2011).

Finally, the focus is not on the transmission of knowledge, but on the development of the potential of the monitors, through the enhancement of local knowledge and encouraging the formation of autonomous individuals acting in collaborative online communities.

Monitoring the Training

During the first eight months of the training program, members of the centers dedicated time and effort to the establishment and strengthening of links between the different actors through the collective initiation and development of community projects. This creativity was motivated by physical meetings with continued discussions via the mailing lists.

According to the dynamics of construction of virtual spaces using the platform of distance education, the content is continually under development and review, following the strategy to co-opt authors as tutors and monitors when appropriate throughout the training based on the content and technology. Thus, members of the centers and monitors share the same spaces, using them to develop and improve their projects. This constitutes the main strategy to promote spontaneous conversation between members of the centers and monitors, favoring the activation of social networks. This training model was designed, initially, to reach around 16 000 monitors and 600 tutors.

To implement and carry out the training course for monitors and activate social networks for the main agents of digital inclusion, the program requires a different type of monitoring. In other words, it is necessary to evaluate:

1. The performance of the monitors on the course, based on their contributions to the development of community projects, and
2. Whether the training contributes to the activation of networks of agents for digital inclusion, and the promotion of connections as social spaces for sharing, solving of everyday problems of the telecenters, and proposal of community projects.

Faced with these premises, to evaluate the effectiveness of the program, it is necessary not only to consider the assessment of learning, but also to assess the indicators that reflect the activities of social interaction among the participants.

To meet these goals, two working groups were established for educational evaluation and monitoring management, respectively. The evaluation group was responsible for the educational development of questionnaires, monitoring, and evaluation of community projects of mentoring, supervision, and others. On the other hand, the monitoring management group was tasked with proposing mechanisms to assess the strategies of network connectivity used throughout the training. Some results of the indicators produced by this group are presented in the next subsection.

Interaction between Actors in the Telecentros.BR Network

To monitor and measure the activation of social networks, the following interactions have been designated for management monitoring:

1. Between members of different centers;
2. Between monitors;
3. Between members of the centers and monitors in their service area, which mainly arise from the strategies adopted by the hubs during the training process.

In principle, one must consider that the current phase is the training program of the Telecentros.BR Network, with records from 12 (twelve) months of interactions between members of different centers (type [1] interactions), and 8 (eight) months of interactions of types (2) and (3).

The distinction between these three levels of interaction enables the initial characteristics of the strategy of connectivity and network evolution to be ascertained. The dimensions suggest that the composition of network activities including various kinds of online communities can be classified according to socialization, and content and knowledge sharing (Hinds & Lee, 2008). For example:

1. Type (1) relationships between members of different centers are mostly concerned with content and collective construction of knowledge sharing and socialization;
2. Type (2) interactions between monitors are mostly concerned with social networking, community projects and knowledge sharing;
3. Type (3) interactions between members of the centers and monitors are mostly concerned with content and sharing of knowledge.

After identifying the relationships between the actors involved and the strategies for training, it is necessary to identify the characteristics of information systems used in the training process.

Characteristics of Information Systems to Support the Training Program

Discussion lists, wikis, blogs, social networking sites, and content sharing systems support collaborative activities of the centers. During the qualification process of the monitors, the Moodle (http://moodle.org) platform was used. It is free, promotes distance learning by providing several resources to browse online content, and also enables interactivity such as chats, discussion forums, instant messaging and blogs (Junco & Cotten, 2011).

Until a few years ago, instant messaging was a multitasking activity that appealed only to adolescents eager to chat with as many friends as possible – often with one hand on the keyboard, and the other on the telephone (Salvetti & Srinivasan, 2005).

Instant messaging is the tool most widely used by the monitors and centers. Based on this observation, various analyses of the structural characteristics of training networks were conducted. Instant messaging data from the 8-month qualification process were extracted from the database logs. This extraction enabled us to observe the interactions within the social networks created during the qualification process.

METRICS TO ANALYZE SOCIAL NETWORKS OF THE MONITORS AND CENTERS

Social Network Analysis (SNA) is a research area that analyzes the structure and relationships of social networks such as density, centrality, and cliques (Scott, 2000). This paper uses SNA to analyze the network based on relationships between the participants of the centers and monitors of the program as well as members of the centers and monitors. For the study conducted in this paper, an actor can be either a monitor of a telecenter, tutor, supervisor, or a participant in the program with an individual login on the Distance Learning Platform (http://ead.telecentros.br.com).

A social network is often initiated and constructed by the daily and continuous communication between people, and therefore includes different types of relationships between individuals or groups (Jin, Matsuo and Ishizuka, 2007). This network consists of two sets (Batagelj, 2009): a set of edges (nodes) representing selected units, and a set of arcs (links) joining two nodes. If the nodes are the same, then the arc becomes a loop. Edges and arcs form a graph that may be directed. Additional data on the nodes or arcs are known as properties (or attributes) (Batagelj, 2009). In this analysis, the graph nodes represent members of the training centers and as attributes each node has a name, age, and state. The network is defined as a graph with a set of associate attributes.

In the Training Network for monitors, message exchanges between actors are directional and can be treated as dichotomous or valued (number of messages) depending on the focus of the analysis.

Due to the volume of messages exchanged between members of centers and monitors, the network is represented as a graph. A computational tool, Pajek (Batagelj & Mrvar, 2003) has been used to visualize clusters formed by subgroups within the network and this tool identifies nodes that belong to the same cluster. Besides determining indicators for the analysis, this software also allows a complex global network to be partitioned into smaller networks without affecting the global context. The combined analyses of the smaller networks may assist in understanding the collaboration in the Training Network . In addition, it allows the user to understand what influence different networks have on one another. Indicators are determined from the set of metrics described in a later section.

The analysis uses the relations between (1) members of different centers, (2) monitors, and (3) the centers and monitors. The results obtained from the applied metrics enable us to analyze and understand the dynamics of the interactions between the participating actors. We represent an instant messaging communication log as a graph where a node represents a person and an edge represents an instant message between two persons.

Centrality of Nodes

Of all the centrality metrics , in the context of SNA, we decided to opt for degree centrality, closeness centrality, and betweenness centrality.

Degree centrality is concerned with the visibility of the node, i.e., the most central node is the one that has the highest degree (Wasserman & Faust, 1994). According to Wasserman and Faust (1994), this metric enables the identification of nodes that are in direct contact with several other nodes, and thus, occupy a central place in the network. On the other hand, a node that is not very central implies that the actor is peripheral to the network.

To understand the metrics for centrality, it is important to understand certain mathematical concepts of graphs. A non-directed graph G (N, L) consists of a set of nodes $N = \{n_1, n_2, ..., n_g\}$, and a set of lines or edges $L = \{l_1, l_2, ..., l_l\}$ between pairs of nodes. N refers to a set with "g" number of actors. A non-directed edge, connecting nodes n_i and n_j, is represented by $l_k = (n_i, n_j)$, such that $l_k = l_q = (n_i, n_j) = (n_j, n_i)$. If we have an ordered pair of actors, n_i and n_j, in which n_i relates to n_j, then the pair is an element of a special collection of pairs referred to as L. We use the symbol L to refer to the set of directed lines and the symbol l to refer to the individual directed lines in the set. In a non-directed graph, degree $d(n_1)$, is the number of incident lines on a node, or similarly, the number of adjacent nodes. The degree of a node may vary from 0, in the case of an isolated node, to $g - 1$, if it is connected to all other nodes. In a directed graph, the in-degree $d_I(n_i)$ and out-degree $d_0(n_i)$, are determined according to the direction of the arcs that enter or leave a node, respectively.

Degree centrality can be defined in terms of the number of edges of a node, i.e., degree centrality of an actor is given by $C_D(n_i) = d(n_i)$. To compare this metric for actors belonging to different networks, the degree must be normalized by dividing it by the maximum degree a node can have, i.e., the number of nodes in the graph minus 1 (the node itself), as expressed by Equation 1 (Wasserman & Faust, 1994):

$$C'_D(n_i) = \frac{d(n_i)}{g-1} \tag{1}$$

Closeness centrality is based on distance and measures the proximity of a node with respect to other nodes (Wasserman & Faust, 1994). An actor is central if it can immediately interact with others, i.e., such actors may be productive when sharing information with the rest as they follow a shorter path to communicate (Wasserman & Faust, 1994). Centrality is inversely related to distance, i.e., the greater the distance from a node to the other nodes, the smaller is the value of its closeness centrality.

To calculate the closeness centrality, we add the geodesic distances (shortest path between two nodes) of a node with respect to all other nodes of the graph. Next, the sum is inverted, since the greater the distance is, the smaller is the proximity, yielding Equation 2 (Wasserman & Faust, 1994):

$$C_C(n_i) = \left[\sum_{j=1}^{g} d(n_i, n_j)\right]^{-1} \tag{2}$$

Normalization, achieved by multiplying $\boldsymbol{C_C(n_i)}$ by $\boldsymbol{g-1}$, yields Equation 3:

$$C'_C(n_i) = \frac{g-1}{\left[\sum_{j=1}^{g} d(n_i, n_j)\right]} = (g-1)C_C(n_i) \tag{3}$$

Interaction between two non-adjacent nodes depends on the nodes that are located on the path, i.e., there is a potential control over the interactions between these two non-adjacent nodes. Thus, to achieve a high betweenness centrality, a node must be on the path between several other nodes.

The degree of betweenness centrality quantifies to what extent a node is on the geodesic paths of other nodes and can be obtained by Equation 4 (Wasserman & Faust, 1994):

$$C_B\left(n_i\right) = \sum_{j<k} \frac{g_{jk}\left(n_i\right)}{g_{jk}}, \tag{4}$$

where g_{jk} is the number of geodesic paths (shorter and of the same size) linking nodes j and k; and $g_{jk}(n_i)$ are the paths, included in the total g_{jk}, that pass through node n_i. Betweenness centrality $C_B(n_i)$ measures, for node n_i, the sum of the probabilities that this node is on the geodesic paths of all other nodes in the graph. To normalize this metric, it must be divided by its maximum, that is, the number of pairs of nodes that do not include n_i, i.e., $(g-1)(g-2)/2$, yielding betweenness centrality normalized per actor (node) as given by Equation 5:

$$C'_B\left(n_i\right) = \frac{C_B\left(n_i\right)}{\left(g-1\right)\left(g-2\right)/2} \tag{5}$$

Network Density

Density of a network is related to the concept defined as strong and weak ties (Granovetter, 1983), in which a distant relationship (weak ties) indicates that involvement is low, whereas strong ties show a higher involvement.

Weak ties indicate a low density of a network, i.e., several relationships are absent. On the other hand, sets that are strongly related are densely linked (Granovetter, 1983). For a family of graphs S, the density of graph G is defined as $\gamma(G) = m(G)/m_{max}(S)$.

RESULTS AND DISCUSSION

Visual Representation of Network Monitors and Centers

We transformed the log into an undirected graph G, where each person participating in a conversation is represented by a node. Two nodes are connected by an edge if they have communicated via an instant message. Each edge carries a weight corresponding to the number of messages exchanged between the two persons. Note that the directionality of the edge is ignored at this stage because we do not consider directionality of the communication exchanged via an instant message.

From a preliminary analysis using the results from Pajek (Batagelj & Mrvar, 2003), it can be seen that networks are formed from the relationships among participants of regional centers (tutors, supervisors, instructional designers, coordinators, and other members) and monitors of each region (Figure 1).

Figure 1 shows the intensity of the relationships between members of the centers and monitors. Another aspect of the analysis shown in Figure 2, is the network established by considering only the relationships between the participants of the regional centers (and not considering their relationships with monitors).

Finally, the network created from relationships between monitors is shown in Figure 3.

Analysis of the figures shows a spatial distribution of the relationships with the greatest density among the centers. However, it is important to point out that quantification of the parameters is needed to compare the relationships with respect to centrality and density.

Thus, the indicators of centrality and diameter enable a quantitative analysis of the relationships.

Network Monitors and Centers: Indicators for Monitoring

Using the indicators of centrality and diameter, it is possible to quantitatively analyze these relationships. Table 2 shows the results.

Figure 1. Network of centers and monitors

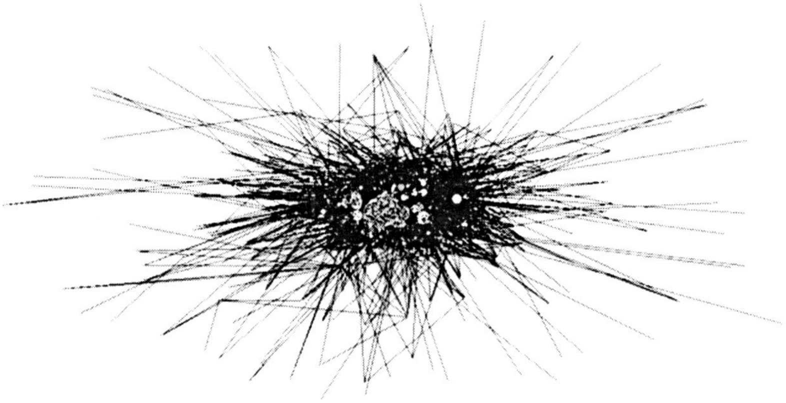

Figure 2. Center network

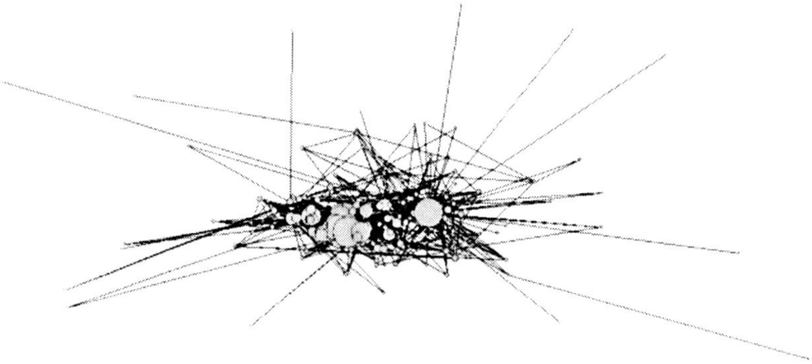

Figure 3. Network of monitors

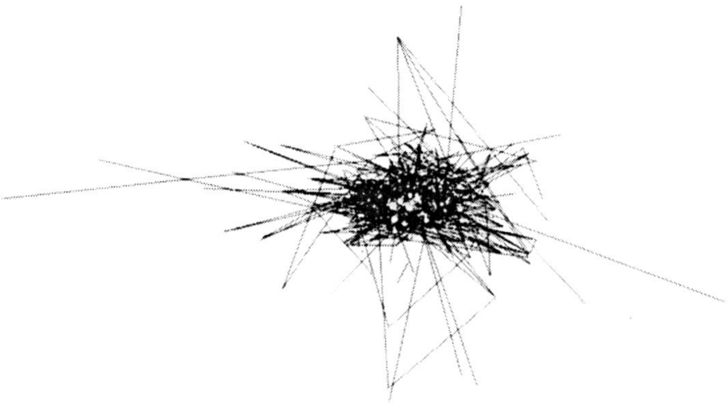

Table 2. Centrality and density indicators for the 3 dimensions of Telecentros.BR

Indicators	Center+ Monitors	Center	Monitors
Density	0.032	0.169	0.01
Average degree centrality	83.85	65.06	18.48
Low degree centrality	0	0	0
High degree centrality	167	122	116
Average closeness centrality	0.2668	0.321	0.1335
Low closeness centrality	0	0	0
High closeness centrality	0.3992	0.4666	0.2772
Average betweenness centrality	0.0016	0.0093	0.0013
Low betweenness centrality	0	0	0
High betweenness centrality	0.0663	0.2586	0.053
Mean distance between elements of each cluster	3.67	3.16	4.04
Longest distance between two vertices	9	7	13

Using Table 2 we can compare and understand the relationships in the 3 dimensions proposed in this paper (centers + monitors, centers only, and monitors only). Models to calculate the indicators shown in Table 2 as well as a comparative analysis of the dimensions are discussed next.

Network Density

An algorithm that analyzes the structural density of a network was used to determine this metric. Structural density is a measure that expresses the coefficient between the existing relationships and possible relationships. This algorithm normalizes the densities according to the maximum number of arcs between classes (ideal for dense networks) (Granovetter, 1983).

Considering the structure, the networking of the centers is 428.13% denser than the networking between "centers + monitors" (0.169 x 0.032). There is a reason for this difference. Members of the centers conducted more face-to-face meetings supported by collaborative technologies to produce content, guidelines, and other material. Density of the "internal" network of the centers (centers only) shows great similarity with the networking based exclusively on monitors and monitors together with members of the centers.

If participation by the members of the centers is not considered, the network density of the monitors decreases by 68.75%. This shows dispersion with respect to the relationships among them.

Degree of Centrality

Compared with the centrality of the network of centers and the network of monitors, the largest indicator for the dimension "centers + monitors", decreases by 26.95% and 30.54%, respectively. This indicator confirms the trend that the highest degree of relationships between participants of the centers and monitors occurs when these actors exchange information intensively. This may be explained by the presence of a tutor (member of a center) who is meant to take care of the monitors by answering their questions and accompanying them during their training.

Closeness Centrality and Betweenness Centrality

These indicators provide an average proximity among the nodes and influence of these nodes, respectively. So, if these values are high, Telecentros.BR depends on the relationships between the centers (tutors, supervisors, coordinators) and the monitors to achieve better qualified monitors.

Networking among centers only is approximately 290% more influential, while networking among monitors only is 20% less influential, considering the nodes that have the potential to control interaction in the network.

Tutors play an important role in the training program. They are the mediators for the monitors under their responsibility. So, the network loses its intensity without their participation.

Monitors naturally develop mediation as they move forward in constructing common strategies, and in communicating among themselves, even without the mediation of the centers. This usually happens when they start using the platform as a means to meet others rather than as an instrument to conduct the training. This aspect needs to be investigated in the future by comparison with different approaches adopted by the centers and monitors.

Average Distance between the Network Nodes

The average distance between the network nodes may be affected, although this may not be significant. However, there is a significant effect when considering only the network of monitors. Table 2 shows that the average distance, with respect to monitors, is 27.9%, which is greater than that in the network of centers, and approximately 10% greater than that in the network for "centers + monitors". Thus, the network is distributed by increasing the distances between monitors. Tutors play a role to mediate connecting monitors, introducing individuals, and presenting ideas and links of interest. This creates the means to promote connections and communication regardless of geographic distance and centers.

FUTURE RESEARCH DIRECTIONS

The work described here not only is related to visualizing the network structure, but also to evaluating the incorporation of some metrics of analysis to construct a methodology for monitoring the training program on a larger scale. In spite of some restrictions, this research has contributed to the understanding of the training processes based on learning using a network. This has enabled us to propose and construct new strategies to activate online community networks.

CONCLUSION

At present, there are movements originating from community telecenters, which may enable these centers to be recognized as important factors for digital inclusion in the country. This may occur not only due to articulation of the communities, but also the need for democratic access to information and public services by means of ICTs to generate and process knowledge to exercise citizenship effectively.

In this context, it is extremely relevant that agents of digital inclusion, in particular monitors, use the most prominent and important facilities of networks of computers for communication between individuals. Telecentros.BR is probably the most important initiative of human resources in the area of digital inclusion. It promotes interaction among individuals, but more importantly raises questions and advertises community activities, besides providing all the necessary support and assistance to develop pedagogic activities.

The Moodle platform is used in the training of human resources for digital inclusion. It has a set of tools that enable connectivity among the agents and between them and centers. The platform also enables the participation of monitors in social networks.

In this paper, we analyzed interactions among actors that are part of the Training Network for Digital inclusion through the Telecentros.BR program. For the analysis, data were extracted from Moodle according to the analysis indicators (centrality and density).

The analysis has enabled the identification of patterns in influential relationships between several actors in the training process. It has also allowed the visualization and quantification of structures that link elements of the network promoting strategies of interaction and sharing of information, which is quite fundamental to the success of the program.

At the current stage in the Training Network, both the densities presented as well as the images for analysis, show the importance of collaborative work taking into consideration the major role played by the centers. The center network is, in fact, denser than that of the monitors. According to the requirements of the management level and based on the volume of information to be analyzed, it is essential that data mining algorithms are used to conduct operations on the process of evaluation and monitoring of the training program.

In particular, with respect to message exchange, the research described in this paper does not consider the semantics of the messages, and thus, ignores the possible identification of the following dimensions: participative, social, interactive, cognitive (Kaye, 1992) and metacognitive (Dewever, Schellens, Valcke, & Vankeer, 2006).

REFERENCES

Amariles, F., Paz, O. P., Russell, N., & Johnson, N. (2006). The impacts of community telecenters in rural Colombia. *Journal of Community Informatics*, *2*(3).

Andrews, S. B. (1995). Structural holes: The social structure of competition by Ronald S. Burt. *Administrative Science Quarterly*, *40*(3), 355–359. doi:10.2307/2393644.

Bailey, A., & Ngwenyama, O. (2011). The challenge of e-participation in the digital city: Exploring generational influences among community telecentre users. *Telematics and Informatics*, *28*(3), 204–214. doi:10.1016/j.tele.2010.09.004.

Balieiro, M. A., Sousa, S. F. Jr, & Souza, C. D. (2008). Análise multidimensional de redes sociais de projetos de software livre. In *Proceedings of Simpósio Brasileiro de Sistemas Colaborativos* (pp. 23–33). Vitória, Brasil: IEEE.

Batagelj, V. (2009). Social network analysis, large-scale. In Meyers, R. A. (Ed.), *Encyclopedia of Complexity and Systems Science* (pp. 8245–8265). Berlin: Springer. doi:10.1007/978-0-387-30440-3_489.

Batagelj, V., & Mrvar, A. (2003). Pajek analysis and visualization of large networks. *Science*, *2265*(19), 8–11.

Becker, J., Bergener, P., Niehaves, B., & Räckers, M. (2008). Social inclusiveness of electronic public service delivery in Germany: A quantitative analysis. *Information Systems Journal*.

Ben-David, J., & Collins, R. (1966). Social factors in the origins of a new science: The case of psychology. *American Sociological Review*, *31*(4), 451–465. doi:10.2307/2090769 PMID:5329541.

Bonacich, P. (1972). Factoring and weighting approaches to status scores and clique identification. *The Journal of Mathematical Sociology*, *2*(1), 113–120. doi:10.1080/0022250X.1972.9989806.

Borgatti, S. P., & Cross, R. (2003). A relational view of information seeking and learning in social networks. *Management Science*, *49*, 432–446. doi:10.1287/mnsc.49.4.432.14428.

Borgatti, S. P., Mehra, A., Brass, D. J., & Labianca, G. (2009). Network analysis in the social sciences. *Science*, *323*(5916), 892–895. doi:10.1126/science.1165821 PMID:19213908.

Bossio, J. F. (2006). *Social sustainability of telecenters from the viewpoint of operators: A case study from São Paulo*. (Unpublished doctoral dissertation). London School of Economics, London, UK.

Bouguessa, M., Wang, S., & Dumoulin, B. (2010). Discovering knowledge-sharing communities in question-answering forums. *Discovery*, *5*(1), 1–49.

Brandes, U. (2001). A faster algorithm for betweenness centrality. *The Journal of Mathematical Sociology*, *25*(2), 163–177. doi:10.1080/0022250X.2001.9990249.

Brin, S., & Page, L. (2006). The anatomy of a large-scale hypertextual web search engine. *Search*, *30*(1-2), 5–10.

Burt, R. S. (2004). Structural holes and good ideas. *American Journal of Sociology*, *110*(2), 349–399. doi:10.1086/421787.

Carleial, L. (2001). *Redes industriais de subcontratação: Um enfoque de sistema nacional de inovação, um estudo das industrias eletrônica, metalmecânica e de confecções da Região Metropolitana de Curitiba*. São Paulo, Brazil: Hucitec.

Cullen, R., & Morse, S. (2011). Who's contributing: Do personality traits influence the level and type of participation in online communities. []. IEEE.]. *Methodology*, *0*, 1–11.

Decree n. 6991, Oct 27, 2009. (2009). National Program to Support Digital inclusion in the communities - Telecentros.BR. DOU n. 206, Sec.1, pp. 3. Federative Republic of Brazil, Brasília, DF. Retrieved Nov 26, 2011, from http://www.in.gov.br/imprensa/visualiza/index.jsp?jornal=1&pagina=3&data=28/10/2009

Department of Digital inclusion - DDI. (2011). *Curso de formação de monitores do telecentros. BR. programa nacional de apoio à inclusão digital nas comunidades: Rede nacional de formação para inclusão digital.* Federative Republic of Brazil. [Documento orientador 2.0]. Brasília, DF: Ministério das Comunicações.

Dewever, B., Schellens, T., Valcke, M., & Vankeer, H. (2006). Content analysis schemes to analyze transcripts of online asynchronous discussion groups: A review. *Computers & Education*, *46*(1), 6–28. doi:10.1016/j.compedu.2005.04.005.

Freeman, L. C. (1996). Some antecedents of social network analysis. *Connections*, *19*(1), 39-42. Retrieved January 01, 2012, from http://www.insna.org/PDF/Connections/v19/1996_I-1-4.pdf

Freeman, L. C. (2004). *The development of social network analysis: A study in the sociology of science*. Canada: Empirical Press.

Galaskiewicz, J., & Wasserman, S. (1993). Social network analysis: Concepts, methodology, and directions for the 1990s. *Sociological Methods & Research*, *22*(1), 3–22. doi:10.1177/0049124193022001001.

Gaved, M. B., & Mulholland, P. (2010). Networking communities from the bottom up: Grassroots approaches to overcoming the digital divide. *AI & Society*, *25*(3), 345–357. doi:10.1007/s00146-009-0259-5.

Gomez, R. (Ed.). (2012). *Libraries, telecenters, cybercafés and public access to ICT: International comparisons*. Hershey, PA: IGI Global.

Gomez, R., & Baron, L. F. (2011). Does public access computing really contribute to community development? Lessons from libraries, telecenters and cybercafés in Colombia. *Electronic Journal of Information Systems in Developing Countries*, *49*(2), 1–11.

Granovetter, M. (1983). The strength of weak ties: A network theory revisited. *Sociological Theory*, *1*, 201–233. doi:10.2307/202051.

Granqvist, M. (2005). Looking critically at ICT-4Dev: The case of Lincos. *The Journal of Community Informatics*, *2*(1).

Grosser, K. (1991). Human networks in organizational information processing. *Annual Review of Information Science & Technology*, *26*, 349–402.

Hanneman, R. A., & Riddle, M. (2005). Introduction to social network methods. [). IEEE.]. *Network*, *1*, 1–322.

Heeks, R., & León, K. L. (2009). *Remoteness, exclusion and telecentres in mountain regions: Analysing ICT-based information chains in Pazos, Peru*. Manchester, UK: Centre for Development Informatics. Retrieved November, 12, 2011, from http://www.sed.manchester.ac.uk/idpm/research/publications/wp/di/documents/di_wp38.pdf

Hinds, D., & Lee, R. M. (2008). Social network structure as a critical success condition for virtual communities. In *Proceedings of the 41st Annual Hawaii International Conference on System Sciences (HICSS'08)*. Waikoloa, HI.

Houaiss, A., & Villar, M. S. (2001). *Dicionário houaiss de língua portuguesa*. Rio de Janeiro: Objetiva.

Huisman, M., & van Duijn, M. A. J. (2003). Software for social network analysis. *Social Science Research*, *27*, 270–316.

Jin, Y., Matsuo, Y., & Ishizuka, M. (2007). Extracting social networks among various entities on the web. In E. Franconi, M. Kifer, & W. May (Eds.), *Proceedings of the Fourth European Semantic Web Conference* (Vol. 4519, pp. 251-266). Springer.

Junco, R., & Cotten, S. R. (2011). Perceived academic effects of instant messaging use. *Computers & Education*, *56*(2), 370–378. doi:10.1016/j.compedu.2010.08.020.

Kaye, A. R. (1992). Collaborative learning through computer conferencing. In Kaye, A. (Ed.), *Computer Conference and Content Analysis* (pp. 117–136). Springer Verlag.

Kermarrec, A.-M., Le Merrer, E., Sericola, B., & Trédan, G. (2011). Second order centrality: Distributed assessment of nodes criticity in complex networks. *Computer Communications*, *34*(5), 619–628. doi:10.1016/j.comcom.2010.06.007.

Kitsak, M., Gallos, L. K., Havlin, S., Liljeros, F., Muchnik, L., Stanley, H. E., & Makse, H. A. (2010). Identification of influential spreaders in complex networks. *Nature Physics*, *6*(11), 888–893. doi:10.1038/nphys1746.

Kleinberg, J. M. (1999). Hubs, authorities, and communities. *ACM Computing Surveys*, *31*(4), 5. doi:10.1145/345966.345982.

Krackhardt, D. (1987). Cognitive social structures. *Social Networks*, *9*(2), 109–134. doi:10.1016/0378-8733(87)90009-8.

Krackhardt, D. (2000). Modeling structures of organizations. In Ilgen, D. R., & Hulin, C. L. (Eds.), *Computational Modeling of Behavior in Organizations: The Third Scientific Discipline*. American Psychological Association.

Krackhardt, D., & Hanson, J. R. (1993). Informal networks: The company behind the chart. *Harvard Business Review*, *71*(4), 104–111. PMID:10127036.

Krebs, V. (2000). Working in the connected world. *IHRIM Journal*, *4*(2), 89–91.

Kumar, R., & Best, M. L. (2006). Social impact and diffusion of telecenter use: A study from the sustainable access in rural India project. *Journal of Community Informatics*, *2*(3), 328–349.

Lemieux, V., & Ouimet, M. (2004). L'analyse structurale des réseaux sociaux. *Recherches Sociographiques*, *47*(1), 179–182.

Lin, N., Cook, K., & Burt, R. (2001). Social capital: Theory and research. *Contemporary Sociology*, *31*, 333.

Lin, N., Fu, Y., & Hsung, R. M. (2001). *The position generator: Measurement techniques for investigations of social capital. Social Capital Theory and Research*. Aldine de Gruyter.

Macías, A. G. (2002). *Redes sociales y clusters empresariales*. Revista Hispana para el análisis de redes sociais, (v. 1, n. 6). Retrieved Dec 01, 2011, from http://revista-redes.rediris.es/html-vol1/vol1_6.htm

Madon, S., Reinhard, N., Roode, D., & Walsham, G. (2009). Digital inclusion projects in developing countries: Processes of institutionalization. *Information Technology for Development*, *15*(2), 95–107. doi:10.1002/itdj.20108.

Matheus, R., Ribeiro, M. M., Vaz, J. C., & De Souza, C. A. (2010). Internet use for social control and participation: What are local governments doing in Latin America? In *Proceedings of the 4th International Conference on Theory and Practice of Electronic Governance* (pp. 333–338). ACM.

Mazur, A., Doran, C., & Doran, P. R. (2010). The use of social network analysis software to analyze communication patterns and interaction in online collaborative environments. In J. Baralt, N. Callaos, W. Lesso, A. Tremante, & F. Welsch (Eds.), Teacher (p. 447). International Institute of Information and Systemics.

McGrath, C., Blythe, J., & Krackhardt, D. (1997). The effect of spatial arrangement on judgments and errors in interpreting graphs. *Social Networks*, *19*(3), 223–242. doi:10.1016/S0378-8733(96)00299-7.

Molina, J. L. (1999). El organigrama informal en las organizaciones: Una aproximación desde el análisis de redes sociales. *Redes Revista Hispana para el Análisis de Redes Sociales*. Retrieved from http://revista-redes.rediris.es/Webredes/textos/organizaciones.doc

Monge, P. R., & Contractor, N. S. (2001). Emergence of communication networks. In Jablin, F. M., & Putnam, L. L. (Eds.), *Handbook of Organizational Communication* (pp. 440–502). Thousand Oaks, CA: Sage.

Montoya, E. V. (2007). Telecentros comunitarios: Un espacio para la participación y formación ciudadana: La experiencia de Manizales, Colombia. *Journal of Community Informatics*, *3*(3).

Moody, J., & White, D. R. (2003). Structural cohesion and embeddedness: A hierarchical concept of social groups. *American Sociological Review*, *68*(1), 103–127. doi:10.2307/3088904.

Mori, C. K., & Assumpção, R. O. (2007). Brazilian digital inclusion public policy: Achievements and challenges. *Journal of Community Informatics*, *3*(3). Retrieved September 30, 2011 from http://ci-journal.net/index.php/ciej/article/view/424

Mullins, N. C. (1972). The development of a scientific specialty: The phage group and the origins of molecular biology. *Minerva*, *10*(1), 51–82. doi:10.1007/BF01881390.

Newman, M. E. J., & Girvan, M. (2003). Finding and evaluating community structure in networks. *Physical Review E: Statistical, Nonlinear, and Soft Matter Physics*, *69*(2 Pt 2), 16.

Otte, E., & Rousseau, R. (2002). Social network analysis: A powerful strategy, also for the information sciences. *Journal of Information Science*, *28*(6), 441–453. doi:10.1177/016555150202800601.

Page, L., Brin, S., Motwani, R., & Winograd, T. (1999). *The Pagerank citation ranking: Bringing order to the web*. Technical Report. Stanford InfoLab. Retrieved Dec 20, 2011, from http://ilpubs.stanford.edu:8090/422/1/1999-66.pdf

Parkinson, S. (2005). *Telecentres, access and development: Experience and lessons from Uganda and South Africa*. Kampala, Uganda: Fountain Publishers.

Parkinson, S., & Lauzon, A. (2008). The impact of the internet on local social equity: A study of a telecenter in Aguablanca, Colombia. *Information Technologies and International Development, 4*(3), 21–38. doi:10.1162/itid.2008.00015.

Parkinson, S., & Ramirez, R. (2006). Using a sustainable livelihoods approach to assessing the impact of ICTs in development. *Journal of Community Informatics, 2*(3).

Pather, S., & Gomez, R. (2010). Public access ICT: A south-south comparative analysis of libraries, telecentres and cybercafés in South Africa and Brazil. In *Proceedings of AMCIS 2010*. AMCIS.

Pick, J. B., & Gollakota, K. (2010). Technology for rural telecenters in India: A model and exploratory study of diffusion of information for telecenter use and sustainability. In *Proceedings of AMCIS 2010*. AMCIS.

Prado, P. (2009). *Bridging digital poverty: Adoption of information and communication technologies at community technology centers in the Dominican Republic*. (Doctoral dissertation). University of Miami, Coral Gables, Florida.

Prado, P., Câmara, M. A., & Figueiredo, M. A. (2011). Evaluating ICT adoption in rural Brazil: A quantitative analysis of telecenters as agents of social change. *The Journal of Community Informatics, 7*(1&2).

Price, D. J. D. S. (1986). *Little science, big science-- and beyond*. New York: Columbia University Press.

Ramanathan, J., Ramnath, R., Singh, N., Xu, Z., & Xu, Y. (2011). Sense-respond cloud mediator architecture for services evolution. In *Proceedings of the 2011 ACM Symposium on Applied Computing - SAC '11*, (pp. 162-169). ACM Press.

Rice Doran, P., Doran, C., & Mazur, A. (2011). Social network analysis as a method for analyzing interaction in collaborative online learning environments. *Journal of Systemics Cybernetics and Informatics*.

Robertson, S. (1998). Telecenters in Mexico: Learning the hard way. *The Journal of Development Communication, 9*(2).

Rocha, C. C. (2003). *Relaciones estratégicas entre pymes: Contraste de hipótesis empresariales mediante ARS*. Revista Hispana para el análisis de redes sociais (v. 4, n. 4, jun. 2003). Retrieved Nov 21, 2011, from http://revista-redes.rediris.es

Rogers, E. M., & Kincaid, D. L. (1981). *Communication networks: Toward a new paradigm for research*. New York: The Free Press.

Rybski, D., Buldyrev, S. V., Havlin, S., Liljeros, F., & Makse, H. A. (2009). Scaling laws of human interaction activity. *Proceedings of the National Academy of Sciences of the United States ofAmerica, 106*(31), 12640–12645. doi:10.1073/pnas.0902667106 PMID:19617555.

Salvetti, F., & Srinivasan, S. (2005). Local flow betweenness centrality for clustering community graphs. *Internet and Network Economics*, 531–544.

Sandoval-Almaz, R. (2007). Digital literacy: Problems faced by telecenter users in Mexico. *Information Systems Journal, 13*(3), 217–232.

Santos, M. B., & Souza, C. D. (2008). Visualização temporal de redes sociais com o OSSNetwork. In *Proceedings of WIVA - Workshop on Information Visualization and Analysis in Social Networks*, (pp. 79-88). Campinas, Brasil: WIVA.

Saxenian, A. (1994). *Regional advantage: Culture and competition in silicon valley and route 128*. Boston: Harvard University Press.

Scott, J. (2000). Social network analysis. *American Ethnologist, 24*(1), 219–220.

Shi, D., Zhu, S., & Liu, L. (2007). Clustering coefficients of growing networks. *Physica A: Statistical Mechanics and its Applications, 381*, 515-524.

Sorj, B. (2003). *Brasil@povo.com: A luta contra a desigualdade na sociedade da informação*. Brasilia, Brazil: Unesco.

Uzzi, B., & Schwartz, M. (1993). Structural holes - The social-structure of competition. In R. S. Burt (Ed.), Contemporary Sociologya Journal of Reviews, 22(2), 155-157. doi:doi:10.2307/2075713 doi:10.2307/2075713.

Wasserman, S., & Faust, K. (1994). *Social network analysis: Methods and applications*. Cambridge, MA: Cambridge University Press. doi:10.1017/CBO9780511815478.

Wellman, B., & Berkowitz, S. D. (1988). Social structures: A network approach. *PsycCRITIQUES, 2*, 513.

Yu, A. Y., Tian, S. W., Vogel, D., & Chi-Wai Kwok, R. (2010). Can learning be virtually boosted? An investigation of online social networking impacts. *Computers & Education, 55*(4), 1494–1503. doi:10.1016/j.compedu.2010.06.015.

Zhang, C. (2008). The institutional framework of the United Nations development programme--Ministry of science and technology (UNDP--most) telecenter project in rural china. *Information Technologies and International Development, 4*(3).

ADDITIONAL READING

Batagelj, V. (2009, July). Pajek: Analysis and visualization of large networks first steps. *Methods (San Diego, Calif.)*, 13–14. PMID:18952176.

Batagelj, V., & Mrvar, A. (2003). How to analyze large networks with Pajek. *Networks*.

Castells, M. (2007). Toward a sociology of the network society Manuel Castells. *Contemporary Sociology, 29*(5), 693–699. doi:10.2307/2655234.

Chen, I.-X., & Yang, C.-Z. (2010). Visualization of social networks. In *Social Networks* (pp. 585–610). New York: Springer.

Coffman, T. R., Suite, J. R., & Marcus, S. E. (2004). Pattern classification in social network analysis: A case study. *Communications, 5*, 3162–3175.

Daming, X., Xiaomei, W., & Wei, L. (2008). Social network analysis. *PLoS ONE, 154*, 132.

Ella, A., Andrea, A. D., Ferri, F., & Grifoni, P. (2010). Computational social network analysis. *Computer Communications, 12*(4), 2–25.

Figueiredo, M. A., Prado, P., Câmara, M. A., & Albuquerque, A. M. (2009). Empowering rural citizen journalism via web 2.0 technologies. In *Proceedings of the Fourth International Conference on Communities and Technologies*. ACM Press.

Gould, E., & Gomez, R. (2010). Community engagement and infomediaries: Challenges facing libraries, telecenters and cybercafes in developing countries. In *Proceedings of the iConference*. Urbana Champaign, IL: iConference.

Henstra, F. (2008). Social network analysis and the eighteenth-century family network: A case study of the Walpole family. *Transactions of the Philological Society, 106*(1), 29–70. doi:10.1111/j.1467-968X.2007.00193.x.

Hutchison, D., & Mitchell, J. C. (2009). *Online communities and social computing*. New York, 5621, 354–363.

Ibrahim, Z., & Ainin, S. (2009). The influence of Malaysian telecenters on community building. *Electronic. Journal of E-Government, 7*(1), 77–86.

Madon, S., Reinhard, N., Roode, D., & Walsham, G. (2009). Digital inclusion projects in developing countries: Processes of institutionalization. *Information Technology for Development*, *15*(2), 95–107. doi:10.1002/itdj.20108.

Marin, A., & Wellman, B. (2010). *Handbook of social network analysis. Network* (pp. 1–23). Sage.

Miller, K. D., Fabian, F., & Lin, S.-J. (2009). Strategies for online communities. *Strategic Management Journal*, *30*, 305–322. doi:10.1002/smj.735.

Notley, T. (2009). Young people, online networks, and social inclusion. *Journal of Computer-Mediated Communication*, *14*(4), 1208–1227. doi:10.1111/j.1083-6101.2009.01487.x.

Preece, J., & Maloney-Krichmar, D. (2003). Online communities. *Online*, *1*(2), 1–63.

Rajalesksmi, K. G. (2007). E-governance services through telecenters: The role of human. *Information Technologies and International Development*, *4*(1), 19–35. doi:10.1162/itid.2007.4.1.19.

Rogers, E. M., & Shukla, P. (2001). The role of telecenters in development communication and the digital divide. *Journal of Development*, *2*(12), 26–31.

Scott, J. (1994). Social network analysis. *Sociology: The Journal of the British Sociological Association*, *22*, 109–127.

Stalder, F. (2006). Manuel Castells: The theory of the network society. *Contemporary Sociology: A Journal of Reviews*, *36*, 255.

Thilagam, P. S. (2010). Applications of social network analysis. *Analysis*, *49*, 637–649.

Varlamis, I., Eirinaki, M., & Louta, M. (2010). A study on social network metrics and their application in trust networks. In *Proceedings of the 2010 International Conference on Advances in Social Networks Analysis and Mining*, (pp. 168-175). IEEE.

Williams, A. L., & Merten, M. J. (2008). A review of online social networking profiles by adolescents: Implications for future research and intervention. *Adolescence*, *43*(170), 253–274. PMID:18689100.

Zaphiris, P., & Ang, C. S. (2009). Introduction to social network analysis. *Network*, *12*, 1–13.

KEY TERMS AND DEFINITIONS

Actor/Node: Any independent social entity (persons, groups, organizations).

Betweenness Centrality: Is a centrality measure of a node within a graph. Nodes that occur on many shortest paths between other nodes have higher betweenness than those that do not.

Centralization: The difference between the number of links for each node divided by maximum possible sum of differences.

Closeness Centrality: Is a centrality measure of a node within a graph. Is preferred to mean shortest-path length, as it gives higher values to more central nodes, and so is usually positively associated with other measures such as degree.

Degree Centrality: Defined as the number of links incident upon a node (i.e., the number of ties that a node has).

Density: A dense graph is a graph in which the number of edges is close to the maximal number of edges. The opposite, a graph with only a few edges, is a sparse graph.

Networks: A set of actors are that related by ties across one or more relations.

Relations: A collection of ties of a specific kind among members of a group.

Social Network Analysis: Is the mapping and measuring of relationships and flows between actors (people, groups, organizations, or other).

Ties/edges: Any persistent communication or exchange relationship between two nodes. Ties (or edges) may be directional and varying in strength.

Chapter 33
Towards E-Government Information Platforms for Enterprise 2.0

Mário Rodrigues
University of Aveiro, Portugal

Gonçalo Paiva Dias
University of Aveiro, Portugal

António Teixeira
University of Aveiro, Portugal

ABSTRACT

Enterprise 2.0 aims to help employees, customers, and suppliers collaborate, share, and organize information. As governments are relevant partners for enterprises (legislation, contracts, etc.) e-government platforms need to be ready for Enterprise 2.0 to what concerns e-government interactions. The public sector holds huge quantities of information and just a small proportion is relevant to each enterprise. Enterprises should only be confronted with relevant information and not flooded with lots of data. This implies data organization with semantic description and services using open standards. The goal is to build a durable information infrastructure for government that can be readily accessed by enterprises. The authors propose a conceptual model for government information provisioning. The rationale for this proposal is to motivate the creation of durable, standard, and open government information infrastructures. The model acquires information from natural language documents and represents it using ontology. A proof-of-concept prototype and its preliminary results are presented.

INTRODUCTION

Enterprise 2.0 aims to help employees, customers and suppliers collaborate, share, and organize information. In McAfee (2006) Enterprise 2.0 was defined as "the use of emergent social software platforms within companies, or between companies and their partners or customers". The idea of Enterprise 2.0 has evolved and is now assumed that important opportunities exist inside and beyond corporate walls, including all stakeholders: businesses, clients, government (Chang & Kannan, 2008).

Government influences the others stakeholders through regulation, taxation, defining of the conditions under which firms compete, and also

DOI: 10.4018/978-1-4666-4373-4.ch033

as a client. Carroll and Buchholtz (2011, p. 347) uses the US federal government's 2011 budget, $3.8 trillion, to illustrate the magnitude of the effect government has on all institutions in society. Adding to this is the influence of state and local governments. This makes governments a very relevant partner for enterprises and thus e-government platforms need to be ready for Enterprise 2.0.

Osimo (2008) acknowledges that governments are knowledge-intensive organizations, that they will become increasingly so in the future and that knowledge management is key to improving the efficiency and effectiveness of government. However, sharing data online is not sufficient to effectively share knowledge. It is necessary to organize the information, provide a semantic description and use open standards that will help information consumers to absorb, analyze, and interpret it. The real opportunity is not the use of temporary tools but the building of a more durable infrastructure for participatory democracy (Leighninger, 2011).

An issue highlighted by McAfee (2006) is the failing practice of knowledge management. He discusses that information technologies used for communication are either channels (e.g. email and instant messaging,) or platforms (e.g. intranets and portals). These technologies are radically different in that channels allow information to be created by anyone but consumed by very few, and platforms contain information that is available to the whole organization and generated by small groups. There is nothing in between. Also, Cook (2008) observes that, with these technologies, the common approach of feeding information to the knowledge management platform is to ask information from people throughout the company and put into a central system for everyone else to access. He further elaborates on this topic writing that this approach is inappropriate: "this method of capturing information neither fits with the way most knowledge workers operate nor reflects what they produce. No wonder then that those trying to locate knowledge within an organization find it so difficult, and when they do find it more often than not it rarely provides the answer to their questions..."

A study requested by the Institute for Prospective Technological Studies, a scientific institute of the European Commission's Joint Research Centre, took the long view to provide input for e-government longer-term strategic planning in the European (Frissen et al., 2007). It did so by identifying emerging trends and opportunities for enhancing governments and governance in 2020. Considering a wide array of all scenarios, the authors of the study foresee empowerment (of citizen and enterprises) as the trend to have the most significant impact in the coming decades. Consequently, "Governments will have to operate in more open and networked constellations with other stakeholders. They will need to ... operate in a flexible, not overtly bureaucratic way..." (Frissen et al., 2007, p. 109).

This perspective of the near future - where concerns as information sharing using open machine readable formats should be addressed - is not exclusive to European Union. The 2010 edition of the United Nations E-Government Survey (UN, 2010) shares a future view that, although not assumed as the United Nations official view, shares the same approach. The idea of "government 2.0" associated with the use of social networks by the public sector should assume a broader definition - government should be viewed as a platform. From this perspective, government should become a provider of data and services that others can also exploit as they see fit, allowing third parties to innovate by building upon government data and applications

The present chapter discusses how government information can be made available taking into consideration government's particularities and proposes a conceptual model for government information provisioning applications. The rationale for a conceptual model proposal is to motivate a framework for application development that facilitates the creation of durable, standard and open information infrastructures. These infrastructures are necessary to the future's view of government as a platform ready for Enterprise 2.0. The chapter also describes of a proof-of-concept prototype and the already achieved results.

BACKGROUND

When discussing the relations between Business and Government, Carroll & Buchholtz (2011, p. 354) acknowledges that government regulation has affected virtually every aspect of how business functions. The influence is felt over the conditions under which firms compete and ranges from the production of goods and services to packaging, distribution, marketing, and service. Governments also have non-regulatory influence over businesses. They typically are among the largest purchasers of goods and services produced in the private sector. Adding to it, they have the power to favor depressed areas and small businesses and can subsidize industries such as agriculture and fishing (Carroll & Buchholtz, 2011, p. 353). Governments are also major competitors in some areas such as postal service, banking, transportation, etc. Health care, education, recreation, and security are more examples of areas where government is a competitor of private held companies.

On an article proposing a research framework on integration and system interoperation in e-government, Hans and Klischewski (2007) shares the view of many that e-government is a solution to minimize the drawbacks of government influence over businesses and society. (World Bank, 2009) defines e-Government as "the use by government agencies of information technologies (such as the Internet and mobile computing) that have the ability to transform relations with citizens, businesses, and other arms of government. These technologies can serve a variety of different ends: better delivery of government services to citizens, improved interactions with business and industry, citizen empowerment through access to information, or more efficient government management. The resulting benefits can be less corruption, increased transparency, greater convenience, revenue growth, and/or cost reductions".

E-government information systems face multiple challenges and a number of serious constraints (Hans & Klischewski, 2007). The problem seems to be the lack of fully understanding the complex nature of e-government and the exact extent of these challenges and constraints regarding integration and interoperability. This topic was also discussed by Misuraca (2009) which claims that the majority of the earlier e-government initiatives, named as e-government 1.0, culminated in failed projects. The introduction of Information and Communication Technologies (ICT) in government was seen as the "silver bullet" that would change the way governments operate but did not produced the expected results. Despite the little amount of data available about the success rates of these projects, which is imputed to political implications, Misuraca (2009) advances a baseline estimation around 70%-80% of total or partial projects failures. The main causes of failure are attributed to the lack of preparation, e-readiness, and poor assessment of the real needs causing unrealistic assumptions. As an effect, governments are trying to take advantage of the success of Web 2.0 technologies (blogs, wikis, RSS feeds, social software, folksonomies, etc.) as a way to reduce risks and understand the barriers to e-government (Misuraca, 2009). This trend is named e-government 2.0.

The view of e-government 2.0 is about having government as a platform, a provider of data and services for others to exploit as they see fit. In this view the role of intermediaries in the context of government will increase as it happen with many businesses that are being aided today by third-party firms acting as intermediaries in providing content and service in the Web 2.0 environment (Chang & Kannan, 2008). The belief is that allowing third parties to innovate by building upon government data and applications it is more likely that information value will be maximized by service provisioning that better respond to users' expectations and needs (UN, 2010). For this to happen it is necessary that governments provide data in a non-proprietary and predictable format. As a consequence, governments will need to rethink how content and services are designed. Content has to be addressable in a granular form, in formats that are open, structured and machine-readable so that intermediaries can pick the appropriate content and application they need to fulfill their service task (Chang & Kannan, 2008; UN, 2010).

A research on e-government held by Institute for Prospective Technological Studies that is monitoring the emerging trends of Web 2.0 since 2005 is presented in (Osimo, 2008). The study addresses four general questions: Are Web 2.0 applications relevant for the government context? If they are, in what way is Web 2.0 likely to have an impact on government? How significant could this impact be? How are Web 2.0 applications implemented in the government context? The study concludes that there is sufficient evidence that Web 2.0 applications are relevant for many different domains of e-government and those Web 2.0 applications contribute to the key goals of better, simpler, joined-up and networked government.

Most of the initiatives found and studied are applied in highly knowledge intensive domains. The wide availability of public data for re-use seems to be an important enabling factor for Web 2.0 applications and the managers of these initiatives agreed that wider availability of public data was their main recommendation to policy makers.

Alongside the optimistic view related to the use of Web 2.0 technologies in e-government, the community reckons that there are some risks. These risks assume particular relevance in the government context because of its institutional role and universal service obligations (Osimo, 2008). Among them are:

- Low participation: the usage of Web 2.0 tools does not lead automatically to greater user involvement;
- Participation restricted to an elite: most Web 2.0 applications are used by the cultural and economic elite and can make societal divides wider by giving more voice to those that already have it. Digital divide refers to the gap between people with effective access and capacity to use ICT and those with very limited or no access or capacity at all;
- Loss of control due to excessive transparency: in a few cases, opening-up the conversation has led to loss of control and loss of credibility. Cases were reported where sensitive information was released in an incorrect and sometimes illegal way;
- Manipulation of content by interested parties: there is a concern that when social media become mainstream, vested interests would take over the content production.
- Privacy issues: Web 2.0 users appear not to be fully aware of the implications of publishing their details on the Web (Hogben, 2007), and Web 2.0 applications in the government context could become a further source of sensitive information being published.

Another related concern, named information asymmetry, is raised by Clarkson, Jacobsen, & Batcheller (2007). Information asymmetry is the lack of information awareness and is another cause of digital divide that can result in negative consequences for both the ones with or without information access. It is not about the possession of means and knowledge to access information but is about knowing that the information exists. Clarkson et al. (2007) explains that "information asymmetry exists when a party or parties possess greater informational awareness pertinent to effective participation in a given situation relative to other participating parties". This problem can be reduced by making systematic and increased information sharing in order to correctly regulate all participants' expectations.

The above issues that affect all tiers of government: national, regional and local. Adding to those, evidence gathered in the 2010 European e-government benchmark survey show that local and regional e-government services are lagging behind when compared to central government (Lorincz et al., 2010). Corroborating these evidences, (Paiva Dias, 2011) conducted a study for municipalities of Portugal, a country that has good classifications in international e-government benchmarks at national level services. The study found that despite the investment made in the last decades in e-government, Portuguese municipalities still exhibit medium level development in what relates information dissemination through the Web. One of the conclusions presented is that "it seems that raising the awareness of both local level politics and civil servants is essential to redirect investments and actual development to achieve more client observable results in terms of e-government". This issue is particularly relevant as municipalities are often the closest point of service for citizens and enterprises (Rodrigues, Dias, & Teixeira, 2010).

RELATED WORK

Given that a systematic review of related work is outside the scope of this chapter, to contextualize the work presented, Tables 1, 2 and 3 present, respectively, relevant research projects, currently deployed government sponsored initiatives and standards definitions efforts made by governments relative to semantic interoperability. A comprehensive search with Publish or Perish (Harzing, 2007) was conducted using the following search

Table 1. Relevant related research projects about government information provisioning

Author	Challenge	Approach	Outcomes
(Chen, 2012)	Incorporates a wide variety of important factors from previous research into a single theoretical framework	A framework for Government 2.0 development and implementation	no practical implementation was discussed
(Hobson et al., 2011)	Municipal employees rely heavily on manual methods for data sharing	Improve interaction and information sharing within and between municipal departments	no practical implementation was discussed
(Wang et al., 2011)	Support ecological and environmental issues such as biodiversity loss, water problems	Monitoring systems based on linked data approach	Web portal
(Fonou-Dombeu & Huisman, 2011)	Strengthen the adoption of semantic technologies in e-government	Combine ontology building methodology with state-of-the-art semantic Web platforms	Government domain ontology
(Mohamed, Saravanan, Muthaiyah, & Arman, 2011)	Improve conventional development processes in terms of time efficiency and collaboration	Conceptual software development technique for building and developing e-government 2.0 portal	Proof-of-concept prototype
(Goodwin, Dolbear, & Hart, 2008)	Represent links between geographic entities in spatial queries	Encoding topological relations between geographic entities over traditional spatial queries	Example dataset for the administrative geography
(Wang, Song, Hamilton, & Curwell, 2007)	Multidimensional information integration, especially spatial information integration	Centralized database approach, accepting various structured data sources and data formats	Integrated multidimensional centralized database

Table 2. Currently deployed government supported initiatives

Name	Domains of Usage in Government	Reference
Procure	Bring together all public local entities for their purchases, give companies a single entry to all tenders,	http://www.eservices-europa.eu/node/122
Show Us a Better Way	Competition about more useful for citizens, businesses and government agencies	UK
OpenPSI	Support government-based information publishers, research communities, and Web developers	http://www.jisc.ac.uk/
Apps for Democracy	Make government data useful for citizens, businesses and government agencies	http://www.appsfordemocracy.org/
GovTrack	Collect data about the U.S. Congress, semantic Web powered services tracking and publishing government data. Provides XML and RDF APIs and SPARQL query endpoint	http://www.govtrack.us/
Regulations.gov	A source for U.S. government regulations and related documents	http://www.regulations.gov
USASpending	Publish data about government spending, increase data quality by adopting a uniform method of identifying the recipients of federal funds	http://www.usaspending.gov/
Govtrack	Integrates information about bill text, floor speeches and votes for both houses of Congress	http://www.govtrack.us/
No given name	Driving conditions and advice to drivers and commuters, combines Mapquest data with realtime traffic data to create "mashup"	http://www.gov.bc.ca/tran/
Data.gov	Improve access to the data generated by the government, uses Linked Data	http://www.data.gov
Eurostat	Improve access to the data generated by the government, datasets organized by themes but not semantically described	http://epp.eurostat.ec.europa.eu

terms: "e-government and enterprise 2.0", "e-government as a platform", "government 2.0" and "semantic government". Some works were discarded in the analysis process as they were too far from the work and objectives established for the conceptual model presented in this chapter.

There has been investment in the development of systems and technologies related to government information provisioning particularly in Europe and USA. Further projects can be found in the literature such as (Osimo, 2008) which contains a list of Web 2.0 initiatives relative to government information domain that were not included here.

UNLOCKING INFORMATION FOR E-GOVERNMENT AND ENTERPRISE 2.0 USING WEB 2.0 AND HUMAN LANGUAGE TECHNOLOGIES

Governments are typically considered knowledge-intensive organizations which make knowledge management a key concern to improve efficiency and effectiveness of government (Organisation for Economic & Development, 2005). In (Osimo, 2008) it is claimed that traditional knowledge management systems cope well with structured knowledge and that Web 2.0 applications - social

Table 3. Standards definitions efforts made by governments relative to semantic interoperability

Name	Technology and Purpose	Country
oeGov	OWL ontologies to enable distributed creation and maintenance of metadata about government data	US
govtalk	Definition of the elements, refinements and encoding schemes to be used by government (XML?)	UK
ADAE	Reference schema, core component, category, or semantic asset	France
InfostructureBase	repository of XMLschemas in the Danish Public Sector about business process descriptions, datamodel descriptions, interface descriptions, and XML schemas from public and private organizations	Denmark
SAGA	XRepository of XML Schemas for documents and a set of codelists	Germany
HKSARG	XML Schema Design and Management Guide	Hong Kong
Joinup	XML and RDF to find, choose, re-use, develop, and implement open source software and semantic interoperability assets	EU
NIEM	Partnership between the U.S. Department of Justice and the Department of Homeland Security to develop, disseminate and support enterprise-wide information exchange standards and processes	US

software, folksonomies, and wiki - are effective with informal and tacit knowledge internally among employees. However, government also produces important documents in natural language that are neither structured, in the sense of have meta-data description associated, or effectively sharable using Web 2.0 applications: the information is not granular, structured, machine-readable, and reusable.

Some works addressed this problem. An ontology based information system named EgoIR used a specific ontology to associate concept instances with documents (Ortiz-Rodriguez, Palma, & Villazón-Terrazas, 2007). The associations were done manually and the authors claimed that the queries returned documents more accurately. No usage examples were demonstrated and the system did not processed or extracted information inside the documents. Leroy and Iriberri (2007) developed a crime reporting system featuring Natural Language Processing (NLP) technologies. NLP was based on Part-of-Speech (POS) tags, lists of words (gazetteers), and semantic tagging with handcrafted rules analyzing witness's narratives to extract the information that was required in standard police reports. The system was developed for police reports domain only. Another work developed an experimental Website, Commentonthis.com, designed to enable having detailed discussions around the contents of major public documents. The Website allows citizens to share their views on the details of some government documents, which have been split into paragraphs in order to make them "commentable."

It is important to push these initiatives further by providing tools that allow efficiently extracting the information inside those natural language documents in order to include it in structured knowledge bases ready for Web 2.0. While doing this, it is important to not expect that governments will change the way they work. Governments are complex organizations with bureaucratic systems designed to have checks and balances to guarantee that powers are divided into separate levels and branches of government (Hans & Klischewski, 2007).

We propose a conceptual model that aims to make available, with semantic description, relevant government information whether it exists in structured formats or in documents written in natural language. This implies the ability to interpret natural language texts, to discriminate which information is relevant, to assign meaning and merge related information. In order to have a tool that can be realistically adopted by government services, it is necessary to support an easy and seamless adaptation to the multiple government actuation domains. Alongside these features, another concern is to keep the model simple and clear.

Requirements

We will now enumerate the general requirements for the proposed conceptual model. The requirements were identified based on the literature review presented in the previous section and on generic concerns regarding information provisioning. Each of the following four subsections elaborates on a requirement: information acquisition from natural language documents, domain adaptation, relevant information identification, and interoperability.

Information Acquisition from Natural Language Documents

Important sources of government information are originally created in natural language plain text documents such as laws, regulations, etc. (Rodrigues et al., 2010). Thus, a requirement for the model is to acquire information from natural language texts. Acquiring information from such documents improves efficiency because it avoids having government services replicating content in various formats. This requirement implies a system able to analyze and understand texts, a task usually called information extraction.

Additionally, the model should be able to obtain information from external structured sources. This would allow complementing government's information with data from sources as relational databases and external sources of information. An example can be a municipal report about streets under repair: alternative to showing a list of street names, this information can be displayed in a map if the coordinates are obtained from a location server as Google Maps Web service.

Domain Adaptation

Different branches of government work with different domains and topics. To build a tool useful to a wide range of applications it is necessary to feature the ability of adapting the information domain. Adapting the information domain means to accept changes in an easily and timely manner, in order to reduce costs and speed up processes. It also means to be able to locate and acquire relevant information for the new domain, doing so without significant system reprogramming or re-engineering. The representation of knowledge about a domain implies the existence of a structural framework for organizing information by its semantic, forming a knowledge representation about the world or some part of it. Such a framework is called ontology. This requierement is very relevant because it is usually cost intensive to keep knowledge bases up-to-date as the domain changes (Bizer et al., 2009).

An important feature of Knowledge Bases (KB) conforming to an ontology is the possibility of performing logic inference. Based on ontology, context-aware computing can exploit various existing logic reasoning mechanisms to infer new facts from already known ones. It is also possible to check and solve inconsistent knowledge that can occur due to imperfect knowledge acquisition

(Wang, Xiong, Zhou, & Yu, 2007). Other benefit of having ontology is that they provide formalized and public application's view of the world and, as such, improve information accessibility, maintainability, and interoperability (Guarino, 1998).

Relevant Information Detection and Integration

Disclosing the large volume of government documentation can create a noise effect and become a way to hide information. Moreover, if not properly addressed, information disclosure can require a lot of time and effort, and can be hard to keep up with all the demands. Surveys across Europe (Colclough & Tinholt, 2009), United States (Reddick, 2005) and other countries (Andersen et al., 2010) show that it's still necessary to improve the capacity of providing government's relevant information to clients and not flood them with random data. This implies the ability to locate and discriminate the relevant parts of the existing information.

Information relevancy is not an absolute value. It depends on several factors as the purpose of the document (law, an informal comment on some topic, etc), the core business of the publisher (for which information the publisher is an authority and which information serves as complement), and the expertise of the target audience on a given subject (what is the appropriate level of detail). These factors make inappropriate to define, a priori and for all government services, the set of information that is (more) relevant in a given context, the same is to say the information domain.

Data Provisioning Using Open Standards

Interoperability is based on agreements between requesters and providers on message passing protocols, procedure names, error codes, etc. Semantic interoperability ensures that these exchanges make sense: that the requester and the provider have a common understanding of the meanings of the requested services and data (Heiler, 1995). Current and future views of e-government urge its information systems to work in networked environments making (semantic) interoperability an important feature to take into account in the proposed conceptual model.

The proposed model needs to provide data using open standard to enable interoperability. As ontologies formalize the application's view of the world, semantic interoperability can be achieved by defining and making public the ontology using an open standard. The use of ontologies allows knowledge sharing because they define the semantic context. The use of context enables computational entities to have a common set of concepts about context while interacting with one another. They also facilitate knowledge reusing. By reusing well defined Web ontologies of different domains (e.g. temporal and spatial ontology), it is possible to compose large-scale context ontology without starting from scratch (Wang, Zhang, Gu, & Pung, 2004).

Conceptual Model and Proof of Concept Prototype

The model is an original proposal, simple and clear, that separates the realms of (natural) language and (semantic) knowledge that complies with the requirements enumerated in the previous section. The architecture is composed by three modules:

1. A knowledge representation module to define the data semantics and provide seed examples of the semantic concepts in natural language texts. The requirement that a change in the knowledge domain cannot cause a software reprogramming/re-engineering implies that the software adapts to (learns) the domain specification;
2. A natural language processing module to extract structured information from natural language texts;

3. A semantic extraction and integration module that creates semantic extraction models from the seed examples, applies them to all natural language texts, and integrates the extracted information with information from structured sources (e.g. databases). This module includes a machine interface for data access using open standards.

The proof of concept implementation follows the proposed conceptual model and was developed aiming public documents of Portuguese municipalities. Therefore, the NLP part was developed to handle European Portuguese documents. It was developed using open source software—adapted to work with European Portuguese—to take advantage of the state of the art approaches and tools. Specific software was developed to integrate the used software in a coherent system. Figure 1 depicts the conceptual model and the way it is designed to work.

Knowledge Representation Module

The component named Knowledge Representation (KR) contributes to both Domain Adaptation and Relevant Information Identification and Integration requirements. Its purpose is to bridge the gap between the realms of natural language and knowledge representation. In order to do so, it containing tools to define data semantics and associate it with output samples of the natural language processing component. The data semantics depends on the application purposes and it is

Figure 1. Conceptual model architecture with the three modules: natural language processing, knowledge representation, semantic extraction and integration. The arrows from 1 to 3 indicate the sequence of the system setup. Arrows 4 and 5 indicate the runtime usage, in which arrow 5 is just used in case of missing information (according to the ontology).

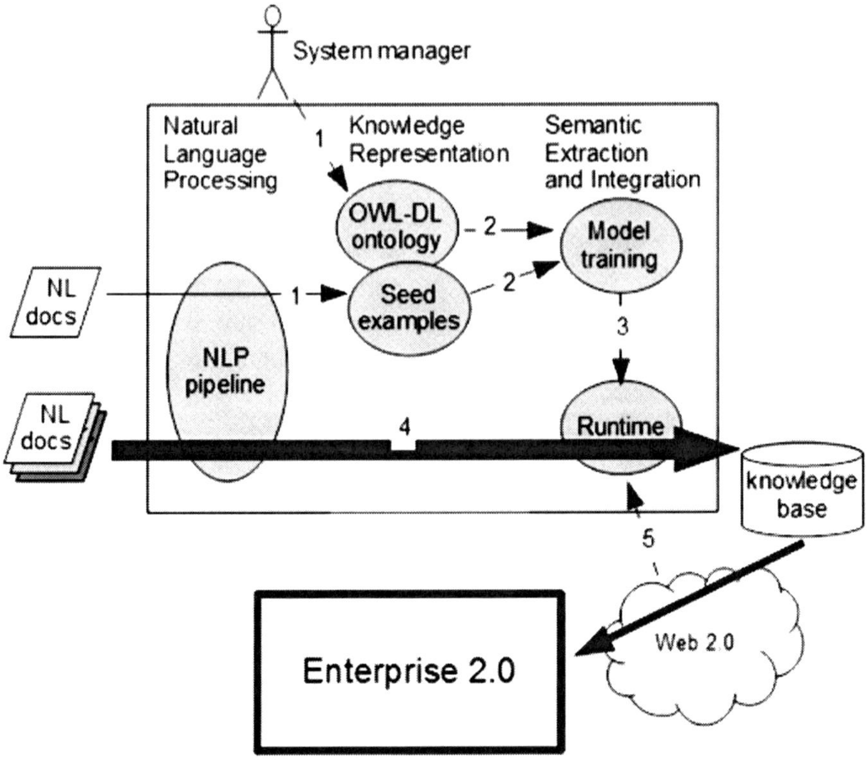

defined via a domain ontology - in this case for government. Alongside the ontology definition, it is necessary to associate ontological classes and relations with output samples of the NLP component. These associations will later be used as learning examples by the Semantic Extraction and Integration (SEI) component. The outputs of this component are the ontology and the associations of ontology classes and relations to the NLP component output.

In the proof-of-concept prototype, the ontology was defined in Web Ontology Language Description Logic (OWL-DL) and created with of Protégé-OWL v4.1. It is a combination of four well known ontologies - Friend of a Friend (FOAF) for identifying persons and its relationships, Dublin Core to encode the documents where the information was found, World Geodetic System (1984 revision) for identifying places latitude and longitude, and GeoNames (full version) to indentify the political organization of places – with a new class named ExecutiveSubject to handle topics relative to municipalities. ExecutiveSubject has six subclasses or specializations and six properties (see Tables 4 and 5). These specializations and properties were defined after assessing which topics were frequent in several municipalities' meeting minutes. Disjunctions between classes and/or relations are defined in the ontology. For instance, Allotment is disjoint with Protocol because protocols are not allotments and vice-versa, but BuildPermit is not disjoint with ConstrContract because they both refer to construction and some overlap is possible.

Table 4. Subclasses of the class ExecutiveSubject

Class Name	Class Description
Allotment	Permissions to perform land allotment or change previous allotments.
BuildPermit	Relative to construction contracts, public or private, already in execution.
ConstrProcess	Announces relative to generic public construction processes: beginning of works, changes in budgets, expropriations, etc.
Exemption	Requests for municipal fees exemptions.
Protocol	Protocols signed with institutions like schools or local clubs.
PublicCalls	Announcements of public contracts to acquire equipment or build some facility.

Table 5. Types of relations for ExecutiveSubject

Relation Name	Relation Description
Deliberation	The outcome.
Identifier	The unique identifier given by services.
Money Amount	Any money amount involved in the process.
Motivation	The motive.
Place	The address of the: construction/allotment, institution that signed the protocol, or entity that requests an exemption or subsidy.
requester	The entity or entities, excluding the municipality, that is/are involved in the process.

The learning procedure is based on associations between text samples and ontology classes and relations. The learning process is explained in the SEI section. The associations are made using AKTive Media ontology based annotator (Chakravarthy, Ciravegna, & Lanfranchi, 2006) and each association must involve at least a relation between two entities. Figure 2 shows the annotation interface. In the top left pane are the ontology classes. Below, after the search widget, a pane shows all relations of the selected class. In the large pane at the right 3 tokens are highlighted: À_Arcel, subsídio and 8.640,00€. Clicking on top of subsídio, in the bottom left pane appears all attribute/value pairs for it. In this case it is visible that the requester is À_Arcel and the moneyAmount is 8.640,00€. The result of annotation is a text file containing the annotation examples. These examples are passed to the Semantic Extraction and Integration part of the system along with the ontology and the texts.

Natural Language Processing Module

The Natural Language Processing (NLP) component accomplishes with the Information Acquisition from Natural Language Documents require-

Figure 2. Screenshot of AKTive media interface. The top left pane shows the ontology classes. Below, after the search widget, a pane shows all relations of the selected class. The large pane at the right shows two words highlighted. Clicking on top of a highlighted word appears all its attribute/value pairs in bottom left pane.

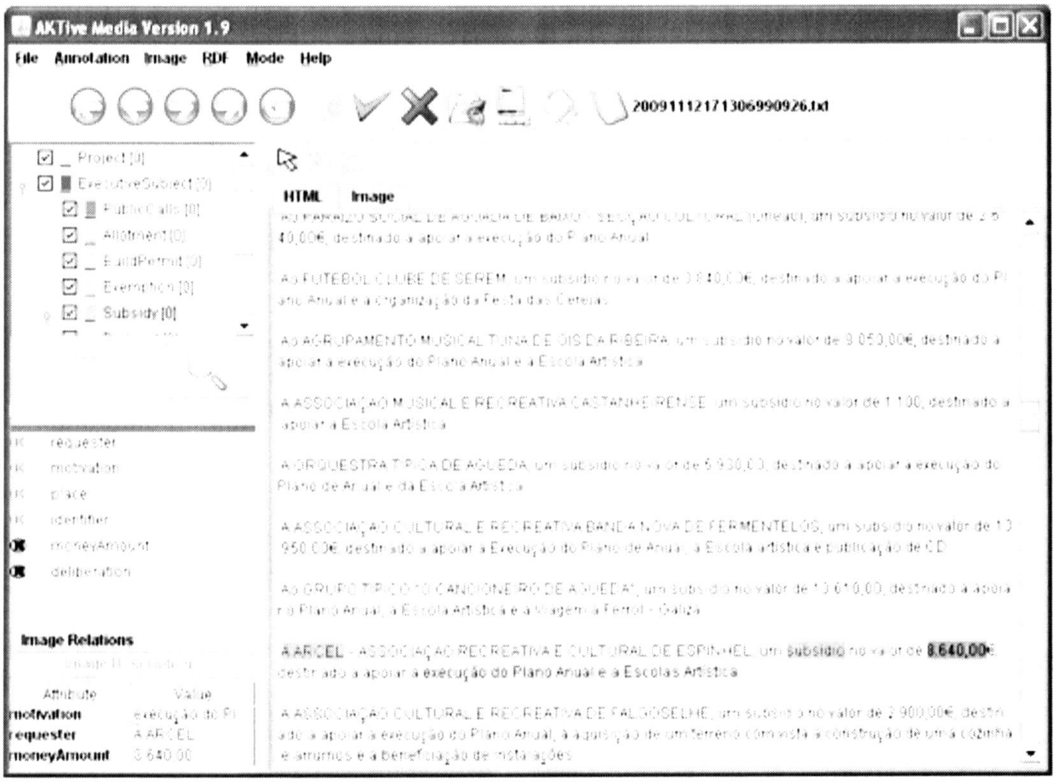

ment and is named Natural Language Processing by being based on technologies from the NLP area. Its goal is to obtain structured data from natural language unstructured texts. For this, it includes tools to obtain documents from the WWW and/or from local file systems and extract their content. Then, it takes these texts as input and produce fixed-format, unambiguous data, as output. The output can be more or less sophisticated but it needs to have enough detail to discriminate sentences with different meanings. This depends on the type of texts to be processed and on application purposes. Taking into account the state of the art in NLP, it is expectable to have an output that identifies named entities and have some kind of syntactic structure associated. This should be the only component of the model to be reprogrammed when changing or adding another natural language (English, French, Portuguese, etc.).

The processing is organized in three sequential steps: First, the text is extracted from the natural language documents and enriched with the inclusion of Part Of Speech (POS) tags – noun, verb, adjective, etc. This is made by TreeTagger (Schmid, 1994), a POS tagger that annotates text with POS and lemma information and has been successfully used to tag several natural languages including Brazilian Portuguese. The tagger was trained with an European Portuguese lexicon in order to be integrated in the system. Second, named entities are discovered and classified. Named entity recognition is based on a system developed for European Portuguese named Rembrandt (Cardoso, 2008). It uses Wikipedia as a raw knowledge resource and its document structure to classify all kinds of named entities in the text. Words belonging to a named entity are grouped. For instance, the names of the person John Stewart Smith become the single token John_Stewart_Smith. Third, sentences are analyzed to determine its grammatical structure. This is done by a dependency parser named MaltParser (Hall, Nilsson, & Nivre). A dependency parser uses a grammar structure that is determined by the relation between a word and its dependents - dependency grammar -, which is distinct from representations based on constituency - phrase structure grammars - as it lacks phrasal nodes. MaltParser was selected because it can be used to induce a grammar from Treebank data and to parse new data. This parser was already successfully used to parse several natural languages as English, French, Greek, Swedish, and Turkish.

Semantic Extraction and Integration Module

The component named Semantic Extraction and Integration (SEI) contributes to both Relevant Information Identification and Interoperability requirements. Its task is to extract, organize and store the output of the NLP component according to the semantic defined by the ontology. It needs to feature machine learning algorithms due to the requirement of supporting domain adaptation. These algorithms learn the associations provided by KR component and produce semantic extraction models that detect relevant information. These models are used in runtime to associate semantic information from all relevant data processed by the NLP component. Missing information - according to the ontology - can be searched in external structured sources. Data input is performed using structured sourced connectors. The existence of structure in the external data makes possible to develop connectors that directly assign appropriate semantics to the data. All information is stored in a knowledge base that conforms to the defined ontology. Data output should be made providing data and it's semantic. This implies to make the ontology public to let third party systems to know the system semantics. Data can be provided via Web services, via query endpoints (Simple Protocol and RDF Query Language (SPARQL), Semantic Web Rule Language (SWRL), etc.), or via other standard mechanisms.

Model Training: the goal of training is to produce a set of statistical classifiers that classify unknown instances based on their similarity with instances of known classes to detect ontological classes and relations in the syntactic structures. The training procedure starts by searching the examples generated with AKTive Media in a training set of documents already processed by the NLP part. The examples found in the training set are collected. A classifier like the ones used by Suchanek, Ifrim, & Weikum (2006) is created for each class or relation found, or updated if it already exists from previous trainings. The classifiers share information according to the ontology specification to improve their performance (Carlson, Betteridge, Hruschka, & Mitchell, 2009): examples for a class or relation will be counterexamples of disjoint classes or relations, respectively; examples for a class or relation will be examples of its super-class or super-relation. These classifiers are stored and used in runtime to assign ontology classes and relations to words in the texts.

Runtime Use: The syntactic structure of every sentence is evaluated by all classifiers. Each classifier performs the evaluation independently of the others. A relation is accepted and stored in the knowledge base if the following two conditions are met:

1. All ontology restrictions are positively evaluated by the classifiers;
2. If the first condition is met, a reasoner checks the coherence between new information and the information already in the knowledge base. The new information is added to the knowledge base when it is coherent with the existing one, otherwise is discarded and a warning is issued.

Reasoning is performed by an open source reasoner called Pellet (Sirin & Parsia, 2004) and the knowledge base is stored and managed by Virtuoso Universal Server (Virtuoso, 2010).

The knowledge base features a mechanism to communicate with external sources of structured information. Information input occurs when some information about some knowledge base record is missing, according to the ontology. As an example, it is being used to get the location of every entity with a fixed physical location (as organizations headquarter) by querying Google Maps Web services. Information output occurs when external systems query the knowledge base. The access can be trough SPARQL queries or raw access to the full knowledge base. For instance, it is possible to combine a SPARQL query with Google Maps in the creation of higher level visualizations of the information available in the system.

First Evaluation Results

Preliminary performance and usability tests were made to the prototype. The proof of concept implementation of our conceptual model was tested with documents from eleven Portuguese municipalities. The objective was to assess if the system retrieves meaningful information from the documents regarding concerns as knowing which subsidies were already granted, which public constructions contracts are being executed, the status of construction processes, the way the municipality money is distributed including which subsidies were granted and which protocols were signed.

Experimental Setup

Documents were retrieved automatically by a Web crawler from the Websites of the following municipalities: Águeda, Albergaria-a-Velha, Anadia, Aveiro, Estarreja, Ílhavo, Murtosa, Oliveira do Bairro, Ovar, Sever do Vouga, and Vagos. Two random sets, one for training other for testing, of 50 PDF documents were selected. The sets had no common documents and only pdf documents were selected because it is more likely to have relevant information in these than in any other type of documents. The training set was manually annotated using the AKTive Media annotator. The annotations provide examples about the type of information that should be extracted regarding subsidies, build permits and protocols. For each topic the following information was also annotated: requester, identifier, motivation, moneyAmount, place, and deliberation (see Table 5 for details). The other set was used as a test set to have knowledge extracted by the system in runtime.

Performance Measurement

Two measures are commonly used to assess information retrieval systems performance: precision and recall. Precision is the ratio between the information correctly retrieved and all information retrieved. Recall is the ratio between the information correctly retrieved and all correct information that actually exists in the sources. Recall calculation implies knowing all information that exists in the documents and, when the test set is large, is a time consuming task. A third measure commonly used is the F-score (F_1) which is the harmonic mean of precision and recall. Table 6 summarizes the results obtained with our test set.

Results show that the system achieves a high precision value. The value 0.95 means that 95% of the extracted information was correct. The recall value of 0.63, meaning that the system identified 63% of all relevant information in the documents, can be explained by the small training

Table 6. Knowledge detected by the system. For each municipality's documents set are presented: the total number of correctly detected information and, between brackets, the total information in those documents. Adding to these information are (¹) 4 building permits incorrectly extracted and (²) 1 protocol incorrectly extracted.

	Municipality									
	a	b	c	D	e	f	G	prec.	recall	F_1
Subsidy	0(2)	3(3)	4(11)	1(1)	1(1)	3(14)	0(0)	1.00	0.44	0.61
Build Permit	3(4)¹	13(13)	47(47)	0(0)	0(0)	4(4)	0(0)	0.94	0.99	0.97
Protocol	3(4)	3(3)	0(3)	0(0)	7(24)	2(7)²	0(0)	0.89	0.20	0.32
Total								0.95	0.63	0.76

set used for this preliminary experimentation. Future improvements and larger training sets should produce a higher recall value. Nevertheless, these values are in line with state-of-the-art information retrieval systems in other areas. Systems such as DBpedia (precision 0.86 to 0.99; recall 0.41 to 0.77), Kylin (precision 0.74 to 0.97; recall 0.61 to 0.96), or YAGO/NAGA (precision 0.91 to 0.99; recall not reported).

Besides specific topics about municipalities' related subjects, these systems can also be useful as tools for other purposes as identifying society dynamics in order to support the definition of public policies and priorities. As an indicator of social dynamics a possible query can be about the location of all activities, with a known location, in a given municipality. As latitude and longitude coordinates are available on the knowledge base, the information can be rendered in a map. Locations without any occurrence would probably be less developed regions and should be looked more carefully by policy makers.

FUTURE RESEARCH DIRECTIONS

An interesting research direction for the proposed conceptual model is to assess how it can help in Government to Government (G2G) relationships. G2G is the online non-commercial interaction between Government organizations, departments, and authorities and other Government organizations, departments, and authorities. The proposed model could provide government information for other branches of government as it provides government information for external businesses. Although not focused here, we do not foresee any technical limitation that would prevent such system to be used in G2G. However it is necessary to further study G2G constraints and challenges before trying to propose and deploy new e-government information provisioning systems.

Another future research direction is the inclusion of a natural language interaction with users. Natural language interfaces are user interfaces that allow people to interact using a human language, such as English, as opposed to a computer language, command line interface, or graphical user interface. Spoken language interfaces are capable of handling spoken human language. As human interaction is based on conversation between persons, recent spoken or written natural language interfaces try to emulate the conversational aspects of human interactions (e.g. turn-taking, speech acts...). In recent years, advances in automatic speech recognition language understanding, language generation, and speech synthesis enabled the emergence of complex conversational spoken language interfaces (Bohus & Rudnicky, 2009). Examples of conversational spoken language interfaces include (Bohus & Rudnicky, 2009): Jupiter that provides up-to-date weather information over the telephone; AdApt that provides real-estate information in the Stockholm area; TRIPS that is a spoken language enabled planning assistant. More advanced conversation systems can make use of technologies from the natural language processing and artificial intelligence fields such as user modeling and knowledge representation.

A third possible future research direction is the extension of the proposed model to include user authentication mechanisms. User authentication is a means of identifying the user and verifying that the user is allowed to access some restricted service or resource. As our proposal was designed for handling public documents and public information, this feature was not required. The lack of user authentication prevents the inclusion of private information in systems strictly conforming to the model. For now, with the current design, it is not possible for a business to access private information related to its interaction with government. Examples of such information are proposals submitted for business contracts. Although not considered in the design, there is nothing in the model that forbids the inclusion of user authentication and custom security implementations.

CONCLUSION

In this chapter, we discussed the current challenges in government information provisioning, and present the description of a new conceptual model able to detect and organize relevant information existing in natural language documents. Driven by the possibility of offering technological solutions that can facilitate the creation of content ready for the Web 2.0 environment, the proposed model assumes itself as an information provisioning system with the main objective of motivating the creation of durable, standard and open information infrastructures that take into account governments' particularities and constraints.

An advantage of our model is that it does not imply a significant change in the way government produces its documentation: the model fits the way government works and not the other way around. This is important because government services should not be diverted to other tasks outside their scope. Based on a modular architecture, the model allows government services define its own knowledge domain without the need of system re-engineering or reprogramming.

Key features of this model are the ability to process natural language texts, to accept a knowledge domain defined by an ontology, and to learn from examples how to extract information. The natural language processing module can also be changed to other natural languages (English, French, etc) without major difficulties as it is based on well known processing technologies. The model also features a structured information entry point to allow the inclusion of information sources that complement the information included in the natural language documents.

From the businesses perspective, values comes from the possibility of accessing more information sources which contain content addressable in a granular form, in formats that are open, structured and machine readable. Adding to the benefit of having better information available, new businesses can arise by adding value over these new information sources.

Results are already available for a reduced number of documents (considered by the authors to be adequate for this stage of development) and obviously are not conclusive. However they provide important cues about the positive and negative aspects of the information provisioning prototype in development. The results show that the system is able to acquire useful, meaningful information. As part of the adopted development methodology, new evaluations will be made after successive refinements of the prototype components, involving a higher number of documents.

REFERENCES

Andersen, K. N., Henriksen, H. Z., Medaglia, R., Danziger, J. N., Sannarnes, M. K., & Enemarke, M. (2010). Fads and facts of e-government: A review of impacts of e-government (2003-2009). *International Journal of Public Administration*, *33*(11), 564–579. doi:10.1080/01900692.2010.517724.

Bizer, C., Lehmann, J., Kobilarov, G., Auer, S., Becker, C., & Cyganiak, R. et al. (2009). DBpedia-A crystallization point for the web of data. *Web Semantics: Science. Services and Agents on the World Wide Web*, *7*(3), 154–165. doi:10.1016/j.websem.2009.07.002.

Bohus, D., & Rudnicky, A. I. (2009). The RavenClaw dialog management framework: Architecture and systems. *Computer Speech & Language*, *23*(3), 332–361. doi:10.1016/j.csl.2008.10.001.

Cardoso, N. (2008). Rembrandt-reconhecimento de entidades mencionadas baseado em relações e análise detalhada do texto. *Encontro do Segundo HAREM, PROPOR 2008.*

Carlson, A., Betteridge, J., Hruschka, E. R., Jr., & Mitchell, T. M. (2009). *Coupling semi-supervised learning of categories and relations.*

Carroll, A. B., & Buchholtz, A. K. (2011). *Business and society: Ethics and stakeholder management.* South-Western Pub..

Chakravarthy, M. A., Ciravegna, P. F., & Lanfranchi, M. V. (2006). *Cross-media document annotation and enrichment.* Paper presented at the SAAW - 1st Semantic Authoring and Annotation Workshop. New York, NY.

Chang, A. M., & Kannan, P. K. (2008). *Leveraging web 2.0 in government.* New York: IBM Center for The Business of Government.

Chen, Y. C. (2012). A framework for government 2.0 development and implementation. In Chen, Y.-C., & Chu, P.-Y. (Eds.), *Electronic Governance and Cross-Boundary Collaboration: Innovations and Advancing Tools* (pp. 350–368). Hershey, PA: IGI-Global.

Clarkson, G., Jacobsen, T. E., & Batcheller, A. L. (2007). Information asymmetry and information sharing. *Government Information Quarterly*, *24*(4), 827–839. doi:10.1016/j.giq.2007.08.001.

Colclough, G., & Tinholt, D. (2009). *Smarter, faster, better e-government-8th benchmarking measurement.* Capgemini, RAND Europe, IDC, SOGETI and DTi

Cook, N. (2008). *Enterprise 2.0: How social software will change the future of work.* Ashgate Pub Co..

Fonou-Dombeu, J. V., & Huisman, M. (2011). Combining ontology development methodologies and semantic web platforms for e-government domain ontology development. *International Journal of Web & Semantic Technology*, *2*(2), 12–25. doi:10.5121/ijwest.2011.2202.

Frissen, V., Millard, J., Huijboom, N., Iversen, J. S., Kool, L., & Kotterink, B. et al. (2007). *The future of eGovernment: An exploration of ICT-driven models of eGovernment for the EU in 2020.* European Comission Join Research Center.

Goodwin, J., Dolbear, C., & Hart, G. (2008). Geographical linked data: The administrative geography of great britain on the semantic web. *Transactions in GIS*, *12*, 19–30. doi:10.1111/j.1467-9671.2008.01133.x.

Guarino, N. (Ed.). (1998). *Formal ontology in information systems: Proceedings of the first international conference (FOIS'98).* IOS.

Hall, J., Nilsson, J., & Nivre, J. (n.d.). Single malt or blended? A study in multilingual parser optimization. *Trends in Parsing Technology*, (pp. 19-33). Academic Press.

Hans, J. S., & Klischewski, R. (2007). E-government integration and interoperability: Framing the research agenda. *International Journal of Public Administration*, *30*(8-9), 889–920. doi:10.1080/01900690701402668.

Harzing, A. W. (2007). *Publish or perish*. Retrieved from http://www.harzing.com/pop.htm

Heiler, S. (1995). Semantic interoperability. *ACM Computing Surveys*, *27*(2), 271–273. doi:10.1145/210376.210392.

Hobson, S., Anand, R., Yang, J., Lee, J., Campos, P., Graham, N., et al. (2011). Towards interoperability in municipal government: A study of information sharing practices. In Human-Computer Interaction – INTERACT 2011 (Vol. 6946, pp. 233-247). Springer. doi:10.1007/978-3-642-23774-4_21.

Hogben, G. (2007). Security issues and recommendations for online social networks. ENISA European Network and Information Security Agency, 80211(1).

Leighninger, M. (2011). Citizenship and governance in a wild, wired world: How should citizens and public managers use online tools to improve democracy? *National Civic Review*, *100*(2), 20–29. doi:10.1002/ncr.20056.

Leroy, G. A., & Iriberri, A. (2007). *Natural language processing and e-government: Extracting reusable crime report information*. Paper presented at the IRI - Information Reuse and Integration. New York, NY.

Lorincz, B., Tinholt, D., Linden, N. V. d., Colclough, G., Cave, J., Schindler, R., et al. (2010). *Digitizing public services in Europe: Putting ambition into action - 9th Benchmark Measurement*. Capgemini, RAND Europe, IDC, SOGETI and DTi.

McAfee, A. P. (2006). Enterprise 2.0: The dawn of emergent collaboration. *IEEE Engineering Management Review*, *34*(3), 38–38. doi:10.1109/EMR.2006.261380.

Misuraca, G. C. (2009). e-Government 2015: Exploring m-government scenarios, between ICT-driven experiments and citizen-centric implications. *Technology Analysis and Strategic Management*, *21*(3), 407–424. doi:10.1080/09537320902750871.

Mohamed, F. Z. M., Saravanan, S., Muthaiyah, O., & Arman, K. (2011). TM: A development technique for e-government 2.0 portals. *WSEAS Transactions on Information Science and Applications*, *8*(2), 96–108.

OECD. (2005). *Modernising government: The way forward*. OECD.

Ortiz-Rodriguez, F., Palma, R., & Villazón-Terrazas, B. (2007). *EgoIR: Ontology-based information retrieval intended for eGovernment*. Paper presented at the 2nd International Applications of Semantic Technologies (AST) Workshop - Informatik 2007.

Osimo, D. (2008). Web 2.0 in government: Why and how. *Institute for Prospectice Technological Studies (IPTS), JRC, European Commission, EUR, 23358*.

Paiva Dias, G. (2011). *Local e-government information and service delivery: A survey of municipal websites in Portugal*. Paper presented at the CISTI 6ª Conferência Ibérica de Sistemas e Tecnologias de Informação. Aviero, Portugal.

Reddick, C. G. (2005). Citizen interaction with e-government: From the streets to servers? *Government Information Quarterly*, *22*(1), 38–57. doi:10.1016/j.giq.2004.10.003.

Rodrigues, M., Dias, G. P., & Teixeira, A. (2010). *Human language technologies for e-gov*. Paper presented at the WEBIST. Valencia, Spain.

Schmid, H. (1994). *Probabilistic part-of-speech tagging using decision trees*.

Sirin, E., & Parsia, B. (2004). *Pellet: An owl dl reasoner*.

Suchanek, F. M., Ifrim, G., & Weikum, G. (2006). *LEILA: Learning to extract information by linguistic analysis*.

UN. (2010). *Government survey 2010 leveraging e-government at a time of financial and economic crisis*. New York: UN.

Virtuoso, O. (2010). *Universal server platform for the real-time enterprise*. Retrieved from http://virtuoso.openlinksw.com/

Wang, C., Xiong, M., Zhou, Q., & Yu, Y. (2007). Panto: A portable natural language interface to ontologies. *The Semantic Web: Research and Applications*, 473-487.

Wang, H., Song, Y., Hamilton, A., & Curwell, S. (2007). Urban information integration for advanced e-planning in Europe. *Government Information Quarterly*, *24*(4), 736–754. doi:10.1016/j.giq.2007.04.002.

Wang, P., Zheng, J., Fu, L., Patton, E., Lebo, T., Ding, L., et al. (2011). A semantic portal for next generation monitoring systems. In *Proceedings of the Semantic Web – ISWC 2011* (Vol. 7032, pp. 253-268). Springer.

Wang, X. H., Zhang, D. Q., Gu, T., & Pung, H. K. (2004). *Ontology based context modeling and reasoning using OWL*.

World Bank. (2009). Retrieved from http://go.worldbank.org/M1JHE0Z280

ADDITIONAL READING

Banko, M., Cafarella, M. J., Soderland, S., Broadhead, M., & Etzioni, O. (2009). *Open information extraction for the web*. Seattle, WA: University of Washington.

Blaylock, N., Allen, J., de Beaumont, W., & Jung, H. (2011). *Towards an OWL-based framework for extracting information from clinical texts*. Paper presented at the First International Workshop on Semantic Applied Technologies on Biomedical Informatics (SATBI). New York, NY.

Bontcheva, K., Davis, B., Funk, A., Li, Y., & Wang, T. (2009). Human language technologies. *Semantic Knowledge Management*, 37-49.

Chatzidimitriou, M., & Koumpis, A. (2008). Marketing one-stop e-government solutions: The European OneStopGov project. *IAENG International Journal of Computer Science*, *35*(1), 74–79.

Contini, F., & Lanzara, G. F. (2009). *ICT and innovation in the public sector: European studies in the making of e-government*. New York: Palgrave Macmillan.

Cook, M. E. (2000). *What citizens want from e-government*. Center for Technology in Government.

Etzioni, O., Cafarella, M., Downey, D., Kok, S., Popescu, A. M., & Shaked, T. et al. (2004). Web-scale information extraction in knowitall. In *Knowledge-Based Systems*. Hershey, PA: IGI Global.

Jurafsky, D., Martin, J. H., Kehler, A., Vander Linden, K., & Ward, N. (2000). *Speech and language processing: An introduction to natural language processing, computational linguistics, and speech recognition*. Cambridge, MA: MIT Press.

Layne, K., & Lee, J. (2001). Developing fully functional e-government: A four stage model. *Government Information Quarterly, 18*(2), 122–136. doi:10.1016/S0740-624X(01)00066-1.

Lee, T. B., Hendler, J., & Lassila, O. (2001). The semantic web. *Scientific American, 284*(5), 34–43. doi:10.1038/scientificamerican0501-34 PMID:11396337.

McQueen, J., Vasques, C., Brakebill, J., Roberts, D., & Parston, G. (2009). *Leadership in customer service: Creating shared responsibility for better outcomes*. Accenture.

Medjahed, B., Bouguettaya, A., & Elmagarmid, A. K. (2003). Composing web services on the semantic Web. *The VLDB Journal, 12*(4), 333–351. doi:10.1007/s00778-003-0101-5.

Moon, M. J. (2002). The evolution of e-government among municipalities: Rhetoric or reality? *Public Administration Review, 62*(4), 424–433. doi:10.1111/0033-3352.00196.

Oteniya, O., Janowski, T., & Ojo, A. (2006). Government-wide workflow infrastructure-enabling virtual government organizations. *Network-Centric Collaboration and Supporting Frameworks*, 573-580.

Paiva Dias, G., & Rafael, J. A. (2007). A simple model and a distributed architecture for realizing one-stop e-government. *Electronic Commerce Research and Applications, 6*(1), 81–90. doi:10.1016/j.elerap.2006.02.001.

Paulheim, H., & Probst, F. (2010). Application integration on the user interface level: An ontology-based approach. *Data & Knowledge Engineering, 69*(11), 1103–1116. doi:10.1016/j.datak.2010.07.005.

Relyea, H. C. (2002). E-gov: Introduction and overview. *Government Information Quarterly, 19*(1), 9–36. doi:10.1016/S0740-624X(01)00096-X.

Sarawagi, S. (2008). Information extraction. *Foundations and Trends in Databases, 1*(3), 261–377. doi:10.1561/1900000003.

Sugumaran, V., & Meziane, F. (n.d.). An architecture to support web-based information extraction using domain ontologies. *Exploring the Grand Challenges for Next Generation E-Business*, 1-9.

Tat-Kei Ho, A. (2002). Reinventing local governments and the e-government initiative. *Public Administration Review, 62*(4), 434–444. doi:10.1111/0033-3352.00197.

Traunmuller, R., & Wimmer, M. (2003). *E-government at a decisive moment: Sketching a roadmap to excellence*. Electronic Government. doi:10.1007/10929179_1.

Wimmer, M., & Tambouris, E. (2002). *Online one-stop government*. Paper presented at the IFIP 17th World Computer Congress. Montreal, Canada.

Yildiz, M. (2007). E-government research: Reviewing the literature, limitations, and ways forward. *Government Information Quarterly, 24*(3), 646–665. doi:10.1016/j.giq.2007.01.002.

KEY TERMS AND DEFINITIONS

E-Government: The use of information and communication technologies to improve government processes and relations with citizens, businesses, and with other branches of government.

Enterprise 2.0: The use of Web 2.0 technologies to improve customer service and enterprises' internal processes.

Human Language Technologies: Research area comprising/addressing speech and natural language processing.

Natural Language Processing: Research area that studies how to analyze and produce human languages, such as English.

Ontology: A structural framework for organizing information by its semantic, forming a knowledge representation about the world or some part of it.

Open Standards: Publicly available standards. A main purpose is to foster system interoperability.

Statistical Classification: Identification of the class of a new, previously unseen element. The identification is based on the similarity between the new element and the individuals used in the training set.

Web 2.0: Set of technologies that make the Web more interactive and its information machine readable: wikis, social software, etc.

Compilation of References

A Wiki of Social Media Monitoring Solutions. (2011). *Monitoring solutions master list*. Retrieved from http://wiki.kenburbary.com

Abascal, J., & Civit, A. (2000). Mobile communication for older people: New oportunities for autonomous life. In *Proceedings of the Worshop on Universal Accessibility of Ubiquitous Computind: Providing for the Elderly* (pp. 255-268). Firenze, Italy: European Research Consortium for Informatics and Matematics.

Abecker, A., & Decker, S. (1998). Organizational memory: Knowledge acquisition, integration and retrieval issues. In *Proceedings of XPS-99* (LNAI), (vol. 1570, pp. 113-124). Berlin: Springer.

Acquisti, A. (2010). The economics of personal data and the economics of privacy. *WPISP-WPIE Roundtable*. Retrieved on November 3, 2011, from http://www.oecd.org/dataoecd/8/51/46968784.pdf

Actuate/BIRT. (2011). *BIRT open source*. Retrieved from http://www.actuate.com/

Adams, M., & Oleksak, M. (2010). *Intangible capital - Putting knowledge to work in the 21st-century organization*. Santa Barbara, CA: Praeger.

Adler, R. (2002). *The age wave meets the technology wave: Broadband and older americans*. Thousand Oaks, CA: Senior Net.

Afuah, A. (1998). *Innovation management*. New York: Harvard Press.

Agarwal, A., Shankar, R., & Tiwari, M. (2007). Modeling agility of supply chain. *Industrial Marketing Management*, *36*(4), 443–457. doi:10.1016/j.indmarman.2005.12.004.

Agarwal, R., & Prasad, J. (1999). Are individual differences germane to the acceptance of new information technologies. *Decision Sciences*, *30*(2), 361–391. doi:10.1111/j.1540-5915.1999.tb01614.x.

AGEMDI. (2011). *IV estudio sobre marketing y publicidad en medios interactivos*. Retrieved November, 20, 2010 from http://www. agemdi.es

Agencia, E. F. E. (2009). BBVA cierra las sucursales de Dinero Express para unificar su negocio con inmigrantes. *Terra News*. Retrieved from http://noticias.terra.es/economia/2009/0519/actualidad/bbva-cierra-las-sucursales-de-dinero-express-para-unificar-su-negocio-con-inmigrantes.aspx

Ahmad, M., & Bowman, I. (2011). Predicting system performance for multi-tenant database workloads. In *Proceedings of the Fourth International Workshop on Testing Database Systems* (pp. 6.1-6.6). ACM Press.

Ahrens, A., & Zaščerinska, J. (2011). Enterprise 3.0 in engineering education. In G. Noviks (Ed.), *Proceedings of the 15th International Student Scientific Practical Conference Human Environment. Technology* Rēzekne: Rēzeknes Augstskolas Izdevniecība.

Ahson, S. A., & Ilyas, M. (2011). *Near field communications handbook*. Boca Raton, FL: CRC Press. doi:10.1201/b11226.

Ajzen, I. (1991). The theory of planned behavior. *Organizational Behavior and Human Decision Processes*, *50*, 179–211. doi:10.1016/0749-5978(91)90020-T.

Akenti. (2009). *Amentia distributed access control*. Retrieved November 29, 2010, from http://dsd.lbl.gov/Akenti

Akhter, S. H. (2003). Strategic planning, hypercompetition, and knowledge management. *Business Horizons*, *46*(1), 19. doi:10.1016/S0007-6813(02)00275-6.

Akkermans, H., & Helder, K. (2002). Vicious and virtuous cycles in ERP implementation: A case study of interrelations between CSF. *European Journal of Information Systems*, *2*, 35–46. doi:10.1057/palgrave.ejis.3000418.

Aksu, A. A., & Tarcan, E. (2002). The internet and five-star hotels: A case study from the Antalya region in Turkey. *International Journal of Contemporary Hospitality Management*, *14*(2), 94–97. doi:10.1108/09596110210419282.

Al Mahmud, A., Mubin, O., Shaid, S., & Martens, J.-B. (2008). Desigining and evaluating the tabletop game experience for seniors citizens. In *Proceedings of the 5th Nordic Conference on Human-Computer Interaction: Building Bridges*. ACM.

Alavi, M., & Leidner, D. (2001). Knowledge management and knowledge management systems: Conceptual foundations and research issues. *Management Information Systems Quarterly*, *25*(1), 107–136. doi:10.2307/3250961.

Alba, J. W., & Hutchinson, J. W. (1987). Dimension of consumer expertise. *The Journal of Consumer Research*, *13*(4), 411–455. doi:10.1086/209080.

Albert, S., & Bradley, K. (1997). *Managing knowledge: Experts, agencies and organizations*. Cambridge, UK: Cambridge University Press. doi:10.1017/CBO9780511582486.

Alcobia, P. (2001). Atitudes e satisfação no trabalho. In Ferreira, J. M., Neves, J., & Caetano, A. (Eds.), *Manual de psicossociologia das organizações*. Lisboa, Portugal: McGraw-Hill.

Aldrich, H. E. (1979). *Organizations and environment*. Upper Saddle River, NJ: Prentice Hall.

Alee, V. (2003). *The future of knowledge: Increasing prosperity through value networks*. Burlington, MA: Elsevier Science.

Alee, V. (2008). Value network analysis and value conversion of tangible and intangible assets. *Journal of Intellectual Capital*, *9*(1).

Alexander, B. (2006). Web 2.0: A new wave of innovation for teaching and learning? *Educause Review*, *41*(2), 32-44. Retrieved May 28, 2011, from http://www.educause.edu/ir/library/pdf/erm0621.pdf

Alfiery, R. (2003). Managing dynamic user communities in a grid of autonomous resources. In *Proceedings of the Conference for Computing in High Energy and Nuclear Physics*. IEEE.

Algesheimer, R., Dholakia, U. M., & Herrmann, A. (2005). The social influence of brand community: Evidence from european car clubs. *Journal of Marketing*, *69*(3), 19–34. doi:10.1509/jmkg.69.3.19.66363.

Allee, V. (1997). *The knowledge evolution: expanding organizational intelligence*. Burlington, MA: Butterworth-Heinemann.

Allen, C., Jazayeri, D., Miranda, J., Biondich, P. G., Mamlin, B. W., & Wolfe, B. A. et al. (2007). Experience in implementing the OpenMRS medical record system to support HIV treatment in Rwanda. *Studies in Health Technology and Informatics*, *129*, 382–386. PMID:17911744.

Allen, N., & Meyer, P. (1990). Organizational socialization tactics: A longitudinal analysis of links to newcomers' commitment and role orientation. *Academy of Management Journal*, *33*(4), 1–18. doi:10.2307/256294.

Al-Mashari, M., Al-Mudimigh, A., & Zairi, M. (2003). Enterprise resource planning: Taxonomy of critical factors. *European Journal of Operational Research*, *146*(2), 352–364. doi:10.1016/S0377-2217(02)00554-4.

Al-Qawabah, M. (2012). *Assessing transformational leadership components as drivers in learning organisations*. (Doctor of Philosophy Dissertation). University of Technology, Sydney, Australia.

Alvesson, M. (2002). *Understanding organizational culture*. London: SAGE.

Alvesson, M. (2004). *Knowledge work and knowledge-intensive firms*. Oxford, UK: Oxford University Press.

AMA. (1985). AMA board aproves new marketing definition. *American Marketing Association News*, *19*(5).

AMA. (2007). *Definition of marketing*. Washington, DC: American Marketing Association.

Amabile, T. M. (1988). A model of creativity and innovation in organisations. *Research in Organizational Behavior, 19*, 123–167.

Amabile, T. M. (1996). *Creativity in context*. Boulder, CO: Westview Press.

Amariles, F., Paz, O. P., Russell, N., & Johnson, N. (2006). The impacts of community telecenters in rural Colombia. *Journal of Community Informatics, 2*(3).

Amoako-Gyampah, K., & Salam, A. F. (2004). An extension of the technology acceptance model in an ERP implementation environment. *Information & Management, 41*, 731–745. doi:10.1016/j.im.2003.08.010.

Anand, G., & Kodali, R. (2010). Development of a framework for implementation of lean manufacturing systems. *International Journal of Management Practice, 4*(1), 95–116. doi:10.1504/IJMP.2010.029705.

Anckar, B. (2008). Omena hotels: Technology towards operational efficiency. In Egger, R., & Buhalis, D. (Eds.), *eTourism: case studies* (pp. 37–47). Oxford, UK: Butterworth Heinemann - Elsevier.

Andersen, K. N., Henriksen, H. Z., Medaglia, R., Danziger, J. N., Sannarnes, M. K., & Enemarke, M. (2010). Fads and facts of e-government: A review of impacts of e-government (2003-2009). *International Journal of Public Administration, 33*(11), 564–579. doi:10.1080/01900692.2010.517724.

Anderson, L. (2004). *E-learning at Augsburg college*. Retrieved April 2011 from http://www.augsburg.edu/eteam/report.pdf

Anderson, L.W., & Krathwohl (Ed.). (2001). *A taxonomy for learning, teaching and assessing: A revision of Bloom's taxonomy of educational objectives*. New York: Longman.

Anderson, P. (2007). What is web 2.0? Ideas, technologies and implications for education. *JISC Technology and Standards Watch*, 2-64.

Anderson, A., McEwan, R., Bal, J., & Carletta, J. (2007). Virtual team meetings: An analysis of communication and context. *Computers in Human Behavior, 23*, 2558–2580. doi:10.1016/j.chb.2007.01.001.

Anderson, E. (2008). *The long tail: Why the future of business is selling less of more*. New York: Hyperion.

Anderson-Lehman, R., Watson, H. J., Wixom, B. H., & Hoffer, J. A. (2004). Continental airlines flies high with real-time business intelligence. *MIS Quarterly Executive, 3*(4), 163–176.

Andersson, S. (2008). Finnair: Innovating interactivity. In Egger, R., & Buhalis, D. (Eds.), *eTourism: Case studies* (pp. 293–303). Oxford, UK: Butterworth Heinemann - Elsevier.

Andreasen, A., Lee, N., & Rothschild, M. (2008). Further thoughts on the 2007 AMA definition of marketing and its implications for social marketing. *Social Marketing Quarterly, 14*(2), 101–104. doi:10.1080/15245000802103575.

Andrews, S. B. (1995). Structural holes: The social structure of competition by Ronald S. Burt. *Administrative Science Quarterly, 40*(3), 355–359. doi:10.2307/2393644.

Andriessen, J. H. E. (2003). *Working with groupware: Understanding and evaluating collaboration technology*. London: Springer-Verlag. doi:10.1007/978-1-4471-0067-6.

Andriole, S. J. (2010). Business impact of web 2.0 technologies. *Communications of the ACM, 53*(12), 67–79. doi:10.1145/1859204.1859225.

Andrus, D. (2005). The wiki and the blog: Toward a complex adaptive intelligence community. *Studies in Intelligence, 49*(3).

Anklam, P. (2007). *Net work - A practical guide to creating and sustaining networks at work and in the world*. Oxford, UK: Elsevier.

Anwer, S., & Ikram, N. (2006). Goal oriented requirement engineering: A critical study of techniques. In *Proceedings of the Software Engineering Conference* (pp. 121-130). IEEE Computer Society Press.

Apache. (n.d.). Retrieved from www.apache.org

Argyris, C. (1993). Education for leading-learning. *Organizational Dynamics*, *21*(3), 5–17. doi:10.1016/0090-2616(93)90067-B.

Argyris, C., & Schön, D. A. (1978). *Organisational learning: A theory of action perspective*. Philippines: Addison-Wesley Publishing Co..

Ariely, D. (2000). Controlling the information flow: Effects on consumers' decision making and preference. *The Journal of Consumer Research*, *27*(2), 233–248. doi:10.1086/314322.

Asunda, P. (2010). Productivity, social networks and net communities in the workplace. *Techniques: Connecting Education and Careers*, *85*(5), 38–41.

Attia, M. (2011). Arab spring from cyberspace to reality. *MultiLingual*, *22*(7), 36–39.

Azevedo, S., Carvalho, H., Cruz-Machado, V., & Grilo, F. (2010). The influence of agile and resilient practices on supply chain performance: An innovative conceptual model proposal. In Blecker, Kersten, & Luthje (Eds.), Innovative Process Optimization Methods in Logistics: Emerging trends, concepts and technologies, (pp. 265-281). Berlin: Erich Schmidt Verlag GmbH & Co. KG.

Azevedo, S. G., Carvalho, H., & Cruz-Machado, V. (2011). A proposal of LARG supply chain management practices and a performance measurement system. *International Journal of e-Education, e-Business, e-. Management Learning*, *1*(1), 7–14.

Azevedo, S. G., Machado, V., Barroso, A., & Cruz-Machado, V. (2008). Supply chain vulnerability: Environment changes and dependencies. *International Journal of Logistics and Transport*, *1*, 41–55.

Baggio, R. (2008). Province of Rimini: Communicating with the customer. In Egger, R., & Buhalis, D. (Eds.), *eTourism: Case studies* (pp. 213–223). Oxford, UK: Butterworth Heinemann - Elsevier.

Bagozzi, R. P., & Dholakia, U. M. (2006). Antecedents and purchase consequences of customer participation in small group brand communities. *International Journal of Research in Marketing*, *23*(1), 45–61. doi:10.1016/j.ijresmar.2006.01.005.

Bailey, A., & Ngwenyama, O. (2011). The challenge of e-participation in the digital city: Exploring generational influences among community telecentre users. *Telematics and Informatics*, *28*(3), 204–214. doi:10.1016/j.tele.2010.09.004.

Bajwa, I. S., Bordbar, B., & Lee, M. G. (2010). OCL constraints generation from natural language specification. In *Proceedings of the 14th IEEE International Enterprise Distributed Object Computing Conference* (pp. 204-213). New York: IEEE Press.

Baker, L., Rideout, J., Gertler, P., & Raube, K. (2005). Effect of an Internet-based system for doctor-patient communication on health care spending. *Journal of the American Medical Informatics Association*, *12*(5). doi:10.1197/jamia.M1778 PMID:15905484.

Balabanis, G., & Vassileiou, S. (1999). Some attitudinal predictors of home-shopping through the internet. *Journal of Marketing Management*, *15*, 361–385. doi:10.1362/026725799784870315.

Balasubramanian, S., & Mahajan, V. (2001). The economic leverage of the virtual community. *International Journal of Electronic Commerce*, *5*(3), 103–138.

Balieiro, M. A., Sousa, S. F. Jr, & Souza, C. D. (2008). Análise multidimensional de redes sociais de projetos de software livre. In *Proceedings of Simpósio Brasileiro de Sistemas Colaborativos* (pp. 23–33). Vitória, Brasil: IEEE.

Ball, S., Eckel, C., Grossman, P. J., & Zame, W. (2001). Status in markets. *The Quarterly Journal of Economics*, *116*(1), 161–188. doi:10.1162/003355301556374.

Baloglu, S., & Mangaloglu, M. (2001). Tourism destination images of Turkey, Egypt, Greece, and Italy as perceived by US-based tour operators and travel agents. *Tourism Management*, *22*, 1–9. doi:10.1016/S0261-5177(00)00030-3.

Baloglu, S., & Pekcan, Y. A. (2006). The website design and Internet site marketing practices of upscale and luxury hotels in Turkey. *Tourism Management*, *27*, 171–176. doi:10.1016/j.tourman.2004.07.003.

Bancroft, N., Seip, H., & Sprengel, A. (2001). *Implementing SAP R/3* (2nd ed.). Greenwich, CT: Manning Publications Co..

Bandopadhaya, S. K., Bhattacharyya, D., Mukherjee, S., Ganguly, D., & Das, P. (2008). Statistical approach for offline handwritten signature verification. *Journal of Computer Science*, *4*(3), 181–185. doi:10.3844/jcssp.2008.181.185.

Bandyo-Padhyay, N. (2002). *E-commerce: Context, concepts and consequences*. New York: McGraw-Hill.

Barabba, V. (2004). *Surviving transformation*. Oxford, UK: Oxford University Press.

Barão, A., & Rodrigues da Silva, A. (2011). A model to evaluate the relational capital of organizations (SNARE-RCO). In *Proceedings of Conference of Enterprise Information Systems* (Centeris'2011). Springer-Verlag.

Barão, A., & Silva, A. (2008). SNARE - Social network analysis and reengineering environment: Architecture overview. In *Proceedings of WEBIST - International Conference on Web Information Systems and Technologies*. Funchal, Portugal: WEBIST.

Barão, A., & Silva, A. R. (2010). The SNARE language overview. In *Proceedings of the 12th ICEIS - International Conference on Enterprise Systems, ICEIS'2010*. INSTICC.

Barão, A., & Silva, A. R. (2011). A model to evaluate the relational capital of organizations SNARE-RCO. In M. M. Crus-Cunha et al. (Eds.), *CENTERIS - Conference on Enterprise Information Systems*, (pp. 400-409). Berlin: Springer.

Barbeira, M. R., & Franco, M. J. (2009). Um sistema de gestão do conhecimento como fomentador de redes estratégicas interorganizacionais. *Revista Ibero-Americana de Estratégia*, *8*(2), 5–29.

Barnard, C. (1938). *The functions of the executive* (2nd ed.). Boston: Harvard University Press.

Barnatt, C. (2008). Higher education 2.0. *International Journal of Management Education*, *7*(3), 47–56. doi:10.3794/ijme.73.250.

Barrett, R., Maglio, P. P., & Kellem, D. C. (1997). How to personalize the web. In *Proceedings of Human Factors In Computing Systems*. New York: ACM Press.

Barrett, R., & Maurice Salles, M. (2006). *Social choice with fuzzy preferences. Center for Research in Economics and Management (CREM), University of Rennes 1*. University of Caen and CNRS.

Bass, B. M. (1985). *Leadership and performance beyond expectations*. New York: Free Press.

Bass, B. M. (1990). *Bass and Stogdill's handbook of leadership: Theory, research, and applications* (3rd ed.). New York: Free Press.

Bass, B. M., & Avolio, B. J. (1990). *Transformational leadership development: Manual for the multifactor leadership questionnaire*. Palo Alto, CA: Consulting Psychologists Press.

Bass, B. M., & Avolio, B. J. (1994). *Improving organisational effectiveness through transformational leadership*. Thousand Oaks, CA: Sage Publications.

Bassus, O., & Wolfgramm, K. (2009). The innovative entrepreneurship training program at Hochschule Wismar University of Technology, Business and Design. In Ahrens & Lange (Eds.), *First Asian Conference on e-Business and Telecommunications* (pp. 36-39). Berlin: Mensch & Buch.

Bassus, O., Ahrens, A., & Zaščerinska, J. (2011). Clustering for the development of engineering students' use of enterprise 3.0. In *Proceedings of the 4th International Conference of Engineering & Business Education and 1st SAFRI Journey to Excellence Conference* (pp. 373-383). Cape Town, South Africa: Cape Peninsula University of Technology.

Bassus, O., Zaščerinska, J., & Ahrens, A. (2011). From enterprise 2.0 to 3.0: Challenges in engineering and business education. In Bassus, , Ahrens, , & Lange, (Eds.), *Information and Communication Technologies in Engineering and Business* (pp. 79-96). Berlin, Germany: Mensch & Buch.

Batagelj, V. (2009). Social network analysis, large-scale. In Meyers, R. A. (Ed.), *Encyclopedia of Complexity and Systems Science* (pp. 8245–8265). Berlin: Springer. doi:10.1007/978-0-387-30440-3_489.

Batagelj, V., & Mrvar, A. (2003). Pajek analysis and visualization of large networks. *Science*, *2265*(19), 8–11.

Bateman, T., & Organ, D. (1983). Job satisfaction and the good soldier: The relationship between affect and employee 'citizenship'. *Academy of Management Journal*, *26*(4), 587–595. doi:10.2307/255908.

Bates, D. W., & Wright, A. (2009). Evaluating eHealth: Undertaking robust international cross-cultural ehealth research. *PLoS Medicine*, *6*(9), e10000105. doi:10.1371/journal.pmed.1000105 PMID:19753106.

Baumol, W. (2001). When is inter-firm co-ordination beneficial? *International Journal of Industrial Organization*, *19*(5), 727–737. doi:10.1016/S0167-7187(00)00091-6.

Baumol, W. (2010). *The micro-theory of innovative entrepreneurship*. Princeton, NJ: Princeton University Press.

Bautista García-Vera, A. (2001). Desigualdades sociales, nuevas tecnologías y política educativa. In Area Moreira, M. (Ed.), *Educar en la sociedad de la información*. Bilbao, Spain: Desclée de Brower.

Beagrie, N. (2005). Plenty of room at the bottom? Personal digital libraries and collections. *D-Lib Magazine*, *11*(6). Retrieved October 22, 2011, from http://www.dlib.org/dlib/june05/beagrie/06beagrie.html

Becker, M. Y., & Sewell, P. (2004). Cassandra: Distributed access control policies with tunable expressiveness. In *Proceedings of the Fifth IEEE International Workshop on Policies for Distributed Systems and Networks* (p. 159). Washington, DC: IEEE Computer Society.

Becker, J., Bergener, P., Niehaves, B., & Räckers, M. (2008). Social inclusiveness of electronic public service delivery in Germany: A quantitative analysis. *Information Systems Journal*.

BECTA. (2001). *The 'digital divide': A discussion paper*. BECTA.

Becta. (2008). *Harnessing technology: Next generation learning 2008-14: A summary*. Retrieved April 2011 from http://www.becta.org.uk

Bédard, F., & Louillet, M. C. (2008). BonjourQuebec.com: A vision, a strategy, a brand. In *R. Egger & D. Buhalis (2008). eTourism: Cases studies* (pp. 200–212). Oxford, UK: Ed. Butterworth Heinemann – Elsevier.

Beek, H. (1964). The influence of assembly line organization on output, quality, and morale. *Occupational Psychology*, *38*(3/4), 161–172.

Been-Lirn Duh, H., Yi-Luen Do, E., Billinghurst, M., Quek, F., & Chen Hsueh-Hua, V. (2010). Senior-friendly technologies: Interaction design for seniors users. In *Proceedings of CHI*. Atlanta, GA: ACM.

Bel, R. (2010). *Leadership and innovation: Learning from the best*. Retrieved frm www.interscience.wiley.com

Belch, G. E. (1981). An examination of comparative and noncomparative television commercials: The effects of claim variation and repetition on cognitive response and message acceptance. *JMR, Journal of Marketing Research*, *18*, 333–349. doi:10.2307/3150974.

Beldarrain, Y. (2006). Distance education trends: Integrating new technologies to foster student interaction and collaboration. *Distance Education*, *27*(2), 139–153. doi:10.1080/01587910600789498.

Bell, M. (2008). *Service-oriented modeling: Service analysis, design, and architecture*. New York: John Wiley & Sons.

Bellotti, V., Dalal, B., Good, N., Flynn, P., Bobrow, D. G., & Ducheneaut, N. (2004). What a to-do: Studies of task management towards the design of a personal task list manager. In *Proceedings of the SIGCHI Conference on Human Factors in Computing Systems* (pp. 735-742). New York: ACM.

Benabou, R., & Tirole, J. (2003). Intrinsic and extrinsic motivation. *The Review of Economic Studies*, *70*(3), 489–520. doi:10.1111/1467-937X.00253.

Ben-David, J., & Collins, R. (1966). Social factors in the origins of a new science: The case of psychology. *American Sociological Review*, *31*(4), 451–465. doi:10.2307/2090769 PMID:5329541.

Benkler, Y. (2006). *The wealth of networks - How social production transforms markets and freedom*. New Haven, CT: Yale University Press.

Bennet, A. (2006). The learning organisation portfolio. *The Journal of information and Knowledge Management Systems*, *36*(1).

Benn, T. (2011). The flowers of the Arab spring grow from buds of free information. *New Statesman (London, England), 140*(5048), 12.

Benson, V., Filippaios, F., & Morgan, S. (2010). Online social networks: changing the face of business education and career planning. *International Journal of e-Business Management, 4*(1), 20-33.

Benson-Armer, R., & Hsieh, T. (1997). Teamwork across time and space. *The McKinsey Quarterly, 4*, 18–27.

Bergeron, B. (2000). Regional business intelligence: The view from Canada. *Journal of Information Science, 26*(3), 153–160. doi:10.1177/016555150002600305.

Berkem, B. (2008). From the business motivation model (BMM) to service oriented architecture (SOA). *Journal of Object Technology, 7*(8), 57–70. doi:10.5381/jot.2008.7.8.c6.

Berkun, S. (2010). *The myths of innovation*. Cambridge, UK: O'Reilly Media.

Berling, R. J. (1993). The emerging approach to business strategy: Building a relationship advantage. *Business Horizons, 36*(4), 16. doi:10.1016/S0007-6813(05)80115-6.

Bernardino, J., & Ribeiro, P. (2011). Open source business intelligence: An alternative to proprietary tools. *International Journal of Electronic Business, 9*(3), 219–237. doi:10.1504/IJEB.2011.042543.

Berry, L. L. (1995). Relationship marketing of services - Growing interest, emerging perspectives. *Journal of the Academy of Marketing Science, 23*(4), 236–245. doi:10.1177/009207039502300402.

Berry, L. L. (2002). Relationship marketing of services - Perspectives from 1983 and 2000. *Journal of Relationship Marketing, 1*(1), 59–77. doi:10.1300/J366v01n01_05.

Bertino, E., Catania, B., Damiani, M. L., & Perlasca, P. (2005). GEO-RBAC: A spatially aware RBAC. In *Proceedings of the 11th ACM Symposium on Access Control Models and Technologies (SACMAT '06)* (pp. 29-37). New York: ACM.

Bertocci, V., Serack, G., & Baker, C. (2007). *Understanding Windows CardSpace: An introduction to the concepts and challenges of digital identities*. Reading, MA: Addison-Wesley.

Bertot, J. C., Jaeger, P. T., & Grimes, J. M. (2010). Using ICTs to create a culture of transparency: E-government and social media as openness and anti-corruption tools for societies. *Government Information Quarterly, 27*(3), 264–271. doi:10.1016/j.giq.2010.03.001.

Beyer, M. (2009a, February). Tutorial: Key roles for successful BI/DW delivery: Business intelligence solution architect. *Gartner*.

Beyer, M. (2009b, April). Fundamentals of data warehousing for the CIO. *Gartner*.

Beynon-Davies, P. (2002). *Information systems: An introduction to informatics in organizations*. New York: Palgrave.

Bhagwat, R., & Sharma, M. K. (2006). Management of information system in Indian SMEs: An exploratory study. *International Journal of Enterprise Network Management, 1*(1), 99–125. doi:10.1504/IJENM.2006.010068.

Bhargav-Spantzel, A., Squicciarini, A. C., & Bertino, E. (2007). Trust negotiation in identity management. *IEEE Security & Privacy, 5*(2), 55–63. doi:10.1109/MSP.2007.46.

Bhattacharya, C. B., Du, S., & Sen, S. (2010). Maximizing business returns to corporate social responsibility (CSR): The role of CSR communication. *International Journal of Management Reviews, 12*(1), 6–19.

Bhatti, R., Bertino, E., & Ghafoor, A. (2007). An integrated approach to federated identity and privilege management in open systems. *Communications of the ACM, 50*(2), 81–87. doi:10.1145/1216016.1216025.

Bianchi, G., Bonola, M., Falletta, V., Proto, F. S., & Teofili, S. (2008). The SPARTA pseudonym and authorization system. *Electronic Notes in Theoretical Computer Science, 197*(2), 57–71. doi:10.1016/j.entcs.2007.12.017.

Bian, Y. (1997). Bringing strong ties back In Indirect ties, network bridges, and job searches in China. *American Sociological Review*, *62*(3), 366–385. doi:10.2307/2657311.

Bierly, P., & Chakrabarti, A. (1996). Generic knowledge strategies in the U.S. pharmaceuticals industry. *Strategic Management Journal of Special Issue on Knowledge and the Firm*, *17*, 123–135.

Bin Husin, M. H., & Swatman, P. M. C. (2010). Removing the barriers to enterprise 2.0. In *Proceedings of the 2010 IEEE International Symposium on Technology and Society (ISTAS)* (pp. 275-283). IEEE.

Birt, J. L., Bilson, C. M., Smith, T., & Whaley, R. E. (2006). Ownership, competition, and financial disclosure. *Australian Journal of Management*, *31*(2), 235–263. doi:10.1177/031289620603100204.

Bishop, M. (2004). *Profit maximisation*. Economist Intelligence Unit.

Bitly. (2011). *Bitly: Shorten, share and track your links*. Retrieved November 15, 2011, from https://bitly.com/

Bizer, C., Lehmann, J., Kobilarov, G., Auer, S., Becker, C., & Cyganiak, R. et al. (2009). DBpedia-A crystallization point for the web of data. *Web Semantics: Science. Services and Agents on the World Wide Web*, *7*(3), 154–165. doi:10.1016/j.websem.2009.07.002.

Blau, P. M. (1964). *Exchange and power in social life*. New York, NY: Wiley.

Blaya, J. A., Gomez, W., Rodriguez, P., & Fraser, H. (2008). Cost and implementation analysis of a personal digital assistant system for laboratory data collection. *The International Journal of Tuberculosis and Lung Disease*, *12*(8), 921–927. PMID:18647452.

Blaze, M., Feigenbaum, J., & Lacy, J. (1996). Decentralized trust management. In *Proceedings of the 1996 IEEE Symposium on Security and Privacy* (pp. 164-173). IEEE Computer Society Press.

Blaze, M., Feigenbaum, J., Ioannidis, J., & Keromytis, A. D. (1999). *RFC-2704: The keynote trust management system version 2*. Geneva, Switzerland: Internet Engineering Task Force.

Blood, R. (2000). *Weblogs: A history and perspective*. Retrieved September 28, 2011, from http://www.rebeccablood.net/essays/Weblog_history.html

Bluma, D. (2008). Teacher education in the context of Bologna process. In Žogla, I. (Ed.), *Association for Teacher Education in Europe Spring University Conference Teacher of the 21st Century: Quality Education for Quality Teaching* (pp. 673–680). Riga, Latvia: University of Latvia.

Blumenstock, J. E. (2008). Size matters: Word count as a measure of quality on Wikipedia. In *Proceeding of the 17th International Conference on World Wide Web*. IEEE.

Blum, V., & Fallon, J. (2002). Welsh visitor attraction web sites: Multipurpose tools or technological tokenism? *Information Technology & Tourism*, *4*, 191–201. doi:10.3727/109830501108750985.

Boateng, R., Mbarika, V., & Thomas, C. (2010). When web 2.0 becomes an organizational learning tool: Evaluating web 2.0 tools. *Development and Learning in Organizations*, *24*(3), 17–20. doi:10.1108/14777281011037254.

Bobek, S., & Sternad, S. (2010). Management of ERP solutions. In Vaish, A. (Ed.), *Recent advances in management and information security* (pp. 31–47). New Delhi: Shree Publishers & Distributors.

Boehm, B., & Turner, R. (2003). *Balancing agility and discipline: A guide for the perplexed*. Boston: Pearson Education, Inc..

Boev, O. V., Kriushova, A. A., Kulyukina, E. S., Surygin, A. S., Freeston, I., Heitmann, G., & Chuchalin, A. I. (2011). *Guidelines on engineering curriculum design aligned with the European qualification framework and European standards for quality assurance of engineering education*. Tomsk: TPU Publishing House.

Bohus, D., & Rudnicky, A. I. (2009). The RavenClaw dialog management framework: Architecture and systems. *Computer Speech & Language*, *23*(3), 332–361. doi:10.1016/j.csl.2008.10.001.

Boisot, M. (1998). *Knowledge assets: Securing competitive advantage in the information economy*. New York: Oxford University Press.

Boldi, P., Bonchi, F., Castillo, C., & Vigna, S. (2011). Viscous democracy for social networks. *Communications of the ACM*, *54*(6), 129–137. doi:10.1145/1953122.1953154.

Bonaccorsi, A., & Lamastra, C. R. (2003). *Altruistic individuals, selfish firms? The structure of motivation in open source software*.

Bonacich, P. (1972). Factoring and weighting approaches to status scores and clique identification. *The Journal of Mathematical Sociology*, *2*(1), 113–120. doi:10.1080/0022250X.1972.9989806.

Bonsón, E., Torres, L., Royo, S., & Flores, F. (2011). *Local e-government 2.0: Social media and corporate transparency in municipalities*. Paper presented at XVI Congreso AECA. Granada, Spain.

Bonsón, E., Escobar, T., & Flores, F. (2006). Online transparency of the banking sector. *Online Information Review*, *30*(6), 714–730. doi:10.1108/14684520610716180.

Bonsón, E., Escobar, T., & Flores, F. (2008). Navigation quality as a key value for the web page of a financial entity. *Online Information Review*, *32*(5), 623–634. doi:10.1108/14684520810914007.

Bonsón, E., Escobar, T., & Martín, M. P. (2002). La mejora del sistema de información contable mediante la integración de tecnologías emergentes. *Revista de Contabilidad*, *3*(6), 21–48.

Bonsón, E., & Flores, F. (2011). Social media and corporate dialogue: The response of the global financial institutions. *Online Information Review*, *35*(1), 34–49. doi:10.1108/14684521111113579.

Bontis, N. (2001). Assessing knowledge assets: A review of the models used to measure intellectual capital. *International Journal of Management Reviews*, *3*(1). doi:10.1111/1468-2370.00053.

Bontis, N., Crossan, M., & Hulland, J. (2002). Managing an organisational learning system by aligning stocks and flows. *Journal of Management Studies*, *39*(4), 437–469. doi:10.1111/1467-6486.t01-1-00299.

Borgatti, S. P., & Cross, R. (2003). A relational view of information seeking and learning in social networks. *Management Science*, *49*, 432–446. doi:10.1287/mnsc.49.4.432.14428.

Borgatti, S. P., Mehra, A., Brass, D. J., & Labianca, G. (2009). Network analysis in the social sciences. *Science*, *323*(5916), 892–895. doi:10.1126/science.1165821 PMID:19213908.

Borgatti, S., & Foster, P. (2003). The network paradigm in organizational research: A review and typology. *Journal of Management*, *29*(6).

Borgman, C. (2003). Personal digital libraries: Creating individual spaces for innovation. *NSF/JISC Post Digital Library Futures Workshop*. Retrieved October 22, 2011, from http://www.sis.pitt.edu/~dlwkshop/paper_borgman.html

Boss, J. (2011). Les nouveaux visages du marketing. *Revue Française du Marketing,* (231), 61-74.

Bossio, J. F. (2006). *Social sustainability of telecenters from the viewpoint of operators: A case study from São Paulo*. (Unpublished doctoral dissertation). London School of Economics, London, UK.

Boudreau, M. C. (2002). Learning to use ERP technology: A causal model. In *Proceedings of the 36th Hawaii International Conference on System Sciences*. Retrieved July 7, 2008, from http://csdl2.computer.org/comp/proceedings/hicss/2003/1874/08/187480235b.pdf

Bouguessa, M., Wang, S., & Dumoulin, B. (2010). Discovering knowledge-sharing communities in question-answering forums. *Discovery*, *5*(1), 1–49.

Boulos, M. N., & Wheeler, S. (2007). The emerging web 2.0 social software: An enabling suite of sociable technologies in health and health care education. *Health Information and Libraries Journal*, *24*(1), 2–23. doi:10.1111/j.1471-1842.2007.00701.x PMID:17331140.

Bove'e, C. L., & Thill, J. V. (2000). *Business communication today* (6th ed.). Upper Saddle River, NJ: Prentice-Hall.

Bovi, A. M. (2003). Ethical guidelines for use of electronic mail between patients and physicians. *The American Journal of Bioethics*, *3*(3), 43–47. doi:10.1162/152651603322874771 PMID:12859845.

Bowers, D. (1964). Organizational control in insurance company. *Sociometry*, *27*(2), 230–244. doi:10.2307/2785719.

Bowers, D., & Seashore, S. (1966). Predicting organizational effectiveness with a four-factory theory of leadership. *Administrative Science Quarterly*, *11*(2), 238–263. doi:10.2307/2391247.

Box, S., & Cosgrove, S. (1968). The productivity of scientists in industrial research laboratories. *Sociology*, *11*(2), 163–172. doi:10.1177/003803856800200202.

Boyd, D. M., & Ellison, N. B. (2008). Social network sites: Definition, history, and schollarship. *Journal of Computer-Mediated Communication*, *13*, 210–230. doi:10.1111/j.1083-6101.2007.00393.x.

Brackett, L. K., & Carr, B. N. (2001). Cyberspace advertising vs. other media: Consumer vs. mature student attitudes. *Journal of Advertising Research*, *41*(5), 23–32.

Bradford, M. (2008). *Modern ERP—Select, implement & use today's advanced business systems*. Raleigh, NC: North Carolina State University, College of Management.

Bradford, M., & Florin, J. (2003). Examining the role of innovation diffusion factors on the implementation success of enterprise resource planning systems. *International Journal of Accounting Information Systems*, *4*(3), 205–225. doi:10.1016/S1467-0895(03)00026-5.

Bradley, J., & Lee, C. C. (2007). ERP training and user satisfaction: A case study. *International Journal of Enterprise Information Systems*, *3*(4), 33–55. doi:10.4018/jeis.2007100103.

Bradley, S. P., & Nolan, R. L. (1998). Capturing value in the network era. In Bradley, S. P., & Nolan, R. L. (Eds.), *Sense & Respond: Capturing Value in the Network Era*. Boston, MA: Harvard Business School Press.

Brandes, U. (2001). A faster algorithm for betweenness centrality. *The Journal of Mathematical Sociology*, *25*(2), 163–177. doi:10.1080/0022250X.2001.9990249.

Bremer, D., & Bryant, R. (2005). *A comparison of two learning management systems: Moodle vs Blackboard*. Paper presented at the 18th Annual Conference of the National Advisory Committee on Computing Qualifications. New York, NY.

Brescia, W., & Miller, M. (2006). What's it worth? The perceived benefits of instructional blogging. *Electronic Journal for the Integration of Technology in Education*, *5*, 44-52. Retrieved September 11, 2011, from http://ejite.isu.edu/Volume5/Brescia.pdf

Bretthauer, D. (2002). Open source software: A history. *Information Technology and Libraries*, *21*(1), 3–11.

Briggs, R., & Hollins, N. (1997). Advertising on the web: Is there response before click-through? *Journal of Advertising Research*, *37*(2), 33–45.

Brin, S., & Page, L. (2006). The anatomy of a large-scale hypertextual web search engine. *Search*, *30*(1-2), 5–10.

Brooks, R. G., & Menachemi, N. (2006). Physicians' use of email with patients: Factors influencing electronic communication and adherence to best practices. *Journal of Medical Internet Research*, *8*(1).

Brown, J., & Adler, R. (2008). *Minds of fire: Open education, the long tail and learning 2.0*. Retrieved May 2011 from http://net.educause.edu/ir/library/pdf/ERM0811.pdf

Brown, K., & Mitchell, T. (1991). A comparison of just-in-time and batch manufacturing: The role of performance obstacles. *Journal of the Academy of Management*, *34*(4), 906–917. doi:10.2307/256395.

Bruner, G. C. II, & Kumar, A. (2000). Web commercials and advertising hierarchy-of-effects. *Journal of Advertising Research*, *40*(1/2), 35–42.

Bryant, S. M., Albring, S. M., & Murthy, U. (2009). The effects of reward structure, media richness and gender on virtual teams. *International Journal of Accounting Information Systems*, *10*, 190–213. doi:10.1016/j.accinf.2009.09.002.

BT. (2004). *The digital divide in 2025*. BT.

Buchanan, F., & Huczynski, A. (2010). *Organizational behaviour*. Harlow, MA: Pearson.

Bucher, T., Gericke, A., & Sigg, S. (2009). Process-centric business intelligence. *Business Process Management Journal*, *15*(3), 408. doi:10.1108/14637150910960648.

Buckinx, W., Moons, W., Van Den Poel, D., & Wets, G. (2003). *Customer-adapted coupon targeting using feature selection*. Gent, Belgium: Universiteit Gent, Faculteit Economie En Bedrijfskunde.

Buckmaster, R. A. (2004). *English for specific purposes on-line course*. Retrieved March 15, 2005, from http://www.sisekaitse.ee/?id=831

Buczek, L. (2011). *The big failure of enterprise 2.0 social business*. Retrieved October 1, 2011, from http://www.lauriebuczek.com

Bueno, S., & Salmeron, J. L. (2008). TAM-based success modelling in ERP. *Interacting with Computers*, *20*(6), 515–523. doi:10.1016/j.intcom.2008.08.003.

Bueren, A., Schierholz, R., Kolbe, L., & Brenner, W. (2004). *Customer knowledge management - Improving performance of customer relationship management with knowledge management*. Paper presented at the 37th Hawaii International Conference on System Sciences. Hawaii, HI.

Bughin, J., & Manyika, J. (2007). *How businesses are using web 2.0: A McKinsey global survey*. Retrieved November 3, 2011, from http://www.mckinseyquarterly.com/article_page.aspx?ar=1913

Bughin, J., Chui, M., & Miller, A. (2009). McKinsey global survey results: How companies are benefitting from web 2.0. *The McKinsey Quarterly*. Retrieved September 3, 2009, from http://www.mckinseyquarterly.com

Bughin, J. (2008). The rise of enterprise 2.0. *Direct. Data and Digital Marketing Practice*, *9*(3), 251–259. doi:10.1057/palgrave.dddmp.4350100.

Bughin, J., & Chui, M. (2011). The rise of the networked enterprise: Web 2.0 finds its payday.[from http://www.mckinseyquarterly.com]. *The McKinsey Quarterly*, *22*, 2–9. Retrieved September 15, 2011

Buhalis, D. (1999). Limits of tourism development in peripheral destinations: problems and challenges. *Tourism Management*, *20*, 183–185.

Buhalis, D. (2000). Marketing the competitive destination of the future. *Tourism Management*, *21*, 97–116. doi:10.1016/S0261-5177(99)00095-3.

Buhalis, D. (2003). *eTourism: Information technologies for strategic tourism management*. Harlow, MA: Pearson Higher Education.

Buhalis, D., & Spada, A. (2000). DMS: Criteria for success – An exploratory research. *Information Technology and Tourism*, *3*(1), 41–58.

Bulik, B. (2000). Ad nauseum. *Business 2.0*, *12*, 112.

Bunt, G. G., Wittek, R. P., & Klepper, M. C. (2005). The evolution of intra-organizational trust networks. *International Sociological Association*, *20*(3), 339–369. doi:10.1177/0268580905055480.

Buono, A. F. (2003). *Enhancing inter-firm networks and interorganizational strategies*. Charlotte, NC: Information Age Publishing Inc..

Burnett, R., & Marshall, D. I. (2003). *Web theory: An introduction*. London: Routhledge.

Burns, J. M. (1978). *Leadership*. New York: Harper and Row.

Burt, R. S. (1992). *Structural holes: The social structure of competition*. Cambridge, MA: Harvard University Press.

Burt, R. S. (2004). Structural holes and good ideas. *American Journal of Sociology*, *110*(2), 349–399. doi:10.1086/421787.

Buttle, F. (2008). *Customer relationship management* (2nd ed.). Boston: Butterworth-Heinemann.

Byun, J.-W., Bertino, E., & Li, N. (2005). Purpose based access control of complex data for privacy protection. In *Proceedings of the 10th ACM Symposium on Access Control Models and Technologies (SACMAT 'O5)* (pp. 102-110). New York: ACM.

Cabot, J., Pau, R., & Raventós, R. (2010). From UML/OCL to SBVR specifications: A challenging transformation. *Information Systems*, *35*, 417–440. doi:10.1016/j.is.2008.12.002.

Cai, H., Reinwald, B., Wang, N., & Guo, C. (2011). SaaS multi-tenancy: Framework, technology, and case study. *International Journal of Cloud Applications and Computing*, *1*(1), 62–77. doi:10.4018/ijcac.2011010105.

Calero, M. ª. R., Martinez, M., Ortega, J. M., & Román, Mª. V. (2005). Impacto de las nuevas tecnologías en los canales de distribución financieros. Madrid, Spain: Dykinson.

Calisir, F., Gumussoy, C. A., & Bayram, A. (2009). Predicting the behavioural intention to use enterprise resource planning systems—An exploratory extension of the technology acceptance model. *Management Research News*, *32*(7), 597–613. doi:10.1108/01409170910965215.

Calvo, S., & Reinares, P. (1999). *Comunicación en internet: Estrategias de comunicación y marketing interactivo*. Madrid: McGraw-Hill.

Camenisch, J., & Van Herreweghen, E. (2002). Design and implementation of the idemix anonymous credential system. In *Proceedings of the 9th ACM Conference on Computer and Communications Security (CCS '02)* (pp. 21-30). New York: ACM.

Camenisch, J., & Pfitzmann, B. (2007). Federated identity management. In Petkovic, M., & Jonker, W. (Eds.), *Security, Privacy, and Trust in Modern Data Management* (pp. 213–238). Berlin: Springer-Verlag. doi:10.1007/978-3-540-69861-6_15.

Cameron, K., & Quinn, R. (2005). *Changing organization culture*. New York: Wiley.

Cameron, K., & Whetten, D. (Eds.). (1982). *Organizational effectiveness: A comparison of multiple models*. New York: Academic Press.

Cameron, S., & Whetten, D. (1986). Effectiveness as paradox: Consensus and conflict in conceptions of organizational effectiveness. *Management Science*, *32*(5), 539–553. doi:10.1287/mnsc.32.5.539.

Campanella, S., Dimauro, G., Ferrante, A., Impedovo, D., Impedovo, S., & Lucchese, M. G. et al. (2008). E-learning platforms in the Italian universities: The technological solutions at the University of Bari. *WSEAS Transactions on Advances in Engineering Education*, *5*, 12–19.

Capozzi, M. (2007). Knowledge management architectures beyond technology. *First Monday*, *12*(6). doi:10.5210/fm.v12i6.1871.

Carbone, F., Contreras, J., & Hernández, J. Z. (2010). Enterprise 2.0 and semantic technologies for open innovation support. *Lecture Notes in Computer Science*, *6097*, 18–27. doi:10.1007/978-3-642-13025-0_3.

Cardoso, N. (2008). Rembrandt-reconhecimento de entidades mencionadas baseado em relações e análise detalhada do texto. *Encontro do Segundo HAREM, PROPOR 2008*.

Cardozo, R. (1965). An experimental study of consumer effort, expectations and satisfaction. *JMR, Journal of Marketing Research*, *2*, 244–249. doi:10.2307/3150182.

Carillo, K., & Okoli, C. (2008). The open source movement: A revolution in software development. *Journal of Computer Information Systems*, *49*(2), 1–9.

Carleial, L. (2001). *Redes industriais de subcontratação: Um enfoque de sistema nacional de inovação, um estudo das industrias eletrônica, metalmecânica e de confecções da Região Metropolitana de Curitiba*. São Paulo, Brazil: Hucitec.

Carley, K., Diesner, J., Reminga, J., & Tsvetovat, M. (2007). *Toward an interoperable dynamic network analysis toolkit*. Retrieved in January 2010, from https://community.bus.emory.edu/dept/ISOM/Shared%20Documents/Hightower%20Speaker%20Papers/KathleenCarley.pdf

Carlota, J., Silva, A. R., & Silva, P. (2009). The learning object pool and the BOA-GPI case study. In *Proceedings of the Iberoamerican Congress on Telematics (CITA-2009)*. CITA.

Carlson, A., Betteridge, J., Hruschka, E. R., Jr., & Mitchell, T. M. (2009). *Coupling semi-supervised learning of categories and relations*.

Carlsson, C., Fedrizzi, M., & Fuller, R. (2004). *Fuzzy logic in management*. Berlin: Springer. doi:10.1007/978-1-4419-8977-2.

Carroll, A. B., & Buchholtz, A. K. (2011). *Business and society: Ethics and stakeholder management*. South-Western Pub..

Carter, S. (2011). *Get social: Using social media to create a new type of social business*. Hoboken, NJ: IBM Press.

Casaló, L. V., Flavián, C., & Guinalíu, M. (2011). Understanding the intention to follow the advice obtained in an online travel community. *Computers in Human Behavior*, *27*, 622–633. doi:10.1016/j.chb.2010.04.013.

Casielles, R. V., Martín, A. M., & Vázquez, A. S. (2004). Cómo usan Internet las líneas aéreas para desarrollar relaciones estables con los clientes. *Universia Business Review*, *2*(2), 34–47.

Castañeda, J. A., Muñoz, F., Luque, T., & Alcántara, J. M. (2005). *Experience moderation effect on the relationship between usefulness, ease of use and website acceptance*. Paper presented at Network and Electronic Commerce Conference. Riva Del Garda, Italia.

Castells, M. (2001). *A galáxia Internet – Reflexões sobre internet, negócios e sociedade*. Lisbon, Portugal: Ed. Fundação Calouste Gulbenkian.

Castilla, E. J. (2005). Social networks and employee performance in a call center. *American Journal of Sociology*, *110*(5), 1243–1283.

Castro, J., Kolp, M., & Mylopoulos, J. (2002). Towards requirements-driven information systems engineering: The Tropos project. *Information Systems*, *27*(6), 365–389. doi:10.1016/S0306-4379(02)00012-1.

Cavaleri, S., Seivert, S., & Lee, W. L. (2005). *Knowledge leadership: The art and science of the knowledge-based organisation*. Alexandria, VA: KMCI Press.

Cavus, N., & Momani, A. (2009). Computer aided evaluation of learning management systems. *Procedia - Social and Behavioral Sciences*, *1*(1), 426-430.

Cechinel & Sicilia. (2011). Evaluating models for automated quality assessment of learning objects inside repositories. In *Proceedings of Laclo2011*. Laclo.

Cechinel, C., & Sánchez-Alonso, S. (2011). *Analyzing associations between the different ratings dimensions of the MERLOT repository*. Interdisciplinary Journal of E-Learning and Learning Objects.

Celaya, J., Vázquez, J. A., Saldaña, I., & García, Y. (2009). *Visibilidad de las ciudades en la web 2.0*. Grupo BPMO.

Cerf, V. (2007). An information avalanche. *IEEE Computer*, *40*(1).

Certo, S., & Certo, T. (2009). *Modern management*. New York: Pearson.

Chadwick, D., Zhao, G., Otenko, S., Laborde, R., Su, L., & Nguyen, T. A. (2008). PERMIS: A modular authorization infrastructure. *Concurrency and Computation*, *20*(11), 1341–1357. doi:10.1002/cpe.1313.

Chaffey, D., Mayer, R., Johnston, K., & Ellis-Chadwich, F. (2000). *Internet marketing strategy, implementation and practice*. Harlow, MA: Prentice Hall.

Chakravarthy, M. A., Ciravegna, P. F., & Lanfranchi, M. V. (2006). *Cross-media document annotation and enrichment*. Paper presented at the SAAW - 1st Semantic Authoring and Annotation Workshop. New York, NY.

Chan, J. O. (2005). Toward a unified view of customer relationship management. *Journal of American Academy of Business*.

Chan, A., Yung, E., Lam, P., Tam, C., & Cheung, S. (2001). Application of delphi method in selection of procurement systems for construction. *Construction Management and Economics*, *19*(7), 699–718. doi:10.1080/01446190110066128.

Chanal, V., & Caron-Fasan, M.-L. (2010). The difficulties involved in developing business models open to innovation communities: The case of a crowdsourcing platform. *M@n@gement*, *13*(4), 318-340.

Chandler, A. (1996). *Strategy and structure: Chapters in the history of the American industrial enterprise*. Cambridge, MA: MIT Press.

Chandon, P., Wansink, B., & Laurent, G. (2000). A benefit congruency framework of sales promotion effectiveness. *Journal of Marketing*, *64*(4), 65–81. doi:10.1509/jmkg.64.4.65.18071.

Chan, F., & Qi, H. (2003). An innovative performance measurement method for supply chain management. *Supply Chain Management*, *8*(3), 209–223. doi:10.1108/13598540310484618.

Chang, A. M., & Kannan, P. K. (2008). *Leveraging web 2.0 in government*. New York: IBM Center for The Business of Government.

Chang, C.-S., & Chang, H.-H. (2007). Effects of internal marketing on nurse job satisfaction and organizational commitment: Example of medical centers in southern Taiwan. *The Journal of Nursing Research, 15*(4), 265–274. doi:10.1097/01.JNR.0000387623.02931.a3 PMID:18080971.

Chang, S. C., & Lee, M. S. (2007). A study on relationship among leadership, organisational culture, the operation of learning organisation and employees' job satisfaction. *The Learning Organization, 14*(2), 155–185. doi:10.1108/09696470710727014.

Chan, K. W., & Li, S. Y. (2010). Understanding consumer-to-consumer interactions in virtual communities: The salience of reciprocity. *Journal of Business Research, 63*(9-10), 1033–1040. doi:10.1016/j.jbusres.2008.08.009.

Chatterjee, P., & McGinnis, J. (2010). Customized online promotions: Moderating effect of promotion type on deal value, perceived fairness, and purchase intent. *Journal of Applied Business Research, 26*(4), 13–19.

Chatterjee, R., & Eliashberg, J. (1990). The innovation diffusion process in a heterogeneous population: A micromodeling approach. *Management Science, 36*, 1057–1079. doi:10.1287/mnsc.36.9.1057.

Chaudhary, S. (2004). Management factors for strategic BI success. In *Business intelligence in digital economy: Opportunities, limitations and risks*. Hershey, PA: IDEA Group Publishing.

Chaudhary, S., Dayal, U., & Narasayya, V. (2011). An overview of business intelligence technology. *Communications of the ACM, 54*(8), 88–98. doi:10.1145/1978542.1978562.

Chen, T., Sun, F., & Lu, Y. (2007). Research on TPL-oriented fuzzy integrated evaluation method for supply chain. In *Proceedings of the Sixth Wuhan International Conference on E-Business*. Wuhan.

Chen, C.-T., Lin, C.-T., & Huang, S.-F. (2006). A fuzzy approach for supplier evaluation and selection in supply chain management. *International Journal of Production Economics, 102*, 289–301. doi:10.1016/j.ijpe.2005.03.009.

Cheng, B., & Atlee, J. (2007). Research directions in requirements engineering. In *Proceedings of the Future of Software Engineering Symposium* (pp. 285-303). IEEE Computer Society Press.

Chen, L., Soliman, K. S., Mao, E., & Frolick, M. N. (2000). Measuring user satisfaction with data warehouses: An exploratory study. *Information & Management*, 103–110. doi:10.1016/S0378-7206(99)00042-7.

Chen, S., & Bouvain, P. (2009). Is corporate responsibility converging? A comparison of corporate responsibility reporting in the USA, UK, Australia, and Germany. *Journal of Business Ethics, 90*(4), 523–536. doi:10.1007/s10551-010-0604-0.

Chen, Y. C. (2012). A framework for government 2.0 development and implementation. In Chen, Y.-C., & Chu, P.-Y. (Eds.), *Electronic Governance and Cross-Boundary Collaboration: Innovations and Advancing Tools* (pp. 350–368). Hershey, PA: IGI-Global.

Chesbrough, H. (2009). *Open innovation: The new imperative for creating and profiting from technology*. Boston: Harvard Business Press.

Cheung, C. M. K., Zhu, L., Kwong, T., Chan, G. W. W., & Limayem, M. (2003). *Online consumer behavior: A review and agenda for future research*. Paper presented at 16th Bled eCommerce Conference. Bled, Slovenia.

Chinowsky, P. S., & Rojas, E. M. (2003). Virtual teams: Guide to successful implementation. *Journal of Management Engineering, 19*(3), 98–106. doi:10.1061/(ASCE)0742-597X(2003)19:3(98).

Chin, W. W. (1998). Issues and opinions on structural equation modelling. *Management Information Systems Quarterly, 22*, 7–16.

Chin, W., Marcolin, B., & Newsted, P. (2003). A partial least squares latent variable modeling approach for measuring interaction effects: Results from a Monte Carlo simulation study and an electronic-mail emotion/adoption study. *Information Systems Research, 14*(2), 189–217. doi:10.1287/isre.14.2.189.16018.

Chou, D. C., Tan, X., & Yen, D. (2004). Web technology and supply chain management. *Information Management & Computer Security, 12*(4), 338–349. doi:10.1108/09685220410553550.

Christensen, P. H. (2007). Knowledge sharing: Moving away from the obsession with best practices. *Journal of Knowledge Management, 11*(1), 36–47. doi:10.1108/13673270710728222.

Christopher, M., & Peck, H. (2004). Building the resilient supply chain. *The International Journal of Logistics Management, 15*(2), 1–14. doi:10.1108/09574090410700275.

Christopher, M., & Towill, D. (2001). An integrated model for the design of agile supply chains. *International Journal of Physical Distribution & Logistics Management, 31*(4), 235–246. doi:10.1108/09600030110394914.

Chui, M., Miller, A., & Roberts, R. P. (2009). Six ways to make web 2.0 work.[from http://www.mckinseyquarterly.com]. *The McKinsey Quarterly*, 1–7. Retrieved April 24, 2009

Chung, T., & Law, R. (2003). Developing a performance indicator for hotel websites. *Hospital Management, 22*, 119–125. doi:10.1016/S0278-4319(02)00076-2.

Chu, R. (2001). What online Hong Kong travelers look for on airline/travel websites? *International Journal of Hospitality Management, 20*(1), 95–100. doi:10.1016/S0278-4319(00)00046-3.

Churchill, D. (2009). Educational applications of web 2.0: Using blogs to support teaching and learning. *British Journal of Educational Technology, 40*(1), 179–183. doi:10.1111/j.1467-8535.2008.00865.x.

Churchill, E., & Halverson, C. (2005). Social networks and social networking. *IEEE Internet Computing, 9*(5). doi:10.1109/MIC.2005.103.

Chu, S. K.-W. (2008). TWiki for knowledge building and management. *Online Information Review, 32*(6), 745–758. doi:10.1108/14684520810923917.

Ciribelli, M. (2003). *Como realizar uma dissertação de mestrado através da pesquisa científica*. Rio de Janeiro, Brazil: Viveiros de Castro Editora.

Clark, J., & Soliman, F. (1997). Application of scoring method for measuring the value of knowledge based systems to key employees. *Journal of Systems and Information Technology, 1*(2), 23–40. doi:10.1108/13287269780000736.

Clarkson, G., Jacobsen, T. E., & Batcheller, A. L. (2007). Information asymmetry and information sharing. *Government Information Quarterly, 24*(4), 827–839. doi:10.1016/j.giq.2007.08.001.

Coates, H., James, R., & Baldwin, G. (2005). A critical examination of the effects of learning management systems on university teaching and learning. *Tertiary Education and Management, 11*(1), 19–36. doi:10.1080/13583883.2005.9967137.

Coelli, T., Prasada Rao, S., O'Donnell, C., & Battese, G. (2005). *An introduction to efficiency and productivity analysis*. New York: Springer.

Coffee, S. (2011, November). *Freshly brewed tweets from Brad and Lee at Starbucks in Seattle, WA*. Retrieved from http://twitter.com/#!/starbucks

Cohen, L., & Manion, L. et al. (2003). *Research methods in education*. London: Routledge/Falmer Taylor & Francis Group.

Cohen, W. M., & Levinthal, D. A. (1990). Absorptive capacity: A new perspective on learning and innovation. *Administrative Science Quarterly, 35*(1). doi:10.2307/2393553 PMID:10106582.

Cohn, M. (2005). *Agile estimating and planning*. Upper Saddle River, NJ: Pearson Education, Inc..

Colclough, G., & Tinholt, D. (2009). *Smarter, faster, better e-government-8th benchmarking measurement*. Capgemini, RAND Europe, IDC, SOGETI and DTi

Cole, A. (2004). *Management*. London: Thomson.

Cole, M. (2007). The networked consumer: A critical review and assessment. *Journal of Customer Behaviour, 6*(1), 5–18. doi:10.1362/147539207X198347.

Coleman, J. S. (1990). *Foundations of social theory*. Cambridge, MA: Harvard University Press.

Coleman, J. S. (1998). Social capital in the creation of human capital. *American Journal of Sociology, 94*(Supplement), S95–S120. doi:10.1086/228943.

Coleman, J. S., Katz, E., & Menzel, H. (1966). *Medical innovation: A diffusion study*. Indianapolis, IN: The Boobs-Merrill Company.

Collins, J. (2001). *Why some companies make the leap ... and others don't*. Sydney, Australia: Random Books.

Collis, B., & Moonen, J. (2008). Web 2.0 tools and processes in higher education: Quality perspectives. *Educational Media International*, *45*(2), 93–106. doi:10.1080/09523980802107179.

Comisión de Mercado de las Telecomunicaciones. (2010). Retrieved from http://informeanual.cmt.es/informe-sector/comunicaciones-moviles

Commission of the European Communities. (2006). *Efficiency and equity in European education and training systems.* Retrieved December 3, 2011, from ec.europa.eu/education/policies/2010/doc/comm481_en.pdf

Company, T. N. (2011). *BlogPulse.* Retrieved September 28, 2011, from http://www.blogpulse.com/

Conger, J. A., & Kanungo, R. N. (1987). Toward a behavioural theory of charismatic leadership in organisational settings. *Academy of Management Review*, *12*, 637–647.

Connolly, T., Conlon, E., & Deutsch, S. (1980). Organizational effectiveness: A multiple-constituency approach. *Academy of Management Review*, *5*(2), 211–217.

Constantinides, E. (2006). The marketing mix revisited: Towards the 21st century marketing. *Journal of Marketing Management*, *22*(3-4), 407–438. doi:10.1362/026725706776861190.

Constantinides, E., Gómez, M., & Lorenzo, C. (2008). Social media: A new frontier for retailers? *Europea Retail Research*, *22*, 1–28.

Constanzo, H. (2009). Web 2.0: A simple concept, a complex solution. *Bank Technology News*, *22*(3), 24.

Conway, S., & Steward, F. (2009). *Managing and shaping innovation.* Oxford, UK: Oxford University Press.

Cook, J., & Wall, T. (1980). New work attitude measures of trust, organizational commitment, and personal need non-fulfillment. *Journal of Occupational Psychology*, *53*(1), 39–52. doi:10.1111/j.2044-8325.1980.tb00005.x.

Cook, N. (2008). *Enterprise 2.0: How social software will change the future of work.* Hampshire, UK: Gower Publishing Limited.

Cooper, C., Fletcher, J., Gilbert, D., & Wanhill, S. (1998). *Tourism: Principles and practice.* London: Prentice Hall.

Cooper, R. B., & Zmud, R. W. (1990). Information technology implementation research: A technological diffusion approach. *Management Science*, *36*(2), 123–139. doi:10.1287/mnsc.36.2.123.

Copper, W. (2008). *Amnesty looks to utilise social media in latest global campaign.* Retrieved October 25, 2011 from http://www.mad.co.uk/Main/Search/MadSearchResults/Articles/2bd0e47f9b3247719c112e0bf3968aaf/Amnesty-looks-to-utilise-social-media-in-latest-global-campaign.html

Corbett, P., & Ward, D. (2006). *Open source reporting solutions for institutional reporting: The BIRT approach. Australasian Association for Institutional Research.* AAIR.

Cordis. (n.d.). retrieved from cordis.europa.eu

Cormode, G., & Krishnamurthy, B. (2008). Key differences between web 1.0 and web 2.0. *First Monday*, *13*(6). doi:10.5210/fm.v13i6.2125.

Corso, M., Martini, A., Pellegrini, L., Massa, S., & Testa, S. (2006). Managing dispersed workers: The new challenge in knowledge management. *Technovation*, *26*, 583–594. doi:10.1016/j.technovation.2005.02.003.

Cossentino, M. (2007). *Open source software.* Retrieved from http://www.pa.icar.cnr.it/cossentino/ICT/ppt/S11%20-%20Open%20Source%20Software.pdf

Costantino, C. (1996). Using interest-based techniques to design conflict management systems. *Negotiation Journal*, *12*(3), 207–214. doi:10.1111/j.1571-9979.1996.tb00095.x.

Coyle, C. L., & Vaughn, H. (2008). Social networking: Communication revolution or evolution? *Bell Labs Technical Journal*, *13*(2), 13–17. doi:10.1002/bltj.20298.

Crainer, S., & Birkinshaw, J. (2008). Who needs employees? *Business Strategy Review*, *19*(3), 18–21. doi:10.1111/j.1467-8616.2008.00547.x.

Cramton, C. D. (1997). Information problems in dispersed teams. Academy of Management Proceedings, 298-302.

Cramton, C. D. (2001). The mutual knowledge problem and its consequences for dispersed collaboration. *Organization Science*, *12*, 346–371. doi:10.1287/orsc.12.3.346.10098.

Cramton, C. D. (2002). Finding common ground in dispersed collaboration. *Organizational Dynamics*, *30*(4), 354–367. doi:10.1016/S0090-2616(02)00063-3.

Cramton, C. D., & Orvis, K. L. (2003). Overcoming barriers to information sharing in virtual teams. In Gibson, C. B., & Cohen, S. G. (Eds.), *Virtual Teams that Work: Creating Conditions for Virtual Team Effectiveness*. San Francisco, CA: Jossey-Bass.

Cress, U., & Kimmerle, J. (2008). A systemic and cognitive view on collaborative knowledge building with wikis. *International Journal of Computer-Supported Collaborative Learning*, *3*(2), 105–122. doi:10.1007/s11412-007-9035-z.

Cristopher, M., Payne, A., & Ballantine, D. (1994). *Relationship marketing*. Boston: Butterworth-Heinemann, Ltd..

Croft, A. C. (2008). Emergence of new media moves PR agencies in new directions: Competitive pressure threatens agencies' livelihood. *Public Relations Quarterly*, *52*(1), 16–20.

Cross, R., & Parker, A. (2004). *The hidden power of social networks: Understand how work really gets done in organizations*. Boston: Harvard Business School Press.

Crowston, K., & Howison, J. (2006). Hierarchy and centralization in free and open source software team communications. *Knowledge, Technology & Policy*, *18*, 65–85. doi:10.1007/s12130-006-1004-8.

Cudanov, M., Jasko, O., & Jevtic, M. (2008). Influence of information and communication technologies on decentralization of organizational structure. *Computer Science and Information System*, *6*(1), 93–109. doi:10.2298/CSIS0901093C.

Cui, C. C., Lewis, B. R., & Park, W. (2003). Service quality measurement in the banking sector in South Korea. *International Journal of Bank Marketing*, *21*(4), 191–201. doi:10.1108/02652320310479187.

Cullen, R., & Morse, S. (2011). Who's contributing: Do personality traits influence the level and type of participation in online communities.[). IEEE.]. *Methodology*, *0*, 1–11.

Cunha, L. (2001). *Introdução ao turismo*. Lisbon, Portugal: Ed. Verbo.

Cunningham, B. (1977). Approaches to the evaluation of organizational effectiveness. *Academy of Management Review*, *2*(3), 463–474.

Cuppens, F., & Cuppens-Boulahia, N. (2008). Modeling contextual security policies. *International Journal of Information Security*, *7*(4), 285–305. doi:10.1007/s10207-007-0051-9.

Cusumano, M. (2010). Cloud computing and SaaS as new computing platforms. *Communications of the ACM*, *53*(4), 27–28. doi:10.1145/1721654.1721667.

Cutlip, S. M., Center, A. H., & Broom, G. M. (2000). *Effective public relations*. Englewood Cliffs, NJ: Prentice Hall.

Dabbagh, N., & Reo, R. (2010). Back to the future: Tracing the roots and learning: Affordances of social software. In Lee, M., & McLoughlin, C. (Eds.), *Web 2.0-Based E-Learning: Applying Social Informatics for Tertiary Teaching* (pp. 1–20). Academic Press. doi:10.4018/978-1-60566-294-7.ch001.

Dabbah, M. A., Woo, W. L., & Dlay, S. S. (2007). Secure authentication for face recognition. In *Proceedings of the IEEE Symposium on Computational Intelligence in Image and Signal Processing* (pp. 121 – 126). IEEE.

Daft, R. (2000). *Management*. Fort Worth, TX: The Dryden Press.

Daft, R. (2003). *Management*. Cincinnati, OH: South-Western College.

Daft, R. (2006). *Organization theory and design*. Cincinnati, OH: South Western College Publishing.

Daft, R. (2007). *Organization theory and design*. Cincinnati, OH: South-Western College.

Daft, R. (2009). *The new era of management*. Cincinnati, OH: South-Western College.

Daghfous, A. (2007). Absorptive capacity and innovative enterprise systems. *International Journal of Innovation and Learning*, *4*(1), 60–73. doi:10.1504/IJIL.2007.011475.

Dahlander, L., Frederiksen, L., & Rullani, F. (2008). Online communities and open innovation: Governance and symbolic value creation. *Industry and Innovation*, *15*(2), 115–123. doi:10.1080/13662710801970076.

Dahlen, M. (1998). *Controlling the uncontrollable: Towards the perfect web sample*. Paper presented at the Worldwide Internet Seminar. Amsterdam: Esomar Publications.

Dalkir, K. (2011). *Knowledge management in theory and practice* (2nd ed.). Cambridge, MA: The MIT Press.

Damacena, C., & Pedron, C. D. (2004). *Estratégia de CRM: O desafio da implantação*. Paper presented at the Congresso Anual de Tecnologia de Informação (CATI 2004). Aviero, Portugal.

Damiani, E., Frati, F., & Monteverdi, C. (2009). *Open source BI adoption*. Retrieved from http://www.ow2.org/xwiki/bin/download/BusinessIntelligence/Documents/OSBIadoption-v10.pdf

Dardenne, A., van Lamsweerde, A., & Fickas, S. (1993). Goal-directed requirements acquisition. *Science of Computer Programming*, *20*(1-2), 3–50. doi:10.1016/0167-6423(93)90021-G.

Davenport, T. (2008). Enterprise 2.0: The new, new knowledge management? *Harvard Business Review*.

Davenport, T. H., Harris, J. G., & Kohli, A. K. (2001). How do they know their customers so well? *MIT Sloan Management Review*, *42*(2), 63–73.

Davenport, T. H., & Short, J. E. (1990, Summer). The new industrial engineering: Information technology and business process redesign. *Sloan Management Review*, 11–27.

Davis, F. D. (1989). Perceived usefulness, perceived ease of use, and user acceptance of information technology. *Management Information Systems Quarterly*, *13*(3), 319–340. doi:10.2307/249008.

Davis, F. D., Bagozzi, R. P., & Warshaw, P. R. (1989). User acceptance of computer technology: A comparison of two theoretical models. *Management Science*, *35*(8), 982–1003. doi:10.1287/mnsc.35.8.982.

Davison, R. (2002). Distribution channel analysis for business travel. In Buhalis, D., & Eric, L. (Eds.), *Tourism distribution channels: Practices, issues and transformations* (pp. 73–86). New York: Continuum.

Dawley, H. (2007). *Coming at you and real soon, web 3.0*. Retrieved January 2011 from http://www.medialifemagazine.com/artman2/publish/New_media_23/Coming_at_you_and_real_soon_Web_3_0.asp

De Ascaniis, S., & Morasso, S. G. (2011). When tourists give their reasons on the web: The argumentative significance of tourism related UGC. In Law, R., Fuchs, M., & Ricci, F. (Eds.), *Information and Communication Technologies in Tourism 2011* (pp. 125–138). New York: Springer. doi:10.1007/978-3-7091-0503-0_11.

De Geus, A. (1988, March-April). Planning as learning. *Harvard Business Review*, 70–74.

De Hertogh, S., Viaene, S., & Dedene, G. (2011). Governing web 2.0. *Communications of the ACM*, *54*(3), 124–130. doi:10.1145/1897852.1897882.

De Pedro, X., Rieradevall, M., López, P., Sant, D., Piñol, J., Núñez, L., et al. (2006). *Writing documents collaboratively in higher education using traditional vs. wiki methodology: Qualitative results from a 2-year project study*. Paper presented at the 4th Internacional Congress of University Teaching and Innovation. New York, NY.

Deal, T., & Kennedy, A. (2000). *Corporate cultures*. Jackson, MI: Perseus Books Group.

Decree n. 6991, Oct 27, 2009. (2009). National Program to Support Digital inclusion in the communities - Telecentros. BR. DOU n. 206, Sec.1, pp. 3. Federative Republic of Brazil, Brasília, DF. Retrieved Nov 26, 2011, from http://www.in.gov.br/imprensa/visualiza/index.jsp?jornal=1&pagina=3&data=28/10/2009

del Arco Carabias, J., & San Segundo Encinar, J. M. (2010). *Los mayores ante las TIC: Accesibilidad y accesiquibilidad*. Fundacion Vodafone España.

Del Chiappa, G. (2011). Trustworthiness of web 2.0 applications and their influence on tourist behavior: An empirical investigation in Italy. In Law, R., Fuchs, M., & Ricci, F. (Eds.), *Information and Communication Technologies in Tourism 2011* (pp. 331–342). New York: Springer. doi:10.1007/978-3-7091-0503-0_27.

Delgado, J., & Nieto, M. J. (2002). Incorporación de la tecnología de la información a la actividad bancaria en España: La banca por Internet. *Estabilidad Financiera*, *3*, 85–105.

Dell. (2012). *Peace of mind! We've got covered!* Retrieved from http://www.dell.com/content/learnmore/learnmore.aspx?c=us&l=en&s=dhs&~id=serv_inspn&~line=notebooks&~lt=popup&~series=inspn&ref=CFG#tn2

DelVecchio, D., Henard, D. H., & Freling, T. H. (2006). The effect of sales promotion on post-promotion brand preference: A meta-analysis. *Journal of Retailing*, *82*(3), 203–213. doi:10.1016/j.jretai.2005.10.001.

Department of Digital inclusion - DDI. (2011). *Curso de formação de monitores do telecentros.BR. programa nacional de apoio à inclusão digital nas comunidades: Rede nacional de formação para inclusão digital*. Federative Republic of Brazil. [Documento orientador 2.0]. Brasília, DF: Ministério das Comunicações.

Deperlioglu, O., & Kose, U. (2010). The effectiveness and experiences of blended learning approaches to computer programming education. *Computer Applications in Engineering Education*.

Derby, E., & Larsen, D. (2006). *Agile retrospectives: Making good teams great*. New York: The Pragmatic Bookshelf.

Dess, G., & Shaw, J. (2001). Voluntary turnover, social capital, and organizational performance. *Academy of Management Review*, *26*(3), 446–456.

Devlin, B. P., & Murphy, P. T. (1988). An architecture for a business and information system. *IBM Systems Journal*, *7*(1), 60–80. doi:10.1147/sj.271.0060.

Dewever, B., Schellens, T., Valcke, M., & Vankeer, H. (2006). Content analysis schemes to analyze transcripts of online asynchronous discussion groups: A review. *Computers & Education*, *46*(1), 6–28. doi:10.1016/j.compedu.2005.04.005.

Dhar, R., & Wertenbroch, K. (2000). Consumer choice between hedonic and utilitarian goods. *JMR, Journal of Marketing Research*, *37*, 60–71. doi:10.1509/jmkr.37.1.60.18718.

Dholakia, R. R., & Kshetri, N. (2004). Factors impacting the adoption of the Internet among SMEs. *Small Business Economics*, *23*(4), 311–322. doi:10.1023/B:SBEJ.0000032036.90353.1f.

Dholakia, U. M., Bagozzi, R. P., & Pearo, L. K. (2004). A social influence model of consumer participation in network- and small-group-based virtual communities. *International Journal of Research in Marketing*, *21*(3), 241–263. doi:10.1016/j.ijresmar.2003.12.004.

Diamond, W., & Campbell, L. (1989). The framing of sales promotions: Effects on reference price change. *Advances in Consumer Research. Association for Consumer Research (U. S.)*, *16*, 241–247.

Dim Mock, N., Belokosztolszki, A., Eyers, D., Bacon, J., & Moody, K. (2004). Using trust and risk in role based access control policies. In *Proceedings of the 9th ACM Symposium on Access Control Models and Technologies* (pp. 156-162). New York: ACM.

Dinis, P., & Rodrigues da Silva, A. (2007). Design experiences with the learning objects board system. In *Proceedings of the 40th of Hawaii International Conference on System Sciences*. IEEE.

Dinis, P., & Rodrigues da Silva, A. (2009). Application scenarios for the learning objects pool. *Journal of Universal Computer Science*, *15*(7), 1455–1471.

Disney, S., Naim, M., & Towill, D. (1997). Dynamic simulation modeling for lean logistics. *International Journal of Physical Distribution & Logistics Management, 27*(3/4), 174–196. doi:10.1108/09600039710170566.

Divitini, M., Haugalokken, O., & Morken, E. M. (2005). *Blog to support learning in the field: Lessons learned from a fiasco.* Paper presented at the Fifth IEEE International Conference on Advanced Learning Technologies. New York, NY.

Dodds, P. S., Muhamad, R., & Watts, D. J. (2003). An experimental study of search in global social networks. *Science, 301*, 827–829. doi:10.1126/science.1081058.

Donaldson, E. A., & Grant-Vallone, E. J. (2000). Longitudinal examination of mentoring relationships on organizational commitment and citizenship behavior. *Journal of Career Development, 26*(4), 233–248. doi:10.1177/089484530002600401.

Donavan, D., Brown, T., & Mowen, J. (2004). Internal benefits of service-worker customer orientation: job satisfaction, commitment, and organizational citizenship behaviors. *Journal of Marketing, 68*(1), 128–146. doi:10.1509/jmkg.68.1.128.24034.

Dösinger, G., Stocker, A., Us, A., & Wagner, C. (2007). The three pillars of 'corporate web 2.0': A model for definition. In *Proceedings of I-MEDIA '07 and I-SEMANTICS '07*. Graz, Austria: IEEE.

Douglas, A., & Mills, J. E. (2004). Staying afloat in the tropics: Applying a structural equation model approach to evaluating national tourism organization websites in the Caribbean. *Journal of Travel & Tourism Marketing, 17*(2/3), 269–293. doi:10.1300/J073v17n02_20.

Dowling, G. R., & Uncles, M. (1997). Do customer loyalty programs really work? *Sloan Management Review, 38*(4), 71–82.

Doyle, S. (2002). Software review: Communication optimisation - The new mantra of database marketing: Fad or fact? *Journal of Database Marketing, 9*(2), 185–191. doi:10.1057/palgrave.jdm.3240074.

Dragoi, G., Draghici, A., Rosu, S. M., & Cotet, C. E. (2010). Virtual product development in university-enterprise partnership. *Information Resources Management Journal, 23*(3), 43–59. doi:10.4018/irmj.2010070104.

Drucker, P. (1946). *Concept of corporation.* New York: Harper and Row.

Drucker, P. (2007). *Management - Tasks, responsabilities and practices.* New Brunswick, NJ: Transaction Publishers.

Dubois, D., & Prade, H. (1987). The mean value of a fuzzy number. *Fuzzy Sets and Systems, 24*, 279–300. doi:10.1016/0165-0114(87)90028-5.

Dubois, D., Prade, H., & Ughetto, L. (1999). Fuzzy logic, control engineering and artificial intelligence. In Verbruggen, , Zimmermann, , & Babuska, (Eds.), *Fuzzy Algorithms for Control*, (pp. 17-57). Dordrecht, The Netherlands: Kluwer Academic Publishers. doi:10.1007/978-94-011-4405-6_2.

Dumas, M., van der Aalst, W. M. P., & ter Hofstede, A. H. M. (2005). *Process-aware information systems: Bridging people and software through process technology.* New York: Wiley. doi:10.1002/0471741442.

Dutta, S. (2010). What's your personal social media strategy? *Harvard Business Review, 88*(11), 127–130. PMID:21049685.

Duval, E. (2005). LearnRank: The real quality measure for learning materials. In Policy and Innovation in Education-Quality Criteria. European Schooet.

Dwyer, C., Hiltz, S., & Passerini, K. (2007). *Trust and privacy concern within social networking sites: A comparison of Facebook and MySpace.* Paper presented at the Americas Conference on Information Systems (AMCIS). New York, NY.

Dwyer, L., Edwards, D., Mistilis, N., Roman, C., & Scott, N. (2009). Destination and enterprise management for a tourism future. *Tourism Management, 30*(1), 63–74. doi:10.1016/j.tourman.2008.04.002.

Dyché, J. (2002). *The CRM handbook: A business guide to customer relationship management.* Reading, MA: Addison-Wesley Pearson Education.

Dyché, J., & Levy, E. (2006). *Customer data integration: Reaching a single version of the truth.* Hoboken, NJ: John Wiley & Sons, Inc..

e-Business W@tch. (2006). *ICT and e-business in the tourism industry.* Retrieved from http://www.ebusiness-watch.org/resources/tourism/SR08-2006 Tourism.pdf

Eclipse/BIRT. (2011). *BIRT project*. Retrieved from http://www.eclipse.org/birt

Editors of the American Heritage Dictionaries (EAHD). (2000). *The American heritage dictionary of the English language*. Boston: Houghton Mifflin.

Egan, J. (2011). *Relationship marketing* (4th ed.). Harlow, MA: Pearson Educational Limited.

Egbu, C., Botterill, K., & Bates, M. (2001). The influence of knowledge management and intellectual capital on organisational innovations. In *Proceedings of ARCOM Seventeenth Annual Conference*, (pp. 547-555). ARCOM.

Egger, R. (2010). Theorizing web 2.0 phenomena in tourism: A sociological signpost. *Information Technology & Tourism, 12*, 125–137. doi:10.3727/109830510X12887971002666.

Egger, R., & Buhalis, D. (2008). *eTourism: Case studies*. Oxford, UK: Ed. Butterworth Heinemann.

Egger, R., & Wörndl, L. (2008). Hotel Sallerhof: Innovations in interaction. In Egger, R., & Buhalis, D. (Eds.), *eTourism: Case studies* (pp. 56–64). Oxford, UK: Butterworth Heinemann - Elsevier.

Eginton, K. (1998). Knowledge management – Law firms can do it too! *Australian Law Librarian, 6*, 247–255.

Eker, M., Eker, S., & Pala, F. (2008). The effects of job satisfaction on organizational commitment among Turkish health care staff: an empirical study. *Journal of Academic Studies, 10*(36), 46–68.

Elgg. (2011). *Elgg - Open source social networking engine*. Retrieved October 4, 2011, from http://elgg.org/

Elia, G., Margherita, A., & Taurino, C. (2009). Enhancing managerial competencies through a wiki-learning space. *International Journal of Continuing Engineering Education and Lifelong Learning, 19*(2-3), 166–178. doi:10.1504/IJCEELL.2009.025025.

Ellison, L. (1999). *The internet changes everything and the CEO of Oracle is living proof*. Retrieved June 2011 from http://money.cnn.com/magazines/fortune/fortune_archive/1999/05/24/260276/index.htm

Ellison, C., Frantz, B., Lampson, B., Rivest, R., Thomas, B., & Ylonen, T. (1999). *RFC-2693: SPKI certificate theory*. Geneva, Switzerland: Internet Engineering Task Force.

Embarcadero Technologies. (2008). *Why data warehouse projects fail*. Retrieved from http://www.embarcadero.com/resources/technical_papers/Why-Data-Warehouse-Projects-Fail.pdf

Embid, P., Martín, M., & Zorrilla, V. (1998). *Marketing financiero*. Madrid, Spain: McGraw-Hill.

Emerson, R. (1962). Power-dependence relations. *American Sociological Review, 27*(1), 31–41. doi:10.2307/2089716.

Encyclopaedia Britannica. (2007). *Britannica concise encyclopedia*. London: Encyclopedia Britannica.

England, E., & Finney, A. (2007). *Managing interactive media: Project management for web and digital media*. Harlow, MA: Pearson Education, Inc..

Ericson, J. (2009). The real thing? *Information & Management, 19*(6), 14–19.

Erol, I., Sencer, S., & Sari, R. (2011). A new fuzzy multi-criteria framework for measuring sustainability performance of a supply chain. *Ecological Economics, 70*, 1088–1100. doi:10.1016/j.ecolecon.2011.01.001.

Estêvão, J. P., Carneiro, M. J., & Teixeira, L. (2011). Destination management systems: Improving the tourism experience by empowering visitors. In *Proceedings of the 4th Advances in Tourism Marketing Conference*. ATMC.

Ettredge, M., Richardson, V., & Scholz, S. (2001). The presentation of financial information at corporate web sites. *International Journal of Accounting Information Systems, 2*, 149–168. doi:10.1016/S1467-0895(00)00017-8.

Ettredge, M., Richardson, V., & Scholz, S. (2002). Dissemination of information for investors at corporate web sites. *Journal of Accounting and Public Policy, 21*, 357–389. doi:10.1016/S0278-4254(02)00066-2.

Etzioni, A. (1997). *Modern organizations*. London: Profile Books.

Europa. (n.d.). Retrieved from europa.eu

European Commission. (2010). *Communication from the commission to the European parliament, the council, the European economic and social committee and the committee of the regions: A Digital Agenda for Europe, L 245*. Brussels, Belgium: European Commission.

European Commission. (2010). *Communication from the commission to the European 2020: A strategy for smart, sustainable and inclusive growth*. Brussels, Belgium: European Commission.

European Opinion Research Group. (2011). *Attitudes on data protection and electronic identity in the European Union. Technical Report Special Eurobarometer 359*. Bruxelles, Belgium: European Commission.

European Parliament and Council. (1995). Directive 95/46/EC of the European parliament and of the council on the protection of individuals with regard to the processing of personal data and on the free movement of such data. *Official Journal of the European Communities, 281*, 31–50.

European Parliament and Council. (1999). Directive 99/93/EC of the European parliament and of the council on a community framework for electronic signatures. *Official Journal of the European Communities, 13*, 12.

European Parliament and Council. (2002). Directive 2002/58/EC of the European parliament and of the council concerning the processing of personal data and the protection of privacy in the electronic communications sector (directive on privacy and electronic communications). *Official Journal of the European Communities, 201*, 37–47.

European Parliament. (2011). *Consumer behavior in a digital environment*. Retrieved 20 November, 2010 from http://www.europarl.europa.eu/document/activities/cont/201108/20110825ATT25258/20110825ATT25258EN.pdf

European Union (EU). (2006). *Implementing the partnership for growth and jobs*. Brussels, Belgium: EU.

European Union. (2003). The new SME definition: User guide and model declaration. *Official Journal of the European Union, 124*, 36.

Eurostat. (2011). Retrieved from http://epp.eurostat.ec.europa.eu/portal/page/portal/eurostat/home/

Evans, D., & McKee, J. (2010). *Social media marketing: The next generation of business engagement*. New York: John Wiley & Sons, Inc..

Evan, W. (1976). Organizational theory and organizational effectiveness. *Organizational and Administrative Science, 7*, 15–28.

Evelson, B., & Hammond, J. S. (2010). *The Forrester Wave™: Open source business intelligence (BI), Q3 2010*. Forrester Research.

Eysenbach, G. (2001). What is e-health? *Journal of Medical Internet Research, 3*(2), e20. doi:10.2196/jmir.3.2.e20 PMID:11720962.

Facebook. (2011). *Statistics*. Retrieved November 15, 2011, from http://www.facebook.com/press/info.php?statistics

Fan, Z. P., Suo, W. L., Feng, B., & Liu, Y. (2011). Trust estimation in a virtual team: A decision support method. *Expert Systems with Applications, 38*(8), 10240–10251. doi:10.1016/j.eswa.2011.02.060.

FAO. (2010). *Organizational evaluation*. Retrieved in January 2010, from http://www.fao.org/docrep/w7510e/w7510e05.htm

Farah, R. M., & Arantes, R. P. (2010). *Novas tecnologias no envelhecimento.*.

Fare, R., Grosskopf, S., & Fukuyama, H. (2004). *New directions: Efficiency and productivity*. Boston: Springer.

Faust, W., & Faust, K. (1994). *Social network analysis: Methods and applications: Structural analysis in the social sciences*. Cambridge, UK: Cambridge University Press.

Fayol, H. (1949). *General and industrial management*. New York.

Felder, R., & Soloman, B. (2011). *Learning styles and strategies*. Retrieved February 2011 from http://csu.edu/unity/lockers/users/f/felder/public/ILSdir/styles.htm

Felder, R. (1993). Reaching the second tier: learning and teaching styles in college science education. *Journal of College Science Teaching, 23*(5), 286–290.

Filev, A. (2007, September 29). *How do enterprise 2.0 technologies make companies more agile?* [Web log comment]. Retrieved from http://www.wrike.com/projectmanagement/09/29/2007/How-Do-Enterprise-2-0-Technologies-Make-Companies-More-Agile

Filev, A. (n.d.). *Project management 2.0: Blending bottom-up and top-down approaches*. Retrieved from http://www.wrike.com/apple_booklet_for_Web.pdf

Filipe, S., & Barbosa, M. (2012). The relationship markeitng under the perception of the client in the context of higher educaton: An exploratory study. *International Business and Economics Review, 3.*

Finkenzeller, K. (2010). *RFID handbook: Fundamentals and applications in contactless smart cards, radio frecuency identificacion and NFC*. New York: Wiley. doi:10.1002/9780470665121.

Fink, M., & Kraus, S. (Eds.). (2009). *The management of small and medium enterprises*. New York: Routledge.

Fishbein, M., & Ajzen, I. (1975). *Belief, attitude, intention, and behavior: An introduction to theory and research*. Reading, MA: Addison-Wesley Reading.

Flick, U. (2004). Design and process in qualitative research. In Flick, U., Von Kardoff, E., & Steine, I. (Eds.), *A Companion to Qualitative Research* (pp. 146–152). London: SAGE.

Flood, R. L. (2009). *Rethinking the fifth discipline: Learning within the unknowable*. London: Routledge.

Florida, R. (2002). *The rise of the creative class*. New York: Basic Books.

Flyvbjerg, B. (2006). Five misunderstandings about case-study research. *Qualitative Inquiry*, *12*(2), 219–245. doi:10.1177/1077800405284363.

Foa, U. G. (1971). Interpersonal and economic resources. *Science*, *29*, 345–351. doi:10.1126/science.171.3969.345.

Fonou-Dombeu, J. V., & Huisman, M. (2011). Combining ontology development methodologies and semantic web platforms for e-government domain ontology development. *International Journal of Web & Semantic Technology*, *2*(2), 12–25. doi:10.5121/ijwest.2011.2202.

Ford, D. V., Jones, K. H., Verplancke, J. P., Lyons, R. A., John, G., & Brown, G. et al. (2009). The SAIL databank: Building a national architecture for e-health research and evaluation. *BMC Health Services Research*, *9*, 157. doi:10.1186/1472-6963-9-157 PMID:19732426.

Fornell, C., & Larcker, D. F. (1981). Evaluating structural equation models with unobservable variables and measurement errors. *JMR, Journal of Marketing Research*, *18*, 39–50. doi:10.2307/3151312.

Foster, M. K., Francescucci, A., & West, B. C. (2010). Why users participate in online social networks. *International Journal of e-Business Management, 4*(1), 3-19.

Fowler, M. (2003). *What is a bliki*. Retrieved October 6, 2011, from http://martinfowler.com/bliki/WhatIsaBliki.html

Fox, S. (2001). *pewInternet*. Retrieved from www.pewInternet.org

Foxall, G. R., Goldsmith, R. E., & Brown, S. (1998). *Consumer psychology for marketing* (2nd ed.). London: International Thomson Business Press.

FP6 IST Project PRIME (Privacy and Identity Management for Europe). (n.d.). Retrieved November 3, 2011, from https://www.prime-project.eu/

FP7 IST Project PrimeLife (Privacy and Identity Management in Europe for Life). (n.d.). Retrieved November 3, 2011, from http://www.primelife.eu/

Franck, E., & Jungwirth, C. (2003). Reconciling investors and donators: The governance structure of open source. *Journal of Management and Governance*, *7*, 401–421. doi:10.1023/A:1026261005092.

Franklin, T., & Harmelen, M. V. (2007). *Web 2.0 for content for learning and teaching in higher education.*

Frappaolo, C. (2010). Implementing enterprise 2.0 within the European Union. *The 2.0 Adoption Council*. Retrieved September 1, 2011, from http://info.newsgator.com

Freeman, L. C. (1996). Some antecedents of social network analysis. *Connections, 19*(1), 39-42. Retrieved January 01, 2012, from http://www.insna.org/PDF/Connections/v19/1996_I-1-4.pdf

Freeman, L. C. (2004). *The development of social network analysis: A study in the sociology of science*. Canada: Empirical Press.

FreshMinds Research. (2010). *Turning conversations into insights: A comparison of social media monitoring tools*. Retrieved from http://shared.freshminds.co.uk/smm10/whitepaper.pdf

Friedkin, N. E. (2011). Spine segments in small world networks. *Social Networks, 33*(1), 88–97. doi:10.1016/j.socnet.2010.11.004.

Friedkin, N. E., & Johnsen, E. C. (1997). Social positions in influence networks. *Social Networks, 19*(3), 209–222. doi:10.1016/S0378-8733(96)00298-5.

Frissen, V., Millard, J., Huijboom, N., Iversen, J. S., Kool, L., & Kotterink, B. et al. (2007). *The future of eGovernment: An exploration of ICT-driven models of eGovernment for the EU in 2020*. European Comission Join Research Center.

Frondizi, R. (Ed.). (1992). *Qué son los valores? Introduccion a la axiología* (3rd ed.). Breviarios del Fondo de Cultura Económica.

Fujitsu. (2009). *Soluciones para el sector bancario*. Fujitsu.

Fukuyama, F. (1995). *Trust: The social virtues and the creation of prosperity*. New York, NY: Free Press.

Fundación Orange. (2010). *eEspaña 2010: Informe anual sobre el desarrollo de la sociedad de la información en España*. Fundación Orange.

Funk, W. (1992). *Word origins: An exploration and history of words and language*. Gravesend, NJ: Bell Publishing Company.

Furst, S. A., Blackburn, R. S., & Rosen, B. (1999). Virtual team effectiveness: A proposed research agenda. *Information Systems Journal, 9*, 249–269. doi:10.1046/j.1365-2575.1999.00064.x.

Furst, S. A., Reeves, M., Rosen, B., & Blackburn, R. S. (2004). Managing the life cycle of virtual teams. *The Academy of Management Executive, 18*(2), 6–20. doi:10.5465/AME.2004.13837468.

Gaffney, J. (2001). The battle over internet ads. *Business 2.0*. Retrieved from http://www.business2.com/articles/Web/0,1653,16546,00.html

Galaskiewicz, J., & Wasserman, S. (1993). Social network analysis: Concepts, methodology, and directions for the 1990s. *Sociological Methods & Research, 22*(1), 3–22. doi:10.1177/0049124193022001001.

Galbraith, J. (2002). *Designing organizations*. New York: Wiley and Sons.

Galbraith, J. R. (1971). Matrix organization designs How to combine functional and project forms. *Business Horizons, 14*(1), 29–40. doi:10.1016/0007-6813(71)90037-1.

Galbrait, J. (1995). *Designing organizations: An executive briefing on strategy, structure, and process*. San Francisco, CA: Jossey-Bass.

Gallagher, R. (2002). *The soul of an organization*. New York: Kaplan Business.

Gallaugher, J. (2010). Get S.M.A.R.T. – Social media awareness & response team. In *Information Systems: A Manager's Guide to Harnessing Technology* (pp. 125–134). Flat World Knowledge.

Gallup Organization. (2008). *Data protection in the European Union: Citizens' perceptions – Analytical report (flash eurobarometer 225)*. Retrieved November 3, 2011, http://ec.europa.eu/public_opinion/flash/fl_225_en.pdf

Gallupe, B. (2001). Knowledge management systems: Surveying the landscape. *International Journal of Management Reviews, 3*(1), 61–77. doi:10.1111/1468-2370.00054.

Ganorkar, S. R., & Ghatol, A. A. (2007). Iris recognition: An emerging biometric technology. In *Proceedings of the 6th WSEAS International Conference on Signal Processing, Robotics and Automation* (pp. 91 – 96). WSEAS.

García Ponce, F. J. (2007). *Accesibilidad, TIC y educación. CNICE*. Centro Nacional de Información y Comunicación Educativa. Ministerio de Educación y Ciencia.

Gardner, W. L., & Avolio, B. A. (1998). The charismatic relationship: A dramaturgical perspective. *Academy of Management Review, 23*, 32–58.

Gartner. (2011). *Gartner says enterprises that harness the power of collective behaviors will be the ultimate winners with social media*. Retrieved February 28, 2011, from http://www.gartner.com

Garvin, D. A. (1993). Building a learning organisation. *Harvard Business Review*, *71*, 78.

Garvin, D. A., Edmondson, A. C., & Gino, F. (2008). Is yours a learning organisation? *Harvard Business Review*, *86*(3), 109.

Gattiker, T. F., & CFPIM. (2002). Anatomy of an ERP implementation gone awry. *Production and Inventory Management Journal*, *43*, 96–105.

Gattiker, T. F., & Goodhue, D. L. (2005). What happens after ERP implementation: Understanding the impact of interdependence and differentiation on plant-level outcomes. *Management Information Systems Quarterly*, *29*(3), 559–585.

Gaved, M. B., & Mulholland, P. (2010). Networking communities from the bottom up: Grassroots approaches to overcoming the digital divide. *AI & Society*, *25*(3), 345–357. doi:10.1007/s00146-009-0259-5.

Gebert, H., Geib, M., Kolbe, L., & Brenner, W. (2003). Knowledge-enabled customer relationship management: Integrating customer relationship management and knowledge management concepts. *Journal of Knowledge Management*, *7*(5), 107–123. doi:10.1108/13673270310505421.

Gefen, D., Benbasat, I., & Pavlou, P. A. (2008). A research agenda for trust in online environments. *Journal of Management Information Systems*, *24*(4), 275–286. doi:10.2753/MIS0742-1222240411.

Gellman, R. (1996). Disintermediation and the internet. *Government Information Quarterly*, *1*, 1–8. doi:10.1016/S0740-624X(96)90002-7.

Getz, D. (1987). Tourism planning and research: Traditions, models and futures. In *Proceedings of the Australian Travel Workshop* (pp. 407-448). Bunbury, Australia: Australian Travel Workshop.

Ghorbel, M., & Mokhtari, M. (2005). Toward an assistive indoor/outdoor living environment for people with disabilities.[Boca Raton, FL: IOS Press.]. *Proceedings of ICOST*, *05*, 237–244.

Giaever, H. (1999). Collecting, storing and utilizing information about improvement opportunities: A discussion of the non-technological barriers to success. In *Proceedings of the 11th International Conference on Software Engineering & Knowledge Engineering*, (pp. 200-202). Kaiserslautern, Germany: IEEE.

Gigerenzer, G. (2004). Mindless statistics. *Journal of Socio-Economics*, *33*(5), 587–606. doi:10.1016/j.socec.2004.09.033.

Gilbert, D. C., Powell-Perry, J., & Widijoso, S. (1999). Approaches by hotels to the use of the Internet as a relationship marketing tool. *Journal of Marketing Practice: Applied Marketing Science*, *5*(1), 21–38. doi:10.1108/EUM0000000004549.

Gleanster. (2010). *Gleansight: Social media monitoring*. Gleanster, LLC

Gloor, P. A., Paasivaara, M., Schoder, D., & Willems, P. (2008). Finding collaborative innovation networks through correlating performance with social network structure. *International Journal of Production Research*, *46*(5), 1357–1371. doi:10.1080/00207540701224582.

Gluesing, J. C., & Riopelle, K. R. (2010). Correlating survey data and network data to understand performance in global virtual teams. *Procedia Social and Behavioral Sciences*, *2*, 6551–6560. doi:10.1016/j.sbspro.2010.04.065.

Goldman, J. et al. (1995). *Competitors and virtual organizations*. London: Van Nostrand Reinhold.

Goldsmith, R. E., & Lafferty, B. A. (2002). Consumer response to web sites and their influence on advertising effectiveness. *Internet Research*, *12*(4), 318–328. doi:10.1108/10662240210438407.

Goldstein, S. Z. (2006). Fast forward: Future trends in corporate communication: A checklist of top priorities for professionals in 2006. *Strategic Communication Management*, *10*(1), 14–17.

Gomez, R. (Ed.). (2012). *Libraries, telecenters, cybercafés and public access to ICT: International comparisons.* Hershey, PA: IGI Global.

Gomez, R., & Baron, L. F. (2011). Does public access computing really contribute to community development? Lessons from libraries, telecenters and cybercafés in Colombia. *Electronic Journal of Information Systems in Developing Countries, 49*(2), 1–11.

Gomis, J. M. (2005). *Tourism, distribution and IT: Strategic approach to the effects of a new paradigm on intermediation.* (Doctoral Thesis). Universitat de Barcelona, Barcelona, Spain.

Gomulka, S. (1990). *Theory of technological change and economic growth.* Florence, Italy: Routledge. doi:10.4324/9780203013052.

Gonzales, M. L., & Wells, D. L. (2006). *BI strategy: How to create and document.* Austin, TX: HandsOn-BI, LLC.

González, J., & Garazo, T. (2006). Structural relationships between organizational service orientation, contact employee job satisfaction and citizenship behavior. *International Journal of Service Industry Management, 17*(1), 23–50. doi:10.1108/09564230610651561.

Gonzalez, P., Sarkis, J., & Adenso-Diaz, B. (2008). Environmental management system certification and its influence on corporate practices: Evidence from the automotive industry. *International Journal of Operations & Production Management, 28*(11), 1021–1041. doi:10.1108/01443570810910179.

Goodman, P., & Penningss, J. (Eds.). (1977). *New perspectives on organizational effectiveness.* San Francisco, CA: Jossey-Bass.

Goodman, R. (1970). Organizational preference in research and development. *Human Relations, 23*(4), 279–298. doi:10.1177/001872677002300403.

Goodrich, K. (2011). Anarchy of effects? Exploring attention to online advertising and multiple outcomes. *Psychology and Marketing, 28,* 417–440. doi:10.1002/mar.20371.

Goodwin, C. (2007). *Getting through.* Retrieved October 25, 2011 from www.directmag.com

Goodwin, J., Dolbear, C., & Hart, G. (2008). Geographical linked data: The administrative geography of great britain on the semantic web. *Transactions in GIS, 12,* 19–30. doi:10.1111/j.1467-9671.2008.01133.x.

Gove, P. (Ed.). (2002). *Third new international dictionary of the English language.* Chicago: Merriam-Webster.

Govindarajan, V., & Trimple, C. (2010). *The other side of innovation.* Boston: Harvard Business Press.

Grabner-Kraeuter, S., & Waiguny, M. (2011). Why users stay in online social networks: Perceptions of value, trust, subjective norm and the moderating influence of duration of use. *American Marketing Association, 22*(1), 240-249.

Grabova, O., Darmont, J., Chauchat, J.-H., & Zolotaryova, I. (2010). Business intelligence for small and middle-sized entreprises. *SIGMOD Record, 39*(2), 39–50. doi:10.1145/1893173.1893180.

Grace, T. P. L. (2009). Wikis as a knowledge management tool. *Journal of Knowledge Management, 13*(4), 64–74. doi:10.1108/13673270910971833.

Graham, J. (1991). An essay on organizational citizenship behavior. *Employee Responsibilities and Rights Journal, 4*(4), 249–270. doi:10.1007/BF01385031.

Granovetter, M. (1973). The strength of weak ties. *American Journal of Sociology, 78*(6), 1360–1380. doi:10.1086/225469.

Granovetter, M. (1983). The strength of weak ties: A network theory revisited. *Sociological Theory, 1,* 201–233. doi:10.2307/202051.

Granovetter, M. S. (1973). The strength of weak ties. *American Journal of Sociology, 83,* 1420–1443. doi:10.1086/226707.

Granovetter, M. S. (1982). The strength of weak ties: A network theory revisited. In Marsden, P. V., & Lin, N. (Eds.), *Social structure and network analysis* (pp. 105–130). Beverly Hills, CA: Sage Publications.

Granovetter, M. S. (1992). Problems of explanation in economic sociology. In Nohria, N., & Eccles, R. G. (Eds.), *Networks and organizations: Structure, form, and action* (pp. 25–56). Boston, MA: Harvard Business School Press.

Granqvist, M. (2005). Looking critically at ICT4Dev: The case of Lincos. *The Journal of Community Informatics*, *2*(1).

Grant, R. (1996). Toward a knowledge-based theory of the firm. *Strategic Management Journal*, *17*, 109–122.

Gray, K., Thompson, C., Clerehan, R., Sheard, J., & Hamilton, M. (2011). Web 2.0 authorship: Issues of referencing and citation for academic integrity. *The Internet and Higher Education*, 112–118.

Gray, P. H., Parise, S., & Iyer, B. (2011). Innovation impacts of using social bookmarking systems. *Management Information Systems Quarterly*, *35*(3), 629–643.

Grebner, O., & Riss, U. (2008). Implicit metadata generation on the semantic desktop using task management as example. In *Proceedings of the Conference on Formal Ontologies Meet Industry* (pp. 33-44). Amsterdam: IOS Press.

Greenberg, G. (1998). Distance education technologies: Best practices for K-12 settings. *IEEE Technology and Society Magazine*, *17*, 36–40. doi:10.1109/44.735862.

Greenberg, P. (2010). *CRM at the speed of light: Social CRM strategies, tools, and techniques for engaging your customers* (4th ed.). New York: The McGraw-Hill Companies.

Greene, D. (1999). *Measuring what matters: The paths of intangible value*. Paper presented at the Institute for International Research. San Diego, CA.

Greene, C. (2009). *Entrepreneurship: Ideas in action*. Mason, GA: South-Western.

Griffith, T. L., & Neale, M. (2001). Information processing in traditional, hybrid, and virtual teams: From nascent knowledge to transactive memory. *Research in Organizational Behavior*, *23*, 379–421. doi:10.1016/S0191-3085(01)23009-3.

Griffith, T. L., Sawyer, J., & Neale, M. (2003). Virtualness and knowledge in teams: managing the love triangle of organizations, individuals, and information technology. *Management Information Systems Quarterly*, *27*(2), 265–287.

Grönroos, C. (1980). Designing a long range marketing strategy for services. *Long Range Planning*, *13*(2), 36–42. doi:10.1016/0024-6301(80)90030-8.

Grönroos, C. (1994). From marketing mix to relationship marketing: Towards a paradigm shift in marketing. *Management Decision*, *32*(2), 4–20. doi:10.1108/00251749410054774.

Grönroos, C. (1997). Keynote paper: From marketing mix to relationship marketing - Towards a paradigm shift in marketing. *Management Decision*, *35*(4), 322. doi:10.1108/00251749710169729.

Grönroos, C. (2006). On defining marketing: finding a new roadmap for marketing. *Marketing Theory*, *6*(4), 395–417. doi:10.1177/1470593106069930.

Grossbart, S., Muehling, D., & Kangun, N. (1986). Verbal and visual references to competition in comparative advertising. *Journal of Advertising*, *15*(1), 10–23. doi:10.1080/00913367.1986.10672984.

Grosseck, G. (2009). To use or not to use web 2.0 in higher education?. *Procedia - Social and Behavioral Sciences*, *1*(1), 478-482.

Grosser, K. (1991). Human networks in organizational information processing. *Annual Review of Information Science & Technology*, *26*, 349–402.

Gruban, B., Verčič, D., & Zavrl, F. (1997). *Pristop k odnosom z javnostmi*. Ljubljana, Slovenia: Pristop.

Gruber, T. (2008). Ontology. In Liu, L., & Ozsu, M. (Eds.), *Encyclopedia of Database Systems*. Berlin: Springer-Verlag.

Grunig, A. L., Grunig, E. J., & Dozier, M. D. (2002). *Inside the organization: Culture, structure, systems of internal communication, gender and diversity V: Excellent public relations and effective organizations*. Hoboken, NJ: Lawrence Erlbaum Associates, Inc..

Grunig, E. J., & Grunig, A. L. (2002). Implications of the IABC excellence study for PR education. *Journal of Communication Management*, *7*(1), 34–42. doi:10.1108/13632540310807232.

Grusky, O. (1963). Managerial succession and organizational effectiveness. *American Journal of Sociology*, *69*(1), 21–31. doi:10.1086/223507.

Guarino, N. (Ed.). (1998). *Formal ontology in information systems: Proceedings of the first international conference (FOIS'98).* IOS.

Guenzi, P., Georges, L., & Pardo, C. (2009). The impact of strategic account managers' behaviors on relational outcomes: An empirical study. *Industrial Marketing Management*, *38*, 300–311. doi:10.1016/j.indmarman.2007.09.011.

Gummesson, E. (1987). The new marketing - Developing long-term interactive relationships. *Long Range Planning*, *20*(4), 10–20. doi:10.1016/0024-6301(87)90151-8.

Gummesson, E. (1997). Relationship marketing as a paradigm shift: Some conclusions from the 30R approach. *Management Decision*, *35*(4), 267. doi:10.1108/00251749710169648.

Gummesson, E. (1998). Implementation requires a relationship marketing paradigm. *Journal of the Academy of Marketing Science*, *26*(3), 242–249. doi:10.1177/0092070398263006.

Gummesson, E. (2008). *Total relationship marketing* (3rd ed.). Oxford, UK: Butterworth-Heinemann.

Gunasekaran, C., & Tirtiroglu, E. (2001). Performance measures and metrics in a supply chain environment. *International Journal of Operations & Production Management*, *21*(1/2), 71–87. doi:10.1108/01443570110358468.

Gunn, C. (1972). *Vacationscape: Designing tourist regions*. Austin, TX: University of Texas.

Gupta, J., & Sushil, S. (2004). *Creating knowledge based organizations*. Hershey, PA: Idea Group Publishing.

Gurumurthy, A., & Kodali, R. (2009). Application of benchmarking for assessing the lean manufacturing implementation. *Benchmarking: An International Journal*, *16*(2), 274–308. doi:10.1108/14635770910948268.

Guttentag, D. A. (2010). Virtual reality: Applications and implications for tourism. *Tourism Management*, *31*(5), 637–651. doi:10.1016/j.tourman.2009.07.003.

Guzzo, R. A., & Dickson, M. W. (1996). Teams in organizations: Recent research on performance and effectiveness. *Annual Review of Psychology*, *47*, 307–338. doi:10.1146/annurev.psych.47.1.307 PMID:15012484.

Hackman, R., & Oldham, G. (1975). Development of the job diagnostic survey. *The Journal of Applied Psychology*, *60*(2), 150–170. doi:10.1037/h0076546.

Hackman, R., & Oldham, G. (1976). Motivation through the design of work: A test of a theory. *Organizational Behavior and Human Performance*, *16*(2), 250–279. doi:10.1016/0030-5073(76)90016-7.

Haenlein, M., & Kaplan, A. (2010). Users of the world, unite! The challenges and opportunities of social media. *Business Horizons*, *53*(1), 59–68. doi:10.1016/j.bushor.2009.09.003.

Hagel, J., & Brown, J. S. (2010). *The enterprise value of social software*. Retrieved September 1, 2011, from http://blogs.hbr.org

Hagel, J. III, Brown, J. S., & Davidson, L. (2010). *The power of pull: How small moves, smartly made, can set big things in motion*. New York: Basic Books.

Haimes, Y. (2006). On the definition of vulnerabilities in measuring risks to infrastructures. *Risk Analysis: An Official Publication of the Society for Risk Analysis*, *26*(2), 293–296. doi:10.1111/j.1539-6924.2006.00755.x PMID:16573621.

Hair, J. F., Ringle, C. M., & Sarstedt, M. (2011). PLS-SEM: Indeed a silver bullet. *Journal of Marketing Theory and Practice*, *19*(2), 139–151. doi:10.2753/MTP1069-6679190202.

Haislip, A. (2006). Question of the day: What's your MySpace strategy? *Venture Capital Journal*, *46*(9), 3–6.

Halic, O., Lee, D., Paulus, T., & Spence, M. (2010). To blog or not to blog: Student perceptions of blog effectiveness for learning in a college-level course. *The Internet and Higher Education*, *13*(4), 206–213. doi:10.1016/j.iheduc.2010.04.001.

Hall, J., Nilsson, J., & Nivre, J. (n.d.). Single malt or blended? A study in multilingual parser optimization. *Trends in Parsing Technology*, (pp. 19-33). Academic Press.

Hall, C. M. (2000). *Tourism planning: Policies, processes and relationships*. Harlow, MA: Pearson Education.

Hall, R., & Clark, J. (1980). An ineffective effectiveness study and some suggestions for future research. *The Sociological Quarterly*, *21*, 119–134. doi:10.1111/j.1533-8525.1980.tb02203.x.

Hammond, K., Mcwilliam, G., & Narholz, A. (1998). Fun and work on the web: Differences in attitudes between novices and experienced users. *Advances in Consumer Research. Association for Consumer Research (U. S.)*, *25*, 372–378.

Ham, S., Kim, W. G., & Jeong, S. (2004). Effect of information technology on performance in upscale hotels. *International Journal of Hospitality Management*, *24*, 281–294. doi:10.1016/j.ijhm.2004.06.010.

Han, K. H., Yoon, D., & Cameron, G. T. (2001). *Web users' attitude and behavior toward online coupons*. Paper presented at 2001 Annual Conference of American Academy of Advertising. New York, NY.

Handy, C. (1995). Trust and the virtual organization. *Harvard Business Review*, *73*(3), 40–50.

Hanneman, R. A., & Riddle, M. (2005). Introduction to social network methods.[). IEEE.]. *Network*, *1*, 1–322.

Hansen, M. T., Nohria, N., & Tierney, T. (1999, March-April). What's your strategy for managing knowledge? *Harvard Business Review*, 106–116.

Hans, J. S., & Klischewski, R. (2007). E-government integration and interoperability: Framing the research agenda. *International Journal of Public Administration*, *30*(8-9), 889–920. doi:10.1080/01900690701402668.

Hanson, K. O. (2011). The long history of conscious capitalism: A response to James O'Toole and David Vogel's "Two and a half cheers for conscious capitalism". *California Management Review*, *53*(3), 77–83. doi:10.1525/cmr.2011.53.3.77.

Hao, W., Jhat, S., Livny, M., & McDaniel, P. D. (2004). Security policy reconciliation in distributed computing environments. In *Proceedings of the 5th IEEE International Workshop on Policies for Distributed Systems and Networks (POLICY'04)* (pp. 137-146). IEEE.

Hardy, Q., Pomerantz, D., & Hill, K. (2010). In mark we trust. *Forbes*, *186*(6), 80–86.

Harker, M. J. (1999). Relationship marketing defined? An examination of current relationship marketing definitions. *Marketing Intelligence & Planning*, *17*(1), 13–20. doi:10.1108/02634509910253768.

Harker, M. J., & Egan, J. (2006). The past, present and future of relationship marketing. *Journal of Marketing Management*, *22*(1-2), 215–242. doi:10.1362/026725706776022326.

Hars, A., & Qu, S. (2002). Working for free? Motivations for participating in open-source projects. *International Journal of Electronic Commerce*, *6*(3), 25.

Harvard Business Review Analytic Services. (2010). *The new conversation: Taking social media from talk to action*. Boston: Harvard Business School Publishing.

Harvey, M., Novicevic, M. M., & Garrison, G. (2004). Challenges to staffing global virtual teams. *Human Resource Management Review*, *14*, 275–294. doi:10.1016/j.hrmr.2004.06.005.

Harzing, A. W. (2007). *Publish or perish*. Retrieved from http://www.harzing.com/pop.htm

Hauser, C. H., Bakken, D. E., Dionysiou, I., Gjermundrod, H. K., Irava, V. S., Helkey, J., & Bose, A. (2008). Security, trust and QoS in next-generation control and communication for large power system. *International Journal of Critical Infrastructures*, *4*(1/2), 3–16. doi:10.1504/IJCIS.2008.016088.

Hay, R., & Gray, E. (1974). Social responsibilities of business managers. *Academy of Management Journal*, *17*(1), 135–143. doi:10.2307/254777.

Haythornthwaite, C. (2005). *Social network methods and measures for examining e-learning*. Graduate School of Library and Information Science.

Healey, J., & Prus, S. (2009). *Statistics: A tool for social research* (First Canadian Edition). Cengage Learning.

Hearn, G., Foth, M., & Gray, H. (2009). Applications and implementations of new media in corporate communications: An action research approach. *Corporate Communications*, *14*(1), 49–61. doi:10.1108/13563280910931072.

Hebert, R., & Link, A. (1989). In search of the meaning of entrepreneurship. *Small Business Economics, 1*(1), 39–49. doi:10.1007/BF00389915.

He, D. D., & Yang, J. (2009). Authorization control in collaborative healthcare systems. *Journal of Theoretical and Applied Electronic Commerce Research, 4*(2), 88–109.

Heeks, R., & León, K. L. (2009). *Remoteness, exclusion and telecentres in mountain regions: Analysing ICT-based information chains in Pazos, Peru*. Manchester, UK: Centre for Development Informatics. Retrieved November, 12, 2011, from http://www.sed.manchester.ac.uk/idpm/research/publications/wp/di/documents/di_wp38.pdf

Heiler, S. (1995). Semantic interoperability. *ACM Computing Surveys, 27*(2), 271–273. doi:10.1145/210376.210392.

Heinonen, K. (2006). Temporal and spatial e-service value. *International Journal of Service Industry Management, 17*(4), 380–400. doi:10.1108/09564230610680677.

Heinonen, K., & Strandvick, T. (2005). Communication as an element of service value. *International Journal of Service Industry Management, 16*(2), 186–198. doi:10.1108/09564230510592306.

Heiskanen, E., Hyysalo, S., Kotro, T., & Repo, P. (2010). Constructing innovative users and user-inclusive innovation communities. *Technology Analysis and Strategic Management, 22*(4), 495–511. doi:10.1080/09537321003714568.

Helms, R., & Buijsrogge, K. (2005). *Knowledge network analysis: A technique to analyze knowledge management bottlenecks in organizations*. Paper presented at the Sixteenth International Workshop on Database and Expert Systems Applications. New York, NY.

Hemetsberger, A., & Reinhardt, C. (2009). Collective development in open-source communities: An activity theoretical perspective on successful online collaboration. *Organization Studies, 30*(9), 987–1008. doi:10.1177/0170840609339241.

Hempel, J., & Kowitt, B. (2009). How Facebook is taking over our lives. *Fortune International, 159*(4), 34–41.

Henseler, J., Ringle, C. M., & Sinkovics, R. (2009). The use of partial least squares path modelling in international marketing. *Advances in International Marketing, 20*, 277–319. doi:10.1108/S1474-7979(2009)0000020014.

Herget, J., & Mader, I. (2009). Social software in external corporate communications - A conceptional approach towards measuring, assessment and optimization of web 2.0 activity. *Information-Wissenschaft und Praxis, 60*(4), 233–240.

Herrero, A. (2005). *El proceso de adopción de nuevos sistemas de venta: Aplicación al comercio electrónico entre particulares y empresas*. Cantabria, Spain: Departamento de Administración de Empresas, Universidad de Cantabria.

Hertel, G., Geister, S., & Konradt, U. (2005). Managing virtual teams: A review of current empirical research. *Human Resource Management Review, 15*, 69–95. doi:10.1016/j.hrmr.2005.01.002.

Hertel, G., Konradt, U., & Orlikowski, B. (2004). Managing distance by interdependence: Goal setting, task interdependence, and team-based rewards in virtual teams. *European Journal of Work and Organizational Psychology, 13*(1), 1–28. doi:10.1080/13594320344000228.

Hickson, D., Hinings, C., Lee, C., Schneck, R., & Pennings, J. (1971). A strategic contingencies' theory of interorganizational power. *Administrative Science Quarterly, 16*(3), 216–229. doi:10.2307/2391831.

Hienerth, C. (2006). The commercialization of user innovations: The development of the rodeo kayak industry. *R & D Management, 36*(3), 273–294. doi:10.1111/j.1467-9310.2006.00430.x.

Highsmith, J. (2004). *Agile project management: Creating innovative products*. Redwood City, CA: Addison Wesley Longman Publishing Co., Inc..

Hiltz, S. R., & Turoff, M. (1993). *The network nation* (Revised Ed.). Cambridge, MA: MIT Press.

Hinchcliffe, D. (2007). *The state of enterprise 2.0*. Retrieved September 1, 2011, from http://www.zdnet.com

Hinchcliffe, D. (2011). *Integration and connection to work are central to social business success*. Retrieved September 15, 2011, from http://www.ebizq.net

Hinds, D., & Lee, R. M. (2008). Social network structure as a critical success condition for virtual communities. In *Proceedings of the 41st Annual Hawaii International Conference on System Sciences (HICSS'08)*. Waikoloa, HI.

Hinton, P. R., Brownlow, C., McMurray, I., & Cozens, B. (2004). *SPSS explained*. London: Routledge Taylor & Francis Group.

Hirota, K., & Pedrycz, W. (1999). Fuzzy computing for data mining. *Proceedings of the IEEE*, *87*(9), 1575–1600. doi:10.1109/5.784240.

Hirschman, E., & Holbrook, M. (1982). Hedonic consumption: Emerging concepts, methods and propositions. *Journal of Marketing*, *46*(2), 92–101. doi:10.2307/1251707.

Hix, B. (2011). Seniors, mobile communication, and health care. Boca Raton, FL: 3CInteractive, LLC.

Ho, G., Lau, H., Chung, S., Fung, R., & Chan, T. (2008). Fuzzy rule sets for enhancing performance in a supply chain network. *Industrial Management + Data Systems*, *108*(7), 947-972.

Hoang, H., & Antoncic, B. (2003). Network-based research in entrepreneurship: A critical review. *Journal of Business Venturing*, *18*(2), 165–187. doi:10.1016/S0883-9026(02)00081-2.

Hobson, S., Anand, R., Yang, J., Lee, J., Campos, P., Graham, N., et al. (2011). Towards interoperability in municipal government: A study of information sharing practices. In Human-Computer Interaction – INTERACT 2011 (Vol. 6946, pp. 233-247). Springer. doi:10.1007/978-3-642-23774-4_21.

Hoek, V., Harrison, A., & Christopher, M. (2001). Measuring agile capabilities in the supply chain. *International Journal of Operations & Production Management*, *21*(1/2), 126–148. doi:10.1108/01443570110358495.

Hoffman, D. L. (2000). The revolution will not be televised: Introduction to the special issue on marketing science and the internet. *Marketing Science*, *19*(1), 1–3. doi:10.1287/mksc.19.1.1.15181.

Hoffman, D. L., & Novak, T. P. (1996). Marketing in hypermedia computer-mediated environments: Conceptual foundations. *Journal of Marketing*, *60*(3), 50–69. doi:10.2307/1251841.

Hoffman, D. L., & Novak, T. P. (2000). How to acquire customers on the web. *Harvard Business Review*, *78*(3), 179–188. PMID:11183979.

Hofstede, G., & Pedersen, P. (2004). *Cultures and organizations*. New York: McGraw-Hill.

Hogben, G. (2007). Security issues and recommendations for online social networks. ENISA European Network and Information Security Agency, 80211(1).

Ho, J. Y. C., & Dempsey, M. (2010). Viral marketing: Motivations to forward online content. *Journal of Business Research*, *63*(9-10), 1000–1006. doi:10.1016/j.jbusres.2008.08.010.

Holbrook, M. B., & Gardner, M. P. (1993). An approach to investigating the emotional determinants of consumption duration, why do people consume what they consume for as long as they consume it? *Journal of Consumer Psychology*, *2*(2), 123–142. doi:10.1016/S1057-7408(08)80021-6.

Holloway, J. C. (2002). *The business of tourism* (6th ed.). London: Prentice Hall.

Holt, D., & Ghobadian, A. (2009). An empirical study of green supply chain management practices amongst UK manufacturers. *Journal of Manufacturing Technology Management*, *20*(7), 933–956. doi:10.1108/17410380910984212.

Holtz, S. (2002). *Public relations on the internet*. New York: Amazon.

Honeycutt, A., & Richards, B. (1989). An organizational transformation model: The road to renewal. *Educational Technology*, *29*(10), 42–45.

Ho, S., Kauffman, R. J., & Liang, T. (2007). A growth theory perspective on B2C e-commerce growth in Europe: An exploratory study. *Electronic Commerce Research and Applications*, *6*, 237–259. doi:10.1016/j.elerap.2006.06.003.

Hossain, L., & Zhu, D. (2009). Social networks and coordination performance of distributed software development teams. *The Journal of High Technology Management Research*, *20*(1), 52–61. doi:10.1016/j.hitech.2009.02.007.

Houaiss, A., & Villar, M. S. (2001). *Dicionário houaiss de língua portuguesa*. Rio de Janeiro: Objetiva.

Hounshell, B. (2011). The revolution will be tweeted. *Foreign Policy*, (187): 20–21.

House, R. (1971). A path goal theory of leader effectiveness. *Administrative Science Quarterly, 16*(3), 321–339. doi:10.2307/2391905.

House, R. (1980). *Evaluating with validity*. Beverly Hills, CA: Sage Publications.

House, R. J. (1977). A 1976 theory of charismatic leadership. In Hunt, J. G., & Larsons, L. L. (Eds.), *Leadership: The cutting edge* (pp. 189–207). Carbondale, IL: Southern Illinois University Press.

Howard, J. A., & Sheth, J. N. (1969). *The theory of buyer behavior*. New York: Wiley.

Howell, J. M., & Avolio, B. J. (1993). Transformational leadership, transactional leadership, locus of control, and support for innovation: Key predictors of consolidated-business-unit performance. *The Journal of Applied Psychology, 78*(6), 891–911. doi:10.1037/0021-9010.78.6.891.

Hozjan, T. (2010). *Spletne skupnosti kot orodja odnosov z javnostmi*. Ljubljana, Slovenia: Fakulteta za družbene vede.

Hsieh, J. J. P. A., & Wang, W. (2007). Explaining employees' extended use of complex information systems. *European Journal of Information Systems, 16*(3), 216–227. doi:10.1057/palgrave.ejis.3000663.

Hu, A., & Hsu, C. (2006). Empirical study in the critical factors of green supply chain management (GSCM), practice in the Taiwanese electrical and electronics industries. In *Proceeding of 2006 IEEE International Conference on Management of Innovation and Technology*. Singapore: IEEE.

Huang, R., Kahai, S., & Jestice, R. (2010). The contingent effects of leadership on team collaboration in virtual teams. *Computers in Human Behavior, 26*, 1098–1110. doi:10.1016/j.chb.2010.03.014.

Huang, S.-L., & Yang, C.-W. (2009). Designing a semantic bliki system to support different types of knowledge and adaptive learning. *Computers & Education, 53*(3), 701–712. doi:10.1016/j.compedu.2009.04.011.

Hubbard, D. W. (2010). *How to measure anything - Finding the value of intangibles in business* (2nd ed.). Hoboken, NJ: John Wiley & Sons, Inc..

Huber, J. T., Walsh, T. J., & Varman, B. (2005). Camp for all connection: A community health information outreach project. *Journal of the Medical Library Association, 93*(3), 348–352. PMID:16059424.

Huffaker, D. (2005). The educated blogger: Using weblogs to promote literacy in the classroom. *AACE Journal, 13*(2), 91–98.

Huisman, M., & van Duijn, M. A. J. (2003). Software for social network analysis. *Social Science Research, 27*, 270–316.

Hull, R. (2008). Lecture Notes in Computer Science: *Vol. 5332. Artifact-centric business process models: Brief survey of research results and challenges* (pp. 1152–1163). Heidelberg: Springer. doi:10.1007/978-3-540-88873-4_17.

Hurlbert, J. S. (2001). Social networks, social circles, and job satisfaction. *Work and Occupations, 18*(4), 415–430. doi:10.1177/0730888491018004003.

Huston, L., & Sakkab, N. (2006, March). Connect and develop: Inside Procter & Gamble's new model for innovation. *Harvard Business Review*, 1–9.

Hutley, R. (2009). *Social networking as a business tool*. Cisco Internet Business Solutions Group.

Hwang, H.-G., Ku, C.-Y., Yen, D. V., & Cheng, C.-C. (2004). Critical factors influencing the adoption of data warehouse technology: A study of the banking industry in Taiwan. *Decision Support Systems, 37*(1), 1–21. doi:10.1016/S0167-9236(02)00191-4.

Hwang, J., Altman, J., & Kim, K. (2009). The structural evolution of the web 2.0 service network. *Online Information Review, 33*(6), 1040–1057. doi:10.1108/14684520911010990.

Hwang, M. I., & Lin, J. W. (1999). Information dimension, information overload and decision quality. *Journal of Information Science, 25*(3), 213–218. doi:10.1177/016555159902500305.

IAB. (2010). *Interactive advertising bureau.* Retrieved from www.iab.net

Iakovou, E., Vlachos, D., & Xanthopoulos, A. (2007). An analytical methodological framework for the optimal design of resilient supply chains. *International Journal of Logistics Economics and Globalisation*, *1*(1), 1–20. doi:10.1504/IJLEG.2007.014498.

IBM. (2006). *The global innovation outlook.* Armonk, NY: IBM.

IBM. (2009). *The new voice of the CIO.* Retrieved from http://www-935.ibm.com/services/us/cio/ciostudy/

Ihator, S. A. (2001). Communication style in the information age. *School of Journalism and Broadcasting*, *6*(4), 199–204.

Ilyinska, L. (2004). *English for science and technology: Course design, text analysis, research writing.* RTU Publishing House.

In Goldsmith, R. E., & Lafferty, B. A. (2002). Consumer response to web sites and their influence on advertising effectiveness. *Internet Research*, *12*(4), 318–328. doi:10.1108/10662240210438407.

Inche, J. L. (1998). Modelos de innovación tecnológica. *Industrial Data*, *1*(2), 9–16.

INE. (2010). *Encuesta de Tecnologías de la Información en los hogares 2010.* Retrieved from www.ine.es

Information Security Forum (ISF). (2007). *The standard of good practice for information security.* ISF.

Information Systems Security Association (ISSA). (2004). *Generally accepted information security principles.* GAISP.

Inmon, B. (2002). *Building the data warehouse* (3rd ed.). New York: Wiley and Sons.

Insiti, M. (2007). ERP end-users business productivity: A field study of SAP & Microsoft. *Keystone Strategy Research 2007.* Retrieved June 12, 2010, from http://download.microsoft.com

International Data Corporation (IDC). (2008). The hyperconnected: Here they come! A global look at the exploding 'culture of connectivity' and its impact on the enterprise. *Framingham USA/MA.* Retrieved February 9, 2012, from www.nortel.com/hyperconnectivity/idc/hyperconnectivity_idc.pdf

International Telecommunication Union. (2005). *Information technology – Open systems interconnection – The directory: Public-key and attribute certificate frameworks.* ITU-T Recommendation X.509. Retrieved November 29, 2010, from http://www.itu.int/rec/T-REC-X.509-200508-I

Internet World Stats. (2011). *Internet users in the world.* Retrieved from http://www.Internetworldstats.com/stats.htm

Ireland, R., & Hitt, M. (1997). Performance strategies for high growth entrepreneurial firms. *Frontiers of Entrepreneurship Research*, *9*(1), 101–104.

Iriana, R., & Buttle, F. (2005). *Strategic, operational and analytical customer relationship management: Attributes and measures (No. MGSM WP 2005-1).* Macquarie Graduate School of Management.

Iriberri, A., & Leroy, G. (2009). A life-cycle perspective on online community success. *ACM Computing Surveys*, *41*(2). doi:10.1145/1459352.1459356.

Ismail, H. S., & Sharifi, H. (2006). A balanced approach to building agile supply chains. *International Journal of Physical Distribution & Logistics Management*, *36*(6), 431–444. doi:10.1108/09600030610677384.

ISO/IEC 27002. (2005). *Information technology - Security techniques - Code of practice for information security management.* ISO/IEC.

Israel, D. (2009). *Data analysis in business research: A step-by-step nonparametric approach.* Thousand Oaks, CA: Sage Publications Pvt. Ltd..

Itmazi, J., Megías, M. G., Paderewski, P., & Gutiérrez, F. L. (2005). *A comparison and evaluation of open source learning management systems*. Paper presented at the IADIS International Conference on Applied Computing. Retrieved September 21, 2011, from http://www.iadis.net/dl/final_uploads/200501C014.pdf

Ives, B., & Gersting, A. (1998, February/March). Implementing knowledge management – Lessons learned. *Knowledge Management*.

Jabbour, K. K. (2011). Web 2.0 tecnology tools for global education in Lebanon. *International Journal of Advanced Engineering Sciences and Technologies*, *7*(1), 151–168.

Jackson, B. (1985). Building customer relationships that last: How close can industrial markets get to their customers - And for how long? *Harvard Business Review*, *63*, 120.

Jain, A. K., Ross, A., & Pankanti, S. (2006). Biometrics: A tool for information security. *IEEE Transactions on Information Forensics and Security*, *1*(2), 125–144. doi:10.1109/TIFS.2006.873653.

Jankowski, N. W. (2009). Creating community with media: History, theories and scientific investigations. In Lievrouw, L. A., & Livingstone, S. M. (Eds.), *Handbook of new media: Social shaping and social consequences of ICT's* (pp. 55–74). Los Angeles, CA: Sage.

Jarvenpaa, S. L., & Leidner, D. E. (1999). Communication and trust in global virtual teams. *Organization Science*, *10*(6), 791–815. doi:10.1287/orsc.10.6.791.

Jarvis, J. (2012). *BuzzMachine*. Retrieved from http://buzzmachine.com/archives/cat_dell.html

Jaspersoft. (2011). *Jaspersoft*. Retrieved from http://www.jaspersoft.com/ Jedox/Palo. (2011). *Open source business intelligence*. Retrieved from http://www.jedox.com/

JavaHispano. (2011, November 15). *Tu lenguaje, tu comunidad*. Retrieved from http://javaHispano.org

Jennings, M. (2005). *Business: Its legal, ethical and global environment*. Brentford, UK: SW Pub..

Jeppesen, L. B., & Frederiksen, L. (2006). Why do users contribute to firm-hosted user communities? The case of computer-controlled music instruments. *Organization Science*, *17*(1), 45–63. doi:10.1287/orsc.1050.0156.

Jiang, Y., Raghupathi, V., & Raghupathi, W. (2009). Content and design of corporate governance web sites. *Information Systems Management*, *26*(1), 13–27. doi:10.1080/10580530802384704.

Jie, W., Arshad, J., Sinnott, R., Townend, P., & Lei, Z. (2011). A review of grid authentication and authorization technologies and support for federated access control. *ACM Computing Surveys*, *43*(2), 12:1-12:26.

Jin, Y., Matsuo, Y., & Ishizuka, M. (2007). Extracting social networks among various entities on the web. In E. Franconi, M. Kifer, & W. May (Eds.), *Proceedings of the Fourth European Semantic Web Conference* (Vol. 4519, pp. 251-266). Springer.

Johnson, E. J., Bellman, S., & Lohse, G. L. (2003). Cognitive lock-in and the power law of practice. *Journal of Marketing*, *67*, 62–75. doi:10.1509/jmkg.67.2.62.18615.

Johnson, P. (2006). Whence democracy? A review and critique of the conceptual dimensions and implications of the business case for organizational democracy. *Organization*, *13*(2), 245–274. doi:10.1177/1350508406061676.

Johnson, P., Heimann, V., & O'Neill, K. (2001). The wonderland of virtual teams. *Journal of Workplace Learning*, *13*(1), 24–29. doi:10.1108/13665620110364745.

Johnston, D., Pan, E., Walker, J., Bates, D. W., & Middleton, B. (2003). *The value of computerized provider order entry in ambulatory settings*. Wellesley, MA: Center for Information Technology Leadership.

Jones, J. (2008). An exploratory study on attitude persistence using sales promotion. *Journal of Managerial Issues*, *20*(3), 401–417.

Jones, M. (2006). Which is a better predictor of job performance: Job satisfaction or life satisfaction? *Journal of Behavioral and Applied Management*, *8*(1), 20–42.

Jordá, C. (2008). Impacto ambiental del transporte aéreo y de las infraestructuras aeroportuarias. *Ingeniería y Territorio*, *83*, 26–33.

Jordan, J., & Ellen, C. (2009). Business need, data and business intelligence. *Journal of Digital Asset Management*, *5*(1). doi:10.1057/dam.2008.53.

Joshi, J. B. D., Bertino, E., Latif, U., & Ghafoo, A. (2005). A generalized temporal role-based access control model. *Journal of IEEE Transactions on Knowledge and Data Engineering*, *15*, 4–23. doi:10.1109/TKDE.2005.1.

Joshi, K., & Curtis, M. (1999). Issues in building a successful data warehouse. *Information Strategy: The Executive's Journal*, *15*(2), 28–35.

Judge, T., Parker, S., Colbert, A., Heller, D., & Remus, I. (2001). Job satisfaction: A cross-cultural review. In Anderson, N., Ones, D., Sinangil, H., & Viswesvaran, C. (Eds.), *Handbook of Industrial, Work and Organizational Psychology* (*Vol. 2*, pp. 25–52). London: Sage Publications.

Junco, R., & Cotten, S. R. (2011). Perceived academic effects of instant messaging use. *Computers & Education*, *56*(2), 370–378. doi:10.1016/j.compedu.2010.08.020.

Jung, D. I., Chow, C., & Wu, A. (2003). The role of transformational leadership in enhancing organisational innovation: Hypotheses and some preliminary findings. *The Leadership Quarterly*, *14*, 525–544. doi:10.1016/S1048-9843(03)00050-X.

Jung, K., & Lee, B. Y. (2010). Online vs. offline coupon redemption behaviors. *International Business & Economics Research Journal*, *9*(12), 23–36.

JupiterResearch. (2011). *Jupiter research report 2006-2011*. Retrieved from www.jupiterresearch.com

Kahneman, D., & Tversky, A. (1984). Choices, values and frames. *The American Psychologist*, *39*, 341–350. doi:10.1037/0003-066X.39.4.341.

Kaldis, K., & Kaldis, E. (2008). Emmantina and Palmira beach hotels: Distribution for independent hotels. In Egger, R., & Buhalis, D. (Eds.), *eTourism: Case studies* (pp. 65–73). Oxford: Butterworth Heinemann - Elsevier.

Kalkan, V. D. (2008). An overall view of knowledge management challenges for global business. *Business Process Management Journal*, *14*(3), 390–400. doi:10.1108/14637150810876689.

Kalla, K. H. (2005). Integrated internal communications: a multidisciplinary perspective. *Corporate Communications: An International Journal*, *10*(4), 302–314. doi:10.1108/13563280510630106.

Kanigel, R. (1999). *The one best way: Frederick Winslow Taylor and the enigma of efficiency*. New York: Viking.

Kanter, R. M. (1983). *The change masters: Corporate enterpreneurs at work*. London: Routledge.

Kaplan, J., & Warren, A. (2009). *Patterns of entrepreneurship management*. New York: Wiley.

Kardoff, E. (2004). Qualitative evaluation research. In Flick, U., Von Kardoff, E., & Steinke, I. (Eds.), *A Companion to Qualitative Research* (pp. 137–142). London: SAGE.

Karjaluoto, H., Mattila, M., & Pento, T. (2002). Factors underlying attitude formation toward online banking in Finland. *International Journal of Bank Marketing*, *20*(6), 261–272. doi:10.1108/02652320210446724.

Kathleen, C. (2003). *Dynamic social network modeling and analysis: Workshop summary and papers*. Washington, DC: National Academy Press.

Katz, D., & Kahn, R. (1987). *Psicologia social das organizações* (3rd ed.). São Paulo, Brazil: Editora Atlas.

Katz, R. (Ed.). (2003). *The human side of managing technological innovation*. Oxford, UK: Oxford University Press.

Kaye, A. R. (1992). Collaborative learning through computer conferencing. In Kaye, A. (Ed.), *Computer Conference and Content Analysis* (pp. 117–136). Springer Verlag.

Kayworth, T. R., & Leidner, D. E. (2000). The global virtual manager: A prescription for success. *European Management Journal*, *18*(2), 183–194. doi:10.1016/S0263-2373(99)00090-0.

Kayworth, T. R., & Leidner, D. E. (2001). Leadership effectiveness in global virtual teams. *Journal of Management Information Systems*, *18*(3), 7–40.

Kear, K., Woodthorpe, J., Robertson, S., & Hutchison, M. (2010). From forums to wikis: Perspectives on tools for collaboration. *The Internet and Higher Education*, *13*(4), 218–225. doi:10.1016/j.iheduc.2010.05.004.

Keating, E., Nagai, E., Hadder, N., & Kowalsky, J. (2007). *The role of the mobile phone in the welfare of aged and disabled people*. Austin, TX: University of Texas / NTT DoCoMo, Inc..

Kekes, J. (1989). *Moral tradition and individuality*. Princeton, NJ: Princeton University Press.

Kelley, H. (2001). *Attributional analysis of computer self-efficacy*. (Unpublished doctoral dissertation). Richard Ivey School of Business, London, UK.

Kelley, D. (2009). Adaptation and organizational connectedness in corporate innovation programs. *Journal of Product Innovation Management*, *26*(5), 487–501. doi:10.1111/j.1540-5885.2009.00676.x.

Kelly, S. (1997). Data marts: The latest silver bullet. *Data Mart Review*, 12-16.

Kennedy, G. E., Judd, T. S., Churchward, A., Gray, K., & Krause, K. L. (2008). First year students' experiences with technology: Are they really digital natives? *Australasian Journal of Educational Technology*, *24*(1), 108–122.

Kermarrec, A.-M., Le Merrer, E., Sericola, B., & Trédan, G. (2011). Second order centrality: Distributed assessment of nodes criticity in complex networks. *Computer Communications*, *34*(5), 619–628. doi:10.1016/j.comcom.2010.06.007.

Kerzner, H. (2010). *Project management best practices: Achieving global excellence* (2nd ed.). Hoboken, NJ: John Wiley and Sons, Inc..

Ke, W., & Zhang, P. (2009). Motivations in open source software communities: The mediating role of effort intensity and goal commitment. *International Journal of Electronic Commerce*, *13*(4), 39–66. doi:10.2753/JEC1086-4415130403.

Khan, Z. H. (2010). *ICT and the changing face of higher education.* Paper presented at the International Conclave of Scientists on Regional Cooperation in Science & Technology: Opportunities and Challenges in the Context of Globalization. New Delhi, India.

Khan, A. (2002). *Implementing SAP with an ASAP methodology focus*. San Jose, CA: Writers Club Press.

Kimball, R., & Ross, M. (2002). *The data warehouse toolkit: The complete guide to dimensional modeling* (2nd ed.). New York: John Wiley and Sons.

Kim, D. H. (1993). The link between individual and organisational learning. *Sloan Management Review*, *35*(1), 37–50.

Kim, H. N. (2008). The phenomenon of blogs and theoretical model of blog use in educational contexts. *Computers & Education*, *51*(3), 1342–1352. doi:10.1016/j.compedu.2007.12.005.

Kim, S.-Y., Jung, T.-S., Suh, E.-H., & Hwang, H.-S. (2006). Customer segmentation and strategy development based on customer lifetime value: A case study. *Expert Systems with Applications*, *31*, 101–107. doi:10.1016/j.eswa.2005.09.004.

King, M. F., & Balasubramanian, S. K. (1994). The effects of expertise, end goal, and product type on adoption of preference formation strategy. *Journal of the Academy of Marketing Science*, *22*(2), 146–159. doi:10.1177/0092070394222004.

Kirkman, B. L., & Mathieu, J. E. (2005). The dimensions and antecedents of team virtuality. *Journal of Management*, *31*(5), 700–718. doi:10.1177/0149206305279113.

Kirkman, B. L., & Rosen, B. (2000). Powering up teams. *Organizational Dynamics*, *28*(3), 48–66. doi:10.1016/S0090-2616(00)88449-1.

Kirkman, B. L., Rosen, B., Gibson, C. B., Tesluk, P. E., & McPherson, S. O. (2002). Five challenges to virtual success: Lessons from Sabre, Inc. *The Academy of Management Executive*, *16*(3), 67–79. doi:10.5465/AME.2002.8540322.

Kirkman, B. L., Rosen, B., Tesluk, P. E., & Gibson, C. B. (2004). The impact of team empowerment on virtual team performance: The moderating role of face-to-face interaction. *Academy of Management Journal*, *47*(2), 175–192. doi:10.2307/20159571.

Kitchen, P. (1997). *Public relations: Principles and practice*. London: International Thomson Business Press.

Kitsak, M., Gallos, L. K., Havlin, S., Liljeros, F., Muchnik, L., Stanley, H. E., & Makse, H. A. (2010). Identification of influential spreaders in complex networks. *Nature Physics*, *6*(11), 888–893. doi:10.1038/nphys1746.

Kleinberg, J. M. (1999). Hubs, authorities, and communities. *ACM Computing Surveys*, *31*(4), 5. doi:10.1145/345966.345982.

Klein, S., Köhne, F., & Öörni, A. (2004). Barriers to online booking of scheduled airline tickets. *Journal of Travel & Tourism Marketing*, *17*(2/3), 27–29. doi:10.1300/J073v17n02_03.

Knight, M. (2011). *BI growth to buck economic trends*. Retrieved July 14, 2011, from http://www.itpro.co.uk/183480/bi-growth-to-buckeconomic-trends

Koch, C. (2003). *Open source - Your open source plan*. Retrieved from http://www.cio.com/article/31768/Open_Source_Your_Opensource_Plan

Koch, M., & Richter, A. (2008). Functions of social networking services. In *Proceedings of COOP '08: the 8th International Conference on the Design of Cooperative Systems*. COOP.

Kojima, S., & Kaplinsky, R. (2004). The use of a lean production index in explaining the transition to global competitiveness: The auto components sector in South Africa. *Technovation*, *24*(3), 199–206. doi:10.1016/S0166-4972(03)00142-1.

Konovsky, M., & Organ, D. (1996). Dispositional and contextual determinants of organizational citizenship behavior. *Journal of Organizational Behavior*, *17*(3), 253–266. doi:10.1002/(SICI)1099-1379(199605)17:3<253::AID-JOB747>3.0.CO;2-Q.

Korten, D. (2009). *Agenda for a new economy*. San Francisco, CA: Berrett-Koehler.

Kositanuri, B., Nqwenyama, O., & Osei-Bryson, K. M. (2006). An exploration of factors that impact individual performance in an ERP environment: An analysis using multiple analytical techniques. *European Journal of Information Systems*, *15*, 556–568. doi:10.1057/palgrave.ejis.3000654.

Kossinets, G., Kleinberg, J., & Watts, D. (2008). The structure of information pathways in a social communication network. In *Proceeding of the 14th ACM SIGKDD International Conference on Knowledge Discovery and Data Mining*, (pp. 435–443). New York, NY: ACM. doi:10.1145/1401890.1401945

Kotler, P., Armstrong, G., Saunders, J., & Wong, V. (1999). *Principles of marketing*. London: Prentice Hall.

Kotler, P., Armstrong, G., Wong, V., & Sauders, J. (2008). *Principles of marketing* (5th ed.). London: Prentice Hall.

Kotler, P., Bowen, J. T., & Makens, J. C. (2003). *Marketing for hospitality and tourism* (3rd ed.). Upper Saddle River, NJ: Pearson Prentice Hall.

Kotler, P., & Keller, K. L. (2006). *Dirección de marketing* (12th ed.). Madrid, Spain: Pearson Education.

Kotler, P., & Keller, K. L. (2009). *Marketing management* (13th ed.). Upper Saddle River, NJ: Pearson Education International.

Kotler, P., & Lee, N. (2004). *Corporate social responsibility: Doing the most good for your company and your cause*. Hoboken, NJ: Wiley.

Koufaris, M., Kambil, A., & Labarbera, P. A. (2002). Consumer behavior in web-based commerce: An empirical study. *International Journal of Electronic Commerce*, *6*(2), 115–138.

Kouwenhoven, T. (1998). Reengineering for learning. *SIGGROUP Bulletin*, *19*(1), 39–45.

Krackhardt, D. (1987). Cognitive social structures. *Social Networks*, *9*(2), 109–134. doi:10.1016/0378-8733(87)90009-8.

Krackhardt, D. (1992). The strength of strong ties: The importance of philos in organizations. In Nohria, N., & Eccles, R. G. (Eds.), *Networks and organizations: Structure, form, and action* (pp. 216–239). Boston, MA: Harvard Business School Press.

Krackhardt, D. (2000). Modeling structures of organizations. In Ilgen, D. R., & Hulin, C. L. (Eds.), *Computational Modeling of Behavior in Organizations: The Third Scientific Discipline*. American Psychological Association.

Krackhardt, D., & Hanson, J. R. (1993). Informal networks: The company behind the chart. *Harvard Business Review*, *71*(4), 104–111. PMID:10127036.

Krebs, V. (2000). Working in the connected world. *IHRIM Journal*, *4*(2), 89–91.

Krebs, V. (2007). Managing the 21st century organization. *IHRIM Journal*, *9*(4), 2–8.

Krogh, G. (1998). Care in knowledge creation. *California Management Review*, *40*(3), 133–153. doi:10.2307/41165947.

Kumaran, S., Liu, R., & Wu, F. Y. (2008). On the duality of information-centric and activity-centric models of business processes. *Lecture Notes in Computer Science*, *5074*, 32–47. doi:10.1007/978-3-540-69534-9_3.

Kumar, N., & Idris, K. (2006). An examination of educational institutions' knowledge performance: Analysis, implications and outlines for future research. *The Learning Organization*, *13*(1), 96–116. doi:10.1108/09696470610639158.

Kumar, R., & Best, M. L. (2006). Social impact and diffusion of telecenter use: A study from the sustainable access in rural India project. *Journal of Community Informatics*, *2*(3), 328–349.

Kumar, V., & Reinartz, W. J. (2006). *Customer relationship management: A databased approach*. New York: Wiley.

Kummervold, P. E., Chronaki, C. E., Lausen, B., Prokosch, H. U., Rasmussen, J., & Santana, S. et al. (2008). eHealth trends in Europe 2005-2007: A population-based survey. *Journal of Medical Internet Research*, *10*(4), e42. doi:10.2196/jmir.1023 PMID:19017584.

Künzle, V., & Reichert, M. (2009). Towards object-aware process management systems: Issues, challenges, benefits. *Lecture Notes in Business Information Processing*, *29*, 197–210. doi:10.1007/978-3-642-01862-6_17.

Kupp, M., & Anderson, J. (2007). Zopa: Web 2.0 meets retail banking. *Business Strategy Review*, *18*(3), 15–17. doi:10.1111/j.1467-8616.2007.00478.x.

Kuratko, D. (2008). *Entrepreneurship: Theory, process, and practice*. Cincinnati, OH: South-Western College.

Kurniawan, S. (2007). mobile phone design for older persons. *Design for Seniors: Innovations for Graying Tmes*, *14*(4), 24–25.

Küster, J. M., Ryndina, K., & Gall, H. (2007). Generation of business process models for object life cycle compliance. *Lecture Notes in Computer Science*, *4714*, 165–181. doi:10.1007/978-3-540-75183-0_13.

Kwahk, K. Y., & Lee, J. N. (2008). The role of readiness for change in ERP implementation: Theoretical bases and empirical validation. *Information & Management*, *45*(7), 474–481. doi:10.1016/j.im.2008.07.002.

Kwan, M., & Ramachandran, D. (2009). Trust and online reputation systems. In *Computing with Social Trust* (pp. 287–311). Berlin: Springer-Verlag. doi:10.1007/978-1-84800-356-9_11.

Kwon, T. H., & Zmud, R. W. (1987). Unifying the fragmented models of information systems implementation. In Boland, R. J., & Hirschheim, R. A. (Eds.), *Critical Issues in Information Systems Research*. New York: John Wiley & Sons.

Lafley, A., & Johnson, M. (2010). *Seizing the white space: Business model innovation for growth and renewal*. Boston: Harvard Business Press.

Lafollette, H. (Ed.). (2005). *The Oxford handbook of practical ethics*. Oxford, UK: Oxford University Press. doi:10.1093/oxfordhb/9780199284238.001.0001.

Lafuente, R. (2005). *Los servicios financieros bancarios electrónicos*. Valencia, Spain: Tirant lo Blanch.

Lai, Y. C., & Ng, E. M. W. (2011). Using wikis to develop student teachers' learning, teaching, and assessment capabilities. *The Internet and Higher Education*, *14*(1), 15–26. doi:10.1016/j.iheduc.2010.06.001.

Lakatos, I., & Musgrave, A. (Eds.). (1970). *Criticism and the growth of knowledge*. Cambridge, UK: Cambridge University Press.

Lambercy, V. (2010). Preaching for aviation 2.0. *PlasticPilot*. Retrieved February 9, 2012, from http://www.plasticpilot.net/blog/2010/11/14/preaching-for-aviation-2-0/

Lambert, D. M., & Cooper, M. C. (2000). Issues in supply chain management. *Industrial Marketing Management*, *29*, 65–83. doi:10.1016/S0019-8501(99)00113-3.

Lambert, D. M., Stock, J. R., & Ellram, L. M. (1998). *Fundamentals of logistics management*. Burr Ridge, IL: Irwin/McGraw-Hill.

Langenwalter, G. (2000). *Enterprise resources planning and beyond: Integrating your entire organization*. Boca Raton, FL: St. Lucie Press.

Larrán, M., & Giner, B. (2002). The use of the internet for corporate reporting by Spanish companies. *The International Journal of Digital Accounting Research*, *2*(1), 53–82.

Laster, J. (2010). Seton Hill to offer iPads to full-time students. *The Chronic of Higher Education*. Retrieved February 2012 from chronicle.com/blogs/wiredcampus/seton-hill-to-offer-ipads-to-full-time-students/22153

Lau, H., Pang, W., & Wong, C. (2002). Methodology for monitoring supply chain performance: A fuzzy logic approach. *Journal of Enterprise Information Management, 15*(4), 271–280.

Lau, K. (2011). Benchmarking green logistics performance with a composite index. *Benchmarking, 18*(6), 873–896. doi:10.1108/14635771111180743.

Lavelle, J., Brockner, J., Konovsky, M., Price, K., Henley, A., Taneja, A., & Vinekar, V. (2008). Commitment, procedural fairness, and organizational citizenship behavior: A multifoci analysis. *Journal of Organizational Behavior, 30*(3), 337–357. doi:10.1002/job.518.

Lawler, E., Worley, C., & Porras, J. (2006). *Built to change: How to achieve sustained organizational effectiveness*. San Francisco, CA: Jossey-Bass.

Law, R., & Hsu, C. H. C. (2005). Customers' perceptions on the importance of hotel web site dimensions and attributes. *International Journal of Contemporary Hospitality Management, 17*(6), 493–503. doi:10.1108/09596110510612130.

Law, R., Leung, K., & Wong, R. J. (2004). The impact of the Internet on travel agencies. *International Journal of Contemporary Hospitality Management, 16*(2), 100–107. doi:10.1108/09596110410519982.

Law, R., & Leung, R. (2000). A study of airlines' online reservation services on the Internet. *Journal of Travel Research, 39*, 202–211. doi:10.1177/004728750003900210.

Lawrence, A., & Weber, J. (2007). *Business and society*. New York: McGraw-Hill.

Lawrence, P. R., & Lorsch, J. W. (1967). *Organization and environment*. Boston: Harvard University Press.

Lawrence, P., & Lorsch, J. (1967). Differentiation and integration in complex organizations. *Administrative Science Quarterly, 12*(1), 1–30. doi:10.2307/2391211.

Lawton, G. (2009). Users take a close look at visual analytics. *IEEE Computer, 42*(2), 19–22. doi:10.1109/MC.2009.61.

Lebacqz, K. (1986). *Six theories of justice: Perspectives from philosophical and theological ethics*. Augsburg, Germany: Augsburg Books.

Lee, A. J., & Yu, T. (2009). Towards a dynamic and composable model of trust. In *Proceedings of the 14th ACM symposium on Access Control Models and Technologies (SACMAT '09)* (pp. 217-226). New York: ACM.

Lee, D. H., Lee, S. M., Olson, D. L., & Chung, S. H. (2010). The effect of organizational support on ERP implementation. *Industrial Management & Data Systems, 110*(1-2), 269–283. doi:10.1108/02635571011020340.

Lee, G. K., & Cole, R. E. (2003). From a firm-based to a community-based model of knowledge creation: The case of the linux kernel development. *Organization Science, 14*(6), 633–649. doi:10.1287/orsc.14.6.633.24866.

Lee-Kelley, L., & Sankey, T. (2008). Global virtual teams for value creation and project success: A case study. *International Journal of Project Management, 26*(1), 51–62. doi:10.1016/j.ijproman.2007.08.010.

Lee, M. R. (2009). E-ethical leadership for virtual project teams. *International Journal of Project Management, 27*, 456–463. doi:10.1016/j.ijproman.2008.05.012.

Lee, M. R., & Lan, Y. (2007). From web 2.0 to conversational knowledge management: Towards collaborative intelligence. *Journal of Entrepreneurship Research, 2*(2), 47–62.

Lefebvre, L., Harvey, J., & Lefebvre, E. (1991). Technological experience and the technology adoption decisions in small manufacturing firms. *R & D Management, 21*(3), 241–249. doi:10.1111/j.1467-9310.1991.tb00761.x.

Leganza, G. (2010). *The top 15 technology trends EA should watch: 2011 To 2013*. Forrester Research, Inc.

Legoinha, P., Pais, J., & Fernandes, J. (2006). *O Moodle e as comunidades virtuais de aprendizagem*. Paper presented at the VII Congresso Nacional de Geologia. New York, NY.

Leighninger, M. (2011). Citizenship and governance in a wild, wired world: How should citizens and public managers use online tools to improve democracy? *National Civic Review, 100*(2), 20–29. doi:10.1002/ncr.20056.

Leiper, N. (1990). *Tourism systems: An interdisciplinary perspective*. Palmerston North, New Zealand: Massey University Printery.

Lemieux, V., & Ouimet, M. (2004). L'analyse structurale des réseaux sociaux. *Recherches Sociographiques*, *47*(1), 179–182.

Lerner, J. (2009). *Boulevard of broken dreams: Why public efforts to boost entrepreneurship and venture capital have failed and what to do about it*. Princeton, NJ: Princeton University Press.

Lerner, J., & Tirole, J. (2002). Some simple economics of open source. *The Journal of Industrial Economics*, *50*(2), 197–234. doi:10.1111/1467-6451.00174.

Leroy, G. A., & Iriberri, A. (2007). *Natural language processing and e-government: Extracting reusable crime report information*. Paper presented at the IRI - Information Reuse and Integration. New York, NY.

Lester, K., & Piore, M. (2004). *Innovation - The missing dimension*. Cambridge, MA: Harvard Business Press.

Leung, H., Lee, A., & Law, R. (2011). Adopting web 2.0 technologies on chain and independent hotel websites: A case tudy of hotels in Hong Kong. In Law, R., Fuchs, M., & Ricci, F. (Eds.), *Information and Communication Technologies in Tourism 2011* (pp. 331–342). New York: Springer. doi:10.1007/978-3-7091-0503-0_19.

Levy, M., & Powell, P. (1998). SME flexibility and the role of information systems. *Small Business Economics*, *11*(2), 183–196. doi:10.1023/A:1007912714741.

Levy, M., Powell, P., & Yetton, P. (2002). The dynamics of SME information systems. *Small Business Economics*, *19*(4), 341–354. doi:10.1023/A:1019654030019.

Lewis, R. (1998). Membership and management of a 'virtual' team: The perspectives of a research manager. *R & D Management*, *28*, 5–13. doi:10.1111/1467-9310.00076.

Leydesdorff, L. (2006). *The knowledge-based economy*. Boca Raton, FL: Universal Publishers.

Li, N., & Mitchell, J. C. (2003). Datalog with constraints: A foundation for trust management languages. In *Proceedings of the 5th International Symposium on Practical Aspects of Declarative Languages* (pp. 58-73). IEEE.

Li, N., Mitchell, J. C., & Winsborough, W. H. (2002). Design of a role-based trust management framework. In *Proceedings of the 2002 IEEE Symposium on Security and Privacy* (pp. 114-130). IEEE.

Li, N., Winsborough, W. H., & Mitchell, J. C. (2001). Distributed credential chain discovery in trust management: Extended abstract. In *Proceedings of the 8th ACM Conference on Computer and Communications Security (CCS '01)* (pp. 156-165). New York: ACM.

Liang, T. P., & Huang, J. S. (1998). An empirical study on consumer acceptance of products in electronic markets: A transaction cost model. *Decision Support Systems*, *24*, 29–43. doi:10.1016/S0167-9236(98)00061-X.

Liao, S. (2006). The effects of nonmonetary sales promotions on consumer preferences: The contingent role of product category. *The Journal of American Academy of Business*, *8*(2), 196–203.

Lim, S., Matolcsy, Z., & Chow, D. (2007). The association between board composition and different types of voluntary disclosure. *European Accounting Review*, *16*, 555–583. doi:10.1080/09638180701507155.

Lin, T. C., Lee, C. K., & Lin, J. C. C. (2010). Determinants of enterprise 2.0 adoption: A value-based adoption model approach. In *Proceedings of the 2010 International Conference on Information Society (i-Society)* (pp. 12-18). i-Society.

Lin, W.-J., Liu, Y.-L., Kakusho, K., Yueh, H.-P., Murakami, M., & Minoh, M. (2006). *Blog as a tool to develop e-learning experience in an international distance course*. Paper presented at the Sixth International Conference on Advanced Learning Technologies. New York, NY.

Lindholm, C., & Keinonen, T. (2003). *Mobile usability: How Nokia changed the FACE of the mobile phone*. New York: McGraw Hill.

Lin, N. (2001). *Social capital: A theory of social structure and action*. Cambridge, UK: Cambridge University Press. doi:10.1017/CBO9780511815447.

Lin, N., Cook, K., & Burt, R. (2001). Social capital: Theory and research. *Contemporary Sociology*, *31*, 333.

Lin, N., Fu, Y., & Hsung, R. M. (2001). *The position generator: Measurement techniques for investigations of social capital. Social Capital Theory and Research*. Aldine de Gruyter.

Linstone, H. A., & Turoff, M. (Eds.). (1975). *The delphi method: Techniques and applications*. Reading, MA: Addison-Wesley.

Lioudakis, G. V., Gaudino, F., Boschi, E., Bianchi, G., Kaklamani, D. I., & Venieris, I. S. (2010). Legislation-aware privacy protection in passive network monitoring. In Portela, I. M., & Cruz-Cunha, M. M. (Eds.), *Information Communication Technology Law, Protection and Access Rights: Global Approaches and Issues*. Hershey, PA: IGI Global. doi:10.4018/978-1-61520-975-0.ch022.

Lippert, S., & Spagnolo, G. (2008). Internet peering as a network of relations. *Telecommunications Policy*, *32*(1), 33–49. doi:10.1016/j.telpol.2007.11.004.

Liu, L., & Ma, Q. (2006). Perceived system performance: A test of an extended technology acceptance model. *Journal of Organizational and End User Computing*, *18*(3), 1–24.

Li, X., & Wang, Y. (2010). Evaluating the effectiveness of destination marketing organisations' websites: Evidence from China. *International Journal of Tourism Research*, *12*, 536–549.

Locke, E. (1968). *What is job satisfaction?* Washington, DC: American Psychological Association.

Locke, E., Latham, G., & Erez, M. (1988). The determinants of goal commitment. *Academy of Management Review*, *13*(1), 23–39.

Lodahl, T., & Porter, L. (1961). Psychometric score patterns, social characteristics, and productivity of small industrial work groups. *The Journal of Applied Psychology*, *45*(2), 73–79. doi:10.1037/h0043379.

Lo, M.-C., & Ramayah, T. (2009). Dimensionality of organizational citizenship behavior (OCB) in a multicultural society: The case of Malaysia. *International Business Research*, *2*(1), 48–55.

López, S. P., Montes Peón, J. M., & Ordás, C. J. V. (2006). Human resources management as a determining factor in organisational learning. *Management Learning*, (37): 215–239. doi:10.1177/1350507606063443.

Lorincz, B., Tinholt, D., Linden, N. V. d., Colclough, G., Cave, J., Schindler, R., et al. (2010). *Digitizing public services in Europe: Putting ambition into action - 9th Benchmark Measurement*. Capgemini, RAND Europe, IDC, SOGETI and DTi.

Lovejoy, W. S., & Sinha, A. (2010). Efficient structures for innovative social networks. *Management Science*, *56*(7), 1127–1145. doi:10.1287/mnsc.1100.1168.

Lubbe, B. (2008). Kulula.com: Low-cost carrier and ICTs. In Egger, R., & Buhalis, D. (Eds.), *eTourism: Case studies* (pp. 282–292). Oxford, UK: Butterworth Heinemann – Elsevier.

Lu, J., Chun-Sheng, Y., Liu, C., & Yao, J. E. (2003). Technology acceptance model for wireless Internet. *Internet Research: Electronic Networking Applications and Policy*, *13*(3), 206–222. doi:10.1108/10662240310478222.

Lūka, I. (2008). Development of students' ESP competence and educator's professional activity in tertiary level tourism studies. In Žogla, I. (Ed.), *Association for Teacher Education in Europe Spring University Conference Teacher of the 21st Century: Quality Education for Quality Teaching* (pp. 689–697). Riga, Latvia: University of Latvia.

Luo, L. (2009). Web 2.0 integration in information literacy instruction: An overview. *Journal of Academic Librarianship*, *36*(1), 32–40. doi:10.1016/j.acalib.2009.11.004.

Lu, R., Sadiq, S., & Governatori, G. (2009). On managing business processes variants. *Data & Knowledge Engineering*, *68*(7), 642–664. doi:10.1016/j.datak.2009.02.009.

Lybaert, N. (1998). The information use in a SME: Its importance and some elements of influence. *Small Business Economics*, *10*(2), 171–191. doi:10.1023/A:1007967721235.

Lymbix. (2011). *Add sentiment intelligence to your applications*. Retrieved from http://www.lymbix.com/

Lynn, G. S., Lipp, S., Akgün, A. E., & Cortez, A. Jr. (2002). Factors impacting the adoption and effectiveness of the world wide web in marketing. *Industrial Marketing Management*, *31*, 35–49. doi:10.1016/S0019-8501(00)00104-8.

Lyons, B., & Henderson, K. (2005). Opinion leadership in a computer-mediated environment. *Journal of Consumer Behaviour*, *4*(5), 319–329. doi:10.1002/cb.22.

Machado, M., & Tao, E. (2007). *Blackboard vs. Moodle: Comparing user experience of learning management systems*. Paper presented at the 37th ASEE/IEEE Frontiers in Education Conference. New York, NY.

Macías, A. G. (2002). *Redes sociales y clusters empresariales*. Revista Hispana para el análisis de redes sociais, (v. 1, n. 6). Retrieved Dec 01, 2011, from http://revista-redes.rediris.es/html-vol1/vol1_6.htm

MacIntosh, R. W., & Goeldner, C. R. (1986). *Tourism principles, practices, philosophies*. New York: John Wiley & Sons INC.

Mackeviciute, A., & Iacubiţchi, S. (2010). *The impact of enterprise 2.0 tools on innovation processes: The case study of incentive at IBS*. (Master Thesis). Jönköping International Business School, Jönköping, Sweden.

Madon, S., Reinhard, N., Roode, D., & Walsham, G. (2009). Digital inclusion projects in developing countries: Processes of institutionalization. *Information Technology for Development*, *15*(2), 95–107. doi:10.1002/itdj.20108.

Magretta, J. (1999). *Managing in the new economy*. Boston: Harvard Business School.

Magretta, J. (2002, May). Why businėss models matter. *Harvard Business Review*, 86–92. PMID:12024761.

Mahmoud, S. S. (2008). *A proposed model for distributing e-courses content through mobile technology architectures*. Paper presented at the word academy of science, engineering and technology. New York, NY.

Malik, M., Nawab, S., & Naeem, B. (2010). Job satisfaction and organizational commitment of university teachers in public sector of Pakistan. *International Journal of Business & Management*, *5*(6), 17–26.

Mangleburg, T. F., Doney, P. M., & Bristol, T. (2004). Shopping with friends and teens' susceptibility to peer influence. *Journal of Retailing*, *80*(2), 101–116. doi:10.1016/j.jretai.2004.04.005.

Mankiw, N. G. (1998). *Microeconomics*. London: Elsevier.

Manso, J. (1996). *Estatística descritiva e previsão* (2nd ed.). Covilhã, Portugal: Universidade da Beira Interior.

Maqsood, T., Walker, D., & Finegan, A. (2007). Extending the knowledge advantage: Creating learning chains. *The Learning Organization*, *14*(2), 123–141. doi:10.1108/09696470710726998.

March, J. G., & Olsen, J. P. (1975). The uncertainty of the past, organisational ambiguous learning. *European Journal of Political Research*, *3*, 147–171. doi:10.1111/j.1475-6765.1975.tb00521.x.

Margaryan, A., Littlejohn, A., & Vojt, G. (2011). Are digital natives a myth or reality? University students' use of digital technologies. *Computers & Education*, *56*(2), 429–440. doi:10.1016/j.compedu.2010.09.004.

Marimin, M., Hatono, I., & Tamura, H. (1998). Linguistic labels for expressing fuzzy preference relations in fuzzy group decision making. *IEEE Transactions on Systems, Man, and Cybernetics. Part B, Cybernetics*, *28*(2), 205–218. doi:10.1109/3477.662760 PMID:18255937.

Marjanovic, O., & Freeze, R. D. (2011). Knowledge intensive business processes: Theoretical foundations and research challenges. In *Proceedings of the IEEE 44th Hawaii International Conference on System Sciences*. New York: IEEE Press.

Mark, G., Grudin, J., & Poltrock, S. (1999). Meeting at the desktop: An empirical study of virtually collocated teams. In *Proceedings of ECSCW'99, the 6th European Conference on Computer Supported Cooperative Work*, (pp. 159-178). ECSCW.

Markkula, M. (1999). Knowledge management in software engineering projects. In *Proceedings of the 11th International Conference on Software Engineering & Knowledge Engineering*, (pp. 20-27). Kaiserslautern, Germany: IEEE.

Marks, O., & Patel, S. (2010). *Accelerating business performance*. Retrieved from http:///www.e2conf.com/downloads/whitepapers/ent2-10_TWwhitepaper.pdf

Marks, O., & Patel, S. (2010). Enterprise 2.0 white paper: Accelerating business performance. *Sovos Group*. Retrieved September 1, 2011, from http://sovosgroup.com

Maroco, J. (2007). *Análise estatística com utilização do SPSS* (3rd ed.). Lisboa, Portugal: Edições Sílabo.

Maroco, J., & Garcia-Marques, T. (2006). Qual a fiabilidade do alfa de Cronbach? Questões antigas e soluções modernas? *Laboratório de Psicologia*, *4*(1), 65–90.

Marshall, B., Choi, J., El-Shinnaway, M. M., North, M., Svensson, L., & Wang, S. et al. (2009). Online and offline social ties of social network website users: An exploratory study in eleven societies. *Journal of Computer Information Systems*, *50*(1), 54–64.

Martin, D., Alzua, A., & Lamsfus (2011). A contextual geofencing mobile tourisdm service. In R. Law, M. Fuchs, & F. Ricci (Eds.), *Information and Communication Technologies in Tourism 2011* (pp. 331-342). New York: Springer.

Martin, R. (2009). *Opposable mind: Winning through integrative thinking*. Boston: Harvard Business Press.

Martins, L., Gilson, L., & Maynard, M. (2004). Virtual teams: What do we know and where do we go from here? *Journal of Management*, *30*(6), 805–835. doi:10.1016/j.jm.2004.05.002.

Masamila, B., Mtenzi, F., Said, J., & Tinabo, R. (2010). A secured mobile payment model for developing markets. *Communications in Computer and Information Science*, *87*(2), 175–182. doi:10.1007/978-3-642-14292-5_20.

Maslo, E. (2007). Transformative learning space for life-long foreign languages learning. In D. Cunningham, D. Markus, J. Valdmanis, et al. (Eds.), *International Nordic-Baltic Region Conference of FIPLV Innovations in Language Teaching and Learning in the Multicultural Context* (pp. 38-46). Rīga: SIA Izglītības Soļi.

Masoumzadeh, A., & Joshi, J. B. D. (2008). PuRBAC: Purpose-aware role-based access control. In *Proceedings of the On the Move to Meaningful Internet Systems: OTM 2008* (LNCS), (vol. 5332). Berlin, Germany: Springer Berlin / Heidelberg.

Matheus, R., Ribeiro, M. M., Vaz, J. C., & De Souza, C. A. (2010). Internet use for social control and participation: What are local governments doing in Latin America? In *Proceedings of the 4th International Conference on Theory and Practice of Electronic Governance* (pp. 333–338). ACM.

Mathews, A. W. (2000). Advertisers find many web sites too tasteless.

Mathies, C., & Weiermair, K. (2003). *Technological change in the accommodation industry - Enhancing and constraining factors of the IT adaptation*. Paper presented at the Biennal Conference: Leisure, Change and Diversity. Sydney, Australia.

Mayring, P. (2004). Qualitative content analysis. In Flick, , von Kardoff, , & Steinke, (Eds.), *A Companion to Qualitative Research* (pp. 266-269). London: SAGE.

Mayring, P. (2007). On generalization in qualitatively oriented research. *Forum Qualitative Sozial Forschung*, *8*(3), 1–8.

Maznevski, M. L., Gomez, C. B., Noorderhaven, N. G., & Wu, P. (1997). *The cultural orientations framework and international management research*. Paper presented at the Academy of International Business Annual Meeting. Monterrey, Mexico.

Maznevski, M. L., & Chudoba, K. M. (2000). Bridging space over time: Global virtual team dynamics and effectiveness. *Organization Science*, *11*(5), 473–492. doi:10.1287/orsc.11.5.473.15200.

Mazur, A., Doran, C., & Doran, P. R. (2010). The use of social network analysis software to analyze communication patterns and interaction in online collaborative environments. In J. Baralt, N. Callaos, W. Lesso, A. Tremante, & F. Welsch (Eds.), Teacher (p. 447). International Institute of Information and Systemics.

McAfee, A. (2006, May 27). *Enterprise 2.0, version 2.0*. [Web log comment]. Retrieved from http://andrewmcafee.org/2006/05/enterprise_20_version_20/

McAfee, A. (2011). *Data from the edge*. Retrieved September 15, 2011, from http://andrewmcafee.org

McAfee, A. (2011). *Putting enterprise 2.0 into context*. Retrieved September 15, 2011, from http://andrewmcafee.org

McAfee, A. (2006). Enterprise 2.0: The dawn of emergent collaboration. *MIT Sloan Management Review*, *47*(3), 21–28.

McAfee, A. (2006). Enterprise 2.0: The dawn of emergent collaboration. *Sloan Management Review*.

McAfee, A. (2009). *Enterprise 2.0: New collaborative tools for your organization's toughest challenges*. Boston, MA: Harvard Business Press.

McAfee, A. P. (2006). Evangelizing in the empty quarter. In *The Business Impact of IT*. New York: Wordpress.

McAfee, A. P. (2008). Some questions you might get asked. In *The Business Impact of IT*. New York: Wordpress.

McAfee, A. P. (2009). *Enterprise 2.0: New collaborative tools for your organization's toughest challenges*. Boston: Harvard Business Press.

McAtamney, G., & Parker, C. (2006). An examination of the effects of a wearable display on informal face-to-face communication. In *Proceedings of the SIGCHI Conference on Human Factors in Computing Systems*. Montréal, Canada: ACM.

McAuley, J., Duberley, J., & Johnson, P. (2007). *Organization theory: Challenges and perspectives*. Harlow, MA: Pearson.

McGrath, C., Blythe, J., & Krackhardt, D. (1997). The effect of spatial arrangement on judgments and errors in interpreting graphs. *Social Networks, 19*(3), 223–242. doi:10.1016/S0378-8733(96)00299-7.

McGraw-Hill Company. (1989). *McGraw-Hill encyclopedia of science and technology*. New York: McGraw-Hill Company.

McGregor, J. (2006, April 24). The world's most innovative companies. *BusinessWeek*, 63-74.

McKnight, D. H., Cummings, L. L., & Chervany, N. L. (1998). Initial trust formation in new organizational relationships. *Academy of Management Review, 23*(3), 473–490.

McLoughlin, C., & Lee, M. J. W. (2007). *Social software and participatory learning: Pedagogical choices with technology affordances in the web 2.0 era*. Paper presented at the Ascilite. Singapore.

McWilliams, A., & Siegel, D. (2001). Corporate social responsibility: A theory of the firm perspective. *Academy of Management Review, 26*(1), 117–127. doi: doi:10.2307/259398.

McWilliams, A., & Siegel, D. S. (2011). Creating and capturing value. *Journal of Management, 37*(5), 1480–1495. doi:10.1177/0149206310385696.

Meder. (1999) Didaktische ontologien: Globalisierung und wissensorganisation: Neue aspekkte fur wissen. *Wissenschaft und Informationsysteme*, 401-416.

Mehrez, A. (2010). *The role of quality gaps in assessing the performance of management programs*. (Ph.D. thesis). University of Newcastle, Newcastle, Australia.

Mehrtens, J., Cragg, P. B., & Mills, A. M. (2001). A model of internet adoption by SMEs. *Information & Management, 39*(3), 165–176. doi:10.1016/S0378-7206(01)00086-6.

Mellor, R. B. (2007). *Innovation nuclei in SMEs involved in Internet B2C e-commerce*. (Tesis doctoral). Retrieved from http://kurir.kingston.ac.uk/mellor2007.pdf

Mellow, P. (2005). *The media generation: Maximise learning by getting mobile*. Retrieved May 27, 2011, from http://www.ascilite.org.au/conferences/brisbane05/blogs/proceedings/53_Mellow.pdf

Mena Tobar, L., Latorre Andrés, P., & Lafuente Lapena, E. (2009). WebA mobile (web analysis mobile), assistance tool for the design and evaluation of website for mobile devices. In *New Trends on Human-Computer Interaction. Research, Development, New Tools and Methods*. London: Springer. doi:10.1007/978-1-84882-352-5_13.

Mendieta, M. M. (2007). Llega la oficina bancaria 2.0. *Cinco días*.

Mentzer, J. T., De Witt, W., Keebler, J. S., Min, S., Nix, N. W., Smith, C. D., & Zacharia, Z. G. (2001). Defining supply chain management. *Journal of Business Logistics, 22*(2), 1–25. doi:10.1002/j.2158-1592.2001.tb00001.x.

Meta Group. (2001). *Integration: Critical issues for implementation of CRM solutions*. Stanford, CA: Meta Group Inc..

Meyer, M., Hannappel, A., Rensing, C., & Steinmetz, R. (2007). Automatic classificaion of didactic functions of e-learning resources. In *Proceedings of 15th International Conference on Multimedia* (pp. 513-516). Augsburg, Germany: ACM.

Meyer, J., & Herscovitch, L. (2001). Commitment in the workplace: Toward a general model. *Human Resource Management Review, 11*(3), 299–326. doi:10.1016/S1053-4822(00)00053-X.

Meyer, K. A. (2010). A comparison of web 2.0 tools in a doctoral course. *The Internet and Higher Education*, *13*(4), 226–232. doi:10.1016/j.iheduc.2010.02.002.

Meyer, P., Stanley, D., Herscovitch, L., & Topolnytsky, L. (2002). Affective, continuance, and normative commitment to theorganization: A meta-analysis of antecedents, correlates, and consequences. *Journal of Vocational Behavior*, *61*(1), 20–52. doi:10.1006/jvbe.2001.1842.

Middleware Architecture Committee for Education (MACE). (2001). *Shibboleth system*. Retrieved November 3, 2011, from http://shibboleth.Internet2.edu/

Mihm, J., Loch, C. H., Wilkinson, D., & Huberman, B. A. (2010). Hierarchical structure and search in complex organizations. *Management Science*, *56*(5), 831–848. doi:10.1287/mnsc.1100.1148.

Milgrom, P., & Roberts, J. (1995). Complementarities and fit strategy, structure, and organizational change in manufacturing. *Journal of Accounting and Economics*, *19*(2-3), 179–208. doi:10.1016/0165-4101(94)00382-F.

Miller, M. (2012). *East Stroudsburg University suspends professor for Facebook posts*. Retrieved February 2012 from chronicle.com/blogs/wiredcampus/east-stroudsburg-u-suspends-professor-for-facebook-posts/21498

Miller, M., Marks, A., & DeCoulode, M. (2011). Social software for business performance. *The Deloitte Center for the Edge*. Retrieved February 23, 2011, from http://www.deloitte.com/

Miller, S. S. (1998). *ASAP—Implementation at the speed of business*. New York: McGraw-Hill.

Mill, R. C., & Morrison, A. M. (1998). *The tourism system: An introductory text* (3rd ed.). Dubuque, IA: Kendall/Hunt.

Mill, S. (2002). *Utilitarianism*. Indianapolis, IN: Hackett Pub..

Milojicic, D. (2008). Interview with Rich Friedrich, Dave Cohen, and Alex Dreiling. *IEEE Internet Computing*, *12*(1), 10–13. doi:10.1109/MIC.2008.15.

Mimno, P. (2002). *How to avoid data mart chaos using hybrid methodology*. TDWI Flash point column.

Mislove, A., Marcon, M., Gummadi, K. P., Druschel, P., & Bhattacharjee, B. (2007). Measurement and analysis of online social networks. In *Proceedings of the 7th ACM SIGCOMM Conference on Internet Measurement*, (pp. 29–42). New York, NY: ACM. doi:10.1145/1298306.1298311

Misuraca, G. C. (2009). e-Government 2015: Exploring m-government scenarios, between ICT-driven experiments and citizen-centric implications. *Technology Analysis and Strategic Management*, *21*(3), 407–424. doi:10.1080/09537320902750871.

Mitchell, V. W., & Vassos, V. (1997). Perceived risk and risk reduction in holiday purchases: A cross-cultural and gender analysis. *Journal of Euromarketing*, *6*(3), 47–79. doi:10.1300/J037v06n03_03.

Mittal, M., & Sethi, P. (2011). The effectiveness of sales promotions tools among Indian consumers: An empirical study. *Journal of Promotion Management*, *17*, 165–182. doi:10.1080/10496491.2011.580693.

Miyazoe, T. (2008). *LMS-based EFL blended learning: Blackboard vs. Moodle*. Paper presented at the JALT2007. New York, NY.

Mobile Web Best Practices Working Group. (n.d.). Retrieved from http://www.w3.org/2005/MWI/BPWG/

MobileOk Checker. (n.d.). Retrieved from http://www.w3.org/2005/MWI/BPWG/Group/TaskForces/Checker/

Moggridge, C. (2011). The evolution of Facebook. *B&T Magazine*, *61*(2734), 14.

Mohamed, F. Z. M., Saravanan, S., Muthaiyah, O., & Arman, K. (2011). TM: A development technique for e-government 2.0 portals. *WSEAS Transactions on Information Science and Applications*, *8*(2), 96–108.

Moisil, I., & Jitaru, E. (2006). E-health progresses in Romania. *International Journal of Medical Informatics*, *75*, 315–321. doi:10.1016/j.ijmedinf.2005.08.013 PMID:16275159.

Molina, J. L. (1999). El organigrama informal en las organizaciones: Una aproximación desde el análisis de redes sociales. *Redes Revista Hispana para el Análisis de Redes Sociales*. Retrieved from http://revista-redes.rediris.es/Webredes/textos/organizaciones.doc

Momparler, A. (2008). *El desarrollo de la banca electrónica en España: Un análisis comparativo entre entidades online y tradicionales en España y estados unidos*. (Doctoral Thesis). Department of Business Organization, Universidad Politécnica de Valencia, Valencia, Spain.

Monge, P. R., & Contractor, N. S. (2001). Emergence of communication networks. In Jablin, F. M., & Putnam, L. L. (Eds.), *Handbook of Organizational Communication* (pp. 440–502). Thousand Oaks, CA: Sage.

Montoya, E. V. (2007). Telecentros comunitarios: Un espacio para la participación y formación ciudadana: La experiencia de Manizales, Colombia. *Journal of Community Informatics*, *3*(3).

Montoya-Weiss, M. M., Massey, A. P., & Song, M. (2001). Getting it together: Temporal coordination and conflict management in global virtual teams. *Academy of Management Journal*, 1251–1262. doi:10.2307/3069399.

Moodle. (2011). *Moodle*. Retrieved June 2, 2011, from http://moodle.org/

Moody, J., & White, D. R. (2003). Structural cohesion and embeddedness: A hierarchical concept of social groups. *American Sociological Review*, *68*(1), 103–127. doi:10.2307/3088904.

Moore, M., & Kearsley, G. (2005). *Distance education: A systems view* (2nd ed.). Belmont, CA: Wadsworth Publishing Company.

Moreira, M. A. (1998). *Desigualdades, educación y nuevas tecnologias*. Quaderns Digitals.

Morgan, J. P. (2011). *Annual report forecasting trend*. Retrieved from http://www.jpmorgan.com

Morgan, G. (1986). *Images of organization*. Beverly Hills, CA: SAGE.

Mori, C. K., & Assumpção, R. O. (2007). Brazilian digital inclusion public policy: Achievements and challenges. *Journal of Community Informatics*, *3*(3). Retrieved September 30, 2011 from http://ci-journal.net/index.php/ciej/article/view/424

Morris, M. G., & Venkatesh, V. (2000). Age differences in technology adoption decisions: Implications for a changing work force. *Personnel Psychology*, *53*(2), 375–404. doi:10.1111/j.1744-6570.2000.tb00206.x.

Motiwalla, L. F., & Thompson, J. (2009). *Enterprise systems for management*. Upper Saddle River, NJ: Pearson Education, Inc..

Moura, R., & Bernardino, J. (2010). Um modelo para a integração de serviços: Moodle e sistemas de gestão Académica. *RISTI- Revista Ibérica de Sistemas e Tecnologias de Informação,* (5), 31-44.

Moura, A., & Carvalho, A. A. (2009). Mobile learning: two experiments on teaching and learning with mobile phone. In Hijón-Neira, R. (Ed.), *Advanced Learning* (pp. 89–100). Academic Press. doi:10.5772/8105.

Mowery, D., Oxley, J., & Silverman, B. (1996). Strategic alliances and interfirm knowledge transfer. *Strategic Management Journal*, *17*, 77–91.

Mulej, M. (2000). *The dialectical systems theory*. Maribor, Slovenia: FEB.

Mulej, M., & Kajzer, S. (1998). Ethics of interdependence and the law of requisite holism. In M. Rebernik & M. Mulej (Eds.), *Proceedings of STIQE 1998* (pp. 24-34). Maribor, Slovenia: FEB.

Mulej, M., et al. (2000). *Dialectical and other soft systems theories*. Maribor, Portugal: FEB.

Mulej, M., et al. (2008). *Management of innovation processes*. Maribor, Slovenia: FEB.

Mulej, M. (1974). Dialectical systems theory. *Our Economy*, *21*(3-4), 207–212.

Mulej, M. et al. (2012). *Dialectical systems thinking and the law of requisite holism*. Phoenix, AZ: ISCE Publishing.

Mullins, R., Duan, Y., Hamblin, D., Burrell, P., Jin, H., Jerzy, G., … Aleksander, B. (2007). A web based intelligent training system for SMEs. *The Electronic Journal of e-Learning, 5*, 39-48.

Mullins, L. (2006). *Essentials of organizational behavior*. Harlow, MA: Prentice Hall.

Mullins, L. (2010). *Management and organizational behaviour*. New York: Prentice Hall.

Mullins, N. C. (1972). The development of a scientific specialty: The phage group and the origins of molecular biology. *Minerva*, *10*(1), 51–82. doi:10.1007/BF01881390.

Muniz, A. M., & O'Guinn, T. (2001). Brand community. *The Journal of Consumer Research*, *27*, 412–432. doi:10.1086/319618.

Munkvold, B. (2003). *Implementing collaboration technologies in industry: Case examples and lessons learned*. London: Springer-Verlag. doi:10.1007/978-1-4471-0073-7.

Munkvold, B., & Zigurs, I. (2007). Process and technology challenges in swift-starting virtual teams. *Information & Management*, *44*, 287–299. doi:10.1016/j.im.2007.01.002.

Murata, T. (1989). Petri nets: Properties, analysis and applications. *Proceedings of the IEEE*, *77*(4), 541–580. doi:10.1109/5.24143.

Murphy, J., Forrest, E. J., Wotring, C. E., & Bryman, R. A. (1996, June). Hotel management and marketing on the internet. *The Cornell Hotel and Restaurant Administration Quarterly*, 70–82. doi:10.1177/001088049603700322.

Musaji, Y. F. (2003). *Integrated auditing of ERP systems*. New York: John Wiley & Sons, Inc..

Mutch, A. (1998). Using information technology. In Thomas, R. (Ed.), *The management of small tourism and hospitality firms* (pp. 92–206). London: Cassell.

My Starbucks Idea. (2011, November). *Share. Vote. Discuss. See. Share your ideas, tell us what you think of other people's ideas and join discussion*. Retrieved from http://mystarbucksidea.force.com/

MySQL. (n.d.). Retrieved from www.mysql.com

Nadhan, E. G. (2008). *Forecast for the next generation enterprise 3.0*. Paper presented at the EDS Distinguished SE Open Group Enterprise Architecture Practitioners Conference. Chicago, IL.

Nadiri, H., Kandampully, J., & Hussain, K. (2009). Zone of tolerance for banks: A diagnostic model of service quality. *Service Industries Journal*, *29*(11), 1547–1564. doi:10.1080/02642060902793425.

Nahapiet, J., & Ghoshal, S. (1998). Social capital, intellectual capital, and the organizational advantage. *Academy of Management Review*, *23*(2), 242–266.

Nah, F. F., Tan, X., & Teh, S. H. (2004). An empirical investigation on end-users' acceptance of enterprise systems. *Information Resources Management Journal*, *17*(3), 32–53. doi:10.4018/irmj.2004070103.

Nazalek, M. (2008). Orbis on line: Internet distribution strategies for a regional hotel group. In Egger, R., & Buhalis, D. (Eds.), *eTourism: Case studies* (pp. 74–82). Oxford, UK: Butterworth Heinemann - Elsevier.

Ndou, V., & Petti, C. (2007). DMS business models design and destination configurations: Choice and implementation issues. *Information Technology and Tourism*, *9*, 3–14. doi:10.3727/109830507779637602.

Neil, Y., Shih, Chao, & Jin. (2010). Ranking metrics and search guidance for learning object repository. *IEEE Transactions on Learning Technologies*, *3*, 250-264.

Nelson, M. R., & Otnes, C. C. (2005). Exploring cross-cultural ambivalence: A netnography of intercultural wedding message boards. *Journal of Business Research*, *58*(1), 89–95. doi:10.1016/S0148-2963(02)00477-0.

Nevin, J. R. (1995). Relationship marketing and distribution channels: Exploring fundamental issues. *Journal of the Academy of Marketing Science*, *23*(4), 327–334. doi:10.1177/009207039502300413.

Newman, A. C., & Thomas, J. G. (2009). *Enterprise 2.0 implementation*. New York: McGraw Hill.

Newman, M. E. J., & Girvan, M. (2003). Finding and evaluating community structure in networks. *Physical Review E: Statistical, Nonlinear, and Soft Matter Physics*, *69*(2 Pt 2), 16.

Newsroom, S. (2011, January). *Starbucks support of the troop$/military*. Retrieved from http://news.starbucks.com/about+starbucks/myths+facts/militarydonations.htm

Ngai, E. W. T., Law, C. C. H., & Wat, F. K. T. (2007). Examining the critical success factors in the adoption of enterprise resource planning. *Computers in Industry*, *59*, 548–564. doi:10.1016/j.compind.2007.12.001.

Nielsen. (2008). *Trends in online shopping*. Retrieved January 01, 2009 from http://www.nielsen.com

Nielsen, J. (1993). *Usability engineering*. Academic Press.

Ni, Q., Bertino, E., Lobo, J., Brodie, C., Karat, C. M., Karat, J., & Trombetta, A. (2010). Privacy-aware role-based access control. *Journal of ACM Transactions Information System Security*, *13*(3), 1–31. doi:10.1145/1805974.1805980.

Nonaka, I. (1991). The knowledge creating company. *Harvard Business Review*, *69*(6), 96–104.

Nonaka, I., & Konno, N. (1998). The concept of ba: Building a foundation for knowledge creation. *California Management Review*, *40*(3), 40–55. doi:10.2307/41165942.

Nonaka, I., & Takeuchi, H. (1995). *The knowledge creating company: How Japanese companies create the dynamics of innovation*. New York: Oxford University Press.

Nonaka, I., & Takeushi, H. (1991). The knowledge creating company. *Harvard Business Review*.

Nonaka, I., Toyama, R., & Konno, N. (2000). SECI, ba and leadership: A unified model of dynamic knowledge creation. *Long Range Planning*, *33*, 5–34. doi:10.1016/S0024-6301(99)00115-6.

Nurcan, S. (2008). A survey on the flexibility requirements related to business processes and modeling artifacts. In *Proceedings of the IEEE 41st Hawaii International Conference on System Sciences*. New York: IEEE Press.

Nussbaum, B., Berner, R., & Brady, D. (2005, August 15). Special report. *Business Week*, 51-68.

O'Connor, P. (2008). InterContinental hotel group: Dealing with online intermediaries. In Egger, R., & Buhalis, D. (Eds.), *eTourism: Case studies* (pp. 15–22). Oxford, UK: Butterworth Heinemann - Elsevier.

O'Mahony, S. (2007). The governance of open source initiatives: What does it mean to be community managed? *Journal of Management and Governance*, *11*(2), 139–150. doi:10.1007/s10997-007-9024-7.

O'Mahony, S., & Bechky, B. A. (2008). Boundary organizations: Enabling collaboration among unexpected allies. *Administrative Science Quarterly*, *53*(3), 422–459. doi:10.2189/asqu.53.3.422.

O'Mahony, S., & Ferraro, F. (2007). The emergence of governance in an open source community. *Academy of Management Journal*, *50*(5), 1079–1106. doi:10.5465/AMJ.2007.27169153.

O'Reilly, T. (2005). What is web 2.0: Design patterns and business models for the next generation of software. *O'Reilly*. Retrieved October 22, 2011, from http://oreilly.com/Web2/archive/what-is-Web-20.html

O'Reilly, T., & Battelle. (2009). Web squared: Web 2.0 five years on. *Web 2.0 Summit*. Retrieved from http://assets.en.oreilly.com/1/event/28/Web2009_Websquared-whitepaper.pdf

O'Reilly, T. (2007). What is web 2.0: Design patterns and business models for the next generation of software. *International Journal of Digital Economics*, *65*, 17–37.

Ochoa, X. (2011). Intercambio social y recomendación de material educativo. *Tutorial LACLO 2011*. Retrieved from www.slideshare.net/xaoch

Ochoa, X., & Duval, E. (2006). Quality metrics for learning object metada. In *Proceedings of World Conference on Educational Multimedia, Hypermedia and Telecommunications 2006* (pp. 1004-1011). IEEE.

Ochoa, X., & Duval, E. (2008). Relevance ranking metrics for learning objects. *IEEE Transactions on Learning Technologies*, *1*(1), 34–48. doi:10.1109/TLT.2008.1.

OECD. (2005). *Modernising government: The way forward*. OECD.

Oganisjana, K., & Koke, T. (2008). Developing students' enterprise. In Maslo, Kiegelmann, & Huber (Ed.), Qualitative Psychology in the Changing Academic Context (pp. 218-233). Tübingen, Germany: Academic Press.

Ohdar, R., & Ray, P. (2004). Performance measurement and evaluation of suppliers in supply chain: An evolutionary fuzzy-based approach. *Journal of Manufacturing Technology Management*, *15*(8), 723–734. doi:10.1108/17410380410565311.

Oliveira, J., & Fazendeiro, P. (2003). On the achievement of both accurate and interpretable fuzzy systems using data-driven design processes. In Casillas, J. et al. (Eds.), *Accuracy Improvements in Linguistic Fuzzy Modeling*. Physica-Verlag.

Oliver, S. (1997). *Corporate communication: Principles, techniques and strategies*. London: Kogan Page.

Olson, G. M., & Olson, J. S. (2003). Groupware and computer-supported cooperative work. In Jacko, J. A., & Sears, A. (Eds.), *The Human-Computer Interaction Handbook*. London: Lawrence Erlbaum Associates.

Olszak, C. M., & Ziemba, E. (2006). Business intelligence systems in the holistic infrastructure development supporting decision-making in organizations. *Interdisciplinary Journal of Information. Knowledge and Management*, *1*, 47–58.

Olugu, E., & Wong, Y. (2009). Supply chain performance evaluation: Trends and challenges. *American Journal of Engineering and Applied Sciences*, *2*(1), 202–211. doi:10.3844/ajeas.2009.202.211.

OMG. (2010). Retrieved in January 2010, from www.uml.org

OMG-BPMN. (2011). *Business process model and notation*. Retrieved October 14, 2011, from http://www.omg.org/spec/BPMN/

OMG-OCL. (2010). *Object constraint language*. Retrieved October 14, 2011, from http://www.omg.org/spec/OCL/

OMG-SBVR. (2008). *Semantics of business vocabulary and business rules*. Retrieved October 14, 2011, from http://www.omg.org/spec/SBVR/

OMG-UML. (2011). *Unified modeling language: Superstructure*. Retrieved October 14, 2011, from http://www.omg.org/spec/UML/

ONTSI. (2011). *La sociedad en red 2010*. Retrieved January 01, 2011 from http://www.ontsi.red.es/estudios-informes

Öörni, A. (2004). Consumer objectives and the amount of search in electronic travel and tourism markets. *Journal of Travel & Tourism Marketing*, *17*(2/3), 3–14. doi:10.1300/J073v17n02_01.

Open, I. (2011). *Open intelligence*. Retrieved from http://www.openi.org/

Open Source. (n.d.). Retrieved from www.opensource.org

OpenSourceInitiative. (2011). Retrieved from http://www.opensource.org/

O'Reilly, T. (2005). *What is web 2.0: Design patterns and business models for the next generation of software*. Retrieved May 18, 2011, from http://oreilly.com/Web2/archive/what-is-Web-20.html

O'Reilly, T. (2006). *Web 2.0 compact definition: Trying again*. Retrieved May 18, 2011, from http://radar.oreilly.com/archives/2006/12/Web-20-compact.html

Organ, D. (1977). A reappraisal and reinterpretation of the satisfaction-causes-performance hypothesis. *Academy of Management Review*, *2*(1), 46–53.

Organ, D., & Lingl, A. (1995). Personality, satisfaction and organizational citizenship behaviors. *The Journal of Social Psychology*, *135*(3), 339–250. doi:10.1080/00224545.1995.9713963.

Organ, D., & Moorman, R. (1993). Fairness and organizational citizenship behavior: What are the connections? *Social Justice Research*, *6*(1), 5–18. doi:10.1007/BF01048730.

Organización Mundial del Turismo. (1998). *Introducción al turismo*. Madrid, Spain: Organización Mundial del Turismo.

Organization for Economic Co-Operation and Development (OECD). (1980). *Guidelines on the protection of privacy and transborder flows of personal data*. Retrieved November 3, 2011, from http://www.oecd.org/document/18/0,3343,en_2649_34255_1815186_1_1_1_1,00.html

Organization for Economic Co-Operation and Development (OECD). (2011). *The evolving privacy landscape: 30 years after the OECD privacy guidelines*. Retrieved November 3, 2011, from http://dx.doi.org/10.1787/5kgf09z90c31-en

Organization for the Advancement of Structured Information Standards (OASIS). (2004). *OASIS eXtensible access control markup language (XACML) TC*. Retrieved November 3, 2011, from http://www.oasis-open.org/committees/xacml/

Organization for the Advancement of Structured Information Standards (OASIS). (2005). *Security assertion markup language (SAML) v2.0*. Retrieved November 3, 2011, from http://docs.oasis-open.org/security/saml/v2.0/saml-2.0-os.zip

Ortenbald, A. (2004). The learning organisation: Towards an integrated model. *The Learning Organization, 11*(2/3), 129. doi:10.1108/09696470410521592.

Ortiz-Rodriguez, F., Palma, R., & Villazón-Terrazas, B. (2007). *EgoIR: Ontology-based information retrieval intended for eGovernment.* Paper presented at the 2nd International Applications of Semantic Technologies (AST) Workshop - Informatik 2007.

Osarenkhoe, A. (2006). Customer-centric strategy: A longitudinal study of implementation of a customer relationship management solution. *International Journal of Technology Marketing, 1*(2), 115–144.

Osimo, D. (2008). Web 2.0 in government: Why and how. *Institute for Prospectice Technological Studies (IPTS), JRC, European Commission, EUR, 23358.*

Osterle, H. (1995). *Business in the information age: Heading for new processes.* Berlin: Springer.

Ostroff, C., & Schmitt, N. (1993). Configurations of organizational effectiveness and efficiency. *Academy of Management Journal, 36*(6), 1345–1361. doi:10.2307/256814.

Otte, E., & Rousseau, R. (2002). Social network analysis: A powerful strategy, also for the information sciences. *Journal of Information Science, 28*(6), 441–453. doi:10.1177/016555150202800601.

Oyelere, P., Laswad, F., & Fisher, R. (2003). Determinants of internet financial reporting by New Zealand companies. *Journal of International Financial. Management and Accounting, 14*(1), 26–63.

Page, L., Brin, S., Motwani, R., & Winograd, T. (1999). *The Pagerank citation ranking: Bringing order to the web.* Technical Report. Stanford InfoLab. Retrieved Dec 20, 2011, from http://ilpubs.stanford.edu:8090/422/1/1999-66.pdf

Page, S. J. (1999). *Transport and tourism.* Harlow, MA: Addison Wesley Longman.

Page, S. J., & Hall, C. M. (2003). *Managing urban tourism.* Harlow, MA: Prentice Hall.

Pagliari, C. (2007). Design and evaluation in eHealth: Challenges and implications for an interdisciplinary field. *Journal of Medical Internet Research, 9*(2), e15. doi:10.2196/jmir.9.2.e15 PMID:17537718.

Paiva Dias, G. (2011). *Local e-government information and service delivery: A survey of municipal websites in Portugal.* Paper presented at the CISTI 6ª Conferência Ibérica de Sistemas e Tecnologias de Informação. Aviero, Portugal.

Palazon, M., & Delgado-Ballester, E. (2009). Effectiveness of price discounts and premium promotions. *Psychology and Marketing, 26*, 1108–1129. doi:10.1002/mar.20315.

Pape, W. (1997). The book of virtuals. *INC Technology, 4*(19), 7–26.

Parkinson, S. (2005). *Telecentres, access and development: Experience and lessons from Uganda and South Africa.* Kampala, Uganda: Fountain Publishers.

Parkinson, S., & Lauzon, A. (2008). The impact of the internet on local social equity: A study of a telecenter in Aguablanca, Colombia. *Information Technologies and International Development, 4*(3), 21–38. doi:10.1162/itid.2008.00015.

Parkinson, S., & Ramirez, R. (2006). Using a sustainable livelihoods approach to assessing the impact of ICTs in development. *Journal of Community Informatics, 2*(3).

Park, Y., & Gretzel, U. (2006). Evaluation of emerging technologies in tourism: The case of travel search engines. In Hitz, M., Sigala, M., & Murphy, J. (Eds.), *Information and communication technologies in tourism 2006* (pp. 371–382). Vienna, Austria: Springer Verlag. doi:10.1007/3-211-32710-X_51.

Parolini, C. (1999). *The value net: A tool for competitive advantages.* Chichester, UK: Wiley.

Parra-López, E., Bulchand-Gidumal, J., Gutierrez-Taño, D., & Díaz-Armas, R. (2011). Intentions to use social media in organizing and taking vacation trips. *Computers in Human Behavior, 27*, 640–654. doi:10.1016/j.chb.2010.05.022.

Parra-Luna, F. (2000). *The performance of social systems.* New York: Kluwer Academic / Plenum Publishers. doi:10.1007/978-1-4615-4251-3.

Parra-Luna, F. (2003). *Elementos para un teoria formal del sistema socia: Una orientacion critica.* Madrid, Spain: Universidad Complutense.

Parveen, M., & Rao, T. (2009). An integrated approach to design and analysis of lean manufacturing system: A perspective of Lean supply chain. *International Journal of Services and Operations Management*, *5*(2), 175–208. doi:10.1504/IJSOM.2009.023232.

Pather, S., & Gomez, R. (2010). Public access ICT: A south-south comparative analysis of libraries, telecentres and cybercafés in South Africa and Brazil. In *Proceedings of AMCIS 2010*. AMCIS.

Paulraj, A. (2009). Environmental motivations: A classification scheme and its impact on environmental strategies and practices. *Business Strategy and the Environment*, *18*(7), 453–468. doi:10.1002/bse.612.

Paulsen, M. (2003). Experiences with learning management systems in 113 European institutions. *Journal of Educational Technology & Society*, *6*(4), 134–148.

Paulus, T. M., Payne, R., & Jahns, L. (2009). Am I making sense here? What blogging reveals about undergraduate student understanding. *Journal of Interactive Online Learning*, *8*(1).

Pava, M. L., & Krausz, J. (1996). The association between corporate social-responsibility and financial performance: The paradox of social cost. *Journal of Business Ethics*, *15*, 321–357. doi:10.1007/BF00382958.

Pavon, F., & Casanova, J. (2006). Telefonía móvil y personas mayores: La accesibilidad como derecho. *Latinoamericana de Tecnología Educativa*, *5*(2), 385–395.

Payne, A. (2005). *Handbook of CRM: Achieving excellence through customer managemen*. Boston: Butterworth-Heinemann.

Payne, A., Ballantyne, D., & Christopher, M. (2005). A stakeholder approach to relationship marketing strategy: The development and use of the six markets model. *European Journal of Marketing*, *39*(7/8), 855–871. doi:10.1108/03090560510601806.

Payne, A., Christopher, M., Clark, M., & Peck, H. (1997). *Relationship marketing for competitive advantage*. Oxford, UK: Butterworth-Heinemann.

Pedersen, P. E., & Nysveen, H. (2003). *Search mode and purchase intention in online shopping behavior*. Retrieved March 10, 2004 from http://citeseer.ist.psu.edu/article/pedersen03search.html

Pedron, C. D., & Caldeira, M. (2005). *Objectivos da adopção do CRM: Um estudo de caso em uma empresa brasileira de telecomunicações*. Paper presented at the 6ª Conferência da Associação Portuguesa de Sistemas de Informação. Aviero, Portugal.

Peixoto, S. (2010). *Web trends - 10 cases made in web 2.0. Gaia*. Comunicarte Publishing.

Pelkonen, T. (2008). Value creation patterns and current trends in digital media service creation: A case study of the Finnish digital media industry. In Bruck, P. A., & Boumans, J. M. (Eds.), *High Performance Multimedia: A Reader on the Technological, Cultural and Economic Dynamics of Multimedia* (pp. 23–65). Amsterdam: IOS Press.

Pennings, J. (1975). The relevance of the structural-contingency model for organizational effectiveness. *Administrative Science Quarterly*, *20*(3), 393–410. doi:10.2307/2391999.

Pentaho Community. (2011). *Pentaho community home*. Retrieved from http://community.pentaho.com/

Pentaho. (2011). *Pentaho open source BI*. Retrieved from http://www.pentaho.com/

People, N. C. (n.d.). *ICT and older people in Ireland: Evidence from a study by the national council on ageing and older people*. Dublin, Ireland: Author.

Peppers, D., & Rogers, M. (2004). *Managing customer relationships: A strategic framework*. Hoboken, NJ: John Wiley & Sons, Inc..

Pereira, P. F. (2003). *Comportamiento del consumidor bancario en internet*. (Doctoral Thesis). Department of Administration and Business Economics, University of Salamanca, Salamanca, Spain.

Perrow, C. (1961). The analysis of goals in complex organizations. *American Sociological Review*, *26*(6), 854–866. doi:10.2307/2090570.

Petersen, C., & Plenborg, T. (2006). Voluntary disclosure and information asymmetry in Denmark. *Journal of International Accounting, Auditing & Taxation, 15*, 127–149. doi:10.1016/j.intaccaudtax.2006.08.004.

Pettinger, R. (2007). *Introduction to management*. Chicago: Palgrave MacMillan.

Pfeffer, J., & Salancik, G. (1978). *The external control of organizations*. New York: Harper & Row.

Philippou, S. (2005). The problem of the European dimension in education: A principled reconstruction of the Greek Cypriot curriculum. *European Educational Research Journal, 4*(4), 343–367. doi:10.2304/eerj.2005.4.4.2.

PHP. (n.d.). Retrieved from www.php.net

Pick, J. B., & Gollakota, K. (2010). Technology for rural telecenters in India: A model and exploratory study of diffusion of information for telecenter use and sustainability. In *Proceedings of AMCIS 2010*. AMCIS.

Pijpers, G. G. M., & Montfort, K. (2006). An investigation of factors that influence senior executives to accept innovations in information technology. *International Journal of Management, 23*(1), 11–23.

Pilevari, N., Hosseini, S., & Jassbi, J. (2008). Fuzzy logic supply chain agility assessment methodology. *IEEE International Conference on Industrial Engineering and Engineering Management*, 1113-1117.

Pinelle, D., & Gutwin, C. (2000). A review of groupware evaluations. In *Proceedings of 9th IEEE WETICE 2000 - Workshop on Enabling Technologies: Infrastructures for Collaborative Enterprises*. WETICE.

Podsakoff, P., & MacKenzie, S. (1997). Impact of organizational citizenship behavior on organizational performance: A review and suggestions for future research. *Human Performance, 10*(2), 133–151. doi:10.1207/s15327043hup1002_5.

Podsakoff, P., & MacKenzie, S., & Fetter. (1993). Citizenship behavior and fairness in organizations: Issues and directions for future research. *Employee Responsibilities and Rights Journal, 6*(3), 257–269. doi:10.1007/BF01419449.

Podsakoff, P., MacKenzie, S., Paine, J., & Bachrach, D. (2000). Organizational citizenship behaviors: A critical review of the theoretical and empirical literature and suggestions for future research. *Journal of Management, 26*(3), 513–563. doi:10.1177/014920630002600307.

Politis, J. D. (2001). *The relationship between self-management leader behaviour, self-leadership worker behaviour and job-related attitudes and perceptions*. (PhD dissertation). University of Technology, Sydney, Australia.

Polk, W. T., Hastings, N. E., & Malpani, A. (2003). Public key infrastructures that satisfy security goals. *IEEE Internet Computing, 7*(4), 60–67. doi:10.1109/MIC.2003.1215661.

Pollock, A. (1995). The impact of information technology on destination marketing. *EU Travel and Tourism Analyst, 3*, 66–83.

Portelli, J. P., & Vilbert, A. B. (2002). A curriculum of life. *Education Canada, 42*(2), 36–39.

Portelli, J. P., & Vilbert, A. B. (2002). Standards, equity, and the curriculum of life. *Analytic Teaching, 22*(1), 4–19.

Porter, M. (1980). *Competitive strategy*. New York: Free Press.

Porter, M. (1998). *Competitive advantage of nations*. New York: Free Press.

Portes, A. (1998). Social capital: Its origins and applications in modern sociology. *Annual Review of Sociology, 22*, 1–24. doi:10.1146/annurev.soc.24.1.1.

Portes, A., & Sensenbrenner, J. (1993). Embeddedness and immigration: Notes on the social determinants of economic action. *American Journal of Sociology, 98*(6), 1320–1350. doi:10.1086/230191.

Potocan, V. (2003). Transition from ethics of independence to ethics of interdependence as a factor of sustainable development. In *Proceedings of the 10th Interdisciplinary Information Management Talks*, (pp. 123-130). Linz, Austria: Universitätsverlag Trauner.

Potocan, V. (2004). *Operations management*. Maribor, Portugal: FEB.

Potocan, V. (2008). Why we need trust in organization?. *Issues in GRBE*, 102-115.

Potocan, V., & Mulej, M. (2007). *From an institutional transition to a real one.* Maribor, Slovenia: FEB.

Potocan, V., & Mulej, M. (2010). *From an institutional transition to a real one into an innovative enterprise.* Maribor, Slovenia: FEB.

Potocan, V., & Rebernik, M. (2002). Achieving synergy of business system via anticipatory system. In *Proceedings of the AIP Conference,* (pp. 441-447). AIP.

Potocan, V. (2005). Efficiency or effectiveness? *Organization, 38*(10), 570–576.

Potocan, V. (2006). Business operations between efficiency and effectiveness. *Journal of Information and Organizational Sciences, 30*(2), 251–262.

Potocan, V. (2009). What culture do we need for economic development? *Business Review (Federal Reserve Bank of Philadelphia), 12*(1), 102–107.

Potocan, V., & Kuralt, B. (2007). Synergy in business: Some new suggestions. *The Journal of American Academy of Business, 12*(1), 199–204.

Potocan, V., Mulej, K., & Kajzer, S. (2005). Business cybernetics: A provocative suggestion. *Kybernetes, 34*(9/10), 1496–1516. doi:10.1108/03684920510614786.

Potocan, V., & Mulej, M. (2006). Ethics of a sustainable enterprise. *Systemic Practice and Action Research, 19*(6), 35–47.

Potter, R. E., & Balthazard, P. A. (2002). Understanding human interaction and performance in the virtual team. *Journal of Information Technology Theory and Application, 4*, 1–23.

Power, D. J. (2007). A brief history of decision support systems, version 4.0. *DSSResources.com*. Retrieved from http://DSSResources.COM/history/dsshistory.html

Prabhakar, S., Pankanti, S., & Jain, A. K. (2003). Biometric recognition: Security and privacy concerns. *IEEE Security & Privacy, 1*(2), 33–42. doi:10.1109/MSECP.2003.1193209.

Prado, P. (2009). *Bridging digital poverty: Adoption of information and communication technologies at community technology centers in the Dominican Republic.* (Doctoral dissertation). University of Miami, Coral Gables, Florida.

Prado, P., Câmara, M. A., & Figueiredo, M. A. (2011). Evaluating ICT adoption in rural Brazil: A quantitative analysis of telecenters as agents of social change. *The Journal of Community Informatics, 7*(1&2).

Prensky, M. (2001). Digital natives, digital immigrants: Do they really think differently? *Horizon, 9*(5), 1–6. doi:10.1108/10748120110424816.

Presenza, A., Sheehan, L., & Ritchie, B. J. (2005). Towards a model of the roles and activities of destination management organizations. *Journal of Hospitality, Tourism and Leisure Science.*

Price, D. J. D. S. (1986). *Little science, big science-- and beyond.* New York: Columbia University Press.

Price, J. (1972). The study of organizational effectiveness. *The Sociological Quarterly, 13*(4), 3–15. doi:10.1111/j.1533-8525.1972.tb02100.x.

Price, L. L., Feick, L. F., & Guskey, A. (1995). Everyday market helping behavior. *Journal of Public Policy & Marketing, 14*(2), 255–266.

Przeclawski, K. (1990). *Le tourisme et le monde de l'unité dans la pluralité. Cahiers du Tourisme (139, Série C).* Aix-en-Provence: Centre des Hautes Etudes Touristiques.

Purvanova, R. K., & Bono, J. E. (2009). Transformational leadership in context: Face-to-face and virtual teams. *The Leadership Quarterly, 20*, 343–357. doi:10.1016/j.leaqua.2009.03.004.

Putnam, R. D. (2000). *Bowling alone: The collapse and revival of american community.* New York, NY: Simon & Schuster. doi:10.1145/358916.361990.

Pyka, A., & Scharnhorst, A. (2009). *Innovation networks.* Berlin: Springer. doi:10.1007/978-3-540-92267-4.

Quick, D., & Nelson, J. (2009). *Principles of organization behavior: Realities and challenges.* Cincinnati, OH: South-Western College.

Quinn, J. B. (1992). *Intelligent enterprise: A knowledge and service based paradigm for industry*. New York: The Free Press.

Quinn, J. B., Anderson, P. Y., & Filkenstein, S. (1996, March-April). Managing professional intellect: Making the most of the best. *Harvard Business Review*, 71–80.

Quinn, R., & Rohrbaugh, J. (1983). A spatial model of effectiveness criteria: Toward a competing values approach to organizational analysis. *Management Science*, *29*(3), 363–377. doi:10.1287/mnsc.29.3.363.

Quintarelli, E. (2011). *Socializing the extended value chain*. Retrieved September 30, 2011, from http://www.socialenterprise.it

Quivy, R., & Campenhoudt, L. (2008). *Manual de investigação em ciências sociais* (5th ed.). Lisboa, Portugal: Gradiva.

Rabassa, B. (1987). *Promoción de ventas: Cómo se prepara una campaña*. Madrid, Spain: Editorial Pirámide.

Rajib, P., Tiwari, D., & Srivastava, G. (2002). Design and development of an integrated supply chain management system in an Internet environment. *Journal of Service Research*, *2*(1), 22–43.

Raju, P. S. (1980). Optimum stimulation level: Its relationship to personality, demographics and exploratory behavior. *The Journal of Consumer Research*, *7*, 272–282. doi:10.1086/208815.

Ramanathan, J., Ramnath, R., Singh, N., Xu, Z., & Xu, Y. (2011). Sense-respond cloud mediator architecture for services evolution. In *Proceedings of the 2011 ACM Symposium on Applied Computing - SAC '11*, (pp. 162-169). ACM Press.

Rao, P., & Holt, D. (2005). Do green supply chains lead to competitiveness and economic performance? *International Journal of Operations & Production Management*, *25*(9), 898–916. doi:10.1108/01443570510613956.

Rasmusson, L., & Janson, S. (1996). *Simulated social control for secure internet commerce*. New York: ACM Press. doi:10.1145/304851.304857.

Ratnasingam, P. (2005). Trust in inter-organizational exchanges: A case study in business to business electronic commerce. *Decision Support Systems*, *39*(3), 525–544. doi:10.1016/j.dss.2003.12.005.

Ravari, A. N., Jafarian, J. H., Amini, M., & Jalili, R. (2010). GTHBAC: A generalized temporal history based access control model. *Journal of Telecommunication Systems*, *45*(2), 111–125. doi:10.1007/s11235-009-9239-9.

Rawls, J. (1971). *A theory of justice*. Cambridge, MA: Harvard University Press.

Raykov, T., & Grayson, D. (2003). A test for change of composite reliability in scale development. *Multivariate Behavioral Research*, *38*(2), 143–159. doi:10.1207/S15327906MBR3802_1.

Raymond, E. (1999). The cathedral and the bazaar. *Knowledge, Technology & Policy*, *12*(3), 23–49. doi:10.1007/s12130-999-1026-0.

Rebelo, T. M., & Gomes, A. D. (2008). Organisational learning and the learning organisation. *The Learning Organization*, *15*(4), 294–308. doi:10.1108/09696470810879556.

Recordon, D., & Reed, D. (2006). OpenID 2.0: A platform for user-centric identity management. In *Proceedings of the 2nd ACM Workshop on Digital Identity Management (DIM'06)* (pp. 11-16). New York: ACM.

Reddick, C. G. (2005). Citizen interaction with e-government: From the streets to servers? *Government Information Quarterly*, *22*(1), 38–57. doi:10.1016/j.giq.2004.10.003.

Rego, A. (2002). *Comportamentos de cidadania nas organizações*. Lisboa, Portugal: McGraw-Hill.

Rego, A., Ribeiro, N., & Cunha, M. (2010). Perceptions of organizational virtuousness and happiness as predictors of organizational citizenship behaviors. *Journal of Business Ethics*, *93*(1), 215–235. doi:10.1007/s10551-009-0197-7.

Reich, K. (2005). *Systemisch-konstruktivistische pädagogik*. Weinheim: Beltz.

Reisenwitz, T., Iyer, R., Kuhlmeier, D., & Eastman, J. (2007). The elderly's internet usage: An updated look. *Journal of Consumer Marketing*, *24*(7), 406–418. doi:10.1108/07363760710834825.

Report, S. M. (2010). *Lightspeed research and the internet advertising bureau UK*. Retrieved from http://www.iabuk.net/en/1/socialmedialanding.html

Rethlefsen, M. L. (2007). Social networking. *Medical Reference Services Quarterly, 26*(sup1), 117-141.

Rezabakhsh, B., Bornemann, D., Hansen, U., & Schrader, U. (2006). Consumer power: A comparison of the old economy and the Internet economy. *Journal of Consumer Policy, 29*(1), 3–36. doi:10.1007/s10603-005-3307-7.

Rezgui, Y. (2007). Exploring virtual team-working effectiveness in the construction sector. *Interacting with Computers, 19*(1), 96–112. doi:10.1016/j.intcom.2006.07.002.

Rhinesmith, S. (1999). *A manager's guide to globalization*. Chicago: Erwin.

Rice Doran, P., Doran, C., & Mazur, A. (2011). Social network analysis as a method for analyzing interaction in collaborative online learning environments. *Journal of Systemics Cybernetics and Informatics*.

Rice, J., & Caniato, F. (2003). Building a secure and resilient supply network. *Supply Chain Management Review, 7*(5), 22–31.

Rico, D. et al. (2009). *The business value of agile software methods: Maximizing ROI with just-in-time processes and documentation*. Fort Lauderdale, FL: J. Ross Publishing.

Ringle, C. M., & Will, A. (2005). *SmartPLS 2.0 (M3)*. Retrieved June 1, 2009, from http://www.smartpls.de

Riss, U. V., Rickayzen, A., Maus, H., & van der Aalst, W. M. P. (2005). Challenges for business process and task management. *Journal of Universal Knowledge Management, 2*, 77–100.

Rist, R. (1997). Challenges faced by the data warehousing pioneers. *Journal of Data Warehousing, 2*(1).

Roberts, J. A., Hann, I. H., & Slaughter, S. A. (2006). Understanding the motivations, participation, and performance of open source software developers: A longitudinal study of the Apache projects. *Management Science, 52*(7), 984. doi:10.1287/mnsc.1060.0554.

Roberts, J. H., & Urban, G. L. (1988). Modeling multiattribute utility, risk and belief dynamics for new consumer durable brand choice. *Management Science, 34*, 167–185. doi:10.1287/mnsc.34.2.167.

Robertson, S. (1998). Telecenters in Mexico: Learning the hard way. *The Journal of Development Communication, 9*(2).

Rocha, C. C. (2003). *Relaciones estratégicas entre pymes: Contraste de hipótesis empresariales mediante ARS*. Revista Hispana para el análisis de redes sociais (v. 4, n. 4, jun. 2003). Retrieved Nov 21, 2011, from http://revista-redes.rediris.es

Rodgers, W., Negash, S., & Suk, K. (2005). The moderating effect of on-line experience on the antecedents and consequences of online satisfaction. *Psychology and Marketing, 22*(4), 313–331. doi:10.1002/mar.20061.

Rodrigues, M., Dias, G. P., & Teixeira, A. (2010). *Human language technologies for e-gov*. Paper presented at the WEBIST. Valencia, Spain.

Roebuck, K. (2011). *Near field communication (NFC), hight-impact strategies - What you need to know: Definition, adoptions, impact, benefits, maturity, vendors*. Emereo Pty Limited.

Roehm, M. L., Pullins, E. B., & Roehm, H. A. Jr. (2002). Designing loyalty-building programs for packaged goods brands. *JMR, Journal of Marketing Research, 39*(2), 202–213. doi:10.1509/jmkr.39.2.202.19085.

Rogers, E. M. (1983). *Difussion of innovations* (3rd ed.). New York: The Free Press.

Rogers, E. M. (2003). *Diffusion of innovations* (5th ed.). New York, NY: The Free Press.

Rogers, E. M., & Kincaid, D. L. (1981). *Communication networks: Toward a new paradigm for research*. New York: The Free Press.

Romero, D., & Molina, A. (2011). Collaborative networked organisations and customer communities: Value co-creation and co-innovation in the networking era. *Production Planning and Control, 22*(5/6), 447–472. doi:10.1080/09537287.2010.536619.

Rosen, A. (2006). *Technology trends: E-learning 2.0 learning solutions*. Retrieved March 2011 from http://www.readygo.com/e-learning-2.0.pdf

Rosen, D., Kim, J. H., & Nam, Y. (2010). Birds of a feather protest together: Theorizing self-organizing political protests with flock theory. *Systemic Practice and Action Research*, *23*(5), 419–441. doi:10.1007/s11213-010-9167-3.

Rosen, D., & Nelson, C. (2008). Web 2.0: A new generation of learners and education. *Computers in the Schools*, *25*(3-4), 211–225. doi:10.1080/07380560802370997.

Ross, J. W., Vitale, M. R., & Willcocks, L. P. (2003). The continuing ERP revolution: Sustainable lessons, new modes of delivery. In Shanks, G., Seddon, P. B., & Willcocks, L. P. (Eds.), *Second-wave enterprise resource planning systems—Implementing for effectiveness* (pp. 102–132). Cambridge, UK: Cambridge University Press. doi:10.1017/CBO9780511815072.005.

Rosu, S. M., Guran, M., & Mateescu, L. M. (2007). E-learning sites development using open source software support in the enterprise. In *Proceedings of the 4th Balkan Region Conference on Engineering Education & MSE* (pp. 98-103). Sibiu, Romania: MSE.

Rosu, S. M., & Dragoi, G. (2011). VPN solutions and network monitoring to support virtual teams work in virtual enterprises. *Computer Science and Information System*, *8*(1), 1–26. doi:10.2298/CSIS100127033R.

Rosu, S. M., Dragoi, G., Rosu, L., & Guran, M. (2010). Virtual enterprise network solutions to support e-learning sites development. In Katalinic, B. (Ed.), *DAAAM International Scientific Book 2010* (pp. 725–742). Vienna, Austria: DAAAM International. doi:10.2507/daaam.scibook.2010.63.

Rotman, J. (2010). *Unite breaks guitars – Case study*. Toronto, Canada: School of Management, University of Toronto.

Rowe, G., & Wright, G. (1999). The delphi technique as a forecasting tool: Issues and analysis. *International Journal of Forecasting*, *15*(4), 353–375. doi:10.1016/S0169-2070(99)00018-7.

Rudman, R. J., & Steenkamp, L. P. (2009). Potential influence of web 2.0 usage and security practices of online users on information management. *South African Journal of Information Management*, *11*(2).

Rudra, A., & Yeo, E. (1999). Key issues in achieving data quality and consistency in data warehousing among large organizations in Australia. In *Proceedings of the 32nd Hawaii International Conference on System Sciences*, (pp. 7012-7019). IEEE.

Rugimbana, R. O., & Iversen, P. (1994). Perceived attributes of innovations. *International Journal of Bank Marketing*, *12*(2), 30–35. doi:10.1108/02652329410052955.

Rusman, E., van Bruggen, J., Sloep, P., & Koper, R. (2010). Fostering trust in virtual project teams: Towards a design framework grounded in a trustworthiness antecedents (TWAN) schema. *International Journal of Human-Computer Studies*, *68*(11), 834–850. doi:10.1016/j.ijhcs.2010.07.003.

Russ-Eft, D., & Preskill, H. (2001). *Evaluation in organizations: A systemic approach to enhancing learning, performance, and change*. Cambridge, MA: MIT Press.

Russell, N., ter Hofstede, A. H. M., Edmond, D., & van der Aalst, W. M. P. (2005). Workflow data patterns: Identification, representation and tool support. *Lecture Notes in Computer Science*, *3716*, 353–368. doi:10.1007/11568322_23.

Ryan, M. (2003). Public relations and the web: Organizational problems, gender and institutional type. *Public Relations Review*, *29*(3), 335–349. doi:10.1016/S0363-8111(03)00040-7.

Rybski, D., Buldyrev, S. V., Havlin, S., Liljeros, F., & Makse, H. A. (2009). Scaling laws of human interaction activity. *Proceedings of the National Academy of Sciences of the United States of America*, *106*(31), 12640–12645. doi:10.1073/pnas.0902667106 PMID:19617555.

Saari, L., & Judge, T. (2004). Employee attitudes and job satisfaction. *Human Resource Management*, *43*(4), 395–407. doi:10.1002/hrm.20032.

Saaty, T. L. (1980). *The analytic hierarchy process*. New York: McGraw Hill Publications.

Saaty, T. L. (1996). *Decision making with dependence and feedback: The analytic network process*. Pittsburgh, PA: RWS Publications.

Sadik, A. (2009). Improving pre-service teachers' visual literacy through flickr. *Procedia - Social and Behavioral Sciences, 1*(1), 91-100.

Salancik, G., & Pfeffer, J. (1974). The bases and uses of power in organizational decision making: The case of a university. *Administrative Science Quarterly, 19*(4), 453–473. doi:10.2307/2391803.

Salvetti, F., & Srinivasan, S. (2005). Local flow betweenness centrality for clustering community graphs. *Internet and Network Economics*, 531–544.

Samad, S. (2005). Unraveling the organizational commitment and job performance relationship: Exploring the moderating effect of job satisfaction. *Business Review (Federal Reserve Bank of Philadelphia), 4*(2), 79–84.

Sánchez, J. R. (1997). *Marketing financiero: Principios y estrategias*. Madrid, Spain: Civitas.

Sánchez, M. J., & Villarejo, A. F. (2004). La calidad del servicio electrónico: Un análisis de los efectos moderadores del comportamiento de uso de la web. *Cuadernos de Economía y Dirección de la Empresa, 21*, 121–152.

Sandoval-Almaz, R. (2007). Digital literacy: Problems faced by telecenter users in Mexico. *Information Systems Journal, 13*(3), 217–232.

Santo, C. D., Colace, F., Santo, M. D., & Vento, M. (2003). *Evaluating on-line learning platforms: A case study*. Paper presented at the 36th Hawaii International Conference on System Sciences. Hawaii, HI.

Santoro, F. M., Borges, M. R. S., & Santos, N. (2006). Patterns for designing planning mechanisms. *International Journal of Computer Applications in Technology, 25*(2/3), 102–115. doi:10.1504/IJCAT.2006.009066.

Santos, A. (2010). *Robust and adaptable platforms of dynamic educational environment content: Contribution to the Portuguese education success in the secondary level*. (Unpublished master dissertation). Open University, Aviero, Portugal.

Santos, M. B., & Souza, C. D. (2008). Visualização temporal de redes sociais com o OSSNetwork. In *Proceedings of WIVA - Workshop on Information Visualization and Analysis in Social Networks*, (pp. 79-88). Campinas, Brasil: WIVA.

Sanz Rodriguez, J. (2010). *Evaluación apriorística de la reusabilidad de los objetos de aprendizaje*. Retrieved from http://dbspace.uah.es/dbspace/handle/10017/8715

Sanz, J., Dodero, J. M., & Sanchez-Alonso, S. (2009). A preliminary analysis of software engineering metrics-based criteria for the evaluation of learning objects reusability. *International Journal of Emerging Technologies in Learning, 4*.

Sashkin, M. (1988). The visionary leader. In Conger, J. A., & Kanungo, R. N. (Eds.), *Charismatic leadership: The elusive factor in organisational effectiveness*. San Francisco, CA: Jossey-Bass.

Saxenian, A. (1994). *Regional advantage: Culture and competition in silicon valley and route 128*. Boston: Harvard University Press.

Sbarcea, K. (1998, March 6). Know what, know how, know why: Implementing a knowledge management system – The Phillips Fox experience. *Australian Law Librarian*, 4-8.

Schegg, R., Liebrich, A., Scaglione, M., & Ahmad, S. F. S. (2008). An exploratory field study of web 2.0 in tourism. In O'Connor, P., Höpken, W., & Gretzel, U. (Eds.), *Information and Communication Technologies in Tourism 2008* (pp. 209–219). New York: Springer. doi:10.1007/978-3-211-77280-5_14.

Schein, E. (1992). *Organizational culture and leadership: A dynamic view*. San Francisco, CA: Jossey-Bass.

Schein, E. (2004). *Organization culture and leadership*. New York: Wiley.

Schermerhorn, J. (2009). *Management*. New York: Wiley-Blackwell.

Schilling, M. A., & Phelps, C. C. (2007). Interfirm collaboration networks: The impact of large-scale network structure on firm innovation. *Management Science, 53*(7), 1113–1126. doi:10.1287/mnsc.1060.0624.

Schmid, H. (1994). *Probabilistic part-of-speech tagging using decision trees.*

Schultz, W. (2001). *The moral conditions of economic efficiency*. Cambridge, UK: Cambridge University Press. doi:10.1017/CBO9780511549649.

Schumpeter, J. (1934). *The theory of economic development*. Cambridge, MA: Harvard University Press.

Schwaber, K. (2004). *Agile project management with scrum* (*Vol. 7*). Redmond, WA: Microsoft Press.

Schwartz, J. (2006). *The magic of thinking big*. London: Simon & Schuster.

Schwarz, A. (2003). *Defining information technology acceptance: A human-centred, management-oriented perspective*. (Unpublished doctoral dissertation). University of Houston, Houston, TX.

Scott, J. (2000). Social network analysis. *American Ethnologist*, *24*(1), 219–220.

Scott, J. E., & Walczak, S. (2009). Cognitive engagement with a multimedia ERP training tool: Assessing computer self-efficacy and technology acceptance. *Information & Management*, *46*(4), 221–232. doi:10.1016/j.im.2008.10.003.

Sears, N. (2009). Measures should be taken to provide granular control over each social networking site. *Engineering & Technology*, *6*, 6.

Seashore, S., & Yuchtman, E. (1967). Factorial analysis of organizational performance. *Administrative Science Quarterly*, *12*(3), 377–395. doi:10.2307/2391311.

Seddon, P., Shanks, G., & Willcocks, L. P. (2003). Introduction: ERP—The quiet revolution? In Shanks, G., Seddon, P. B., & Willcocks, L. P. (Eds.), *Second-wave enterprise resource planning systems—Implementing for effectiveness* (pp. 1–19). Cambridge, UK: Cambridge University Press. doi:10.1017/CBO9780511815072.001.

Semple, E. (2007). *Survey proves 90% of managers are clueless*. Retrieved September 1, 2011, from http://www.fastforwardblog.com

Senge, P. M. (1990). *The fifth discipline: The art and practice of the learning organisation*. New York: Doubleday.

Seokwoo, S., Nerur, S., & Teng, J. T. C. (2008). Understanding the influence of network positions and knowledge processing styles. *Communications of the ACM*, *51*(10), 123–126. doi:10.1145/1400181.1400208.

Serrano, C., Fuertes, , & Gutiérrez, B. (2007). Online reporting by banks: A structural modelling approach. *Online Information Review*, *31*(3), 310–332. doi:10.1108/14684520710764096.

Serusi, M. (2011). Customer service 2.0: Top 10 airlines and airports performing customer service through social media. *SimpliFlying*. Retrieved February 9, 2012, from http://simpliflying.com/2011/customer-service-2-0-top-10-airlines-and-airports- performing-customer-service-through-social-media/

Seyedhoseini, S., Jassbi, J., & Pilevari, N. (2010). Application of adaptive neuro fuzzy inference system in measurement of supply chain agility: Real case study of a manufacturing company. *African Journal of Business Management*, *4*(1), 83–96.

Shachaf, P. (2008). Cultural diversity and information and communication technology impacts on global virtual teams: An exploratory study. *Information & Management*, *45*(1), 131–142. doi:10.1016/j.im.2007.12.003.

Shadbolt, N. (2006). *Problemas sociales, eticos y legales: ¿Cómo afecta el aumento al acceso al conocimiento a nuestra sociedad?* Paper presented at Memories for Life: The Future of our Pasts. London, UK.

Shah, S. K. (2005). Motivation, governance & the viability of hybrid forms in open source software development. *SSRN eLibrary*. Retrieved from http://papers.ssrn.com/sol3/papers.cfm?abstract_id=898247

Shane, S. (2008). *The handbook of technology and innovation management*. New York: Wiley-Blackwell.

Shankar, C., & Bellefroid, V. (2011). *Microsoft dynamics sure step 2010: The smart guide to the successful delivery of Microsoft dynamics business solutions*. Birmingham, UK: Packt Publishing.

Shapiro, D. L., Furst, S. A., Spreitzer, G. M., & Von Glinow, M. A. (2002). Transnational teams in the electronic age: Are team identity and high performance at risk? *Journal of Organizational Behavior*, *23*, 455–467. doi:10.1002/job.149.

Sherman, K. (1998, November 1). Let the seller beware. *CIO Magazine, 1*.

Sheshimski, E., Strom, R., & Baumol, W. (2007). *Entrepreneurship, innovation, and the growth mechanism of the free-enterprise economies*. Princeton, NJ: Princeton University Press.

Sheth, J. N., & Parvatiyar, A. (1995). Relationship marketing in consumer markets: Antecedents and consequences. *Journal of the Academy of Marketing Science*, *23*(4), 255–271. doi:10.1177/009207039502300405.

Sheth, J. N., & Parvatiyar, A. (2002). Evolving relationship marketing into a discipline. *Journal of Relationship Marketing*, *1*(1), 3–16. doi:10.1300/J366v01n01_02.

Shi, D., Zhu, S., & Liu, L. (2007). Clustering coefficients of growing networks. *Physica A: Statistical Mechanics and its Applications, 381*, 515-524.

Shiels, M. (2011). Twitter co-founder Jack Dorsey rejoins company. *BBC News*. Retrieved from http://www.bbc.co.uk/news/business-12889048

Shih, Y. Y., & Huang, S. S. (2009). The actual usage of ERP systems: An extended technology acceptance perspective. *Journal of Research and Practice in Information Technology*, *41*(3), 263–276.

Shimp, T. A., & Bearden, W. O. (1982). The use of extrinsic cues to facilitate product adoption. *JMR, Journal of Marketing Research*, *19*(2), 229–240. doi:10.2307/3151623.

Shim, S. S. Y., Bhalla, G., & Pendyala, V. (2005). Federated identity management. *IEEE Computer*, *38*(12), 120–122. doi:10.1109/MC.2005.408.

Shin, Y. (2005). Conflict resolution in virtual teams. *Organizational Dynamics*, *34*(4), 331–345. doi:10.1016/j.orgdyn.2005.08.002.

Shivers-Blackwell, S. L., & Charles, A. C. (2006). Ready, set, go: Examining student readiness to use ERP technology. *Journal of Management Development*, *25*(8), 795–805. doi:10.1108/02621710610684268.

Shi, Y. Z., Cheung, K. M., & Prendergast, G. (2005). *The effectiveness of sales promotion tools: A Hong Kong study*. Hong Kong: Hong Kong Baptist University.

Shum, S. B., Motta, E., & Domingue, J. (2000). ScholOnto: An ontologybased digital library server for research documents and discourse. *International Journal on Digital Libraries*, *3*(3), 237–248. doi:10.1007/s007990000034.

Shu, W., & Chuang, Y.-H. (2011). Why people share knowledge in virtual communities? *Social and Personality*, *39*(5), 671–690. doi:10.2224/sbp.2011.39.5.671.

Sicilia, M., Ruiz, S., & Munuera, J. L. (2005). Effects of interactivity in a web site: The moderating effect of need for cognition. *Journal of Advertising*, *34*(3), 31–45. doi:10.1080/00913367.2005.10639202.

Siegel, J., & Shim, J. (2000). *Accounting handbook*. New York: Barron.

Sigala, M. (2002). Modelling e-marketing strategies: Internet presence and exploitation of Greek hotels. *Journal of Travel & Tourism Marketing*, *11*(2), 83–103.

Sigala, M. (2008). Web 2.0, social marketing strategies and distribution channels for city destinations: Enhancing the participatory role of travelers and exploiting their collective intelligence. In Gascó-Hernández, M., & Torres-Coronas, T. (Eds.), *Information Communications Technologies and City Marketing*. Hershey, PA: Information Science Publishing.

Sigala, M. (2011). Preface – Special issue on web 2.0 in travel and tourism: Empowering and changing the role of travelers. *Computers in Human Behavior*, *27*, 607–608. doi:10.1016/j.chb.2010.04.005.

Sigala, M., & Marianidis, D. (2010). DMOs, e-democracy and collaborative destination management: An implementation framework. In Gretzel, U., Law, R., & Fuchs, M. (Eds.), *Information and Communication Technologies in Tourism 2010* (pp. 235–246). New York: Springer. doi:10.1007/978-3-211-99407-8_20.

Siggelkow, N., & Rivkin, J. W. (2005). Speed and search: Designing organizations for turbulence and complexity. *Organization Science*, 101–122. doi:10.1287/orsc.1050.0116.

Siika, A. M., Rotich, J. K., Simiyu, C. J., Kigotho, E. M., Smith, F. E., & Sidle, J. E. et al. (2005). An electronic medical record system for ambulatory care of HIV-infected patients in Kenya. *International Journal of Medical Informatics*, *74*(5), 345–355. doi:10.1016/j.ijmedinf.2005.03.002 PMID:15893257.

Silva, A., & Gardesani, R. (2005). *Impactos do CRM no relacionamento da empresa com clientes*. Paper presented at the Congresso Anual de Tecnologia da Informação. Aviero, Portugal.

Silva, P., & Silva, A. (2007). Design experiences with the learning objects board system. In *Proceedings of the Hawaii International Conference on System Sciences (HICSS-40)*. IEEE Computer Society.

Silva, P., & Silva, A. R. (2009). Application scenarios for the learning objects pool. *Journal of Universal Computer Science*, *15*(7).

Simões, D. (2010). *Enterprise data warehouses: A conceptual framework for a successful implementation*. Paper presented at the Canadian Council for Small Business & Entrepreneurship Annual Conference (CCSBE 2010). Calgary, Canada.

Simões, D., & Soares, A. L. (2003). *Redes organizacionais e desenvolvimento de sistemas de informação*. Paper presented at the 4ª Conferência da Associação Portuguesa de Sistemas de Informação (CAPSI'03). Porto, Portugal.

Simões, D., Ferreira, H., & Soares, A. L. (2007). *Ontology engineering in virtual breeding environments*. Paper presented at the 8th IFIP Working Conference on Virtual Enterprises (PRO-VE'07). New York, NY.

Simões, D., & Soares, A. L. (2007). Knowledge communities and inter-organizational networks. In Putnik, G. D., & Cunha, M. M. (Eds.), *Encyclopedia of Networked and Virtual Organizations*. Hershey, PA: Information Science Reference.

Simon, C. J., & Warner, J. T. (1992). Matchmaker, matchmaker: The effect of old boy networks on job match quality, earnings, and tenure. *Journal of Labor Economics*, *10*(3), 306–330. doi:10.1086/298289.

Simon, H. (1976). *Administrative behavior: A study of decision-making processes in administrative organizations*. New York: Free Press.

Simon, S. J., & Paper, D. (2007). User acceptance of voice recognition technology: An empirical extension of the technology acceptance model. *Journal of Organizational and End User Computing*, *19*(1), 24–50. doi:10.4018/joeuc.2007010102.

Singer, P. (1999). *Practical ethics*. Oxford, UK: Oxford University Press.

Sirin, E., & Parsia, B. (2004). *Pellet: An owl dl reasoner*.

SITA. (2007). *Airline ICT trends survey 2007 executive summary*. Retrieved from http://www.sita.aero/NR/rdonlyres/2C464901-6574-4AA0-B4E317199B9B8D45/0/AirlineIT07Booklet.pdf

Sittig, D. F., King, S., & Hazlehurst, B. L. (2001). A survey of patient-provider e-mail communication: What do patients think? *International Journal of Medical Informatics*, *61*(1), 71–80. doi:10.1016/S1386-5056(00)00134-9 PMID:11248604.

Skarzynski, P., & Gibson, R. (2008). *Innovation to the core*. Boston: Harvard Business Press.

Skoog, R., Von Lehmen, A., Clapp, G., Gannett, J. W., Kobrinski, H., & Poudyal, V. (2004). Metro network design methodologies that build a next-generation network infrastructure based on this generation's services and demands. *Journal of Lightwave Technology*, *22*(11), 2680–2692. doi:10.1109/JLT.2004.836748.

Skrt, R. (2007). *Spletne socialne mreže*. Retrieved October 25, 2011, from http://www.mojmikro.si/preziveti/kar_tako/spletne_socialne_mrezenavidezna_indija_koromandija

Sledgianowski, D., & Kulviwat, S. (2009). Using social network sites: The effects of playfulness, critical mass and trust in a hedonic context. *Journal of Computer Information Systems*, *49*(4), 74–83.

Sliger, M., & Broderick, S. (2008). *The software project manager's bridge to agility*. Boston: Pearson Education, Inc..

Small, G. (2009). *El cerebro digital*. Barcelona, Spain: Ediciones Urano.

Smith, A., & Peck, B. (2010). The teacher as the `digital perpetrator': Implementing web 2.0 technology activity as assessment practice for higher education innovation or imposition?. *Procedia - Social and Behavioral Sciences, 2*(2), 4800-4804.

Snowden, D., & Boone, M. (2007). A leader's framework for decision making. *Harvard Business Review, 85*(11), 68–76. PMID:18159787.

Social Business Systems. (2011). *Success factors for enterprise 2.0 applications*. Retrieved October 30, 2011, from http://www.aiim.org

Soliman, F., Innes, C., & Spooner, K. (1999). Managing the human resources' knowledge. In *Proceedings of the Seventh Annual Conference of the International Employment Relations Association*, (pp. 497-510). Christchurch, New Zealand: Lincoln University.

Soliman, F. (2009). Modelling the appraisal of quality management programs. *The Employment Relations Record, 9*(2), 73–83.

Soliman, F. (2010). Role of human resources management as a CoP match-maker. *The International Employment Relations Review, 16*(1), 69–81.

Soliman, F. (2011). Could one transformational leader convert the organisation from knowledge based into learning organisation, then into innovation? *Journal of Modern Accounting and Auditing, 7*(12), 1352–1361.

Soliman, F. (2011). Globalisation as driver for transforming organisations from knowledge to learning and then to innovation. In Srivastava, R., Pandy, T., Kumar, N., & Singhal, R. (Eds.), *Business Competitiveness in the 21st Century* (pp. 42–52). New Delhi: MacMillan Publishers India Ltd..

Soliman, F. (2011). Modelling the role of HRM in the innovation chain. *The Employment Relations Record, 11*(2), 1–20.

Soliman, F., & Spooner, K. (2000). Strategies for implementing knowledge management: Role of human resources management. *Journal of Knowledge Management, 4*(4), 337–345. doi:10.1108/13673270010379894.

Soliman, F., & Youssef, M. (2003). The role of critical information in enterprise knowledge management. *Industrial Management & Data Systems, 103*(7), 484–490. doi:10.1108/02635570310489188.

Solomon, C. M. (1995). Global teams: The ultimate collaboration. *The Personnel Journal, 74*(9), 49–53.

Solomon, C. M. (2001). Managing virtual teams. *Workforce, 80*(6), 60–64.

Solove, D. J. (2006). A brief history of information privacy law. In Wolf, C. (Ed.), *Proskauer on Privacy: A Guide to Privacy and Data Security Law in the Information Age* (pp. 1–46). New York, NY: Practising Law Institute.

Somers, M. T., Nelson, K., & Karimi, J. (2003). Confirmatory factor analysis of the end-user computing satisfaction instrument: Replication within an ERP domain. *Decision Sciences, 34*(3), 595–621. doi:10.1111/j.1540-5414.2003.02428.x.

Somers, T. M., & Neslon, K. G. (2004). A taxonomy of players and activities across the ERP project life cycle. *Information & Management, 41*(3), 257–278. doi:10.1016/S0378-7206(03)00023-5.

Sood & Adams. (1984). Model of management learning styles or predictor of export behavior and performance. *Journal of Business Research, 12*, 169–182. doi:10.1016/0148-2963(84)90004-3.

Sorj, B. (2003). *Brasil@povo.com: A luta contra a desigualdade na sociedade da informação*. Brasilia, Brazil: Unesco.

Soule, A. (2010). *Fighting the social media wildfire: How crisis communication must adapt to prevent from fanning the flames*. (Thesis). University of North Carolina at Chapel Hill, Chapel Hill, NC.

Sousa, L., & Gomes, R. (2010). Strategy 2.0 to a teaching and learning process in higher education. In *Proceedings of the 2010 International Conference on E-Education, E-Business, E-Management and E-Learning: Ic4e 2010*, (pp. 484-489). Los Alamitos, CA: IEEE Computer Soc.

So, W. C. M., Wong, T. N. D., & Sculli, D. (2005). Factors affecting intentions to purchase via the internet. *Industrial Management & Data Systems, 105*(9), 1225–1244. doi:10.1108/02635570510633275.

Spago, B. I. (2011). *Spago business intelligence*. Retrieved from http://www.spagoworld.org/

Spivack, N. (2007). *How the WebOS evolves?* Retrieved February 2011 from http://novaspivack.typepad.com/nova_spivacks_Weblog/2007/02/steps_towards_a.html

Splichal, S. (1997). *Javno mnenje: Teoretski razvoj in spori v XX*. Ljubljana, Slovenia: Fakulteta za družbene vede.

Spruit, M., & Abdat, N. (2012). The pricing strategy guideline framework for SaaS vendors. *International Journal of Strategic Information Technology and Applications*, *3*(1), 38–53. doi:10.4018/jsita.2012010103.

Srivastava, S. (2007). Green supply-chain management: A state-of-the-art literature review. *International Journal of Management Reviews*, *9*(1), 53–80. doi:10.1111/j.1468-2370.2007.00202.x.

Stanforth, N. F., Lennon, S. J., & Moore, S. (2000). *Perceived risk and purchase intent associated with television shopping*. Paper presented at Frontiers in Direct and Interactive Marketing Research. New York, NY.

Starbucks (Producer). (2011, October 28). *The create jobs for USA fund* [informative video]. Retrieved November 15, 2011, from http://www.youtube.com/user/Starbucks

Starbucks. (2011). *LinkedIn*. Retrieved November 15, 2011, from http://www.linkedin.com/company/starbucks

Starbucks. (2011). *Facebook*. Retrieved November 15, 2011, from http://www.facebook.com/Starbucks

Stata, R. (1989). Organisational learning-the key to management innovation. *Sloan Management Review*, *30*(3), 63–74.

Staw, B. (1986). Organizational psychology and the pursuit of the happy/productive worker. *California Management Review*, *28*(4), 40–53. doi:10.2307/41165214.

Steckle, N., & Fondas, N. (1995). Building team leader effectiveness: A diagnostic tool. *Organizational Dynamics*, *23*(3), 20. doi:10.1016/0090-2616(95)90023-3.

Steenkamp, J. E. M., & Baumgartner, H. (1992). The role of optimum stimulation level in exploratory consumer behavior. *The Journal of Consumer Research*, *19*, 434–448. doi:10.1086/209313.

Steers, R. (1975). Problems in the measurement of organizational effectiveness. *Administrative Science Quarterly*, *20*(4), 546–558. doi:10.2307/2392022.

Steers, R. (1977). *Organizational effectiveness: A behavioral view*. Santa Monica, CA: Goodyear.

Steffen, A. (2006). *Worldchanging: A user's guide for the 21st century*. New York: Harry N. Abrams.

Stepper, J. (2011). *Don't retweet the revolution*. Retrieved October 1, 2011, from http://johnstepper.com

Sterne, J. (2010). *Social media metrics: How to measure and optimize your marketing investment*. New York: John Wiley & Sons, Inc..

Stevenson, J. S., Bruner, G. C. II, & Kumar, A. (2000). Webpage background and viewer attitudes. *Journal of Advertising Research*, (January): 29–34.

Stewart, D., & Grout, J. (2001). The human side of mistake-proofing. *Production and Operations Management*, *10*(4), 440–459. doi:10.1111/j.1937-5956.2001.tb00086.x.

Stoitsev, T., Scheidl, S., & Spahn, M. (2007). A framework for light-weight composition and management of ad-hoc business processes. *Lecture Notes in Business Information Processing*, *4849*, 213–226.

Strange, K. F. T. (2009). *Making BI and data warehousing strategic: The key issues, LE-19-4691*. Gartner Group.

Strasses, S., Eveland, J., Cummins, G., Deniston, L., & Romani, J. (1981). Conceptualizing the goal and systems models of organizational effectiveness – Implications for comparative evaluation research. *Journal of Management Studies*, *18*(3), 321–340. doi:10.1111/j.1467-6486.1981.tb00105.x.

Straub, D. (1989). Validating instruments in MIS research. *Management Information Systems Quarterly*, *13*(2), 147–169. doi:10.2307/248922.

Student, K. (1968). Supervisory influence and work group performance. *The Journal of Applied Psychology*, *52*(3), 188–194. doi:10.1037/h0025886 PMID:5659502.

Suchanek, F. M., Ifrim, G., & Weikum, G. (2006). *LEILA: Learning to extract information by linguistic analysis*.

Su, F., & Beaumont, C. (2010). Evaluating the use of a wiki for collaborative learning. *Innovations in Education and Teaching International*, *47*(4), 417–431. doi:10.1080/14703297.2010.518428.

Sum, S. M. (2008). *Internet technology and social capital: how the Internet affects seniors' social capital and wellbeing*. Sydney, Australia: University of Sydney.

Sung, Y., Kim, Y., Kwon, O., & Moon, J. (2010). An explorative study of korean consumer participation in virtual brand communities in social network sites. *Journal of Global Marketing*, *23*(5), 430–445. doi:10.1080/08911762.2010.521115.

Sun, P. Y. T., & Scott, J. L. (2003). Exploring the divide-organisational learning and learning organisation. *The Learning Organization*, *10*(4), 202–215. doi:10.1108/09696470310476972.

Sun, Y., Bhattacherjee, A., & Ma, Q. (2009). Extending technology usage to work settings: The role of perceived work compatibility in ERP implementation. *Information & Management*, *46*, 351–356. doi:10.1016/j.im.2009.06.003.

Sun, Y., & Chen, C. (2011). Towards coequal authorization for dynamic collaboration.[LNCS]. *Proceedings of Active Media Technology*, *6890*, 229–240. doi:10.1007/978-3-642-23620-4_26.

Sveiby, K.-E. (2010). *Methods for measuring intangible assets*. Retrieved in July 2010, from www.sveiby.com/articles/IntangibleMethods.htm

Swafford, P., Ghosh, S., & Murthy, N. (2008). Achieving supply chain agility through IT integration and flexibility. *International Journal of Production Economics*, *116*(2), 288–297. doi:10.1016/j.ijpe.2008.09.002.

Swanson, M., & Guttman, B. (1996). Generally accepted principles and practices for securing information technology systems. Washington, DC: National Institute of Standards and Technology (NIST).

Tamashiro, R. (2002). *Pros and cons of online learning: Conflicting perceptions among teacher education students*. Retrieved January 2011 from http://www.hiceducation.org/edu_proceedings/Roy Tamashiro.pdf

Tang, C. S. (2006). Robust strategies for mitigating supply chain disruptions. *International Journal of Logistics: Research and Applications*, *9*(1), 33–45. doi:10.1080/13675560500405584.

Tan, S. T. (1999). Strategies for reducing consumers' risk aversion in internet shopping. *Journal of Consumer Marketing*, *16*(2), 163–180. doi:10.1108/07363769910260515.

Taylor, D. G., Lewin, J. E., & Strutton, D. (2011). Friends, fans, and followers: Do ads work on social networks? *Journal of Advertising Research*, *51*(1), 258–275. doi:10.2501/JAR-51-1-258-275.

Teichmann, K., & Zins, A. (2008). Information elements on DMO-Web sites: Alternative approaches for measuring perceived utility. In O'Connor, P., Höpken, W., & Gretzel, U. (Eds.), *Information and Communication Technologies in Tourism 2008* (pp. 209–219). New York: Springer. doi:10.1007/978-3-211-77280-5_19.

Tenenhaus, M., Vinzi, V. E., Chatelin, Y. M., & Lauro, C. (2005). PLS path modelling. *Computational Statistics & Data Analysis*, *48*, 159–205. doi:10.1016/j.csda.2004.03.005.

The Liberty Alliance Project. (2005). *Liberty alliance identity federation 1.2 (ID-FF 1.2) specifications*. Retrieved November 3, 2011, from http://www.projectliberty.org/liberty/resource_center/specifications/liberty_alliance_id_ff_1_2_specifications/

Themistocleous, M., & Chen, H. (2004). Investigating the integration of SMEs' information systems: An exploratory case study. *International Journal of Information Technology and Management*, *3*(2-4), 208–234. doi:10.1504/IJITM.2004.005033.

This WeekIn Startups (Producer). (2011, January 4). *This week in startups - Frank Speiser, founder of SocialFlow.com* [informative video]. Retrieved November 15, 2011, from http://thisweekin.com/thisweekin-startups/this-week-in-startups-105-frank-speiser-founder-of-socialflow-com/

Thompson, L., & Cupples, J. (2008). Seen and not heard? Text messagind and digital sociality. *Social & Cultural Geography*, *9*(1), 95–108. doi:10.1080/14649360701789634.

Thompson, R., Compeau, D., & Higgins, C. (2006). Intentions to use information technologies: An integrative model. *Journal of Organizational and End User Computing, 18*(3), 25–46. doi:10.4018/joeuc.2006070102.

Thorbjornsen, H., & Supphellen, M. (2004). The impact of brand loyalty on website usage. *Journal of Brand Management, 11*(3), 199–208. doi:10.1057/palgrave.bm.2540166.

Tidd, J., & Bessant, J. (2009). *Managing innovation: Integrating technological, market and organizational change*. Chichester, UK: Wiley.

Top, E., Yukselturk, E., & Inan, F. A. (2010). Reconsidering usage of blogging in preservice teacher education courses. *The Internet and Higher Education, 13*(4), 214–217. doi:10.1016/j.iheduc.2010.05.003.

Torrent-Sellens, J., Castillo, D., Gabaldón, P., Ruiz, E., & Sainz, J. (2010). *Hacia la banca multicanal*. Madrid, Spain: ESIC.

Townsend, A., DeMarie, S., & Hendrickson, A. (1998). Virtual teams: Technology and the workplace of the future. *The Academy of Management Executive, 12*(3), 17–29.

Treville, S., & Antonakis, J. (2006). Could lean production job design, be intrinsically motivating? Contextual, configurational, and levels-of-analysis issues. *Journal of Operations Management, 24*(2), 99–123. doi:10.1016/j.jom.2005.04.001.

Trevino, L., & Nelson, K. (2006). *Managing business ethics: Straight talk about how to do it right*. New York: Wiley.

Tsui, A. (1990). A multiple-constituency model of effectiveness: An empirical examination at the human resource subunit level. *Administrative Science Quarterly, 35*(3), 458–483. doi:10.2307/2393313.

Turban, E. Aronson, Liang, & Sharda, R. (2007). Decision support and business intelligence systems (8th Ed.). Englewood Cliffs, NJ: Prentice Hall.

Turban, E., King, D., Lee, J. K., & Viehland, D. (2004). *Electronic commerce 2004: A managerial perspective* (3rd ed.). Englewood Cliffs, NJ: Prentice Hall.

Turban, E., Sharda, S., Aronson, J. E., & King, D. (2008). *Business intelligence: A managerial approach*. Upper Saddle River, NJ: Pearson Prentice Hall.

Tversky, A., Sattath, S., & Slovic, P. (1988). Contingent weighting in judgement and choice. *Psychological Review, 95*, 371–384. doi:10.1037/0033-295X.95.3.371.

Twidale, M., Randall, D., & Bentley, R. (1994). Situated evaluation for cooperative systems. In *Proceedings of Computer-Supported Cooperative Work Conference – CSCW'94*. Chapel Hill, NC: CSCW.

Ullrich, C., Tan, X., Borau, K., Shen, L., Luo, H., & Shen, R. (2008). Why web 2.0 is good for learning and for research: Principles and prototypes. In *Proceedings of the 17th International World Wide Web Conference*, (pp. 705-714). IEEE.

Umble, E. J., Haft, R. R., & Umble, M. M. (2002). Enterprise resource planning: Implementation procedures and CSF. *European Journal of Operational Research, 146*(2), 241–257. doi:10.1016/S0377-2217(02)00547-7.

UN. (2010). *Government survey 2010 leveraging e-government at a time of financial and economic crisis*. New York: UN.

Universal McCann. (2010). *The socialisation of brands – Social media tracker wave 5*. Retrieved December 01, 2011 from www.mccannworldgroup.com/

Usluel, Y. K., & Mazman, S. G. (2009). Adoption of web 2.0 tools in distance education. *Procedia - Social and Behavioral Sciences, 1*(1), 818-823.

Uysal, M., Chen, J. S., & Williams, D. R. (2000). Increasing state market share through a regional positioning. *Tourism Management, 21*, 89–96. doi:10.1016/S0261-5177(99)00082-5.

Uzoka, F. M. E., Abiola, R. O., & Nyangeresi, R. (2008). Influence of product and organizational constructs on ERP acquisition using an extended technology acceptance model. *International Journal of Enterprise Information Systems, 4*(2), 67–83. doi:10.4018/jeis.2008040105.

Uzzi, B., & Schwartz, M. (1993). Structural holes - The social-structure of competition. In R. S. Burt (Ed.), Contemporary Sociologya Journal of Reviews, 22(2), 155-157. doi:doi:10.2307/2075713 doi:10.2307/2075713.

Vala, J., Monteiro, M., Lima, L., & Caetano, A. (1995). *Psicologia social das organizações: Estudos em empresas portuguesas*. Oeiras, Portugal: Celta Editora.

ValueNetworks. (2010). *What is value network analysis (VNA)?* Retrieved in December 2010, from www.valuenetworks.com

Van den Bulte, C., & Stremersch, S. (2004). Social contagion and income heterogeneity in new product diffusion: A meta-analytic test. *Marketing Science*, *23*(4), 530–544. doi:10.1287/mksc.1040.0054.

Van Den Bulte, C., & Wuyts, S. (2007). *Social networks and marketing*. Cambridge, MA: Marketing Science Institute.

van der Aalst, W. M. P., Pesic, M., & Schonenberg, H. (2009). Declarative workflows: Balancing between flexibility and support. *Computer Science -. Research for Development*, *23*(2), 99–113.

van der Aalst, W. M. P., Weske, M., & Grünbauer, D. (2005). Case handling: A new paradigm for business process support. *Data & Knowledge Engineering*, *53*(2), 129–162. doi:10.1016/j.datak.2004.07.003.

Van der Merwe, L. F., Pitt, L.P., & Abratt, R. (2005, Spring). Stakeholder strength: PR survival strategies in the internet age. *Public Relations Quarterly*, 39-48.

Van Dyne, L., Graham, J., & Dienesch, R. (1994). Organizational citizenship behavior: Construct redefinition, measurement and validation. *Academy of Management Journal*, *37*(4), 765–802. doi:10.2307/256600.

Vanilla. (2011). *True open source BI platform*. Retrieved from http://www.bpm-conseil.com/

Varadharajan, V. (2009). A note on trust-enhanced security. *IEEE Security & Privacy*, *7*(3), 57–59. doi:10.1109/MSP.2009.59.

Varian, H. R. (2002). Market structure in the network age. In Brynjolfsson, E., & Kahin, B. (Eds.), *Understanding the digital economy: Data, tools, and research*. Cambridge, MA: MIT Press.

Varner, P. E. (1999). *The economics of open source software*. Retrieved from http://www.cs.virginia.edu/~pev5b/writing/econ_oss/

Vázquez, J. A., Saldaña, I., & Celaya, J. (2009). La visibilidad de los museos en la web 2.0. *Portal Cultural Dosdoce.com*. Retrieved October 17, 2011, from http://www.dosdoce.com/articulo/estudios/3071/la-visibilidad-de-los-museos-en-la-Web-2-0/

Venkatesh, V. (1998). *User acceptance of information technology: A unified view*. (Unpublished doctoral dissertation). University of Minnesota, Minneapolis, MN.

Venkatesh, V., & Bala, H. (2008). Technology acceptance model 3 and a research agenda on interventions. *Decision Sciences*, *39*(2), 273–315. doi:10.1111/j.1540-5915.2008.00192.x.

Venkatesh, V., & Davis, F. D. (2000). A theoretical extension of the technology acceptance model: Four longitudinal field studies. *Management Science*, *46*(2), 186–205. doi:10.1287/mnsc.46.2.186.11926.

Venkatesh, V., Morris, M. G., Davis, G. B., & Davis, F. D. (2003). User acceptance of information technology: Toward a unified view. *Management Information Systems Quarterly*, *27*(3), 425–445.

Virkus, S. (2008). Use of web 2.0 technologies in LIS education: Experiences at Tallinn University, Estonia. Program: Electronic Library and Information Systems, 42(3), 262 - 274.

Virtuoso, O. (2010). *Universal server platform for the real-time enterprise*. Retrieved from http://virtuoso.openlinksw.com/

Viswesvaran, C. (2001). Assessment of individual job performance: A review of the past century and a look ahead. In Anderson, N., Ones, D., Sinangil, H., & Viswesvaran, C. (Eds.), *Handbook of Industrial, Work and Organizational Psychology* (*Vol. 1*, pp. 110–126). London: SAGE Publications. doi:10.4135/9781848608320.n7.

von Hippel, E. (2005). Democratizing innovation: The evolving phenomenon of user innovation. *Journal für Betriebswirtschaft*, *55*(1), 63–78. doi:10.1007/s11301-004-0002-8.

Vossen, G. (2009). Web 2.0: A buzzword, a serious development, just fun, or what? In J. Filipe, D. A. Marca, B. Shishkov, M. van Sinderen (Eds.), *ICE-B 2009 - Proceedings of the International Conference on e-Business*, (pp. 33-40). Milan, Italy: INSTICC Press.

Vygotsky, L. S. (1978). *Mind in society: The development of higher psychological processes*. Cambridge, MA: Harvard University Press.

Wagner, J., & Schneider, B. (1987). Legal regulation and the constraint of constituency satisfaction. *Journal of Management Studies*, *24*(2), 189–200. doi:10.1111/j.1467-6486.1987.tb00943.x.

Walsh, J. P., & Ungson, G. R. (1991). Organizational memory. *Academy of Management Review*, *16*, 57–91.

Wang, C., Xiong, M., Zhou, Q., & Yu, Y. (2007). Panto: A portable natural language interface to ontologies. *The Semantic Web: Research and Applications*, 473-487.

Wang, P., Zheng, J., Fu, L., Patton, E., Lebo, T., Ding, L., et al. (2011). A semantic portal for next generation monitoring systems. In *Proceedings of the Semantic Web – ISWC 2011* (Vol. 7032, pp. 253-268). Springer.

Wang, X. H., Zhang, D. Q., Gu, T., & Pung, H. K. (2004). *Ontology based context modeling and reasoning using OWL*.

Wang, H., Song, Y., Hamilton, A., & Curwell, S. (2007). Urban information integration for advanced e-planning in Europe. *Government Information Quarterly*, *24*(4), 736–754. doi:10.1016/j.giq.2007.04.002.

Wan, L., & Zhao, C. (2007). Construction of a knowledge management framework based on web 2.0. *Wireless Communications. Networking and Mobile Computing*, *12*, 5341–5344.

Warner, M., & Witzel, M. (2004). *Managing in virtual organizations*. London: Thomson.

Wasko, M. M., & Faraj, S. (2005). Why should I share? Examining social capital and knowledge contribution in electronic networks of practice. *Management Information Systems Quarterly*, *29*(1), 35–57.

Wasserman, S., & Faust, K. (1994). *Social network analysis: Methods and applications*. Cambridge, MA: Cambridge University Press. doi:10.1017/CBO9780511815478.

Wasserman, S., & Galaskiewicz, J. (1994). *Advances in social network analysis: Research in the social and behavioural sciences*. Thousand Oaks, CA: Sage Publications.

Watch, S. (2002). *Older people and information society technology: A comparative analysis of the current situation in the European Union and of future trends*. Academic Press.

Waterman, R., & Peters, T. (1982). *In search of excellence*. New York: Harper Collins.

Watson, H. J. (2009). Tutorial: Business intelligence –Past, present, and future. *Communications of the Association for Information Systems*, *25*(39).

Watson, H. J., Gerard, J. G., Gonzalez, L. E., Haywood, M. E., & Fenton, D. (1999). Data warehousing failures: Case studies and findings. *Journal of Data Warehousing*, 44–55.

Watson, H. J., & Wixom, B. H. (2007). The current state of business intelligence. *IEEE Computer*, *40*(9), 96–99. doi:10.1109/MC.2007.331.

Watts, D. J. (1999). Networks, dynamics, and the small-world phenomenon. *American Journal of Sociology*, *105*, 493–527. doi:10.1086/210318.

Weber, M. (1968). *Economy and society*. Totowa, NJ: Bedminster Press.

Webster Dictionary (WD). (1928). *An American dictionary of the English language*. Retrieved September 16, 2011 from http://www.cbtministries.org/resources/Webster1828.htm

Webster, F. E. Jr. (1992). The changing role of marketing in the corporation. *Journal of Marketing*, *56*(4), 1–17. doi:10.2307/1251983.

Weeks, S. (2001). Understanding trust management systems. In *Proceedings of the 2001 IEEE Symposium on Security and Privacy* (p. 94). Washington, DC: IEEE Computer Society.

Wei, S., Ruys, F., van Hoof, H. B., & Combrink, T. (2001). Uses of the internet in the global hotel industry. *Journal of Business Research*, *54*, 235–241. doi:10.1016/S0148-2963(00)00117-X.

Wellman, B., & Berkowitz, S. D. (1988). Social structures: A network approach. *PsycCRITIQUES*, *2*, 513.

Welti, N. (1999). *Successful SAP R/3 implementation—Practical management of ERP project*. Boston: Addison-Wesley Longman Publishing Co..

Were, M. C., Sutherland, J. M., Bwana, M., Ssali, J., Emenyonu, N., & Tierney, W. M. (2008). Patterns of care in two HIV continuity clinics in Uganda, Africa: A time-motion study. *AIDS Care*, *20*(6), 677–682. doi:10.1080/09540120701687067 PMID:18576169.

Werther, W., & Chandler, D. (2005). *Strategic corporate social responsibility: Stakeholders in a global environment*. London: SAGE.

Werthner, H., & Klein, S. (1999). *Information technology and tourism – A challenging relationship*. New York: Springer Verlag. doi:10.1007/978-3-7091-6363-4.

Werthner, H., & Klein, S. (2000). ICT and the changing landscape of global tourism distribution. *EM-Electronic Markets*, *9*(4), 256–262.

Weske, M. (2007). *Business process management - Concepts, languages, architectures*. Berlin: Springer.

What Is, R. S. S. (n.d.). *RSS explained*. Retrieved October 14, 2011, from http://www.whatisrss.com/

White, J. (2005). *Contemporary moral problems*. Surrey, UK: Wadsworth.

Wikström, S., Carlell, C., & Frostling-Henningsson, M. (2002). From real world to mirror world representation. *Journal of Business Research*, *55*(8), 647–654. doi:10.1016/S0148-2963(00)00205-8.

Wiley, D. (2000). *Connecting learning objects to instructional design theory: A definition, a metaphor, and a taxonomy*. Retrieved from http://reusability.org/read/chapters/williams.doc

Wiley, D. (2001). Peer-to-peer and learning objects: The new potential for collaborative constructivist learning online.[ICALT.]. *Proceedings of ICALT*, *2001*, 494–498.

Williams, J. B., & Jacobs, J. (2004). Exploring the use of blogs as learning spaces in the higher education sector. *Australasian Journal of Educational Technology*, *20*(2), 232-247. Retrieved September 28, 2011, from http://www.ascilite.org.au/ajet/ajet20/williams.html

Williams, K. T. (2009). Case study: Dell hell: The impact of social media on corporate communication. Hoboken, NJ: CorpCommCollab.

Williams, L., & Anderson, S. (1991). Job satisfaction and organizational commitment as predictors of organizational citizenship and in-role behaviors. *Journal of Management*, *17*(3), 601–617. doi:10.1177/014920639101700305.

Wilson, S. (2008). Public key superstructure it's PKI Jim, but not as we know it! In *Proceedings of the 7th Symposium on Identity and Trust on the Internet (IDtrust '08)* (pp. 72-88). New York: ACM.

Wilson, H. J., Guinan, P. J., Parise, S., & Weinberg, B. D. (2011). What's your social media strategy? *Harvard Business Review*, *89*(7/8), 23–25.

Wixom, B., & Watson, H. J. (2001). An empirical investigation of the factors affecting data warehousing success. *Management Information Systems Quarterly*, *25*(1), 17–41. doi:10.2307/3250957.

Wold, H. (1982). Soft modelling: The basic design and some extensions. *Systems Under Indirect Observations*, 1–52.

Wolfinbarger, M., & Gilly, M. (2001). Shopping online for freedom, control, and fun. *California Management Review*, *43*(2), 34–55. doi:10.2307/41166074.

Wollan, R., Smith, N., & Zhou, C. (2011). *The social media management handbook: Everything you need to know to get social media working in your business*. New York: John Wiley & Sons, Inc..

Womack, J., Jones, D., & Roos, D. (1991). *The machine that change the world*. New York: HarperCollins Publishers.

Woodman, R. W., Sawyer, J. E., & Griffin, R. W. (1993). Toward a theory of organisational creativity. *Academy of Management Review*, *18*, 293–321.

World Bank. (2009). Retrieved from http://go.worldbank.org/M1JHE0Z280

World Tourism Organization Business Council. (1999). Introduction. In *Marketing tourism destinations online: Strategies for the information age*. Madrid, Spain: World Tourism Organization.

World Tourism Organization. (2001). *E-business for tourism – Practical guidelines for tourism destinations and businesses*. Madrid, Spain: World Tourism Organization.

Wren, D. (2004). *The history of management thought*. New York: Wiley.

Wyld, D. C. (2008). Management 2.0: A primer on blogging for executives. *Management Research News*, *31*(6), 448–483. doi:10.1108/01409170810876044.

Xiaowei, L. (2006). A test on the systematic fuzzy measures of the key degree for the core employees' performance traits. *Canadian Social Science*, *2*(5), 38–43.

Xie, G., Yang, Y., Liu, S., Qiu, Z., Pan, Y., & Zhou, X. (2007). EIAW: Towards a business-friendly data warehouse using semantic web technologies. In K. Aberer, et al. (Eds.), *ISWC/ASWC '07: Proceedings of the 6th International Semantic Web Conference and 2nd Asian Semantic Web Conference* (LNCS), (vol. 4825, pp. 851-904). Berlin: Springer Verlag.

Xinyi, H., Yang, X., Chonka, A., Jianying, Z., & Deng, R. H. (2011). A generic framework for three-factor authentication: Preserving security and privacy in distributed systems. *IEEE Transactions on Parallel and Distributed Systems*, *22*(8), 1390–1397. doi:10.1109/TPDS.2010.206.

Yammarino, F. J., Spangler, W. D., & Bass, B. M. (1993). Transformational leadership and performance: A longitudinal investigation. *The Leadership Quarterly*, *4*, 81–102. doi:10.1016/1048-9843(93)90005-E.

Yang, H., Lim, S., King, J., & Helal, A. (2006). Open issues in nomadic pervasive computing. In *Proceedings of UbiSys'06 (LNCS)*. Berlin: Springer.

Yang, T., & Lai, H. (2006). Comparison of product bundling strategies on different online shopping behaviours. *Electronic Commerce Research and Applications*, *5*, 295–304. doi:10.1016/j.elerap.2006.04.006.

Yao, Y. (2006). Three perspectives of granular computing. *Journal of Nanchang Institute of Technology*, *25*(2), 16–21.

Yau, S., & Chen, Z. (2008). *Security policy integration and conflict reconciliation for collaborations among organizations in ubiquitous computing environments. Ubiquitous Intelligence and Computing (LNCS)* (*Vol. 5061*, pp. 3–19). Berlin: Springer.

Yaxley, H. (2008). *How PR practitioners should engage with social networking*. Retrieved October, 25, 2011 from http://greenbanana.wordpress.com/2008/02/28/how-pr-practitioners-should-engage-with-social-networking/

Yelmo García, J. C., San Miguel González, B., & Martín García, Y. S. (2007). *Análisis del potencial de las comunicaciones móviles para la mejora de los servicios proporcionados por la administración pública a las personas con discapacidad*. Retrieved from http://www.tecnimap.es

Ye, Q., Law, R., Gu, B., & Chen, W. (2011). The influence of user-generated content on traveler behavior: An empirical investigation on the effects of e-word-of-mouth to hotel online bookings. *Computers in Human Behavior*, *27*, 634–639. doi:10.1016/j.chb.2010.04.014.

Yeung, J., Chan, A., Chan, D., & Li, L. K. (2007). Development of a partnering performance index (PPI) for construction projects in Hong Kong: A Delphi study. *Construction Management and Economics*, *25*(12), 1219–1237. doi:10.1080/01446190701598673.

Yeung, T. A., & Law, R. (2004). Extending the modified heuristic usability evaluation technique to chain and independent hotel websites. *Hospital Management*, *23*, 307–313. doi:10.1016/j.ijhm.2003.03.001.

Yi, Y. M., Fiedler, K. D., & Park, J. S. (2006). Understanding the role of individual innovativeness in the acceptance of IT-based innovativeness: Comparative analyses of models and measures. *Decision Sciences*, *37*(3), 393–426. doi:10.1111/j.1540-5414.2006.00132.x.

Yongchareon, S., & Liu, C. (2010). Lecture Notes in Computer Science: *Vol. 6426*. *A process view framework for artifact-centric business processes* (pp. 26–43). Heidelberg: Springer. doi:10.1007/978-3-642-16934-2_6.

Yoo, K. H., & Gretzel, U. (2008). Understanding differences between online travel review writers and non-writers. In T. Hara (Ed.), *Proceedings of the 13th Annual Graduate Education and Student Research* (pp. 21-29). Orlando, FL: GESR.

Yoo, K. H., & Gretzel, U. (2010). Antecedents and impacts of trust in travel-related consumer-generated media. *Information Technology and Tourism*, *12*, 139–152. doi:10.3727/109830510X12887971002701.

Yoo, K. H., Lee, Y., Gretzel, U., & Fesenmaier, D. R. (2009). Trust in travel-related consumer generated media. In Höpken, W., Gretzel, U., & Law, R. (Eds.), *Information and Communication Technologies in Tourism 2009* (pp. 49–59). New York: Springer. doi:10.1007/978-3-211-93971-0_5.

Young, J. (2012). *College 2.0: Teachers without technologies strikes back*. Retrieved February 2012 from chronicle.com/article/College-20-Teachers-Without/123891/

Youngberg, E., Olsen, D., & Hauser, K. (2009). Determinants of professionally autonomous end user acceptance in an enterprise resource planning system environment. *International Journal of Information Management*, *29*, 138–144. doi:10.1016/j.ijinfomgt.2008.06.001.

Young, K. (2011). Social ties, social networks and the Facebook experience. *International Journal of Emerging Technologies and Society*, *9*(1), 20–34.

Youssef, H., Sait, S. M., & Khan, S. A. (2002). Topology design of switched enterprise networks using a fuzzy simulated evolution algorithm. *Engineering Applications of Artificial Intelligence*, *15*, 327–340. doi:10.1016/S0952-1976(02)00066-0.

Yu, A. Y., Tian, S. W., Vogel, D., & Chi-Wai Kwok, R. (2010). Can learning be virtually boosted? An investigation of online social networking impacts. *Computers & Education*, *55*(4), 1494–1503. doi:10.1016/j.compedu.2010.06.015.

Yu, C. S. (2005). Causes influencing the effectiveness of the post-implementation ERP system. *Industrial Management & Data Systems*, *105*(1/2), 115–132. doi:10.1108/02635570510575225.

Yuchtman, E., & Seashore, S. (1967). A system resource approach to organizational effectiveness. *American Sociological Review*, *32*(6), 891–903. doi:10.2307/2092843.

Yuki, G., & Howell, J. M. (1999). Organisational and contextual influences on the emergence and effectiveness of charismatic leadership. *The Leadership Quarterly*, *10*(2), 257–283. doi:10.1016/S1048-9843(99)00014-4.

Yun, T. W., & Lee, W. (2001). *Psychological antecedents of amount of attention to web sites – An exploratory study*. Paper presented at 20th Annual Advertising and Consumer Psychology Conference, Online Consumer Psychology: Understanding and Influencing Consumer Behavior in the Virtual World. Seattle, WA.

Zablah, A. R., Bellenger, D. N., & Johnston, W. J. (2004). An evaluation of divergent perspectives on customer relationship management: Towards a common understanding of an emerging phenomenon. *Industrial Marketing Management*, *33*, 475–489. doi:10.1016/j.indmarman.2004.01.006.

Zaccaro, S., & Bader, P. (2003). E-leadership and the challenges of leading e-teams: Minimizing the bad and maximizing the good. *Organizational Dynamics*, *31*(4), 377–387. doi:10.1016/S0090-2616(02)00129-8.

Zack, M. H. (1999). Developing a knowledge strategy. *California Management Review*, *41*(3), 125–145. doi:10.2307/41166000.

Zadeh, L. (1976). The concept of linguistic variable and its application to approximate reasoning. *Information Sciences*, *8*, 199–249, 301–357. doi:10.1016/0020-0255(75)90036-5.

Zadeh, L. (1997). Toward a theory of fuzzy information granulation and its centrality in human reasoning and fuzzy logic. *Fuzzy Sets and Systems*, *90*, 111–127. doi:10.1016/S0165-0114(97)00077-8.

Zadjabbari, B., Wongthongtham, P., & Hussain, F. K. (2008). Towards an ontological intellectual capital based model in sustainable business performance. In *Proceedings of CIMCA*. IEEE.

Zafiropoulos, C., Vrana, V., & Paschaloudis, D. (2006). The Internet practices of hotel companies: An analysis from Greece. *International Journal of Contemporary Hospitality Management*, *18*(2), 156–163. doi:10.1108/09596110610646709.

Zaidi, M. A. (2006). Is Google the best search engine marketing solution? *SearchMarketing-UK.com*. Retrieved from http://www.searchmarketing-uk.com

Zammuto, R. (1982). *Assessing organizational effectiveness: Systems change, adaptation and strategy*. Albany, NY: SUNY Press.

Zammuto, R. (1984). A comparison of multiple constituency models of organizational effectiveness. *Academy of Management Review*, *9*(4), 606–618.

Zaščerinska, J. (2010). Conditions, criteria, indicators and levels of forming communicative competence. In *Proceedings of International Scientifical Conference Society, Integration, Education of Rezekne Higher Education Institution*. Rēzekne, Latvia: Rēzeknes Augstskolas Izdevniecība.

Zaščerinska, J. (2010). *Efficiency of English for academic purposes activity in student language education: developing the system of the external and internal perspectives*. Paper presented at the European Conference on Educational Research Education and Cultural Change. Helsinki, Finland. Retrieved December 3, 2011, from http://www.eera-ecer.eu/ecer-programmes/conference/ecer-2010/contribution/465-2/?no_cache=1&cHash=3b88f1a563

Zaščerinska, J., & Ahrens, A. (2011). *Components of languaging in tertiary studies*. Paper presented at the European Conference on Educational Research 2011 Urban Education. Berlin, Germany.

Zaščerinska J. (2009). Designing teaching/learning activities to promote e-learning. In AhrensLange (Eds.), First Asian Conference on e-Business and Telecommunications (pp. 22-35). Berlin, Germany: Mensch & Buch.

Zaščerinska, J. (2011). Social dimension of web 3.0 in engineering education. In Bassus, , & Ahrens, , & Lange (Eds.), *Information and Communication Technologies in Engineering and Business* (pp. 101-130). Berlin, Germany: Mensch & Buch.

Zaščerinska, J. (2011). How to teach content: Existing concepts and prospects for development. *Changing Education in a Changing Society*, *1*, 134–149.

Zaščerinska, J., Ahrens, A., & Bassus, O. (2011). Enterprise 2.0 and 3.0 in education: Engineering and business students' view. In Cruz-Cunha, M. M., Putnik, G. D., Lopes, N., Gonçalves, P., & Miranda, E. (Eds.), *Business Social Networking: Organizational, Managerial, and Technological Dimensions* (pp. 472–494). Hershey, PA: IGI Global. doi:10.4018/978-1-61350-168-9.ch025.

Žbogar, D. (2010). *Vpliv družbenih medijev na prakso odnosov z javnostmi*. Ljubljana, Slovenia: Fakulteta za družbene vede.

Zeinstejer, R. (2008). The wiki revolution: A challenge to traditional education. *TESL-EJ*, *11*(4). Retrieved September 28, 2011, from https://tesl-ej.org/~teslejor/ej44/m1.html

Zeisser, M. (2010). Unlocking the elusive potential of social networks. *The McKinsey Quarterly*, (3): 28–30.

Zenko, Z., Mulej, M., & Marn, J. (2004). Innovation before entry into the EU: The case of Slovenia. *Post Communist Economies*, *16*(2), 169–189. doi:10.1080/1463137042000223877.

Zhang, C. (2008). The institutional framework of the United Nations development programme--Ministry of science and technology (UNDP--most) telecenter project in rural china. *Information Technologies and International Development*, *4*(3).

Zhang, X., Song, M., & Huang, G. Q. (2009). Tourism supply chain management: A new research agenda. *Tourism Management*, *30*, 345–358. doi:10.1016/j.tourman.2008.12.010.

Zhou, S.-M., & Gan, J. (2008). Low-level interpretability and high-level interpretability: A unified view of data-driven interpretable fuzzy system modelling. *Fuzzy Sets and Systems*, *159*, 3091–3131. doi:10.1016/j.fss.2008.05.016.

Zigurs, I. (2003). Leadership in virtual teams: Oxymoron or opportunity? *Organizational Dynamics*, *31*(4), 339–351. doi:10.1016/S0090-2616(02)00132-8.

Zolin, R., Hinds, P., Fruchter, R., & Levitt, R. (2004). Interpersonal trust in cross-functional, geographically distributed work: A longitudinal study. *Information and Organization*, *14*(1), 1–26. doi:10.1016/j.infoandorg.2003.09.002.

zur Muehlen, M., & Indulska, M. (2010). Modeling languages for business processes and business rules: A representational analysis. *Information Systems*, *35*, 379–390. doi:10.1016/j.is.2009.02.006.

About the Contributors

Maria Manuela Cruz-Cunha is currently an Associate Professor in the School of Technology at the Polytechnic Institute of Cavado and Ave, Portugal. She holds a Dipl. Eng. in the field of Systems and Informatics Engineering, an M.Sci. in the field of Computer Integrated Manufacturing and a Dr.Sci in the field of Production Systems Engineering. She teaches subjects related with Information Systems, Information Technologies, and Organizational Models to undergraduate and post-graduate studies. She supervises several PhD projects in the domain of Virtual Enterprises and Information Systems and Technologies. She regularly publishes in international peer-reviewed journals and participates on international scientific conferences. She serves as a member of Editorial Board and Associate Editor for several International Journals and for several Scientific Committees of International Conferences. She has authored and edited several books and her work appears in more than 120 papers published in journals, book chapters and conference proceedings. She is the co-founder and co-chair of several international conferences: CENTERIS – Conference on ENTERprise Information Systems and ViNOrg – International Conference on Virtual and Networked Organizations: Emergent Technologies and Tools. She is editor-in-chief of the *International Journal of Web Portals*.

Fernando Moreira graduated in Computer Science (1992), M.Sc. in Electronic Engineering (1997), and Ph.D. in Electronic Engineering (2003), both at the Faculdade de Engenharia da Universidade do Porto. He is a member of the Dep. Informatics at Universidade Portucalense since 1992, currently as Associate Professor. He is a (co-)author of several scientific publications with peer-review on national and international conferences. He has already regularly serves as a member of the Programme and Organizing Committees of national and international workshops and conferences, namely CAPSI, ISEIS, CISTI, and CENTRIS. He conducts his research activities in Communication Networks, Quality of Services, eLearning, and m-Learning. He is the coordinator of the M.Sc. of Informatics. He is associated with NSTICC, ACM, and IEEE.

João Eduardo Varajão is a professor of Information Systems Management, Project Management and Software Engineering at the University of Trás-os-Montes e Alto Douro and a visiting professor at the University of Porto Business School. He is also a researcher of the Centro Algoritmi at the University of Minho. Born and raised in Portugal, he attended the University of Minho, earning his Undergraduate (1995), Masters (1997), and Doctorate (2003) degrees in Technologies and Information Systems. In 2012, he received his Habilitation degree from the University of Trás-os-Montes e Alto Douro. His current main research interests are in Information Systems Management and Project Management. Before joining academia, he worked as an IT/IS consultant, project manager, information systems analyst, and software developer, for private companies and public institutions. He has supervised more than 50 Masters and Doctoral dissertations in the Information Systems field. He has published over 250 works, including refereed publications, authored books, edited books, book chapters, and communications at international conferences. He serves as editor-in-chief, associate editor, and member of the editorial board for international journals and has served in numerous committees of international conferences and workshops. He is co-founder of CENTERIS – Conference on ENTERprise Information Systems and other events.

* * *

Andreas Ahrens was born in Wismar, Germany, in January 1971. He received the Dipl.-Ing. degree in electrical engineering from the University of Rostock in 1996. From 1996 to 2008, he was with the Institute of Communications Engineering of the University of Rostock, from which he received the Dr.-Ing. and Dr.-Ing. habil. degree in 2000 and 2003, respectively. In 2008, he became a Professor for Signal and System theory at the Hochschule Wismar, University of Technology, Business, and Design, Germany. His main field of interest includes error correcting codes, multiple-input multiple-output systems, iterative detection for both wireline and wireless communication as well as social computing.

Ana Margarida Almeida holds a PhD in Sciences and Technologies of Communication and is an Assistant Professor at the Department of Communication and Arts, University of Aveiro, Portugal. She is also the first cycle degree Director (New Communication Technologies Degree) and member of the Cetac.media research unit direction board. Her present research interests are related to multimedia projects management, communication, and health and digital inclusion.

Helena Alvelos graduated in Electronics and Telecommunications Engineering, received a MSc degree in Management (MBA) and a PhD in Engineering Sciences. She is currently an Assistant Professor in the Department of Economics, Management, and Industrial Engineering at the University of Aveiro and teaches subjects in the fields of Applied Statistics and Quality. She has published in several conferences and journals, and currently she is a researcher at the Governance, Competitiveness, and Public Politics (GOVCOPP), and her current research interests include data analysis, quality management, and statistical quality control.

Anna Antonakopoulou is a PhD candidate of the Intelligent Communications and Broadband Networks Laboratory (ICBNet) of the National Technical University of Athens (NTUA), Greece. She received her diploma in Electrical and Computer Engineering from the University of Patras in 2006. As a research fellow of the NTUA since 2007, she has participated in several European and national research projects. Her research interests include Internet Technologies, Information Security & Privacy, Semantic Web, Object-oriented software design and development, QoS in IP networks, Transport and control protocols; she has eight publications related to these fields.

Susana Garrido Azevedo (Ph.D in Management) is Assistant Professor of Logistics and Management at University of Beira Interior (UBI) – Portugal. She is member of the Research Unit UNIDEMI. Her research interests include: logistics, ICT in logistics (RFID), and supply chain management. She has published in several international journals and has published books in Operations Management, Logistics and Competitiveness areas. Also, she has collaborated as reviewer with many journals and also international conferences. She has published in several international journals and is also associate editor of The *International Journal of Management Science and Information Technology* (IJMSIT) and member of the editorial board of the *International Journal of Business Performance and Supply Chain Modelling* (IJBPSCM).

Zélia Baptista is a Portuguese and French language teacher and is currently the head of the Portuguese language department at the Macau Portuguese School. She received her degree in Romanic Languages from the University of Coimbra in 1979. Since 1976 until 1995, Zélia worked as a teacher for the public educational system in Portugal where she held several coordination positions in different schools. Afterwards, she moved to the Special Administrative Region of Macau where she has been teaching for the past two decades both Portuguese curricula and Portuguese as a foreign language (UMAC, IPM, IPOR). Zélia has worked at the Macau Portuguese School since its very beginning and has devoted much of her late career to translational pedagogy using the territory's unique characteristics as a learning platform. Zélia co-authored three trilingual publications with her students and is currently a Master in Education student at the University of Saint Joseph.

Alexandre Humberto dos Santos Barão is teacher of Portuguese Education Ministry and researcher of Instituto de Engenharia de Sistemas e Computadores - Investigação e Desenvolvimento (INESC-ID) Lisboa. As a teacher, he was responsible for several disciplines such as: object oriented programming, Web development, algorithms and data structures, and information systems modeling. He is the Social Network Analysis and Reengineering Environment (SNARE) operational coordinator. SNARE is a research project developed at the Information System Group, INESC-ID. He has interests in the following areas: Modeling and Metamodeling, Oriented Objects Programming, Hypermedia, Social Computing and Organizational Knowledge Management, Learning Objects, Social Software, and Collaborative Learning Platforms.

Salvador Del Barrio-García has a Ph.D. in Business Administration from University of Granada (Spain). He is an Associate Professor of Marketing and Market Research Department at this University. His area of specialization are the Integrated Marketing Communication (IMC), Online Consumer Behaviour, and Marketing for Higher Education. He has published several books as author and co-author on these matters. He has also published various peer-reviewed papers in prestigious journals such as *European Journal of Marketing, Cities, EURE, Public Relations Review, Industry and Higher Education, Journal of Marketing Trends, European Marketing Academy, Spanish Journal of Marketing Research.* He has directed research projects with businesses and the public administration and has taught master and doctoral studies in various universities. He is referee for several international journals: *European Journal of Marketing, CyberPsychology and Behavior, Cornell Hospitality Quarterly, Innovar Journal, Journal Research Science Teaching, European Marketing Academy.*

Olaf Bassus was born in Wolfsburg, Germany, in January 1956. He received the Dipl.-Oec. degree in Business Administration from the University of Economics, Berlin, in 1981. From 1981 to 1985, he was with the Institute of Business Administration of the University of Economics, Berlin, from which he received the Dr. Oec. degree in 1985. From 1986 to 1990, he worked as the Head of the Operative Planning Division and Deputy Head of the Finance Division in the machine building company NILES in Berlin. From 1990 to 1994, he worked as an assistant scientific director of the Institute of Financing, Taxation, and Auditing at the University of Technology and Economics in Berlin, and as freelance lecturer and management consultant in Berlin and Brandenburg. In 1994, he became a Professor for Accountancy and Auditing at the Hochschule Wismar, University of Technology, Business, and Design, Germany.

Roberto Berjón (PhD.). Received a PhD. in Computer Science from the Universidad de Deusto in 2006. At present, he is Professor at the Universidad Pontificia de Salamanca (España). He obtained a degree in Engineering in Computer Sciences at the Universidad de Deusto in 1993. He has been a member of the organizing and scientific committee of several international symposiums such as IWAAPAMS, SPEDECE, etc., and has co-authored papers published in a number of recognized journals, workshops, and symposiums. He is currently developing applications for mobile environments, focusing his work on Android.

Jorge Bernardino is Coordinator Professor at ISEC (Instituto Superior de Engenharia de Coimbra) of Polytechnic of Coimbra, Portugal. He received his MsC degree in Systems and Technologies of Information and PhD Degree in Computer Engineering from University of Coimbra, in 1994 and 2002, respectively. He was President of Scientific Council of ISEC during 2003–2005 and President of ISEC from 2005–2010. He is member of Software and Systems Engineering (SSE) group of Centre for Informatics and Systems of the University of Coimbra (CISUC) research centre. His research interests are in the areas of data warehousing, business intelligence, database knowledge management, e-business, and e-learning.

Samo Bobek is a professor of Information Systems at the Faculty of Economics and Business at University of Maribor. He teaches courses in undergraduate level (Introduction to Information Systems, Information Systems in Finance and Banking), Master of Science program (Information Systems Management, Management Information Systems, Information Systems in Service Organizations), and MBA program (Information Management). Professor Bobek's research areas are Strategic Information Systems Planning, Information management, and Banking technology. He has published several books in Slovene language. His bibliography includes more than 200 articles, conference papers, research reports etc. Professor Bobek is head of Information and organization systems department. Professor Bobek also acts as consultant to several corporations, banks, and insurance firms in Slovenia.

Silvana Rossy de Brito, Cyberspace Institute, Federal Rural University of Amazônia (UFRA), Brazil. Silvana R. Brito received the BS degree in computer science from the Federal University of Pará (1993), and she is a doctoral student in the same university. Her current research is focused on monitoring and evaluating training programs for large-scale digital inclusion.

Giorgio Bruno is an Associate Professor at Politecnico di Torino, where he teaches courses on software engineering and object-oriented programming. His current interests concern the operational modeling of business processes and collaborative services, and the design of information systems and workflow systems. He has authored two books and over 140 technical papers on the above-mentioned subjects.

María del Mar Sánchez Cañadas, Doctorate in Accounting and Professor of the Department of Business Administration and Management at the University of Almería. She teaches subjects related to the area of Financial Economics and Accounting at the Master and Doctorate. She is member of the research group New Approaches in Finance and Business Information Systems as well as several research projects with public funding. She has published articles in national and foreign magazines and has presented conference papers both nationally and internationally, as Congress of AEDEM, AECA, ASEPUC, etc.

Vera Silva Carlos graduated in Work and Organizational Psychology and took a Master's degree in Marketing. Currently, she is a Ph.D. Student in Business at the University of Beira Interior (Portugal) and she is teaching 'Marketing' and 'Electronic Commerce and Web Marketing' in this university. She is also a researcher at the Research Centre on Enterprise Science (NECE – Núcleo de Estudos em Ciências Empresariais). Her research interests are mainly focused on Internal marketing, Online social networks and Quality management, specifically on their influence on the individual's attitudes and behaviours at work. She is now investing in publishing her research papers in international journals and in books.

Maria João Carneiro is Assistant Professor of Tourism at the University of Aveiro (UA) (in Portugal) and researcher at the Governance, Competitiveness, and Public Policy (GOVCOPP) research unit at this University. She holds a Degree in Tourism Management and Planning from UA, an MBA from New University of Lisbon and a PhD in Tourism from UA. She is the Director of the degree program (licenciatura) in Tourism of the UA. She has published papers in several journals and conference proceedings, and has also presented several works in conferences and seminars. Her research interests are competitiveness of tourism destinations, consumer behaviour in tourism and destination marketing.

Maébh Coleman (MeBus, BSc) is a researcher in the College of Engineering and Informatics at the National University of Ireland, Galway. Her current research interests include green innovation and enterprise, open innovation, e-business, and technology transfer. Maébh has over ten years' international experience in the areas of ICT, project management, marketing and communications, and high-tech procurement.

Kathryn Cormican (Ph.D.) is a lecturer in the College of Engineering and Informatics at the National University of Ireland Galway. Her research interests lies in the areas of enterprise integration and analysis and technology innovation management. Kathryn leads a number of research projects in this area. She has published over 70 papers at international conferences and peer reviewed journals. Kathryn works closely with many leading organisations and SMEs helping them to diagnose, develop, and deploy new processes and systems.

Carolina Costa graduated in Teaching of Mathematics and in Applied Mathematics and Computation and received a MSc degree in Information Management. Currently she is pursuing a PhD in the Information Systems area from University of Aveiro. She has worked in technology applied to the teaching and learning process. During her studies, she has published in several conferences.

João Crisóstomo Weyl Albuquerque Costa, Applied Electromagnetism Laboratory, Federal University of Pará (LEA-UFPA), Brazil. João C. W. A. Costa received the B.Sc. (Elect.) degree from the Federal University of Pará (UFPA), the M.Sc. degree from the Catholic University of Rio de Janeiro in 1981, and 1990, respectively. He received the Doctor Degree in Electric Engineering in 1994 from the State University of Campinas, São Paulo. He is a researcher of the Brazilian National Research Council (CNPq) since 1994.

Esmeralda Crespo-Almendros has a Ph.D. in Business Administration from University of Granada (Spain). She is an Assistant Professor of Marketing and Market Research Department at this University. Their areas of specialization are the Marketing Communication, Online Consumer Behaviour and Marketing Online. She has published peer-reviewed papers in prestigious Spanish journals such as Revista Europea de Dirección y Economía de la Empresa and she has participated in prestigious congress such as EMAC, American Marketing (AM), ICORIA, ICMC.

V. Cruz-Machado Ph.D. in Industrial Engineering in CIM (Cranfield University, UK). He is an Associate Professor of Industrial Engineering at Faculdade de Ciências e Tecnologia, Universidade Nova de Lisboa, Portugal. He coordinates Postgraduate programmes in industrial engineering, project, and lean management. He teaches operations and production management and has published more than 150 papers in scientific journals and conferences, in addition to having supervised 50 MSc and PhD students. His main scientific activities are directed to the design of lean supply chains. He is the President of UNIDEMI (R&D Unit in Mechanical and Industrial Engineering) and the President of the IIE Portugal Chapter.

José C. Delgado is an Associate Professor at the Computer Science and Engineering Department of the Instituto Superior Técnico (Lisbon Technical University), in Lisbon, Portugal, where he earned the Ph.D. degree in 1988. He lectures courses in the areas of Computer Architecture, Information Technology, and Service Engineering. He has performed several management roles in his faculty, namely Director of the Taguspark campus, near Lisbon, and Coordinator of the B.Sc. and M.Sc. in Computer Science and Engineering at that campus. He has been the coordinator of and researcher in several research projects, both national and European. As an author, his publications include one book, several book chapters, and more than 40 papers in international refereed conferences and journals.

Gonçalo Paiva Dias holds a PhD in Computer Engineering from the University of Aveiro. He is currently the Director of the School of Technology and Management of Águeda of the University of Aveiro and researcher at the Research Unit for Governance, Competitiveness, and Public Policies (GOVCOPP) of the same University. He is a member of the International Editorial Review Board of the *International Journal of Electronic Government Research* (IJEGR), the Scientific Committee of the *Iberian Journal of Systems and Information Technology* (RISTI), and the Coordinating Committee of the Iberian Conference on Information Systems and Technologies (CISTI). He has more than thirty internationally published papers in the areas of electronic government, information society and systems and information technology.

George Dragoi received the B.S. in Electronics & Telecommunications and Dr. Eng. degrees and in Industrial Informatics from University "Polytechnica" of Bucharest, Romania, in 1982 and 1994, respectively. From 1982-1986, he was an Associate Researcher of the Romanian National Research Center in Telecommunication of Bucharest. From 1986 to 1990, he was a Research Assistant, from 1990 to 1993 lecturer, from 1993 to 1998 associate professor, and from 2006 to present, professor at the "Politehnica" University of Bucharest. He has been active in the fields of the industrial robots control, industrial informatics, computer-integrated enterprise, computer networks and telecommunications, virtual enterprise, and collaborative design systems. Since 1998, he has been associated with the Institute National Polytechnic at Grenoble, France, as Associate and Visiting Professor. He received the Romanian Academy Award "Aurel Vlaicu" in 1993, and it has served as a member of the National Council for Technological Education and Innovation after 1999.

João Vaz Estêvão is a researcher in the area of tourism studies. He completed his BA in Tour Operating Management at the Estoril Higher Institute for Hotel and Tourism Studies, in Portugal. In 2004, João Estêvão completed his MSc in Local Tourism Destination's Management at the University of Barcelona, Spain. João Estêvão is currently undertaking a PhD in Tourism at the University of Aveiro, Portugal. His PhD research subject is the adoption of Information Technologies by tourism destinations. Regarding his current professional activity, João Estêvão is a Professor at the School of Tourism and Hospitality Management of the Polytechnic Institute of Guarda, in Portugal, where he lectures subjects in the areas of tour operations, tourism planning, and development and Information Technologies in Tourism. He has presented papers in more than ten national and international conferences and workshops.

Paulo Fazendeiro received the Ph.D. in Computer Science and Engineering (2010), the equivalence of M.S. degree in Computer Science (2001), and the B.S. degree in Mathematics and Informatics (1995, with honors) all from the University of Beira Interior, Portugal. Currently, he is an Assistant Professor at the Informatics Department of the University of Beira Interior. His research interests encompass Computational Intelligence and Granular Computing including the application of fuzzy set theory and fuzzy systems, knowledge discovery and data mining, evolutionary algorithms and their parallelization, multi-objective optimization and clustering techniques with applications to image processing. Dr. Fazendeiro is member of the Pattern and Image Analysis group of the Portuguese Telecommunications Institute and is also a member of the Informatics Laboratory of the University of Algarve.

Carlos Figueroa was born in San Juan, Puerto Rico in 1959. He received the B.S. degree in computer science in 1981, and Master's degree from Jackson State University, USA, in 1991. He is currently Associate Professor of Information Systems at University of Turabo. His research interests are in database design, object business applications and social media influence in society. He is a freelance system analyst and has imparted many different courses and seminars in various topics to the public and private sector.

Sandra Filipe is an Invited Assistant Professor at the Higher Institute of Accounting and Administration of Aveiro University (ISCA-UA), Portugal, since 1999. She teaches Management and Marketing to undergraduate and postgraduate courses. She obtained her Master's Degree in Management by Business School of Lisbon University Institute (ISCTE–IUL), Portugal, in February 2000, and is a doctoral student of Marketing since 2009 at the same school (ISCTE-IUL). Currently, she is a researcher at the Research Unit of Governance, Competitiveness and Public Policy (GOVCOPP) of Aveiro University. Her main research interests are digital marketing, corporate social responsibility, relational marketing, consumer behavior, and marketing research. She has published in scholarly journals.

Juan A. Fraile is a PhD. in computer science from the University of Salamanca, Spain. He obtained the Engineering in Computer Sciences degree at the Pontifical University of Salamanca in 2000. He has been involved in the development of automated systems in the Everis Group company and the Data Processing Centre (Pontifical University of Salamanca). He has also been a co-author of papers published in recognized journals, workshops, and symposiums.

Carlos Renato Lisboa Francês, Laboratory of High Performance Networks Planning, Federal University of Pará (UFPA), Brazil. Carlos R. L. Francês received the BS degree in Computer Science from the Federal University of Pará (1995), master's degree in Computer Science from the University of São Paulo (1998), and Ph.D. in Computer Science and Computational Mathematics at the University of São Paulo (2001). Has experience in Computer Science, acting on the following subjects: Last mile networks, performance models (Markovian and simulation), and Bayesian networks. He is currently a professor of Computer Engineering at the Federal University of Pará and a researcher of the Brazilian National Research Council (CNPq).

Monique Goepel, M.A. in International Business Studies, is a research assistant at the Chair of Strategic Leadership and Global Management at the Berlin Institute of Technology. Her current research interests include innovation management and effective decision making in adaptive organizations. Previous engagements include Ernst & Young Australia and Audible GmbH.

Fotios Gogoulos is a PhD candidate of the Intelligent Communications and Broadband Networks Laboratory (ICBNet) of the National Technical University of Athens (NTUA), Greece. He received his diploma in Electrical and Computer Engineering from the NTUA in 2007. As a research fellow of the NTUA since 2007, he has participated in several European and national research projects. His research interests include Information Security and Privacy, Semantic Web, IPTV, Service Discovery Protocols, System Modelling and Simulation, P2P Networks; he has seven publications related to these fields.

Jacqueline Gladys Guzmán Sequeira is a Student Mastery of Computer Engineering in the Information Systems area. The studies and research have been performed in the Engineering Faculty of the Republic,Uruguay. She is member of the research group Semantic Information Systems of the University. She is interested in the following areas: Modeling, Semantic Web, Ontology, and problems related with interoperability and integration. In the last years she has worked in e-Learning. She has experience in teaching, she has been teaching in presential courses as well as in distance courses, and she has coordinated teaching areas.

Martin Heitmann is a research assistant at the Chair of Strategic Leadership and Global Management at the Berlin Institute of Technology. His main research interests are business development and company-community interaction in the software industry. Previous engagements of his include Deutsche Städte Medien-GmbH and Deutsche and Deutsche Telekom Laboratories.

Damjana Jerman received a Ph.D. in Marketing in 2008 from the Faculty of Economics at the University of Ljubljana. She is an Assistant Professor of Marketing at the International Business School Ljubljana. She also worked as an Assistant Professor at Faculty of Tourism Studies University of Primorska. In addition to teaching and researching, she is primary responsible for public relations and managing marketing communications programs in the logistical company Intereuropa Ltd. Co. where she oversees the management of public relations and marketing communications. Her research interests include empirical and theoretical issues in business-to-business marketing communications, public relations, consumer behavior and marketing communication strategy and implementation. She has published articles in domestic and international journals.

Dimitra I. Kaklamani is a Professor at the School of Electrical and Computer Engineering (SECE) of the National Technical University of Athens (NTUA). She has received the Diploma and Ph.D. degrees from the SECE, NTUA. She has published over 150 journal and conference papers and led and participated in several EU and national research projects. Her research interests span across different fields and include the use of Object-Oriented methodologies and middleware technologies for the development of distributed systems and privacy-aware infrastructures, and the development of visualisation and real-time simulation techniques for solving complex, large scale modelling problems of microwave engineering and information transmission systems.

Francisco J. Liébana-Cabanillas is an Assistant Professor in the Marketing and Market Research Department at the University of Granada (Spain) and holds a Ph.D. Business Sciences in this university. He has a degree in Business and Administration Science and a Master in Marketing and Consumer behavior, from the University of Granada. His main area of research and interest the field is the effectiveness of the mobile and online banking, the results of which are reflected in various papers, which have been presented at the AEMARK, JORNADAS HISPANOLUSAS. He is currently working on different research projects in Internet social networks, Internet ad effectiveness, and new technologies acceptance.

Georgios V. Lioudakis is a senior research associate of the Intelligent Communications and Broadband Networks Laboratory (ICBNet) of the National Technical University of Athens (NTUA), Greece. He received his Dr.-Ing. degree in Electrical and Computer Engineering from the NTUA in 2008. As a research fellow of the NTUA since 2000, he has participated in several European and national research projects. His research interests include privacy protection, mobile networks and services, software engineering, middleware and distributed technologies; he has several publications related to these fields. Since 2009, George is also an adjunct lecturer at the Department of Telecommunications Science and Technology, University of Peloponnese, Greece.

Dalton Lopes Martins, University of Sao Paulo (USP), Brazil. Dalton L. Martins received the B.Sc. (Elect.) degree from the State University of Campinas (2002), master degree in Computer Engineering from the State University of Campinas (2004) and he is a doctoral student in the Information Science from the University of São Paulo. Her current research is focused on Social Network Analysis (SNA).

Francisco Vitorino Martins is Economist Ph.D. in Management Science by University of Paris IX-Dauphine. Professor of Faculty of Economics of the University of Porto from 1981, and, of the Research Centre CEPESE-Management Studies. He is Professor and Researcher on Econometrics, Applied Statistics, Forecasting Methods, and Marketing Research. Author of the book *Econometrics* (1997, McGraw-Hill).

Montserrat Mateos (PhD.) at the present is a Professor at the Pontifical University of Salamanca, Spain. She received a Phd (with distinction) in Computer Science and Languages and Systems from the University of Salamanca in 2006. She obtained a degree in Engineering in Computer Sciences at the University of Salamanca in 2001. She has participated in several research projects related to Mobile and NFC technology, in some of them as main researcher; also she has published in a number international conference proceedings and has co-authored of papers in several recognized scientific journals. She currently is researching and developing applications for mobile environments, focusing her work on smartcards and NFC.

Sandra Morley is a quality engineer and holds a Masters Degree in Operations and Quality Management from the National University of Ireland Galway. She has worked for a large multinational medical device organisation in Galway in various roles over the last 15 years. In her current role of Senior Quality Systems Engineer, she has been involved in a large number of multi-site, multi-discipline teams. This involvement has prompted an interest in the theory of 'virtual teaming' and in the desire to understand how the work of these dispersed teams can be better supported and more appropriately structured.

Regina Motz holds a PhD in Computer Science from the Technische Universität Darmstadt, Germany (2004) and a Master in Computer Science from Universidade Federal Pernambuco, Brazil (1990). She obtained her degree on Computing Engineer Systems at the University of the Republic Uruguay (1988). She currently serves as Full Professor at Institute of Computing Faculty of Engineering of the University of the Republic, Uruguay.

Matjaz Mulej was born on Jan. 1941, in Maribor, Slovenia. Living in Maribor, Slovenia. Retired from University of Maribor, Faculty of Economics & Business, Maribor, as Professor Emeritus of Systems and Innovation Theory. He has published +1,500 publications in +40 countries. Visiting professor abroad for 15 semesters. Author of the *Dialectical Systems Theory* (see: François, 2004, International Encyclopedia) and Innovative Business Paradigm for catching-up countries. Member of New York Academy of Sciences (1996), European Academy of sciences and Humanities, Paris (2004), president of IFSR (International Federation for Systems Research with 37 member associations). M.A. in Development Economics, Doctorates in Systems Theory and in Management.

Francisco Muñoz-Leiva is Associate Professor in Marketing and Market Research at the University of Granada (Spain). He has a first-cycle degree in Statistics from the University of Jaén, a second-cycle degree in Research and Market Techniques and holds a Ph.D. in Business Sciences from the University of Granada. Although his main research interest is Internet consumer behavior and e-banking acceptance, he has also published papers other topics. His recent works have appeared in *Information & Management, Online Information Review, Cities, Quality & Quantity, The Service Industries Journal, Computers in Human Behavior, Defense and Peace Economics, International Journal of Internet Marketing & Advertising*, and communications in international conferences.

Zlatko Nedelko, born 1983, is an Assistant Professor at the Faculty of Economics and Business, Department of Organization and Informatics, University of Maribor (Slovenia). He has published over 40 texts, many of them abroad. The fields of his research interests include organization and management. Recently, he was involved in researching managerial values. He is also a member of many scientific committees at several international conferences.

João Negreiros took his Computer Science licentiate degree in Lisbon, Portugal (1989), MBA in San Diego, CA (1993), PhD in Lisbon, Portugal (2004), and Post-Doc in Almeria, Spain (2009). He worked for several Portuguese and American institutions during his stay in those previous countries while he published over fifty articles for conferences and research magazines worldwide and seven books regarding Geographical Information Systems (GIS), UNIX, and Processing of Digital Image by several publishers. Currently, he is an Associate Professor at Saint Joseph University, Macau, China.

Abraham Otero was born in Orense, Spain in 1978. He received the B.S. degree in physics in 2000 (with honors), and Ph.D degree from the University of Santiago de Compostela, in 2006. He is currently an Associate Professor of Computer Science and Artificial Intelligence at University San Pablo CEU. His research interests include fuzzy temporal knowledge representation and reasoning, biosignal processing, fuzzy constraint satisfaction problems, patient supervision, and the impact of social media. He is author of over 50 scientific papers in these fields.

Carmen Caba Pérez, Doctorate in Accounting and Professor of the Department of Business Administration and Management at the University of Almería. She teaches subjects related to the area of Financial Economics and Accounting at the Master and Doctorate. She is currently Deputy Dean of the

Faculty of Economics and Business Administration. She has published numerous articles in magazines including American and European ISI as well as in national magazines. She has published chapters in books published in North America and has presented papers at national and international conferences, such as the InterAmerican Accounting Conference, AEDEM, AECA, ASEPUC, European Association Accounting, CIGAR, etc. She is responsible for a research group and director of research projects with public funding.

Vojko Potocan, born 1962, is a Full Professor of organization and management on the Faculty of Economics and Business (FEB), Department of Organization and Informatics, University of Maribor, Slovenia. He teaches (on the graduate level, on the undergraduate level, and in doctoral program) in three universities in Slovenia and in three universities abroad (Germany, Croatia, and Czech Republic). He is also the head of postgraduate study of Management and Organization in FEB. He takes part in different foreign scientific conferences and realized a number of study visits on abroad. He was 10 times a visiting professor abroad and gave about eight further seminars at foreign universities. He has published +450 texts (+350 in foreign languages in 32 countries), including 8 books, and edited proceedings and textbooks. His research interests include Management, Organization, and Business Ethics.

Cláudio Alex Jorge da Rocha, Laboratory of High Performance Networks Planning, Federal University of Pará (UFPA), and University of Amazônia (UNAMA), Brazil. Cláudio A. J. da Rocha is graduated in Data Processing from the University of Amazônia (1991), masters in Computer Science and Computational Mathematics at the University of São Paulo (2001) and Doctor Degree in Electric Engineering from the Federal University of Pará (2009). He is currently a professor of Computer Science (University of Amazônia) and professor of Postgraduate Electrical Engineering (Federal University of Pará).

Mário Jorge Ferreira Rodrigues is a Teaching Assistant at the School of Technology and Management of Águeda of the University of Aveiro. He received his BSc degree in Applied Mathematics in 2000, from the University of Porto, and his MSc degree in Electronics and Telecommunications Engineering in 2004, from the University of Aveiro Electronics Telecommunications and Informatics Department. Currently, he is a PhD student in Computer Engineering in the same department. His current research interests include Human Language Technologies, namely Natural Language Processing and Knowledge Representation, and Electronic Government. He has been involved in European and national funded research projects.

Ricardo Gouveia Rodrigues has a Ph.D. in Business and teaches Marketing Research, Entrepreneurial Marketing and Data Analysis to undergraduate, master and doctoral students at the University of Beira Interior, Portugal. He is also a researcher at the Research Centre on Enterprise Science (NECE – Núcleo de Estudos em Ciências Empresariais). His main research interests are Entrepreneurial Marketing and Entrepreneurship Education, but he is also interested in studying the impact of marketing efforts on themes such as physical activity, children behaviour, online gaming addiction, and happiness. Ricardo Gouveia Rodrigues has published several books and book chapters, as well as peer-reviewed papers in international journals.

Arturo Haro de Rosario, research fellow in the department of Business Administration and Management at the University of Almería. He teaches subjects related to the area of Financial Economics and Accounting. He is member of the research group New Approaches in Finance and Business Information Systems as well as several research projects with public funding. He has published articles in national and foreign magazines such as the Spanish Venture Capital Journal and the Accounting and administration Journal. He has presented conference papers both nationally and internationally, as Congress of AEDEM, AECA, ASEPUC, Conferences Hispanic Lusas Scientific Management, etc.

Sebastian Marius Roşu received the B.E. in Aerospace Construction and in Informatics from University "Polytechnica" of Bucharest, in 2000 and University "Dunărea de Jos" of Galaţi in 2002, respectively. In 2009 obtained doctoral degree in Automatics from University "Polytechnica" of Bucharest. From 2001-2004, he was a Researcher in Machines and Thermal Equipment at the GRUP ROMET Buzău. Since 2004, he was Quality Surveillance Receiving Inspector and Pressure Test Supervisor at the Nuclear Power Plant Unit Two Site of Cernavodă. Since as 2006 he is telecommunications engineer at the Romanian Special Telecommunications Service. He has been active in the fields of the thermodynamic, design, nuclear systems, quality control, industrial informatics, computers, computer integrated enterprise, computer networks, radio communications network and collaborative design systems. Since 2005, he has been associated with the PREMINV Research Laboratory at the Polytechnic University of Bucharest, as PhD Student.

Miguel A. Sánchez (PhD.) Associate Professor at the Pontifical University of Salamanca (Spain). At present he is Director of the "Máster en Informática Móvil y Tarjetas Inteligentes" (MIMO – www.upsa.es/mimo) and Director of Innovation Projects based on Mobile Technology. He received a PhD. in Computer Science from the Pontifical University of Salamanca (Madrid campus) in 2007. He obtained an Information Technology degree at the Pontifical University of Salamanca (Madrid campus) in 1999 and an Engineering in Computer Sciences degree at the Pontifical University of Salamanca in 1993. He has been member of the organizing and scientific committee of international symposiums such as SPDECE, IWPAAMS, and IWANN, and co-author of more than 20 papers published in recognized journals, workshops and symposiums. He has worked on several Artificial Intelligence (AI) and Mobility Research projects sponsored by Spanish public and private Institutions, in 3 of them as main researcher.

Neide Santos earned a Master of Education degree from the Federal University of Rio de Janeiro (Brazil) in 1989 and a DSc degree in Engineering of Production at the same university in 1994. Since 1999, she is an associate professor in the Department of Computer Science at the State University of Rio de Janeiro. Currently, she is the assistant coordinator of graduate studies in Computer Science. She published nearly 30 papers in international journals and more than 50 papers in international and Brazilian conference proceedings. In addition, her main areas of interest are Knowledge Representation, Ontologies and Semantic Web, Computer-Supported Cooperative Work, Computer-Supported Cooperative Learning, Artificial Intelligence and Education, and Web-Based Education.

Alberto Manuel Rodrigues da Silva is Associate Professor of Information Systems at the Computer and Information Systems Department at the Technical University of Lisbon (Instituto Superior Técnico – IST/UTL) Lisbon, Portugal. He is also a senior researcher at INESC-ID Lisboa, and a partner at the SIQuant – Engenharia do Território e Sistemas de Informação company. He has interests in the following areas: Modeling and Metamodeling, Model Driven Engineering, Requirement Engineering, Social Computing and Organizational Knowledge Management with a particular emphasis on Software Engineering, Social Software, Learning and Cultural application domains. He is the author or co-author of 5 technical books and more than 150 peer-reviewed scientific communications and he has served on program committees of several international conferences and workshops. He is member of the ACM, PMI, and the Portuguese Ordem dos Engenheiros.

Aleksandra do Socorro da Silva, Cyberspace Institute, Federal Rural University of Amazônia (UFRA), Brazil. Aleksandra S. da Silva received the BS degree in computer science from the Federal University of Pará (1994) and she is a doctoral student in the same university. Her current research is focused on metrics to social network analysis to extract indicators from interaction networks and their correlation with indicators of participation in learning environments.

Ana Silva is currently responsible for Digital Marketing and Social Media at a large international manufacturing group, following a vast experience in the area of Competitive Intelligence and also of Collaboration Management. She holds a Management degree from the University of Porto (Portugal) and post-graduation studies in the areas of Marketing and Information Management and Marketing Intelligence. She teaches Enterprise 2.0 at the Porto Business School and is particularly interested in the future trends affecting work and the workplace. Ana is also involved in the organization of conferences that discuss the impact of social tools and platforms, and also of new concepts such as crowdsourcing or mass collaboration, in businesses, citizenship and society as a whole.

Marisa Silva graduated from Superior Institute Miguel Torga in Social Work. She has also a Master Degree in Family and Social Systems from the same Institute and has a PhD, with mention of European Doctor from the University of Salamanca. Presently she is teaching at The Polytechnic Institute of Viseu – School of Technology and Management of Lamego (ESTGL). She is the scientific coordinator of the Postgraduate studies in Centre Management and Social Services and one of the directors of GAADS – Office of Social Development and Monitoring. She collaborated on the project "Support to Education via Internet," held at ESTGL.

Dora Simões received her PhD in Informatics Engineering from the Faculty of Engineering of Porto University (FEUP-UP), Portugal, in 2008. She is Adjunct Professor, in informatics area, at the Higher Institute of Accounting and Administration of Aveiro University (ISCA-UA). Portugal. She is member of the Advisor Board of the *Journal Studies of ISCA-UA*. Currently, she is researcher at the Research Unit of Governance, Competitiveness, and Public Policy (GOVCOPP) of Aveiro University. As part of her doctoral work, she worked as a invited researcher at the Institute of Engineering and Computer Systems of Porto (INESC Porto), between 2003 and 2008. Her current research interests include information and knowledge management, organizational information systems (CRM – Customer Relationship Management), and collaborative virtual networks. She has published in various conferences and journals, nationals and internationals.

Fawzy Soliman graduated with a PhD degree and Master of Engineering Science degree from the University of New South Wales, Australia, and a Bachelor of Engineering degree from the University of Sydney. Published in international journals in excess of twenty-six papers, six book chapters, and three books, and in excess of fifty-two conference proceeding papers. Former editor of *Journal of Knowledge Management*. Guest editor of *Journal of Knowledge Management and Journal Operations Management*. His publication citations is in excess of 593 with an author impact h-index of 9 and I10-index of 9. Supervised 9 PhD graduates. Convenor of Australia's first conference on Knowledge Management KNOW'99 held on 26-27 November 1999. Taught in a number of international business schools in Australia and overseas. Invited speaker in a number of prestigious conferences. Prior to joining academia, he has held various positions in large Australian organisations.

Ana Filipa Sousa is a communication designer from Aveiro, Portugal. She has a bachelor's degree in New Communication Technologies and a master's degree in Multimedia Communication (Interactive Multimedia Specialization) both by University of Aveiro. During her academic journey, she developed projects within a variety of technological and social fields and became an enthusiast for project management. Besides previous research works in agile management, she has also explored the online education thematic. Furthermore, Filipa has undergone a specialized training in drawing and illustration and currently works as a freelance professional developing Web and graphic design projects.

Simona Sternad is senior lecturer of Information Systems at the Faculty of Economics and Business at University of Maribor. She has a PhD in the field of management information science. Her research areas are Business process reengineering, ERP solutions and e-business solutions, implementation of ERP solutions and maintenance of ERP solutions. Her bibliography includes more than 70 articles, conference papers, research reports, etc. She collaborates in several courses in undergraduate level (E-business, Introduction to Information Systems, E-Finance and E-Banking, Enterprise Resource Planning Solutions, E-Business Information Systems) and several courses in master of science program (Business Information Solutions, Strategic Management Issues in E-Business). Simona Sternad also cooperates with some companies in Slovenia as a consultant.

António Joaquim da Silva Teixeira is Assistant Professor at University of Aveiro Electronics Telecommunications and Informatics Department. He received his BSc and Master in Electronics and Telecommunications Engineering in 1991 and 1993, and his PhD in Electronics Engineering in 2000, all from the University of Aveiro. He is Chair of the Special Interest Group on Iberian Languages of the International Speech Communication Association (ISCA) and the Director of the Master in Speech and Hearing Sciences. His main research activity is in the area of Speech Processing and Multimodal Human-Machine Interaction. He is involved in several national funded research (LUL, AAL4ALL, Smartphones for Smart Seniors) and in a starting European project (AAL Paelife), has supervised 4 concluded PhDs and more than 35 Masters, supervises more than 10 PhD projects and co-authored more than one hundred publications (books, book chapters, international journals, and proceedings of international conferences).

Leonor Teixeira graduated in Management and Industrial Engineering, received an MSc degree in Information Management and a PhD in Health Information Systems area. She is currently an Assistant Professor with the Department of Economics, Management, and Industrial Engineering at the University of Aveiro and teaching in Technology and Information Systems areas. She has published in several conferences and journals, and currently she is researcher at the Governance, Competitiveness, and Public Politics (GOVCOPP) and of the Institute of Electronics and Telematics Engineering (IEETA) of Aveiro research units.

Ana Torres is a Ph.D. candidate at the Faculty of Economics of University of Porto, and recently finished her thesis. She holds a Master of Science in Management Science from the Faculty of Economics of University of Porto, in 2003. She was assistant Professor of Marketing at the University of Aveiro, and presently she teaches at University Portucalense, Portugal. Her previous work experience was in market research and marketing consultancy, having worked with several industries and services. She has published and presented several papers at the international conferences on Internet and leading technologies. Her current research interests are in digital economy, networks analysis, e-marketing strategy, e-commerce, consumer behavior, and quantitative marketing models. Her research is empirical in nature and makes extensive use of structural equation modeling.

Iakovos S. Venieris is a professor at the School of Electrical and Computer Engineering of the National Technical University of Athens since 1994. He received the Dipl.-Ing. degree from the University of Patras, Greece, in 1988, and the Ph.D. degree from the National Technical University of Athens, in 1990, all in Electrical and Computer Engineering. His research interests are in the fields of distributed systems, service engineering, agent technology, multimedia, mobile communications, and Intelligent Networks, Internetworking, signalling, resource scheduling, and allocation for network management, modelling, performance evaluation, and queuing theory. He has over 150 publications in the above areas. Prof. Venieris has received several national and international awards for academic achievement. He is a member of the IEEE and the Technical Chamber of Greece.

Jeļena Zaščerinska received the diploma in Russian Philology in 1994 from the Daugavpils University, Daugavpils, Latvia, Master Degree in English Philology in 2002 from the University of Latvia, Riga, Latvia. In 2011, she was awarded Dr. paed. Degree for her promotion thesis "Development of Students' Communicative Competence in English studies for Academic Purposes." In February 2012, Jeļena Zaščerinska was awarded expert rights in pedagogy by the Latvian Council of Science, Riga, Latvia. Jeļena Zaščerinska worked for a number of years at the interface of pedagogy and philology, and is now a senior researcher at the Centre for Education and Innovation Research, Riga, Latvia. She is a founding member and the Chair of the Board of the Centre for Education and Innovation Research, Riga, Latvia. She is author or co-author of some 40 contributions on teacher, engineer, and language education.

Bruno Završnik is a Professor of Marketing in the Faculty of Economics and Business. He received his PhD in Marketing from the same Faculty. He teaches a variety of courses at the undergraduate and graduate levels at Faculty of Economics and Business. His research interests include empirical and theoretical issues in B2B marketing communications, effectiveness of purchasing, retailing strategy, and implementation. He has published articles in domestic and international journals.

Index

E

F

G

H

I

J

K

L

M

N

O

P

R

S

CPSIA information can be obtained at www.ICGtesting.com
Printed in the USA
BVOW06*1633021214

377175BV00001B/1/P

2 370004 9437